Emanuel Swedenborg

SWEDENBORG STUDIES NO.14

MONOGRAPHS
OF THE
SWEDENBORG FOUNDATION

Emanuel Swedenborg

VISIONARY SAVANT IN THE AGE OF REASON

BY
ERNST BENZ

Introduced and Translated by
Nicholas Goodrick-Clarke

This work was originally published as
Emanuel Swedenborg: Naturforscher und Seher.
Edited by Friedemann Horn. Second edition.
Zurich: Swedenborg Verlag, 1969. First publication 1948.

Swedenborg Studies is a scholarly series published by the Swedenborg Foundation.
The primary purpose of the series is to make materials available for understanding
the life and thought of Emanuel Swedenborg (1688–1772) and the impact
his thought has had on others. The Foundation undertakes to publish
original studies and English translations of such studies and to republish
primary sources that are otherwise difficult to access. Proposals should be
sent to: Senior Editor, Swedenborg Studies, Swedenborg Foundation,
320 North Church Street, West Chester, Pennsylvania 19380.

Library of Congress Cataloging-in-Publication Data

Benz, Ernst, 1907–1978
[Emanuel Swedenborg. English]
Emanuel Swedenborg : visionary savant in the age of reason / by
Ernst Benz ; translated by Nicholas Goodrick-Clarke.
p. cm.—(Swedenborg studies ; no. 14)
Includes bibliographical references and index.
ISBN 0-87785-195-6
1. Swedenborg, Emanuel, 1688–1772. I. Title. II. Series.
BX8748 .B3913 2002
289'.4'092—dc21

2002001156

Edited by Mary Lou Bertucci
Cover design by Karen Connor
Interior design by Sans Serif, Inc., Saline, MI
Set in Galliard by Sans Serif, Inc., Saline, Michigan

Printed in the United States of America.

Contents

Part Three: THE VISIONARY

Part Four: THE DOCTRINE

Part Five: SWEDENBORG AND THE CHURCH OF HIS TIME

Introduction

By any estimate, Emanuel Swedenborg (1688–1772) claims an exceptional place in history, both as famous scientist and as visionary. Born at the end of a troubled century, Swedenborg spans the crucial construction of the modern worldview based on reason, science, and material progress. Before he was yet twenty-five, the precocious Swedish genius had already worked alongside Sir Isaac Newton, Edmund Halley, and other leading scientists in England, France, and Holland. From 1680 to 1715, when Swedenborg first came to London and Paris, the new sciences of astronomy, physics, chemistry, and biology were forged by such figures as Christian Huygens, Robert Boyle, Robert Hooke, and Hermann Boerhaave. Meanwhile, philosophers such as René Descartes and Benedictus de Spinoza supplied a philosophy that was geometric, mechanistic, and optimistic concerning the rational and beneficial order of the universe. Between 1700 and 1740, European science rapidly developed a rational understanding of nature to harness its powers for human purposes. This rapid accumulation of scientific knowledge and its application in navigation, engineering, and industry unleashed an unprecedented wave of economic growth in Europe and laid the basis of European colonial expansion.

Swedenborg inhabited this mental world, working on a fast-revolving stage of new discoveries, inventions, machines, and large engineering projects. He traveled widely through Europe and published pioneering works in such diverse fields as astronomy, physics, engineering, chemistry, geology, anatomy, physiology, and psychology. At the same time, he played a prominent role in Swedish public institutions concerned with mining, finance, and politics. These worldly, rational interests totally absorbed Swedenborg. Until his fiftieth birthday, he appeared uninterested in religion and hardly participated in organized church worship. Then, at the peak of his powers, a renowned figure of European science and member of the

Swedish Academy of Sciences, Swedenborg's life changed forever in the spring of 1744.

While traveling through Holland during Easter week, Swedenborg underwent an emotional crisis culminating in a nocturnal vision of Christ. He fell from his bed, found himself resting on Jesus' chest, and felt he had been divinely commissioned to a special task. In the following months, Swedenborg sought direction and focus for his new religious feeling. He kept a revealing dream diary and wrote *Worship and Love of God*, an extraordinary blend of mythology and science. Then, in the spring of 1745, while a resident in London, he had his first vision of the spiritual world and its inhabitants. The Lord God appeared to Swedenborg and told him his mission was to "explain to men the spiritual meaning of Scripture."

Henceforth, Swedenborg possessed the gift of vision into the spirit world and received constant inspiration for his new vocation. In 1748, he began working on *Arcana Coelestia*, a major eight-volume visionary work, which heralded a stream of books devoted to theology and biblical exegesis, including *Earths in the Universe, The Last Judgment, New Jerusalem and Its Heavenly Doctrine*, and his most famous book *Heaven and Hell*, all published in 1758. During the 1760s, he continued to publish substantial works, all based on an interpretation of Scripture, which the angels explained to him through spirit vision in palaces and parks, in lecture halls, colleges, and conferences among wonderful or ominous landscapes. Swedenborg's visionary faculty was unique. Rather than raptures, mystical union, and ascent experiences common to the famous English, German, and Spanish mystics from the Middle Ages to the seventeenth century, Swedenborg's visions were always related to the meaning of Scripture, which lends his writing an astonishing matter-of-factness. We read a prosaic yet compelling record of encounters with spirits who offer detailed information concerning God, heaven and earth, humankind's purpose, the Last Judgment, and the life to come. Never before had a Christian visionary written with the intellectual training and achievements of a leading European scientist.

If Swedenborg had already won European renown as a scientist in several fields, his new visionary career now made him notorious. If Swedenborg's birth dovetailed with the rise of modern European thought, his new spiritual vocation seemed quite at odds with its climax in the Enlightenment. By mid-century, the worship of nature and reason, so prominent in the thought of Voltaire, Rousseau, and Kant signaled the advent of a secular post-religious era. Swedenborg necessarily attracted controversy, and sides were quickly taken. In 1760, Friedrich Christoph Oetinger (1702–1782), the prominent German Pietist and church prelate, defended Swedenborg's work and invited him to Germany. Meanwhile, Kant wrote a scathing and, by his later admission, unjust work, *Dreams of a Sprit-Seer* (1766), which damaged Swedenborg's reputation among Enlightenment thinkers. While Swedenborg's visions were the talk of England, France, and Germany, ecclesiastical controversy broke out in his native Sweden, and steps were taken to declare his work heretical. Eventually, this storm blew over: Swedenborg was "rehabilitated" and died at the age of 84 in London in 1772. By the end of the century, his many followers in England had founded the New Church to promote his doctrines, which spread through missions to the United States and other countries in the nineteenth century. In 1908, Swedenborg's body was re-interred at Uppsala Cathedral. He is revered as a famous son of his country, and his earthly remains lie besides those of kings and other leading figures of Sweden.

Such is the rare trajectory of Swedenborg's life and works. Given the controversy he aroused, the powerful revelation he disclosed, and the enthusiastic following his doctrines attracted, it is unsurprising that his story has been told many times. Swedenborg's visions, his biblical exegesis, and his biography have been minutely examined by numerous authorities. Major biographies within the Swedenborgian community by Benjamin Worcester (1883), Martin Lamm (1915), Signe Toksvig (1948), Cyriel Sigstedt (1952) and Inge Jonsson (1971) have contributed greatly to our knowledge and understanding of this extraordinary mind. The Japanese philosopher D. T. Suzuki called him the "Buddha of the North," while the French scholar of esotericism Henry Corbin has compared his work to Islamic mysticism.

The biography you now hold in your hands was written over fifty years ago by Ernst Benz, the eminent German theologian and church historian. On reading Benz's monumental biography, one

walks with Swedenborg through his own age. Benz locates Swedenborg in this eighteenth-century world with its remarkable characters,
extraordinary advances, and burning issues. We experience the
young man's inspiration and towering ambition, his passionate appetite for the new mathematical sciences, and prodigious capacity for
research and work. We see his public life and political activity as a
noble in the Swedish upper house, and we travel with him across the
rutted roads of Europe to Amsterdam, Leipzig, Paris, Rome, and
London. But there is more. Benz's work has not dated; indeed, its
publication in English has become ever more urgent. Benz has performed a cardinal service to the estimate of Swedenborg's importance in European religious thought. As a non-Swedenborgian, Benz
has deployed his massive scholarship in the history of religion to
place Swedenborg securely in the mainstream of the Western esoteric
tradition and the history of Christian visionaries.

Born at Friedrichshafen on Lake Constance, Ernst Benz
(1907–1978) initially studied classical philology and archaeology,
while mastering an impressive number of modern European languages. In 1929, he took his doctorate at Tübingen University.
However, he was then motivated to study theology following an encounter with Ernesto Buonaiuti (1881–1946), the Italian theologian
whose practical engagement in Christianity deeply impressed him.
He began his university teaching career at the University of Halle in
1932, and after a year at Dorpat (Estonia), he was appointed professor of Church History at the Philipps University of Marburg in
1935. Benz began his postdoctoral studies in Protestant theology by
focusing on Gottfried Arnold and the mysticism of the seventeenth
and eighteenth centuries, which in due course led to his major books
on Jacob Boehme and Emanuel Swedenborg, including this volume.

Ernst Benz's scholarly bibliography is remarkably extensive, embracing hundreds of learned articles and some fifty books, ranging
from studies of the Eastern Orthodox Churches and Asian religions
to Friedrich Wilhelm Joseph Schelling, the German Romantic and
neo-Platonic philosopher, and Franz Anton Mesmer, the founder of
animal magnetism. As a pupil of Rudolf Otto, Benz regretted the
process of secularization and the loss of transcendence in Western society and counted among his close scholarly friends Leopold Ziegler,

the follower of René Guenon, and the eminent theologian Pierre Teilhard de Chardin. Together with Hans-Joachim Schoeps, the prominent intellectual historian, Benz founded the highly respected *Zeitschrift für Religions- und Geistesgeschichte* in the late 1940s. In 1953, he joined the Eranos Conference at Ascona, a prestigious forum for religion and philosophy since 1933, whose regular participants included Martin Buber, Carl Gustav Jung, Karl Kerényi, Gilles Quispel, Henry Corbin, Gershom Scholem, Mircea Eliade, and Daisetz Suzuki.[1]

Benz addresses the central question that any study of Swedenborg begs. How and why did this paragon of science and secular thought metamorphose into the famous mystic and visionary? While some commentators have invoked psychological interpretations of Swedenborg's change by positing a life crisis and psychosis, Benz makes short shrift of such reductionist efforts. Swedenborg's own mental state is no more material to the importance and influence of his ideas in European thought than, say, a psychiatric report on St. Augustine or St. Ignatius Loyola would be to an estimate of their effect on the history of Christianity and the West. In the best traditions of historicism, that legacy of nineteenth-century German scholarship, Benz relates Swedenborg's life and the development of his thought to the temper of his times, the intellectual and religious currents, the challenges and hopes of the age of reason.

The manifest readiness of thinkers and scientists to embrace a new secular, material worldview at the beginning of the eighteenth century is a key clue to Swedenborg's own appetite for the new science. The year 1710, the date of Swedenborg's first arrival in England, brings to mind images of an elegant Hanoverian London. Here stood the newly built St. Pauls Cathedral of Christopher Wren, the Greenwich Observatory under John Flamsteed, Astronomer Royal, and the gracious mansions built by successful Whig magnates in the reign of Queen Anne. The Bank of England had opened its doors in

---

1. Fridrich Wilhelm Kantzenbach, "Ernst Benz—wie ich ihn sehe und verstehe: Eine Laudatio zum 17.11.1977," in *Zeitschrift für Religions- und Geistesgeschichte* 29 (1977): 289–304; Hans Thomas Hakl, *Der verborgene Geist von Eranos: Unbekannte Begegnungen von Wissenschaft und Esoterik. Eine alternative Geistesgeschichte des 20. Jahrhunderts* (Bretten: scientia nova, 2001), 301–303.

1694, joint stock companies were founded daily, and trade was expanding across Great Britain and Europe. But this comfortable, even complacent era was a relatively recent and hard-won phenomenon. Only a quarter century earlier, Europe had finally emerged from an age of religious wars, which had lasted from 1559 to 1689. During that period, the continent was riven by the French civil wars, the Dutch revolt, the Scottish rebellion, the Spanish Armada against England, the Thirty Years War in Germany, and the Puritan Revolution and Civil War in England. All these conflicts had their origins in the religious controversy unleashed by the Reformation in the early sixteenth century, but their legacy had seared Europe for more than one-and-a-half centuries. The memory of martyrs, crusaders, superstition, intolerance, denominational strife, and hymn-singing armies was only too recent. Not until these ideological conflicts had finally burned out in the 1680s did European politics return to its secular pattern.[2] Henceforth, people were only too happy to embrace the mundane but comfortable worlds of business and investment, science and social improvement.

However, Swedenborg was born and brought up in that recent past, in another country, where things were done differently. He was the son of a powerful and impressive bishop in the Swedish Lutheran Church. Jesper Swedberg (1653–1735) also traveled widely to England, France, and Germany in his youth, anticipating his son's travels across Europe forty years later. Swedberg had encountered English Puritanism, French Catholic charitable works, and above all German Pietism, a powerful new religious movement initiated by Johannes Arndt (1555–1621) and led by Philipp Jakob Spener (1635–1705) and August Hermann Francke (1633–1727). These men blended their Lutheran faith with a piety of the fiery heart in good works involving improving books, orphanages, schools, and social welfare.[3] Swedberg was especially influenced by Pietism. As a Lutheran in his high offices as bishop, rector, and theology professor, he sought to

---

2. Richard S. Dunn, *The Age of Religious Wars 1559–1689* (London: Weidenfeld & Nicolson, 1971), ix.
3. For an excellent introduction and bibliography of Pietism, see *Pietists: Selected Writings*, edited by Peter C. Erb (New York: Paulist Press, 1983).

soften Lutheran orthodoxy and reliance on the doctrine of justification by faith alone through pastoral development. A pious believer in angels, spirits, and the efficacy of exorcism, Swedberg also saw a mortal struggle of God and the Devil for every human soul, including his own in the numerous trials, especially fires, that plagued his life. This was Emanuel Swedenborg's formative environment.

Young Emanuel's move toward the humanities under the tutelage of his brother-in-law, Erik Benzelius, in whose household he lived from 1703 to 1709, represented a major shift away from the stark religious choices and pieties of his father's house. A brilliant young professor at Uppsala, Benzelius encouraged Swedenborg's interest in the new learning and may have been instrumental in launching him among a wide network of bright young students whom he had earlier sent to Western European centers for advanced studies unavailable in Sweden. In any case, by the time Emanuel came to London, he was avidly consuming the works of Isaac Newton, Nicolas Malebranche, John Norris, and Robert Boyle. Benz shows how Swedenborg appears to have forsaken effectively church-based Christianity in his new devotion to the mathematical explanation and prediction of nature.

But while the bishop worried that his son had fallen among atheists and "freethinkers," Swedenborg appears to have found a religion in the scientific study of nature. Benz recalls the contemporary idea of nature as a second book of God beside the Bible and how Swedenborg was strongly influenced by Jan Swammerdam (1637–1680), the Dutch natural historian, and his beautifully illustrated *Biblia naturae* (1737). Swedenborg's scientific thought in his major scientific work *First Principles of Natural Things* (1734) is still geometric and mechanistic. However, already in this work and the treatise *The Infinite and the Final Cause of Creation* (1734), Swedenborg exempted the "Infinite"—a term used to describe a "preceding cause" as a reservoir that supplies the universe with an inexplicable source of energy that streams into the human soul. Here he seems to be moving with the English Deists, a movement that began with John Toland (1670–1722) and Matthew Tindal (1655–1733) among "religion-hungry rationalists" and also, more controversially, in the wash of Arianism. This ancient heresy, originating in the fourth century AD, had dispensed with the Trinity and relegated the divinity of Christ to that of the Father, the one supreme God. The emergence of a mechanistic and mathematical worldview made Arian ideas again attractive to the leaders of the scientific Enlightenment in Hanoverian England, notably Sir Isaac Newton (1642–1727) and his disciples William Whiston (1667–1752) and Samuel Clarke (1675–1729), whose spectacular breaches with the Church occurred during Swedenborg's first stay in London.[4]

Under the influence of the German Enlightenment thinkers, Swedenborg would soon abandon the geometric mechanical world picture in favor of an organic and vitalist conception, which regarded nature as a living, animate whole. Gottfried Wilhelm Leibniz (1646–1716), Christian Wolff (1679–1754), and Andreas Rüdiger (1673–1731) reintroduced teleological concerns to science and rational philosophy. As a professor of philosophy at Halle and Leipzig, Rüdiger was close to Pietist thought. In his critique of the use of mathematical method in philosophy, Rüdiger initiated a new current of academic philosophy in eighteenth-century Germany. Together with his young colleague Christian August Crusius (1715–1775), Rüdiger opposed the dominant influence of Wolff and inspired Immanuel Kant in his precritical phase. Swedenborg was especially inspired by Rüdiger's *Divine Physics* (1716), which subordinated the mechanical insights of science to an organic philosophy of nature deriving from Henry More (1614–1687), the Cambridge Platonist.

Swedenborg's *Economy of the Animal Kingdom* (1740–1741) and *The Animal Kingdom* (1744–1745) demonstrated the new cast of his thought. These two massive works devoted to human physiology and psychology document their author's quest for the seat of the soul. In his discussion of these books, Benz shows how Swedenborg's ideas of the *archeus* (primal energy) and *vis formatrix* or *vis plastica* (energy of formation) describe a metaphysical cosmos and an unfolding implicate order linking the macrocosm of God and heaven with the microcosm of an individual creature. Through Swedenborg's acknowledged debt to Henry More and Johann Baptista van

4. Maurice Wiles, *Archetypal Heresy: Arianism through the Centuries* (Oxford: Oxford University Press, 1996), 77–134.

Helmont (1577–1644), Benz uncovers his membership in the long tradition of *Naturphilosophie* ranging from Albertus Magnus and Nicholas of Cusa, through Paracelsus (1493–1541), who had coined the term *archeus*, and Jacob Boehme (1575–1624) to the Rosicrucians and Robert Fludd (1574–1637). This linkage had already been explored by Martin Lamm in his pioneering study, which established Swedenborg's interest in neo-Platonism and also showed that his scientific worldview was not essentially changed by his religious revelations.[5] Following Lamm's lead, Ernst Benz thus consolidated the scholarly recovery of Swedenborg from a contested hagiographical context and located his scientific writings in the mainstream of the Western esoteric tradition deriving from neo-Platonic and Hermetic ideas concerning the relation of God and the soul.

By demonstrating that these esoteric and mystical notions relating God, nature and man, macrocosm and microcosm, through divine emanations, correspondences, and hierarchies of intelligence were already evident in Swedenborg's later science, Benz shows the essential continuity of Swedenborg's scientific and theological thought. Swedenborg's crisis of 1744 and his gift of vision into the world of spirits remain unique, astonishing, and transformative events in his life; but with Benz's guidance, we glimpse the way in which his scientific and philosophical ideas were already leading him. His visionary works based on the conversation of spirits and angels further explored the doctrine of correspondences, in which he also used Marsilio Ficino's translation of Plotinus and *The Theology of Aristotle*, a pseudepigraphic neo-Platonist text. After his vision of vocation in 1745, this doctrine of correpondences became a doctrine of the divine Word, in which Holy Scripture appeared to him as the visible representation of divine truth, tailored to the sensory status of man, in the manner of Goethe's dictum: "Du gleichst dem Geist, den du begreifst" (*Faust, Part I*). Other visionary themes included the animation (ensoulment) of the whole universe by God's creative love, to form a living, coherent, and implicate whole, another

---

5. Martin Lamm, *Swedenborg. En studie öfver hans utveckling till mystiker och andeskadare* (Stockholm: Hugo Geber, 1915), translated as *Emanuel Swedenborg: The Development of His Thought* (West Chester, Pa.: Swedenborg Foundation, 2000).

continuity with the esoteric tradition from neo-Platonism up to con-temporary ideas of Gaia and the "New Physics."

Thanks to Benz placing Swedenborg in the history of the West-ern esoteric tradition, this issue has since become central to his eval-uation as scientist and mystic. Inge Jonsson also followed Lamm in tracing the philosophical continuity between the later scientific work and the visionary theology. However, he sought to minimize the in-fluence of Renaissance neo-Platonism, the Cambridge Platonists and the *Naturphilosophie* tradition of Paracelsus and Johann Baptist van Helmont on Swedenborg, by emphasising his debt to Cartesian and Enlightenment thought.[6] Jonsson argues that Swedenborg only needed to make a few changes in his psychophysical speculations in *Economy of the Animal Kingdom* to arrive at the ideas he later re-ceived in spirit vision.[7] Inclined to the notion of unmediated revela-tion, Swedenborgians had also noted the visionary's canonical sayings that he had never read the Christian theosophists Jacob Boehme and William Law, preferring to keep his mind clear for spir-itual instruction. Indeed, his visionary works eschew any references save to Scripture, whose exposition was his divine commission. This discussion would therefore counter Benz's view and tend to present Swedenborg as an essentially scientific mind, whose later visions wrongly caused him to be stigmatized at best as an "esotericist" in the wake of a rejected tradition of *Naturphilosophie*, at worst as a "spirit-seer" and throwback to a superstitious age.[8]

Evidence related by Marsha Keith Schuchard also emphasizes Swedenborg's deep roots in the Western esoteric tradition. She has assembled proofs of Leibniz's interest in Rosicrucianism and

---

6. Inge Jonsson, *Emanuel Swedenborg* (New York: Twayne, 1971), 61–62, 81–82. This long-out-of-print work has recently been issued in a second edition as *Vision-ary Scientist: The Effects of Science and Philosophy on Swedenborg's Cosmology* (West Chester, Pa.: Swedenborg Foundation, 1999).

7. Inge Jonsson, "Emanuel Swedenborgs Naturphilosophie und ihr Fortwirken in seiner Theosophie," in *Epochen der Naturmystik: Hermetische Tradition in wis-senschaftlichen Fortschritt*, edited by Antoine Faivre and Rolf Christian Zimmermann (Berlin: Erich Schmidt, 1979), 251.

8. Wouter J. Hanegraaff, *New Age Religion and Western Culture: Esotericism in the Mirror of Secular Thought* (Leiden: E. J. Brill, 1996), 424–425.

Christian Cabala and how he influenced his brilliant Swedish colleague Eric Benzelius, encouraging him to visit the alchemist and Cabalist Francis Mercurius van Helmont (1618–1698). We of course already know Benzelius as young Swedenborg's mentor and beloved brother-in-law, in whose household he lived as a schoolboy and university student at Uppsala.[9] Schuchard's research suggests a continuity in Swedenborg's life-long interest in esoteric subjects, including Rosicrucianism, Freemasonry, and especially Christian Cabala. A particularly provocative suggestion is that Swedenborg may have had long-term involvement with an esoteric circle in London, headed by Samuel Jacob Falk, a mysterious Jewish alchemist and Cabalist, a group that, at various times in its history, included William Blake and the notorious adventurer and esoteric entrepreneur Cagliostro. The picture of Swedenborg drawn by Benz as a man not only interested in many aspects of spiritual insight but also a man engaged in worldly and social activity lends credence to this startling possibility.[10]

As the holder of the first university chair devoted to mystical and esoteric studies in Europe, Antoine Faivre has accomplished the scholarly classification of the Western esoteric tradition as an integral and coherent current of Christian theology. Faivre, who was a close friend of Ernst Benz, identifies key elements of this Hermetic tradition, expressed most simply in the words "As above, so below," in notions of correspondences between God, heaven, earth, and humanity, namely, macrocosm and microcosm; the idea of a living nature; the mediation of imagination and intermediaries on hierarchies of ascent between the planes; and the transmutation

9. Marsha Keith Schuchard, "Leibniz, Benzelius, and Swedenborg: The Kabbalistic Roots of Swedish Illuminism," in *Leibniz, Mysticism and Religion*, edited by Allison P. Coudert, Richard H. Popkin, and Gordon M. Weiner (Dordrecht: Kluwer, 1999), 84–106. However, see Jane Williams-Hogan, "The Place of Emanuel Swedenborg in Modern Western Esotericism," in *Western Esotericism and the Science of Religion*, edited by Antoine Faivre and Wouter J. Hanegraaff (Leuven: Peeters, 1998), 201–252, particularly 209–211.
10. Marsha Keith Schuchard, "Yeats and the Unknown Superiors: Swedenborg, Falk and Cagliostro," *The Hermetic Journal* 37 (Autumn 1987): 14–20; "Swedenborg, Jacobitism, and Freemasonry," in *Swedenborg and His Influence*, edited by Erland J. Brock et al (Bryn Athyn: Academy of the New Church, 1988), 359–379; "The Secret Masonic History of Blake's Swedenborg Society," *Blake: An Illustrated Quarterly* 26, no. 2 (Fall 1992): 40–51.

of the human soul.[11] Faivre and Benz also became close friends through the Eranos Conference, and it is interesting that their ideas have received a joint evaluation in the matter of Swedenborg. Jane Williams-Hogan, the leading Swedenborgian scholarly authority, has assessed Swedenborg's scientific and visionary work in the light of Faivre's categories. While the first, third, and fourth of Faivre's conditions of esotericism were fulfilled by Swedenborg's theology, Williams-Hogan noted that Swedenborg, qua post-Cartesian scientist, saw nature as having "no life of its own, even though it mirrors and can reveal the spiritual, and corresponds to it."[12] This reading suggests that Swedenborg saw a higher spiritual world of life mirrored by a lower material world, which is dead. As Wouter Haanegraaff has commented, the implications are again quite momentous for an understanding of Swedenborg's position and modernizing influence in the Western esoteric tradition.

Through scientific endeavors in anatomy, neurology, and psychology, Swedenborg had penetrated nature to the smallest elements without finding the seat of the soul on the material plane. Attempts to find traces of the divine in nature had brought him to an intellectual dead end, or in his own words, "an abyss."[13] Swedenborg's original debt to Descartes, Spinoza, and English science for a geometric, mechanical world picture was indeed later qualified by the influences of Christian Wolff and especially Andreas Rüdiger, who gave Swedenborg the organic, vitalist idea of an entelechy or intelligent hierarchy underlying the divine plan of evolution in all creation. However, the fundamental dualism of the transcendent and the natural can still be discerned in Swedenborg's conception of the natural world as a Cartesian *res extensa*. It had brought Swedenborg to

---

11. Antoine Faivre, "Introduction I," in *Modern Esoteric Spirituality*, edited by Antoine Faivre and Jacob Needleman (London: SCM Press, 1993), xi–xxii; *Access to Western Esotericism* (Albany: State University of New York Press, 1994), 10–15.
12. Jane Williams-Hogan, "The Place of Emanuel Swedenborg in Modern Western Esotericism," in *Western Esotericism and the Science of Religion*, edited by Antoine Faivre and Wouter J. Hanegraaff (Leuven: Peeters, 1998), 201–252, particularly 220.
13. Ibid., 222.

the limits of science. He essentially solved this impasse through a religious crisis followed by initiation into a world of spirits. Their salvific theology taught Swedenborg that a postmortem conjunction between the living Creator and his creation is possible in a place that is neither divine nor natural, but in a realm of the imagination known as heaven. Benz shows how this notion represents a major pastoral advance on Protestant and Catholic theology regarding the Last Judgment and resurrection. But through its residual dualism (contrary to the monist pansophy of early modern *Naturphilosophie*), we see the dawn of spiritualism, scientific occultism, and a new phase in the Western esoteric tradition.

Swedenborg's life and works document a long and immensely rich journey through the scientific and religious issues and movements of his age. It was a journey that began in his father's house of spirits and pious readings of Arndt's *True Christianity* and other improving books of the German Pietists. In his youth, the new sciences seized his imagination and beckoned him into a seemingly crystal clear world of mathematical calculation, technical invention, and engineering precision. Here God became a divine clockmaker, the transcendent master of a geometric, mechanical, and rational universe, whose second "Bible" was nature itself, to be read, discovered, and exploited by humankind. While Swedenborg sat beside Isaac Newton, William Whiston, and Samuel Clarke in his London years, their Arianism may have contributed to his early philosophical thinking. The influences of Germany, so important in Benz's explorations of Swedenborg's life, again intervened; and his readings of Leibniz, Wolff and Rüdiger brought Swedenborg a new resolution of Cartesian and Christian dualism, which was then compatible with his later "spiritualist" Christianity. As we know, Arianism could not be farther from Swedenborg's mature conception of the Trinity: he objected to its interpretation as three persons as tantamount to polytheism and believed there is a divine trinity, "but it is in the one person of the Lord, its distinguishable aspects being understood as soul, body, and resultant activity. . . . The unity of God in which there is a trinity, or the one God in whom there is a trine, does not exist separately in the Father or the Holy Spirit, but in the Lord alone, since the 'Father' or

'soul' of God and the 'Spirit' or 'activity' of God exist in and come
forth from the Lord only."[14]

The visionary and the scientist both lie on an intellectual and
spiritual continuum, which we today might describe in terms of conflict, growth, and individuation, to use the terminology of Carl Gustav Jung. Like all individual journeys, its coloration is highly
personal. The scientific years had brought Swedenborg into contact
with the Arian heresy, when his father feared for his son's soul
among the freethinkers of London. It is therefore most suggestive
that his religious crisis should involve images of reconciliation and
homecoming. Dreams of acceptance by his father culminated in an
archetypal experience of Pietism. At Easter 1744, Swedenborg fell
off his bed and found himself gazing into Jesus' face, radiant with
warmth and love. This was the new starting point for his individuation, culminating a year later in spirit vision and a commission from
God to give humankind a new religious revelation. This combined
an esoteric view of God, heaven, and earth with a strong desire for a
pietist reform of Lutheran orthodoxy. This remarkable body of writings has remained the lasting monument of the visionary savant in an
age of reason.

Note on the Text and Translation

This work was completed in the immediate aftermath of World War
II. Bomb damage, constraints on the freedom of movement, Allied
occupation, and postwar shortages in Germany inevitably left their
mark upon a work that had its genesis in the world of Weimar liberal
scholarship. The first edition of Verlag Hermann Rinn of Munich in
1948 was published under a Military Government Information Control License, which ensured that literature conformed with Allied requirements on re-education and de-Nazification. The license was
also necessary for paper allocations, given the severe restrictions of
Germany's war-ravaged economy prior to the currency reform.

Informed by the publisher that there was not sufficient paper to
print footnotes, Benz abandoned his referencing of the work. When

14. William Ross Woofenden, *Swedenborg Explorer's Guidebook: A Research Manual*
(West Chester, Pa.: Swedenborg Foundation, 2002), 278.

the second, revised edition of the work was published by the Swedenborg Verlag in Zürich in 1969, Benz attempted to complete the notes that he had prepared more than twenty years earlier. However, many of the quoted works were no longer available to him, and his former doctoral student Friedemann Horn (1921–2000), then editor-in-chief of Swedenborg Verlag, assisted him in this task of reconstitution. Horn has written widely on Swedenborg, including a major study of Schelling's engagement with Swedenborg's works.

This first English edition of Benz's book uses the second edition as the basis of the text, although reference has been made to the first edition where this was considered helpful to the reader. The footnotes provided by Benz and Horn in the second edition have been used and supplemented wherever this has been possible, including providing references to English translations where Horn had provided references only to German works.

NICHOLAS GOODRICK-CLARKE
2002

PART ONE:

The Path to Science

1

The Father's House

Emanuel Swedenborg was the scion of old established Swedish families of miners and ministers. [1] His heredity combined the miners' practical, technical capacity and knowledge of the mysteries of nature with the refined education of heart and spirit proper to old Swedish Lutheranism. The two clearly differentiated periods of his life, the first as an assessor of mines and the second when he devoted himself to theology, can be seen as the development of his dual ancestry.

His paternal grandfather, Daniel Isaacson, was a miner and pit owner who owned Sveden, an estate approximately a Swedish quarter mile from Falun. He had made a considerable fortune through the successful exploitation of a derelict and flooded mine in the Great Copper Mountain. Swedenborg's mother was also descended from an old family of miners. She was born Sarah Behm

---

1. For the following, see Immanuel Tafel, *Sammlung von Urkunden betreffend das Leben und den Charakter Emanuel Swedenborgs*, Bd. 1 (Tübingen, 1838), as well as *Bischof Jesper Swedberg, der Vater Emanuel Swedenborgs* (Frankfurt a.M., [c.1880]), hereafter cited in the text as *Swedberg*, a free translation from R. L. Tafel, *Documents concerning the Life and Character of Emanuel Swedenborg* (London, 1875).

(1666–1696), daughter of Albrecht Behm, assessor of the Board of Mines. The theological tradition was represented by his maternal great-grandfather, Master Peter Bullernaesius, pastor of Swärdsjö, who played a leading role among the clergy in the Great Copper Mountain district. Swedenborg's father, Jesper Swedberg, held him in especial esteem, even though Bullernaesius had been suspected by his peers of heretical papistic tendencies. Swedenborg owed his religious and theological inheritance especially to his father, later Bishop Jesper Swedberg (1653–1735).

Jesper Swedberg was one of the most prominent figures of his day. He lived during a great era of Swedish history, characterized politically by the deeds of King Charles XI and King Charles XII and religiously by the clashes of Lutheran orthodoxy with the revivalist movements of Pietism, enthusiasts, and other inspired groups. His education and training placed him in that current of the Swedish Lutheran Church that was receptive to the reforming ideas of German Pietism and that encouraged personal religious experience, combined with a practical manifestation of faith through a life of penitence and active neighborly love. Many aspects of the father's talent and outlook recur, albeit transformed, in the character of the son. The perennial conflict between father and son was also a highly significant factor in Swedenborg's development. For this reason, it is necessary to sketch the religious and spiritual life of the father, an unusually dynamic personality who stamped his own pious and spiritual life upon his surroundings and his family circle. Alongside his numerous other works, Jesper wrote a one-thousand page autobiography at the end of his life. This is a mine of information, not only for his personal life but also for the religious, ecclesiastical, spiritual, and political life of his era.

Two original traits are discernible in Bishop Swedberg's pious personality: first, an emphasis on the practical side of the Christian religion and, second, a direct visionary experience of the influence of the heavenly world upon the mundane, an experience expressed in his belief in angels and devils. According to his autobiography, these traits were already evident in his early youth.

Under the guidance of his mother, whom he described as a similar influence to Monica on St. Augustine, Jesper Swedberg early cultivated a strong personal piety, which colored his inner and outer development. In his youth, he fell into the millstream near his father's farm and was taken for dead when extricated from the mill-wheel. This incident confirmed his belief in the presence of a guardian angel. From this time on, he commended himself morning and evening to the protection of God and his holy angels, and he kept this resolution up until his death. Prompted by such experiences, he accustomed himself from an early age to read the Bible piously for himself and also to others while picking hops or at other opportunities on the paternal farm. "It always gave me the greatest pleasure to preach to people," he admitted. His theological studies in Lund acquainted him with orthodox scholasticism, which dominated the teaching of the theological faculties in all Protestant lands at that time and which chiefly oriented itself towards the logical and dialectical writings of German orthodoxy such as Scheibler's *Opus Logicum et metaphysicum*. Yet Jesper found little pleasure in this sort of scholastic methodology. After his initially secular life, he appears to have experienced a kind of conversion under the influence of Professor Brunner, dean of the faculty of Uppsala. Henceforth, he abandoned his fashionable clothes and wore a simple dark grey cloak. "In Brunner's house," he wrote, "I learned much of value, both in respect of morals and literary education. I learned especially how to lead a pious, respectable and serious life, for he [Brunner] was spiritually minded both in conversation and social interaction, in his clothing and above all in his whole being."

Angelic manifestations also continued to influence Jesper's development and steered him towards German Pietism and Reformed orthodoxy. "God protected me from bad company during my whole student life. My society and my greatest pleasure were the holy men of God, who wrote the Bible, and the many other men who have achieved high regard in God's Church and whose names are widely known in the scholarly world. God's angel stood next to me and said: 'What are you reading?' I answered: 'I am reading the Bible, Scriver, Lütkemann, Johann Arndt, Kortholt, Großgebau, J. Schmidt and others'" (*Swedberg*, 12).[2]

---

2. Swedenborg continually used the Bible translation of Sebastian Schmidt, who belonged to the Strasbourg orthodox reformers.

"The angel said further: 'Do you understand what you are reading in the Bible?' I answered: 'How can I understand without anyone explaining it to me?' The angel then said: 'Purchase Geier, J. and S. Schmidt, Dietrich, Tarnow, Gerhardi and Crell's *Biblical Concordance!*'" (*Swedberg*, 85) Thus, Swedenborg's father developed a great piety based on personal conversion, a contrite life, a practical application of faith, and the service of one's neighbor. He followed the angel's advice and became a student of the leaders of German Reformed orthodoxy.

His marriage to Sarah Behm had brought him a significant dowry and enabled him to travel abroad. This journey took him to England, France, Germany, and the Netherlands; and he became acquainted with the current trends of religious and ecclesiastical life in those countries. In England, the puritanical church life, especially the scrupulous observance of Sunday, made a deep impression upon him. In France, the charitable activity of the upper-class Catholic laity made him revise his previous criticism of popery. In Germany, he was particularly attentive to the leaders of Reformed orthodoxy and Pietism. Journeying from Strasbourg, he tried without success to visit Philipp Jacob Spener (1635–1705), the father of German Pietism, in Frankfurt. The unloving spirit of Lutheran and Reformed orthodoxy he met in the course of his journey made a frightful impression on him. He described the Hamburg orientalist Dr. Jean Esdras Edzardi, with whom he stayed two and a half months, as the most delightful acquaintance of his travels in Germany, saying: "I can barely describe what a holy and earnest life this man led!"

On his return, an ecclesiastical post enabled him to express his pious spirituality. Jesper was appointed army chaplain to the Royal Guard regiment in Stockholm. Like the pietistic padres of the Prussian soldier-king Frederick William I, the patron of August Hermann Francke, he felt he had a duty to educate his soldiers in practical Christian conduct. He did not limit himself to preaching but also gave religious instruction to his regiment. "According to royal decree, I examined them closely on the catechism at every review and at all their assemblies, albeit in the most mild and moderate fashion possible. Previously unaccustomed to such a thing, they told me later they trembled each time they saw me coming even more than when they were advancing toward the enemy. But once I had begun to speak amicably and gently with them, telling them stories from the Bible and strengthening them in faith and Christian life, the first company did not disperse when the second arrived, but they all thronged around me and almost overwhelmed me. Even the officers sat down voluntarily around the table and began to converse with me about good, useful and edifying things" (*Swedberg*, 18f).

When the regiment was occasionally posted to Upland, Jesper had to deputize for the court preacher in Stockholm and later succeeded to his appointment. In this office he proved his dauntless integrity and unbending character. In the style of the pietistic court preachers of Württemberg, who understood their office as a vocation to confront contemporary moral decline before princes and the court, he did not shy from openly censuring the abuses at court and in the land and urging their redress. Once he reproved the severity with which the king had handled the reduction of landlords' privileges. Immediately the commissioner of the reduction commission protested to the king. However, the king continued to favor the upright court preacher up until his death because, as Jesper wrote, "He liked to see when a serious, zealous servant of the Lord preached the truth in a pointed fashion and boldly stepped forward with no reserve to prove everything clearly by the word of God and without doing any violence to the same" (*Swedberg*, 23).

Others who felt personally attacked by his sermons were less generous. In one court sermon, Swedberg inveighed against the desecration of Sunday and laid the burden of blame on those whose duty it was to uphold the royal decrees concerning the sanctity of the day of rest. The high governor, Count Gyllenstjerna, felt personally attacked by this and directed vengeful glances upon the preacher during the service. "Before the sun could set on his anger," he arraigned Jesper and a wearisome lawsuit ensued, which ended with no disadvantage for the valiant champion of truth.

After serving for a short time in Vingåker, he was appointed by the king to the third professorial chair of theology at the University of Uppsala. Swedberg had already refused a series of high positions and did not want this high honor either, partly because of his lack of experience in the exercise of academic duties and partly because of his aversion to the scholarly disputes among the theologians of Uppsala. Among these, he said "there was one Bilberg, who did not even follow God's word sufficiently to acknowledge his authority in natural things but defended the view that Holy Scripture was only written for the mob." When Swedberg finally accepted the post at the request of the king, the rumor of his pietistic zeal preceded him, and there was already talk in university circles that no student would be permitted to wear a sword or a wig once this pietist arrived. There was good reason for this concern. Swedberg stood for the simple unpretentious customs of old times and stormed against the new luxurious fashions. "Only with sorrow in his heart" did he regard the elegant pastors of the new century, "going around in long powdered wigs, so that their silk coats were snow white over the shoulders and back." In a similar fashion, he opposed "the annoying ladies' headgear known as *fontange*, highly offensive to God, the angels, and every God-fearing Christian." Even his own family felt his disapproval. He wrote of his wife: "When everyone wore the sinful and shameless headgear known as *fontange*, she and her children followed the crowd, but when they heard that a cow in Gotland with great pain, torment and heart-breaking roaring had given birth to a calf with a *fontange*, she took her own *fontange* and that of her daughters and threw them onto the fire and vowed solemnly that neither she nor her daughters, so long as they stood under her sway, would ever wear such a thing again" (*Swedberg*, 92).

At the university, Jesper directed his reforming activity toward more important things than the swords and wigs of the students. He knew how to reconcile quarrelling parties, uphold the order and discipline of academic life with a strong hand, and was soon appointed rector of the university to guide the academic life of Uppsala. His simultaneous nomination as dean of Uppsala Cathedral gave him a comparable influence over the citizenry and public life. He now became extremely active. His professorship and his preaching appointment required him to give many lectures, services, catechisms, debates, and speeches. His lectures on the New Testament and moral theology had a predominantly practical and improving note. They were given in a lively fashion and exhorted the students again and again to practice a sober, practical Christianity. He was tirelessly active as a pastor and preacher. He preached every Friday, on Sundays in the morning and evening, and at all church festivals during the week. Between early prayers and the morning service, he held catechism lessons for the youth of the town and the students.

Even after the accession of the "young lion," King Charles XII, Swedberg continued preaching before the court with his usual fearlessness. When Charles demanded from the clergy a further tenth of their incomes in addition to the extraordinary taxes already levied in order to finance his military plans, no one dared to present the complaint of the clergy to the monarch. Even Swedberg became cautious, but the proven spiritual combatant found a way around the king. In the petition that he handed to the king after his audience, he wrote under his signature: Genesis 47:22. The king had the quotation looked up and found the words: "The only land he did not acquire belonged to the priests, for the priests received an allowance from Pharaoh and lived on the allowance that Pharaoh gave them." Thereupon Charles declared: "Leave the clergy in peace and give them what they usually have!" (*Swedberg*, 53) When Jesper sought out the king on this occasion in Kungsör, a great masked ball was in preparation for the following days. He asked the minister of Kungsör to "preach the masked ball out of the heads of the king and his nobles." When the minister refused, Jesper ascended the pulpit himself and zealously explained to the assembled congregation that it was no time to amuse oneself in such pleasures and that the sanctity of Sunday permitted no Christian to participate. The masked ball was actually cancelled, a success that Jesper glossed with the words "a zealous Samuel or Nathan signifies the welfare of a land, but a flattering Uriah causes much misery" (*Swedberg*, 53).

In 1702, Jesper was appointed Bishop of Skara and moved to Brunsbo. There he embarked on a busy life filled with the practical care of souls in all circles and estates of his diocese. In this last phase of his life, he came to epitomize the figure of a truly classical and popular Swedish bishop. He also took on educational matters—as bishop he was simultaneously head of the Skara Grammar School—public and private welfare, and ecclesiastical morals with a strong hand and practical understanding. He remained a loyal adviser not only to Charles XII but also to Queen Ulrike Eleonore. Indeed, he

publicly distinguished himself in a political matter under Ulrike
Eleonore. The military campaigns of Charles XII had brought the
whole country to the brink of ruin, and so the nobility pressed for a
restriction of royal absolutism, but Swedberg raised the strongest objection against such a measure.

The cleverness with which Swedberg sought to incorporate the
reformist tendencies of Pietism within the established Church
proved favorable for the ecclesiastical development of Sweden.
Pietism had appeared in Sweden with strongly separatist tendencies.
The strict laws proclaimed against the Pietist communities confirmed
their view that the established Church was truly Antichrist and the
demonic Babel and that one should abandon it to save one's soul.
With his insistence on personal conversion and a practical Christian
life, Swedberg was close to Pietism, and he sympathized with the
criticism of orthodox excesses too keenly not to regret such a development most profoundly. When various measures were decided at
the Imperial Diet of 1723 to limit the spread of Pietist meetings, he
visited one such congregation in the house of Chamberlain von Wol-
cker and was convinced that nothing contradicted the spirit of true
Reformed Christianity. He closed the meeting with an address: "I
am happy to have seen and heard how these meetings are conducted.
Furthermore, I can only approve them and must say that it would be
desirable if every father held similar meetings in his house" (*Swedberg*, 73). In conclusion, he drew the assembly's attention to several
matters which could lead to abuses and misinterpretations. Above
all, he disputed the view of several present that, when a clergyman
had not been converted, his office was empty. He shared the impressions he gained here with the Imperial Church Council and achieved
a more considerate treatment of Pietist aspirations.

Besides his practical activity, which took him on annual visits
through all the parishes of his see and also to Lund, Stockholm, and
Uppsala, he found time for literary work, whose volume overshad-
ows everything that the theologians of his century, themselves great
writers, achieved. Jesper himself derived his fondness for writing
books from an interpretation of his Christian name, which means in
Hebrew "he shall write." He asserted that ten carts could scarcely
hold everything that he had written and printed, "and yet," he

added, "there is almost as much unpublished material." The printing press that had been set up at his request in Brunsbo largely served to publish his own works. These were mostly practical writings for improvement, especially collections of sermons, whose titles take the form of puns and alliterations, e.g., *Ungdomsregel och ålderdomsspegel* (Rules for the Young and a Mirror for the Old) and *Casa Pauperum et Gaza Divitum* (House of the Poor and Treasure of the Rich). He also authored school books, among them his *Book of Sentences* in seven parts for elementary and grammar schools, with whose help one could learn Latin, Greek, and some Hebrew "in a pleasant fashion almost as a game." At the same time, biblical works played a great role, like his *Biblia Parva*, an abridged popular Bible, for which he received a royal privilege for nine years and ten thousand reams of duty-free paper, as well as several practical Bible commentaries (*Swedberg*, 80f).

Swedberg's literary style reflected the blunt, realistic cast of his thought and piety. It was quite different from contemporary academic sermons due to its lack of dogmatic polemic, its support for practical moral life, and a strongly personal note. The usual long, abstract discussions were replaced by sermons full of stories drawn from his own life to illuminate the text and, even more importantly, reports of miracles and revelations that had befallen him. It is a living expression of his piety wholly rooted in personal outlook and experience.

However, his literary works caused him much vexation. In 1686, he was appointed by the king as a member of the commission to oversee the revision of the Swedish translation of the Bible. He immediately took on the main task, produced a meticulous revision of the entire text of the Bible, and advanced the sum of 50,000 copper thalers belonging to his wife and children to the printer for paper and type. But the other members of the commission became jealous. When the printing was already underway, the chairman declared the old Swedish Bible translation superior, saying "there was nothing in it that required alteration." So Jesper forfeit not only effort but also money. His attempts to improve the Swedish psalter and hymnal took a similar turn. Once again, Jesper bore the brunt of the work and the costs. But when the revised edition appeared in print, there was a storm of complaint and intrigue despite the previous approval of the work by the authorities. The end result was that the edition remained unsold, and Swedberg once again lost a fortune of 30,000 thalers.

One of his works deserves special mention. In his *Schibboleth*, Jesper had proposed a plan to purge all foreign influences from the Swedish language. The director of the Board of Mines, Urban Hjärne, criticized this work, caricaturing in numerous witty and spiteful examples Swedberg's effort to restore the strong biblical coloration of the old Swedish language in opposition to the modern influence of French language and vocabulary. The king, who staunchly supported Swedberg's linguistic purism, said to him: "Does one speak Swedish in France? Then why should we speak French in Sweden?" He then drew Swedberg's attention to Hjärne's polemic and lent him his copy. Jesper read it through, wrote his objections to Hjärne on half a sheet of paper, and stuck this page at the front of the king's copy. Here he expressed his amazement that the censors had permitted the printing of a book which "was filled with personal and coarsely comical remarks" and thus violated the royal censorship laws. But he was informed by a "highly placed gentleman" that Hjärne's text would have turned out far more unseemly if the censors had not already deleted the most violent attacks.

The life and thought of Swedberg are permeated by a true religious realism akin to early Christianity. God, Christ, the Devil, the angels, heaven and hell, the Last Judgment—these are the realities that rule all human life. The world is the battlefield on which God struggles with the Devil for the souls of men. The whole realm of existence is interwoven with the powers of heaven and hell. The longing for redemption from the dominion of the Devil and sin extends to the depths of creation. St Paul's description of the sighing of all living creatures possessed a literal truth for Swedberg: he believed he heard everywhere how the animals and even inanimate things complained about the sins of men. Insentient nature also had feeling, reason, and voice in his view. If a thief steals a fish from a lake, the fish withdraw from it. If apples are stolen from a tree, it no longer brings forth in abundance. Even furniture complains about the sins of men. "When one unexpectedly hears chests and wardrobes cracking, it seems that something experiences pain within them. The utensils are anxious and sigh about the godlessness gaining ground, angering God and deceiving the angels."

Heavenly powers are mediated to human beings by the angels. Jesper speaks of God and the angels almost always in the same breath. The heavenly world of God is represented here on earth through the angelic spirits, which execute the dominion of God on earth and protect his rights. Humanity is linked to heaven by the angels. They are continually ascending and descending between heaven and earth, as on the ladder of Jacob's dream. They are dispatched as serving spirits to watch over humankind. Every person has one or more such guardian angels to protect him or her when the Devil is abroad "like a roaring lion" and threatening to ensnare that person. They protect people even when they are unconscious and have lost control of themselves, "just as drunkards and intemperate men often do things, that would cause their death even if they had ten lives, if they were not protected by the angels around them."

In Jesper's case, these thoughts were no abstract speculations but derived from personal experience. He felt his angel was watching over him when he fell into the mill-wheel, and his angel had guided him during his studies. His ordination as minister and later consecration as bishop had only fortified his belief in angels. "We priests," he once exclaimed, "I say this with tears, have sworn on our knees before the altar of the Lord and in the presence of the holy angels to maintain the laws of the Church." He sensed the presence of God's angels in church services. They stood around the altar and hovered around the pulpit. He related how, when he was preaching one day in 1663 in the Hoby Church in the seminary at Lund, loud voices singing hymns could be heard in the church, which at that time had no organ. Everyone in the village heard them. From this time on, he felt an even deeper reverence for public worship and the priestly office, which strengthened his conviction that "God's angels perpetually attend this holy office." Following his consecration he celebrated the anniversary of this day, calling it "the great festival of a great sinner" (*Swedberg*, 84f).

Such experiences induced him to explain the relations between angels and humanity in terms of rationalism—hence Swedberg's statements about the angelic language, which recur in the visionary theology of his son. When, in the course of his journey overseas in 1685, Jesper was taking his leave in Hamburg from his friend Edzardi, he discussed with him what language they would speak with each other when they met again in heaven. As Edzardi fell silent, Swedberg continued: "I believe, we will speak the angelic language. As the angels speak Swedish with the Swedes, German with the Germans, and English with the English, I will speak Swedish one day with Abraham, Isaac, and Jacob, and they will answer me in the same language. I cannot believe that we should not speak in heaven. Talking is truly characteristic of mankind" (*Swedberg,* 86). Similar ideas also occur in his later sermons. In a Lenten sermon, he told his congregation that in heaven "we will speak with tongues and learn such things as would have cost us much toil and trouble on earth." "And I believe that when we speak for example with Abraham and he with us, we will be talking in our Swedish language, which he understands, and he will answer in Hebrew, which we will understand. When we speak with St. Peter, we will be speaking our Swedish, while he will speak in his Syriac or Greek."

As in the case of the angels, Jesper Swedberg formed his own mental image of the deceased in heaven. He was firmly convinced that the dead continued to share in the lives of their relatives on earth. They retained their earthly memory, but it was "more pure, refined and clear" above. Whenever someone is converted on earth, that person's dead relatives dwelling in heaven experience a blessed feeling. Jesper was even of the opinion that the deceased intercede with God for their relatives on earth. This belief was based on personal experience. He asked his eldest son Albrecht, who died shortly after his mother in 1696, on his deathbed what he would do in heaven and he replied, "I will pray for my father and mother." This answer affected the father most profoundly. In the name of his children, he composed an inscription for the gravestone of his spouse, in which he expressed this idea of the intercession of the dead for the living. One of his opponents copied the inscription and denounced Jesper to the king, saying the professors in Uppsala were about to become Catholics and pray to the saints. Swedberg justified himself before the king in a subtle manner, asking him "whether His Majesty did not believe that the late Queen Mother in heaven prayed for him and his children?"

(*Swedberg*, 86). The matter was not mentioned again. Later Jesper intended to hold a debate on this subject for the award of a doctorate in theology, but he renounced the subject in deference to the king's reproof. As with the intercession of the dead for the living, he firmly believed that the dead might appear to the living by God's leave. Only religious deniers and the godless, he thought, could contest the fact "that there were spiritual apparitions."

Like the angels, the Devil was a reality for him, with whose power he had to reckon at every moment. He lived in the firm conviction that the Devil was making an attempt on his life for fear that Jesper's militancy in God's cause would do too much damage to the satanic realm. He saw his own biography as a history of failed assassinations that Satan had undertaken against him, in order to destroy him, the champion of the kingdom of God. It was the Devil who had pushed him as a seven-year-old child into the millstream, the Devil who had caused him all possible misfortune in later life and gave him no peace. Shortly before Jesper's appointment as bishop of Skara, God made it known to him through a dream that Satan would also oppose him in Västergötland and furiously rush upon him in order to kill him. In the dream, he saw the Devil jeering with a spear in hand as he followed the episcopal carriage. When he awoke from this dream, he had the unmistakable sensation that the Evil One "was standing visibly in his bedroom." Swedberg lived in a perpetual struggle with the Devil and punished him with prayers and psalms. But the threats of Satan did not impress him, and he retained a rock-solid conviction that the Devil could find no fault in him. In 1719, when he was fiercely attacked by his ecclesiastical and political opponents, he declared with an elevated sense of election, "At least I know that God has commanded my angel to keep a crown in readiness for Him to place upon my head when I depart from this place and enter the kingdom of God" (*Swedberg*, 86).

The more external misfortunes afflicted him, the more Swedberg was convinced that the Devil could find no inner flaw in him. Jesper had every reason to believe in such hidden motives of his destiny. Strangely enough, he was bedevilled by fires throughout his whole life. His home in Uppsala was burnt down twice. He attributed the cause of the great fire of 1702 to "the many grievous sins of the people," on account of which the Devil was empowered to light the blaze. In 1710, he was struck by the great fire of Skara. In 1712, the episcopal residence in Brunsbo was burned to the ground, and all his books and manuscripts were destroyed. But he interpreted even this misfortune as a punishment of God, who had given Satan power over him: "I sorrowfully confess my sins, which fanned God's anger; but I am grateful that I could endure it in good spirits" (*Swedberg* 59). However, he received a comforting sign on the occasion of this fire: "What a marvel! Johann Arndt's *Little Garden of Paradise* and my own *Exercises in Catechism* were discovered in the ashes, their bindings merely charred! I deduce that God has not wholly rejected my modest work and I feel heartened to continue my previous work so far as God's grace allows" (*Swedberg*, 60). A copper medal bearing the likeness of the bishop also survived and upon it his son Emanuel later engraved the following verse:

> In the heat of the flames, this image remained intact,
> When your house was consumed by fire in the night.
> So, father, will your name and memory be with us
> A loving bequest beyond fire and the grave.
>
> (*Swedberg*, 97)

In 1730, the seventy-seven-year-old was once more afflicted by a fire, and, as in 1712, he lost all he owned. However, he did not survive this blow of fate unscathed, and thenceforth he was shaky and had difficulty in writing.

Jesper's early Christian and charismatic faith gave him the firm conviction that he could rely on the power and assistance of God to combat the Devil, wherever he appeared in the form of sickness and possession. Like the later Swabian Pietists, especially Johann Christoph Blumhardt (1805–1880), Jesper was a powerful exorcist and achieved impressive results in this respect. Several people suffering severe depressions with suicidal inclinations assured him that he had healed them by his prayer and powerful exhortation. It is no wonder that, in the years 1712 and 1713, a rumor spread "through the whole country, even as far as Holland, England and other places" that "the Devil had come to me in Brunsbo in the shape of a cavalier to discuss the situation of Sweden and the outcome of the war, whereupon I drove him out through a small hole in the window pane" (*Swedberg*, 89). He once took into his service a maid who had suffered fits and been healed by him. Following an unexpected argument with another maid, a fit overwhelmed her, and she went into the drying room to suffocate herself. The bishop, sitting over his books, was suddenly troubled by a strong feeling of anxiety inexplicably linked to this maid. Involuntarily he yielded to this anxiety, enquired after the maid, and found her face down, mute and motionless, in the drying room. "We laid her on the bed like a stick of wood. I began to sob and cried out in a loud voice: 'Kerstin, awake and rise up, in the name of Jesus Christ!' Immediately she came to, became active, raised herself and began to speak. Afterwards I strengthened her with the Word of God and gave her a good draught of Rhine wine, whereupon she stood up and went about her work" (*Swedberg*, 88f). On another occasion, a female sinner was brought to him who was to pay for her misdeeds on the gallows. He took her into his study, awoke her heartfelt remorse, and gave her absolution, whereupon "she cheerfully went to her death the next day" (*Swedberg*, 90). Soon afterwards, a possessed man was brought to him. The Devil in this person shouted at the bishop: "You grey, old short-haired man, you have played a trick on me, you have stolen my roast joint—you will have to do me a penance" (*Swedberg*, 90). This was actually a reference to the old woman, whom the bishop had converted before her death. The words "You must do me a penance!" came back to the bishop when his house in Brunsbo was burnt down in February 1712. The fire started in the very same room where he had converted the sinner and driven the Devil out! The cheated Devil revenged himself on Jesper in the same spot. "But the Devil gained little by it. Since then God has restored everything to me twofold, like Job, and has given me a much more comfortable house and residence" (*Swedberg*, 90f).

Such a charismatic personality naturally drew kindred spirits to himself. Possessed persons were brought to him, maids speaking in tongues came to him, and wherever a miracle became known in the land, one called upon the Bishop of Skara. He it was, who drove out the Devil through prayer, the laying on of hands, exhortation, and exorcism, he who awakened true repentance in all who believed themselves lost to Satan, and he who healed all those who felt that they had earned God's punishment through especially grievous sins.

His belief in the existence of angels and the Devil had been confirmed from childhood in visions, dreams, and revelations. He actually saw the angels and spoke with them. At the age of thirteen, he had his first vision of heaven and hell. The Savior was standing in a great bath filled with lukewarm water, washing all those whom he wished to redeem, and admitted them into a heavenly chamber on his right side. There sat the elect, "naked in their communal joy and rapture, in holy harmlessness and complete innocence." On his left side was hell, where the damned performed ugly and lewd dances in a pit, whence sulphurous vapors were rising. "And however much they tried with all their power to climb out of the pit, I fancied they were driven back and pushed with fire forks amidst plaintive howling and terrible whining into the abyss." In the first year of his university studies, he had such a remarkable dream that he did not know whether he should regard it as a revelation. "No human tongue can utter and no angel describe what I saw and heard on that occasion." Such experiences continued throughout his whole life and strengthened him in a belief in the miraculous interpenetration of the world and the supernatural, the cause of all mystery in life.

Swedberg influenced the life of his family and his closer acquaintances in the most fervent fashion. But the seriousness and solid dignity of his personality was softened at home by an amiable kindness. The daily house prayers did not take the strict form then customary among most orthodox families. They had the character of "spiritual refreshment," in common with the title of a famous pietistic book of improvement. These evening sessions also assumed a special atmosphere through an artistic touch. The bishop was a great music lover and considered it a special grace of God that he had sent a distinguished musician to his house in the person of Dr. Hesselius, who "had mastered the cello and played such beautiful and divine songs on it every evening, whereupon I can retire with calmness and joy." Swedberg had composed or translated a series of beautiful hymns himself, including Melanchthon's hymn to the holy angels, which totally expressed his religious viewpoint. A further kindly aspect of his nature, evident in his daily life, was the lack of any vengefulness

or resentment. Whenever he sat at table in company, he never omitted to drink the health of his enemies. For all his severity, he was
never intransigent, and he always showed this benevolent side of his
nature in the education of his children and in family life.

2

Schooldays and University Years

Jesper Swedberg still held the office of army chaplain when his son Emanuel—the third of eight children that his first wife bore him—was born in Stockholm on 29 January 1688. At that time, all members of the family bore the name Swedberg. It was only in 1719 that the family of Bishop Swedberg was raised to the hereditary nobility and henceforth bore the name Swedenborg. Extraordinarily little is known about the youth of Emanuel. His father gave him the name Emanuel to remind him constantly of the goal and duty of his life. "The name of my son, Emanuel, means 'God-with-us,' so that he shall always be mindful of God's presence and possess that righteous, holy, secret union which links us through faith with our benevolent and merciful God." Thus wrote Jesper in his autobiography and he surely influenced his son to live up to this name.

It is likely that Swedenborg inherited his visionary gifts from his father. A pronounced religious gift was already evident in the child, conspicuous to his parents and the family's circle of acquaintances. Swedenborg himself spoke of his youth in two references: in his *Spiritual Diary* and in a letter to his friend and student Dr. Gabriel Beyer, dated 14 November 1769. In both, he indicated an intense religious life from an early age, in which fervent prayer and mystical experiences played a part.

In his *Spiritual Diary*, he speaks of the "inner breath," which he believed linked him with angels and spirits. He mentioned how he first became accustomed to this method of breathing at morning and evening prayer. A second comment in the quoted letter indicates that his religious life bore a strongly speculative trait in his early years and that religious reflections occupied his thoughts to a large degree. "From my fourth until my tenth year, my thoughts were constantly occupied with God, salvation and the spiritual conditions of men. I often uttered things which made my parents wonder and think that angels must be speaking through my mouth."[1] In conclusion, he reported how he had proclaimed the fundamental thoughts of his later visionary knowledge of God already as a boy in conversations with clergy.

However, both remarks must be treated with caution: Swedenborg reinterpreted his own youthful piety in the light of his later outlook and sought to demonstrate the inner continuity and direct divine guidance of his development into a visionary. There is no mention of Emanuel's precocious religious gift in the diary of his father, who noted all wonderful events in the sphere of family life.

Nonetheless, one can certainly deduce from the autobiographical remarks of the later Swedenborg that he had a strong tendency toward visionary experience in his childhood, which was significantly encouraged by his religious education and the spiritual milieu of his father's house. At this time, he developed a special sense of the reality and physical presence of the transcendental world, which played such a great role in the religious outlook of his father in the form of angels and the Devil, spirits and demons. He grew up in an

---

1. Letter to Dr. Beyer, dated Nov. 14, 1769, printed in *Leben und Lehre Emanuel Swedenborgs. Eine Sammlung authentischer Urkunden über Swedenborgs Persönlichkeit, und ein Inbegriff seiner Theologie in wörtlichen Auszügen aus seinen Schriften*, ed. I.G. Mittnacht (Frankfurt a.M., 1880), 61f. Hereafter cited in text as LL.

[The letters cited in this text under "LL" can be found in English translation in R. L. Tafel, *Documents concerning the Life and Character of Emanuel Swedenborg*, 2 vols. in 3 parts (London: Swedenborg Society, 1875–1877).]

atmosphere in which all blessings or blows of fate, all illnesses, conflagrations and floods were perceived as the action of either heaven or hell. Miracles, apparitions and dreams played an important role. With such a charismatic father, it is small wonder that young Emanuel should constantly direct his religious imagination towards such things. To him, the heavenly world appeared even more real than this earthly one, and his religious outlook from an early age grew to embrace this miraculous world.

Yet there must have been a conscious break with the religious attitude of his early youth by the time he went to school. During his time at school and university, there are no expressions of a particularly religious life or speculations. Even later he makes no mention of visionary experiences during this period. From the moment when his father moved to Brunsbo upon his appointment as Bishop of Skara in 1702 and left the son to continue his studies in Uppsala, Emanuel devoted all his gifts and energies to the sciences, with which he believed he could conquer the earthly world. For several decades, all expressions of religious speculation and the exercise of personal piety abated almost completely. He would be fifty years old before being swept into a powerful religious crisis.

In Uppsala, the young student was entrusted to his brother-in-law Erik Benzelius the Younger (1675–1743), under whose supervision he pursued his studies at the university. He could not have found a better teacher. Although Benzelius was thirteen years older and was already at the peak of his fame as a brilliant ornament of Swedish humanism, the family and scholarly contact between the scholar and the young student soon deepened into a personal friendship. Emanuel was not only a receiver but also a giver who influenced his teacher with an abundance of ideas. His father followed the intellectual development of the student with misgivings, and Erik Benzelius appears in the letters, which Emanuel later wrote to him from London and Paris, as the intermediary between father and son.

The world of science that opened for Swedenborg under the guidance of Erik Benzelius was the world of Swedish humanism. By the turn of the seventeenth and eighteenth centuries, European scholarship in Germany, France, England, and the Netherlands had long since specialized in the individual disciplines of history, literature, and language. The claims to pre-eminence of humanistic scholarship had already been shaken by the triumphant arrival of the new natural sciences of mathematics, astronomy, geology, and physics. However, in Sweden, humanism still flourished in its older universalist form because it had appeared later here than in continental Europe. The research of Erik Benzelius retained this early humanist, universalist character. It embraced all branches of traditional scholarship: history, including that of the ancient world, philosophy, and the Christian Church; ancient and modern literature; comparative studies of language; the study of ancient documents and—as a particular feature of Swedish humanism—Nordic antiquity with its investigation of Germanic traditions. The humanistic style of his research was characterized by his learned correspondence with the leading scholars of Europe concerning all these branches of learning. He also founded the first learned society of Sweden, the "Collegium curiosorum" and actively helped advance gifted young researchers by recommending them to his learned friends overseas for further study abroad.

However, Benzelius' research was not limited to the old Erasmian disciplines of literature and history. He combined his studies in the arts with a busy involvement in all the problems and findings of modern natural science, to whose advancement he energetically contributed at the University of Uppsala.

Swedenborg was introduced to the world of humanism by Benzelius and learned to command classical studies so swiftly that he mastered their most important tenets and was capable of writing good Latin prose and composing Latin poems of learned content for various family or patriotic occasions. Reverence for humanistic scholarship impressed him so deeply that, on arriving in London, he paid homage to the great humanist Isaac Casaubon (1559–1614) at his grave in Westminster Abbey. He felt himself "seized by so great a love for this learned hero" that he kissed his gravestone and wrote some Latin stanzas in praise of his fame (LL, 37).

However, his heart was not so much in the old humanities but in mathematics, geometry, astronomy, and technology. We do not know whether it was solely Erik Benzelius who awakened and encouraged this love. In the letters that Swedenborg wrote to

Benzelius from England and France, he describes him generally as the adviser and patron of his studies, but the student appears more the stimulus and pioneer of scientific studies than a pupil. Olof Rudbeck (1630–1702), another great Swedish humanist, has also been suggested as the stimulus for Swedenborg's scientific studies. In his later writings on geology and physics, Swedenborg often refers to the theories of Rudbeck, according to which Sweden was once "Attland's great island" and the cradle of humankind. But in his letters from England, he does not mention Rudbeck in connection with his scientific studies, but rather a circle of friends in Uppsala who shared an interest in the new sciences. Apart from Erik Benzelius, these were mostly mathematicians, especially Pehr Elvius, the professor of mathematics and astronomy. The question remains unanswered as to which scholars in Uppsala inducted him into the mysteries of modern science. It is only certain that his personal efforts were increasingly directed toward the scientific disciplines and that he was attracted by the promise of their technical application.

Swedenborg especially admired Christopher Polhem (1661–1751) as the model of the new learning in Sweden. As the leading representative of the mechanical and technical sciences in the land, this man was known as the "Machaon of the North." Charles XII discovered this engineer and called upon him for the execution of military, mining, and shipbuilding projects. Polhem must have seemed the true sovereign of mechanics, who was able to transform the calculation of degrees and numbers into technical inventions and to subdue nature with the aid of her own laws. Swedenborg was bent on making personal contact with Polhem and, if possible, becoming his assistant. In accordance with Emanuel's wish, his father Jesper wrote to Polhem asking if he might take his son into his house, but the request was initially turned down. In June 1710, Jesper, together with Benzelius, repeated his request to Polhem, and this time he received an assent indicating that the famous engineer already assumed significant technical knowledge on the part of the student. He wrote that he would appreciate Swedenborg's presence "in order that he may assist me in my current mechanical project and carry out the necessary experiments. On this subject I am more obliged to him than he to me."

However, this offer came to nothing, as Swedenborg had meanwhile persuaded his father to realize a wish even closer to his heart: a study journey to England. Polhem might well be a great researcher in his field, but the foundations and development of the new science were not taking place in Sweden but in England. There Isaac Newton, Edmund Halley, and John Flamsteed were teaching; there stood the great new observatories, laboratories, and technical workshops; there was the Royal Society, which embraced the leaders of the modern sciences, over which the king presided. Swedenborg felt powerfully drawn to England. Yet even later in England, he had not given up his plan of staying with Polhem, as his letter of 13 October 1710 makes clear: "I have not completely dismissed from my mind the thought of a journey to Polhammer, the Machaon of our age; I have only postponed it until I return with God's help to my fatherland. I would be guilty not only of indifference but also ingratitude, if I failed to take advantage of so great a man's teaching, unique in our country" (LL, 37).

Erik Benzelius gave his young brother-in-law much support in his preparations for the journey to England and also gave him numerous introductions to his English contacts. Emanuel also asked him for a recommendation to the Collegium Anglicanum, in order to complete his studies in mathematics, physics, and natural history. The journey to England provides, for the first time, a greater insight into the life and intellectual development of Swedenborg. While abroad, he wrote numerous letters to Erik Benzelius, which represent the oldest authentic documents for his biography and show the unfolding of his mental activity and the variety of his knowledge and endeavor.

The very first letters demonstrate the remarkable, proud self-confidence of youth. The student felt superior to his Swedish teachers in the new sciences and already had great plans prior to his departure for England. "As it was always my wish to devote myself to useful ends while completing my studies, in pursuance of which I sought your advice and approval, I believe I shall shortly undertake an object, which I can perform over time, while combining it with much that I will observe and read in foreign lands. I have always applied this method to my reading, and now, before my departure,

I am planning to compile a mathematical reader."[2] This work was intended to contain not only the mathematical advances of the preceding two centuries but also future discoveries and "include all
branches of mathematics, and I hope it will be of much use on my
travels, as I can incorporate everything I note in regard to mathematics." Somewhat presumptuously, he asked Benzelius to persuade
Polhem to keep him abreast of his latest inventions, even before
showing them to anyone else. He wanted to include these inventions
in his summary; indeed, Polhem's applied mechanics would be the
crown of the whole work! Filled with such plans and expectations,
Swedenborg traveled to England at the end of September 1710.

---

2. R. L. Tafel, *Documents concerning the Life and Character of Emanuel Swedenborg*,
vol. 1 (London: Swedenborg Society, 1875), 200ff; hereinafter cited in the text as
Tafel. Volume number will also be cited in text.

3

Study Years in England

England was the first destination of the young Swedenborg, eager for scientific knowledge. It was also the country where the first congregation of admirers and disciples would gather round the later visionary. However, this land offered no friendly reception to the new arrival. Just as in old tales, the prince must undergo many trials before he reaches the land of his heart's desire and opens the gates of the enchanted castle, so all kinds of opposing forces hindered the young student from entering the land of Newton, Halley, and Flamsteed. The ship carrying him from Göteborg to London ran aground on a sandbank off the English coast in thick fog, "whereupon all believed themselves lost as the ship's keel was only a quarter fathom from the bank." The ship was then boarded by a privateer, whose crew passed themselves off as Frenchmen, "while we took them for Danes." The situation was further complicated when the English coastguard vessel, receiving a report of the privateer, mistook the Swedish sailing ship for the pirate vessel and fired a broadside, mercifully without inflicting much damage.

But this was not the end of the adventure. A rumor had spread in England that plague had broken out in Sweden, and the coastal authorities gave instructions to hold all Swedish ships for six weeks' quarantine. Swedenborg saw himself in the unpleasant situation of having to spend six weeks with the other travellers confined on the cramped sailing ship with the promised land right before his eyes. When several members of the Swedish colony in London learned of their compatriots' plight, they had some fun in rowing out to the quarantine ship. Naturally, the enterprising student was among those lured into going secretly ashore. Thus, it came about that Sweden-borg was arrested by the English police immediately after his arrival in London. His youthful eagerness had landed him in the most un-pleasant situation imaginable. The English police considered it their medical and social duty to hang such violators of quarantine, espe-cially when it was a matter of the plague. The student was finally saved from the gallows by the intercession of influential members of the Swedish colony. He was acquitted with a severe reprimand and the solemn assurance that the next Swede to break the quarantine would be hanged without fail (LL, 48).

By 1710, England had overcome the crises of the Glorious Revo-lution and was about to claim world hegemony, confident of its grow-ing power and newly won empire. The political importance of the overseas possessions, conquered for the motherland by bold and en-terprising seafarers, was becoming more and more obvious. The East India Company earned enormous profits; the South Sea Company had just been founded; the produce of the world flowed into Eng-land. The expansion of England's political and economic power was accompanied by its intellectual world conquest. The new knowledge that Swedenborg encountered in the observatories, at academy lec-tures, and in the conversation of learned and aristocratic circles, pro-claimed that the mystery of the universe was contained in its numbers. Geometry, mathematics, physics, and mechanics were keys to the knowledge of reality and all the riddles of life, not only the movement of the stars but even the enigmas of the human mind and soul. The advanced methods of calculation, worked out by Newton and Leibniz, supported the refined optical apparatus of telescopes and microscopes that contemporary scientists were constantly seeking to improve. Mechanics was the inseparable companion of the mathemat-ical study of nature. If mathematics was the art of calculating the numbers and dimensions underlying all motion and states of matter, mechanics was the application of this science to master reality and to make it useful to all. The calculation of numbers and dimensions, which underlay the structure and motion of bodies, enabled inventors to apply this knowledge and suborn matter and space to human power with machines. The discovery that all was dimension and number encouraged human beings to shake off their numinous terror of the universe. In their infancy, modern mechanics and technology were considered akin to medieval magic and sorcery and attended by the fear of demons. The old masters still feared that they were illicitly disturbing the firm foundations of God's sacred order with their machines and that human beings should not change things. But once the mysterious reality of nature could be deduced from number, dimension, and simple mathematical laws, it lost its terror and could be put to the service of humanity without misgivings.

The new science and technology spurred each other on. Science taught technology to make nature more pliant to its bold plans; technology encouraged science to forge ahead in the conquest of the universe. However abstract modern science might appear, it implicitly sought practical application. For instance, it is no coincidence, but rather symbolic, that the Greenwich Observatory was built with pirate booty. There was an unexpected link between them. On the basis of his observation of the stars, Flamsteed discovered a better method of determining the position of ships at sea. This enabled English privateers to navigate better and thus facilitated their pirate expeditions. The proceeds served to build an observatory, in which more precise astronomical measurements could be undertaken, better instruments built and better telescopes devised. The practical returns brought benefit to science—and others too.

At the time of Swedenborg's arrival in London, the Royal Society had gathered the leading brains of the new sciences and counted Newton, Halley, and Flamsteed among its most prominent members. Swedenborg immediately endeavored to make contact with these great men in the fields of astronomy, natural science, mechanics, and medicine.

Sir Isaac Newton (1642–1727) was then at the peak of his fame. He had already retired from his professorship at Trinity College,

Cambridge, to which he had been appointed in the fall of 1669. In January 1672, he had been formally accepted as a member of the Royal Society. In 1695, he was appointed master of the Royal Mint. In 1701, he became a member of Parliament for the University of Cambridge and, on 16 April 1705, he was knighted by Queen Anne. When Swedenborg made Newton's acquaintance, he had already been living for seven years in London where he fulfilled his duties in Parliament and at the Royal Mint.

Newton's house was the focal point of high society. There, leading scholars and philosophers met gentlemen from politics, led by Queen Anne's most influential minister, Charles Montague, Earl of Halifax, since 1700. Montague's friendship with Newton went back to the 1690s in Cambridge, where the young, talented student had founded a philosophical society together with Newton. In London, he formed an intimate circle of scholars anew, at whose disposal he placed both his political influence and wealth and to which William Congreve, Edmund Halley, Matthew Prior, Thomas Tickell, Richard Steele, and Alexander Pope belonged. Halifax was attracted to Newton's house both by his friendship and by more romantic links. The large single-storied brick house next to Orange Street Chapel in St. Martin Street with its built-on observatory also accommodated Newton's delightful and intelligent niece, Mrs. Catharine Barton, the widow of Colonel Barton. She managed Newton's household and social life. Following the death of the earl's first wife, Mrs. Barton became the object of his most attentive interest and courtship.

The student from Sweden now came into contact with this learned circle. It was typical that he should carefully prepare himself for these visits rather than introducing himself as a curious dilettante. He had already worked through Newton's works, especially the *Principia* (1687), before he went to see him. "I study Newton daily and I am very anxious to meet him. I have provided myself with a small stock of books for the study of mathematics, and also with a number of instruments which are both a help and an ornament in the study of science," he wrote to his brother-in-law, Erik Benzelius, on 13 October 1710 (LL, 37). He became so familiar with Newton's work that, with his youthful self-confidence, he believed he understood him better than the English and that he was above the contemporary controversies for and against Newton. Already in January 1712, he wrote in a postscript to Benzelius: "Professor Elvius asks what is the opinion of the English concerning Newton's *Principia*. However, one shouldn't ask an Englishman about this matter, because they are blind in their own affairs. But it would be a crime to call the *Principia* into question" (LL, 39).

As well as frequenting Newton's circle, Swedenborg also contacted Flamsteed, the little invalid who lived in the Royal Observatory at Greenwich where, solitary and bitter, he measured the stars with his newly constructed sextants and quadrants. This man had taken on the enormous job of surveyng God's Creation and preparing a map of all fixed stars with the most detailed calculation of their location. His marvels and his paranoia were the subject of the strangest stories in Newton's circle. John Flamsteed (1646–1719), the astronomer royal, had held his unique office from 1675. Plagued by illness from youth, he had been too weak to go to school and had educated himself in astronomy by following his own personal bent. The observation of the solar eclipse of 12 September 1662 stimulated him to build a quadrant, with which he prepared a table of the sun's altitudes. In Cambridge, he had made the acquaintance of Newton and Isaac Barrow and had impressed King Charles II with a work that must have appeared particularly important to the sovereign of an island realm. This was a table of high and low tides, calculated for the use of shipping on behalf of the king.

The practical use of this science stirred Charles II to promote a man of such merit to the Royal Admiralty. Flamsteed worked initially in the observatory of Jonas Moore, the author of *A New System of Mathematics* (1681). After he had once more aroused the king's interest and gratitude through the invention of a new method of calculating ships' positions at sea, Flamsteed was formally appointed astronomer royal on 4 March 1675 and moved to Chelsea. He received the assignment from the king "to correct the tables of heavenly movements and the fixed stars with the most precise detail, care and zeal, and also to discover longitude for the perfection of navigation," which clearly emphasized the practical duty of his science. Greenwich Park's peace and remoteness made it an appropriate place for a new observatory, and the building was erected swiftly according to the design of Christopher Wren, the architect of St. Paul's Cathedral. Flamsteed moved in with his instruments and undertook the great work of figuring out a completely new star table with correct names and altitudes, as all previous heavenly tables used in astronomy and by the navy had proved erroneous. The whole scientific world was eager for the results of this work. The continued progress of research and observations in all fields of astronomy depended on the precision of Flamsteed's measurements.

The solitary man was not very accessible. An atmosphere of mystery surrounded him and lent his fame a certain sensation. He was one of the curiosities of London and had been disturbed in his work by many inquisitive important people. Even Czar Peter the Great paid him a visit at the Royal Observatory in February 1698. The many errors in the earlier astronomical tables made Flamsteed neurotically meticulous in his work. He also shared with many scholars an inclination to keep his researches to himself. His only warm friendship was with Newton, the greatest man of his time. It led to a chain reaction, which disturbed this man who only wanted time for research.

In London, Swedenborg personally experienced the highly emotional quarrel between Newton and Flamsteed, which reached its climax in the years 1710–1712 due to the publication of the astronomical map. Flamsteed had first made Newton's acquaintance in 1670, and their friendship continued after his own appointment as astronomer royal. Newton often visited Flamsteed's observatory where the two researchers discussed their most recent observations and tried out their instruments. From a publishing point of view, Newton appears to have been indebted to Flamsteed. Newton used and printed, in his *Principia*, Flamsteed's data concerning the great comet, which he had observed between 22 December 1680 and 15 February 1681. A dispute then arose over the definitive publication of these results.

Newton had actually advised Flamsteed in 1691 to publish a provisional catalogue of the most important stars. But Flamsteed wanted to publish a complete catalogue with precise tables and rejected the idea of a partial work. He suspected a ruse on Newton's part to make premature use of his results and saw Halley as the author of this intrigue. He hated Halley especially as he had pointed out a computational error in Flamsteed's table of tides and thus aroused Flamsteed's vengeance. In 1691, he took the greatest trouble to frustrate Halley's hopes of a professorship. Flamsteed perceived Halley's kind of criticism as infamous and rejected all efforts at reconciliation. His relations with Newton improved when he turned again to his moon theory, and their personal communications grew more frequent. In September 1694, Newton visited the Royal Observatory again. Flamsteed forgot all earlier friction, treated him as a friend and handed over all his observations concerning the positions of the moon to check his lunar theory, on condition that Newton should make no public use of this material without his prior agreement.

The newly cemented friendship lasted for one and a half years before new jealousies disturbed their solidarity. Flamsteed was often ill and constantly overwhelmed with work so that he could not always fulfill Newton's requests for new measurements. For his part, Newton felt put off by his friend. The more Newton urged, the more Flamsteed withdrew, finally explaining that he felt in no way obliged to hand over the laboriously gathered results of his own research to someone, "who inconsiderately seemed to claim as a right what was intended as a courtesy." He ceased his observations of the moon, which he had undertaken for Newton, and dedicated himself entirely to the fixed stars. In an aggrieved fashion, he relinquished the moon to his rival. But many opportunities repeatedly brought the two together. Newton used these visits to ascertain the progress of the star catalogue whose imminent publication had already been announced. When he urged an early publication, just as thirteen years before, he promised Flamsteed to recommend the work to Prince George of Denmark whom he knew personally. But even now Flamsteed did not want to be hurried in his work. Like many scholars preparing an extensive work, he thought himself immortal and again suspected that Newton intended to reap the fame of his researches for himself. Now the real battle was to begin.

Newton was not to be diverted from his plan to force the fearful Flamsteed into a swift publication of the star map, awaited by the whole learned world. Newton used a tactic that scholars have always used with success in such cases. He had Prince George found a commission for the publication of the star catalogue, which included three other scholars—Christopher Wren, John Arbuthnot, and David Gregory—besides Newton and Flamsteed. The commission provided for the speedy publication of the researches. This forced alliance with Newton under princely supervision stirred up an endless sequence of suspicions and complaints. Flamsteed, who increasingly regarded the heavens as his private property threatened by an evil rival, felt assaulted and robbed of his life's work by the forceful Newton. He seems to have developed extreme paranoia, jealous of his astronomical calculations that he could prove had only been achieved by means of his own inventions. He even expressed the fear that Newton had only meddled in his work in order to sabotage it. He had scarcely handed over his first sheets of manuscript when he regretted ever sharing his researches and delayed the printing by postponing the correction of proofs for so long that the members of the commission sent him an ultimatum. As a result, Flamsteed described the other members as robbers. At Christmas 1707, the first volume finally appeared, containing the observations made with Flamsteed's sextant. The second volume provoked worse conflicts, which were unexpectedly terminated by the death of the patron on 28 October 1708. The printing of further researches was suspended.

Flamsteed was quite delighted to have his stars to himself again and locked himself up in his observatory. But the peace did not last long. Once again he was startled by a commission, and once again it was the evil Newton who wanted to force the progress of publication in this manner. But Newton had also learned his lesson from this long-standing wrangle. This time the commission was not chaired by a benevolent princely dilettante: instead Newton had alerted the queen and instigated an official regulation by pointing to the importance of the publication for English navigation and the empire. On 12 December 1710, a royal order summoned the hostile scholars to the Greenwich Observatory. This order authorized Newton, as president of the commission, now strengthened by further members of the Royal Society, to supervise the edition. Newton stepped forth thus not only as Flamsteed's principal but also as his judge, since the order authorized him to make official note of Flamsteed's lapses.

The latter was furious to find his former friend acting as his superior, accuser, and judge in his observatory. Should he surrender his secret to the "robber" in his very own sanctuary? But his raging protest was of no avail. Newton robed himself in silence, and the only answer the infuriated scholar received was the cold reply of the well-primed secretary that "the Queen would be obeyed."

Cooperation was no longer possible. Despite the royal command, Flamsteed went on strike, and the commission published his star catalogue without his collaboration. It is no surprise that Flamsteed's researches did not emerge unscathed from this struggle. The manuscripts presented to the first commission in 1706 and 1708 were intentionally left incomplete, and they comprised only three-quarters of his whole work. The cunning inventor delivered the new machine in accordance with the high command, but he retained several little cogwheels, without which it did not function. Moreover, Flamsteed had handed over a sealed copy of his first manuscript and felt justified in complaining about Newton's "treachery." As president of the second commission, Newton had broken the seal of the work he received as a "referee" of the first commission and published Flamsteed's works without the latter's knowledge. But owing to Flamsteed's mistrust, the manuscript available to Newton was incomplete, and Flamsteed still possessed some cogs of the machine. In April 1711, Newton sent Arbuthnot to induce Flamsteed to give up the missing part of his researches. After many entreaties, the insulted scholar was almost persuaded to agree, when his suspicion was once more aroused. He heard that the hated Halley was to edit the publication. Halley as the editor of his life's work! In March, he finally gave a written refusal to Arbuthnot in which he protested the relegation of his person and research as a matter of national interest and appealed to the queen and the people. He concluded his letter with the remark: "The disrespect and abuse of my person dishonors the Queen and the nation and its authors will be censured in due course."

The upshot of his refusal was a summons to appear before the president and the other members of the commission in the rooms of the Royal Society in Crane Court. Flamsteed fought for his work with bitter fury and once again stood by his original position. The meeting ended in a tirade of abuse. Initially Newton maintained a cold irony and replied to Flamsteed's jealous tapping of his instruments: "How nice, to have neither observatory nor instruments." But finally he was affected by Flamsteed's irritation and hurled scorn at his complaints: "So we are now the robbers of your works!" Flamsteed remarked that it hurt him to have to affirm this, but Newton himself must admit that this was the case. "After that," Flamsteed continued, "Newton simply raged. He showered me with insults. I tried to soothe his temper and subdue his passion by thanking him for all the bad names he called me."

One can imagine what a sensation such a scene caused in polite society. The battle for the stars was no less topical than the battle for India, the South Sea Islands, and the American possessions. Predictably, the official viewpoint was triumphant. Flamsteed's petition to the queen to prevent the "underhand" publication of the star catalogue was rejected. The work appeared under the title *Historia coelestis* in 1712 with all the omissions caused by Flamsteed's refusal to hand over his recent researches and had to be subsequently corrected and completed without his collaboration.

The sick hermit of Greenwich was not even spared the last insult. He saw his own researches, incomplete and full of errors, edited by his archenemy Halley. The latter insulted him further by sitting in Child's coffeehouse, glorying in how much trouble he had in correcting Flamsteed's mistakes, as well as immortalizing his scorn for the plundered author in his foreword to the book. Thereupon, Flamsteed publicly declared Halley a lazy and malicious thief. However, he could not protest the treatment of his person and work without causing royal displeasure. His rancor continued unabated until a violent outbreak in 1714. On 1 August, the queen died, shortly followed by Halifax, Newton's patron. The new lord chamberlain was a friend of Flamsteed and now the words of Exodus 1:8 applied to Newton: "Then there came to power in Egypt a new king who knew nothing of Joseph." A memorandum from the lord of the treasury directed that the three hundred remaining copies of *Historia coelestis* should be delivered to Flamsteed on the orders of Sir Robert Walpole. Flamsteed then organized a solemn incineration, which he described "as a sacrifice to heavenly truth" and concluded with words "about the ingratitude of two compatriots, who had treated him worse than anyone had ever treated the noble Tycho de Brahe in Denmark." The battle over the "history of heaven" was a very base affair.

The literary feud between Newton and Leibniz was another scholarly dispute that took place with the most passionate partisanship of learned circles during Swedenborg's stay in London. Gottfried Wilhelm Leibniz (1646–1716), the brilliant German polymath and rationalist philosopher, had published two treatises on the foundations of his differential and integral calculus in *Acta Eruditorum* at Leipzig in 1684 and 1686. The following year Newton's chief work *Principia mathematica philosophiae naturalis* appeared, in which he developed an astonishingly similar method of calculation, which he called fluxions. The coincidence of these publications immediately raised the question of who should be credited with the original discovery. This debate over priority was fought by both sides with great passion and engaged not only the scholars at the academies of Europe but also the courts, masonic lodges, and social circles. From the outset, Newton charged Leibniz with plagiarism. Eventually the matter came before a proper court of arbitration. Both researchers appealed to the Royal Society as referee, as more and more intermediaries and subsidiary issues began to confuse the scientific debate, and the battle of the scholars was threatened by political complications. The question was meticulously examined and was the subject of daily conversation of educated London society in the years 1710 until 1712, when the Royal Society published its verdict. As might be expected, the decision went against Leibniz. It was confirmed that Newton and Leibniz were using the same method of calculation and that Newton had discovered it considerably earlier. Documents were appended to the judgment, in a sort of scientific blue book, which seemed to show that Leibniz was the second inventor of differential and integral calculus, because he had inferred the method from references in Newton's letters. Swedenborg followed this demonstrative proclamation of the English scholarly world against Leibniz with the most eager interest.

Swedenborg's visits to Flamsteed were motivated not only by his own intellectual curiosity, but also on behalf of his friends in Sweden, especially the members of the Literary Society of Uppsala. They

urged him to introduce himself to Flamsteed and see how his instruments "were made, how the division of minutes was indicated,
whether he used a telescope instead of a diopter, to look at everything relating to his instruments, how they were moved and how he
used them in darkness or by candlelight etc." Elvius in particular
kept pressing him, and in a letter of 28 July 1711, he gave him the
most precise instructions: "Under all circumstances, you must strive
to be present when Flamsteed makes his observations and you must
note how he does this. You must describe his instruments with all
their attachments. Pay attention to the diopters, to see whether they
are fitted with a moving edge like that of Hedraeus or a crosshair as
in the instrument of Tycho de Brahe, which Robert Hooke recommended contrary to the opinion of Elvius, and see whether he uses a
telescope instead of a distance-glass and how it is mounted."

The student meticulously carried out all these commissions,
which were not easy and cast him in the role of a scientific detective.
They assumed not only an excellent scientific training on his part but
also sharp faculties of observation and technical knowledge. He
managed to disarm Flamsteed's customary and well-justified mistrust
towards visitors and watched him at his nocturnal researches. As requested, he delivered to the Uppsala faculty an exact description of
Flamsteed's observatory and his astronomical instruments, as well as
Flamsteed's request for the Swedish scientist Bilberg's work *Sol inoc-
cidens* containing his studies of the Arctic Circle. Flamsteed also appears to have told Swedenborg much about his life and the progress
of his researches. The student could inform his Swedish friends that
the Russian czar had bought the great quadrant from Halley for
eighty pounds. With this instrument, he discovered various unknown
stars of the southern sky from St. Helena. Swedenborg also conversed with Flamsteed about the general state of astronomical research and the progress of other scholars' investigations and clarified
various matters to his friends in Uppsala. The letters that they sent
him were veritable questionnaires: "What has become of Hooke's
observation, on whose basis he wanted to check the annual motion
of the earth, which he wrote about in his treatise, *An attempt
to prove the motion of the earth* (1674)? Has it been confirmed by
scholars and have others continued observations?" Many of these

questions were discussed at the Greenwich Observatory by the scholar and the eager student.

Swedenborg also became acquainted with Flamsteed's rivals. Sir Edmund Halley (1656–1742), famous for his mathematical and astronomical discoveries as well as the practical application of his geometrical arts, lived in Oxford, where Swedenborg stayed for several months. In 1702, Halley was commissioned by the king to survey the English Channel and its coasts and published a chart of great value for English navigation. Emperor Leopold summoned him to Vienna on the basis of this achievement to discuss the expansion of navigation in the Adriatic Sea. In Leopold's service, he ascertained the best possibilities of landing and harbors on the eastern shore of the Adriatic and supervised the construction of the harbor and military defences of Trieste. In 1703, he took up the Savilian Professorship of Geometry at the University of Oxford. At the time of Swedenborg's visit, he was working in friendly collaboration with Newton on his lunar theory. Swedenborg may have already made his acquaintance in London, where Halley often stayed at Newton's house and where he lectured at the Royal Society, to which he was appointed secretary in succession to Hans Sloane in 1713.

Halley was very hospitable toward Swedenborg and told him a great deal about his astronomical researches. Swedenborg expressly mentioned Halley reporting to him "he was the first to observe the variation of a pendulum beneath the equator." He immediately seized on Halley's hints and developed them independently. He was much occupied with Halley's theory about the motion of the moon. In this respect, he wrote to Uppsala that "with the help [of this theory] an important determination of geographical longitude can be found, for he has discovered that the movement of the moon has up until now been incorrectly determined and all theoretical lunar tables are very imperfect." He was so bold as to set up a new method of calculating longitude at sea on the basis of Halley's observations of the moon and planned to print this discovery in London and present it to the Royal Society—barely a year after his arrival in London. The young researcher was reaching for the stars. Although still in the early stages of his scientific career, he aspired to the most famous learned academy of his time.

Swedenborg gradually became acquainted with other important personalities of the Royal Society, thanks to his tireless enthusiasm and the recommendations that many scholars gave to the notable young heaven-stormer. His acquaintance with Sloane dates back to his first visit to London. Hans Sloane (1660–1753) had travelled to the West Indies as a physicist and zoologist in the service of the Duke of Albermarle, governor of Jamaica, and acquired an unusual wealth of botanical, geographical, and zoological knowledge on his numerous study trips to Madeira, Barbados, and St. Christopher. Between 1693 and 1713, he was the secretary of the Royal Society, and in this capacity, he played a significant role in the dispute between Newton and Flamsteed and in the arbitration of the conflict between Newton and Leibniz. Following Newton's death in 1727, Sloane became president of the Royal Society. He showed Swedenborg his large collections of living and dried plants from all over the world and appeared to think well of him and remembered him with goodwill. It was Sloane who invited Swedenborg to become a member of the Royal Society following the appearance of his first scientific work and introduced him to this Olympus which the student had revered from afar fourteen years earlier.

Swedenborg also became familiar with quite a different kind of science through his acquaintance with Woodward, whose theories and results were attracting the closest attention of contemporaries. John Woodward (1665–1728) was England's leading geologist and the actual founder of this science. He had become known primarily through his fundamental studies of fossils, which he collected on his travels and used to determine the evolution of the earth. In *An Essay towards A Natural History of the Earth* (1695), he proved for the first time the importance of soil and mineral strata for the understanding of the earth's evolution and tried to deduce the stages of our planet's history from the formation of sediment. He was the first to develop systematically the idea that fossils were the actual remains of plants and animals of earlier epochs. He hypothesized that these prehistoric animals and plants had been mixed up with the debris of soil and minerals washed up by the primeval flood and that their weight determined their position in higher or lower layers of sediment once the flood had receded.

Woodward's theories provoked violent opposition. John Harris especially attacked his theory concerning the formation of the earth in his work *Remarks on some late Papers relating to the Universal Deluge* (1697), which also aroused great interest in Germany and was published in Latin by E. Camerarius in Tübingen. In order to rebuff his opponents' objections, Woodward published his *Naturalis historia telluris* (1714), which contained his whole theory of the earth's formation. He was busy elaborating this work when Swedenborg visited him. He not only explained the foundations of his geological researches to Swedenborg but also found such pleasure in him that he introduced him to various scholars and members of the Royal Society. The rules of his *Brief Instructions for Making Observations in All Parts of the World: As Also for Collecting, Preserving and Sending Over Natural Things* (1696) were of the greatest significance to Swedenborg and opened his eyes to the proper observation of natural phenomena on his extensive journeys to the mines of Europe. Woodward opened his eyes to the wonders of nature.

Swedenborg also had close personal relations with John Chamberlayne, an extraordinarily versatile man who played a leading role in the learned and courtly world of London. He held high court offices under Queen Anne and King George I, was secretary of the Bounty Commission, and a fellow of the Royal Society from 1702. He wrote the original work *The Manner of Making Coffee, Tea, and Chocolate. As It Is Used in Most Parts of Europe, Asia, Africa, and America* (1685), which exercised an important influence on the social culture of England. He was the son of a more famous father, Edward Chamberlayne (1616–1703), the author of a fundamental and ingenious representation of English history, *Angliæ Notitia, or the Present State of England* (1669), a widely read mirror of the early empire. Following his father's death, John continued the work that aroused such interest among the politicians and intelligentsia of England that it ran through five editions. He was also busy as a Church historian and introduced the ideas of the famous German jurist Samuel Pufendorf (1632–1694) into English ecclesiastical politics with his translation of *The History of Popedom* (1691). Later he brought out his *History of the Reformation in the Low Countries* in four volumes (1719–1723). Swedenborg claimed that he was "very well acquainted with him."

Special attention must also be given to Swedenborg's acquaintance with the technical inventors and mechanics of contemporary England. This field, where the human spirit freely and fearlessly mastered nature for the first time through mechanical means, caught his imagination. Swedenborg's Swedish friends had commissioned him to follow up the further development of Robert Hooke's pioneering theories and discoveries, but Hooke had died in 1703. Swedenborg names none of the famous living technicians and inventors, but he used his stay in London to educate himself in all kinds of technical skills and arts.

Swedenborg also witnessed in London the first great trial in which modern science collided with Church doctrine. Such a conflict was not intended by English scientists, many of whom were themselves clergymen. Robert Boyle, the founder of modern chemistry, bequeathed a special foundation with whose means leading representatives of natural science would give regular public lectures, the Boyle Lectures, in order that science should not oppose the truths of faith but illuminate and confirm them. The scientist Thomas Bray (1656–1730) founded a society for the spread of Christian knowledge with similar motives. Nevertheless, there were conflicts, and one in particular concerned one of Newton's pupils.

Like many of his talented contemporaries, William Whiston (1667–1752) had found time in his clerical career to familiarize himself with the modern sciences. Newton's *Principia* had impressed him most profoundly. Under Newton's influence, he turned to mathematics and cosmology and wrote his own manuscript under the title *A New Theory of the Earth* (1696), which essentially reflected Newton's thought. At Newton's request, John Locke looked at the work and, with praising words, encouraged Whiston in further research. In this work, Whiston tried to harmonize Newton's teachings with the biblical story of creation by suggesting that the Flood had been caused by the earth's collision with a planet.

In 1701, Whiston was proposed as Newton's successor at Cambridge and took up his chair in 1703, lecturing on Newton's theories in a more popular form, while remaining in constant friendly contact with his teacher whose *Arithmetica universalis* he edited in 1707. At Cambridge, he was chiefly concerned to harmonize the new scientific worldview with the Christian idea of God. However, one particular obstacle appeared to bar his way—the Church doctrine of the Trinity, which taught that God was a unity in three persons. How could this doctrine be rationally linked with a theology based on the number and orders of the universe? On the basis of old Church documents, some newly discovered and edited for the first time, he tried to prove historically that the trinitarian dogma was a later development of Christian doctrine arising from the influence of neo-Platonic metaphysics and a debasement of the original Christian idea of God. Whiston thought that the new scientific worldview could not be reconciled with the trinitarian idea but only with the early Christian notion of God's essence.

Whiston was accused of Arianism, just as Michael Servetus (1511–1553) had been decried and condemned as an Arian for criticizing the Trinity in the light of nature one-and-a-half centuries earlier. The accusation of heresy cost him his professorship at the University of Cambridge, and he was obliged to resign on 30 October 1710. The same year he moved with his family to London. Whiston's originality, intellectual liveliness, and his popular style of teaching made him widely known in London. He added to the excitement of his lectures by displaying the mysteries of laboratories to an inquisitive public and bustling among steaming retorts and all kinds of apparatus to the delight of London. His first lecture on astronomy, with the assistance of Joseph Addison and Richard Steele, took place at Button's Coffee House and led to a series of witty public lectures. He knew how to get publicity for his views and popularize his teachings in an entertaining fashion by debating them in the "best attended coffee houses."

But Whiston gained public attention for a further reason: he was interested in apocalyptic prophecy as well as in scientific and ecclesiastical studies. Together with his teacher Newton, he studied the prophecies of the Old and New Testaments and proved that the Last Times had already begun by interpreting current events or personalities as the fulfilment of biblical prophecy. He also assimilated the great political events of his time into his apocalyptic considerations. When Prince Eugene came to London in 1711–1712 in the course of the negotiations leading to the Treaty of Utrecht, Whiston printed a new dedication for his *Essay on the Revelation of Saint John* (1706), proving that Prince Eugene had now fulfilled several of St. John's promises in the Book of Revelation. Eugene sent Whiston fifteen guineas but also informed him "that he did not wish the honor of St. John's acquaintance."

The ecclesiastical complaints against Whiston still continued in London. At Queen Anne's command, a convocation of the Church of England was called on 4 February 1711 to discuss the reasons for the spread of Deism, Socianism, and Arianism. This assembly ended with the condemnation of Whiston, who contested the right of the convocation to pass a verdict on him. The trial involved the whole learned world as Whiston was friends with famous scholars such as Samuel Clarke, Francis Hawksbee, Francis Hare, and Benjamin Hoadly. Several members of the convocation objected that the proceedings against Whiston did not follow the traditional course of a heresy trial. On the advice of a small majority of high judges, the queen finally ordered that the convocation should proceed to examine the accused. But Whiston had clever ways of constantly raising questions of competence and pointing out procedural errors, so that the trial was repeatedly obstructed. Every session brought demonstrations of his supporters and his accusers lost all interest in the trial after the death of the queen. The trial motivated him to publish his views on early Christianity and its later decay as *Primitive Christianity Revived* at the end of 1711, which inflamed the dispute anew. Swedenborg took great interest in these debates, and his own criticism of the Trinity, so powerfully expressed in his later visionary writings, was doubtless influenced by Whiston's ideas, especially as both men linked their view of God with a scientific conception of the universe.

Whiston aroused Swedenborg's interest for another reason. In certain respects, Swedenborg regarded Whiston as a rival in the calculation of longitude, a special interest of his London period under the influence of Flamsteed. While Swedenborg was using Flamsteed's lunar observations to determine longitude on sea and land, Whiston was working on this problem with Humphrey Ditton, but the method he published in 1714 was initially rejected. Swedenborg closely followed Whiston's studies from Paris, as he feared the latter's discovery could pip him at the post. Whiston found his improved method in 1720 and submitted it at the same time as Swedenborg in 1721, after the king had announced a public competition for the solution of longitude with a personal prize of a hundred pounds and a total of four hundred and seventy pounds. When Swedenborg's method did not win the prize—he naturally considered it the best—he complained in Paris that it was not easy for a foreigner to gain recognition in England.

The findings of modern science were forged in this atmosphere of passionate conflict. The favor of the court, the intrigues of ministers, the rivalry of colleagues, the competition for university chairs, personal dislike and self-justification, social concerns, political cabals and covert influences, the pride and triumph of inventors, human weakness, gossip and convention all played their part in this drama. The battle for the stars in a quiet observatory between jealous scholars, the rivalry over integral calculus and the reconciliation of science and Church dogma became social dramas and a national affair. This must always be remembered if one is to grasp the enthusiasm and involvement of young Swedenborg in these skirmishes. He experienced this atmosphere as a spur to his own scientific genius and threw himself into the fray, to make use of his gifts not only in discovering new things but in applying them practically. In his letter of 30 April 1711, he informed Benzelius that he was daily visiting the best mathematicians of the city and wrote of himself: "You encourage me to continue my studies, but I feel I need to be restrained, so immoderate is my love, especially for astronomy and mechanics" (LL, 38).

Swedenborg led a full life in London. Already before to his journey to England, he had obtained several instruments for his mathematical studies. Once there, he endeavored not only to use these instruments for his researches and test the results of great scholars, but we also find him making efforts to train himself as a technician. Because there were no technical schools or public laboratories, he thought of a cunning yet charming course of action: "I make use of my landlords and change them frequently. First I stayed with a clockmaker, then with a cabinet-maker, and now I am lodging with a maker of mathematical instruments. Thus, I poach the secrets of the craft, which will be useful to me later," he wrote in April 1711 to his brother-in-law. Thus the student eager for knowledge moved from room to room and used his leisure time to observe his landlords surreptitiously at their trade. Soon he was able to provide for his own scientific needs and proudly wrote home in January 1712: "I have learned so much from my landlords regarding the art of making measuring instruments, that I have manufactured many for my own use" (LL, 38).

Such technical work not only demanded the mastery and manipulation of materials but also called for training in draughtsmanship. An agreeable landlord also helped out here. Swedenborg took rooms with an engraver and, by the beginning of 1712, was writing most self-confidently to Sweden: "I have already made such progress in the engraving art that I think I have a gift for it. I am enclosing a sample of my art in the letter to my father. It shows some of my inventions and is the first of my efforts." Swedenborg took a detailed interest in architecture. On his first journey, he never viewed a larger building without carefully studying its style and design—a habit he maintained in all his travels. Shortly after his arrival in London, he witnessed a most significant architectural event: the inauguration of St. Paul's Cathedral, just completed by Christopher Wren. On 13 October 1710, he reported on this to his Swedish friends.

In the course of all this activity, he not only found time to write Latin odes but also to read English literature and to gain an overview of the great poets of the land. Among others he mentioned John Dryden, Edmund Spenser, Isaak Walton, John Milton, Abraham Cowley, Francis Beaumont, John Fletcher, William Shakespeare, Ben Jonson, John Oldham, Ambrose Philips, and John Smith in his letters. However, he did not refer to any personal meetings with contemporary poets.

4

Encounter with Continental Science in Holland and France

Emanuel Swedenborg did not regard himself as a mere student in his scientific fields of study. In England, he was no blind adherent to any one scientist but undertook independent work as soon as he had familiarized himself with a subject. He never lost his need for intellectual autonomy and independence. Even in his apprentice years, he displayed astonishing self-confidence, even youthful arrogance. Within a few months of his stay in England, he felt far superior to the old-fashioned scholarship of his homeland. He could not help exhibiting his new knowledge in his letters, especially to Benzelius, who must have read them with amusement. He added the intentionally casual postscript to the letter to Benzelius (30 April 1711): "For my own entertainment I have recently drawn up several useful tables for all solar and lunar eclipses on the latitude of Uppsala, which will occur between 1712 and 1721." He clearly wished to show his teacher that whatever takes the Swedes a great deal of trouble and exertion, is a mere diversion in England. When describing in a later letter his newly acquired knowledge of how to make measuring instruments, he could not help adding, "If I were in Sweden, I would not need anyone to make the meridians for the globe and other apparatus" (LL, 38).

This exaggerated sense of superiority led him to indulge in superlatives: "I have made such progress in astronomy as to have discovered much that I think will be useful in its study. Although in the beginning it made my brain ache, long speculations are no longer difficult for me. I have examined closely all the schemes for finding the terrestrial longitude but could not find a single one satisfactory. I have therefore originated a method by means of the moon which is unerring, and I am certain that it is the best that has yet been advanced. I have also discovered many new methods for observing the planets, the moon and the stars. I am now busy working my way through algebra, and I intend to make such progress as to be able in time to continue Polhammer's discoveries" (LL, 38). This constant "I am, I can, I will" indicates the arrogance, which would lead him to make surprising suggestions to his Swedish patrons at the end of his travels.

His new attitude affected relations with his family. In Sweden, he had lived entirely within the sphere of his family clan and was related by blood or marriage to many scholars and church leaders. These ties now began to loosen. Initially he felt homesick in his new surroundings. In a letter of 13 October 1710, he wrote somewhat plaintively to his brother: "You ask me, dear brother, how I fare and I would answer: I know that I am still living, but I am not happy, for I miss you and the homeland." However, he quickly overcame this mood and was soon wholly absorbed in the new life that London's observatories, academies, learned circles, glass grinderies, metal workshops, and coffee houses offered. His father was not pleased by this estrangement: he feared that his son would turn away from his Christian upbringing and embrace the free-thinking of England as well as its science. When Benzelius, in agreement with the father, exhorted the student to return home soon, the latter replied somewhat irreverently: "I am not thinking of returning home much before 1715—that is in three years time!" His aversion towards old-fashioned Sweden also affected his behavior towards his compatriots. In order to lose no time for his studies, he threw himself into

English society and distanced himself from his fellow Swedes. He even wrote the letters to his teacher exclusively in English.

The portrait of the young student has both amusing and questionable aspects. Here was a highly talented and versatile young man profoundly stimulated by science. Despite all his theorizing, he was equipped with a practical understanding of utility and advantage. Inspired by a philosophical appetite for truth, he displayed astonishing diligence and self-discipline in the management of his daily work for a student of his age. Utterly dedicated to whatever was new and inspired by naïve self-confidence, he prided himself on the discovery of new knowledge and his own achievements with a certain arrogance towards his former authorities. This is the portrait of the young gentleman in London.

Bishop Jesper tried to cure the intellectual arrogance of his son with the tried and trusted means used by fathers of students down the ages—he sent him less money. But this means was not effective. Swedenborg became even more arrogant and implied that his father was sinning against the sanctity of science by hindering his son's progress through stinginess. At the end of a long description of his new inventions, he wrote indignantly to Benzelius in January 1712: "I cannot understand why my father does not provide better for me. He gave me only two hundred Reichsthalers to live on for sixteen months. He knows that I promised not to bother him with requests for money, but no money has been sent for the last three or four months! It is hard to live without food and drink, like a poor peasant in Schonen" (LL, 39). He enlisted his brother-in-law to change his father's mind. He wrote in a letter of 15 August 1712: "Your great friendliness and kindness give me confidence that your advice and letters will make my father favorable and send me the necessary funds, so that I will win new passion to continue my studies. Believe me, the desire to bring honor to you and my father's house is greater in me than in you" (LL, 39). But the bishop remained adamant.

Despite his lack of money in England, Swedenborg was not depressed by material want but managed to the best of his ability. He not only resided in London but traveled around the country and stayed in Oxford, where the great Halley was teaching, and extended his learned contacts. But his purse was getting ever thinner. If he wanted to see another part of Europe with his dwindling means, he would have to think of curtailing his stay in England earlier than he intended.

Paris enticed him most on the continent. Its Académie Royale boasted an august company of mathematicians, geometricians, physicists, astronomers, and technicians comparable to the Royal Society in London. However, Holland detained him on his journey to France. His reports of his stay in the Netherlands are very brief, so that one cannot precisely establish which scholars and universities he visited there. An entry in his travel diary shows that he used his time there well to pursue his studies thoroughly in mathematics, physics, and mechanics: "It would be too long-winded, to mention all the learned men, with whom I became acquainted during these travels, because I never missed an opportunity to visit libraries, collections and other things of interest" (LL, 39).

In Utrecht, Swedenborg brushed with world politics. The congress was meeting there to secure peace between the European powers in the east and west following the long War of Spanish Succession (1702–1713). If Swedenborg had cared about politics, he would have met Prince Eugene, who had also stayed in London for the preparation of the peace congress. But the Wars of Spanish Succession seemed to have concerned him as little as the peace treaty that ended them—he lived entirely for his science and his arts. The only politician mentioned in his letters was the Swedish ambassador, Palmquist, a great expert in algebra, who daily invited his diligent countryman to his table throughout his stay in Utrecht. Palmquist also made his numerous connections with Dutch scholars available to Swedenborg and obtained permission for him to make astronomical observations in the well-equipped observatory at the University of Leiden, whither he planned to return as soon as possible from Paris. Although Swedenborg stayed only briefly at this important place of research, he used his time there to learn its highly developed craft of lens grinding for the manufacture of astronomical instruments. The lens grinding bench is still to be seen in Spinoza's little house in The Hague. At a time when scholars produced the instruments of their own invention, Swedenborg must have been especially proud when he could write home: "I learnt lens grinding in Leiden, and I now possess all the instruments and tools for this purpose." He probably also saw Jan Swammerdam's scientific collections in Leiden and became acquainted with the doctor and physicist Hermann Boerhaave (1668–1738), who later edited Swammerdam's *Biblia naturae* (1737).[1] Swammerdam's work on insects, illustrated with the author's own copper engravings, exercised an enormous influence on Swedenborg's scientific outlook and induced him to write an extensive commentary for it. In his later scientific works, he gives special acknowledgment again and again to Boerhaave's writings.

His longing for Paris was stronger than anything that could detain him in the university towns of the Netherlands. By way of Brussels and Valenciennes, he traveled to the city of Blaise Pascal (1623–1662), where he remained for over a year.

Swedenborg did not write about the usual things of interest to visitors to Paris at this time. He does not mention the social and courtly life, the death of the Sun King, or the great men of French politics. With an obsessive single-mindedness, he had eyes only for the Paris of science, mathematicians, astronomers, and learned societies, which disputed priority in mathematical and astronomical discoveries with their English colleagues. He gave himself up to this world with the same ardor that marked his efforts in England. He carried the recommendations of Swedish and English friends, which gave him access to the exclusive company of the leading minds of the Académie Royale. Here he was no longer a pupil, but the personal acquaintance of great rivals on the other side of the channel, with whom the Parisian gentlemen were locked in keen debate. He was able to describe the latest discoveries made in England to these inquisitive opponents of Flamsteed, Newton, and Halley (Tafel, doc. 45, 227). He was able to report, pass judgment, and compare and was himself an object of curiosity because this national feud between French and English scholars did not concern him. He cleverly used his neutral status to learn from all and weigh both sides.

---

1. In 1743, Swedenborg wrote a commentary on parts of Swammerdam's *Bibliae naturae*. See Tafel, *Documents concerning . . . Swedenborg*, doc. 313, no. 70, p. 737. For Swedenborg's verdict on Swammerdam, see also Tafel, doc. 299, p. 750, and *Heaven and Hell* §§39, 108–109, 567.

Swedenborg was driven by a sense of urgency in Paris. In view of the short time he had to stay, he feared missing anything useful for his scientific progress, a feeling exacerbated by an illness that prevented him filling his days with work. "Since my arrival here I have been hindered in my work by a six-week period of sickness which has upset my studies and other useful endeavors," he wrote on 19 August 1713. "But finally I am recovered and am beginning to make the acquaintance of the most learned men of this city. I am avoiding any conversation with Swedes and keep away from all those who could interrupt my studies in the slightest. Whatever I hear from scholars, I immediately write up in my diary" (LL, 39).

This diary is no longer preserved. But various letters as well as the reports of Nicolaus Collijn, rector of the Swedish Church in Philadelphia, who often conversed with him, confirm that Swedenborg met several of the most important Parisian mathematicians, especially "the great astronomer and well known geometer" Philippe de La Hire and "the greatest geometer" Pierre Varignon.

To form an impression of the lively scientific life of Paris with its inventions, researches, experiments, and of the personal and professional rivalries of the Paris Academy at that time, it is best to refer to the short but apt biographical sketches published by Bernard le Bovier de Fontenelle in his *Eloges des Académiciens* (1731), which is based on the author's personal acquaintance with the scientific and social life of his subjects.

Philippe de La Hire (1640–1718) surely earned Swedenborg's especial admiration, because he was not only a mathematician and geometrician but also practiced as an engineer, architect, and land surveyor. Jean Baptiste Colbert and François Michel le Tellier de Louvois had already given de La Hire state commissions, and he had prepared the famous map of France together with Jean Picard. This "worthy successor of Pascal" had already published his principal achievement, the two books on conical sections, in 1673 and 1685. On the basis of these studies, he had already worked out a pioneering system of gear-wheels that offered the least friction in a machine. At the command of King Louis XIV, he published his astronomical tables in 1687, followed by his treatise on mechanics in 1695. He was simultaneously a good draughtsman and an architect in much demand with a professorship at the Académie d'Architecture, so that Fontenelle could rightly call him *"une académie entière des sciences."* Thanks to his versatile achievements, de La Hire enjoyed the personal confidence of Louis XIV, who frequently visited him at work and talked with him when he exhibited two great globes in the Pavillons de Morli. When Swedenborg was staying in Paris, de La Hire held the chair of mathematics at the Collège de France as well as the professorship of architecture. He led the life of a learned hermit, whose only physical recreation consisted in walks from the Observatory of the Académie des Sciences to the Académie and the Collège. Like Pascal, he combined scientific thought with a deep Christian faith, which colored his whole life.

Pierre Varignon (1654–1722), fourteen years his junior, distinguished himself in the fields of both physics and mathematics. Jean Baptiste Duhamel and de La Hire led him to publish his *Outline of a New Mechanics* in 1687. Two years after his appointment as professor for mathematics at the Collège Mazarin, he brought out his epoch-making *New Conjections on the Cause of Gravity*, in which he derived the weight of a body from the pressure of air upon it. In 1704, he gained the chair of philosophy as Duhamel's successor at the Collège de France. When Swedenborg visited him, he was absorbed in the debate over differential calculus. The leading Basle mathematician Jacob Bernouilli had just published his latest researches in the *Publications de l'Académie Royale*, on which Varignon would comment in his *Eclaircissments* of 1725. Varignon was totally absorbed in his researches and worked all day without recreation or distraction. Whenever he was attacked, his temper was explosive; he defended his position as the leader of French geometry with energy and zeal right up to the end.

The young researcher was enormously impressed by his meetings with such men, who devoted every minute to their science and who often led an unhealthy lifestyle through their passion for scientific knowledge. He acquired their ethos of tireless research and retained it throughout his scholarly career. Varignon was the image of a researcher consumed by science. Due to constant overwork, he had become incurably ill after 1705, and the doctors had forbidden him to read. Although aware of his condition, he ignored the prohibition, reading and writing secretly on his sickbed and hiding the books under his pillows whenever friends visited.

Swedenborg's encounter with the temperamental and methodological differences between French and English science caused him to take the liveliest interest in the debate of the London and Paris academies and to form his own opinion. There are various hints in his letters. "There prevails great jealousy and rivalry between the mathematicians here and those in England. At Oxford Halley declared he was the first to observe the variation of a pendulum beneath the equator; here this is passed over in silence. On the contrary, the astronomers here assert that Cassini had published on this subject, before Halley undertook his expedition to the island of St. Helena, and so forth" (LL, 39).

Thanks to personal recommendations, Swedenborg also became acquainted with another circle of contemporary French science: the scholars of the Catholic orders, the Oratorians and Dominicans. Benzelius had given Swedenborg a letter to take to the Abbé Jean-Paul Bignon (1662–1743), who received the young researcher in the most friendly fashion. In addition to the universal humanistic, scientific, and historical education of his time, Abbé Bignon had an outstanding gift for preaching. Trained in the severe scholarly spirit of the Congrégation de l'Oratoire, he had long held the position of court preacher at the court of Louis xiv. Following the death of Abbé Camille le Tellier de Louvois, he was appointed the king's librarian and elected to the Académie Royale. He held the learned world of France in thrall with his memoirs, which he continuously published in the *Journal des Savants*. Through its pages, Swedenborg could observe not only the scientific achievements of contemporary French researchers but also the peculiarities of their private lives in the courtly society of Paris and Versailles. During his time in Paris, Swedenborg also met two leading figures in French historiography and theology. Through Abbé Bignon, he became acquainted with the great historian and mathematician Jacques Lelong (1665–1721), who also belonged to the Oratorians. Initially a lecturer in mathematics at the Collège de Juilly, Lelong became librarian of the seminary of Notre Dame des Vertus and later headed the library of the Oratorium in Paris. He too was a researcher body and soul, who sat all day over his books and manuscripts without sleeping. He belonged to that rare breed of universal librarians who are the living incarnation and expression of all the knowledge stored up in folios and manuscripts on their library shelves and whose spirit enables this dead knowledge to lead a rich, profound, and gracious life. When Swedenborg saw him, he had already completed his collection of every single Bible edition and translation, which formed the basis of biblical philology for the whole century. He was at that moment busy working on his historical sketch of the principal polyglot editions of the Bible. Lelong also overworked at his studies, and in 1721 he died of consumption, brought on by his unhealthy regimen.

In this theological circle, Swedenborg met a third researcher who erroneously believed that a lover of science can go without food and sleep. The Dominican Michel Le Quien (1661–1733), like Lelong, devoted himself to the study of the early Bible with the aid of modern philology. The monastic discipline of his order also led Le Quien towards an extraordinary intensification of his scholarly efforts. He never left his study or his books. Le Quien spent his whole life in the order-house in Rue Saint Honoré and died there in 1733. Amid the noisy life of Paris, he was a veritable anchorite of biblical scholarship, whose studies of the Hebrew text and Latin translations of the Bible are still significant today. His three-volume work on the Christian East is the most important study of the Christian antiquities of the Eastern Churches in that period.

We do not know why Swedenborg broke off his stay in Paris. Did his father summon him? Was his money at an end? Did he need to regain his composure after a surfeit of impressions and want to escape the dangerous freedom of universal research by taking an appointment? In the early summer of 1714, he left Paris. He does not appear to have followed up his earlier plan to carry out astronomical studies in the observatory at the University of Leiden. Instead, he planned to meet Leibniz as the conclusion and climax of his study trip. Swedenborg had heard of this mysterious man living in Hanover as Newton's great rival over the discovery of calculus. He had been the ambassador of the Hanoverian court at Paris where he had presented his ideas for a new European economic order. He presented a plan for French colonial policy to Louis XIV, which assigned the whole of the North African coast including Egypt to the French Empire. This man worked for a reunification of the Roman Catholic and Protestant churches, despite all disappointments and intrigues. He canvassed for a new European currency and customs policy and elaborated a new doctrine about mankind and the universe. He also worked on plans to enable the Russian Czar Peter to exploit the natural resources of his enormous empire. As his sovereign's supervisor of mines, he found time to devise new machines for pumping water out of mines and galleries and to contribute to the progress of technology and mechanics through new inventions. He was the most universal spirit of his age, and a meeting with him would crown Swedenborg's studies on the continent. But this wish was not fulfilled. When Swedenborg arrived in Hanover, Leibniz was in Vienna, planning the foundation of an Imperial Academy and the execution of his Russian projects, and thus they never personally met.

In September 1714, Swedenborg arrived at Greifswald, then in Swedish Pomerania. According to his custom, he visited the university and made the acquaintance of the teachers in his favorite disciplines. But once he had stepped onto the soil of the Swedish king and compared a Swedish university with London and Paris, he gave vent to all the intellectual arrogance of one who has heard and seen far more abroad. His diary entry on returning to Swedish territory after a five-year absence characterizes the mood of the home-comer: "Greifswald is a miserable university. Papke, the professor of mathematics, is better suited for anything but this science."

5

Technical Inventions

Swedenborg had spent almost five years abroad and had carried out his plan despite all obstacles. He had visited the principal centers of modern science, met their leaders and spokesmen, acquired the major European languages and contemporary culture, and had trained himself in the necessary arts and skills to continue his scientific studies. More than this, he had formed his own opinion of contemporary scientific research, had glimpsed the context of its intellectual debates, and had an abundance of plans. He had achieved more than anyone else could have in his situation. He might have been content, yet he was assailed by doubt. His ambition was not satisfied. He brought plans and ideas back home with him, but no achievements in the form of proven discoveries.

The finished works in his baggage were hardly sensational. These were his Latin odes, largely composed in London, more an offering to the tradition of learning and humanist convention than a work of spontaneous poetic inspiration. "As my speculations often made me less sociable, than was good for me, I fled for a while into the study of poetry in order to relax. I intend thereby to gain some recognition on this or that occasion," he wrote home from London on 15

August 1712 (LL, 39). He now produced these occasional poems and prepared them for printing, in order to return home at least with a book of his own. At the beginning of September 1714, he revised them once more in Rostock. "I now have time, to arrange my poetic efforts. They are fables, akin to those of Ovid, dealing with events of the last fourteen or fifteen years in Europe. In this fashion, I could while away the time on serious things and amuse myself with the heroes and great men of our fatherland" (LL, 39f). He had these poems printed by the publisher Daniel Benjamin Starck in Greifswald under the traditional title: *Heliconian Pastimes or Miscellaneous Poems*. These poems simply confirm that he had mastered the humanistic foundations of contemporary education. Such odes or poems of homage might be expected of any pastor or schoolmaster. In his academy speech on the death of Swedenborg, Samuel Sandell rightly dismissed these poems with the following words: "His printed collection of Latin verses, written around 1710 and thereafter on various occasions, resemble the efforts of others at this age. In any case, poetry was not his chief concern or occupation" (Tafel, I, 1f). Besides this little book of poetry, Swedenborg brought home drawings and plans of mechanical inventions made during his travels in England, Holland and France. These were intended to be the real surprise of his homecoming and the basis of his future activities in Sweden. He therefore used his last station in Rostock and Greifswald to finish them off carefully. "I am very pleased to be in a place," he wrote from Rostock, "where I have time and leisure to collect all my works and thoughts, which have been hitherto scattered here and there on scraps of paper. I have always wanted the necessary time and place to compile them. Now I have begun this work and will soon have completed it" (LL, 39f).

The fruits of his journey show the general trend of his thought at that time. There are inventions in the fields of mechanics and technology, mostly applicable to mining, marine and inland navigation, military science, and coastal defense in Sweden. These technical designs reflect the peculiar combination of imagination and craftsmanship that characterized the beginnings of modern technology. It is difficult to imagine a time when the machines, which play such a significant part in our daily life, were not yet invented. This was the era when our technically minded ancestors sat in front of a boiling kettle and pondered whether the steam could be exploited for mechanical purposes. Precisely because the technical possibilities were unknown, the imagination set no limits to technology. A glimpse into the physical order of nature, the laws of its motion, and its ratios encouraged scientists to realize the boldest technical dreams of humankind. Locomotion on land, water, and in the air, the transport of loads, and the means of killing were the first challenges of modern mechanics. The great inventions of modern technology, the airplane, the car, the machine-gun, are not the final but initial ideas of technical development. Even Leonardo da Vinci mused on all three problems.

As Swedenborg approached the end of his journey, mechanical projects piled up before him in an almost alarming fashion. He was wholly absorbed by the findings and possibilities of modern science. Despite the discomforts of his stay in foreign countries, the constant change of location, and the difficulties of traveling on sea and land, he always found time to put his technical ideas on paper. He worked them out and drew them with great ability, as well as pursuing his mathematical, astronomical, and philosophical studies and making efforts to train in various crafts. Shortly before his return from Rostock, he proudly sent his brother-in-law Benzelius a statement in a fair draft of fourteen mechanical inventions as a proof of his achievements. But his lack of experience in mechanics still pained him: he could show only plans and designs rather than finished machines and models. "I am to some extent ashamed when I think how much I have spoken of my plans and ideas and yet have nothing to show. My travels and all its discomforts are to blame" (LL, 41). But he planned great things in Sweden. First, to fulfill a promise to his father, he wanted to publish an academic thesis, "for which he would choose one of his mechanical inventions" (LL, 40). He wanted to publicize his inventions further. Now he had "organized them for publication, when the occasion permits. An algebraic and numerical calculation accompanies them all, from which one may deduce all their ratios, movements, times and other properties" (LL, 41).

An examination of these inventions reveals that they are not as original as they might first appear. They largely concern technical appliances and machines, which the great mechanics, physicists, and mathematicians of the age, such as Leibniz, had already worked on. Nevertheless, many of them deserve respect, especially as Swedenborg actually tried out several of these youthful projects when, as assessor of mines, he introduced them to mining technology.

Swedenborg claimed the design for a submarine as his own. He described this as "a ship which can travel with its crew beneath the sea, wherever it wishes, and can inflict great damage on its enemy's navy" (LL, 40). This project belongs to a long series of inventions, conceived by the seafaring Dutch and English, including the ship's clock, the compass, the barometer, the sextant, and the water pump. The submarine was already known to Swedenborg's contemporaries. Christiaan Huygens, Robert Boyle, and Gottfried Leibniz give accounts of experiments carried out by a certain Cornelius Drebbel on the Thames at the beginning of the seventeenth century. Drebbel, a Dutchman from Alkmaar, devised a ship powered by twelve oars and carrying a number of passengers. It dived below the surface of the Thames and reappeared at a distant place. Drebbel was also reported to have in his possession a mysterious essence, which constantly renewed the air in the vessel during its submergence.

The experiments of the famous Papin were better known and more reliable than these legends. He constructed a submarine on the Thames in 1690; after its initial failure, his second attempt in 1692 was of great interest to Leibniz. Papin was still alive during Swedenborg's time in London, and it is quite possible that Swedenborg met the polymathic Frenchman, who died in the year of Swedenborg's departure, 1712, or at least that he received reports of Papin's attempts. Denis Papin, the son of Protestant parents, was born at Blois in 1647. He gained a doctorate of medicine at Angers and established contact with Huygens at Paris in 1671. There he carried out experiments on the latter's air pump and improved its construction. He then went to England, where he tried out and improved Boyle's mechanical inventions and invented a double-pedalled air pump. In 1680, he became a member of the Royal Society and was nominated its "provisional curator of experiments" after a short visit to Italy. When the Edict of Nantes made it impossible for Huguenots to return to France, he followed the call of Landgraf Karl of Hesse and took a professorship at the Philipps University of Marburg, before moving to the sovereign's court at Cassel in 1695. In 1707, he returned to London, hoping to carry out experiments there with a steam machine and a steamship, the inventions he had not been able to test on the River Fulda at Cassel. He had originally planned to travel to England in his own steamship. He died in poverty in London in 1712.

Papin's submarine possessed remarkable technical appliances. It used a centrifugal ventilator of his construction for the air supply to its passengers. The openings for the oars were carefully made watertight with leather. A special construction enabled it to destroy hostile ships or to lift objects from the sea floor. The boat was shaped like an oval barrel and had mounted on its side a large copper tube, in which a man could be accommodated lying down. Once this unfortunate man had taken up his position, the tube was sealed off from the main vessel, and the air pressure within the tube was increased by means of a pump. This enabled the man to open a lid at the front end of the tube, through which he could stretch his arm and drill the hull of a hostile ship, cut ropes or pick up objects. The escaping high pressure was supposed to prevent water from entering the tube.

Papin's first attempt, to which a large learned audience was invited, failed at the outset. The crane, made by a London carpenter, broke while lowering the vessel into the water because of a fault. The second attempt, made privately in May 1692, was much more successful. "The ship," the Cassel librarian Haas wrote to Leibniz on 13 October 1693, "is an oval drum and could carry three men, although M. Papin had only one companion besides himself. It did not remain long underwater, although those inside did not experience the slightest discomfort." Papin emerged with the burning light he had taken on board and the experiment was accounted a complete success. Probably Swedenborg's designs followed Papin's construction and, like Papin, he especially emphasized the military uses of the vessel. However, he did no further work on this project.

Several other inventions Swedenborg claimed as his own also point in the direction of Papin's experiments. The first concerned "a new construction of air-gun, thousands of which could be set off in the same instant by means of a single lever" (LL, 40, no. 5). During his last stay in London, between 1707 and 1712, Papin had constructed two air-guns, one of which functioned by the use of compressed air, the other by a vacuum. Swedenborg had evidently picked up these ideas and developed them further by linking several air-guns together with an air compressor, so that all the guns could be fired at once by a single hand, a precursor of the modern multiple-barrel gun.

Some of Swedenborg's other ideas were clearly based on Papin's steam machine and various pumps, which were themselves indebted to earlier suggestions of the military engineer Thomas Savery, who died in 1715. Swedenborg writes about "new machines, which compress and pump air by means of water, likewise a new pump which operates by water and mercury, which has more advantages and works better than ordinary pumps. Besides these, I still have further new designs for pumps" (LL, 40, no. 7). One of these especially recalls Papin's suggestions: "a machine driven by heat to expel water and a method which could be employed near hammer works, where water is standing rather than falling. The fire and the furnace would deliver sufficient water for the wheels" (LL, 40, no. 5). In the history of eighteenth-century inventions, the problem of raising large amounts of water had an elegant origin. While designing his fountains at Versailles, which Swedenborg admired on his visit, Louis XIV wished to see the waters of the River Seine raised up to the level of his pleasure-grounds and gave this commission to the great physicist Huygens, one of the first members of the Paris Academy. The latter entrusted his collaborator Papin with the manufacture of the necessary mechanical apparatus. First, a machine was built that produced sufficient air pressure to raise the water by burning gunpowder. Although Papin's experiments in the presence of Colbert demonstrated good results, this method proved impractical. Papin then replaced the gunpowder with water, and by heating it "a more complete vacuum was produced than could ever have been achieved by gunpowder."

Papin's princely patron, the Landgraf of Hesse, was interested in his projects because he was anxious to pump water up the Hercules Mountain near Cassel, on whose slopes his own fountain displays, still a great sight today, had been laid out. In 1698 Papin erected a machine on the bank of the River Fulda to perform this miracle, when an unusually early freeze destroyed everything. This stroke of bad luck was fateful for Papin since it caused the Landgraf to lose faith in the machine. The loss of his patron's favor robbed Papin of a further chance to prove his invention. Although many inventions are stimulated by full bottles of wine, Papin discovered his steam pump by observing how an empty wine bottle on his stove filled up with steam and then, to his amazement, sucked in water when the neck was immersed. He received a patent for fourteen years on the machine, which he constructed on this principle, and renewed it for a further twenty-one years in 1699. In 1704 Leibniz sent Papin a drawing of a similar machine, invented by Savery, which Papin immediately laid before the Landgraf. Heartened by Leibniz's authority, the Landgraf regained confidence in Papin and commissioned him to build a machine to pump standing water onto a wheel and thereby drive a flour mill. Swedenborg later claimed the solution as his own, except that he was concerned with hammer works rather than power for mills. Papin's new machine was successfully tested in the presence of the Landgraf, as Papin reported to Leibniz on 19 August 1706. However, the rising tube was not watertight, because the workers had used poor-quality putty despite Papin's warnings to connect the tube parts. Water streamed out of the cracks but even so the water was raised to a height of twenty meters. As assessor of mines, Swedenborg continued to improve pump technology successfully, together with Polhem.

These examples confirm that Swedenborg's inventions were concerned with mechanical problems, on which the great minds of his time were already working and whose solution was probably partly known to Swedenborg. They were suggested by the current requirements of court and industry and chiefly concerned garden design, mining, and navigation. Various physicists and mechanics were stimulated by the same demands for similar inventions. The progressive discovery of new physical principles and mechanical laws produced a convergence in the solution of problems. When Leibniz assumed his ministerial appointment with the elector of Hanover, he was also entrusted with the supervision of the mines in the Upper Harz Mountains. Water was to be pumped out of the pits with the aid of water power, but the primitive machinery that he found on-site left much to be desired. He was moved "to rescue the mine with an advantageous invention." By means of pumps driven by windmills, the water flowing from the wheels was raised onto a higher level, whence it fell again onto the wheels. At first the workers refused to operate these "advantageous" machines. Similar problems can be found in Swedenborg's list of inventions. He mentioned "a new plan for an elevator, by which large volumes of water could be quickly raised to higher localities" (LL, 40, no. 2). Later as a mining expert, he made practical use of this plan.

Swedenborg's listing of a "discovery of new methods for manufacturing springs with their properties" (LL, 41, no. 14) is also related to contemporary mechanical questions in clock-making and instrument-making, once Huygens, Pascal, Hooke, and Leibniz began working on clocks. Swedenborg applied his discovery extensively in later works on steel production and processing.

The problem of sluices and canal locks had long been a concern of the great inventors due to the geography of Holland and England, and Polhem had made new inventions in Sweden in Swedenborg's time. It is therefore unsurprising to find this theme in the wide range of Swedenborg's inventions. The fourth invention on his list "was to build locks through which ships could be raised as high as necessary in one or two hours" (LL, 40). As the collaborator of Polhem, he later had an opportunity to test his ideas on the largest sluice system of his time.

Contemporary inventors were chiefly exercised by problems of improving the transport of people and loads, namely, the mechanical carriage. The court alchemist Johann Joachim Becher (1635–1682) attributed to Leibniz the invention of a stagecoach, which could travel from Hanover to Amsterdam in six hours. Even if Leibniz was not the inventor of the automobile, he made a detailed study of how to move carts swiftly over soft ground. To this end, he invented moveable rails, which ran of their own accord under the wheels, a principle that appears in a somewhat modified form in modern caterpillar-tracked vehicles. Pascal himself did not only theorized on transport problems but also invented the Paris horse-tram system. He accomplished its operation and had a tram-stop placed near his residence, so that he could use his own invention in comfort. Swedenborg also took up the problem of the automatic carriage, which could move in ways based on the motion of a horse. As his twelfth invention, he listed "a mechanical carriage, which contained all kinds of driving-gear set in motion by the horse's own pace" (LL, 40, no. 12). It would be interesting to know he imagined this carriage in a gallop, but this plan has been lost and he did not resume this juvenile project.

Swedenborg published several of his earliest notes and designs relating to inventions in aviation. A flying model constructed according to his plans was displayed in the Swedish pavilion at the Chicago Exhibition of 1939, where it aroused great interest.[1] His reports to Benzelius spoke of "a machine, with whose aid a man could rise into the air and travel aloft." Polhem laughed Swedenborg to scorn, when he presented his plan, saying, "I think you had better drop that. I consider such an attempt on a par with the Philosopher's Stone or perpetual motion." But Swedenborg did not drop it and discussed the question in his own technical journal, *Daedalus Hyperboreus*. In the accompanying sketch, there is a light wing covered with a strong sail and equipped with two broad oars or blades, which move around a horizontal axis and drive the air under the wing. The blades are so constructed that they fold together with upward motion, in order to cause no air resistance, but they unfold with downward motion and press the air under the wing. Swedenborg never claimed that he could really fly with this machine, but he wanted to contribute his ideas to the problem of flight, which he believed would be solved one day. He wrote, "It seems easier to talk about such a machine than to manufacture it in reality, for it requires a greater motive power and a lesser weight than the human body possesses. Mechanical science may perhaps find a means, perhaps a strong spiral spring."[2] Following his description of the basic conditions necessary for hovering in

1. The flying machine model can be seen in the Smithsonian Institute. In *Wings of Man* (1959), the editor, Scandinavian Airlines System, writes as follows: "The model was built in its full dimensions in 1897 by Jesse A. Burt of Glenview, Illinois. According to eye-witnesses, whose statements are preserved in the library of Columbia University in New York, fifteen running men and boys pulled the machine to start, as if it were a dragon. It rose about fifteen metres and flew thirty metres, before it crashed—but it had flown."
2. *Daedalus Hyperboreus* (1716), p. 81. Reprinted in *Machine att Flygga I Wädret* (Stockholm: Bokförlaget Facsimilia, [1960]), 45.

the air, he continued, "If these advantages and requirements are noted, then perhaps someone in future will be able to use our suggestion and make the necessary improvements to realize what is only an idea in my case. There are sufficient proofs and examples in nature to show that flight can be achieved without danger. All the same, at one's first attempts, one will have to pay for one's tuition and risk life and limb." He closed with a quote from Fontenelle: "Do we wish to claim that we have already discovered everything and our knowledge has reached the point, at which nothing can be added to it? Merciful God, let us agree that that there are still things to do in coming centuries."[3]

Swedenborg's long list of inventions also includes a water-clock, a drawbridge that can be shut within gates or walls, and a mechanical method for reproducing silhouettes and prints. Alongside such practical and useful matters there are also plans, which betray the technical imagination of the Baroque, such as the design of "A Universal Musical Instrument, by the Aid of Which the Most Unskilled in Music Can Play All Kinds of Harmonies That Are Found in the Score." We hear no more of such ideas from him.

Swedenborg's "A Method of Ascertaining the Inclinations and Affections of Men's Minds" deserves special mention. The fact that he included his psychoanalytical method among mechanical inventions shows how completely he was absorbed in the new English mechanistic and mathematical worldview. Here he was following the example of English philosophy in understanding the function of the soul as a process based on mathematical and mechanical principles. Even the life of the mind and the soul is but motion and number and can be deduced, as Leibniz would say, by an "advantageous" method. Swedenborg felt so securely possessed of a key to the mystery of numbers and movements in the cosmos that he could suggest a technical explanation for humanity's wildest dreams.

A survey of the young Swedenborg's inventions demonstrates the practical cast of his mind, important for his entire subsequent development. Whatever his gift for the abstract sciences, he always had a sense of their usefulness in daily life. He was no abstract theoretician

---

3. *Machine Att Flygga*, 46.

but combined practical talent with a highly developed intelligence and always kept in mind the utility of his knowledge. This trait, evident throughout his life, makes him comparable with Leibniz. He too combined his theoretical knowledge of the natural sciences and philosophy with their practical and administrative use in the economy, mining, navigation, and postal communications. Swedenborg was very much aware of this particular talent, for he keenly felt the lack of practical thinking among Swedish scientists. From Brunsbo, he wrote of them to Benzelius shortly after his return: "I wonder at your friends, the mathematicians, who have lost all energy and desire to follow up such a clever plan which you suggested to them about building an observatory. It is a fatal flaw of mathematicians that they remain mostly in theory (LL, 40, no. 9). I have thought that it would be a profitable thing if to every ten mathematicians there were assigned one thoroughly practical man by whom the others could be led to market. In that case, this one man would gain more renown and be of more use than all the ten together. If I could contribute to carrying out this plan, I would not mind how much work it took" (LL, 42).

6

Homecoming and Disappointment

Swedenborg had made efforts to become Polhem's assistant before his departure overseas. Now, following his return, he wanted to become a second Polhem and assume the leadership of Swedish science and technology. Given his youthful self-confidence, he may have intended from the outset to supplant his teacher. Does not the list of his inventions sound like a challenge? His first intention on returning was "to take Polhem's inventions, make drawings and descriptions and test them by means of physics, mechanics, hydrostatics, and hydraulics as well as algebraic calculus." He returned not as the pupil but as the critic and judge of his teacher (LL, 41).

He had an extraordinary desire for autonomy and independence. Initially, he had no thought of tailoring his studies to a professional career—to his father's great regret—but planned to work as an independent researcher. This ideal owed much to the great men of science encountered during his travels. Flamsteed, sitting in his Greenwich Observatory, was not even distracted from his work by the visit of monarchs. Newton waged war with Leibniz and sensitive colleagues in Paris, while his mathematical skills were required by the Treasury whenever the English currency wavered. These were the models for Swedenborg's own career path. Such an independent scholar's life might have been his, had he been given a university professorship. However, there was no chair in his field, and this was the start of his difficulties on his return home. Swedenborg was himself to blame for these difficulties because he arrogantly expected such an appointment because of his genius; he neither sought a professorship nor tried to work his way up through attainments and publications. He had certainly acquired no modesty abroad. On 14 February 1716, he suggested that Benzelius should obtain for him a professorship of mechanics at the University of Uppsala. He not only offended the professors' dignity, but even thought that the salary of a new appointment could be raised by a corresponding reduction in the pay of the other professors!

Swedenborg tirelessly forged new plans for a position worthy of his genius. On 4 March, he sent Benzelius a statement of how his professorship could be financed with a memorandum on the reorganization of the entire faculty structure. He suggested the formation of a Faculty of Natural Science and a reduction in the Faculty of Arts, thereby anticipating university developments by a century. "Because a mathematics and science faculty are just as necessary and useful as an arts faculty owing to manufacturing, mining and navigation, a seventh of the university budget should be spent on the creation of such a faculty." This new faculty should have a professor of mechanics (six hundred silver thalers), a secretary (three hundred silver thalers) and four fellows. For these appointments, Swedenborg had in mind Walerius, Elvius, Roberg, and Bromelt, who held professorships in the arts faculty. All professors of the university should forgo a seventh part of their income, in order to raise the necessary three thousand silver thalers to establish this faculty.

This headstrong attack on the old humanistic foundations of the university provoked the greatest resistance on the part of the professors, who felt their peace and pockets were both threatened. Swedenborg complained of "prejudice." Therefore, he presented a new plan on 20 March 1716, which must have even further outraged those affected. One of the "less important professorships of theology or medicine" could be dropped in order to establish his own professorship of mechanics, or else the professorship of oriental languages could be combined with a professorship of theology or Greek language, thus releasing a chair that could be converted into a professorship of mathematics. But as it was obvious to him by now that the holders of these "less important" chairs would not agree to such a plan, he added in a note of resignation that this could take six to ten years, thereby speculating on the demise of several older colleagues. He asked Benzelius to think of another way of helping him find a professorship. Benzelius made a counter-suggestion: Polhem should become assessor of the Board of Commerce and give up his post as director of the Board of Mines; the laboratory of the Board of Mines should be transferred to Uppsala and the directorship made equivalent to a professorship. At the beginning of April 1716, Swedenborg doubted that Polhem would agree.

Another of Swedenborg's ideas aroused the opposition of the conservative professors. The spirit of the new science in Sweden, hitherto represented solely by Polhem, the "Archimedes of the North," needed a focus of more general activity. Swedenborg was filled with such admiration for the Royal Society in London and the Académie Royale in Paris that he decided "to start a society for learning and science in Sweden, on the excellent basis of Polhem's inventions." Once again he failed to take into account the prestige of Swedish academicians, who refused to be suddenly reorganized by a young man.

Swedenborg was no less impetuous with his third plan. He wanted to vie with the English and French and found an observatory in Sweden. Once again he did not ask whether the appropriate specialists agreed. Shortly after his arrival from Brunsbo, he traveled to Kinnekulle in the mountains south of the Väner Lake "to select a site for a small observatory where I intend toward winter to make observations about our horizon, and to lay a foundation for those calculations by which my method of finding longitude may be confirmed" (LL, 44). But first he wanted to travel to Uppsala to obtain the necessary instruments and equipment.

While the young university reformer tirelessly thought up new professorships and directorships for himself, he was soon made aware of his real situation. To begin with, the meeting with his father upset his calculations. Bishop Jesper, already irked by his son's long absence and stubborn behavior, was hardly impressed by his vaulting ambition. His son returned from abroad with plans for airplanes, submarines, and automobiles; and he wanted to found a learned society of physicists and mechanics, overturn the old faculties and establish a new faculty of sorcerers at the expense of theologians and philosophers. Such a son must have appeared a decided fantasist in his eyes. Had his son not squandered his good money on experiments and arts, which might even be the work of the Devil?

There were serious arguments between father and son. The bishop displayed his entire mistrust of his son's personal behavior and science, while Swedenborg reacted to his annoyed parent with all his youthful arrogance. He stuck to his plans despite all reproaches of his reckless behavior, his unusual and exaggerated ideas, and his financial difficulties. His disappointed father refused to put further means at his disposal. In December 1715, Swedenborg turned again to Benzelius and asked him to mediate. The resentment of the misunderstood genius is evident from his letter: "A single word from you to my father will be worth more than twenty thousand remonstrances from me. You can without comment inform him of my project, and of my zeal in my studies; and that he need not imagine that in the future I shall waste my time and his money. One word from another is worth more than a thousand from me. He knows very well that you have the kindness to interest yourself in my behalf, but he knows also that I am still more interested in my own behalf. For this reason he will distrust me more than you, my dear brother" (LL, 42).

The tension with his father continued, although Emanuel had a "sapphic song" printed for the bishop's sixty-third birthday on 28 August 1716, containing a homage to his father. But Jesper remained in ill humor and gave his son only two mentions in his extensive and exhaustive autobiography.

Swedenborg's only success at this time was renewed contact with Polhem. It took a considerable effort to allay the mistrust of the cunning and ambitious scholar, who was not inclined to foster his future rival. On 19 December 1715, Polhem sent a friendly invitation, asking Swedenborg to visit him in Stjärnsund. The foundation of a learned society was postponed, and the modest fruit of Swedenborg's exalted plans was the establishment of a scientific journal with the title *Daedalus Hyperboreus*. The legendary ancient architect of the labyrinth became the patron saint of technological progress in the far north. This periodical appeared in six volumes at various intervals between 1716 and 1718.[1] The cover can hardly have satisfied Swedenborg's ambition, for Polhem did not suffer his name to be included in the subtitle: "New Mathematical and Scientific Experiments and Observations, made by Assessor Polhem Esquire and other Ingenious Men in Sweden, and which are to be occasionally published for the public good." Given this sole outlet for the publication of his ideas and discoveries, Swedenborg worked enthusiastically on the journal and published a series of essays dealing with all kinds of machines, including his article on aviation.

Swedenborg's excessive hopes were not fulfilled in the year following his arrival in Sweden. At loggerheads with his father, cold-shouldered by most mathematicians and physicists at the universities, or dismissed as a greenhorn or dreamer, he had to submit to the authority of Polhem, to whom he already felt himself superior. His plan for a learned academy found no support; his project to erect an observatory with his own means could not be realized; he even had to conceal his name behind the authority of the powerful Polhem when he presented his own achievements in a scientific journal. Moreover, his money was running out, as his father refused to finance his seemingly incomprehensible plans. Now Emanuel directed his attention to more modest and useful things. In April 1716, he enquired about the white clay used to make pottery and pipes in Holland and England because he thought he had discovered in Vestergyllen a clay of identical quality. "If this were so, it would be worth many thousand thalers. But keep it quiet!" (LL, 42) Should the career that began with such ambitious plans end with the manufacture of clay pipes for Swedish sailors and fishermen?

---

1. Cf. Swedenborg's letters to his brother-in-law Benzelius from the end of December 1716, 26 June 1717, 14 January 1718, and 14 September 1718 (LL, 42–44).

7

Meeting with Charles XII

It took the political genius of Sweden, King Charles XII, to discover the genius Swedenborg. His universal mind not only embraced political tasks but seized upon the mathematical and scientific sciences with an intuitive passion for the achievements of the age. Swedenborg had followed the rise of the king and the bold start of his political program with great interest. His coronation was marked by a strange omen. On Christmas Day 1697, Charles put the crown on his head before he proceeded to church, but it fell from his head to the ground as he mounted his horse. The young prince reigned for three years in Sweden, then waged war against Russia and Poland, gathered an army of 8,000 men in Livonia, and won a total victory over an army of 80,000 Russians at Narva on 20 November 1700. This destroyed the threat to the Swedish empire from the east, Russian pressure on Finland and the Baltic countries was neutralized, and the Baltic Sea was open for the development of Swedish trade. It only remained to smash Polish pretensions of power. On 9 June 1701, he defeated the Saxon army besieging Riga and vanquished the Polish and Saxon troops at Klissow on 9 July 1702 and again at Pultusk on 21 August 1703. He conquered Torun and, on 6 February 1704, declared that the Polish king had forfeit his throne. The palatine of Poznan, Stanislaus Leszczynski, was elected king of Poland and crowned on 24 September 1705. A campaign in Silesia forced Augustus the Strong, the Great Elector of Saxony, to renounce his claims to the Polish crown and to recognize and even congratulate Stanislas on his election.

Meanwhile, the Russians had seized the Baltic provinces and occupied Dorpat, Narva, and Ivangorod. The Swedish generals Schlippenbach and Cronjort could not prevent this advance with their meager troops. Charles, still in Saxony with his army of 43,000 regular troops, transferred 6,000 men to Stanislas and marched with the main part of his army against the Russians. General Lewenhaupt, commander of all Swedish units in Riga, received orders to join Charles with all troops at his disposal. This operation miscarried. Lewenhaupt lost more than half his men and supplied only 5,000 men to the king, who had pitched camp at Smolensk. Charles XII's invasion of Greater Russia was a pretext for Mazeppa, the hetman of the Cossacks, to desert the czar and incite a rebellion of the Ukrainians. The armies of Mazeppa and Charles united near Poltava, in order to defeat the main Russian force. But this decisive encounter brought no victory but the defeat of the Swedes and Mazeppa. The date 27 June 1709 marks the turning point in the triumphant rise of the Swedish king. His beaten army was scattered in the Russian wastes. Two days after his defeat, the king crossed the Dneiper with a small retinue and rode through Turkish territory to Bendery in Moldavia, where he arrived at the end of July 1709. The rest of the Swedish army, so far as it was still intact, surrendered to Marshall Mentchikov. The surrender was signed on 29 June at Vorschla on the Dneiper. Revolts broke out in Sweden and Poland at the news of Czar Peter's victory and Charles' flight into Turkey. The conservative Swedish nobles had from the outset been mistrustful of Charles' tyrannical extension of royal power, and they exploited the catastrophe to extend their own political rights and restrict the royal prerogative. The peasantry, which had borne the main burden in blood and taxes for these costly foreign wars, became rebellious. The sight of such revolts, in which several royal officials had been murdered, was Swedenborg's last impression of his country when he travelled abroad. "God protect us from a revolution here, but it looks as if we will have one," he wrote in his farewell letter to Benzelius.

Disturbances also broke out in Poland, threatening to destroy Charles' work. The king answered with thunderbolts from Bendery. He protested against his alleged deposition and claimed the full maintenance of his rights in Poland. Meanwhile, the king's absence benefited all Sweden's enemies. Scarcely had the Swedish army been destroyed in Russia, when France invaded Sweden from Denmark with an army of 17,000 men. The governor of Skåne, Count Stenbok, hurriedly summoned all men fit for military service in the Swedish provinces; and, through a victory at Helsingborg on 28 February 1710, he forced the Danes to withdraw across the Sund. At the command of the absent king, the estates decided to continue the war, but not without opposition in the country. While Charles conducted fruitless negotiations with the Sublime Porte to induce the Turks to declare war on Russia, Peter the Great reconquered the entire Baltic Sea coast between Viborg, Reval, Dünamünde, Pernau, and Riga in 1710 in just three months. Sweden lost all her possessions in Livonia, Estonia, Finland, and Karelia at a single stroke. Plague overtook Stockholm the same year, raging from 10 August 1710 until February 1711, and snatched away almost 30,000 people. During the summer, the armies of Sweden's enemies united before Stralsund. Stanislaus, Charles' vassal, preferred to leave the continent and crossed over to Karlskrona, staying some time in Kristianstad, before making his solemn entry in Stockholm on 1 October 1711. He swore to the Riksdag that he would send new troops and army supplies to Pomerania. Through enormous efforts, the exhausted country succeeded in raising the means for an expedition to Poland, but the undertaking failed under the leadership of Count Stenbok. Stanislaus saw himself compelled to sue for a separate peace and renounce the Polish crown. Now the last basis of Swedish power in Poland was lost. Stanislaus traveled to Bendery, where Charles was still waiting for the decision of the porte.

Filled with new plans, Charles could not understand Stanislaus' behavior, refused to agree to the renunciation of the throne, and sent him to the court of the Duke of Zweibrücken, where he was to await a favorable turn of events. Finally, the porte became ill at ease with Charles's residence in Bendery. Istanbul did not think the time was right for a military solution to the Russian question and induced Charles to leave, first by courteous means and then by force.

Now began a legendary phase in the life of Charles. When the seraskier of Bendery and the khan of the Tartars tried to enforce his departure, he fortified himself with his small retinue in his house at Warniza. There he was finally compelled to surrender and was brought captive to Bendery and then taken to Dimotika near Adrianople (Edirne). Finally persuaded that his plans were hopeless, he decided to return on 1 October 1714. He left his following in Piteşti in Wallachia on 14 October 1714 and set off for his homeland on horseback with only two companions, Captains Düring and Rosén. Equipped with false passes in the name of three Swedish captains, the three rode day and night, with a led horse beside each steed. After Hermannstadt (Sibiu), Rosén sank unconscious to the ground. But the king and Düring rode on, without a break, without sleep and rest through Budapest, Vienna, Regensburg, Nuremberg, Bamberg, Würzburg, Hanau, Cassel, Göttingen, Brunswick, and Güstrow until they came to Stralsund. On the fourteenth day after leaving Wallachia, at one o'clock in the middle of the night, the king reached the gates of Stralsund. The gatekeepers made difficulties and did not want to admit the dusty, exhausted officers, although the king, to maintain his disguise, claimed he had dispatches from King Charles for the governor of the fortress. When the commandant was finally roused and gave permission to admit the urgent messenger, Charles hurried to the house of his devoted Dücker. He found the general waiting on his doorstep in the moonlight to receive in person the embassy of his master. He recognized his master at first sight. Charles had no clothes besides the filthy uniform, in which he had ridden forth from Wallachia, and owing to a severe chafing wound on his foot—he had not removed his boots for eight days—he was lame. For the first few days after his arrival, he could not leave his room. So great was joy over his return among the townsfolk and soldiers of Stralsund that the clamor reached his ears. Princes, ministers, and generals hurried to Stralsund to discuss plans for the future with the king, now he had finally returned. Even Swedenborg followed the fortunes of the king with great interest. During his stay in Paris, he received news from Hendrik Benzelius in Adrianople, who informed him that he had stayed six months with the king in Turkey. Now the legendary king had suddenly surfaced in his immediate neighborhood. All his thoughts and hopes were directed towards the monarch, whose deeds and fortunes had so long occupied his imagination. Swedenborg composed an ode of celebration in Latin, *Festive Applause on the Arrival of our Monarch Charles XII in Pomerania on 22 November 1714.* He had it printed in Greifswald and handed it to the king in Stralsund. Even he can have hardly guessed at that time how closely his subsequent fate would be linked with the king.

After his return, Charles XII found no time to step on Swedish soil but immediately rushed into new wars on the continent. From Stralsund, he opened hostilities against Prussia and occupied Wolgast, Usedom, and Wollin, in order to reconquer Stettin for the Swedish crown. Old enemies then united with new in order to subdue the northern king. A Danish, Prussian, and Saxon army besieged Stralsund and invaded the town in the night of 24/25 October, but without gaining possession of the fortress. During this night, Charles was fighting on Rügen against an enemy landing. He hurried from the violent turmoil, during which a cannonball struck down his horse and a spent bullet hit him in the chest without injury, and hastened back to Stralsund in order to save the fortress and the inner city. During the ensuing struggle, in which he personally fought night after night among the soldiers and the citizens, his loyal Düring, whom he had promoted colonel, fell in battle. Once the sea and the moat, the natural defense of Stralsund, had frozen over in the deep cold, it was no longer possible to hold the town. The ride from Turkey to Stralsund was now followed by an adventurous flight from Stralsund itself. Two fast sailing-ships, the galliot *Snarensven* and the brigantine *Snappupp,* were ordered from Karlskrona to collect the king, but wind and ice floes kept them off the Pomeranian coast. Then Charles decided to travel over the ice towards the ships. After the ice had been broken up with huge effort, he boarded a boat in the night of 22 December 1715, accompanied by only six oarsmen, two officers, and his page, while the chancellery secretaries followed in two other old boats. Soon the boats were caught in the ice. The occupants had to hack a groove through the ice sheet, while fire from batteries on both coasts wounded and killed several people. The king and the rest of his company, struggling with the wind and pack ice, finally reached the *Walfisch*, an old sailing-ship on the open sea. He landed on the coast of Schonen near Trelleborg, where, after fifteen years' absence, he climbed onto land at four o'clock in the morning on Christmas Day 1715, the anniversary of his coronation. He proceeded with his small following to Ystad, while Stralsund fell on the same day.

Returning to Sweden at the very end of 1714, Swedenborg found his fatherland in great excitement. News of Charles' arrival had swiftly quelled the people's discontent. The proximity of the king, whose personality cast a spell on the whole people, quietened the nobles, who had raised their voice against absolutism and supported the government's transfer to Princess Ulrike Eleonore. The divisive parties now sneaked away. But the king's stay in Stralsund and his new military entanglements were leading to fresh unrest.

All through the year 1715, Swedenborg was deeply impressed by his meeting with the monarch in Stralsund. As letters show, he followed his undertakings with the greatest interest. "We have heard the best and the worst news concerning the king; but there is exaggeration and coloring on both sides. Few people know anything with certainty about the king's person. Some claim he was trapped in Stralsund, without the possibility of escape; others take vain delight in his return and expect him every evening. Carriages stand ready at the court to drive to meet him. In general, people believe that he escaped and that, after his horse was shot from beneath him, he ran for two thousand paces before finding another battle-horse. This would redound to his honor. The Dutch say the Swede is the best soldier in the world, when he knows how to make good his escape" (LL, 41).

To be sure, this enthusiastic interest in the fate of the king was overlain by personal worries. But now his stay with Polhem brought him again into the presence of the king. Charles loved to be surrounded by outstanding men of art and science. He was untroubled by the censure of professors or the absence of academic titles. Once he had recognized Polhem's technical gifts, he had raised him to a higher rank. Soon after Charles' arrival in Sweden, Polhem was ordered to attend him in Lund. During their numerous discussions, he did not fail to notice the inventor's brilliant assistant. The king often drew Swedenborg into conversation, whenever he was explaining his most recent technical projects to Polhem, and Swedenborg also had an opportunity to speak of his own plans. The king granted him what scholars had refused. He appreciated the value of a learned scientific society as in London, Paris, and Berlin, which could benefit the training and prosperity of the whole nation. The king was also fascinated by the boldness as well as the economic and military usefulness of his technical ideas. Charles became one of the keenest readers of *Daedalus Hyperboreus*, which often stimulated further discussions of Swedenborg's inventions and his multifarious experiments in physics and mechanics.

Many contemporary monarchs kept astronomers for reasons of representation, but Charles XII was mathematically talented and so knowledgeable that scholars had to watch that they were not shown up by the king's acumen. Scientific conversations with the king made an indelible impression on Swedenborg. Almost four decades later, when describing the life of the monarch to Dr. Norberg in 1746, he could remember such a meeting down to the last detail.

The main topic of the king's conversations with Polhem and his assistant Swedenborg concerned the laws of motion and the treatment of general mathematical problems. At one time, they talked about the usefulness of the customary decimal system. This was not an idle question. As Boutroux put it, "Pascal had already the temerity in 1654 to criticize our decimal system as a mere convention." In 1670, Caramuel y Lobkowicz had publicly presented his philosophical critique of the decimal system. The king's particular interest was how the system actually arose. Swedenborg suggested to him that originally people had counted on their fingers and began again with one, once they had counted up to ten. Numerical sequences were established and named according to this custom and "thus a method of calculation arose on the basis of the fingers." The king approved of this explanation but then thought that this primitive way of calculating might not be the best and one could find a better one. He enumerated the inconveniences of the decimal system: When one halved 10, one had an odd, rather than an even number, whose further division led to fractions rather than the number 1. Thus, when calculating financial sums and measurements in practical life, one always had to deal with complicated fractions rather than simple integers. Moreover, the number 10 was neither the square, cube, or fourth power of any number, so that one had many difficulties in working out its square and cube root. In view of these deficiencies, it would be better to introduce an eight- or sixteen-number system instead of the decimal system. These numbers, when progressively halved, led back to the elementary number 1, without producing a fraction (16, 8, 4, 2, 1) and would also be more suitable for coinage and measures.

The king thereupon commissioned the scholars to devise a system based on another number than 10. When Polhem and Swedenborg objected that this would work only if they invented completely new numbers and names, they were instructed to work out such a system with new numbers and names. "In accordance with royal command," they developed an eight-number system with new symbols and names, together with a method of calculation and its application to monetary units and measurements. This plan was "most humbly submitted" to the king, but he found the solution too simple. The inventors then realized "that their master would have preferred a more extensive and complicated calculation, so that he would have an opportunity to display his great intellect and sharp judgment." The king then suggested they think up a system with a number that was both a cube and a square and that could be reduced to the number 1 on being successively halved. The two mathematicians suggested the number 64, but then they immediately thought of all the poor schoolchildren who would have to learn enormous multiplication tables. They ventured to observe that the replacement of the decimal system through a sixty-four-number system would be too complicated because people would then have to remember tables with 4,096 numbers, besides knowing sixty-four numbers by name and symbol. These objections enticed the monarch to develop the system more than ever, and he volunteered to work out the new method of calculation. The following morning, he handed his scholars a finished plan in which he had not only invented new names and symbols for the numbers from 1 to 64, but also worked out corresponding methods of addition, subtraction, multiplication, and division (LL, 43).

The technical projects that Charles wanted to tackle in the promotion of trade and transport in Sweden were also discussed during the days at Lund. As Polhem was completely taken up with preparing plans and preliminary organization, the king used this opportunity to put Swedenborg's collaboration on a firmer foundation. Swedenborg received the assignment "to give aid to Commercial Counselor Polhem" and was appointed extraordinary assessor at the Board of Mines, with the provision that he should remain at Polhem's disposal for some time (LL, 43f).

Until now Swedenborg had concerned himself with mining occasionally and for pleasure, as his father owned several pits in iron mines. Although he had already made some mining-related inventions, he had not applied himself systematically to the subject. When the king offered him a choice between a technical appointment or a university position, Swedenborg greatly preferred a technical appointment because he had already seen that academics regarded him as merely a talented outsider, not as a colleague. The distinguished gentlemen responsible for the management of the Swedish war and peacetime industry, and the royal mint, were greatly amazed when the young Swedenborg was appointed by the king to the Board of Mines without any customary training, overriding all normal procedures. Their amazement was all the greater on learning that the new postholder would receive the full salary of his appointment without having to work at the Board of Mines.

Swedenborg now had to justify the confidence of the king, who had granted him such a position of responsibility without any formalities. In his present circumstances, this appointment was the best conceivable solution for him. There were neither workshops nor laboratories in the universities or anywhere else in Sweden where a young physicist and mechanic could have occupied himself. Only in the mining industry were such workshops installed, where stones were tested for their ore content, physical and chemical tests were undertaken, models of machines were built, and new technical inventions were tried out. Leibniz also tested his inventions in the workshops of the Hanoverian mines of the Harz. The Swedish Board of Mines even possessed its own laboratory. Now an official state appointment had fallen into the researcher's lap. In collaboration with the greatest technician of the land, he could freely develop his genius for discovery and invention and use his knowledge for the benefit of his nation.

The unusual nature of his appointment immediately gave rise to a cabal, initiated by the vice president of the Board of Mines, Urban Hjärne, the founder of the first chemical laboratory in Sweden. Politically speaking, Hjärne was a convinced opponent of royal absolutism and was among those who deeply regretted the return of the restless and authoritarian monarch. Hjärne declared Swedenborg's appointment to be an illegitimate interference of the king in the affairs of the Board of Mines and took the view that the institution should not stand for this arrangement. Moreover, the young man thus imposed on the board was in no way objectively qualified. In order to counter Swedenborg, he attacked the whole family with a highly insulting review of Bishop Jesper's *Schibboleth* on the subject of Swedish spelling (*Swedberg*, 65). The hostility of such an energetic and tough opponent was very threatening. Would the king support Swedenborg if the Board of Mines made his appointment a matter of political controversy?

Charles quelled the intrigue, welcoming a contest to impose his absolutist conception of royal rights. His faith in the genius of the newly discovered young mathematician was stronger than the objections of his opponents to Swedenborg's inexperience. Hjärne had to yield, and Swedenborg wrote triumphantly in late autumn 1716: "What delights me most is that His Majesty expressed such a favorable and gracious opinion of me and defended me against those who thought the worst of me. I have already received direct and indirect proofs of his promise of further favor and protection. Once his majesty had made sufficient enquiry concerning my character, studies, and such like, and I was so fortunate as to receive good recommendations, he offered me three posts and offices to choose from, and afterwards decreed me the rank and post of an extraordinary assessor. But my enemies made too many intrigues over this decree and wrapped it up in ambiguous conditions. I therefore sent the decree back to his majesty with several comments, knowing I depended on him, whereupon a new decree and a gracious letter to the Board of Mines were granted. My opponent had to sit down at the king's own table and prepare the decree in two versions, for the king to choose the better one. Those who sought to hurt me were happy to preserve their honor and good name; they nearly burnt their fingers" (LL, 43).

Hjärne never forgave Swedenborg for this defeat, especially after Swedenborg declared Hjärne had "a weak grasp of the principles of chemistry." The suppressed enmity broke out immediately after the death of Charles XII. Hjärne revenged himself on the king by publicly and privately demanding a constitutional limitation of royal powers. In his later visionary reports, Swedenborg placed Hjärne in hell, where he encountered him in the company of particularly evil spirits.

Polhem's commissions concerned technical undertakings on a scale hitherto unknown in Europe: the construction of a ship's dock near Karlskrona and the erection of locks on the Göta Canal, which runs from the Väner Lake to Göteborg and flows into the Kattegat. Here the Trollhättan waterfalls had to be surmounted, "one of the greatest mechanical enterprises ever carried out in the world," as Swedenborg proudly declared. He worked on these projects as Polhem's assistant, conducted the land surveys, and helped prepare the technical drawings and calculations. But soon he had an opportunity to show the king an independent sample of his art. In 1718, the conflict with Norway led to a siege of Fredrikshald. When the heavy Swedish artillery could not be brought up by road, Swedenborg used a method of his own invention to transport two galleys, five large boats, and a small boat on rollers for twenty-one miles across hills and valleys from Strömstad to the border town of Iddefjol. "The king was thus enabled to carry out his plan and brought up by barges much heavier artillery than would have been possible by road to the walls of Fredrikshald."

This kind of feat increased Charles' affection for the sorcerer's apprentice of new technology and extended their friendship to daily intellectual exchanges. "Every day I had some mathematical matters for his majesty," wrote Swedenborg with delight on 14 September 1718 from Vänersborg, the starting point of the sluice construction on the Göta Canal. "The king deigned to be pleased with all of them. When the eclipse took place, I went out with him to see it and talked much to him about it. This, however, is a mere beginning. I hope in due time to be able to do something in this quarter for the advancement of science, but I do not wish to bring anything forward now except what is of immediate use" (LL, 44).

Charles XII understood, as few monarchs do, how to attract, stimulate, and utilize these special gifts and talents for himself and his country. Not only Polhem had to achieve the utmost. Royal encouragement for the practical use of his knowledge bestirred Swedenborg to an inconceivable intensity of work between his meeting with Charles at Lund and the latter's death in November 1718. During this time, Swedenborg assisted Polhem with complicated sluice and dock works; produced drawings, calculations, and land surveys; and calculated the fluctuations of water level in various lakes and watercourses related to the canal project. He also prepared a report on the tin industry of Stjärnsund with a description of the production process and the manner of tin plating. He also produced an expert report "Concerning the Support of Trade and Manufacture" and suggested to the king a state-controlled plan for the extraction, processing, and export of Swedish ores. In another submission, he mentioned the establishment of a salt works and then, encouraged by the king, took his own plans in hand. The king decided to grant the salt industry important privileges, "which would perhaps induce many keen persons to invest their means in the salt business."

A further report served to improve and expand Swedish paper manufacture. Swedenborg compiled his experience in dock construction at Karlskrona and the sluice project between Vänersborg and Göteborg as "Information on Dockyards, Canal Locks and Salt Works." Simultaneously he published his observations on the survey of the Väner Lake in the form of a treatise: "On the Rise and Fall of the Väner Lake and the Extent to Which This Is Caused by the Inflow of Water as Well as the Outflow through Rivers." This work was published in *Acta Literaria Sueciae*, the publication of the subsequently founded Swedish Academy.

During this period, whenever opportunity permitted, he familiarized himself with his duties as an assessor of mines and produced an eighty-four-page-long "Description of Swedish Iron-Smelting and the Smelting Process." In the same year, he composed a manuscript entitled "New Guidelines for the Discovery of Mines, or Hitherto Unknown Tips for the Discovery of Mines and Treasures Hidden Deep in the Earth." Besides these writings, he filled the running issues of *Daedalus Hyperboreus* with a mass of treatises on physical and mechanical experiments and technical inventions.

His treatise "On the Nature of Fire and Furnaces," chiefly concerned with new and more profitable methods of ore smelting, also served mining science and practice. Swedenborg wrote of this in a letter of 3 November 1719: "I collected everything that I could gather from smiths, charcoal burners, ore smelters, and smelting inspectors for the basis of my theory of fire. I hope that many of these discoveries will prove useful in time. For example, a fire can be stoked in a new furnace, in which wood and coal normally lasting only one day is sufficient for six days and produces more heat" (LL, 45).

Swedenborg's scientific genius was not exhausted by works useful to his country. His practical work constantly led him on to general and fundamental problems. His earlier interest in rock formation had taught him to see the testimony of earlier geological periods in the mussel and snail fossils he found in limestone and thus to read the prehistory of the earth, a science to which John Woodward had introduced him in London. Over the following years, he tirelessly continued his researches into the earth's prehistory at all locations in Sweden, where he travelled in the service of the king and compiled them in his work *On the Height of Water and the Strong Tides in the Primeval World* (1719). In this work, he included proofs of changes in the northern horizon and demonstrated that Sweden was an island in prehistoric times.

Swedenborg did not neglect his mathematical and astronomical studies during this period. This field was of great interest to the king, and new speculations on these subjects constantly arose from their frequent discussions. He wrote up these studies in 1717 as a 400-page manuscript with contributions to geometry and algebra. At this time, he also published at Uppsala an algebra textbook of ten volumes in the Swedish language.

Despite all opposition, Swedenborg had not given up his old plan for an observatory in Sweden. In 1717, he presented a report on "the importance of establishing an astronomical observatory in Sweden, together with a plan for carrying this out." Here he described everything that he had found of note at Flamsteed's observatory and the other places of research he had visited abroad. However, he still had no luck with this project. Because such a building demanded larger resources and because the king "did not like to hear" of financial needs, as Swedenborg himself well knew, he handed his project not to the king, but to his secretary Cederholm (LL, 44). The latter raised administrative concerns that the plan stemmed not from the faculty in Uppsala but from an outsider and was dismissive. "We must watch for another opportunity," wrote Swedenborg from Lund on 26 July 1717, but this opportunity never arose (LL, 43).

Nevertheless, Swedenborg continued his astronomical studies with the means at his disposal. He considered his observations on the changes in the earth's motion around the sun and their effect on the seasons as a particularly important discovery. He collected these studies in his work *The Motion and Position of the Earth and Planets in Which Are Some Conclusive Proofs That the Earth's Course Decreases in Rapidity, Being Now Slower Than Heretofore, Making Winter and Summer Days and Nights Longer in Respect of Time Than Formerly.* He had similarly distributed his *Experiment to Find Eastern and Western Longitude by Means of the Moon, for the Consideration of the Learned among Contemporaries.* Printed at Skåra in 1718, this was based on his solution of longitude prior to his return to Sweden. Swedenborg's method was adopted by mariners and enabled many captains and navigators to work out their position well into the nineteenth century.

He finally included the world of organic life within his universal mechanistic worldview and wrote a small anatomy of the life force. His *Anatomy of Our Most Subtle Nature, Showing That Our Moving and Life Force Consist of Vibrations* (1719) did not simply repeat Descartes' mechanistic theory of trembling movements but was based on his own anatomical studies. "For this purpose I have thoroughly familiarized myself with the anatomy of nerves and membranes and have proved a correlation exists between this and the interesting geometry of tremulations." The Royal Medical College must have been astonished to receive from an assessor of mines a treatise that substantiated Descartes' abstract and controversial theory with thorough anatomical observations.

Far from disappointing his royal patron, Swedenborg abundantly justified his anomalous appointment to high office with his achievements. Many projects and inventions that the young researcher had brought home with him were now maturing. Swedenborg had developed his admirable universality in the most unfavorable external circumstances. On constant journeys with the wandering king's retinue or accompanying Polhem, on study trips to the mining districts or in surveys of the Baltic Sea, the Kattegat, and the Väner Lake, he had recorded, viewed, compared, and methodically classified everything with strict scientific self-discipline, to glean the inner laws of nature. He did not speculate on a metaphysical view of reality but studied the natural world without preconceptions. The displacement of stones through flooding suggested prehistoric continental drift, when ebb and tide were much stronger. Mussel and snail fossils told him of the formation of the earth's crust at a time when mountains were raised and waters covered the continent of today. His measurements of the earth's motion in relation to the other planetary orbits explained the change in the length of the day and seasons in the course of the earth's history. By means of physical observations of tremulations, he interpreted the functions of nerves and fibers in the brain. His experience of the multifarious realms of nature all around him led him to fathom the ultimate principles of life. He was never a hostage to his theory and preconceived schemes but learned from things and advanced his view of the universe, the more he studied its manifestations in detail. What a noticeable contrast to the philosophical attitude of a theoretician such as Descartes, who withdrew behind a stove in Germany one whole winter long, in order to conceive of the nature of the universe! Swedenborg climbed into the mines, measured ebb and tide, pounded rock fragments from shafts and quarries, collected drift stones in the valleys and gravel from the rivers, compared the metallic traces of various ore-containing rocks,

calculated the movements of the stars, and the changes of the horizon, and allowed things to lead him to their essence. He himself
sensed the growth of his knowledge and thus wrote at the conclusion of the full years under the star of Charles XII: "The profound
study, with which I endeavored to grasp these subjects, caused me
to have a low estimation of everything I had previously published"
(LL, 45).

His universality was also evident in his combination of theory
with practical talent and the way in which he could draw material
benefit from his scientific insights: witness his suggestions for the
conversion of Swedish finance by increasing the productivity of copper mines for coinage and his reports on Swedish finance and trade.
Again, he is comparable with Leibniz, who demonstrated a similar
universality in all scientific and technical fields together with new insights, practical suggestions, and inventions.

8

After the Death of Charles XII

Charles XII's death was a severe hindrance to Swedenborg's mete-oric development. The early demise of the king, who like Gus-tavus Adolphus fell in battle shortly before the attainment of his goals and whose work faded with the decease of its creator, had a similar effect on Swedenborg's career as on the general course of Swedish history. Genius can never reconcile itself to convention, no more than the extraordinary can with the mediocre. There is no scale to measure whether and how long a genius is beneficial to a country. It is only certain that a genius's work will endure only to the extent that succeeding generations will tolerate it. This applied to Charles' political ideas as well as all his other achievements. Thus the work on the sluice system between Vänersborg and Göteborg ceased immedi-ately after his death.

The king had treated the young Swedenborg as a friend. Once his royal patron was dead, he was greatly discouraged. To be sure, he retained his position as assessor: his scientific and practical achieve-ments had long since vindicated his appointment. However, there was now no enthusiasm for his ideas. The establishment of an astro-nomical observatory was shelved once the king no longer promoted it. The scientific and astronomical discoveries, which had so inspired his royal friend, were now rejected by the university in an instinctive defense of its traditions. He had to stand by and watch as academics founded the Society of Sciences at Uppsala without him. He who had wanted to found such a society for the advancement of the new sciences was not admitted until 1729. He was kept waiting five years until the academic consistory at Uppsala finally summoned him "for the benefit of the young and the glory of the academy" to take up the professorship of higher mathematics vacated by Nils Celsius. However, by this time he had long ceased to regard a Swedish university as an appropriate field for his activity. He declined this offer with great conviction and suggested three other colleagues in his reply. "My own subjects are geometry, metallurgy, and chemistry, and there is a great difference between these subjects and astronomy. It would be unpardonable for me to give up a career in which I can be useful. Moreover, I have no gift for teaching. You know my difficulties in speaking. I therefore hope that the academy will not propose me. My thoughts are no longer directed towards an academic life, and I would no longer find satisfaction in it."

After the death of Charles, the letters of the thirty-year-old showed traces of bitter resignation, which overtook him in the midst of his tireless scientific works. "Throughout the summer," he wrote from Stockholm in November 1719, "I have spent some time jotting down what will probably be the last of such speculations and arts in Sweden. For these are condemned to death by a party of political idiots, who regard such ideas as mere scholastic subjects, over which their allegedly sublime ideas and intrigues should take precedence" (LL, 44f). In a letter dated 1 December 1719, the tone is even more bitter: "I am sending you a small work dealing with the decimal system of our coins and measures. This is the last that I will publish myself because I have already worked myself into poverty. I have been singing long enough; let us see whether anyone will come forward and hand me some bread." He saw himself as minstrel or begging musician, ignored and unpaid.

Wearied by scholarly rejection in his own country, his mind turned again to England and France, where he had discovered his ideals. In Charles XII's reign, Sweden had opened its doors to him, but, in the post-Carolingian period, he felt excluded in his own country. However, he did not want to return to foreign lands as a pupil but as a recognized scholar. He therefore decided to prepare his return to the wider world carefully. He had published his journal and his scientific publications as well as his reports and practical guides in Swedish and thus forgone European fame. While working for Charles, he never thought of any higher recognition than that of the king. Now he wanted to translate his works into Latin or French and send them to Holland and England, in order to make his mark in the academic debates of Europe at Paris, London, and Berlin.

There was another important change. He did not want to wander abroad as a scientific adventurer. He knew he was a master of mining science and hoped to acquire a leading position abroad as a mining expert. What the king's generosity had provided by way of a title and a pension, he now recognized as his real vocation. This career led him to discover new natural phenomena and constantly forced him to apply and extend his immense knowledge of mathematics, physics, chemistry, and technology. This career kept directing him towards fundamental questions such as the birth of our planet and its evolution and, beyond these, the origin of the universe and of life itself.

Specialization in mining and emigration were the two other themes of his new program. In a letter of 1 December 1719, he wrote:

Secondly, I now believe I sufficiently understand the mechanical equipment in mines to be able to say better than anyone what is new and what is old. I also understand the theory of fire and stones, in which I have made a number of discoveries. I therefore intend to use all my time promoting mining and to gather as much knowledge as possible upon these foundations. Thirdly, once I have gathered the means and acquired some credit through preparations and publications abroad, I propose to go abroad and seek my fortune in the management and equipment of mines. For he is nothing short of a fool who is independent and at liberty to do as he pleases, and who sees an opportunity for himself abroad, and yet remains at home in darkness and cold, where the Furies, Envy and

Pluto have taken up their abode and assign the rewards, and where labors such as I have performed are rewarded with misery. The only thing I would desire until that time is to find a sequestered place where I can live secluded from the world. I think I may find such a corner in the end, either at Starbo or at Skin(skatte)borg. But because this would take four or five years, I am ready to admit that long-term plans are like long-term building projects, which are always interrupted through unforeseen circumstances. Man proposes, but God disposes. But I believe a man should know what he is doing and devise an orderly plan to carry out what is most practical in his life. (LL, 47)

This is the practical philosophy that the unexpected death of Charles XII had taught him. Necessity and self-knowledge enabled him to overcome the typical crisis of a genius in a positive way. The universality of his greatness was his danger. Would he scatter himself in the abundance of his gifts and the variety of his knowledge, or would he win through to a firm sense of self-limitation? He regained his self-possession and surmounted the crisis, at least for the time being, by deciding on a firm career.

The quarrel with Polhem also came at this time. Given the circumstances, it was inevitable. Polhem had introduced the young researcher to Charles XII and had seen the unexpected rise of his talented pupil and his astonishing successes. Above all, he had witnessed the deepening friendship between the king and Swedenborg. The commercial counselor, an autodidact who had worked himself up from the lowest social class, found the dazzling rise of his young colleague hard to bear. When Swedenborg was officially assigned as his paid assistant by royal command, he became cautious: he did not want to give too much away to the bright young man or support him too much in his plans. Already in June 1717, Swedenborg wrote, "The commercial counselor is determined to bother himself with nothing but his own concerns, as he has noticed that he has been entrusted with many new things he does not understand" (LL, 43). These words show that the rivalry between master and pupil had already reached a disagreeable point. However, Polhem's caution was not unfounded, as Swedenborg clearly played the superior towards his principal. The arrogant self-confidence of the student had only increased.

After Charles' death, Polhem no longer felt obliged to promote the pupil who had grown into a rival. He no longer supported him in the ensuing conflicts with the university and submitted no further contributions to *Daedalus Hyperboreus.* The external circumstances of their separation are not precisely known. Polhem, that is Polhem's spirit, does not reappear until the *Spiritual Diary* of 1750. There Swedenborg describes him as a cunning atheist and victim of his godless ideas who is forever condemned to construct mechanical cats in hell. This contrast in the estimation of his formerly esteemed teacher suggests a major argument and final break after Charles' death.

A family matter may have accelerated the break. During his rise, Swedenborg fell in love with one of Polhem's daughters, and a love story ensued, which is best captured in the patriarchal words of Tubeck:

> When Commercial Counselor Polhem was building the sluices of Trollhättan and Karlskrona, the young Emanuel Swedberg lived in his house as a collaborator and mathematics pupil. Here he fell passionately in love with Polhem's second daughter, Emerentia Polhem, who was subsequently given in marriage to High Court of Justice Counselor Rücersköld. But because the girl was only thirteen or fourteen years old and did not want Swedberg, she could not be persuaded into an engagement. But because her father liked Swedberg so much, he gave him a written contract for her, which she had to sign in filial obedience. But she succumbed to such daily mental anguish that her brother, Chamberlain Gabriel Polhem, seized with sympathy, secretly stole the contract from Swedberg. As the latter's sole recreation was to read this through daily, he soon discovered its loss. His misery was so obvious that old Polhem entreated him to explain its cause and then offered to replace the lost contract through his paternal authority. But when Swedberg finally saw what misery he was causing his loved one, he dropped his claim and took his leave with the solemn oath that he would never think of women nor enter a marriage contract again. Thereupon he travelled abroad. It is also worth noting, that Swedenborg assured the daughters and sons-in-law of his former loved one, when they

visited him in old age in his garden, that he could speak with their deceased mother, as often as he wished.

This story is by no means legendary, although research has proved conclusively that the betrothed was not Emerentia but another of Polhem's daughters. Swedenborg himself later recounted the incident (Tafel, no. 255; LL, 70). When he was entertaining ladies at a party in the house of General Tuxen around 1770 and confessed that he had always enjoyed the company of ladies, the general half-jokingly asked him if he had ever married or wished to be. Swedenborg denied the first and then related how he had nearly married in youth, when King Charles XII recommended Polhem to give him his daughter in marriage. "But she did not want me, as she had already given her pledge to another whom she liked." Here Swedenborg avoided speaking of his love and laid the blame for this plan on the king. If Swedenborg were not veiling his grief at unrequited love, one might conclude that Charles' death also had consequences here. Once the illustrious advocate of Swedenborg's union with the house of Polhem had died, Polhem was no longer keen to become his rival's father-in-law. He may have decided to distance himself from a matter that had caused only vexation, ill-humor, and tearful scenes in his house.

9

The Assessor of Mines: Career and Research Travels

Swedenborg did not emigrate from Sweden, as he had intended in times of ill humor and disappointment following the death of Charles XII. His appointment at the Board of Mines was not affected despite the attempts of several opponents. His scientific and technical achievements were also recognized by the new monarch. Swedenborg immersed himself completely in his career. But the life he led during his appointment as royal assessor of mines showed little of a man at peace with himself, his work, and the world. He was driven by a restless zeal for work, which must have disconcerted his more easy-going colleagues. Owing to his headstrong drive for knowledge and his strong ambition for European fame, he constantly saw his professional activity as a brake on his genius. How could both be reconciled? On the one hand, his hubris dreamed of making his name among European scholars; on the other, he could not deny that his work at the Board of Mines offered him not only a secure income but also an opportunity for research scarcely to be found elsewhere. Where else would he encounter this wealth of metals, this variety of geological formations, and this unique accumulation of natural phenomena in the Swedish mountain districts? The tension between his desire for European acclaim and the love of his work determined the rhythm and course of his life until his vocation as a visionary. He could never remain long in Sweden, working at the Board, in the mines, laboratories, and iron-works of his homeland. Again and again, Europe summoned him. The records of the Board of Mines show a pattern in Swedenborg's requests to the king: to grant him leave for a longer journey to complete scientific studies or to have a larger work printed abroad. Such a journey simultaneously gave him an opportunity to visit mines and metal industries abroad. The other gentlemen of the board led a quieter life, contenting themselves with rare and short visits to England and the Netherlands. Leaves of several years' absence, as requested by Swedenborg, were not customary. Nevertheless, his travel requests were regularly granted, and the king even ordered that his salary should continue to be paid, reduced by a half in order to pay a deputy in his absence. This measure represented an extraordinary concession at a time when officials enjoyed no right to regular pay. The fact that Swedenborg managed to have new scientific works printed abroad on every visit and always returned with new inventions and knowledge of benefit to his country's industry and economy may well have caused his colleagues and the king to meet his exceptional requests. It gradually became evident that Swedenborg's mistrust was misplaced and the Swedish "darkness" did not only hold "Furies" (LL, 47).

Once he had gone, he did not soon return. As the records show, on several occasions after being abroad for six months or a whole year, he sent requests for a further extension on the grounds that his works were not yet completed. Even in these cases, he met with sympathy. The tendency to comply with his requests grew in proportion to his scientific reputation. In this fashion, he found a balance between the two basic drives of his nature, between the open fields of European fame and the practical application of his knowledge in the service of his country. As a result, his life was unusually mobile and constantly gave him opportunities to use his speculative and practical inclinations.

A short survey may indicate the course of these varied years. Swedenborg's first journey after the death of Charles XII led him in early May 1720 via Copenhagen, Hamburg, and Amsterdam to the mines of the present-day Belgian-Rhineland industrial district between Louvain and Aachen. He travelled then to Cologne and neighboring areas and from there to Leipzig and the mining districts of Saxony. Returning to Hamburg, he decided not to voyage back to Sweden just yet. He visited the mines of Hanover and Brunswick, travelling via Brunswick and Goslar to visit the Harz mountains, where he viewed the most important pits and works. Not until July 1722 did he return to Stockholm via Hamburg and Stralsund.

A second journey led him in May 1733 from Stralsund to Berlin, and thence via Dresden to Prague, everywhere on the trail of the most important pits and metal works. Using Karlsbad as a base, he visited the whole area of the Bohemian mining industry and returned through Dresden to Leipzig in order to have his *First Principles of Natural Things* (1734) printed there. Then he turned towards the mining district of Hesse, visited Cassel and all the mines between this town and Schmalkalden. He studied the basalt outcrops near Marburg, the Frauenberg, the Amöneburg, and other striking geological features of Hesse. He then travelled through Gotha to Brunswick, embarking from Hamburg to Stockholm, where he arrived in July 1734.

A third journey took him away from his homeland and his office for three years. It lasted from 1736 to 1740 and his destination this time was Rome, which he reached by way of Paris, Venice, and Bologna.

In 1743 he began yet another long journey. On 21 July, he left Stockholm and visited in Stralsund the old places associated with Charles XII: the house the king had occupied on his return from Turkey and other sites that had acquired a historical significance at the siege of Stralsund in 1715. Then he travelled on to The Hague, where he had his book *The Animal Kingdom* (1744) printed. There commenced the religious crisis, which led to the efflorescence of his visionary gift. On travelling on to England, this crisis reached its climax in his vocational vision at London in April 1745. He returned from an absence of two years, having decided to resign his office and to live according to his spiritual knowledge.

One should emphasize a hitherto neglected point about these numerous travels, namely, Swedenborg's relations with Germany. He was the personal friend of several German princes, especially Ludwig Rudolf, the second son of Anton Ulrich, Duke of Brunswick-Wolfenbüttel. After the latter's death in 1714, the duchy was divided between August Wilhelm and Ludwig Rudolf, whereby the former received Brunswick and the latter Blankenburg with its numerous mines. When Swedenborg visited the Harz in 1722, Blankenburg was the seat of Ludwig Rudolf, who was most friendly towards Swedenborg and showed him the most generous hospitality. The duke may have initially thought it useful to draw a distinguished foreign mining expert to his court, but he soon recognized the universal mind of his Swedish guest, and their relations deepened into personal friendship. Swedenborg dedicated to his patron the fourth part of his *Miscellaneous Observations concerning Natural Things*, which was published in 1722 at Schiffbeck near Hamburg. Following the death of his brother in 1731, the duke also ruled over Brunswick-Wolfenbüttel. Swedenborg visited him a second time on his journey of 1734 and expressed his gratitude in the form of a dedication to the duke in the first volume, *Principia* or *First Principles of Natural Things*, of his major work *Philosophical and Metallurgical Works*, published at Dresden and Leipzig in 1734.[1]

The German travel reports show Swedenborg as a truly universal scholar, who methodically educated his versatile mind to see and study all the peculiarities of nature and art. His chief interest was naturally mining, as his profession demanded. He tirelessly descended the shafts and pits of the Harz and the mines of the Rhineland, Hesse, Saxony, and Bohemia. He examined rock samples and studied the various forms of drainage, smelting, furnaces, bellows, combustion processes, and alloys. He wrote up his observations on rock formations, the incidence of petrification, and crystals. His scientific works were based on his personal observation of European and German mining in a way that was unique for his time.

---

1. For Swedenborg's journeys, see Tafel, II, 3 ff, partly reprinted in LL, 48–52.

Samuel Sandel was quite right when he said in 1772, "No one can accuse Swedenborg of reorganizing another's work, adding a little and then publishing it under his own name. We are aware that he never relied on others but followed his own ideas and made observations found in no other author before his time."[2] He directed his attention towards everything worth knowing, which fell within the scope of his multifarious interests. He sought to acquaint himself with scientific collections and laboratories, which were at that time in the private collections of princes and scholars. In 1733 he visited the laboratory of Dr. Neumann in Berlin, "which is equipped with small fireplaces and ovens for chemical experiments and for distillation in water baths and sand baths, with everything installed in a highly inventive and exact way."[3] In Leipzig, he visited the Museum for Natural History with Michaeli and Rüger, two mine inspectors, and took a particular interest in the fossils from Ilmenau, which later inspired Goethe's theories of evolution. In the same year, 1734, he visited the scientific collection of the Clementinum, the Jesuit college in Prague. He gave precise descriptions of the numerous clocks and instruments and the automaton on display there, "a young man who beats a drum and simultaneously opens and closes his eyes by means of an inner mechanism." He was also shown a German Bible from the pre-Reformation period, the translation of Rüdiger printed at Nuremberg in 1483.

In Hans-Jürgenstadt, he studied the collection of precious and rare stones, which the mine director Derfler had spent fifteen years collecting for King Augustus the Strong (1670–1733) of Saxony. Returning to Leipzig, in the company of the Saxon mining director Henkel he visited the collection of ores, shells, and fossils assembled by the famous chancellor Trier, also a director of mines in Saxony. Here Swedenborg especially admired a shale slab containing the skeleton of a long-tailed monkey. Hermann Lang, professor of physics and mathematics at the University of Halle, showed him his

---

2. *Sammlung von Urkunden betreffend das Leben und den Charakter Emanuel Swedenborgs,* ed. Imanuel Tafel (Tübingen, 1838), I, 1ff; R. F. Tafel, *Documents,* I, 2; reprinted in LL, 6ff.

3. Swedenborg's stay in Germany of 1733–1734: Tafel, II, 6ff. The description of his various journeys between 1733 and 1743 fills 142 pages in *Documents,* II, 6–147.

curiosity cabinet and gave his famous visitor several fossils. Magister Semler, lecturer in physics and chemistry, also showed him his collections, among which Swedenborg particularly noted instruments for measuring magnetic deflection and well as various types of special ovens. Finally, he visited the famous collections exhibited in the orphanage of the German Pietist leader August Hermann Francke (1663–1727). Here there were gifts from missionaries in Tranquebar, images of Indian deities, rare plants, stones, domestic implements, and boats from Tamulenland. There was also a planetarium showing the Ptolemaic and Copernican cosmology in the form of a great globe in which one could sit and view the movements of the planets and stars on the surface of the globe. But the travel reports also contain numerous lengthy descriptions of churches and buildings with a meticulous record of their ground plan, architectural principles, style, and artistic decoration.

On all his journeys, Swedenborg endeavored to acquaint himself with the most recent developments of science in each country he visited. He was constantly busy confirming the insights gathered from books in conversations with friends and acquaintances. He never spared himself the labor of making extensive excerpts from new books on science, cosmology, and metaphysics encountered on his way. In 1733, at Leipzig he worked through Jacob Bernouilli's *Entwurf einer neuen Theorie der Schiffs-Steuerung* and Julius Berhard von Rohr's *Compendieuse Haushaltungsbibliothek*, and made extracts of the latter's chapters on mining. In July 1736 on his journey to Hamburg, he made extracts from Christian Wolff's *Philosophia prima, sive Ontologia* (1729) and *Cosmologia generalis* (1731), "especially from such sections, which I needed en route to test his basic philosophical principles." He had first sight of Wolff's *Cosmologia generalis* in 1733 when visiting the house of the mining secretary Rüger at Leipzig and studied it very carefully.

He also tried to make the personal acquaintance of leading scholars in contemporary Germany. On his way home from Paris to Sweden in 1715, he had travelled through Hanover in the hope of meeting Leibniz there. When he visited Hanover during his journey to Germany in 1721, Leibniz had been dead five years. In the meantime Swedenborg had established relations with Christian Wolff

(1679–1754), one of Leibniz's most important pupils. The documents do not reveal whether this derived from a personal meeting. In his memorial speech, Samuel Sandel reported the well-established fact that Swedenborg was corresponding with Christian Wolff. The Prussian king's banishment of Wolff from Halle had stirred the entire learned world of Europe, and it is perfectly possible that Swedenborg met the famous philosopher on his visit to Marburg in 1734.

Among Wolff's former colleagues, Swedenborg became acquainted with Andreas Rüdiger (1673–1731), whose ideas on science, cosmology, and theology were strikingly similar to his own and may have directly influenced him. During his stay at Halle in 1733 he visited Rüdiger, who held the professorship of philosophy at the university there. While there, he also met the famous theologian and canon law theorist Christian Thomasius (1655–1728) and talked at length with him. Any assessment of the strong influence of the Leibnizians Wolff and Rüdiger on Swedenborg's scientific and metaphysical views must take account of his vital, personal impression of these scholars.

During his journeys, Swedenborg's active mind constantly transmuted the stream of impressions and events he experienced into fruitful applications. Anything new suggested new combinations linked in a higher unity. He was extraordinarily productive as an author, especially when he was travelling. Not only anthologies such as the *Miscellanea*—observations of natural objects—or essays on specific scientific questions grew from his thousands of notes but also his large systematic works. The most important chapters were written while resting and during longer stays at inns in German towns, where he recuperated from his tiring journeys by coach over the rough roads of the German petty states. He stayed at "The Black Eagle" in Hamburg and "The Golden Star" in Halle, and these colorful details of his life enrich our historical imagination. His custom of supervising the printing of his works on the spot also brought him the acquaintance of the great publishers of his age. During his first journey, his *First Principles of Natural Things Deduced from Experiments and Geometry* was published by Jan Osterwyck at Amsterdam in 1720. This work went into a second edition at Amsterdam in

1727 and a third with J.G. Hanisch at Hildburghausen in 1754. In 1721 Osterwyck also published his *New Observations and Discoveries respecting Iron and Fire* and his *New Method of Finding the Longitudes of Places, on Land, or at Sea by Lunar Observations*, as well as his *New Mechanical Plan for Building Docks and Dykes, and a Method for Mechanically Testing the Power and Properties of Ships of Various Kinds and Construction.*

Miscellaneous Observations concerning Natural Things, especially Minerals, Fire and Mountain Strata, parts 1–3, were published in Leipzig, part 4 by H.H. Holle at Schiffbeck near Hamburg in 1722. The three folio volumes of his *Philosophical and Metallurgical Works*, containing his *First Principles of Natural Things*, came out in 1734 with Friedrich Heckel in Dresden and Leipzig, as did his *Outlines of a Philosophical Argument on the Infinite, and the Final Cause of Creation*. His *Economy of the Animal Kingdom* was published by François Changuion in Amsterdam and London, the first part in 1740 and the second in 1741. The first two parts of *The Animal Kingdom, considered anatomically, physiologically and philosophically*, Swedenborg's last scientific work, was published in 1744 by Adrian Blyvenburg at The Hague, the third part appearing in 1745 through an unknown publisher in London.

On his journeys, Swedenborg was both a receiver and a giver in all directions. He gathered the wealth of his impressions into a series of significant scientific works, which brought him European fame. The learned periodicals of all lands discussed his new books; the academies opened their doors to him; and he had come closer to his goal of being received within the Olympus of European learning than he had ever hoped. But at this point, he received a higher calling to cast off his scientific and philosophical work as human vanity and to prepare himself for the proclamation of a higher form of outlook.

10

The Development of a Religious Worldview

Swedenborg the visionary presents a riddle to the student of his life and intellectual development. Until his fortieth year, religion seems to play little role in the life of a man who would devote himself fully to religious contemplation after his vocation. He scarcely mentions religious matters in his correspondence, nor in the many books he wrote leading up to the great works of the 1740s. Nowhere does he speak of his personal religious attitude, his position with regard to the Church, dogma, or the confessions. He gives the impression of religious indifference, astonishing even at this early period of rationalism.

Only Swedenborg's later statements refer to his religious attitude in youth. When his friend Gabriel Beyer asked him for his verdict on the writings of the mystic Jacob Boehme in February 1767—that is, nearly a quarter of a century after his vocation—he replied, "I cannot judge Boehme's writings. I have never read them because I was forbidden to read anything besides dogmatic and systematic theology before heaven opened itself up to me. Otherwise, unfounded opinions and inventions could easily have stolen up on me, and these would have been difficult to eradicate." Two years later, in December 1769, he wrote to the same friend: "From my sixth until my twelfth year, it was my greatest delight to talk about the faith with clergymen. I often said to them, loving kindness or love was the life of the faith, and this loving kindness or love was nothing but the love of one's neighbor. God grants everyone this faith, but it is only accepted by those who really practice loving kindness. In those days, I knew no other faith except that God was the Creator and provider of nature and that he had given men reason, good propensities and other gifts. I knew nothing of that systematic or dogmatic kind of faith, that God the Father imputes the justice or the rewards of his Son to each as he wishes, and if he wishes, even to the unrepentant. And if I had heard of this kind of faith, it would have been completely incomprehensible to me." Swedenborg gave a similar account of himself twice in the same year. Beyer found this so remarkable that he reported it to the Protestant Pietist Friedrich Christoph Oetinger (1702–1782) of Württenberg, the champion of Swedenborg's teachings in Germany (LL, 61f).[1]

Swedenborg's statements indicate that the traditional ecclesiastical form of Christian theology and dogma did not concern him in his youth. This is confirmed by his letters and the writings of his scientific period. But Swedenborg gives a remarkable interpretation of this fact. It was not lack of interest that kept him from ecclesiastical theology, but a divine dispensation to prepare him for his later vocation as a visionary. God himself ensured that he was not shackled by traditional Church doctrine. A new conception of the truth of the Gospel could thus develop freely in the mind of the child like a *tabula rasa*. Later in life, the same mysterious providence also kept from him the theological books that might have acquainted him with

---

1. An extensive description of the debate between Oetinger and Swedenborg, their correspondence and the various defenses Oetinger wrote of Swedenborg, as well as the legal case of the Stuttgart Consistory against Oetinger for publishing his work *Swedenborgs irrdische und himmlische Philosophie*, is found in Ernst Benz, *Swedenborg in Deutschland: F.C. Oetingers und Immanuel Kants Auseinandersetzung mit der Person und Lehre Emanuel Swedenborg, nach neuen Quellen bearbeitet* (Frankfurt a. Main, 1947).

current disputes and thus led him astray from the new faith dawning within him.

This account is typical of a religious person's revision of their own development from the viewpoint of their later vocation. But how accurate was this view? It is simply untrue that Swedenborg never came into contact with the dogmatic teachings of theology during his youth. Swedenborg grew up in a profoundly religious house. Soon after the birth of his son Emanuel, Jesper Swedberg took up his episcopal appointment and became the focus of religious, ecclesiastical, and theological life in his diocese. Severe religious discipline prevailed at home, and the children were instructed in Church teaching from an early age by their father. Prayers united the family mornings and evenings, before and after meals, and on all the important occasions of life. The family attended frequent church services. Several uncles and other relatives were pastors and bishops; pastors even predominated among the family's acquaintances and friends. If topical theological and ecclesiastical questions were discussed anywhere in Sweden, they would be discussed in the house of Bishop Jesper. At table and on family walks, the young Swedenborg could learn more of these matters than any Swedish boy of his time. But was he interested?

In the statement cited above, he did not claim indifference to the clergy's conversations in his parental home. On the contrary, he listened with pleasure and liked talking with the pastors. He did, however, remark that he opposed their dogmatic conception of faith with another one. With bold self-assurance, he projected the basics of his later doctrine back into his early youth. He described his dispute with the pastors according to the analogy of Jesus' conversation with the priests in the temple: the child instructs the wise. The spirit of the later revelation already speaks from the child.

But this tendentious description of youth contains a grain of truth. It was not the spirit of contemporary Lutheran orthodoxy, but the spirit of Pietism that prevailed in the house of Bishop Jesper. In his sermons, the bishop was always storming against the attitude of churchgoers who contented themselves with possessing the right faith and agreeing with the external teachings of Holy Scripture, without having a spark of Christian love in their hearts. Among his parishioners and clerical colleagues, and in his own case, the bishop always stressed a duty to fulfill the faith morally in a life of love and saw the only sign of a truly living faith in the practice of Christian love. Precisely this aspect of his religious preaching remained in Emanuel's heart.

Bishop Jesper had begun to have doubts about the religious attitude of his compatriots on his journey to France. He discovered that the French Catholics performed many more charitable works than the severe Lutherans of his homeland, who arrogantly believed they could forgo "good works" by relying on justification by faith. He wrote in his diary: "In the error of their faith, the Catholics simply comply with the command of Christ. By contrast, we neglect the works of charity in our orthodoxy." During his episcopate, he ceaselessly tried to shake the self-assurance of his flock and pastors and turn their formal life of faith into a life of love. He fought most strongly against "mere faith," as he used to call it, "which is a belief of the brain and not the heart, a lifeless shadow, a dead rather than a living faith, a Devil's faith." Sluggish hearts were lulled by the admonishment: "Just go to church and the Lord's Communion at the appointed time, and you can carry on living in all your sinful, carnal desires. Don't worry! *Sola fides*, faith alone, orthodoxy is sufficient!" This attitude also moved him to strengthen his son in a practical piety of the heart and not to burden him with dogmatic disputes, which dominated the religious textbooks. There is no reason to doubt that the young Swedenborg expressed this attitude in conversation with the numerous clergy visiting his father's house, just as he described in his old age.

Bishop Jesper was himself decried as a Pietist—a term of abuse and almost heresy in those times—and repeatedly complained that one could not lead a godly life, keep the sabbath holy, and oppose drunkenness without hearing pastors say: "You are a Pietist!" The urge to renew the Church sometimes assumed a revolutionary tone in Jesper's sermons. However little he thought of introducing innovations into prevailing ecclesiastical practice, he hoped that such a renewal of Christian life would occur in the future. Occasionally, he made predictions about the coming of a new reformer who would again fill the orthodoxy of contemporary Lutheranism with the spirit of love. "O my God! You who once awakened Luther and armed him with your spirit of courage, to reintroduce the Christian doctrine of faith. Awaken now a new Luther, who will courageously introduce a Christian life!"[2]

The devotional books read at family prayers must have also strengthened the young Swedenborg's piety. These were Johannes Arndt's *True Christianity* (1605) and Christian Scriver's *The Treasure of the Soul* (1675). Arndt's book had been translated into all European languages, including Russian, and served all confessions in European countries as a much-read book of improvement throughout the eighteenth century. The famous thirty-ninth chapter of Arndt's book deeply impressed Jesper and his son: "The sincerity of the teaching and the divine Word is not maintained only by disputes and many books, but with true repentance and a holy life." Arndt says, "It is easy to write, preach, and dispute against heretics and the rabble to uphold the pure doctrine and true religion; but this has become such an abuse that Christian living, true repentance, godliness, and Christian love are forgotten in all the violent disputes, sermons, writing, and counterblasts. It is as if Christianity existed only in disputing and the multiplication of polemics rather than in the transformation of the Holy Gospel and Christ's teaching into a holy life."

What Swedenborg later prized as divine providence, protecting him from dogmatic polemics during his youth, may have been attributable to his father's preference for pietistic books of improvement over controversial compendiums of contemporary orthodoxy. The young Swedenborg was educated in a form of Christianity that awakened his aversion to this polemic theology of the period. This was not a fully developed theoretical point of view on the part of a boy, but rather his unconscious response to an upbringing in Arndt's "Christianity of the heart."

His later statement concerning his youthful piety also contains another seed of truth. As we have seen, he once said he had "no other faith except that God was the Creator and provider of nature, and that he had given men reason, good propensities and other gifts" (LL, 42). This trait also stems from the piety encountered in Johann

---

2. Johann Arndt, *Wahres Christentum*, fifteenth printing (Reutlingen: Enßlin), 161.

Arndt and other improving books of pietistic mysticism. In Johannes Arndt's piety, one finds the old teaching of Raimund von Sabunde and Jacob Boehme about the two books of resurrection, which will inaugurate a new era of religious contemplation of nature. According to this doctrine, there is besides the written book of divine revelation, the Bible, a second divine book, namely, nature. Nature is also a revelation of God, the visible realization and representation of divine love and wisdom. This idea became the religious basis of modern science. When Johannes Kepler exchanged his clerical career for an appointment as mathematician and astronomer, he justified this step by saying that he served the glory of God no less when he proclaimed his fame from the book of nature than from the Bible. Jan Swammerdam understood his scientific researches as a holy priesthood and entitled his study of the marvelous world of the insects *Biblia naturae* (1737). This idea of the priestly task of the scientist recurs in the great physiologists of the age such as Hermann Boerhaave and the important mathematicians like Newton and Leibniz. The scientist interprets the wonders of God in the book of nature and proclaims the honor of God by establishing the mysterious orders of the universe and its motions. Not only the heaven of the angels and saints glorifies God's eternal honor, but also the heaven of the stars, the planets, the earth, and all creatures, the animals, even the insects that Swammerdam describes, so that even a flea can reveal the splendor of God. Even the greatest doctors of the period understood the investigation of the human organism as a holy office for the glorification of God. Lorenz Heister (1683–1758), one of the most famous German doctors of the eighteenth century, whose *Compendium der Anatomie* (1717) Swedenborg frequently quotes in his principal works, wrote about anatomy in the same way as Swammerdam: "The purpose of anatomy is manifold, but its chief purpose is the knowledge and admiration of the wonderful works of the highest Being in the body of man and other creatures. The contemplation of the highly artistic organism and the form, link, communication, effect, and effectiveness of each of its parts proves not only the existence but also the immense and stupendous wisdom of God, to the scorn of all atheists, and invites us to prayer and reverence. Therefore, the chief purpose of anatomy must be the glorification of God. In this sense, anatomy can be called a philosophical, physical and theological science, which is of the greatest benefit for all true lovers of wisdom and theology."

Young Swedenborg's religious development continued in this form of piety, and he maintained these views during his studies. This attitude could well lead to his distancing himself from external church life. It could assume the character of a "private Christianity" that gave priority to the Book of Nature over the Bible for the time being. Nevertheless, Swedenborg remained inwardly convinced that there was no fundamental contradiction between the two forms of God's revelation in his Word and in his creation. He believed that it must be possible to harmonize the Bible with the findings of the new science.

Swedenborg's "private Christianity" and lack of church involvement during his studies may also have been a reaction to the ecclesiastical atmosphere of his upbringing. In any case, there is scant evidence of his participation in church life during the period of his study travels. This is not attributable to any lack of personal information. If the Church had been important to him, he would surely have given at least some indication of this in his diaries and letters. But these reveal a completely different picture: a truly religious ardor animates his study of the wonders of nature through mathematics, chemistry, geology, and mechanics, but he remains indifferent to the Church.[3]

His father regarded this development with the greatest concern. His constant entreaties to return home were not only rooted in financial problems but also the fear that his son might become an atheist under the influence of new sciences abroad. His concern must have been all the greater, when his son's letters never made any mention of church activity. Among the famous men whom he visited in London and Holland, he never mentioned a single theologian, except for the "heretical" William Whiston. At a time when the controversy over the deism of John Toland and Matthew Tindal was raging, John Locke's work on the rationalism of biblical Christianity was arousing debate, the European question of religious tolerance

---

3. Concerning Swedenborg's chemical experiments, see his letter from Brunsbo, 2 May 1720 [Swedenborg to Benezelius: Tafel, doc. 93, 325–326].

was being fought from the pulpits of England and Holland, François Fénelon was preaching in Paris, and Leibniz was advocating the union of Protestants and Catholics in Germany, Swedenborg did not write a single word about the religious questions that stirred all Europe. Concerning ecclesiastical events in England, he only reported in October 1710 the bitter struggle between the Anglican and Presbyterian churches, "which are inflamed by an almost mortal hatred for each other. The firebrand and trumpet of this uproar is one Dr. Sacheverell, whose name is on everyone's lips on every street corner, the subject of leaflets in every bookshop" (LL, 37). However, his words indicate no involvement in these events; at most, they suggest an aversion to this unchristian wrangling. In his description of Westminster Abbey, he makes no mention of a church service but gives an avid account of the homage he paid to the grave of the humanist Casaubon. His saints were not those of the Church but of scholarship and science.

Reports of Swedenborg's later journeys show the same lack of interest in the Church. He visited churches as if they were museums, with an artistic and architectural motive. He never mentioned a preacher, and yet he could have heard the most famous theologians of the age in Holland, France, and Germany. Travelling through Copenhagen in 1736, he found the town "infected with Pietism or Quakerism." He only mentioned the fact because this piety produced an epidemic of suicides. His heart and mind were not engaged in ecclesiastical matters but in the modern arts and sciences.

Nevertheless, it would be wrong to interpret this attitude as a lack of religious sentiment and to attribute his ostensible rejection of the Church to his contact with the representatives of science. The great scholars whom he met were deeply devout men who tried to harmonize their private Christianity and personal piety with the traditional ecclesiastical form of religion. There was not a single opponent of Christianity or a single atheist among the scientists whom Swedenborg met in England. Sir Isaac Newton himself was ecclesiastically minded and a convinced Christian. Besides the studies and experiments he carried out in preparation for his work on optics at the beginning of the 1690s, he still found time to write a commentary on the prophet Daniel and the Book of Revelation. The destruction of his early work on optics was even the result of his attending church. While he was at the early morning service on a winter's morning in 1693, his little dog Diamond upset a candle on his desk, and the papers containing his years of study on optics were burned. Nor had French mathematics at the time Swedenborg was staying in Paris lost the legacy of Blaise Pascal's inner connection of science with the Christian faith.

According to Swedenborg's later statements, only Christopher Polhem appears to have belonged to that group of modern scientists who had inwardly broken away not only from the Church but from the Christian faith altogether. In the reports of his visions, Swedenborg described him as an atheist, firmly convinced that there was no God and that all incidents of life are of a purely mechanical nature: human beings and animals were "machines filled with air." But this assertion does not fit the facts, as Polhem's own letters give a different picture of his religious attitude. His correspondence with the younger Benzelius, the teacher and friend of Swedenborg, makes it clear that, even as a scientist, he adhered to the Bible. "It behoves no Christian," he wrote, "to doubt the words of Moses, which were dictated by the Holy Spirit, let alone Christ's own words." Like his German and English contemporaries, he also understood his scientific research as a rational exposition of the divine Word according to the "Book of Nature" and as a confirmation of salvation through the works of creation. He emphasized, "that there was not the least contradiction between the words of Moses and the properties of nature, once a few rules of reason were conceded to men, without which they would be soulless brutes." Even if his application of "rules of reason" to the words of Scripture might seem rather arbitrary, he never demonstrated hostility towards the faith or the Church.

Such a piety based on a new sensitivity to nature was a living force in Swedenborg and permeates the scientific writings of his youth. God is no empty concept for him, no mere philosophical idea, but the eternal foundation and Creator of all being, all life and all motion. The reality of life is not exhausted in nature and the visible universe but is nourished by the eternal and aims at the infinite. "Geometric motion and shape or construction derive from that which is least constructed, and this in turn derives from the simple and pure motion and shape. But the simple and pure derive from the infinite. The infinite has its basis in itself, and this is nothing else but God and the Divine, the origin and being of all things!"

These words recall neo-Platonic ideas, but they are filled with a new feeling for the world, once modern science had offered a glimpse into the immeasurable dimensions of the universe. The telescope and microscope had disclosed new realms of life, infinitely deepened humanity's reverence for the wonders of creation, and simultaneously appointed humankind a wholly new position within the newly discovered universe. After describing the immense expansion of the heavens visible to all people, Swedenborg expressed the shift in worldview when he wrote, "This immeasurably distant firmament is perhaps only a particular sphere, of which our own solar system is but a single particle, because this finite universe rests in the infinite. There may be countless similar heavenly spheres, which are perhaps so numerous and great, that our firmament is but a point in comparison with them. But all these firmaments together, however many there may be, because they are finite and limited, they will not even be a speck in comparison with the infinite. If all spheres and the armies of heavens are not even a speck in comparison with the infinite, and the whole firmament, which appears so immeasurable to our eyes is but a point in comparison with the finite universe, and if our solar system is in turn only a small part of this firmament, and our Earth is only a small part of our solar system, what should a man think of himself? Is he really still what he thinks he is? You complacent creature, why do you think so highly of yourself and consider everything less important than you? You worm, why do you brag and boast? If you observe the scale of the firmament and simultaneously compare yourself, oh, you are just a tiny particle of the heaven and earth, you tiny little man! Your greatness can only consist in your worship of the greatest One and the infinite!" Thus God looms larger for him through his discovery of the greater universe. The greatness of humankind, however, which has shrivelled to nothing when confronted with a new understanding of the greatness of the universe, is only justified by the worship of God, who has created this immeasurable universe.

On the basis of this belief in God, Swedenborg tried to reconcile the knowledge gleaned from the Book of Nature with the teachings of Holy Scripture. "Neither religion nor morals nor the state has anything to fear from true knowledge." This principle underlying Christian Wolff's ontology and cosmology was a determining factor in Swedenborg's *First Principles of Natural Things* (1734) and became the axiom of the early Enlightenment.

The doctrines of revelation that motivated him to study the Book of Nature are particularly significant for an understanding of Swedenborg's later development. It was primarily questions about the evolution of our Earth that led him to study the biblical story of Creation. He never criticized biblical teachings and notions, nor used them as a basis for his research, but he occasionally noted when one of his scientific insights confirmed the biblical view.

His work *On the Height of Waters and the Strong Tides in the Primeval World* (1719) was intended "to lend authority to the Divine Word and the truth of the matter." He was similarly trying in his *Miscellaneous Observations* (1722), which are chiefly concerned with the origin and evolution of the earth, "to reconcile his theories about the primal chaos and the formation of stars and planets with the divine oracles" and to illuminate the words of Scripture through natural science. In his work *On the Motion and Position of the Earth and Planets* (1719), he attempted to compare his astronomical theory that the earth was travelling more slowly in its orbit than previously with Old Testament accounts of the greater longevity of the oldest generations of human beings. He showed how his calculations concerning the gradual lengthening of summer accorded with Holy Scripture. This theme later recurs in his visions: the doctrine of paradise. Swedenborg proved that the discovery of Earth's longer orbits around the sun could scientifically explain the tradition of paradise and referred to the ancient myth of the golden, silver, bronze and iron ages in illustration:

> It is possible that a vast garden once stretched over the whole earth, or that the whole surface of the earth was once adorned with marvelous gardens. For in those days the earth completed its annual orbit around the sun in a relatively short time. The seasons

followed one another at short intervals. Autumn quickly succeeded the summer, winter the autumn, and summer the spring. The glowing heat of the sun during the summer was immediately softened by the autumnal coolness, but the cold of winter did not endure but was immediately compensated by the mildness of spring and the heat of the following summer. The short daily revolutions around the sun additionally created a complete equalization of temperature: the nocturnal cold was foiled by the heat of the day and vice versa, so that neither exceeded a certain temperature. Scarcely had the cold begun to increase after sunset, when a new dawn and sunrise ensued and neither the cold of the night nor the heat of the day had sufficient time to spread. It therefore follows from our theory that prevailing conditions at that time must have resembled paradise.

Reflections on the Golden Age moved Swedenborg to a poetic hymn, which provided the keynote to his work *Worship and Love of God* (1745). In this first age, "Nature showed her most friendly face in conditions of sweetness and delight. There was nothing in the world, which did not bloom in the full power of youth. But in the following age, these joys and games of young Nature turned to sadness. The earth gradually moved further and further away from the sun. The annual and daily revolutions of the earth around the sun lengthened. The intervals between winter and summer, day and night got longer. The cold was harder in winter, and the heat more intense in summer in comparison with earlier." Gradually the world entered "old age," a state "in which we live with less joy, even if we are ourselves still young."

This tone of discontent with the world in a purely scientific work betrays a particular sentiment of great importance for his later religious development. The scholar eagerly trying to decipher the wonders of this world does not really feel comfortable in this world. His heart holds an image of paradise lost, which makes the present old world seem depressing with its tensions and conflicts. His spirit is directed towards the spiritual world in the sun, where opposites are overcome and the blessed live together without cares.

His speculations on paradise continued in *First Principles of Natural Things*. On the basis of calculations concerning the swifter succession of summer and winter in earlier epochs, Swedenborg developed his doctrine of the eternal spring of the paradisiacal first epoch. This spring "prevailed over the whole globe and was most ideal for the reproduction and creation of things. Without such a continual May neither the seeds would have sprouted nor would plants and animals of all kinds come forth. Thanks to this eternal spring the whole earth was adorned like a paradise. Everything was in the bloom of youth and an age of cheerful play. It was the Golden Age." This description ends in a prayer: "Keep adoring and wondering at the providential infinite with amazement. All things are signs of its providence, all effects are overwhelming proofs of its prophecy."

These speculations show how scientific study, religious intuition and imagination blended in the thought of the young Swedenborg. But where would science be without imagination? Not even today's specialized science can succeed without this creative energy that enables the researcher to see connections in nature, to summarize great periods of development, and to trace paths in unexplored fields. Imagination played a much greater and more universal role in the early phases of science. How could men like Newton and Flamsteed, exploring the starry heavens with sophisticated instruments for the first time, conceive of the unity of the universe without imagination? How could Hawksbee or Woodward reconstruct the evolution of the earth from fossils and geological strata without imagination? How could Swammerdam grasp the evolution of life in the lower animal world without imagination?

Swedenborg tried to illuminate a second area of biblical doctrine through his scientific insights: the doctrine of the realm of the dead and the postmortem state. This problem, whose solution he later found in the "opening of inner vision," had already surfaced in his earliest scientific period. In a letter sent to Benzelius from Stockholm on 26 November 1719, he used his observations of vortices and the effect of centrifugal and centripetal energy to confirm several teachings of Scripture:

> Regarding the place of the damned and whether this may be the sun, I have completely opposite thoughts: to my mind, the sun is

rather the place of the blessed. My reasons are the following: Firstly, the sun is the central point of our whole planetary system and motion together with the existence of everything within its sphere has its origin in this central point. Secondly, the planetary heaven is always directed towards the sun; every ascent within a solar orbit always occurs in the direction of the sun. But below it is always in the direction of the extremes of the vortex, in the direction of Saturn and Uranus. Thirdly, the principal light and clarity is in the sun; on the contrary, when the sun is furthest away and where one can hardly see the sun, gloom and other terrors prevail. But the fourth reason is the chief one: the sun contains the purest air and the subtlest substance of all, consisting of the fewest elements. For the nearer we come to the sun, the subtler everything becomes. At its center, we would probably find such a degree of purity and subtlety that the parts would scarcely cohere and would lose the quality of matter, as well as form, gravity, and other properties. It is also probable that the subtlest beings will be in the place of greatest subtlety. God, the angels, anything which has nothing material in its substance will be in their element there. Like seeks like, and the more subtle naturally does not seek the more coarse. There are therefore more grounds for believing that God has his seat in the sun, as the Bible says. With regard to fire, it is too coarse a notion to suggest that the bodies of the damned are tortured there, for the pains of burning do not naturally occur without causing destruction. When fire burns, it causes a feeling of being torn apart, dissolved, and destroyed. Where there is no destruction, no pain can exist as a result of burning. The pangs of conscience should be a sufficiently hot fire for this purpose. I hope that my philosophising on this matter will not be misunderstood, for it is based on God's Word. (LL, 46)

Here an otherwise hidden feature of his religious thought suddenly gleams through: the realm of the dead, the realm of the damned, the fires of hell are unshakeable facts for him. They mean so much to him that he tries to reconcile them with his scientific understanding of matter and the movements of the universe. Two major problems of his later visionary works are the existence of a spiritual world of the dead and the damned, and the nature of their corporeality. Already Swedenborg was developing a view of the spiritual world that lacks the properties of material existence but that never-theless possesses a real corporeal character. These ideas also antici-pate a third idea in his later vision of the spiritual world: the fire of the damned is not physical hellfire but the spiritual fire of conscience that burns the damned without destroying them. Swedenborg's thought shows that it is already directed towards the mysteries of the transcendental world. He is still seeking to unveil them by means of scientific knowledge, but he will later understand them more clearly on the path of intuition.

11

The Development of a Scientific Worldview

Two periods may be distinguished in Swedenborg's intellectual development before his religious crisis: a first phase of purely mechanistic thought and a second of organic and vitalist thought. Both phases find their expression in his standard scientific works of European renown. His mechanistic worldview is represented in the *First Principles of Natural Things* (1734), while his organic-vitalist worldview is evident in his *Economy of the Animal Kingdom* (1740) and his *Animal Kingdom* (1744–1745). The differentiation of these two phases and worldviews appears self-evident. Nevertheless, they do not directly follow one another. One sees rather an inner continuity of development, a transition from mechanistic to organic thinking, in which the history of ideas was reflected in the history of science of his century.

The mechanistic worldview that Swedenborg encountered in England exercised a powerful spell over him. The science he met in the new mathematics, astronomy, and mechanics impressed him as a science of number and dimension. By their mastery, he not only hoped to glimpse the innermost order of the universe but also expected to conquer nature through the command of their dimensions and laws by technical means. His attempt to explain spiritual and mental events as mechanical movements also coincides with the period of his technical projects. There are two particular works from the early phase that contain such a mechanical interpretation of life: "Proof That Our Life Force Mostly Consists of Small Vibrations, i.e,. Tremulations," published in *Daedalus Hyperboreus* in 1718, and a manuscript from the following year *The Anatomy of Our Most Subtle Nature Showing That Our Moving and Life Force Consist of Vibrations.*

The idea that all signs of life are ultimately movements of a mechanical nature did not originate in Swedenborg's theory of tremulations. It first appears with the Italian researcher Giovanni Alfonso Borelli (1608–1679), especially in his work *De motu animalium* (1680–1681) and was then further developed in the philosophy of René Descartes and the medical science of Giorgio Baglivius, before influencing the thought of Polhem, Swedenborg's teacher. Swedenborg knew the work of his predecessors and extended it, confident of proving their theories more completely, "because I consider my proofs to be new and my own, while the opinions themselves stem from others."

In the above quoted works, Swedenborg tried to crown the mechanistic worldview with the "unshakeable proof" that all organic life, even our thought processes, is motion and subject to the same mechanical laws as the movements we can perceive with the aid of our senses. Such a proof can prevail only within a materialist view of spiritual things. Thoughts are only movements, waves, or radiations of a subtle material; they have "the same effect as our outer senses, they are influenced by eating, they can work and become tired. This shows that they must be material, as all effects must occur through matter, however subtle this may be. Whenever the air vibrations touch our hearing, or light waves touch our sight and activate them, why should not some matter more subtle than ether activate our thoughts or their organs in our brain?"

Swedenborg's teacher Polhem had already expressed such speculations. He also imagined a kind of thought-matter, more subtle than air or ether, a most subtle matter, whose movements are thoughts, in the same way that light waves are the movements of the ether, sound waves are the movements of air, save that the speed of the movements of this thought-matter is even more rapid. Polhem adduced this theory to confirm telepathic phenomena. Just as sound penetrates the wall, and light shines through the hardest diamond, so thought vibrations penetrate everywhere in a faster and more intense fashion. "This accounts for the movement that two people linked by strong ties of friendship can feel from each other at a distance of many miles, especially parents and children. Thus, it happens that, when people experience great grief, anxiety, or joy and simultaneously think of an absent friend, a feeling is transmitted often, though not always, to this latter person." Dreams in which one learns of the misfortune or well-being of another may also be traced to this movement of thought-matter between two persons linked by close ties of love.

Swedenborg took these ideas from Polhem and developed them further. He was initially interested in the spiritual life of irrational animals, whose thoughts were only "tremulations" caused by external sense perceptions. But he appears to have also explained human perception in the same materialistic and mechanistic way as Polhem. He refers to his anatomical studies, which are supposed to have revealed the mystery of this mechanism to him. "Whenever one tests, explores and exposes the sense impressions in the human body, one sees that a certain mechanism controls the body in its whole extent. This is primarily evident in the eye, which is adapted to the reception of wave movements streaming through the senses. However great the number of the nerves, links, and connections may be in the eye, the one maintains and affects the other." Thus it is with the whole body. A glance at the mysterious connection of fibers, muscles, meninges, nerves, and blood vessels with their countless different functions indicates that something mechanical underlies all sense perceptions, with the sole difference "that one organ receives the wave movements of a subtler element in its variations, while the other organ receives the coarser wave movements." The individual sense organs like the eye and ear are accordingly formed more subtly or more coarsely and adapted to a particular sensitivity. The subtler the matter, the subtler the organ for the reception of its movements, while the impression is also subtler.

On this basis, one can understand the strange reference in the 1719 letter, where Swedenborg commented on the realm of the dead. Here Swedenborg appears to have related his notion of God to his theory of a most subtle matter as a vehicle of the spirit. God also works and lives in a most subtle materiality, which no longer has structure, form, or weight, and which can no longer be described as matter. But Swedenborg does not carry these thoughts to their conclusion. Is God ultimately this most subtle and simple matter? Or is this only the material basis of his omnipresence in the world? What is clear is that Swedenborg has taken the mechanistic view of the world very far indeed.

In *First Principles of Natural Things*, Swedenborg develops a cosmology and tries to explain the origin of the universe according to these mechanistic principles. His hypothesis is expressed in the sentence: "The whole world of elements, minerals, plants, and animals is purely mechanical." This cosmology attempts to derive the origin of all existence and life from the mathematical point, by proving that nature obeys the laws of geometry and that everything in nature is geometrical. The mathematical point is the origin and starting point of all other points and particles of nature. It represents an indivisible unity without spatial dimensions and therefore stands midway between the infinite from which it is created and the finite world, which proceeds from this mathematical point. This first indivisible unity "can be compared to the double-faced Janus, who simultaneously looks in two directions, turning his face towards both the infinite and finite universe." The first movement proceeds from this point, forming the first finite points, their combination into compound forms and new centers of movement. The mathematical point is simultaneously the medium, through which the infinite completes its entire development.

All forms of existence develop through movement, which is present as an inner potential, a striving (*conatus*) in the first mathematical point, but first activated in the movements of the first finite points. This follows the analogy of heavenly movements: the first finite particles are conceived as tiny planets, moving in spirals and turning on their own axis. The laws of heavenly movements, obeying geometrical and mechanical principles, are mirrored throughout the universe down to its smallest particles. The same mechanical laws that dictate the orbits of the planets activate the bodies of men and animals through the muscles, nerves, and fibers. The heart operates as a blood pump, the lungs as bellows; even the sense perceptions can be mechanically explained likewise.

After his *First Principles of Natural Things* (1734), Swedenborg published a shorter work entitled *Outlines of a Philosophical Argument on the Infinite* (1734), which extended his geometrical and mechanistic worldview into the realm of the soul. As all creation obeys the laws of geometry and mechanics, so too must the soul. Even if humanity's blunt methods of perception were not yet capable of explaining the mechanism of the soul, there was no reason to doubt that it would eventually be possible. Just as the world is ultimately a large machine moving according to mechanical laws, so the soul is a machine containing its own principle of life and movement. Because it operates in the physical realm, it must be able to extend itself through a material constitution. It is located throughout the body, but its actual throne is where the tissues are finest, in the brain and the spinal cord. Its functions consist of movements in the brain tissues and the fine fluid that they contain. Here Swedenborg is already approaching the research of the soul through the anatomy of the brain. His contemporaries were amazed by his findings, which are in turn still recognized by specialists.

Here Swedenborg's thought appears to merge with pure materialism for which contemporary reviewers reproached him. However, he did not eliminate God and the immortality of the soul. Rather, he wanted to find more certain proofs of their existence. He was one of the few minds of his era to grasp the significance of the new science for the solution of the inner connections between mind and reality. At this time, the scholastic Cartesian view prevailed that the soul was a purely spiritual essence and thoughts abstract concepts. Swedenborg considered this view inadequate for understanding the combination and mutual influence of soul and body in a human being, God, and the world in the universe. If one attributes a purely abstract being to the mental world, this implies doubt as to its reality.

His scientific approach was thus intended as an antidote to a rationalist or idealist philosophy, which devalued the mental world through abstract conceptions. The new science could show how the mental sphere operated in the corporeal, how it forms organs and becomes active with the aid of these organs. It could even prove the immortality of the mental sphere. Once the soul has been proved the finest, subtlest substance of the body, it follows that it cannot be destroyed by coarser elements and is thus immortal. It is not the mechanistic, scientific explanation of the mental and divine worlds that promotes atheism, but rather the old metaphysical attempt to present everything spiritual as something abstract and far removed from our senses.

Although the mechanistic and geometric principle seems complete in the writings of the younger Swedenborg, it already contained the germ of his organic and vitalist worldview. His view of motion provided the starting point. The first mathematical point is created by the motion of the infinite. This is pure motion and not yet subject to mechanical laws. This striving (*conatus*) towards movement exists as an inner potential in the mathematical point, which still has nothing substantial in itself that could be moved. The activation of this impulse towards movement leads to the first created particles and points, which then become centers of their own motion within a more general movement. Movement is thus seen as energy, potential and kinetic. The pure motion of the infinite is realized through the first mathematical point as a kinetic energy, which constantly develops new movements and brings new combinations of the first finite particles into motion, until the whole universe is formed and set in general motion.

Swedenborg's concept of movement increasingly turns into the concept of life, while his mechanistic and geometric worldview was transformed into a vitalist worldview. The process in which the first finite particles proceed from the first mathematical point and pure motion constantly activates its potential energy in the impulse of new movements generates a hymn to the creative life of nature in the *First Principles of Natural Things*. He described this vision as "the wrathful," a concept found in the natural philosophy of Jacob Boehme. Swedenborg wrote of this life of nature: "It is simultaneously possessed of a powerful anger and a violent ambition. It is never at rest but always expanding further and further out. Its ambition is to expand into the universe and the larger it grows, the wilder and more ambitious it is. It seeks to extend its dominion into the infinite, where there are no boundaries and where it can multiply itself without limit." The life of nature is always creating new worlds and planetary systems. New stars and planets are constantly formed, enter their period of youth, develop the abundance of their life forms, mature, and finally sink into old age. Here a new organic worldview emerges from the mechanistic cosmology, anticipating *The Economy of the Animal Kingdom* (1740), his second major scientific work.

The transmutation of his mechanistic worldview also had a second starting point. Swedenborg tried to explain the life of the soul, the presence of God, and his effectiveness in the world in geometric and mechanical terms. In so doing, he reached the limits of human knowledge. In *Outlines of a Philosophical Argument on the Infinite*, he hoped that it would be possible, with finer means of detection, to understand the mechanical and geometric laws of motion in the soul. In the *First Principles,* he curbed this exaggerated expectation characteristic of the intellectual tenor of his age. René Descartes and Pierre Gassendi had tried to reduce the whole universe to mathematical formulae. Swedenborg asserted the contrary: it is impossible to comprehend the infinite altogether by mechanistic and geometric means. Even where we can comprehend the effectiveness of the infinite by these means, we must still assume a powerful superabundance of the infinite over the finite. The infinite works in the finite, but is neither exhausted by it nor identical with it.

In the *First Principles,* Swedenborg arrives at this insight by considering the nature of the soul. The course of spiritual life might well occur through movements, whose later course may be deduced by geometric and mechanistic principles, but the innermost life of the soul streams into our world from the infinite and its origin cannot be comprehended through geometry:

> Granted, the world is mechanical and consists of a series of finite things, which have resulted from the most varied contingencies; granted, the world can accordingly be investigated by experience

and with the aid of geometry. However, it does not follow that everything in the world is subject to the sceptre of geometry. The infinite cannot be comprehended by geometry because it is its preceding cause. There are many other things, which stem from the infinite and were coeval with the world, which geometry and rational philosophy cannot penetrate, for instance, the mental principle, which exists in a creature or determines its life. If this mental principle in the soul is not of a mechanical nature itself but only in the way it works, what is this something in the soul, which is nothing mechanical and what are the appropriate means of understanding it?

It was precisely Swedenborg's attempt to geometrize the whole world according to Descartes and Gassendi that led him to see the limits of this approach to knowledge. A dual mystery always remained, God and the soul, and this mystery is basically a single one. Even if it were possible to comprehend the course of motion and the chain of cause and effect in the world through geometry and mechanics, the question of the origin of all motion, all energy, all life, and all order would remain unsolved.

Thus, the attempt to interpret the world mechanically and geometrically did not end in consistent materialism, but rather in a critique of the scope of mechanistic and geometric explanation and a reverence for the abundant, incomprehensible abundance of the infinite. Evidently our science is not sufficient to comprehend the world altogether. The presence of the infinite in the world brings our knowledge to a standstill. This is the point at which Swedenborg's thought suddenly changed from mechanistic philosophy into theosophy. Where human knowledge fails, only revelation, intuition, and wonder can help. This infinite is always an inconceivable superabundance of energy, ideas, and life over visible, finite reality. The creation is not a world-machine that has exhausted itself, but works with inconceivable inexhaustibility upon the universe, directing the course of movements, the chain of cause and effect, and the mutation of life forms. Thus "all those who regard nature as the origin of all things to the exclusion of the infinite or who confuse the infinite with nature are but lesser minds and have scarcely reached the lowest threshold of true philosophy. For nature is only an effect of the infinite; the infinite is her cause. The faith in miracles is not buried by true philosophy."

The sustained influence of the German Enlightenment on his scientific thought, chiefly represented by the schools of Leibniz and Wolff, was responsible for this change in Swedenborg's intellectual development. One particular influence deserves especial emphasis. Although Swedenborg never personally met Leibniz and Wolff, in 1734 he visited Wolff's important pupil, Andreas Rüdiger, professor of philosophy, at Halle. Rüdiger was the author of a famous work entitled *Göttliche Physik, ein rechter Weg zwischen dem Aberglauben und dem Atheismus, der zu der natürlichen und sittlichen Seligkeit des Menschen führt* (1716). This work contained ideas that induced Swedenborg to move from his earlier mechanistic and materialist thought towards his later organic and vitalist worldview.

As the title suggests, Rüdiger's struggle was directed against two opponents. On the one hand, against superstition, which idolizes the things of this world and misuses them for sorcery and magic; on the other, against modern atheism, which seeks to explain the whole world mathematically and mechanically and no longer concedes a space in nature to God. Both trends, superstition and atheism, are false paths that lead from true insights to a false conclusion. Neither possesses the right notion of the presence of the infinite in the finite. The first unduly idolizes the finite, while the other ousts the infinite from the finite. Modern science arose as a learned front against the superstition of the uneducated but has been misled into expelling God from the world and destroying faith together with superstition. Through the one-sided application of its principles, modern science has sunk into atheism and into the opposite evil.

Rüdiger attempts to correct this error with a new science, which can properly comprehend the infinite in the finite and the divine in nature. This science is "divine physics." Its concern is "to link the mechanical principles with the vital, life-giving principles and thereby to understand nature." Historically speaking, Rüdiger saw his task as linking the organic *Naturphilosophie* of English theosophists such as Henry More, who were influenced by Rosicrucians like Robert Fludd and the English followers of Boehme, with the mathematical and mechanistic thought of English and French natural philosophy.

Rüdiger simultaneously undertook to harmonize modern science with biblical accounts and to relate the new cosmology to the biblical story of creation. He set out on the same path which divine providence would later lead Swedenborg. According to Rüdiger's doctrine, the true divine physics is in the Bible, especially in the Book of Genesis. Moses, the divinely inspired scribe of the creation story, still possessed knowledge of the true divine physics. "If one would prefer to read the principles of true physics rather than research them for oneself, one will find no better source than the memorials of Moses." This archphysicist mastered the ancient Egyptian and Phoenician occult sciences, whose insights were also reflected in Greek myths. Just like Swedenborg's work *Worship and Love of God*, Rüdiger also tried to relate the Mosaic tradition to the creation myths of all ancient religions. Rüdiger further taught that the divine physics entered a state of decadence when polytheism developed out of the true old doctrine. Christ restated the true physics, but there was a new decline following him, when physics passed to the Arabs. From them it returned as false Aristotelian physics into the Latin West and experienced an efflorescence in the Middle Ages, before sinking into superstition, against which modern science has arisen, only to decay in turn into atheism.

The main theme of *Göttliche Physik* is a meticulous clarification of the validity of mathematical principles that serve modern science. This clarification leads Rüdiger to a critique of Descartes and Gassendi. With these thinkers, mathematics has overstepped its boundaries and elevated itself to the sole guiding principle of the whole universe. This presumption has led to atheism. Mathematics cannot conceive all reality because it is based only on quantities that it can count and measure according to its own basic structure. By contrast, the object of physics is the divine first cause of things and its realization in the emergence of individual forms. Physics therefore is concerned with a more divine subject than mathematics—namely, nature and the essence of things—"while mathematicians are concerned with a far less noble object in the consideration of quantity." It is therefore perverse to want to explain the entire reality of things by mathematics, as this science relates only to created being, and moreover only to its quantities. Precisely this overestimation of mathematics has led to modern atheism, while the universal application of mathematical principles ultimately leads to the fact that "nothing remains in nature that is capable of convincing the intellect of the existence of a supreme *noumenon*." Rüdiger plays Newton off against Descartes in a very subtle fashion. Newton's clear insight into the limits of mathematics allowed one to recognize the intellectual absurdity of Descartes, "who shamelessly declared that there were no other physical principles besides those of mathematics." In opposition, Newton established the limits of mathematics in his *Philisophae Naturalis Principia Mathematica* (1687) and limited himself to the calculation of the mass of bodies, their movements and their forces of repulsion and attraction. This wise limitation of mathematics to its proper sphere was a lesson to "all contemporary idiots" who wanted to make mathematical observation the basis of judging all phenomena and who saw in mathematics the foundation of all disciplines, even philosophy and physics.

In contrast to the extravagant claims of mathematics, Rüdiger regards physics as the science most suited to comprehend the divine principles of nature. Physics does not concern itself with quantities but rather the nature and essence of things and is thus able to grasp the hidden energies and forms of life. It is "the science with which we can probably understand the intangible principles God used to form sensuous nature. Whenever dealing with an object of nature, we will thus be able to proceed with intelligence and resolutely oppose both superstition and Godlessness."

Rüdiger's understanding of space was fundamental to his attempt to grasp the relationship between God and the world, between spirit and reality on the basis of physics. Henry More, whom he frequently quotes, had argued that Descartes was wrong in asserting that only material was capable of extension. Space is also real and exists outside our body and our thought. More had used this view in order to construct an entire theosophical system of the present, describing the movement of the spirits in space, and a series of speculations about the fourth dimension. Rüdiger has a similar view of space. Everything mundane, even spirit, has a spatial extension. God is universal space, comprising all finite spaces in himself but simultaneously permeating all of them. He is not space in the sense that he and space are one and the same, but in that he is the substance, the cause, and the Father. He encompasses and simultaneously fulfills everything, in such a way that one must qualify the customary distinction between empty and full space in the universe. A glance at the starry firmament causes the observer to think that there are enormous empty spaces between the individual stars, but even this ostensibly empty space "is not denuded of every substance, for God is present everywhere, and although he cannot be enclosed in a space, no empty space is so empty, as to not be filled by the divinity."

An extension also applies to the spirit and the soul. Rüdiger emphasizes just this thought—like Swedenborg—in order to explain the presence and effectiveness of the mental and spiritual spheres in the realm of creation and thereby oppose a devaluation of the mental sphere. It is inappropriate to define the body as a spatially extended substance because the spirit is also a spatially extended substance. The difference between mind and matter does not lie in extension but in the nature of their substantiality. Here Rüdiger emphasizes that Holy Scripture does not presuppose the scholastic view of a nonspatial abstract essence of the spirit. Like Swedenborg, Rüdiger proves the necessity of the spirit's extension as a basis for its development. It would be absurd to identify the soul with the natural point, for this would deny it any possibility of effect. Rüdiger similarly proves the immortality of the soul by stating that the subtle, fine character of its substance precludes its destruction by a natural cause.

These ideas of Rüdiger strongly influenced the young Swedenborg. He had previously followed Descartes in trying to explain all reality according to mathematical and mechanistic principles. He had based his cosmology on the Cartesian theory of vortices and his psychology on the Cartesian theory of tremulations. His own religious outlook might well have warned him against extending the limits of geometry too far and tending toward pure materialism. The encounter with Newton, whose *Principia* he knew in detail, had hardened this view. Now he found in Rüdiger an exact systematic and historical explanation of the problems that were so important to him. He realized how right he was in not subjecting the Infinite to geometric principles. Like Rüdiger, he now tried to blend mechanistic with vitalist principles and thus transmute his worldview according to vitalist and organic precepts. His concepts of the Infinite, as the energy of motion and life having a constant effect upon the whole universe, and of the soul's extension provided the essential starting points for the new direction of his thought. He now rejected a purely mechanistic and geometric worldview and began to study the hidden divine mysteries in the development of life.

Swedenborg now chiefly focused on anatomy, investigating the mysteries of the structure and variation of the animal and human organism with his dissection knife. These new researches were represented by the works *Economy of the Animal Kingdom*, whose first part was published in 1740, the second in 1741 by François Changuion in London and Amsterdam, and *The Animal Kingdom, considered anatomically, physiologically and philosophically* (1744–45). During their preparation and printing, he entered the religious crisis that preceded his conversion. The first part of the latter work treats of "The Entrails of the Abdomen or the Organs of the Lower Region," the second part "The Entrails of the Chest or the Organs of the Higher Region" and both parts were published at The Hague in 1744. The third part, published at London in 1745, treats of "The Skin, the Senses of Feeling and Taste and the Organic Forms in General." The fourth part on the brain was not completed, but the studies of the brain are preserved in manuscript form. The treatise on the soul, intended as the sixth part of this work, was published from manuscript notes by J.F.I. Tafel in 1849.

The *Economy of the Animal Kingdom* still preserves the cosmological model of *First Principles of Natural Things* (1734) in its derivation of all being from the natural point. But the origin of being is no longer understood mechanically and geometrically but in an organic and vitalist sense. The idea that pure motion is effective as a striving (*conatus*) and unfolds in the form of spiral motion and in the creation of the first finite points and particles has been transformed into the idea of the creative primal energy. This primal energy radiates from the first substance of nature, the natural point, and is effective in all things as their creative, forming and maintaining principle "leading right down to the lowest realm of life." This idea of active energy—*vis formatrix*—still seems entirely based on the ancient Aristotelian worldview, which divides all things into form and matter. But this division is only conceptual: form is an active principle of effect, which cannot operate without a corporeal basis; matter is a passive principle, which cannot exist by itself but "longs for form, as a woman longs for man." One can, therefore, distinguish form and matter in theory, but in reality they can only exist together and in each other. Form is inherent in the active urge to realize itself in matter and represent itself physically. The creative primal energy operates in every individual form, leading to the unfolding of life in an inconceivable abundance of forms. By grounding all living forms in a primary universal formative energy, Swedenborg joins the great tradition of mystical *Naturphilosophie*, ranging from Albertus Magnus and Nicholas of Cusa, through Paracelsus and Jacob Boehme, then through the English Behmenists and Rosicrucians like Robert Fludd, to the great researchers like Johann Baptista van Helmont and Henry More, whom Swedenborg so frequently quoted. The terms he used to describe the creative energy of nature already indicate that he knew the tradition of this idea. He called it *archeus, vis formatrix* (formative energy), *vis plastica* (energy of formation), thereby emphasizing his debt to Helmont, who had also adopted Paracelsus' term *archeus* for this primal energy of nature. He was also obliged to the English mystical natural philosophers Ralph Cudworth and Henry More, who spoke of a "plastic force," and to German scholars like Rüdiger, who characterized the primal energy as *idea formatrix* (formative idea). Helmont appears to have inspired him especially and even stimulated his speculations about the Adamic intellect. Helmont had described the *archeus* as a "life aura" (*aura vitalis*), which "produces all things and keeps them alive." In his organological and medical studies, he repeatedly suggested that this aura in animal life is embodied in the most subtle part of the blood, which he calls "life spirit" or "life fluid." Swedenborg likewise taught that the life force in animal life resided in a most subtle spiritual fluid (*fluidum spirituosum*), dictating the course of life and its functions.

An organic worldview based on a metaphysical notion of life thus replaced the mechanistic picture. The origin of all life is not an abstract point but a living formative energy, which pushes towards ceaseless activity and multiplication. The formative energy cannot be grasped with ordinary concepts. Within the microcosm, which it creates, it rules like a kind of god or genius of its world. It is the seed of its microcosm, containing and gradually unfolding all the stages of its growth from its origin to its final destination. But this primal form does not possess its own energy. It emerges from nature itself; it is the image of its creator, and is complete only insofar as it is an image. This applies not only to every individual organic microcosm but to nature as a whole, which ultimately represents a unique, living, organic form as the macrocosm, in which the primal energy and primal idea are realized. This *archeus* or primal form thus assumes the same position as the figure of the heavenly Sophia in the theosophy of Jacob Boehme. She is the mirror of God, the first form, through which the formless God unfolds into the form of urgent, powerful life.

With this doctrine of the *archeus*, Swedenborg attempted to understand the inner connection and structure of all organic forms of the universe. Everything in the universe is connected to its origin and its final destination. Swedenborg called the development from higher to lower life forms, from simple to compound substances, the doctrine of series and degrees. The geometric steps in the development of the first movement, as described in *First Principles of Natural Things* (1734), now appear as evolutionary stages in the descent and unfolding of all life. The whole realm of nature can be seen as a system of series, which unfold in various degrees. Just as a root gives rise to a tree, which forms a series of branches, each branch a series of twigs, and each twig a series of leaves, so the first simple substance gives rise to the series of six realms of nature, each one of which in turn represents a series divided into various degrees. The first substance of each series is its simplest and basic substance. It creates the whole series and all its degrees, which are dominated by the *archeus* of the first substance right up to the last ramification of its multiplication. These series describe the entire organic linkage of the universe. Not only visible, external life but also spiritual life is subject to the law of series. The natural forms unfold in such series, while our knowledge of them arises through our own ascent in the series and degrees from the lowest forms to their first substance and *archeus*. All sciences and all forms of government consist of series. We understand, think, talk and act through series. Where no series exist, nature is destroyed, for there is nothing outside the formative energy that unfolds in series and degrees.

The whole universe is a living organism, in which all parts, functions, and movements correspond down to the last detail of life. The same harmonious diversity prevails in every organic microcosm and in the macrocosm. As the law of series is valid for all realms of life, it is possible to rise from a lower to higher degree and to penetrate more deeply into the mysteries of nature with the aid of experience and analogy.

Swedenborg also follows the tradition of mystical *Naturphilosophie* in his particular notion of the development of the *archeus*. The universe comprises four atmospheres or auras—namely, air, ether, the magnetic fluid, and the highest aura, whence flows the spiritual fluid, the most subtle, supreme life force. All organisms maintain their form, motion, and coherence, as the auras' influence streams down upon them. Not until the auras influence the animal organism and microcosm are these alive in a higher sense. The life absorbed by such a microcosm is not its own life nor the life of nature, but the life which streams forth from the infinite, for even nature in its totality is only an organ of life. "Considered alone, nature is dead and serves life only as an instrumental cause."

Swedenborg's metaphysics of life will remain the dominant idea of his visionary theology: all life flows from God, the source of wisdom and eternal light. Instead of the impersonal "infinite," which produced the first mathematical point according to the *First Principles of Natural Things*, Swedenborg now refers to the living God or the "spiritual sun." Instead of the "pure motion" of the Infinite, Swedenborg now describes God, whose spiritual life streams into the organs of the universe and its living realms, activating new life forms in its descent through nature, without ever exhausting itself. The universe with all its forms is the organism in which the divine life incarnates itself through descent.

Such was Swedenborg's new worldview. During his mechanistic phase, Swedenborg had been chiefly concerned with apprehending the infinite in the finite. At the beginning of this phase, he had attributed locality and extension and even the subtlest materiality to God. He had emphasized the spatial extension of the soul to prove the direct, omnipresent influence of God on the world and the soul on the body. He also wanted to avoid reality's rupture into a world of abstract spirituality and a world of dense matter. Whereas he had formerly materialzed God and the soul, the whole realm of life was now spiritualized by the idea of God as the spiritual sun and the *archeus* as the subtlest life force in the universe. In its origin and its supreme form, all life is spiritual life, a formative energy that pervades matter and creates organs for its realization in matter. The mystery of life's descent is called incarnation, the mystery of its ascent spiritualization.

Here one may already discern the outlines of his later theosophical system. His portrayal of the animal kingdom describes the descent of life and its differentiation in the most varied organs within the individual series and degrees of animal life. By contrast, his visionary writings describe the ascent of life to God, an ascent that is fulfilled through humankind, the supreme spiritual creature, and that passes from the theater of this earth through the realm of spirits and angels to the vision of the spiritual sun.

This idea suggests a new relationship between spirit and reality. Everything spiritual is basically life that strives for realization—namely, incarnation—and wants to create physical organs for achieving this. But these organs need not be material in the sense of earthly matter. There are various kinds of corporeality, and there are various steps in the incarnation of the divine life. Every lower thing can become the body of a higher thing, and the whole spiritual and natural universe is only the body and organ of the divine life, realized by the *archeus.*

This new outlook is clearly presented in the doctrine of the soul in the *Economy of the Animal Kingdom.* In *First Principles of Natural Things,* Swedenborg had traditionally distinguished between the vegetative life (*animus*) and rational life (*mens*) of the soul. He now proposed another structure for the soul. The *anima,* the intuitive power of the soul, stands at the highest point in the series of spiritual life. This *archeus* of all spiritual life encompasses all the individual spiritual functions, the power of understanding, the power of will, and the power of sensory perception that are still undivided. The *anima* is the spiritual fluid because substances cannot be separated from their functions nor actions from their organ in these highest units of a series. The *anima* is simultaneously the operational center and organ of the supreme life. The second degree of this series is *mens*, the reason of the soul. It has created for itself a physical instrument of its realization, the cortical substance of the brain. This idea led Swedenborg to investigate the distribution of specific mental events on specific areas of the cortex, and his discoveries were first confirmed through modern brain research. The third degree of the series, the *animus*, embraces vegetative life. The organs of sense and movement in the body constitute the fourth degree, so that the soul represents a series of four degrees in total.

Here contemporary psychology is moving beyond the rationalism of the Enlightenment. The reasoning ability is not the highest power of the soul but rather the intuitive capacity of the soul. Within it reside all spiritual functions, all higher and lower degrees, still unfolded, and by its means the most subtle, most spiritual life force can be activated.

Swedenborg refers to rationalist psychology to check the correctness of his views on experience. We know that a higher power of the soul, quite distinct from reason, is at work in us because we often unconsciously "feel moved as by the threads of fate to particular actions. In such cases we then speak of fate, destiny and chance" and do not suspect that a mysterious supreme principle of the soul is working in our breast, dictating our thoughts and wishes. Our conscience similarly indicates the existence of such a higher life of the soul. Reason often cannot grasp the disquiet of conscience, which springs from a deeper level of the soul than rationality. Our reason is a lower degree in the series of the soul and is unaware that the *anima* is the inner ruler of its realm. The innermost life of the soul is unknown to us because it lies above reason and cannot be grasped in words and concepts. We can speak of it only in derivative concepts and images. It is the origin of all spiritual being, the purest life, the purest knowledge, the purest desire and love and the ground of all influence and understanding. This may also explain why our reason "develops from the outset of our perceptions an extremely rational philosophy and logic, which seems innate to us." Without ever having heard of logic, we are accordingly able from childhood onwards to order our impressions and perceptions and construct a rational worldview for ourselves. This fact presupposes a power within us, whose activity is knowledge. Intuition, unknown to us, precedes thought.

Even the *anima* is not an abstract essence as the organ of the most subtle, spiritual fluid. It is rather the inner form of humankind; it possesses spatial extension and lives in the tissues of the body, building its instruments of activity from the fibers, muscles, and nerves. Only at death does it become free in its spiritual form, although it does retain the image of its corporeality. Here is the starting point for the later states of the soul after death and for the education of the spiritual person in the next world.

The old distinctions of the traditional doctrine of the soul no longer apply to this new view of the relationship between the spirit and reality. Swedenborg states that one could call the *anima* both material and immaterial. Considered as the most subtle spiritual fluid, linked with the fibers, nerves and humors of the human organism, the *anima* belongs to the realm of matter. But if one considers the *anima* in the light of its origin, as an emanation of the divine spirit, as life from divine life, it dispenses with its material nature. The old abstract way of looking at things no longer applies to this new view of reality. Everything that is substantial is subject to extension and can therefore be termed matter, even the soul. But in the degree to which it possesses being and life, it also shares in the uncreated and the divine and can no longer be called material. With regard to its life, even the body cannot be said to be material.

Swedenborg thus revives the metaphysics of the soul of Meister Eckhart (c. 1260–1327), who was also not understood by his contemporary critics. In his doctrine of the *anima*, the intuitive capacity of the soul superior to reason, Swedenborg describes the same mystery of the soul that Eckhart indicated in his teaching of the "uncreated," the "spark" and "the castle of the soul." He also described the organic, creaturely character of the soul as a created thing. But Eckhart also spoke of the uncreated aspect of the soul, illuminated by the light of the divine sun and divine intellect. Both Swedenborg and Eckhart rank the uncreated aspect, the small spark of the divine, above the rational ability of the soul in the spiritual series. Will, reason, and all other degrees of the spiritual life are still undivided in the small spark of the divine, when the divine light shines into the soul. The union with God also occurs at the ascent of the soul in this "ground." The intellect reascends back into its uncreated aspect and experiences contact with God. Swedenborg also knew this mystical path of ascent, in which the soul rises above consciousness and the will to a pure knowledge and love of God.

This touches on the clearest manifestation of Swedenborg's transition from scientific thought to mystical theology: his view of knowledge.

12

Scientific and Intuitive Knowledge

The greatness of humankind consists in its reverence for God. This insight of the young Swedenborg forms a crucial link in his development from scientist to visionary. However extreme the contrast between Swedenborg the scientist and Swedenborg the visionary may seem, deeper examination shows that the same image of humankind and the same view of human knowledge is common to both. He tried to answer the same fundamental question regarding the nature of life with two distinct types of knowledge in these two ostensibly irreconcilable phases of his career. Swedenborg embarked on the path of empirical research with the aid of mechanics, physics, and geometry but soon reached the limits of this type of knowledge. He then sought a higher type of knowledge, intuition, which he dimly sensed toward the end of his scientific period. After his vocation, its stirring became so insistent that he ended by believing he could dispense with empirical knowledge.

The inner link between Swedenborg's scientific and visionary way of looking at things is attested by the fact that a mystical image of humankind and a mystical theory of knowledge already underlay his scientific researches before his conversion. Swedenborg was not alone in this respect. German and English science during the eighteenth century was imbued with the spirit of mysticism and emerged from a new view of humankind and the universe. The original form of this new view can be clearly seen in Paracelsus (1493–1541) and Jacob Boehme (1575–1624), while its influence extended from the works of Boehme through the mediation of the English philosophers Robert Fludd (1574–1637) and Henry More (1614–1687) and led directly to the speculations of Newton.

The fundamental idea of this mystical image of humankind is that God, human beings, and the world stand in a pictorial relationship to each other. The same idea is found in Swedenborg and in Boehme and his circle of English followers in their speculation about the archetypal human, or Adam, in the biblical language of these mystics. In these speculations about the archetypal human, the connection between humans, God, and the universe is substantiated by the assertion that both human beings and the universe are an image of God. "God created man in the image of Himself, in the image of God He created him," says the creation story of the Bible. This passage became the starting point of profound insights for the theosophists of the seventeenth and eighteenth centuries. In humanity, God created his counterpart, a spiritual creature, in which he mirrored himself. Humankind is the only creature who carries within him- or herself this imprint of God's image. This is expressed by each individual's being a person. Each is a person because God himself is a person in the original sense and because each person carries within him- or herself the image of God, who alone can say of himself: "I am, that I am." Only humans have this "I am," this imprint of personal being as a gift and reflection of the Creator, the "I am, that I am." But the world is also the image of God, even if in a different, lower sense. All energies, forms and ideas, which are in God, unfold in the world, thus outside God and in themselves. They mirror themselves there in material existence. The world is the image of God because God incarnates himself materially in it. The world is the body of God in the sense that the abundance of the divine life realizes itself in a visible, corporeal particularization of the individual forms and energies of God in the world. Thus, each person, who as a person is the image of God, is simultaneously also an image of the world because all energies and elements of the universe are gathered in him or her as the highest creature. The structure of the universe reflects itself in the structure of its corporeality and its form. The whole world, the highest and the lowest thing, helps construct the form of the perfect creature, the human being.

Swedenborg had already met this ancient mystical idea of humankind as the microcosm in Johann Arndt's books of true Christianity, and it informed his scientific observations and determined his theory of knowledge. Swedenborg had expressed it in an elementary form in the *First Principles of Natural Things*, where he gathered the chief results of his scientific work. However, the ancient mystical doctrine of humankind appears here in a new guise, defined by his theory of the subtle vibrations of membranes and nerves. As Swedenborg explained in his preface, he wishes to speak not of the individual human, but "of man in his original and perfect state." He defines the most important property of the archetypal human as the inner connection of his mind-body nature, so that every stimulus acting upon the human being from without can communicate itself without any weakening of its vibrations "to his subtlest being." Every movement from without streams into this person; even the gentlest impression passes into his innermost center. Each person is an image of the universe, for everything in the universe enjoys an uninterrupted inner connection, from the sun down to our terrestrial atmosphere. "Movements around the sun or rays pass in an instant and a continuous flow through the ether into the air and finally into the eye. By virtue of the inner connection, they operate as movements in the present." This connection between the inner and outer side of humanity is the reason that every movement in the outer world is completely present in the inner world. In this way, humanity is the sensor of the world, the center of cognition, in which all movements and incidents in the universe are faithfully reflected.

The archetypal human described by Swedenborg possesses complete, pure, and clear understanding. "When, according to God's providence, the finest atom of man clothed itself in the body and gradually grew part by part, the subtlest movements in the outer world necessarily passed to the inner world." This human, "in whom all parts co-operated," was by necessity perfect, "for there reigned within him a permanent inner connection of all goals and all means, leading to these goals." Because his finest sensor absorbed unchanged all movements and impressions that streamed upon him, he had no need of glasses, telescope, or microscope: he possessed "the natural philosophy." All things were revealed to him, precisely as they were in their being. Their understanding occurred through the things themselves without any distortion. This "natural philosophy" is not a reflection of things, but the human being experiences the things through the things themselves, which carry their being to his inner world. His senses are infallible, for "whatever could penetrate his sense, immediately streamed into his simplest and most efficient First Being. Whatever entered his eye, immediately flowed through the finest vibrating membranes to his most subtle center. The same applied to his sense of smell and taste." All knowledge thus had the character of the most sensitive and accurate experience. Humans could thus "take delight in the most complete, intact, and detailed cognitive ability. They became fully and immediately conversant with every movement of the elements on the basis of their observation or use." They needed no teachers to impart knowledge through derived concepts, because their "soul could directly sense phenomena and objects." They could "simultaneously be at the center and take in the circumference of the world with a single glance."

This is the image of the perfect human. Just as God stands in the center of the world and takes in all events from a speck of dust to the circle of the stars, so humankind stands in the center of the perceived world and understands the connection and essence of all things with an intuitive glance.

Thus, Swedenborg described his fundamental doctrine of humankind and the highest goal of his cognitive ambition. The archetypal form of knowledge is not abstraction but intuition, not a concept but a vision of essence. These ideas recall the speculations of Jacob Boehme, for whom the fundamental act of human understanding was intuition, "the view into the essence of all essences," "the view into the center of nature." As Swedenborg emphasizes, this view embraces the vision of the present, that is, the order and movement of things as they present themselves to the human being at the instant of their contemplation. But this view also simultaneously includes the vision of the origin and the completion of things, a view into the past and the future. Everything discloses to the viewer not only its present form but also its earlier and future development. The sage looking at the present is at the same time the historian, who sees how the present came about, and the prophet, who beholds the future fulfilment of the present. Swedenborg justified this connection by reference to causality. A strict sequence of cause and effect prevails in the course of movements. Whoever looks at something in the present can know what causes have led to its formation, what influences presently lie hidden within it, and how these will work out in the future. The scientist is simultaneously a visionary. This is the key to Swedenborg's personal development between his scientific and visionary periods.

As a counterimage, Swedenborg then describes his view of the natural, mundane human, "the depraved and imperfect state of man, into which we are born today." The complete view of the perfect human is lacking in this state. Things no longer speak their own language directly to the person; they no longer disclose themselves to intuition. With great exertion, the path of understanding must instead be constantly renewed "through ceaseless experience and with the aid of geometry and the capacity to think." This understanding is no longer "the view into the essence" but is derivative conceptual thinking and an abstraction. The purity of the movements flowing from the outer to the inner world is disturbed by alien movements that cause degeneration. These alien movements proceed from the selfish urges of human beings "and furrow the inner tissue, so that the inner connection is torn apart and confused and no longer flows continuously as before."

A remarkable view of the relation between mind and body in the human being underlies these reflections. In the archetypal human, the body is a perfect instrument of the mind. The senses are capable of relaying the finest stimuli to the center of the soul through all vessels and tissues of the body. The membranes of the body are the most delicate devices for relaying all vibrations without any alteration. From a physiological point of view, this body is the most perfect image of the person's spiritual form, the pure organic representation of the inner model. This purity is destroyed in the "depraved" human. The disordered movements proceeding from the appetites disorganize the delicate construction of the bodily organs. Swedenborg proves this by reference to the changes in human facial expression due to emotional disturbances. The appetites are able to twist the fine fibers, muscles, and nerves, so that the individual passions are reflected in the contortion of the facial muscles or the expression of the eyes. The subtle translation of impressions from the outer world to the inner world is disordered, deflected, and obstructed by different vibrations proceeding from the emotions. The primal sin, selfishness, has a physical as well as a mental effect. It is therefore "no surprise that contemporary man needs aids for thinking. But even with the aid of analytical rules akin to geometry and which he has to be taught, his thought still cannot penetrate to the most subtle Being."

Swedenborg turns from this image of depraved humanity back to the perfect archetypal human. The "view" of the archetypal human is not only a scientific but also a religious intuition. Thanks to his intuitive capacity, the perfect human possesses not only a complete understanding of nature but also a complete understanding of God. Amid the abundance of impressions streaming out of the universe upon him, "the most distant infinite" is revealed to him and he sees that everything is resolved therein and proceeds from it. The highest perception leads to the highest devotion, and the chain of his intuitions is accompanied by an uninterrupted act of piety and prayer. The vision of the universe leads to the vision of God; knowledge of the essence of things encompasses the worship of the Creator and Lord of these things. Every act of perception and cognition is accompanied by an act of revering God. "The more profound the wisdom, the more profound the worship of the *noumenon*" and also the deeper the gratitude towards this divine essence, which reveals its mystery anew with every glimpse to the viewer.

This anticipates the later development of Swedenborg. His scientific and theological ideas are not opposed to each other and his inner development shows no break. The understanding of nature leads to the understanding of God and awakes in him the love of the Lord, who called this world into being from himself and incarnated himself in its manifold variety. "The wiser a man, the more he reveres the *noumenon*, and the greater his love of it. The supreme reverence and love of the *noumenon* cannot exist without the supreme cult of the *noumenon*. What, in the present state of the human soul, could be more delightful and more worthy of achievement than ceaselessly honoring the supreme Being, bound so closely to man through ties of love."

Swedenborg was not the first of his age to dream of an "Adamic understanding," which could surpass empirical understanding through intuition. This dream has inspired all Western intellectual history. The founders of the modern view of nature pursued their laborious researchers while filled with a longing for higher intuition. Let us consider the image of Adamic understanding developed by the elder Helmont. Johannes Baptista van Helmont (1577–1644), lord of Merode, Royenborch, Orrschot, and Pellines, who worked as a physician in the Netherlands, was descended from old Dutch nobility and belongs to a series of universal geniuses, who were so numerous in the Baroque period. At the age of seventeen, he was lecturing on surgery, had developed the doctrines of Paracelsus, and occupied himself with mathematics, geometry, philosophy, and ethics. Under the influence of the writings of the German mystics Johannes Tauler (c. 1300–1361) and Thomas á Kempis (1380–1417), he experienced a conversion, which led to his renunciation of scientific research. Helmont shares with Swedenborg not only a juvenile universality and thirst for knowledge but a conversion that fundamentally altered their attitude to the sciences.

There is a work among the late writings of this remarkable man that clearly shows how his spirit was inflamed by the biblical account of Adam's creation. This tract *Intellectus Adamicus* (Adamic Understanding) develops the same ideas as Swedenborg. Helmont sets forth his view of the original nature of intuition on the basis of the biblical account, which describes how God presented the animals to Adam, in order that he could name them. Adam was able to give the right names to the creatures because he possessed "an inner or intuitive knowledge" of things. This intuition, the *adeptum naturae*, was applicable not only to the animals but equally to herbs, minerals, and stars, disclosing to him a universal understanding of nature. This came about because every object that came before his eyes revealed its innermost properties and its true essence. Helmont also speaks of this Adamic understanding in his work *The Law of the Duumvirate*. "The first-created man cannot be thought ignorant and foolish before his Fall, because he gave all creatures their own and essential names." His immortal spirit contemplated everything in an intuitive fashion, reflected everything in itself, and inwardly within itself recognized all the creatures around him. Only after Adam's Fall did sensuality darken the intuitive understanding of the spirit.

Just like Swedenborg, Helmont also explains the disappearance of this vision as a result of sin, the Fall, which consists in humankind's egotistical self-assertion contrary to God. In this context, he discusses an important question. Scholars used to argue, he reports, whether traces of the original intuitive understanding of the archetypal human still remained in fallen humankind or whether human beings finally lost this gift of vision after the Fall. Life had taught us a severe lesson. He relates how he had not wanted to accept that this vision had finally vanished. "O, I have tried everything, in order to achieve the Adamic understanding!" His spirit was driven by the same longing for higher knowledge that burnt in Swedenborg, and he strived for this understanding by advancing beyond the analytical sciences to essential vision. But he had to learn that the pursuit of intuition was in vain and that Adamic intuition was lost. Fallen humankind cannot gain this vision by its own efforts but can receive it only as a gift of divine grace.

This insight caused Helmont to experience profound inner turmoil, which finds plaintive expression in his work *On the Image of the Spirit*. The human spirit toils away with numbers, calculations, and analysis, yet never achieves a true, direct vision and never penetrates into the essence of things. However, this higher understanding might be the only way to protect humankind from falling into godlessness! "It would be my supreme wish, that the unbelievers should be permitted, at least for a single moment, to enjoy to the full intellectual contemplation and feel the immortality of the spirit. As far as I am concerned, I do not know the rules or method to illuminate the spirit of another. But I am extremely sorry that men who seek the truth in constant research never attain this degree of knowledge."

Despite the presentiment of higher understanding in his heart, Helmont sees himself relegated to the lower level appointed to fallen humanity. "After I had absorbed the knowledge of a long life and the causes of death in my soul, I now know that Adam's spirit, as long as he was immortal, directly animated and led his body, indeed so far, that he recognized in a perfect fashion everything spread around him according to the words of Scripture." Through the awakening of the sensitive soul, which emerged after the Fall, Adam's life moved from his spirit into his soul, and only fleeting memories of his earlier knowledge remained in the form of "dark and discursive thought." This new state is our inevitable human destiny. But at this point, Helmont's Christian faith arises. This fall into a lower cognition has awakened God's love of us. Grace can restore humanity to higher cognition and, through God's revealed truths, set us on the level of higher vision, although this is vouchsafed on earth in only a very few mysterious exceptions.

Helmont and Swedenborg travelled along the same path. They both described all the ways in which the science of their time revealed a knowledge of being. Both felt the limitations of this science most acutely. Both surmised the possibility of higher intuition and desired the magic wand that could awaken this higher light in the souls of those lost in error. Both regretted the lost paradise and felt the keenest guilt for the fall into error. Yet their path did not lead to the same destination.

At the end of his busy scholarly life, Helmont humbly renounced the idea of pure intuition. Faith was the appropriate form of intuition for men in this world:

> Whoever strives towards a higher degree of love endeavors as far as his talents permit to hasten through acts of love to the truths of faith. He does this until he feels that his spirit is bathed in a supernatural light through the grace of unremitting practice and by constant advance in humility and love. Human beings should not attempt to jump over the path of understanding appointed to fallen humankind. Only by faith in the revealed truth, which the grace of God awakens in man, can he advance to a higher cognition. God does not wish human beings to possess the knowledge of angels. Precisely the poverty of human understanding serves the glorification of redeeming love. God wishes there to be differences in understanding. He created the angels, so that they might worship him

in the spirit of understanding without the distractions of bodies. He relegated humanity a little beneath the angels, but nevertheless made man his first choice as the image of God for his glory and worship.

The only path of understanding given to the human being on this earth is the path of faith and love. If he follows this path in true love to the end, he will be raised over the angels and promoted to the temple of wisdom.

Helmont's tract on Adamic intuition does not, therefore, conclude as Swedenborg did with a glorification of paradisiacal understanding but with a eulogy of the earthly human being in his fallen state, indeed with a eulogy of the Fall itself, for through *felix culpa* this opens the abundance of grace to humanity. "The condition of mortal man is far more fortunate than that of the immortal Adam. For this poverty of spirit is in truth knowing full of wisdom, understanding full of knowledge, believing full of trust, and man thereby truly feels and humbly admits that he is subject to all errors as a useless and wicked servant. Along this path man approaches the ineffable Kingdom of God, the ocean of light, which illuminates our intellect beyond all desire and brings us much more sublime things, than could answer the prayers of angels." This testimony is an act of truly pious resignation, born of the same spirit as *The Imitation of Christ* by Thomas á Kempis. Helmont ultimately scorns the wisdom of the angels and descends into the depth of human error, in order to partake of the whole wealth of grace and to experience elevation above the angels.

Proceeding from the same experience as Helmont, Swedenborg arrived at a different conclusion. His reflections on the relationship between scientific understanding and intuition anticipate in several places his subsequent path leading from his scientific to his visionary period. Like Helmont, he had dedicated himself with loving devotion to the natural science of his time. But the more he started independent research in the various branches of this science, the more clearly he felt the inadequacy of this endeavor, and the more brilliantly the image appeared before him of the archetypal human, who gleaned the truth by contemplating things without trouble, teachers, geometry, and analysis. But he did not cease striving for the wisdom of Adam and the angels. What he experienced eleven years later was nothing less than his divine vocation. He then knew that he had been advanced to the condition of the archetypal human and his Adamic understanding, which he had so long imagined and desired. He felt translated into a higher form of vision. The spiritual world opened itself to him alone among men upon earth. He saw himself raised to the throne, from which Adam was cast down after his Fall. The portals of heaven and hell opened up before the gaze of his illuminated eyes. The scientist became a visionary, who saw the present, past, and future of things because he possessed the "vision into the essence." From now on, he spoke with the figures of prehistory and saw the future birth of the heavenly kingdom. His vocation fulfilled his yearning for initiation into the cognitive state of paradise lost. But this initiation was not the result of headstrong desire and methodical training. He achieved it only after the collapse of his self-consciousness and as the conclusion of a crisis, which first led him to repentance and self-abasement before God.

PART TWO

The Vocation

13

Visionary Experiences before the Vocational Vision

The vocational vision, from which Swedenborg dated his visionary gift, did not overtake him unexpectedly. It was the climax of
a long religious crisis, beginning in autumn 1736 and leading to a
series of remarkable inner experiences. Swedenborg's scant descriptions of his extraordinary experiences prior to his vocational vision
may clarify these phenomena. On 27 August 1748, he wrote in his
Spiritual Diary:

> Before my senses were opened to enable me to communicate with
> spirits, I had such assurances for several years that I now wonder
> why I did not realize that the Lord was leading me through the
> mediation of spirits. For several years, I had not only dreams
> through which I was taught about the very things I was just writ-
> ing about, but I also experienced changes in my state while writing,
> in that an extraordinary light appeared in the things I wrote. Later
> I had various visions with closed eyes and wonderful illuminations.
> I also experienced influences from spirits, so clear to the senses, as
> if it was occurring bodily. I experienced varied visitations by
> evil spirits whenever I was in temptation, and whenever I wrote

something which the spirits disliked, I was almost possessed by them and felt like shivering. I saw burning lights and heard conversations in the early morning besides many other things, until a spirit spoke some words to me, and I was amazed that he could read my thoughts.

The process thus began with "assurances," with experiences, which overtook him while working on his scientific works. Insights suddenly appeared certain to him and their correctness was confirmed by special phenomena. From his later viewpoint, these assurances appeared to him as influences of the spiritual world upon his life. However, he emphasized that he did not initially recognize the links with the spiritual world. The onset of such experiences conforms to his own theory: intuition first supplements "geometric" understanding, corroborates it, and ultimately replaces it altogether.

Swedenborg says dreams were the first form of such assurance experiences. Typically, they related to the scientific researches on which he was currently working. These dreams confirmed the correctness of his understanding, which he was committing to paper. The early occurrence of such dreams explain a comment from the year 1746 in his *Adversaria*, where he reported that he "has had dreams over many years and partly understood their meaning." These dreams must have greatly concerned him, for he began to write up his dreams and visions in 1736, the same year that he began writing about the dynamics of the soul's domain. Unfortunately, the entries for the years 1736–1740 are torn out of the manuscript in which they were written. Although a note on the surviving pages indicates that they passed to the Swedenborg family, they have not yet come to light.

However, the character of these dreams can clearly be deduced from later diary entries. Twelve dreams and visions are noted, among other things, in his dream diary of 1744. He regards all these dreams as mysteriously connected to his work *The Animal Kingdom*. They warn, confirm, or encourage him to continue his studies in a certain way, or they illustrate links in organic life, on whose laws he is presently working. He connected his dream of being enmeshed in the wheel rods of a machine with his studies on the development of the lung of an embryo in the womb. On 25/26 March, he dreamed of a key, with which he opens a locked door. The doorkeeper examines the key, while he is arrested and put under guard. Swedenborg connected this dream to the second part of *The Animal Kingdom*, which was then being printed. The dream confirmed to him the accuracy of his description of the lung artery because "it is the key to the lung and consequently to the movement of the whole body."

A dream of 11/12 April gave him particulars of the thymus gland and its connection to the adrenal glands, which he was discussing in *The Animal Kingdom*. A dream of 14/15 April 1744 relates to his researches on muscles. Another of 3/4 July is connected with the conclusion of a chapter in his work dealing with the senses and with the beginning of the next part on the brain. He understood a dream of 8/9 August as an indication that a particular medical discussion in the third part of *The Animal Kingdom* was incomplete, while a dream of 1/2 September confirmed that the conclusion of his first chapter on the sense of taste was "correct and satisfactory." In a dream of 29/30 September, he similarly finds corroboration of his explanations of organic forms in general and of his concluding chapter in particular. On 6/7 October, he had a dream concerning his work *Worship and Love of God*, in which he learned it was "a divine book."

The dreams thus accompanied the particular divisions of his scientific research. The dream operated as a kind of censor of his daily scientific labors and either confirmed his results or demanded a more careful treatment of the subject. His diary entries also confirm his later assertion that he only partly understood the meaning of his dreams. Swedenborg frequently juxtaposed several possibilities and left open the final interpretation.

The history of science can produce many examples of dreams reflecting the day's work with the dream illuminating and directing the scholar's work in progress. Swedenborg himself distinguished between ordinary and special dreams. He perceived their impressiveness, accompanying mood, and subsequent effect on consciousness after waking as special spiritual events. He later developed a theory of dreams, which distinguished between fantastic and signifying dreams. While fantastic dreams originate in the normal activity of the imagination in the human soul, signifying dreams may be traced back to the influence of a higher nonhuman power such as God, the angels, or the spirits. Swedenborg developed this theory of dreams under the impression of his vocational vision; it cannot be dated back to the beginnings of his visionary experiences. However, it is certain that by 1736 he was already distinguishing between ordinary dreams stemming from fantasy and "higher" dreams. He accorded the latter an objective meaning for his life and his scientific work and allowed himself to be led by them long before he understood them as revelations and the angelic guidance of his life.

In the same way that Swedenborg related his dreams to his scientific work, he later related his visions to the text of Holy Scripture, which he was currently reading. Whereas his dreams contributed to the clarification and evidence of his scientific research, his visions are similar assurances, clarifying and confirming his exposition of Scripture or his current meditation on certain doctrinal questions.

There are visions of light besides the dreams in this first period of the crisis. They also have the quality of assurances, relating to his scientific studies for *The Animal Kingdom*. While writing his works, he felt a "change in his state." He perceived "a certain extraordinary light in the things being written down." In a flash of inner illumination, he received confirmation of a particular insight in the field of organic, human, or animal life, over which he was laboring. At such moments, scientific knowledge became intuition. While investigating the function of the lungs, the glands, or specific parts of the brain, it suddenly dawned on him: "That's it—it can only be that!"

Even this experience can assume various forms. At its simplest, Swedenborg felt an inner illumination while writing down certain thoughts. But such an illumination could also be connected with external manifestations of light: then he actually saw a light or a flame before him. He was constantly accompanied by such light visions in his later visionary period. In an entry of his *Spiritual Diary* of 1744, he explained that a flame meant confirmation in a spiritual sense and continued: "Something of this kind often appeared to me through divine mercy, in various sizes, colors and brightness, so that for months scarcely a day passed, without a flame appearing to me as living as the flame on the hearth. At that time, this was a sign of confirmation, and it occurred before the spirits began to talk with me in voices."

There is an analogy between assurances given in the form of illumination and changes of state, combined with visions of light, and assurances in the form of dreams. The former predate his visionary writings and already accompany the work on his last scientific books, especially *The Animal Kingdom*. At the end of his treatise on the corpuscular philosophy, written in 1740, one finds the noteworthy comment: "*Verum est, quia signum habeo*—That is true, for I have a sign."

Swedenborg also took this experience of confirmatory illuminations into account in his theory of knowledge. In the preface to his *Economy of the Animal Kingdom*, whose composition coincided with his first visionary experiences—the preface was written on 6/7 September 1736 according to the entries in his travel diary—he discusses a series of questions in the theory of knowledge raised by his own personal experiences. Here the path of understanding is described as the gradual opening of the organs of perception. "We are born in deepest ignorance and insensitivity. Gradually our organs are opened; initially we perceive hazy images and concepts; the whole universe presents itself to the eye as an indeterminate chaos: but everything becomes clearer with time, and finally there is the test of reason. Reason comes late to us. One can only know the cause of things or truths by experience. For whenever the spirit strays alone without this companion, how easily it falls into error, then worse error and finally into the worst error of all. One cannot derive experience from firmly established principles, but one must proceed from experiences to the principles. If we let ourselves be led by syllogisms, we are like blindfolded children led the long way round."

Swedenborg applies this insight in evident self-criticism to his own development and earlier works, in which he too readily followed his constructive reason rather than his experience. He resolves to yield less to his egoism and to content himself with sharing his discoveries with others because egoism and vanity are the deadliest enemies of science. "Bad scholars, who practice their profession for self-interest and without a true inner liking, build castles in the air for general admiration. However, born scholars possess the rare

ability to find the cause of things from given phenomena. This demands a good memory and strong powers of imagination and intuition. Whenever such born thinkers find a truth at the end of a long
train of thought, they feel an enlivening light, a sort of confirmatory
flash, which illuminates the sphere of their reason, a certain secret radiance, which traverses the holy temple of the brain. In this fashion,
a voice of reason reveals itself and gives the sign that the soul is summoned to a kind of inner connection; in this moment it falls back
into the golden age of its original state." He concludes these explanations by observing that, once the soul has experienced this delight,
it "regards as meager all bodily delights."

Here Swedenborg has evidently systematized his own experiences of assurance. When he describes the enlivening light, the confirming flash, the secret radiance, or the sign of inner connection as
an indication of intuitive knowledge, it reflects his own change of
inner state frequently described in his diaries. Again he takes up the
doctrine of the original state of human understanding and Adamic
intuition, already discussed in the introduction to his *First Principles
of Natural Things*. Intuitive knowledge was predominant in the
golden age of humankind. At that time, the human center of cognition was still inwardly connected to the essence of things, and the ray
of divine truth directly illuminated the temple of the human spirit.
But now the researcher can achieve intuition only in exceptional
cases.

In *First Principles of Natural Things*, Swedenborg expressed his
deep desire to recover the original form of knowledge. In the meantime, he had experienced the first signs of such an illumination and
flashes of intuition, first in dreams and then in manifestations of an
enlivening and confirming light. From now on, he was completely
absorbed in striving for this higher knowledge. He progressed along
these lines until he experienced his vocational vision. Whatever he
had experienced before in fleeting illuminations and corroboration
then became a permanent and predominant form of vision.

Individual intuitive illuminations occurred in varying intensity
and duration and could lead to longer periods of illumination combined with extreme euphoria. Swedenborg's visions in 1736 began
with such an illumination, connected with the composition of his

work *Economy of the Animal Kingdom*. On 27 October 1743, Swedenborg wrote in his *Spiritual Diary*: "In the morning, when I awoke, I was overcome by a similar bout of dizziness or *deliquium*, as I had when I began *Oeconomia Regni Animalis*, only much more subtle, so that I thought I was near to death. But when I saw the light, the dizziness gradually passed and I fell into a light sleep, so that this *deliquium* was more inward and deep but passed more quickly. As before, it meant that my head was liberated and purified of any obstruction to my thoughts and gave me penetration." This experience of illumination during his stay at Amsterdam from 17–20 August was also linked with an inner dissolution (*deliquium*), a liberation from obstructive thoughts, an inner purification, and a gift of penetration into the true essence of things. The haze, the lack of clarity, has disappeared; he sees things in their original form and idea, and this vision is accompanied by an ecstatic feeling of exultation and happiness.

Swedenborgian research has already indicated the close relationship that exists between the intuition theory of Swedenborg and Locke. In the chapter of *Economy of the Animal Kingdom* dealing with the *anima* as the actual organ of intuition, Swedenborg refers to "the famous Locke" and quotes a sentence from his *Essay concerning Human Understanding* (1690), in which Locke supposes that the angels and spirits of honest men will in a future life have an understanding resembling our intuition. This idea stimulated Swedenborg's understanding of his own experiences. After the opening of his inner sight, he regarded his new understanding as comparable to the cognition of angels and spirits. His explanation of his own experiences thus begins to combine with his doctrine of the spirit realm and the world of angels.

Some of Swedenborg's statements suggest that these experiences were connected with specific physical states and exercises. In 1747, he wrote in his *Spiritual Diary* about "the inner breath":

> I first became accustomed to this breathing in my childhood, while saying my morning and evening prayers, and occasionally later while I was studying the activity of the heart and lungs, and particularly during the writing of *Oeconomia Regni Animalis* and *De*

Regno Animali. I noticed for several years that a quiet breathing was present, scarcely perceptible. Later I thought and talked about this. I was therefore accustomed from my childhood to such respiration, particularly through intensive speculations, when customary breathing ceases. Intensive speculation on truth is not otherwise possible. Also later, when heaven had opened itself to me, so that I could speak with spirits, I accustomed myself so completely to this respiration that I sometimes drew no breath for a whole hour. I had inhaled only so much air, as I needed to think. In this way, I was introduced to the inner breath by the Lord. Perhaps also in dreams, for I repeatedly noticed that I stopped breathing after I had fallen asleep, and gasped for air when I awoke. This kind of breath stops, whenever I observe, write or reflect on things not spiritual. These means were given to me to meet the spirits.

Here Swedenborg indicates that his mental absorption was already combined with a certain breathing technique at his childhood prayers, which he first practiced unconsciously but later used as a means of concentration and withdrawal: the outer breath stops and the inner breath starts. To my knowledge, this is the only known form of Western Christian piety in which meditation and concentration exercises are linked to a certain breathing technique. These methods are of course systematically developed in the practice of Indian yogis as well as in the "heart prayer" of the Hesychasts at Mount Athos. With Swedenborg, the breathing technique evidently consisted in the suppression of the outer breath, which intensified and concentrated his mental activity and gave a free train of thought.

In *Economy of the Animal Kingdom,* Swedenborg gave a physiological proof of his theory and practice of inner breath. "Whenever the brain is eagerly active, reflects deeply, or is busy with anxious thoughts, the lungs breathe quietly and softly. The chest expands only to a certain degree for fear it might disturb the peace of the brain by too deep an inhalation. It contracts and allows only a small quantity of air to penetrate. Whenever the brain is cheerful and merry, then the lungs expand and unfold." He similarly writes: "Whenever the brain reflects and its thinking capacity is active, it wants to be calm and breathe quietly, as is usual with people who reflect intensively." A year later he writes in *Divine Love and Wisdom*:

Everyone can note in their own case that the reason corresponds to the lungs . . . , for no one can think, without his breath keeping pace and being in harmony with his thought. When he thinks quietly, he breathes quietly, and when he thinks deeply, he breathes deeply. He inhales and exhales in harmony with his thinking. He contracts his lungs and expands them . . . slowly, fast, impetuously, gently, or straining. If he holds his breath altogether, he cannot think except in his spirit, whose breath is hardly perceptible.

These statements suggest that Swedenborg was probably accustomed to holding his breath unconsciously and unintentionally when praying during childhood. However, he then noticed an intensification of his prayer and later retained this habit in his intellectual work, reflecting on certain scientific topics. Once he became conscious of the phenomenon, he developed a proper breathing technique in his meditations. If he had not personally experienced these links between mental activity and breathing, he would hardly have considered them in such detail in his scientific works on the activity of the brain and the lungs. One cannot dismiss the possibility that Swedenborg's varied visionary experiences of illuminations, flames, confirmations, and penetration are related to this phenomenon of the inner breath.

This is confirmed by a further entry in the *Spiritual Diary* from the year 1744, where he reports the following:

When inhaling, the thoughts are constrained by the body. When exhaling, it is as if they were expelled or made straight, so that true thoughts have their rhythm like the breathing of the lungs. At each breath, the thoughts are subject to this rhythm. If evil thoughts enter my mind, I only have to hold my breath to drive them forth. This is why the lungs are maintained in a state of equilibrium when one thinks deeply, and why the breath is inhaled quicker than it is exhaled, precisely contrary to what is usual. Likewise, why thoughts are absent as in sleep from a person who is in a state of ecstasy and whose breath is held back. The same can be shown of the brain, where thoughts begin. All the inner organs are in a state of expansion together with the brain during inhalation.

His link between visionary experiences and a certain kind of breath later received a theological interpretation in *Arcana Coelestia*. There Swedenborg attempts to generalize his doctrine of the two kinds of breath in the light of his own experiences. Every person has an outer and an inner breath; the outer is from this world, while the inner breath is from heaven. This breath depends on one's state of salvation—by which Swedenborg means states of love and understanding—so that the breathing of the angels is of an inner nature, while the occupants of hell have an outer breath. Here again, Swedenborg relates this to his experiences with the spiritual world. In the foreword to *Arcana Coelestia*, he compares the breathing and understanding of the angels with the first humans: like the angels, the people of the Old Church had an inner breath, which changed according to their inner state. After the gradual extinction of angelic qualities in prehistoric humans, the inner breath ceased. "They could no longer breathe with the angelic heaven, which was the real reason for their destruction. From this time on, the inner respiration and the link with heaven ceased, and the outer respiration replaced it." This theological explanation confirms that higher understanding, the link with heaven and inner breath, were all connected in Swedenborg's mind.

Swedenborg's visionary experiences understandably produced severe inner conflicts. His profession was exact science, empirical research, and the meticulous observation of natural phenomena. But as the introduction to *First Principles of Natural Things* already shows, this laborious discovery of knowledge no longer satisfied him; he already yearned for a higher knowledge, the understanding of Adam and the angels. It is possible that he was already encouraged in this pursuit by particular experiences. Since he had begun writing *Economy of the Animal Kingdom*, such higher experiences and intuitions occurred more and more frequently: first as an overwhelming experience of illumination, penetration, and purification, then in shorter or longer visions of light, confirmations, assurances, and sudden flashes of illumination. At the time that he was writing his laboriously collected observations concerning the organic world, the animal kingdom, and human physiology, he increasingly felt involved in a realm of higher understanding and direct mode of viewing. If the truth flew to him in such intuitions, if such a direct path into the realm of knowledge were opened to him, was it then still necessary to grope along the laborious path of empirical experiment? But if there was an inner temple and the inner person could receive a flash of illumination through a direct ray of divine truth, was he worthy of such illumination? Was his inner temple ready and pure to receive the divine truth?

The assurance experiences marked the start of a religious crisis, in which Swedenborg began to question his personal worthiness, the sanctity of his personal life, and the continuation of his scientific career. After attaining a higher form of understanding, science must have appeared more of an obstacle than a path to true knowledge. The sheer abundance of empirical detail seemed to weigh his spirit down and deterred his direct inner link with the spiritual world. The religious crisis exploded dramatically in 1743–1744 as a struggle between his inner vocation and his outer career.

14

The Religious Crisis

Swedenborg committed the story of his conversion to private diaries, not intended for publication. Here he answered to himself and to God, recording the gradual transformation of his old identity. In describing the most intimate spiritual experiences, he sought to understand the uncanny and confusing event now taking place in himself.

These diaries plainly show that his religious crisis ran its course as a profound convulsion of his personality. The crisis did not merely lead to a change in his thought but in his whole life, even to a physical transformation. It ended with his conversion, which carried all the signs of repentance, and with a vision of Christ. How did this change come about in Swedenborg's lively mental life?

Let us imagine the mood in which Swedenborg was writing his introduction to *The Animal Kingdom.* He was preparing the publication of a large scientific work, containing his researches into the structure of the soul's domain, the organic forms of life, animal and human anatomy, and the functions of inner and outer organs—the brain, the lungs, and the circulation of the blood. This work was supposed to serve the understanding of God and the glorification of his almighty power: he wanted to illuminate God's truth and greatness from the Book of Nature. This concern did not lead him beyond the deistic piety of his age. In none of the scientific works or his letters hitherto was there the slightest reference to the person of Christ or to his personal religious views on salvation and atonement. The whole sphere of Christian piety and experience of God appeared not to exist for him in his scientific period—and then all at once he is powerfully drawn into it.

This strange process is clearly connected with a profound disturbance of his self-confidence, scientific ambition, and pride. The various assurance experiences, dreams, and illuminations, which began with the sense of an inner purification and "penetration" in 1736, greatly undermined his scientific self-assurance. The young man in possession of the new natural sciences had believed he could storm heaven and already saw himself at the pinnacle of European renown. Now he suddenly realized that his previous researches touched only the outer shell of being but had not introduced him to the inner life of things. True understanding of being had not come to him in calculations, measurements, and experiments but in fleeting flashes of intuition. Like Locke and Leibniz, he understood these illuminations as the breath of the spiritual world, as a personal contact with the realm of truth itself. His former scientific self-confidence dissolved in this contact. Previously he had been proud of his achievements, but now it was clear to him how unfounded this pride was. He saw how far removed human understanding is from the genuine understanding of the truth, despised by vain scholars and accessible only to the humble through the gift of inner illumination. His previous life's foundation began to crumble.

There is still no sign of such a crisis in his travel reports during the years 1736 to 1739. Even the diary of the journey undertaken in 1743 to have *The Animal Kingdom* printed began in the customary style of earlier descriptions of travel. He described the stages of the journey, his meetings with important personalities, and his visits to museums, institutions, and other buildings. However, the entries describing his journey, beginning at Stockholm on 21 July, via Stralsund, Wisum, and Hamburg to Groningen, suddenly break off.

When they resume, they show him already in the grip of violent agitation, which will end with his conversion and vocational experience.

His interpretation of his dreams and visionary experiences initially influenced this transformation. He understood his inner experiences not as a natural process of his inner life but as the effect of a spiritual power, as the supernatural intervention of the Divine. For the first time, he begins to have a presentiment of the meaning of grace. He understands this revelation of a higher certainty and understanding of the truth as a sign of God's special grace towards him. He realizes a new aspect of God, which brings him closer to the Christian notion of God.

During his scientific period, he had been honest enough to import only those elements of his faith into the new worldview that seemed to him proven by the investigation of nature and his observation of the human soul. These concerned the belief in God as the Creator and upholder of the world, the Lord of life, the origin of all ideas and forms, the founder of all laws, ordinances, numbers, and dimensions, the source of being, who was worthy of supreme reverence and glorification. Now he experienced another form of the divine reality: he felt how this distant God entered his life and met the defects of human reason with the grace of illumination. God appeared to him as the personal God, who incomprehensibly transforms and elevates the seeker. He learned to understand this experience in the same way that he had learned in his youth from his father and from the writings of Arndt, Scriver, and other teachers of conversion. It would be an exaggeration to say that the scholar reverted to his childhood faith under the impact of his visionary experience. However, it is possible that the forgotten and repressed pietistic family tradition of his youth helped him to understand his inner transformation as a conversion experience. There are many indications for this.

Swedenborg was accustomed to describe his transformation entirely in expressions used by Pietism to portray the process of conversion. Under the impact of his visions, he finds his way back to the Church and the Bible, neither of which had previously fulfilled his thoughts and feelings. Even more persuasive is the major role his father plays in his dreams and visions during the period of crisis. His father did not agree with the direction of his son's intellectual thought in England, and the conflict between father and son was never finally settled during his father's lifetime. When Swedenborg began to feel God's grace in the prime of his life, his late father appeared to him in a radiant light as a guide on the new path and the dreams in which he met his father assumed a special meaning. After his vision of Christ in the night of 6/7 March 1744, he sees his father in a reddish robe.[1] His father hails him, embraces him, and urges him to change and take up the spiritual vocation. On another occasion, his late father appears to him at a party, which Swedenborg wants to join but finds his way barred. In the night of 14/15 April 1744, Swedenborg the dreamer hurries down a staircase, hardly touching the steps. Then he hears the voice of his father: "You are making such a [fuss], Emanuel!" On 20/21 June, the dreamer sees his whole life and all the chasms he has been led past. He is brought into a marvelous grove, then into a palace, where he chooses a room for himself. The following night, the dream resumes, and he is admitted to a party, from whose midst his father walks up to him and says that the son's treatise on providence is the best work he has yet written. This treatise, which Swedenborg never printed and which is lost, was the sole theological work of his scientific period. On 27/28 July, Swedenborg dreams that his father is standing in a wonderful surplice before an assembly. "He spoke kindly to me and wanted to take me to a person in an inner room, one who appeared to be asleep, to tell him about me. I left, afraid of waking him up." Swedenborg related this dream to the fact that he was now beginning to read the Bible again every evening. His father appears to him as the guide who leads him to the Word—the sleeping man in the inner room—and wants to acquaint him with Holy Scripture. During his life, Jesper Swedberg had been the angry representative of Reformed orthodoxy, who saw only atheists in the new scientists and quarrelled with his son who had taken their side. Now he approached Emanuel as the guardian angel of a new outlook on life.

---

1. Swedenborg's journal of dreams has been translated into English; see Lars Bergquist, *Swedenborg's Dream Diary,* translated by Anders Hallengren (West Chester, Pa.: The Swedenborg Foundation, 2001). Where a date is not provided, the number of the dream is cited in the text. —*Editor*

The process of Swedenborg's inner transformation is revealed in his diary. The travel diary of 1743–1744 contains entries from which one can deduce that Swedenborg has already experienced violent spiritual turmoil, evoked in short keywords. The corresponding notes show that he has experienced an inner purification, comparable to his first great illumination of 1736. This is accompanied by a profound critique of his former life and scientific achievement, perceived not only as a purification of his intellect but as a moral purge.

The nullity of his former life is presented in a mass of shocking dreams of anxiety and persecution. For example, he writes: "How I saw hideous specters, without life, in horrible shrouds within which they moved. With a beast that attacked me but not the child" (*Dream Diary* §15). Such anxious dreams of a large dog biting him occur frequently in the later entries for the year 1744. One such dream is described as follows: "I seemed to be reclining on a rocky mountain, beneath which there was a chasm. Lying there among the knobby cliffs, I tried to get onto my feet by holding onto a rock, without a foothold; an abyss beneath" (*Dream Diary* §16). Here the spiritual situation is clear: Swedenborg sees himself confronted with the fall into the void. He tries to save himself but has no means of doing so, and the awareness of his own impotence increases his fear and sense of threat. He interpreted the dream himself the same way: "This signifies that I wished to rescue myself from the precipice all by myself, and that was not possible."

He continued to explain his various illuminations during this period—"my ecstasies before and after sleep; my clear thoughts about things"—as an influence of the divine spirit. He perceived the increasingly frequent phenomena as gifts of God's grace, attempting to elevate him to a higher plane of understanding.

The moral purge, which he felt as a consequence of this spirit, is equally significant. He experienced in himself the beginning of the miracle of sanctification. Under the influence of the new spirit of God, he now recognized the true danger of the things that had previously filled his life: egoism and ambition, scientific vanity, and sexual lust. He saw through the selfish pride, which had previously dominated his mental attitude, and felt with amazement how the spirit of arrogance now deserted him. "I was astonished at myself, that I no longer bothered about my own honor." He realized that a majority of his works contained errors, and especially in those places where "they opposed the power of the Holy Spirit," and that all mistakes stemmed from him, "but all the truths from the Holy Spirit." His scientific self-confidence, formerly so conspicuous, was now tottering. On arrival at The Hague, he felt to his amazement how selfishness and egoism increasingly dissipate in him. He noticed "that I was not inclined toward sexual relations, which I had been all my days" (*Dream Diary* §12) and "how the inclination toward women, which had been my chief passion, so suddenly ceased" (*Dream Diary* §14).

Swedenborg felt in himself the mysterious unfolding of a completely new and unknown principle of life. However, it became clear to him that he had not reached a completed state. This was only the prelude to an inner struggle, in which the old identity resists with all its energy the grace of new life. There are also short references to this: "How I used to oppose the spirit and how pleased I was to do this before I found that this was nonsense, without life and meaning. Sometimes I became impatient and thought I wanted to rebel, when everything did not proceed with the ease that I wished; afterwards, I did nothing just for my own sake."

The diary breaks off on 8 December 1743 and resumes on 1 March 1744. The new entries show the inner struggle continuing violently. The anxious dreams become more and more frequent. In one dream, he is standing beside a machine that is set in motion by a wheel. He is caught in the spokes and borne upwards so that he cannot escape and wakes full of fear. He interpreted this dream to mean "that I must be kept in further difficulty" (*Dream Diary* §18). In another dream, he hurries cheerfully down a broad staircase, at whose end stands a ladder. The ladder leads down into a hole of great depth. He fears that he could fall into the hole while trying to reach its far side, although several people standing there stretch out their hands to help him. "This is the danger . . . of falling into the abyss unless I receive help" (*Dream Diary* §20).

Other dreams are dominated by a feeling of inner impurity, by the desire to escape his oppressed situation and by the longing for complete purification. In his dream he sees a garden with many pretty flowerbeds. "I looked around to see if there was any other path; I saw one and thought of another. There was someone who was picking away at a heap of invisible creeping things and killed them; he said they were bugs that someone had carried thither and thrown in, infesting the entire place. I did not see them, but saw some other crawling creature, which I dropped on a white linen sheet beside a woman; it was the impurity which ought to be rooted out of me" (*Dream Diary* §19). Again the situation is very characteristic: he finds ugly faults—insects—in the pretty, neatly kept flowerbeds of his science. He seeks an exit from the garden but cannot find it, even though he laid it out himself. The longing for inner purity is expressed very clearly in a dream of recovery during the night of 25/26 March 1744. "I asked for a cure against my illness, and I was offered a heap of rags to buy [one prepared lint as a bandage from rags in those days]. I took half of them and selected from the other half, but finally I gave back all the rags. He said that he would himself buy me something that would lead to a cure. The rags were my corporeal thoughts by which I wished to cure myself, but they were good for nothing." His own knowledge, his researches and studies, upon which he had formerly looked with so much pride and self-confidence and for which he would have given anything, now appear to him as rags, useless for healing his disease. The cure, he surmises, must come from something else.

The feeling of inability to help himself by his own efforts, which expressed itself in all kinds of anxieties, gives way to thoughts of his utter vileness. He feels that God has a hand in his strange transformation and wants to direct him towards a certain goal, but he finds himself unprepared and unworthy of all divine grace. He becomes particularly conscious of this in a dream of 2/3 April: "Two persons came and entered a house which, although built, was not yet in order. They went about it, but did not seem favorably impressed. We saw that our power was gone and feared them. One of them came up to me and said that they intended to inflict a punishment on me the following Maundy Thursday, unless I took flight. I did not know how to get out, but he told me he would show me the way. Woke up. Meant that I had invited the highest to visit me in an unprepared and untidy hut and that they had found it untidy and that I ought to be punished, but I was most graciously shown the way by which to escape their wrath." The unknown man increasingly appears as the representative of God, who wishes to heal him, who shows him an exit, who gathers up and kills the insects in his garden. It is highly significant that this figure is already indicated in his dreams; for, in a hallucination immediately prior to the vocational vision, the unknown man appears again and shouts to him, "Don't eat so much!" The images of his dreams and his visions are related to each other and form a continuous series.

The Easter week brought the crisis to a climax. Swedenborg had been threatened with punishment from God for Maundy Thursday. In his distress, he again found his way to the Church and the Bible. In order to allay his inner fear, he prepared himself to receive Communion on Easter Sunday, but this brought no relief from agitation. On the contrary, the feeling of unworthiness and guilt escalated to a sense of eternal damnation, as he shows in his entry of 5/6 April: "Easter Day was on 5 April; and then I went to God's table. The temptation was persistent, mostly in the afternoon up to six o'clock. There was nothing definite, but an anxiety as if one were damned and in hell; and yet all the time remained the hope which the Holy Ghost inspired, and very strongly so, according to Paul's Epistle to the Romans, V:5" (*Dream Diary* §38). In his extremity, he clearly refers to the passage "And this hope is not deceptive, because the love of God has been poured into our hearts by the Holy Spirit which has been given us." Like Job, he feels he has been delivered up to Satan, who harasses him through diverse thoughts. "The temptation came in the afternoon [of Easter Sunday], in an entirely different manner, but strongly; for I was assured that my sins were forgiven, but yet I could not govern my wayward thoughts to restrain some expressions opposed to my better knowledge. It was from the Evil One, by permission [of God]. Prayer gave some relief, and also the Word of God; faith was there entirely, but confidence and love seemed to be absent. Went to bed at nine; the temptation and the trembling continued until 10:30. Then I fell into a sleep, where all my temptation was represented to me" (*Dream Diary* §39–40).

He finally experienced an unexpected deliverance from this torment. Having already received during the day the assurance that his sins were forgiven, he experienced during the night a complete inner purification "in wonderful and indescribable upheavals" and in experiences which fell into a "mystical series." The temptation ended in ecstasy and an encounter with God, which led to the most profound convulsion of his whole being. Immediately following the temptation he had assuring dreams, which offered answers to his tormenting thoughts of the day. These were such "that there was a life and a glory in the whole of it that I cannot in the least describe, for it was all heavenly. At the time, it was clear to me, but now, afterwards, I cannot express anything. In short, I was in heaven, and I heard a speech that no human tongue can utter, nor can anyone describe the glory and bliss of that life. Apart from this, I was awake, in heavenly ecstasy, which is ineffable, too. At nine o'clock, I went to bed and arose between nine and ten, having been in bed from twelve to thirteen hours. To the Highest be praise, honor, and glory! Hallowed by His Name, Holy, Lord God Zabaoth!" (*Dream Diary* §§44–45) The feeling of bliss continued throughout the whole of the following day: "Had also in my mind and my body a kind of sensation of indescribable delight, so intense that, had it been increased, the body would have been, as it were, dissolved from delight alone. This took place in the night between the first and second day after Easter, and during the whole of [Easter] Monday" (*Dream Diary* §48).

Swedenborg was already on the same path that many pious people have traversed before and after him. The first encounter with the Holy One awoke in him the feeling of imperfection and unworthiness and made him scream for purification and deliverance by divine grace. He experienced in himself the unfolding of a new life and spirit, but this stirring of the new persona inflamed the opposition of his old persona and unleashed temptations, which led to feelings of deepest damnation and depravity. The temptation was overcome in an ecstasy, which led him to the threshold of self-dissolution.

The ups and downs of this inner struggle, which brought him to the edge of total physical exhaustion, repeated itself the following day, in the night between Easter Monday and Easter Tuesday. The temptation now consisted in thoughts that overcame him while reading Holy Scripture and made him doubt the truth of God's Word. After he had withstood this struggle, an even greater exaltation followed: he saw the face of Christ, the living Lord. This vision of Christ, which assumed the greatest importance for his further religious development and missionary consciousness, he described as follows:

> 6/7 April 1744. NB NB NB In the evening, I came into another sort of temptation, namely, between eight and nine in the evening, while I read about God's miracles performed through Moses. I observed that something of my own understanding interfered and made it impossible for me really to believe this as I should; I both believed and not believed at the same time. I thought that this is the reason that the angels and God showed themselves to shepherds and not to philosophers, who let their understanding enter into these matters: then you can always ask why God made use of the wind to call together the locusts, why he hardened the Pharaoh, why he did not set to work at once, and other such things, at which I smiled to myself, but which nevertheless made me incredulous.

He now tried to subdue the temptations, which beset him. "I looked at the fire"—he was sitting beside the hearth—"and said to myself":

> Thus, I should not believe that the fire exists, because the external senses are more fallacious than the words of God, which are truth itself and which I should believe more than in myself. With such musings, I spent some hour and a half and inwardly smiled at the tempter. . . . At ten o'clock, I went to bed and felt a little better. After half an hour, I heard some din under my head, and then I thought that the tempter left. Immediately a shiver came over me, starting from the head and spreading throughout the body, with some rumbling, coming in waves, and I realized that something holy had befallen me. Whereupon I went to sleep, and about twelve o'clock, or perhaps it was at one or two in the morning, such a strong shivering seized me, from my head to my feet, as a thunder produced by several clouds colliding, shaking me beyond description and prostrating me. And when I was prostrated in this way, I was clearly awake and saw how I was overthrown. I

wondered what this was supposed to mean, and I spoke as if awake
but found that the words were put into my mouth. I said, "Oh,
thou almighty Jesus Christ, who of thy great mercy deigns to come
to so great a sinner, make me worthy of this grace!" and I clasped
my hands and prayed. Then a hand emerged, which pressed my
hands firmly. In a little while, I continued my prayer, saying, "Thou
hast promised to receive in grace all sinners; thou canst not otherwise than keep thy word!" In the same moment, I was sitting in his
bosom and beheld him face to face, a countenance of a holy mien.
All was such that I cannot describe. He was smiling at me, and I
was convinced that he looked like this when he was alive. He spoke
to me and asked if I have a health certificate; and to this I replied,
"Lord, thou knowest better than I." He said, "Well then, do!"—
that is, as I inwardly grasped this, "Do love me" or "Do as promised." God give me grace thereto! I found it beyond my powers
and woke up shuddering. *(Dream Diary §§50–54)*

This vision brought about the decisive turning point of his life.
Until now, Swedenborg had striven for scientific knowledge in all
fields of empirical research. But now it was plain to him: one cannot
achieve fulfillment and bliss through the understanding of science but
only through the understanding of salvation. This knowledge of salvation was granted to Swedenborg in the vision of Christ. Previously
God had appeared to him in an impersonal form, as the dark background of all being and life and as the hidden law of all nature. Now
God was revealed to him in the image of the Son, not as a law of nature, not as destiny, not as an idea, not in an impersonal, abstract form,
but in a physical, personal figure, turning his face towards all people, as
the Son, as Christ the Lord, as the heavenly humanity of God.

From now on, Christ, as he had seen him face to face, was the
focus of Swedenborg's piety, his thought, and his vision. The secret
source of being, the fount of life—for him, this is the meaning of the
new revelation—is not a dark, intangible divine power, a distant,
mysterious God beyond the stars, but the personal God who approaches us in his human aspect, in Christ the Lord, as Redeemer. In
Christ, humankind receives a new life, a new understanding, and a
new access to truth, while experiencing a renewal of his human
image.

Swedenborg perceived this encounter with the Lord as an over-whelming flow of divine grace into his life. It threw him to the ground. He felt his complete nullity, his total surrender to this power, which had surprised him. The words that he spoke were not his words, for his ego had vanished in contact with the Lord. It was Christ himself who put the words of confession and a plea for mercy into his mouth.

Here Swedenborg was describing an essentially Christian experience of repentance. In the course of his religious crisis, he arrived at a point where his former self-confidence and his pride in his scientific achievements collapsed. In this abyss of self-examination, he realized that Christ is the path to true life and true understanding. His report of his vision indicates that he had already promised to love Christ and commit his life to him but had found that he could not achieve this by his own powers. But now the Lord himself leads him out of the abyss of his temptations, looks him in the face, presses his hands together, and puts the words of prayer into his mouth.

It is striking how old images from Swedenborg's youth surface in this shattering experience. When Christ asks him if he has a "health certificate," this recalls the first great adventure of his youth, the voyage to England. After many dangers, he had finally reached the coast of the promised land. Although he had arrived from Sweden where the plague was raging, he had illegally slipped into England without a certificate of health. This violation had almost cost him his life on the gallows. Now, after his inner spirit has suffered manifold temptations and dangers, he is standing on the coast of his spiritual longing and hears the warning question of the guardian of the threshold: "Have you a clean bill of health?" This means, "Are you worthy and pre-pared to enter this land? Have you got through the quarantine of temptations and purges? This is obligatory for everyone wishing to come from the plague country of the world into this realm. Or does the plague of selfishness, vanity, and willfulness that rages in your for-mer homeland still cling to you?" With self-confidence and untrou-bled high spirits, he had entered England, the land of scientific knowledge. Now that he had progressed to the limits of natural understanding and was cast into the deepest despair, he feels himself carried to the shore of the land of divine truth by the waves of divine grace. Here the angels and spirits proclaim to him the true essence of things.

The vision of Christ understandably plunged Swedenborg into deepest thought and critical reflections. The most important question for him was whether the vision was genuine. Was it not after all the product of his own fantasy or a delusion? Thus, the old persona immediately began to express its doubts. But with the recent impact of religious revelation, this critical question about the authenticity of the vision seemed a blasphemy. Was not doubting the manifestation of the living Lord a fresh and even greater outrage to be guilty of? Would he not forfeit the new grace through this doubt?

He was torn hither and thither by these doubts:

> I thought: What can this really be? Have I seen Christ, the Son of God? But it is a pity that I doubt this. However, as we are commanded to try the spirits, I carefully thought all this over; and from what had occurred during the night, I concluded that the Holy Spirit had been purifying me all night and that it had encompassed and preserved me, preparing me for this. And from the facts that I fell on my face; that the words I spoke and the prayer did not come from myself, but that the words were put into my mouth, although it was I who spoke; and that everything was holy, I saw that it was the Son of God himself who descended with such a resounding noise that I was spontaneously prostrated, offered up the prayer, and said it was Jesus in person. (*Dream Diary* §55)

Swedenborg thus saw the events of the previous and current night in the continuous context of preparation and fulfillment. His initial doubts yielded to certainty that it was the Lord himself who had revealed himself to him. The principal proof for him was the fact that the prayer, in which he addressed the apparition as Christ, did not stem from him but was put into his mouth by the Lord. He understood this as a self-proclamation of the Lord, who thus names himself and reveals the true nature of the apparition.

Now all his misgivings vanished:

> I prayed for my long-term doubts to be forgiven and that in my thoughts I had demanded miracles, which I now saw was not reasonable. Thereupon, I fell in prayer, and I prayed only for grace.

That was all I could express, but afterwards I added that I pray for love, which is the work of Jesus Christ and not mine. When I said this, tremors repeatedly passed over me. Later, at dawn, I fell asleep when having all this in mind, considering how Christ binds himself to people, and then sacred thoughts emerged that I cannot get down in writing, nor what then passed: I only know I had such ideas. (*Dream Diary* §§56–57)

The vision of Christ was the start of a new life and new understanding for Swedenborg. He had labored his whole life to understand the truth and yearned for the highest level of knowledge. He had researched and experimented; he had striven for truth in the depths of the mines, in the oceans, lakes and rivers, in the stones and rock strata of the mountains, in fossils, and in the anatomy of plants, animals, and the human body. Everywhere he had discovered that the whole ultimate truth is not accessible through things. Now he had been granted the fundamental religious experience, which told him the highest and whole is given only to a human being through grace. Everything is grace and nothing comes through the work of the individual. It is not the arrogance of knowledge but the humility of ignorance and self-surrender that lead to perfection. He therefore wrote in conclusion about his vision of Christ: "This I have now learned of the spiritual: that the only thing is to humble oneself to the grace of Christ, in all humility to ask for no more than that. I had added something of my own—to receive love—but that was presumptuous. Because when one delivers oneself to the grace of God, one is at the mercy of Christ and acts according to his wishes. One is happiest when in God's grace" (*Dream Diary* §61).

This vision of Christ represents the preparation for his vision of vocation in 1745. At first, Swedenborg had no clear idea where this vision was leading and what it meant for his life. But in the following weeks, he realized that he was being prepared for special work and that God planned something particular for him. Under the impact of new visions, he started to manifest his later vocational and missionary consciousness. He felt empowered by the forgiveness of his sins and the outpouring of the Holy Spirit, which initially led to naive and impulsive forms of expression. In a state of exaltation following his meeting with Christ, he wanted to become a martyr and take all possible sufferings for Christ upon himself. He saw his new task of fighting Satan in the power of the received spirit, and this resolution was strengthened in the following weeks through his reading of the Bible. He reported that the twelfth chapter of the Book of Revelation, in which the pursuit of the woman clothed by the sun by the dragon is described, awoke in him a violent desire, "I wished I could be instrumental in killing the dragon; but that is not in my power but that of God alone" (*Dream Diary* §227).

It was initially a highly romantic but vague task to which Swedenborg thought himself called, and his mood was touched by an exuberance unusual in a fifty-five-year-old man with a long scholarly life behind him. At this time, his religious self-consciousness was so great that, under the direct influence of his vision of Christ, he thought he might be taken for a saint, "if anyone took me for a holy man, and therefore esteemed me, yes, as with some simpleminded people, not merely to venerate but also to adore a putative holiness or a saint" (*Dream Diary* §72). However, he perceived this thought as a new temptation of his arrogance and a stirring of his old persona. Nevertheless, this idea stirred him so violently that he even considered what he would do in order to prevent the worship of his person. "I then perceived that . . . I would be willing to inflict upon [people who worshipped me] every evil, even unto the extreme, rather than any such sin cleave to [them]. And that I must entreat out Lord with earnest prayers that I may not have any share in so damnable a sin. . . ."

In the light of such considerations, Swedenborg initially decided not to tell anyone about his visionary pardon. Evidently, the observations that he wrote on this point subsequently seemed foolhardy, for they are carefully crossed out. However, the following can be deciphered: "I . . . [did not dare] to tell . . . what high grace had been conferred upon me; for I discerned that this could serve no other purpose than to make people think this or that about me, according to the pros and cons of each, nor perform any use. . . . The best comparison I could make of myself was with a peasant who had been given the power of a prince or king, so that he would posses everything his heart could wish for. . . . But from the comparison one finds that [it is] thy gracious hand which causes the great joy. Still I was distressed because I feared that he cannot maintain that grace with me" (§80–81). He actually carried out his intention of concealing his inner transformation because, on the 7/8 April, he notes in his diary, "During all this, I remained in the company of my former associates, and no one could [discern] the least change with me, which was God's grace."

The day laborer raised to the royal throne—this image reflects the mood of Swedenborg most clearly. He perceives an incomparable exaltation, a vocation to a supreme and most holy task. Ever more clearly he understands that he has been chosen by God as an instrument for great work. An apparition in the night of 18/19 April tells him "that I will obtain sound and noble knowledge, on which I may use my time." In the night of 28/29 April, a new dream suggests "that I ought to employ my remaining time upon what is higher and not write about worldly things, which are far beneath, but about that which concerns the very center of all and concerning Christ. May God be gracious and enlighten me further regarding my duty, for I am still in some obscurity as to whither I should turn."

The explanation of this dream indicates that he already appreciates the transformation of his former inner state will also demand a change of his profession and position in the world. Now that Christ himself has shown him the path of salvation, should he waste his time further searching for grains of mundane truth upon the old path of empirical research?

This question greatly occupied Swedenborg. Even after his vision of Christ, he continued to relate certain dreams and illuminations to the scientific researches on which he was presently working, especially his work on *The Animal Kingdom*. For a time, he felt his vocation consisted in completing this work, in order to understand the secret principle of vitality in the animal and human organism. But he soon decoded that the spirit was driving him in another direction, and he sensed a new task. In a dream of 15/16 April, two women appeared to him, one older and one younger, who followed him to a green wall. "I kissed the hands of both and did not know which one of them I should make love to." According to his own explanation, the older woman signified his previous research, the younger, his work of the spirit. To which should he now apply himself?

In the night of 19/20 April, this question is clarified in a new visionary dream. There he is granted the insight "that, by the grace of God, I have gained the battle and that the blood and merit of Jesus have helped me and that, in my studies, I shall gain my object. . . . I was so angry with Satan that I wanted to fight him with the weapons of faith." In the night of 21/22 April, he finally decided to devote himself completely to God and the true knowledge of God. A final crisis preceded this decision: he wanted to flee from his divine task and thought of traveling home in order to evade what had befallen him in such a confusing and inescapable fashion.

> Afterwards, I came into a state of hesitation because I seemed to be so far estranged from God that I could not yet think of him in a living manner, and whether I should not turn my journey homewards. There came a mass of complex reasoning and motions of the body, but I gathered courage and concluded that I had come here [Holland] to do my very best and to promote the glory of God, that I have got the talent, that everything aimed in this direction, that the spirit has been with me from my youth unto this end, and I considered myself unworthy to live if I did not stick to the right way. And, accordingly, I smiled at the other seductive ideas. Thus, as to pleasure, wealth, and rank, which I had pursued, I perceived that all was vanity and that he is the more happy who is devoid of such things and is nevertheless contented than the one who does possess them. And therefore, I smiled at all [arguments to the contrary], and thus by the help of God I came to a resolution. May God help me.

A triumphant new consciousness arises in him that he has received a new profession from God, which consists in promoting the glory of God, not his own. His whole previous life already appears to him as a unique, mysterious preparation for the hour of illumination. After much trouble and torment, he resolved to devote himself henceforth to God and live the new gift of spirit, which has been given to him. An outer sign confirmed the decision: "I seemed to hear a hen clucking, as she does when she has laid an egg."

After the "egg has been laid," he freed himself from his last remaining doubts concerning his decision during his voyage from Holland to England in the early days of May. He felt his thoughts "wildly racing round," but "with the aid of the spirit I killed them and was thereby acquitted." A dream revealed to him the change in his understanding: "My speculation, which was previously a posteriori, was from this moment onwards transformed into an a priori understanding." He thus took a decision concerning his previous scientific and professional career. Speculation a posteriori defined his scientific, chemical, biological, and mathematical studies, which were constructed upon an empirical investigation of the external reality. He now wished to devote himself exclusively to a priori understanding or intuition, which was granted him by God through the gift of the spirit. After arrival in England, he wrote on 6 May these significant closing words in his diary: "[This is the sum of all.] (1) Only grace can save us. (2) Grace is in Jesus Christ who is the throne of grace. (3) It is the love of God in Christ by which salvation is effected. (4) And that one then allows oneself to be led by the spirit of Jesus. (5) Everything that comes from ourselves is dead and is nothing but sin and worthy of eternal damnation. (6) For nothing good can come except from the Lord."

To be sure, this did not solve the practical question: how should he continue to lead his life? Was he not ultimately sacrificing his scientific and professional activity for an illusion? What would his relatives, friends, and colleagues say about his transformation? Even in July doubts assailed him concerning the path he had to take. "I do not know, whether I must pursue another method for my work and whether I must be prepared for something else. I am still in the dark over this." But through all his doubts, he remained conscious that he had previously erred, and his dreams and visions confirmed him in this view. In the night of 7/8 October, a dream taught him "that I have been on the wrong path and have followed my reason in a fog, where one is afraid even of one's own people, as it they were enemies; but when on the right track, one is afraid of no one."

The last vision entered in his diary contains a final confirmation of his decision to live for the Lord from now on. He sees a marvelous loaf of bread offered to him on a plate, "which was a premonition that the Lord himself was going to instruct me, since I have now finally come into such a state that I know nothing, and that all preconceived opinions have been taken away from me, which is the beginning of learning, namely, that one first must become a child, and then be nurtured into knowledge, as is now, I think, happening to me."

We leave Swedenborg in this state at the end of the year 1744. Determined to surrender himself to the new, dark, mysterious life beginning to stir in him, ready to sacrifice his old knowledge and scientific vanity to the new understanding from God, he awaited the Lord's instruction. He believed this would bring him a complete understanding of what was already stirring his spirit through intermittent illumination. He had experienced in himself what the apostle Paul had described: "Our knowledge is imperfect, and our prophesying is imperfect. But once perfection comes, all imperfect things will disappear. Now we are seeing a dim reflection in a mirror, but then we shall be seeing face to face. The knowledge that I have now is imperfect, but then I shall know as fully as I am known"(1 Corinthians 13: 11–12). But, unlike the apostle, Swedenborg did not hope for perfection in a future life, but in this life itself, and moreover in the near future. He then experienced the fulfillment of this high-flown expectation in the vision of God granted to him in London in 1745.

The course of Swedenborg's inner transformation can be discovered from the medley of dream accounts, reports of visions, feelings, reflections, doubts, and temptations as he described them chronologically in his diary. But this development was by no means continuous. Feelings and thoughts ran to and fro in an illogical and contradictory tangle of personal and objective motives. Nevertheless, the principal themes of his later piety and visionary theology are already evident. Above all, the entries confirm that the basic attitude of his piety is an authentic Christian mysticism, as practiced by many devout mystics of the medieval and Baroque periods. It is not the intellectual mysticism of Meister Eckhart but the loving myticism of St. Bernard of Clairvaux that recurs in Swedenborg's vision of Christ. He did not know the writings of St. Bernard, but he had very similar experiences. Christ was and remained from now on the center of his piety, subsequent theology, and philosophy of religion.

Whenever temptations and doubts assailed him, he concentrated his thoughts upon the image of Christ. He described this in his notes of 8 April in the following way: "I was also in such a temptation that my fancies went out of control, yes, with such a force that I could think only of keeping a close check on them, to counter the spiritual power, which is heading in another direction; yes, with such a force that had not God's grace been even stronger, I'd have fallen or been driven crazy. At times, I was not able to focus on Christ at all, whom I had seen, but for a little while. The power and agitation of the spirit fell upon me so strongly that I would rather become insane." It was not an external image of Christ or a theological concept of Christ to which he clung in his contemplation but the face that had appeared to him in his first vision of Christ and remained inextinguishable within him. Now this Christ appeared to him as the living center of the universe. In a vision on the morning of 9 April 1744, he saw the whole world interwoven by this center. "Thee was an inward joy that could be felt all over the body. Everything seemed in a consummate way to be fulfilled, flew upwards as it were, concealing itself in something infinite, as a center, where love itself was, and it seemed as if it issued thence round about and then down again, thus moving around in incomprehensible circles from a center that is love, and back."

Having seen the radiant Lord in his first vision of Christ, Swedenborg later saw the crucified Christ, whose image played a large part in his spiritual exercises. On 14 April 1744, he wrote: "I was all day in equivocal thoughts, which tried to destroy the spiritual by contemptuous abuse to the extent that I felt that the temptation was very strong. By the grace of the Spirit, I managed to focus my thoughts on a tree, then on the cross of Christ, and on to the Crucifixion; and as I did so, all other thoughts fell flat to the ground, as if by themselves. I pushed this thought so far that it seemed to me I was pressing down the tempter by means of the cross and driving him away; and then, after a while, I was free. Afterwards, I had to fix my thoughts upon [the cross] so intently that, whenever I let it slip out of my thoughts and internal vision, I fell into temptation-thoughts." These experiences were concluded by a vision of the crucified Christ on the following night. Just as Bernard of Clairvaux had a face-to-face vision of Christ, culminating in a holy kiss, so Swedenborg had an experience in the night of 14/15 April, which he described as follows:

On awakening, I had before me Jesus crucified and his cross. The spiritual came upon me with all its heavenly, almost ecstatic life, and I was ascending so high and permitted to go higher that, had I proceeded, I would have been dissolved by this veritable life of joy. It then appeared to me in the spirit that I had gone too far; that in my thoughts I had embraced Christ on the cross, when I kissed his feet and that I then removed myself thence, falling upon my knees and praying before him crucified. It seemed that the sins of my weakness are forgiven as often as I do this. It occurred to me that I might have the same idol before the eyes of my body, but I found that this would be far from right and, indeed, a great sin.

A second consequence of Swedenborg's religious crisis was that he practiced an intensified piety, not only in frequent meditation and contemplation, but in regular prayer, reflections on his visions, and especially in reading Holy Scripture and the frequent taking of Communion. Swedenborg also appears to have practiced self-punishment, not only by restricting his eating and drinking but even by self-flagellation, for he noted on 20 April: "This day I was in the most severe temptation, so that, when I thought of Jesus Christ, there came at once ungodly thoughts, which I thought were not my fault. I beat myself, but I can confess that I was never of better courage than this day and was not in the least downhearted or pained as on previous days, although the temptation was most severe. The reason is that our Lord has given me the firm faith and confidence that he will help me for the sake of Jesus Christ and on account of his promise, so that I then experienced the workings of such a faith."

In its various images, Swedenborg's new state can be interpreted as anticipating his subsequent ideas on rebirth and the inner life. He had the strange experience of seeing his own conversion in a vision. On 8 April, he described his state as a day-laborer who is crowned king of the world. The true meaning of this elevation became clear to him on 16 April: "The most remarkable fact was that I now represented the internal man." This is the theological explanation of his rebirth: the center of his life, his feeling, and thought have shifted from his outer person into his inner. He is no longer identical with his outer being but represents his inner person, the spiritual person, the archetypal image, that has been renewed in him by Christ. He has been restored to wholeness. His archetypal form, which was destroyed by his guilt, now emerged as a new being in him and became his new self. Now he was actually a different person. He considered his earlier thoughts as those of a stranger and was "afraid of them." The accusations he made against his old persona seem directed against a stranger. "So now there has been a change: I represent the internal man, who is opposed to another person, for I have prayed to God that I may not be my own, but that God may please to let me be his."

These deliberations tie in with a dream experience in which he heard the name Nicholas being called (*Dream Diary* §133). He interpreted this to mean this was his new name. This is also a typical experience of conversion and rebirth. The converted person loses his old name with his old persona and receives a new one—Saul becomes Paul. The change of name for a novice who makes his vows is an established institution of monastic life.

Swedenborg's inner transformation made itself apparent to him through further manifestations. In Leiden on 24 April, he heard the words "*Interiorescit, integratur*" [he is growing more inward, he is being made whole], "which signifies that, by my infestations, I am becoming more purified." In a vision of 9/10 July, he felt himself received into the company of the children of God. In the night of 15/16 June, he saw himself transported to a magnificent palace in a heavenly grove. "I desired to take lodgings to have the prospect of the grove and the moats always in view. A window was open far down in one of the wings, and I thought I would like to have my room there." Already he felt admitted to heavenly regions. But the inhabitants of this realm were still silent. Only after his vision of God in London did they begin to speak with him.

The link between the conquest of his carnal life and his vision of Christ deserves special mention. Many Swedenborgians have sought to transform Swedenborg into a saint, using all manner of arguments to suggest that he never ate Eve's apple either before or after his conversion. Such apology seems to be a fundamental error. These apologists are confounded by Swedenborg's own claim that he had a lover in Rome on his Italian journey. What is certain is that Swedenborg never married and that, after his conversion, he led a life in which he had obviously surmounted carnal desire. To claim apologetically that he never knew carnal desire, because a saint may not be a sinner at any time in his life, is simply to deny the profound character of conversion and his hard-won inner transformation, which he understood as an inconceivable act of grace. There is no conversion without the recognition of sin and no recognition of sin without experience of sin. The illustrious community of saints has always been recruited from the ranks of sinners and not from the class of pharisees.

On this point, Swedenborg's own testimony is more reliable than his apologists. Even if he had not confided in his diary that his passion for women was the strongest of his life, his numerous erotic dreams and visions assert this. The leaves of his diary, perhaps torn out by an apologist, could probably give more information on this point. It is impossible to establish how much he lived his passions to the full, and the report about his lover in Rome has been challenged. But it is decisive that his conversion intervened in the sphere of sexual desire, a fact frequently found in the conversions of great sinners and saints. Swedenborg's vitality was unbroken by his conversion. His friends still describe the youthful energy of the seventy-year-old and the amazing health he enjoyed until his last days. Apart from his illness as a student in Paris, there is no mention of a serious illness until the cold that killed him at the age of eighty-four. Throughout his life, he retained his fresh, cheerful temperament and a great energy for work. Right up to his last years, he undertook strenuous journeys on sea and land. He radiated vitality and an exciting sense of dynamism. But after his conversion, he had the same experience as the hot-blooded Augustine and many other sinners and subsequent saints. They all found that, after their decisive encounter with God, their vitality developed on a spiritual plane. As Adolf von Harnack says of St. Augustine, "it was easier for them afterwards in this respect."

In the struggle between the new and old forms of Swedenborg's life and thought, it is significant that he had no more power over the temptations than over the spiritual experiences that overcome him. He saw himself torn by an inner conflict, in which God and Satan fought over him and in which he frequently failed to impose his own will. Such a struggle immediately followed his vision of Christ. "I was also in such a temptation that my fancies went out of control . . . to counter the spiritual power, which is heading in another direction; yes, with such a force that had not God's grace been even stronger, I'd have fallen or been driven crazy" (*Dream Diary* §65). Several days later he wrote: "I was continually in dissension with double thoughts, opposed to one another. I pray thee, O Almighty God, to grant me the grace to be thine and not my own! . . . I pray for the grace of being permitted to be thine and that I may not be left to myself" (*Dream Diary* §118).

The entries show that these temptations concerned doubts about the authenticity of his vocation, just as they surfaced after his vision of Christ, but also concerned thoughts suggesting he renounce his vocation due to personal unworthiness. In order to oppose these temptations, Swedenborg applied an old mystical practice: *resignatio ad infernum*, complete surrender to the divine will in an act of blind, unreflective faith, allowing the storms of contradictory thoughts to pass overhead. On 11 April, he wrote: "Afterwards, when I was awake, I began to consider if this might not be sheer fantasy. Then I realized that my faith was faltering, and I prayed with clasped hands that I might be strengthened in my faith, which also happened at once. I also fell into thoughts about my being more worthy than others; but I prayed in a similar manner, and then these ideas vanished at once." Thus he learned to conquer his attacks by means of faith.

An experience on 18 April made him contemplate this leap into faith.

> At last, it was granted me by the grace of the Spirit to receive faith without reasoning, a real assurance of it. Then, I saw my own confirmatory thoughts as it were beneath me and smiled at them in my mind, and still more at those thoughts that offended and opposed them. Faith then appeared to me far above the reach of reason. . . . This is pure faith; the rest is impure as far as it blends with our own understanding: we must make our understanding captive to the obedience of faith . . . This faith, therefore, is purely the gift of God, which an individual receives if he lives according to the commandments of God and diligently prays to God for it.

This doctrine of pure faith, understood in a mystical rather than an orthodox sense, is particularly striking because it seems to contradict Swedenborg's subsequent standpoint. His later writings are full of polemic statements against the teaching that one's reason must be the hostage of faith. But in these later writings, he criticizes faith as the historical confession of faith of the individual churches. He attributes the decline of the Christian confessions to their subjection of reason to a historical form of dogma devoid of spiritual understanding. In contrast, he demands a faith based on illuminated reason, showing the advance in his own religious development. In 1744, he had not yet experienced the London vision of God that led to the opening of his inner vision. The reason he describes here is not the illuminated reason of the inner person but the reason of the outer person opposed to spiritual understanding. The object of faith is not historical dogma but the presence of Christ, just as he has experienced it, the living faith that he perceived as the fulfillment of his life and understanding. Regarding this kind of faith, one must suppress the rebellious, mundane reason with its temptations and blasphemous thoughts in order that the lower life may not smother the higher life. This is the highest act of his self-renunciation. One must bind one's own will, the source of all selfishness, and also one's own reason in order that no trace of egoism remains. The individual then confronts God in pure self-surrender, ready to become God's instrument, willing to give up his or her own form in order to receive the new form from God's hand. Swedenborg continues in the same reflection: "We must make our understanding captive to the obedience of faith . . . This is perhaps what is meant by the teaching that we should be like children."

This renunciation of human reason expressed the strongest upheaval in his former ways of understanding. Swedenborg had believed that he could advance towards God on the path of analytical thought and all his scientific work was a grand expression of this attempt. Once he has been thrust into the abyss of self-knowledge through his encounter with God, he saw that even the noblest thoughts of natural person are tainted by selfishness. He saw that the highest flight of human reason is burdened with the original sin of the human being in wanting to be like God. Thus he wrote on 12 April:

> Subsequently, I found . . . that in every thought, yes, even in those we believe to be pure, there is concealed an endless quantity of sin and impurity, as also in every desire that comes from the body into the thoughts. . . . It is therefore best to acknowledge every hour and moment that one deserves the punishment of hell and to trust that the grace and mercy of God, which are in Jesus Christ, over- look it. Yes, I have also observed that our whole will, which we have inherited and which is ruled by the body and introduces thoughts into the mind, is opposed to the spirit. For this reason, there is a continual strife, and there is no way for us to unite our- selves with the spirit, which by grace is with us. And hence it is that we are, as it were, dead to all that is good, but to the evil we are ourselves. A person should, therefore, at all times account himself guilty of innumerable sins, for the Lord God knows everything, and we know only a little. . . .

Thus Swedenborg experienced an inner conversion in all its rev- olutionary power. Confronted by God, he felt guilty, recognized the rebellion of his will and reason against God, and saw that this rebel- lion began in the desire for self-assertion. He understood that, by his own efforts alone, he could never escape the spell of egotistical life and bend his will and reason back to God, the ground and goal of all being and life. His new life thus seemed to him a gift of pure grace and his new understanding revealed itself as pure faith.

These inner upheavals did not occur without affecting his outer conduct. He had concealed the experience from his friends, but the encounter with the most Divine induced him to give way to this re- demption in his outer life. He began to examine his whole life and considered what was worthy of God. This great self-confession re- vealed a number of lapses. Long-forgotten things arose and accused his soul. "I found things emerging in my thoughts, which had long previously sunk into oblivion. I saw the truth of God's word con- firmed, that God knows the slightest word and thought and that we will have to answer for it." He began to make resolutions so that he could avoid relapses into his past way of life.

He first decided to combat his egoism, most conspicuous in his literary vanity and scientific complacency. His arrogance often struck him in forceful ways. While on a walk, he saw a bookstore and "immediately the thought struck me that my work would have greater effect than the works of others; but I checked myself at once by the thought that one person serves another and that our Lord has many thousand ways of preparing everyone, so that every book must be left to its own merits. . . . Nevertheless, pride immediately pushed itself forward. May God control it, for the power is in his hands" (*Dream Diary* §78).

He then rationed his eating and drinking and tried to free himself of contemporary excesses, which he had previously all too willingly enjoyed. On 10 April 1744, he reported: "All day . . . I was in prayers, songs of praise, reading the Word of God, fasting. . . ." Any deviations from his self-restraint he saw as a relapse. Thus he is warned in a dream during the night of 30 April/1 May, "that I had drunk more than I should, which is not spiritual but carnal, and accordingly sinful." He is similarly commanded to eat less. "On the following day, I was more on my guard, but I came into a rather strong temptation—that now and henceforth I must forcibly govern my appetite. This brought me into a strange condition and, as it were, into a state of chagrin; but I was quickly released after I had prayed and sung a hymn, particularly since I do not wish to be my own, but to live as a *novos homo* in Christ."

The mention of his appetite is important, insofar as an angel declared in his vision of vocation: "Don't eat so much!"[2] Even here zealous apologists have tried to reinterpret the literal sense of this admonishment, in order that the later visionary should not be guilty of a human weakness prior to his conversion. It seems more important to me that Swedenborg found it hard to give up heavy Swedish breakfasts. Is that not truly human? The conversion did not occur in a weakling but a man whose powerful vitality was transformed through a process of conflict into spirituality.

---

2. The vision in which Swedenborg is commanded to "not eat so much!" is recounted in Robsahm's memoirs (Tafel, doc. 5, 35).

A changed attitude to the Church was also evident in the outer transformation of his life. He had long had no inner connection to the Church; but after his vision of Christ, he was now wondering whether he should not give up his profession and become a clergyman. He may have been influenced by the example of his father. He soon realized that he must remain a layman: clerical status would be more of a hindrance than a help in his new life. His father appears to him in a dream, wearing a radiant robe, and holds him by the sleeve, on which he notices the lace cuff customarily worn by the nobility. "That I was wearing cuffs meant that I did not belong to the clergy but am, and should be, a civil servant." In his dream, he replies to his father's question "according to my conscience, that one should not be allowed to change one's estate . . . , of whatever kind it may be" (*Dream Diary* §58–59).

It was clear to Swedenborg that his vision of Christ had fundamentally changed his external relationship to the Church. He recognized "that we should return to the Church for the glory of God, in one way or another. This will also perhaps happen to me." Here he clearly says that he had been estranged from the Church up until now. The vision of Christ itself took place after an Easter Communion, which he had decided to take as a result of his inner struggles. Later visions are also associated with taking Communion. After his vision of Christ, Swedenborg appears to have taken the sacrament more frequently. But from the very outset, it is questionable which of the various existing confessions might correspond to his pietistic experience. For a while, he wondered whether he should join the Moravian Brethren, the community that regarded Jan Amos Comenius (1592–1670) as their purest and noblest spiritual leader and whose scientific universalism resembles that of Swedenborg. But Swedenborg found no access to this community. Even the Swedish Church in London, which he initially attended, did not satisfy him. He felt that his own religious experience did not accord with the contemporary orthodoxy of Swedish Lutheranism in its liturgy or its sermons. As his conviction grew that he had been called by the Lord, he realized ever more clearly that none of the existing churches matched his understanding of religion.

This is expressed in a dream during the night of 21/22 July 1744. "I pushed my way through a crowded congregation. I wanted to get out in time, but it was packed. I made my way through and came to an empty bench that had a cloth upon it, with which I wanted to cover myself. This meant that I wished . . . to come into that congregation, while remaining unknown!" This already sounds like his later conduct towards the Church of his own country. He never seceded from the Church, but he went his own way, which led him against the tide. He constantly maintained his "incognito" as a visionary towards the Swedish Church, by printing his visionary writings abroad, first anonymously and in Latin, so that they might be accessible only to scholars and not to the broad church-going public.

While he considered an organized Church necessary as a vehicle for the divine Word between heaven and earth, in the weeks following his vision of Christ, Swedenborg began to wonder if he personally needed the terrestrial Church. Even while taking the sacraments, doubts arose in his mind whether this practice was necessary for him. On the evening before Sunday, 5 August 1744, he wrote: "I planned to go to God's table the next day, but thus finding that no human being but God alone can grant absolution, I gave up going; and on this account, it was also give to me to comment upon confession."

Swedenborg looked well on the way to becoming a separatist enthusiast, claiming that he could dispense with the organized Church on account of his inner illumination. During the whole of August 1744, this question of the Church occupied him greatly. At this time, he was seized repeatedly by melancholy and remorse for his sins, his sense of guilt oppressed him, and he feared that he had not received forgiveness. He finally suspected that his wrong attitude to the Church and his separatist impulses were to blame for these afflictions. Thereupon he experienced deliverance and forgiveness and felt certain that he was granted grace. In the night of 1/2 September, he received a final inspiration concerning his attitude to the Church: "Now I hear, as if [God] inspirited me, that I should not leave the Church of Christ and go for the Lord's Supper over yonder, since then I would again become spiritually dead. The rest I could not grasp, so there is a mystery under this. I refrained from attending, and it was kindled by the Holy Spirit, as is generally the case when I act according to command."

This vision gave him guidelines for his conduct towards the Church, which he observed until his death. It represented a compromise between orthodox and separatist standpoints. He regarded the orthodox Church on earth as necessary and valued his membership in it because the Church must at all times facilitate the meeting of heaven and earth. But he saw himself in a special category, subject to his illuminations and direct access to God. Thanks to the inner light, he believed he no longer needed the Church for salvation. His inner transformation therefore did not lead him back to his national Church or to any other. As Friedrich Christoph Oetinger said, he assumed the role of "*ecclesia monadica*."[3]

Swedenborg's abstention from Communion appeared to have a specific cause in his nocturnal vision of 12/13 October, when a marvelous loaf of bread was offered to him on a plate. "[That] was a premonition that the Lord himself was going to instruct me, since I have now finally come into such a state that I know nothing, and that all preconceived opinions have been taken away from me. . . ." From God's very own hand, he receives the holy bread of the divine Word and relates this to his direct illumination. Why should he now need to take Communion from the hand of a priest? He believed he now received directly from God that which had previously been granted as a symbol.

In another respect, he distanced himself from the Church after an initial rapprochement. He resisted the influence of Lutheran dogma as a key to understanding his religious experiences. This also demonstrates an enthusiastic, separatist tendency, which marked the entire inspirational movement of the eighteenth century and its leaders such as Johann Konrad Dippel, Ernst Christian Hochmann von Hochenau, Johann Petersen, and the Philadelphians. As he had been promised that God wanted to instruct him, he sought to escape his former opinions and also to distance himself from all theological doctrine. In the night of 25/26 April, "it also was represented in a

---

3. K. C. E. Ehmann, *F. C. Oetingers Leben und Briefe* (Stuttgart, 1859), no. 564, p. 684.

certain way that I should not contaminate myself by reading other books on theological and related theses, because this I have in the Word of God and from the Holy Spirit." He later developed this idea, saying God had even prevented his familiarity in youth with theological opinion in order to make him a pure instrument for his revelation.

The experiences immediately following his great vision of Christ thus contained the seeds of his subsequent religious self-understanding, his missionary consciousness, and his special attitude towards the established Church, which lasted until his death.

15

The Vision of Vocation

Swedenborg's religious crisis ended with his experience of vocation. Although this event is not recorded in his diary, two extant reports describe its chief features. Swedenborg biographers usually rely on the report of his friend Carl Robsahm, who recounts the vision of vocation as a narrative by Swedenborg told in the first person. According to this report, the vision of vocation occurred as two consecutive visionary experiences on the same day. First, an experience of purification took place around midday at Swedenborg's eating house in London. The same night in his room he received a vocation to disclose the inner sense of Holy Scripture and the opening of his vision into the world of spirits, heaven, and hell.

This vocation took him unawares at London in the middle of April 1745. Between May 1744 and April 1745, the third volume of *The Animal Kingdom* and the first and second parts of his work *Worship and Love of God* had been printed. He was still uncertain what course his new life would take and how his new understanding would be expressed when the decisive event occurred, here recounted in the words of Robsahm's memoirs:

I was in London and dined rather late at the inn where I was in the habit of dining, and where I had my own room. My thoughts were engaged on the subjects we had been discussing. I was hungry, and ate with a good appetite. Towards the close of the meal I noticed a sort of dimness before my eyes: this became denser, and then I saw the floor covered with the most horrid crawling reptiles, such as snakes, frogs and similar creatures. I was amazed; for I was perfectly conscious, and my thoughts were clear. At last the darkness increased still more; but it disappeared all at once, and then I saw a man sitting in the corner of the room; as I was then alone, I was very much frightened at his words, for he said: "Eat not so much." All became black again before my eyes, but immediately it cleared away, and I found myself alone in the room.

Such an unexpected terror hastened my return home; I did not let the landlord notice anything; but I considered well what had happened, and could not look upon it as a mere matter of chance, or as if it had been produced by a physical cause. I went home, and during the night the same man revealed himself to me again, but I was not frightened now. He then said that He was the Lord God, the Creator of the world, and the Redeemer, and that He has chosen me to explain to men the spiritual sense of Scripture, and that He Himself would explain to me what I should write on this subject; that same night also were opened to me, so that I became thoroughly convinced of their reality, the world of spirits, heaven and hell, and I recognized there many acquaintances of every condition in life. From that day I gave up the study of all worldly science, and labored in spiritual things, according as the Lord had commanded me to write. Afterwards the Lord opened, daily very often, my bodily eyes, so that, in the middle of the day I could see into the other world, and in a state of perfect wakefulness converse with angels and spirits. (Tafel, I, doc. 5, 35–36)

The two episodes are distinguished from each other by time and content: first, a visionary purification of appetite; second, a divine commission to interpret Holy Scripture in a spiritual sense, coupled with the opening of the spiritual eye and vision into the other world. The connection and sequence of these visions are beyond all doubt. However, their form and content have several characteristics that do not accord with Swedenborg's other reports of visions. It is useful to consider both parts of this visionary sequence separately.

The purification is directly linked to the earlier visionary experiences of his religious crisis and concludes them. His spiritual development, the preparation of his vocation, and new spiritual task had been completed as a liberation from his former dominant earthly desires. Swedenborg expressly mentions the sudden cessation of his passion for women and sexual urges, and he similarly describes his struggle against greed, in which he often relapsed but from which he now feels freed. Fortunately, there is an authentic report in Swedenborg's *Adversaria* §1957, in which he describes the same visionary experience in quite another context:

> At lunch an angel said to me that I should not pander too much to my stomach. Then it seemed as if a visible vapor like steam rose from the pores of my body and sank to the floor. The vapor settled on a carpet and turned into all kinds of worms, which gathered on the table, and were suddenly burnt with a pop. A fiery light then appeared there and a rustling was audible. It felt as if all the worms produced by an immoderate appetite had been expelled and burnt, and I had been purged of them. One sees from this, what a luxurious lifestyle can incur. April 1745.

Compared with Robsahm's report, Swedenborg's account carries the sure stamp of authenticity. Robsahm writes about a kind of mist spreading over Swedenborg's eyes, which becomes thicker and the room grows darker. In the darkening room, he sees the floor covered with abominable reptiles like snakes and toads. The darkness increases but then suddenly disappears, and even the reptiles vanish from the floor. It is suddenly light again, and Swedenborg is terrified to see a man sitting in the corner of the room, "a man, who says: Eat not so much!" This report does not match the usual content and course of Swedenborg's visions.

In his *Adversaria* account, Swedenborg describes how a vapor streams out of his pores and sinks to the floor like visible steam. He is therefore aware that something bad is leaving him. The vapor appears initially on the floor as a vaguely patterned carpet, which then changes into worms. The worms conglomerate on the table and burn, accompanied by light, popping, and rustling, acoustic and optical phenomena suggesting a fire.

The admonition occurs not at the end but at the beginning of the manifestation. The vision describes the warning of the angel in the form of a "correspondence." The speaker is not a man but an angel whose warning that Swedenborg should not pander to his stomach (he could very well have said "Eat not so much") actually produces the experience of the sweated vapor and ensuing events. In conclusion, we have Swedenborg's clear interpretation of the experience: "It felt as if all the worms produced by an immoderate appetite had been expelled and burnt, and I had been purged of them."

That is the form and course of a visionary experience, which corresponds to Swedenborg's similar experiences of this kind during his religious crisis. In a dream during the night of 30 April/1 May 1744, he was warned—it is not clear whether this was through a voice or a visible angelic apparition—"that I had drunk more than I should, which is the work of the flesh rather than the spirit and therefore sinful." He is likewise warned afterwards to curb his appetite: "On the following day, I was more on my guard, but I fell into sore temptation. While thinking I should curb my appetite, my mood grew contrary and angry. However, I was delivered from it after I had prayed and sung a hymn, especially as I no longer wanted to belong to myself but wanted to live in Christ as a new creature."

Swedenborg's own writings give no full account of the second vision, the opening of his inner sight and his vocation. However, there is such an account in a letter that Swedenborg's friend Dr. Gabriel Beyer addressed to C.F. Nordenskjöld on 25 March 1776. He wrote: "The information respecting the Lord's personal appearance before the assessor, who saw him, in imperial purple and majestic light, seated near his bed, while He gave Assessor Swedenborg his commission, I had from his own lips at a dinner-party in the house of Dr. Rosén, where I saw the old gentleman for the first time. I remember that I asked him, how long this lasted; whereupon he answered, About a quarter of an hour: also, whether the strong light did not affect his eyes: when he said, No" (Tafel, II, doc. 254, 426).

Here the nocturnal part of the vocational vision is described as a vision of the Lord that corresponds to Swedenborg's other visions of the Lord. All statements that Swedenborg subsequently made about his vocation concur with this. Moreover, Swedenborg frequently spoke of his vocational experience in most of his later works. For him, it was the exact date of the beginning of his new life as an interpreter of the spiritual meaning of Holy Scripture. He regularly recalls the two main points mentioned by Robsahm: his election as the spiritual interpreter of the Bible and the opening of his vision into the world of spirits, heaven, and hell.

Robsahm was mistaken in linking the visionary experience of purification with the opening of spiritual sight. In this way, he made the "man," who appears as a warning figure in the corner of the dining room, reappear as God the Creator and Redeemer at the beginning of the vision of election. This does not correspond to Swedenborg's other visionary experiences. He himself mentions the purification vision as the manifestation of an angel. But the main figure in his vocation to interpret the Bible and the opening of his spiritual sight is no angel, but the Lord himself. At all events, this vision of election was described in all Swedenborg's later works as a vision of the Lord. For his own missionary consciousness, the nocturnal vision of vocation is quite distinct as a vision of the Lord in degree, experience, and content from any of the preceding visions of preparation and purification. This vision produced a final, massive, and profound upheaval and actually created him anew, with new understanding, new eyes and a new life.

The inner connection between the two experiences of purification and vocation can no longer be precisely reconstructed. It is sufficient to establish that Robsahm's coupled visions are distinct as a vision of an angel and a vision of the Lord and that the vision of the Lord was a decisive turning point, the beginning of his new life, his new office, and a new understanding.

The incident appears to be a genuine prophetic experience of vocation, which is by no means unique in the history of Christian piety. It is an important fact in the history of the Christian Church that free utterances of the spirit in prophecy and vision were suppressed from the second century and their place was taken by the priestly office and Church doctrine. The Church no longer tolerated free prophecy and the spontaneous revelation of the spirit but restrained them by fixing the oral and written apostolic tradition in Scripture and doctrine. At the beginning of the second century, a new wave of free prophecy by Montanus and his followers referred to new revelations from the angels, but this was rejected by the Church as error and an offense against the apostolic tradition. Further revelation on the basis of inspiration was unacceptable. The only form of prophecy tolerated by the Church was a form of prophecy based on the literal content of the Bible. Swedenborg's experience is thus typical of later Church prophecy. In the thirteenth century, the prophetic Abbot Joachim of Fiore perceived his "spiritual understanding" as a decipherment of the Bible's secret meaning, and he wrote down his revelations as a prophetic interpretation of the biblical books. Even his prophecy had its origin in an experience of vocation he was granted at Whitsun, the festival of the outpouring of the Holy Spirit.

But vocational experiences were also known among the German Pietists. Devout individuals have deciphered Scripture and unexpectedly understood the secret inner connection of divine revelation. They have been so powerfully affected by this experience that it marked the beginning of a new life for them. The prophetic interpretation of the Book of Revelation by Johann Albrecht Bengel (1687–1752), the Württemberg prelate, originated in a similar experience. This was accompanied by a sudden spiritual illumination, which showed him the inner coherence of the entire history of salvation. Jacob Boehme's "glimpse into the essence of all essences" can be traced to a prophectic interpretation of Holy Scripture. His principal work *Mysterium Magnum* (1623) is a prophetic exegesis of the biblical account of creation, granted to him by the opening of mystical vision.

Swedenborg experienced this vision of vocation as the conclusion of his crisis. In the course of his struggles, he sensed that God had chosen him for special work, and he had prepared himself inwardly and outwardly for this purpose. Now he finally understood what this work was to be. If he had previously striven in his science to establish divine revelation in the Book of Nature, he was now directed towards the Holy Scripture as the supreme form of divine revelation. He felt empowered to lift its inner meaning from the images and allegories of its outer words. His new task was the decipherment of the spiritual revelation of the Bible. He felt empowered for this task through the gift, which represented the fulfillment of all his former hunger for knowledge. He experienced how the spiritual world was opened up to him. He was granted the vision of Adam. This is the special aspect of his vocation: the heavenly world begins to open to him, and spirits and angels instruct him in the hidden ground of Being. Swedenborg's piety is not unique in his prophetic interpretation of the Bible: devout visionaries such as Joachim of Fiore, Jacob Boehme, and Johann Albrecht Bengel preceded him in this. What is special about Swedenborg is that this prophetic theology is based on a vision of the spiritual world.

At this time, there was still a living belief in the existence and corporeality of the spirits and angels among church-going people as well as among the great thinkers of the eighteenth century. For Leibniz and Pascal, the existence of an angelic and spirit world was even more real than the existence of the table on which they wrote their works or the room in which they were sitting. Not even the Enlightenment of Christian Wolff eliminated this belief. The existence of the world of spirits was more real than that of the terrestrial world for the leaders of German Idealism. Only after the Left Hegelians transformed their master's idealism into dialectical materialism did the sense of the transcendent world disappear from modern thought. In Swedenborg's era, it was by no means peculiar that he believed in a world of angels and spirits: he shared this belief with all his great contemporaries and with all pious Christians. His speciality lay in his claim to immediate access to this world and the ability to talk while fully awake to the angels and spirits as with his own kind.

Swedenborg's sense of the transcendent world had already been stimulated by his religious upbringing. In his father's house, he had learned to interpret the incidents of inner and outer life as the influences of good or evil spirits. His childhood faith saw a terrestrial world permeated with angels and demons, and the sermons and attitude of his father must have confirmed this view. This world of angels, devils, and spirits was no world of romance but a reality that determined his own life. He already had a clear notion of the angels' form, language, and activity. During his scientific research, he had tried to justify his belief in a world of angels, devils, and demons on scientific and philosophical grounds. Under the impact of his subsequent visionary experiences, these notions acquired a new meaning.

During the onset of his religious crisis in 1743–1744, Swedenborg had understood his visions, dreams, and illuminations as an encounter with the spiritual world. The spiritual world had been self-evident to him since childhood. He now felt directly related to this world and felt its influence upon him. He was transported into heavenly landscapes of the spirits. His deceased father appeared to him in a radiant state. He found himself accepted in the company of the dead. He looked around for a dwelling place in heavenly palaces. Before his inner eye, there appeared hosts of the redeemed with crowns on their heads. He understood his visions as a result of the restoration of the broken link between heaven and earth. He even regarded his temptations as assaults of demonic powers in the course of his spiritual development.

Following his vision of Christ, we find Swedenborg already inwardly prepared to attain a higher and more perfect understanding of the spiritual world. Now, in his vision of vocation, he felt he had been granted that which he had long desired: the intuition of Adam, the original understanding of man, the unhindered vision of the spiritual world, the conversation of angels and spirits. These would introduce him directly to the insights and revelations of the higher world. With this, his life received a new content and a new form. He now hastened to divest himself of his former lifestyle and devote himself completely to his new vocation. The scientist had become the visionary.

16

The Development of
Religious Self-Consciousness

Swedenborg's experience of vocation in London had a decisive effect on his understanding of his prophetic gift and commission. His religious self-consciousness became ever stronger throughout his visionary period right up until his death. But in *Adversaria*, his first work following his vocation, Swedenborg was not yet fully convinced of the revelatory character of his visions. "I cannot yet so confirm what I have written that I could attest it thorough God, for I cannot know whether the words of my account exactly match my vision; therefore, they must be improved, if God is willing, so that I will be telling the whole truth." Here Swedenborg expressly rejects the conclusive nature of his revelations and admits the possibility of further development in his spiritual understanding. But later he was so confident of the pure revelatory character of his notes that he could assert that all his writings stemmed from the Lord and literally contained the whole and pure truth. The revision of his revelatory writings he initially thought necessary was no longer undertaken.

In the *Spiritual Diary,* one still finds indications of growth in his inner understanding after his vision of vocation. In an entry of 31 August 1747, he wrote: "For nearly three years, I was permitted to feel and know the effect of the spirits, not through a kind of inner sight but through a sensation connected with a kind of dim sight, through which I observed their presence, their approach, and withdrawal besides many other things." This "dim sight" was later purified into a brighter and clearer sight. His awareness of the meaning of his mission and the revelatory nature of his writings also assumed a greater clarity. His earlier idea of revising his revelations ultimately receded before the claim that he was the visionary of his age, chosen to proclaim the whole truth of heaven.

This notion recurs frequently in the history of Christian prophecy. The visionary does not perceive his vocation as a chance intervention of God but as the goal toward which his life is unfolding according to a hidden plan of God. He regards his election as evidence of divine intention, which embraces his whole life from birth. When the Lord speaks to his prophet Jeremiah in the vision of vocation, "Before I formed you in the womb I knew you; before you came to birth I consecrated you; I have appointed you as prophet to the nations," this expresses the essence of prophetic vocation proper to all authentic prophecy and missionary consciousness. Through his vocation, Swedenborg was also induced to regard his whole life from the viewpoint of divine election. In hindsight, he saw the course of his life dictated by a mysterious law and rhythm. He regarded many events of his life and many changes in his personality as occurrences whose meaning was first disclosed in his vocation. In *Adversaria* he wrote: "We are not aware of the spiritual meaning of events in our life, as God wills, sometimes until much later. Much has happened to me through the mercy of God, which I did not understand when it was happening, nor what the events in my life signified; but later I was instructed in many things, whence I deduced that the reins of divine providence had guided the events of my life from childhood onwards. I ultimately arrived at this end through the knowledge of the things of nature and by divine grace so I could serve as an instrument to reveal the innermost mystery of the word of God. What was not previously revealed is now evident." The idea of his whole life's being subject to divine guidance increasingly dominates his thoughts in his later years, especially between 1765 and 1771 when the Churches of England, Sweden, and Germany expressed their opposition to his work.

Friedrich Christoph Oetinger (1702–1782), the Württemberg pietist, was the most inspired supporter of Swedenborg in Germany who endured violent persecution by the Stuttgart consistory on account of his work *Swedenborgs irdische und himmlische Philosophie* (1765). In a letter of 13 October 1765, Oetinger asked Swedenborg for information concerning his visionary gift and the nature of his vocation. On 23 September 1766, Swedenborg replied that Oetinger could already see from his work *Arcana Coelestia* "that I speak with the angels, as there is not a single verse in the Book of Revelation which can be understood without this revelation. I can solemnly swear that the Lord appeared to me and that he sent me to do what I am doing. For this reason, he opened my inner spirit, that is my spiritual man, in order that I might see and hear things in the spiritual world, as I have now for these past twenty-two years" (LL, 59f).

In a second letter of 11 November 1766, Swedenborg gives a detailed description of his own development under divine guidance and answers the question "Why do I feel chosen as a philosopher to reveal the secrets of heaven?"

> This has happened, in order that spiritual matters revealed in the present can be taught and understood in a natural and rational way. For the spiritual truths correspond to natural truths: they have their end and basis in them. For this reason, I was first introduced to the natural sciences during the years from 1710 to 1744 by the Lord, when heaven was opened to me. Everyone is led through the natural to the spiritual realm, for man is born naturally, brought up morally and later begotten spiritually by the Lord. But the Lord granted me to love the truths spiritually, not for the sake of honor or profit, for the sake of the truths themselves. (LL, 61)

The question of the inner meaning of his career, namely, whether science had been a wrong path or a necessary stage on the way to true understanding, greatly preoccupied Swedenborg in these years. He discussed this especially in his work *Intercourse Between the Soul and Body* (1769). "I was once asked how I, a philosopher, became a theologian. I answered that this happened in the same way that fishermen were made disciples and apostles by the Lord, that I too was a spiritual fisherman from my youth. When my companion heard this, he asked what a spiritual fisherman was. I answered that in the Word, a fisherman in the spiritual meaning indicated a person who hunts out and teaches natural truths, and afterwards spiritual truths in a rational way." Like many other devout persons before and after him, Swedenborg elevated his own conversion to a general principle. As a philosopher who has become a visionary, he proposes that an understanding of spiritual truths must lead through the understanding of natural truths.

These ideas served as the basis of the autobiographical letter that he wrote in 1769 at the insistence of Oetinger and Thomas Hartley.[1] Through his divine mission, his career is transformed into the life of a saint, where everything indicating his later vocation override all other details of his life. Even the contents of his later doctrine are projected by hindsight into his childhood. This is a typical occurrence in the history of Christian autobiography and the lives of the saints: the saint must have been holy as a child, the prophet already prophetic as a child and thus have stood out from the mass of his contemporaries from the outset. The logic of sainthood demands this. However, this logic can dominate an autobiography so that memory models itself on religious self-consciousness. The later Swedenborg remembers the young Swedberg as a theologizing, pious lad, who, like Jesus in the temple, elaborates all the wisdom of the later visionary before the amazed theologians of the land. Autobiographies frequently present the story of the author not as he was, but as he should have been, in order to legitimize his later role.

In Swedenborg's last great work *True Christian Religion* (1771), this idea of divine preparation is again discussed on a higher plane in the world of spirits. There several spirits from the underworld ask him the question, which he had often heard from his contemporaries: "Why has your Lord revealed the mysteries to you as a layman and not a member of the clergy?" Swedenborg replies: "This lay in the pleasure of the Lord, who prepared me for this office from my

---

1. Tafel, I, doc. 5. See also Tafel, I, doc. 3, p. 10.

earliest youth. But I want to ask you a question in return: Why did the Lord, when he was on earth, choose fishermen for his disciples, and not some from among the lawyers, scholars, priests or rabbis? Think about that and you will discover the reason!" (*True Christian Religion* §771).

The comparison of himself with the apostles indicates a new feature of his religious self-consciousness. In his writings, Swedenborg frequently tried to prove that his own kind of prophecy was comparable to the truth and authority of the revelations of prophets in the Old and New Testaments. In Swedenborg's opinion, ancient prophecy also occurred through the opening of inner vision and a glimpse into the mysteries of the heavenly world. The correspondence between ancient prophetic visions and his own was based on the idea that they both behold one and the same heavenly reality and the same inner sense of the Word. Swedenborg laid down a fundamental doctrine of prophecy to establish the similarity of his prophecy with that of the ancient prophets (*Apocalypse Revealed* §36). The ancient prophets said that they "were in the spirit," when the mysteries of the heavenly world were shown to them. "By the spirit of a man one understands his soul and so by 'being in the spirit' one understands the state of the soul separated from the body. Because the prophets saw things, which existed in the spiritual world, in this state, this is called 'a vision of God.' They were thus in the same state that spirits and angels are in that world. That is the same state I have now known for twenty-six years." On the basis of his doctrine of "being in the spirit," Swedenborg repeatedly indicated the affinity of his visions with those of the ancient prophets and equated his state with that of Jacob, Ezekiel, Daniel, Zechariah, St. John, St. Peter, and St. Paul.

There is even a reversal of the relationship, which is highly significant for his religious self-consciousness. He does not regard his own visions as a modest commentary on the sublime experience of God, as did the ancient prophets, but vice versa: the visions of the ancient prophets must serve to confirm the truth of his own revelations. Thus he writes in *True Christian Religion* concerning his own visionary experiences: "The same things described in the *Memorabilia* really appeared in the heavens and this is clearly shown by similar things which John saw and described in the Book of Revelation, as well as such things that the prophets saw and described in the Old Testament." Here Swedenborg is not simply the interpreter of ancient prophecy, but the visionary who explains the earlier prophetic visions of the Old and New Testament through new and clearer visions. Whatever the prophets saw veiled in images and allegories, Swedenborg now presents as a rational, coherent teaching on the basis of a clearer vision. He is not *a* visionary among others but *the last* visionary, who removes the seals from the mysteries of all preceding prophecy.

Swedenborg's claim is also expressed in another way. Just as St. Paul traced his revelations back to the Lord whenever he wanted to assert the authority of his teaching so that his gospel would be upheld, even if an angel came from heaven and proclaimed another gospel, so Swedenborg emphasizes that his revelation stems from the Lord and not from the angels—that is, from the source of truth and not from its intermediaries. "That the Lord manifested himself before me, his servant, and sent me to this office, that he afterward opened the eyes of my spirit and thus introduced me into the spiritual world and granted me to see the heavens and the hells, and to talk with angels and spirits, and this now continuously for several years, I affirm in truth; as also from the first day of that call I have not received anything whatever pertaining to the doctrines of that Church from any angel, but from the Lord alone" (*True Christian Religion* §779).

This is usually stated in the prefaces of his prophetic writings, as in the preface to his *Apocalypse Revealed*: "Everyone can see that the Book of Revelation can be explained by no one else but the Lord alone, for the individual words contain secrets, which no one could ever know without special illumination and revelation. It therefore pleased the Lord to open the face of my spirit and to teach me. One should not think that I have taken this from myself or from an angel, but only from the Lord." Swedenborg even attributed to himself a special distinction, which helped him in his revelations and protected him from deception. "It was given to me, to clearly understand what comes from the Lord and what from the angels. Whatever came from the Lord, I wrote down, but not what came from the angels."

In terms of the history of religion, there is an important difference between Swedenborgian visions and those of the Old and New Testament. Ancient prophecy consisted in seeing heavenly figures and hearing heavenly words. In Swedenborg's case, the visions and auditions serve to expound the Bible. His visions are related to the Bible and have the character of biblical commentaries, which seek to reveal the inner meaning of Scripture. The hidden spiritual sense of the Word is imparted to him through the vision of heavenly things, conversations with angels and spirits, and attendance at heavenly schools and academies. His visions are therefore not free revelations but relate to Scripture. Swedenborg is no prophet in the sense that he pronounces new, mysterious promises of curses or blessings, but he is a visionary who reveals the hidden meaning of promises already concealed in Scripture. Hence, he could write to Oetinger that he was no prophet but a visionary because he brought no new promises in images and riddles but because he saw what lay hidden in riddles and allegories in the Word of Scripture.

Swedenborg did not rest content in comparing himself with the prophets and apostles. In his final works, he dared to suggest that his writings fulfilled the promise, described in the New Testament and above all in the Book of Revelation as the Second Coming of Christ. This claim was the logical development of his vocation. The older he grew, the more his vocation appeared to him as a gift of grace unique in the history of humankind's redemption. He alone could see with waking eyes the things of heaven and earth, the angels and spirits spoke to him alone, and the Lord revealed the inner sense of the Word to him alone. He must therefore have been granted a very special station in the history of redemption. What station might this be? The interpretation of Scripture helped him further here. According to Swedenborg, all events and persons of the Bible can be understood spiritually, as well as in a physical and historical sense. Thus Christ's return is not to be imagined as his bodily and physical descent through the clouds, as described by St. John, but as a spiritual event. The first time Christ came in the body, but at his return he will come spiritually, and moreover in the form revealed by the inner sense of the Word. Through this spiritual opening, all the pictorial and allegorical veiling of Scripture, as if "looking in a glass" is stripped away, and replaced by the spiritual vision of heavenly things in their pure and undisguised reality.

> One reads in many places that the Lord will come "on the clouds of heaven." But no one has known up until now, what is understood by the clouds of heaven. One used to believe He would appear in person on these clouds. But it has remained concealed that the clouds of heaven have a literal meaning, while the spiritual meaning is that he will also come in power and glory. But as the Lord has revealed to me the spiritual sense of the Word and I simultaneously received the gift of speaking with angels and spirits in their world as one of them, it was revealed to me that the "cloud of heaven" should be understood as the "power" and "glory" of the Lord in a spiritual sense. The reason why He does not appear in person, is that he was transfigured into the state of his radiant humanity after his ascent to heaven, and he can appear to no man in this state, unless he first opens the eyes of their spirit. (*True Christian Religion* §776)

The Lord does not come again in person, but in the unveiling of the inner sense of his Word—this is the precondition for the last stage of Swedenborg's religious self-understanding and the height of his prophetic enthusiasm. There was a veiled indication of this in Swedenborg's work on the last days and the coming of the New Church, *Apocalypse Revealed, wherein the secrets, which are foretold in the same and had been previously hidden are now revealed* (1766). The introduction of this compendious work is written in the full spirit of Swedenborg's high-flown missionary consciousness. "There have been already many people, who have endeavored to interpret the Book of Revelation, but the spiritual sense of the Word was previously unknown, so they could not see the hidden secrets therein." He is the first to whom the Lord has revealed the true meaning. "Everyone can see that the Book of Revelation can be explained by no one else but the Lord alone, for the individual words contain secrets, which one would never know without special illumination and revelation. It therefore pleased the Lord to open the face of my spirit and to teach me."

In *Apocalypse Revealed*, Swedenborg first attempted to establish the soteriological significance of his mission. "Since the Lord cannot manifest himself in person . . . and nevertheless has foretold that he was to come and establish a new church . . . it follows that he will do this by means of a man, who is able not only to receive these doctrines in his understanding but also to publish them by the press" (*True Christian Religion* §779). "In order that the true Christian religion might be developed, it was necessary for someone to be introduced to the spiritual world and hear the truths of the Word from the mouth of the Lord." He then applied this general rationale to his own person and vocation: "That the Lord manifested himself before me, his servant, and sent me to this office . . . I affirm in truth" (*True Christian Religion* §779).

This self-explanation means that Swedenborg saw in his mission the fulfillment of redemption. He thus ascended the highest peak of prophetic exultation. However humble and modest he was in his daily life, his nature, and in relationships with people, his consciousness is utterly exalted regarding the mission with which God has honored him. In the history of religion, there is a certain analogy with the missionary consciousness of Mohammed, except that he understood himself as the last of the prophets, while Swedenborg linked his tidings to the promise of the Second Coming. He was a complete mystic in his total surrender to the exaltation of his mission, however unmystical his experience and thought might otherwise be. "Apart from the clearest proofs that the spiritual sense of the Word has been openly stated by the Lord through me, who else has had such experiences, since the Word was revealed in the writings of Israel? And this sense is the actual holiness of the Word. The Lord himself is with his divinity in this sense, and in a natural sense with his humanity. Not one iota of the same can be revealed, save through the Lord himself. This surpasses all revelations that have been made since the creation of the world!"

In this connection, it should be noted that Swedenborg made a handwritten note on the cover of his *Brief Exposition of the Doctrine of the New Church* (1769): "*Hic Liber est Adventus Domini, scriptum ex mandato.*" Depending on how one wants to translate it, this means either "This book is the Coming of the Lord; that is written by order" or "This book belongs to the Coming of the Lord etc." At any rate, the handwritten note provides an insight into the growth of

Swedenborg's missionary consciousness. While he was in the spirit, Swedenborg is told that something of the Lord's Coming is realized in the book he has written. Because this disclosure appeared so presumptuous, he added "written by order," that is, on the express command of the Lord during his "being in the spirit."

While this self-understanding is barely hinted at in *Apocalypse Revealed* (1766), it completely permeates his work *True Christian Religion* (1771) and culminates in the glorification of his own mission. Swedenborg expressed this exalted self-understanding quite clearly in the first section of the work. "It is here brought to notice that, in the New Heaven, which is just being founded by the Lord, this faith (which is to be portrayed in the following work) is the outline, portal, and short summary." As in *Apocalypse Revealed*, he teaches here that the promise of Christ's Second Coming on the clouds of heaven does not relate to a personal return but to the opening of the inner meaning of the divine Word. The final chapters of the work are to prove that Swedenborg's age is actually the last days, that the end of the present form of the Christian Church has arrived, and that he, Swedenborg, is leading forth the New Church of the millennium. "Since the Lord cannot manifest himself in person, as shown just above, and nevertheless has foretold that he was to come and establish a new church . . . it follows that he will do this by means of a man who is able not only to receive these doctrines in his understanding but also to publish them by the press. That the Lord manifested himself before me, his servant, and sent me to this office, that he afterward opened the eyes of my spirit and thus introduced me into the spiritual world and granted me to see the heavens and the hells, and to talk with angels and spirits, and this now continuously for several years, I affirm in truth; as also from the first day of that call I have not received anything whatever pertaining to the doctrines of that church from any angel, but from the Lord alone while I have read the Word" (*True Christian Religion* §779).

The way for the New Church should be prepared and the decline of Christianity halted on earth through a printed book, therefore, through his book. Thus Swedenborg felt that he was inaugurating a new world era. Accordingly, he concludes with a "fact worthy of mention": "After this work [*True Christian Religion*] was finished, the Lord called his twelve disciples together, who had followed Him in the world, and on the next day he sent them all out into the whole spiritual world, to preach the gospel, that the Lord God Jesus Christ reigns, whose kingdom will endure for ever, according to the prophecy in Daniel (7:13–14) and the Book of Revelation (11:15), and that all those are blessed, who come to the marriage feast of the Lamb, Book of Revelation (19:9). This happened in the month of June on the 19th day in the year 1770." Swedenborg's book therefore also has an influence in heaven. Even in the spiritual world, the gospel is revealed; and on behalf of the Lord, the apostles assume the task in heaven, which has been assigned to Swedenborg on earth: to proclaim the true meaning of the Word.

In order to avoid any misunderstandings, Swedenborg expressly repeated this exalted claim in a letter accompanying a copy of *True Christian Religion*, which he sent in 1771 to Ludwig XII, Landgraf of Hesse-Darmstadt. Encouraged by Oetinger, the Landgraf had written to Swedenborg to ask him for further information following his mysterious announcement in 1768 about the forthcoming appearance of the doctrine of the New Church. Immediately after his book was published, Swedenborg wrote to him on 18 June 1771 from Amsterdam:

> I waited (with my answer), until I had received the recently printed theological work from the press. Entitled *True Christian Religion*, it contains the entire theological learning of the New Church, which is foretold by the Lord in Daniel (7:13–14) and in the Book of Revelation (21:1–2ff). I have sent two copies to you, most illustrious duke, by the stagecoach, which leaves this city twice a week for Germany. The Lord our Savior foretold through the evangelists as well as in the Book of Revelation that he would could come again and establish the New Church. Because he cannot come in person, this must happen through a man who not only grasps the teachings of this Church through his understanding but who can also publicize them through the press. And because the Lord has prepared *me* from my childhood onwards, so he has manifested himself in person to me, his servant, and has given me this commission. This happened in the year 1743 and afterwards he opened my spiritual vision and introduced me to the world of spirits, and permitted me to see the heavens and their wonders, and also hell at

the same time, and to speak with the angels and spirits, and this has now continued for twenty-seven years. That this happened to me is quite unique and only on account of the New Church, of which I have just spoken. (LL, 63)[2]

Through his prophetic exaltation, Swedenborg felt elevated to the rank of a messianic figure. This development can be traced through the writings, letters, and personal accounts of the Nordic visionary, with a vividness unique in the history of Western religion. It is the key to both an understanding and a critique of his visionary literature. It was at this point that the Swedish Lutheran Church, to which Swedenborg belonged all his life, began to dissent. A community was already gathering around him during his lifetime, from which the present New Church has proceeded. Their congregations have spread all over the world, and they see their founder in Swedenborg, while appropriating his self-interpretation as the basis of their preaching of the spiritual meaning of the Word.

2. See also *True Christian Religion* §851, where the twenty-seven years are also mentioned.

17

The Consequences of Vocation

Swedenborg experienced his vocation as God's command to begin a new work. The emergence of his new spiritual gift, with its clarity of spiritual understanding and vision into the spiritual world, made all else in his life pale into insignificance. Let others sit on the Board of Mines, make plans for the minting of copper, invent new pumps; let others fathom the mystery of nature from shells in limestone, fossils in shale and underground channels: the spirit of truth had now spoken to him. Angels proclaimed the highest secrets to him, the spirits endeavored to instruct him, and the Lord himself spoke with him. With the opening of his vision, his old life fell away. The old pattern of ambitious striving for scientific renown, with its methods of research and time-consuming demands, appeared as an obstacle to his new task. This was to live according to his inner vision, to keep his inner eye open for the wonderful revelation of the spiritual world, and not to waste a moment in revealing the true inner meaning of the divine Word to the world.

However, Swedenborg only gradually disassociated himself from his career. He remained in his office at the Board of Mines for two years after his London vision. After Chancellor Bergenstjerna resigned as councillor of the Board of Mines in spring 1747, the board unanimously proposed Swedenborg as his successor in recognition of his scientific and practical achievements. But Swedenborg used this crowning success as an opportunity to hand in his resignation. He did not speak openly about his vocation. He justified his retirement by suggesting that he felt obliged "to complete the work, for which I have been commissioned." This formulation, comprehensible to him in its real sense, allowed others to think that he wished to withdraw in order to add a new volume to his series of scientific works. This wording of his resignation must have been all the less remarkable, as he had earlier justified his journeys abroad with reference to his having to complete a scientific work. As with his earlier requests for leave, he linked his request for dismissal with his terms of pay. He asked the king that he might continue to receive half his salary, "in order that I can complete the important work, for which I have been commissioned." The king granted his request in a decree of 12 June 1747, discharging him from his duties to give him the opportunity "to complete the work, for which he has been commissioned," while expressing the hope that this work like his others would "contribute to general benefit and welfare." On 15 and 17 June, Swedenborg took part in meetings of the board, whose members expressed regret at his resignation, and he was asked to keep the board in mind. His formal discharge followed on 17 June, when his colleagues gave a speech of thanks, wishing him a safe journey and a return in good health. He then traveled to England to have his *Arcana Coelestia* printed, which he had written already prior to his resignation.

Nevertheless, his inner transformation could not remain a secret. However little Swedenborg boasted of his spiritual experiences to his contemporaries after his vocation, however much he tried to keep his lifestyle and speeches unobtrusive, he could not deceive himself about the destiny that would befall him on account of his newly acquired gifts. He would be regarded as insane if the true reason for his resignation were to become known. Swedenborg willingly accepted this destiny of all visionaries because he knew that the visionary is regarded as a fool and madman in all ages.

However, in comparison with earlier centuries, no age of

European intellectual history was more disposed to regard prophets and visionaries as insane than the age in which Swedenborg stepped forth with his visions. This was the age of the Enlightenment, which was beginning to dominate Western thought with its happy faith in the excellence of the world and humankind. This was the age when the European spirit conquered the earth with power. The ideas of French sensualists, English empiricists, and materialists, spread by hundreds of enlightened journalists, daily fortified European citizens in the conviction that they had finally escaped the one-and-a-half-thousand-year dominion of monks, enthusiasts, and prophets and that they did not need to believe in heaven or hell, for the simple reason that neither existed. Prophets had never been so offensive nor a visionary so ridiculous as in this age, which had scarcely surmounted the previous age of religious intolerance, wars, and endemic enthusiasm and recalled the past century only with horror. Swedenborg would not have attracted particular notice in the century of St. Hildegard of Bingen, when one strove for the grace of prophetic vision behind monastic walls; he might have been burned as a heretic, not because he had visions—others had visions and were canonized—but because he deviated from Church doctrine. The eighteenth century especially regarded the visionary as the antithesis of its own ideals, especially when the prophet had previously worn the intellectual costume of the enlightened sage and scholar, as in Swedenborg's case. A scholar who had attained an international reputation through his researches in the most modern fields of science gives up his influential position at the moment he is offered a high office in his country, in order to converse undisturbed with spirits! In the judgment of the age, only a madman could occupy himself with such nonsense in such a splendid era when magic, demons, and spirits were consigned to the past.

Swedenborg had foreseen this reaction to his revelations with a certain calm. The fact that he resigned his office to follow his new vocation, fully aware of the fatal consequences of this step, makes his decision appear even more significant. It is proof of his unconditional honesty and confirms that his zeal for his new task was stronger than any fear of ridicule and scorn that might arise from it.

Antoine-Joseph Pernety (1716–1796), a member of the Royal

Academy of Sciences in Berlin, reported a memorable conversation between Swedenborg and Imperial Councillor Count Anders von Höpken, his friend and spokesman at the Swedish court. The imperial councillor asked Swedenborg why he had actually published his visionary writings, which would be condemned by so many people as empty visions and lies. Swedenborg replied: "I was commanded by the Lord to write and publish them. Do not believe that without this express command I would have thought of publishing things, which I knew in advance would make me look ridiculous and many people would think lies. But if I had assured them that I received this command, they would not believe me. But at least I have the satisfaction that I have obeyed the commands of my God and I will answer them with the words of St. Paul to the Corinthians: 'Here we are, fools for the sake of Christ, while you are the learned men in Christ' (1 Corinthians 4:10), and 'When we are mad, we are mad with God.'"

This statement shows that Swedenborg clearly understood that he would not be spared the fate of the prophet, and that he submitted to this fate—truly a sign of humility. For what could be worse for a scholar of his time than the curse of ridicule? And what did this curse mean to a scientist of Swedenborg's rank? That Swedenborg published his visionary writings despite the certain prospect of European mirth, he regarded as proof of the authenticity of his mission and the truth of his proclamations. If he had wanted to flatter his personal vanity, he would have done everything to avoid ridicule. In defiance of all worldly learning, he expressed his revelations in the consciousness of divine command, and this consciousness helped him to bear the hostility of his contemporaries. Therefore he also said to Höpken: "As a man of advanced years, why should I want to make myself ridiculous for the sake of pure fantasies and lies?"

With his book *Dreams of a Spirit-Seer* (1766), Immanuel Kant became the arbiter of Swedenborg's destiny as a prophet, whom he ridiculed to contemporaries with cutting wit and fierce invective.[1] *Dreams of a Spirit-Seer* made it impossible for anyone in academic circles to utter an appreciative word about Swedenborg without making

---

1. Immanuel Kant, *Dreams of a Spirit-Seer*, ed. Kehrbach (1912) in Reclams Univ. Bibl. No. 1320. Kehrbach published *War Kant Spiritist?* (1880) on Kant's relationship to second sight.

himself ridiculous. Friedrich Christoph Oetinger experienced this for himself after his *Swedenborgs irdische und himmlische Philosophie* was published in 1765. In a personal letter to Swedenborg in 1766, he reported: "O my dear Sir, you will scarcely believe how much I have had to suffer on your account for translating the first part of your book." In his reply, Swedenborg consoled him by remarking that these persecutions were proper to a witness of the truth and fortified him with these words: "What must suffer more that the truth these days? How many people are there, who only see what they wish to see? Therefore tire not and be a defender of the truth!" These words greatly encouraged Oetinger in his respect for Swedenborg and the truth contained in his writings. In his next letter, he told Swedenborg of his keen advocacy against his many detractors, who derided "a philosopher, who weighs and measures things in a geometric fashion according to Wolff and all at once turns into a fool."

His contemporaries' suggestion that he was mad—even Kant refers him to the asylum—threatened Swedenborg's work and even his life. During the Riksdag of 1769, the "Swedenborg case" was discussed. As Robsahm reports in his memoirs, several clergy tried to arraign Swedenborg, as his new doctrines were offensive to them. It was planned to have him first interrogated, in order to declare that he had lost his senses through religious brooding and was now so insane as to represent a danger to society. He should therefore be deprived of his freedom and confined in an asylum. A friendly imperial councillor, probably Count Höpken, informed Swedenborg by letter of his opponents' attack and advised him to travel abroad. "Swedenborg was very depressed at this but soon went into his garden, knelt down, and prayed to God, asking what he should do. He received the comforting assurance that no harm would come to him." Even his enemies in London did not shrink from alleging his insanity in their polemics against him. But Swedenborg never provoked his enemies through either his behavior or his speeches. It is a guarantee of the authenticity of his prophetic exultation that he never indulged the role of holy madness or intentionally played the holy fool. In his manner of living and speaking, he retained the social customs of the nobility and the upper-middle classes.

PART THREE:

The Visionary

18

Swedenborg's Private Life

After resigning his offices under the impact of his vocation, Swedenborg's outer life conformed to the pattern of a quiet scholarly existence. Stage effects and self-importance were quite foreign to the nature of this amiable person. He led the life of a bachelor philosopher with all its eccentricities.

His residence was a small house in a pretty garden near Stockholm. The living rooms were fairly narrow, without any conspicuous display. The furnishings matched Swedenborg's simple lifestyle. According to his trusted friend Carl Robsahm, the director of the Swedish Bank, "it was no doubt comfortable for him, but not for anyone else" (Tafel, doc. 5, pp. 31–32). In 1767, he had a pretty little summer-house with two wings constructed in the garden for occasional guests. His library was deposited in one of the wings, while garden tools were kept in the other. He later had another garden house built, a rectangular design with four doors, so that he could sit with the doors open as in a pavilion in the open air and enjoy a view into the garden from all sides. For the amusement of himself and others, he had a maze of green hedges laid out in the garden; it delighted him whenever his guests, especially the children, got lost in its tortuous paths. He had a small flowerbed planted in front of the main house, which he adorned at great expense. It was planted with box-trees in the Dutch manner, which were cut into marvelous figures. There was also the obligatory factotum for such a scholarly household: the gardener, to whom he gave the garden's entire produce. The gardener's wife took care of the residence and kept the household in order, which was not always simple given the peculiar lifestyle of its master.

Even allowing for the legends that have gathered around the visionary, his lifestyle was still quite peculiar. He worked by day and night alike and made no formal distinction between working hours and rest. He did not maintain bourgeois customs. His principle was, "When I am sleepy, I go to bed." His private division of time thus was frequently at odds with that of society. Because he could not expect a servant to keep such irregular hours, he served himself. He demanded no other service from his maid, the gardener's wife, than that she should make his bed and place a large pitcher of water in the front room. In order to lead his independent lifestyle, he limited his demands for food and drink to a minimum. Like Balzac, he chiefly lived on coffee, which he prepared himself on the fire of his private room and which he took without milk or cream but with much sugar, and with which he frequently roused himself by day and night. Whenever he ate at home, his nourishment consisted of a bread roll in warm milk. He almost never drank wine at home. He rarely ate dinner at home. In order to brew coffee at all times, a fire was always lit on the hearth of his study. His bedroom was unheated even in extreme cold. According to the severity of the winter, his bed was covered with three or four English woolen blankets, and only on the very coldest days did he have it placed in his study. As soon as he awoke, he went into his study, where he found glowing coals on the hearth. Dry wood and birch bark, which he had bought in bundles, served to kindle the fire. He prepared his own coffee and then sat down to write. In the little-used drawing room there stood a marble table with a splendid inlay work, which he later gave to the Board of Mines. Even this room was simple and furnished without ostentation.

Swedenborg also dressed very simply. During the winter, he wore a fur coat of reindeer skins, and in the summer, he wore a dressing gown at home, "both rather worn out, as becomes a philosopher," as his friend Robsahm reported (Tafel, 33). If he went out, he exchanged his dressing gown for a suit of black velvet. He shared a certain hapless neglect of the small things in life with the learned bachelors of all ages. If he went to a party without first submitting to the critical gaze of his maid, he often overlooked details on his suit or that one shoe had a jeweled buckle, the other silver. This neglect often amused ladies in society, which he then acknowledged with philosophical calm.

Apart from the Hebrew and Greek Bibles, all books were banned from his study. After the secret meaning of Scripture had been revealed to him, the Book of Books was sufficient. On his desk lay the registers and indexes of his works in his own hand. He started these to spare himself constant reference in his numerous works and to check at any time what he had already written. This method of working with indexes is visible in the style of his works. It is expressed in the numerous cross-references, which were made easier by Swedenborg's division of his works with pedantic precision into continuously numbered short sections, so that in any cross-reference he needed to give only an abbreviated title of the relevant work with the corresponding number. Thus we find at numerous places where specific doctrines are mentioned whole numerical series of references to passages in his other works, where the same doctrine is discussed.

Swedenborg enjoyed excellent health with this simple lifestyle. In eighty-four years, he was almost never ill and still moved with a youthful briskness and vigor, which amazed everyone. The few short illnesses he suffered he attributed to spiritual crises and upsets. He ascribed these to the influence of demons, with which he had to wrestle, and therefore he refused medical treatment. He especially attributed the toothaches that sometimes plagued him to the influence of demons. When his friend offered him a remedy against toothache, he declined this on the grounds that his pain did not stem from the nerves of his teeth but from the influence of hell and from particular demons who caused him this plague. He consoled himself about his pains after he was informed in a vision that the pains would soon cease. Thus, he reached the age of eighty-four without a doctor and died of a chill without the care of a doctor.[1]

It amazed his contemporaries that, in contrast to most scholars of his time who followed the splendid and expensive fashions of their era, he had no debts and never lacked for money to pay for his numerous voyages to England and Holland or the expenses of printing his works, which he financed from his own resources. However, this is not so surprising in view of his thriftiness and simple lifestyle. On the basis of a royal decree, he received half his salary in pay from the resignation of his office until the end of his life. This income was increased by the revenues from the sale of his books; moreover, he had come into a considerable inheritance on the death of his father—the bishop had owned iron mines—so that he remained financially independent and could devote himself to his higher calling without external cares. He could afford to decline several offers of well-paid honorary appointments.

Despite this solitary and independent lifestyle, Swedenborg did not withdraw from social life. He received and paid many visits. As the harbinger of such amazing visions, he was also pestered by the curious. It is a sign of the purity of his religious feeling that he was never tempted to use his remarkable gift for financial gain or to exploit gullible people. How easily he could have played the part of a Cagliostro! Because his opponents sought to twist his words and misrepresent him, he was in the habit of never receiving strangers on his own. Especially when ladies were visiting, he regularly called the gardener or his wife into the room.

His visitors fell into various groups. First, there were the Swedish or overseas family friends, who frequently visited and by whom he was also often invited. Then there were the foreign scholars and travelers, who knew him from his numerous travels and visited him in his homeland; others were attracted by his books and reputation and wanted to make the personal acquaintance of the strange man. Visitors from these two groups were always welcome.

---

1. For Swedenborg's excellent state of health, see *Sammlung von Urkunden betreffend das Leben und den Charakter Emanuel Swedenborgs*, ed. Immanuel Tafel (Tübingen, 1838), 29.

He found it more difficult to protect himself from visitors of another kind. There were persons of rank who saw Swedenborg only as a spirit-seer and wanted to inquire after their late relatives. There were ladies and gentlemen who simply took him for a soothsayer and asked him to explain bizarre things, out of pure curiosity, to test him, or just to amuse themselves. These visitors were of no account to him. If such visitors succeeded in gaining admittance and their class and rank excluded a simple rebuff, then one of the servants always had to be present. "Women are crafty; they could say that I sought their better acquaintance, and one also knows that such people turn things round and twist whatever they hear and do not understand." He did not hesitate to send people away who wanted to consult him as a soothsayer or use his clairvoyant gifts for purposes of detection.

Swedenborg understood and spoke fluent Latin, English, Dutch, French, Italian, and German, but he always conducted conversations at home in Swedish, so that the servants present could understand, for "I want witnesses to my speech and conduct, in order to foil any malicious gossip or slander." The gardener's wife told the scholar Pernety of one characteristic episode. One day the visionary received a visit from Bishop Hallenius, his father's successor, who was surrounded by much gossip of irregularity in the conduct of his office. The conversation turned to the subject of church sermons. In the course of the discussion, Swedenborg reproached the bishop for spreading lies in his sermons. Given this turn in the conversation, the bishop was embarrassed by the presence of the gardener's wife and sent her out of the room. But Swedenborg ordered her to remain. The conversation continued. The two men referred to the Hebrew and Greek Bibles to clarify their views. The dispute led to personal insults that ended with Swedenborg accusing the bishop of greed and injustice. He finally said to him: "You have already reserved your place in hell. But I prophesy to you that in several months you will suffer a serious illness, during which the Lord will seek to convert you." In point of fact, the bishop did shortly fall ill and mended his ways in the course of this trial (Tafel, doc. 6, pp. 67–68).

However much Swedenborg avoided the visits of strangers and

knew how to protect himself from the throng of the curious, he greatly loved the company of his friends. He delighted all with his cheerfulness, while his pleasant and interesting conversation never lacked for fun. The eighty-year-old always treated ladies with a chivalrous and courteous amiability. His bright conversation freely and playfully ranged over the whole wealth of learning he had acquired in his studies and on his travels. He was generally commended as a merry and agreeable companion, never surly or ill-tempered. He was quite free of that common scholarly failing of wanting to talk only about his own ideas and doctrines. He spoke about his own experiences only when directly asked and only when he thought the questioner was personally interested. By contrast, when people asked him impertinent questions or wanted to make a fool of him, he knew perfectly well how to lead them up the garden path and reduce them to silence with a choice retort.

He occasionally enjoyed playing a *partie l'hombre* with his contemporaries. However, he regulated his sociability. At evening parties, he was accustomed to rise from the table at seven o'clock, even if he was enjoying himself. Among his close friends, he relaxed his ascetic lifestyle and dined with a good appetite and even drank some wine, which according to his housekeeper "he preferred to sweeten strongly, by filling the conical wine-glass half full with sugar."

His conversation was occasionally hindered by his congenital tendency to stutter, to which he had referred when declining his appointment as a professor. For this reason, he always spoke in a slow and measured fashion, which emphasized the dignity of his appearance and drew attention to the content of his speech. When he spoke, all other conversations tended to fall silent and everyone listened to him—a fact reported by others who made his acquaintance by chance in company at London or Amsterdam. The very presence and power of his personality reduced scoffers to silence. "I was frequently amazed," one Dutch citizen recorded of him, "whenever I took him to large parties, where mockers had come with a view to making a fool of the old man. They would forget their laughter and taunts and listen open-mouthed to him whenever he related in a slightly child-like and reserved manner the most marvelous things from the world of spirits. His eyes possessed the power to make everyone silent."[2] Whenever he spoke about his visions, he did it without presumption or arrogance, with modest simplicity and as a matter of course. His words bore a stamp of such authentic personal experience and conviction, that he always won the trust of his listeners. An English friend of Kant, who visited Swedenborg at his behest, described him as a "reasonable, pleasant and candid man and scholar" (Tafel, II, doc. 272, p. 627).[3]

Swedenborg spent a large part of the years between 1745 and 1772 on overseas journeys lasting several months, during which he often stayed in Holland and England. He undertook these journeys in order to deliver his manuscripts to publishers in Amsterdam and London and to discuss with them the printing of his new works, which he partly supervised. Even on his travels, Swedenborg maintained his peculiar lifestyle, adopted ever since his vocation. Whenever he left Sweden, he usually traveled in an open carriage from his home in Stockholm to Göteborg, where he embarked for England or Holland. As far as possible, he used the same ships and the same accommodation and gathered a loyal circle of friends around him in Amsterdam and London. The descriptions of his acquaintances in Amsterdam include the most personal and intimate testimonies to the life of the visionary.

Even the captains with whom he sailed had many stories of him and may well have woven a few sailor's yarns about their unusual passenger over time. As the friend of two such regular captains, Robsahm learnt many singular things about Swedenborg. Both of them unanimously reported that Swedenborg remained abed in his cabin almost the whole of the voyage but talked to himself as if he were in company, which struck the crew as most uncanny. A cabin boy on Captain Harrison's ship was the first to notice Swedenborg's strange conversations with himself and reported them to the helmsman.

---

2. *Aufzeichnungen eines Amsterdamer Bürgers über Swedenborg*, ed. A. Scheeler (Hanover, 1858); reprinted in part in LL, 73.

3. Letter from Immanuel Kant to Charlotte von Knobloch, 1763, reprinted in most editions of Immanuel Kant, *Träume eines Geistersehers* (1766); see also LL, 91. For a recent translation that includes this letter, see *Kant on Swedenborg: Dreams of a Spirit-Seer and Other Writings*, translated by Gregory Johnson (West Chester, Pa.: Swedenborg Foundation, 2002).

Growing uneasy that their passenger had lost his reason, they reported the matter to the captain. The latter made a real sailor's decision: "He may or may not be out of his wits, but as long as he is calm, I have no authority over him. He is always clever and reasonable in conversation with me, and apart from this, you see that we have the best wind. If this weather lasts, I will never have made a faster voyage."

On his journeys, Swedenborg could not conceal his unusual habits and especially his visionary states as well as he could in his solitary home in Stockholm. Not only cabin boys surprised him in a state of ecstasy, but even his friends. Once, due to unfavorable winds, the ship that was to take Swedenborg to Amsterdam lay for four days at anchor in the Kattegat several miles off Helsingör. Swedenborg's friend there, General Tuxen, took a boat out to the ship in order to visit Swedenborg. When the door of the cabin was opened, he found him sitting in his dressing gown, elbows resting on the table, his face propped on his hands, with his eyes open and turned upwards. Unheralded and wanting to surprise his friend, Tuxen walked up to him with words of heartfelt greeting. Too late he noticed from the rigid, entranced posture of his friend that he had surprised him in a state of rapture. As a result of the sudden disturbance, Swedenborg gradually came to his senses, stood up with every sign of confusion, took several wavering and unsteady steps, and slowly recovered. Finally restored, he bade his guest welcome and asked whence he came. Tuxen invited him to come ashore and dine with him, to which Swedenborg immediately agreed. He took off his dressing gown and slippers and "got dressed as nimbly and cheerfully as a youth of twenty-one."

This report shows that Swedenborg did not always have an easy time traveling. Nevertheless, sailors' tales elaborated his journeys. Numerous anecdotes report that a favorable wind blew and that the voyage proceeded swiftly and with helpful circumstances whenever Swedenborg was on board. The legend of the spirit-seer claims that he is led gently over the sea by good spirits. The legend even makes the coffee ration the object of his marvels: higher powers ensure that he will not run out of his favorite drink on board. A Swedish innkeeper in London called Gerbström, responsible for

Swedenborg's supplies on voyage, asked him for how many days he should pack ground coffee. Swedenborg told him six days. Gerbström was amazed and replied: "That is too little; it is impossible that the Assessor will be back in Stockholm in so short a time." Then Swedenborg declared he should pack coffee for seven days. "And what happened?"—the legend continues—"after six days the ship was in Dalarön and on the seventh in Stockholm." On his return to London, the English captain is said to have reported that he had never had such a favorable wind as on this occasion; every time they changed course, the wind followed suit. The stories that captain and crew told in taverns about their strange passenger offered the most amiable portrait of Swedenborg.

On land, Swedenborg tried as far as possible to continue his home regimen. The notes of an Amsterdam citizen named Christian Cuno describe how he rented two rooms in the Kälberstrasse below the Oude Kerk in Amsterdam in November 1768 (Tafel, II, doc. 256, pp. 445–446; LL, 72ff). When Cuno asked in astonishment why he had no servant to wait on him in his advanced years, Swedenborg replied that he required none. On his travels, he had no fears for himself because his angel was constantly talking with him and watching over him. The couple he was staying with were young merchants who ran a shop selling calico, handkerchiefs, and such things and had quite a quite a number of children. "I asked the landlady," Cuno continued, "whether they had to do much for the old gentleman. 'Almost nothing' was her answer. 'My maid has nothing to do with him other than lighting the fire on the hearth in the mornings. He goes to bed every evening as the clock strikes seven and gets up the next morning at eight o'clock. We don't have to do anything further for him. He keeps the fire going himself the whole day. When he goes to sleep, he ensures that his fire will do no damage. He dresses and undresses himself and attends to all his needs, so that we do not know whether we have someone staying or not. I really wish he would spend the rest of his life with us. My children will miss him most, for he never goes out without bringing them something to nibble.'"

While traveling, he also maintained his home diet. Coffee, chocolate, and rusk were his usual midday meal in his room at

Amsterdam, "and his landlord, landlady and their children had to eat most of it." If he had a greater appetite, he went to an eating house on the Heilige Weg. These things are not mentioned as curiosities but because they serve to correct the current eccentric image of Swedenborg "the spirit-seer" and paint him in his true colors. This man was no charlatan. Given his abilities, his contacts, knowledge, and experience of men and the world, how easy it would have been for him to play the brilliant and profitable role of magician at the courts of his time! How obvious the temptation must have been to use his visionary gifts as a comfortable and secure route to wealth, power, and fame. He resisted all these temptations and led the life of a scholar up to his death. He declined all lucrative offers in order to have the necessary peace for his sacred commission, the interpretation of the inner meaning of Scripture and the opening of the world of spirits. He lived his mission in all simplicity and modesty.

19

Swedenborg's Public Life

The preceding portrait of a quiet scholarly life needs some qualification in order to present the full scope of his versatile character. Even after renouncing his former career, Swedenborg did not wholly break with science but occasionally donned the robes of his former erudition, fully aware of his superiority. His seat in the Swedish Academy of Sciences gave him such opportunities. It was with a certain irony that the seer presented a lecture in 1763 entitled "Description of the way that marble slabs are inlaid for tables and other ornaments," which was published in the academy journal. In his youth, he had hoped to reform the world through an academy of scholars. Now that he possessed inner vision, he gave the academy, idol of his youth, a mere trifle of his former scholarship.

In his visionary period, Swedenborg produced a second scientific work in the old style. His many voyages had awoken in him the old passion of calculating a method to determine one's position at sea. Indeed, the safety of ocean navigation depended on it. His first juvenile work, which he had presented to Halley and Bignon, thereby acquired a new significance for him. In 1766, he used his stay in Amsterdam, while he had *Apocalypse Revealed* printed, to publish a new edition of *New Method of Finding Longitude*. He sent this study off simultaneously with copies of *Apocalypse Revealed*. For example, he sent a copy of these "*lucubrations de ma jeunesse*" to Archbishop Menander of Sweden with the remark that the work had "been subject to examination by scientific societies and academies." He requested that he send it to the professor of astronomy at Åbo, "in order that he may deign to give it practical application, if he finds the method to his taste and considers its realization appropriate" (LL, 57). But these scientific works are mere detours beside his visionary writing, now his real career. More significant by contrast are his attempts to intervene in public life through politics, economics, and education at key moments in Swedish history.

Swedenborg's political attitudes were already formed prior to his experience of vocation. He had grown up during the reign of Charles XII and had experienced royal absolutism in a form highly advantageous to himself. Nevertheless, Swedenborg was no supporter of absolutism. In the person of Charles XII, he had experienced how dangerous it is for a country to be subject to the power of an autocrat. His personal misfortunes after the death of Charles may well have confirmed this view. Charles XII had not trimmed his political plans according to the military and economic capacities of the people but had squandered them in martial improvisations. Swedenborg was well aware how much the country suffered from the consequences of unsuccessful wars; and after Charles' death, he advocated a policy to spare his country further foreign adventures.

He had already stated this view publicly before his conversion in 1734. Under Peter the Great, Russia had seized the Baltic provinces from the Swedish crown in the Nordic War, whereupon a war party in Sweden pressed for their reconquest. In this view, Swedish foreign policy should resume the great plans of Charles XII and aim to make the Baltic Sea a Swedish lake by eliminating Russia and involving Poland in Swedish continental policy. In a revanchist war against Russia, the Swedish war party banked on the promise of French assistance. In the decisive year 1734, Swedenborg was a member of the secret committee of the Riksdag and the crown council dealing with this question. In this capacity, he worked on a memorandum for the other members, in which he opposed a declaration of war on Russia. This far-seeing memorandum helped the peace party maintain the upper hand, albeit for only a few years. In 1738, the Swedish prime minister, Count Horn, had to yield to the party eagerly preparing for war with Russia and war was declared in 1741. Sweden paid for defeat two years later with the loss of a large part of Finland, as Swedenborg had anticipated.

The collapse of Charles XII's policy had made the people aware of the damaging effects of royal absolutism. Swedenborg had personally welcomed the curtailment of absolutism with utmost conviction. In the years 1760–1761, however, an absolutist party wanted to expand the powers of the king again and suspend the constitution. In 1761, Swedenborg addressed the Riksdag with a speech that compared the advantages of the existing constitution with absolutist tendencies. In a virtual paean of praise, he described the political conditions created by the constitution as an ideal accommodation of the various political forces in the country:

> Everything in our fatherland is ordered with wisdom; everything concerning the administration of justice is cleverly fitted together as in an unbroken chain from the man in the highest position down to him, who has the lowest function. Everything with us is subordinated to a firm hierarchy. The district judge is subject to the county-court judge, and both are subject to the high court; but this office is again subject to royal review, and this in turn to the imperial estates. In the same way, the lower and higher officials are subject to the provincial governor, he is responsible to the high court and the imperial colleges, and these to the imperial council. The imperial council, the high court and all imperial colleges are responsible to the four estates of the realm, who nominate committees in each annual session to examine their conduct. Additionally, every employee is responsible to the treasury and the procurator, and ultimately the imperial estates have to answer before God, if they do not uphold the laws as their one and only sovereign. (LL, 53f)

This exposition of the Swedish constitution sounds more democratic than it actually is in word and spirit. The real purpose of this speech was the strengthening of the constitutional element. Swedenborg continued to emphasize that in Sweden, "no one can arbitrarily do as they like, but in every dispute everyone may enjoy their rights and may be certain of the issue, as long as the law is on his side." He emphasized that in Sweden "every estate may enjoy its freedoms and special privileges" and concluded, by cleverly describing an aspiration as reality: "None of us is a slave, but whoever lives as a good and righteous citizen can enjoy all their due rights and is completely free." He wished the Riksdag to take special care to forestall all discontents "which certain restless spirits and hotheads would like to incite against the existing form of our government both in the provinces and in the present assembly of the imperial estates."

Swedenborg's political views correspond to the convictions he had gathered on his journeys. In France, he had seen royal absolutism; in Holland, republican freedom; and in England, the balance of both systems. His real sympathy lay not with absolutist states but with the free Netherlands and its republican constitution. He wrote of his journey there in a letter of 21 August 1736:

> I have considered why it has pleased our Lord to bless such an uncouth and avaricious people with such a splendid country; why he has preserved them for so long a time from all misfortune; has caused them to surpass all other nations in commerce; and made their country a place with most of the riches, not only of Europe but also of other places flow. The principal reason seems to me to have been that it is a republic, in which the Lord delights more than in monarchical countries. The result is that no one deems himself obliged to accord honor and veneration to any human being, but considers the low as well as the high to be of the same worth as a king, as is also shown by the native bent and disposition of everyone in Holland. The only one for whom they entertain a feeling of veneration is the Lord, putting their trust in flesh. When the highest is revered and no human being is in his place, it is most pleasing to the Lord. Besides each enjoys his own free will, and from this his worship of God grows. Each is, as it were, his own king under the government of the Highest. From this it follows that they do not out of fear or timidity or excess of caution lose their courage and their independent rational thinking but in full freedom they are able to fix their souls upon the honor of the Highest, who is unwilling to share his worship with any other. (Tafel, II, doc. 206, p. 86)[1]

---

1. For an account of Swedenborg's experiences with the Dutch in the next life, see *True Christian Religion* §§800–805.

Given his liberal inclinations, Swedenborg also set great value on the maintenance of the Swedish constitution, which balanced the power of the king, the estates and the people following the collapse of absolutism. Because an absolutist party demanded the expansion of royal prerogatives at the very moment that he addressed his speech to the Riksdag, he described the existing order as ideal and declared: "I would like to say that the best and wisest form of government presently exists in our fatherland."

As a scholar, Swedenborg had a particular reason for his sympathy with the liberal constitution. The political conditions in the Netherlands must have appeared ideal to the learned writer. For the first time in European history, religious tolerance had been achieved and constitutionally guaranteed there. Only there did freedom of speech and the press prevail. The severe censorship in his homeland made these foreign freedoms particularly admirable. To avoid conflict with the Swedish censors over the publication of his numerous writings, he regularly traveled to have his books printed in the liberal countries; he had his entire theological works printed in Amsterdam and London, after the greater part of his scientific works had already been published abroad. He was thus spared many difficulties right up to the last years of his life and did not encounter any conflict with Swedish censorship provisions until 1769.

Only once did he attempt to have a book printed in France. Where the freest spirits risked their necks under the most absolutist rule of Europe, censorship existed in its most oppressive form, but only according to the letter.

The censors administered their office very lightly, as many of them already sympathized with the free spirit of the age. When Swedenborg applied for a printing permit for *True Christian Religion*, the Paris censor immediately realized that, if this work appeared in Paris, it would incite the violent opposition of the clerical authorities, leading to a legal suit against author and printer. But because the censor did not wish France to lag behind the advances in intellectual freedom already won by the Dutch and English, he suggested a current expedient to Swedenborg. He should have the book printed in Paris but give Amsterdam or London as the place of publication on the title page, so that it could be sold in France as a foreign book. The upright Swedenborg was appalled by this elegant circumvention of censorship and rejected the generous suggestion. He did not want to get his revelations into print through deception and thus preferred to have his book appear in free Amsterdam.

Not only the models of England and Holland strengthened his aversion to absolutism, for he had also seen the depressing effect of absolutism on the intellectual life of the German princely courts. Although his travel diary gives no specific accounts, his eloquent descriptions of the Germans are reminiscent of Gotthold Ephraim Lessing's battle against the German censor. His description of the life of the Germans in the intellectual world, included in *True Christian Religion* §§813–816, gives a faithful reflection of the conditions of contemporary Germany, as he knew it. He shows "an empire parcelled up into many territories. There is an emperor, but the prince of each territory enjoys tyrannical rights. There are larger and smaller principalities, and each prince is an autocrat in his own territory." Moreover, religion is divided by confession: in several principalities there are "so-called Evangelicals," in others Reformed, and in others Papists. "Given the variety of their government and religion, the Germans cannot be as easily described by their temperament, interests and lifestyle as other peoples: but it is still possible to see the common spirit which prevails in the same language."

Swedenborg saw the absence of freedom of speech, "as the Dutch and British have," as a special shortcoming of intellectual life in Germany, which he regarded as a consequence of German absolutism. In criticizing these conditions, Swedenborg expressed his political conviction much more freely and clearly than he would have been able to do in a Riksdag speech. "Whenever the freedom to speak and write is restricted, the freedom to think, the ability to penetrate matters comprehensively and exhaustively, is also set within bounds. It is like a spring, which is enclosed by a sealed container. If the container is full, the spring no longer flows. Thought is like the spring, and speech, which springs from it, is like the container. In a word, the inflow adjusts to the outflow, and reason has the same degree of freedom that thoughts have to be uttered and acted upon." According to this simile, censorship not only hinders the freedom of speech and the press but blocks the living source of thoughts themselves. In a closed space without egress, neither the word nor the idea can ever develop, and the source of the spirit runs dry.

Swedenborg explains the general state of German scholarship in his century by this lack of freedom of speech and writing. German scholarship is no longer directed towards free speculation but towards history because historical scholarship can better adapt itself than the free development of thoughts to the limits of censorship. The truth can be more easily presented in a historical garb than in its philosophical form. "This noble nation therefore devotes itself to the objects of memory rather than reasoning. They are thus devoted to the history of literature. In their writings, they put their trust in men who have a scholarly reputation and whose opinion they can copiously quote and subscribe to." Swedenborg condenses this criticism of the dependent character of German scholarship into a telling image. German scholarship is symbolized by a man with a book under his arm. To anyone disputing something, he says, "I will give you the answer to that!," whereupon he produces the book from beneath his arm and reads a passage out.

Swedenborg similarly describes the circumstances of German theologians. "While they are students, the clergy fill their notebooks from the mouths of the university professors, and they keep these as arsenals of erudition. Once they have taken holy office or are employed in the schools, they borrow these lectures from their notebooks for presentation from the pulpit or rostrum." Swedenborg blames all this on absolutism, which makes the people unfree and prevents them from "rising to a higher understanding" but "only admits them to a lower understanding." According to this criterion of the freedom of intellectual life, he divides the free from the unfree nations, who are as different "as the eagle which soars aloft from the swans in the river, or as the great deer with antlers freely running through the fields and forest are from the deer kept in parks to please the prince, or as different as winged horses of the ancients are from horses with fine harness in the stables of kings."

These statements show that Swedenborg understood freedom as the religious and intellectual freedom of the individual, a privilege the English and Dutch dissenters had achieved in their tenacious struggles for religious freedom. This was the fundamental reason for his rejection of absolutism. In his second speech to the Riksdag in 1761, he justified the maintenance of the constitution by reference to the consequences of an absolutist royal prerogative on the religious question. "We live in the extreme north, which one might call the end of the world; if unrestricted absolutism were to be reintroduced, there would be as little counterbalance or opposition on the part of the people as in Russia or in the Asian lands." Nobody could rein or suppress even a single passion on the part of the sovereign in the absence of an opposition. Swedenborg only hinted at one of the "countless terrors" that could result: the Babylonian whore, namely, "the papistical religion," could come and bewitch the Swedish heir to the throne. It had tempted the ruling princes of Saxony, Cassel, and Zweibrücken, and England before the accession of the House of Hanover, "just as it had tempted the ruling King of Prussia, when he was still heir to the throne, and King Sigismund and Queen Christine of Sweden." If, in an absolutist constitution, "this whore, who knows how to act and adorn herself like a goddess" entered the cabinet of a Swedish king, neither the army nor the clergy nor the peasantry could prevail "against the violence and passions of the sovereign and the cunning of the Jesuits. This and every other kind of slavery must be feared in future, if our present excellent form of government and invaluable freedom were suspended."

Besides these general views, Swedenborg also made concrete suggestions for Swedish foreign policy at the Riksdag of 1761. Even if he could not accomplish these proposals, they show that the opening of his inner vision had not clouded his understanding of the country's political needs. On the contrary, he displayed a shrewd and expert judgment of the situation whenever he found himself opposing the party view prevailing in the country.

His other statements on political questions in the Riksdag concerned monetary policy and public health. His incorruptible uprightness and altruism guided him in both areas, and he endeavored to realize his ethical views in practical measures for the benefit of the whole people.

Swedish industry as well as Swedish finance was indebted to Swedenborg. Besides its iron mines, Sweden possessed great deposits of copper and silver. At the beginning of his career, Swedenborg had made a major contribution to the discovery and exploitation of these resources through his observations of the ore-containing rocks. After the discovery of the copper and silver deposits, the Swedish industrial elite tended to give priority to the exploitation of silver seams over iron-mining. From the outset, Swedenborg was opposed to this emphasis on precious metal mining at the expense of iron production. In his time, raw iron was mined in Sweden but then shipped to Dutch industrial towns to be manufactured into steel by secret methods before resale. In this way, the main profit of the iron trade eluded Sweden. On his journeys to Holland, Swedenborg made a precise study of steel manufacture; in 1734, he published a work on this subject, which was reprinted by the French Academy. At the same time, he designed plans for new blast furnaces with an exact calculation of coal consumption and steel production from year to year, in order to guarantee the profitability of the process. After iron production was neglected in favor of the extraction of precious metals, Swedenborg opposed this one-sided preference in several memoranda written even after resigning from his office at the Board of Mines. He pointed out that the Swedish economy would derive greater benefits by expanding iron-mining to its greatest potential rather than producing precious metals. He demonstrated the financial advantages of this practice, as well as developing a wider view of public economy by showing that increased iron production would employ a far greater proportion of the population than the exploitation of a few precious metal mines, whose profit benefited only their owners. "One should not only consider the nobility of the metal, but also the public good, that is to say all those particulars and circumstances which cause one kind of work to benefit the country in time more than another, or that the work is noble even if the metal is not."

Not only the Swedish iron-masters but also the pioneers of prohibition and the state control of liquor could count Swedenborg among their apostles. In 1755 in the Swedish House of Nobles, a whole century before the spread of prohibition laws in Europe, Swedenborg demanded the introduction of state control over liquor production for reasons of economy and public health. As every Swedish peasant or townsman could distill as much liquor at home as he wished, its consumption had risen inordinately among the common people. Swedenborg was greatly concerned by this trend, whose effects he regularly saw in public and family life. A leaf among his theological manuscripts reads, "The immoderate enjoyment of liquor will be the ruin of the Swedish people." Since his conversion, he refrained from alcoholic beverages at home, although, as Robsahm relates "in company he could drink the *poculum hilaritatis*, albeit in moderation." Swedenborg considered such moderation beneficial to his compatriots. In a submission to the House of Nobles in 1755, he showed that Sweden imported more goods than it exported, which had to be balanced by an increased export of ores, for which there was sufficient demand. But this demanded a greater efficiency in the mining industry. The people were incapable of higher achievement while this evil drinking habit and the inordinately high consumption of alcohol persisted. This would hardly decrease as long as people might produce as much liquor as they wanted at home. The general right to produce liquor must therefore be withdrawn by the state and granted to a few individual producers against payment of a high tax. The state would thus retain control of the amount of liquor produced as well as gain the advantage of increased taxes. Swedenborg went so far as to demand that liquor should no longer be served in taverns but only handed out through a sliding window onto the street. In 1761, the same year that Swedenborg wrote *Summaries of the Internal Sense of the Prophets and Psalms*, he brought the proposal on liquor production once again before the House of Nobles.

All these proposals and expert opinions of a political and economic nature show that Swedenborg was never a solitary eccentric forgetful of the reality of life after his conversion. Here was a man who used the full breadth of his knowledge and experience to solve general questions and tasks in the life of his people and whose suggestions were decades ahead of their time. Given the one-sided impression of the "spirit-seer" current since the time of Kant, it is important to consider this practical side of his activity. This historically accurate portrait of his personality enables one to understand the development of his visionary life and literature.

20

The Prelude to a New Work

The prelude to Swedenborg's visionary literature is represented by *Worship and Love of God* (*De cultu et amore Dei*) which, although a fragment, is stylistically and intellectually the most impressive and individual product of his genius. This fragment combines his scientific, speculative, and artistic talent in such a fascinating way that Per Atterbom, the Swedish Romantic poet, declared, "It is written with a poetic inspiration, which if shared among a dozen poets would still suffice to make them a star of the first magnitude in the firmament of poetry." This work was produced immediately after the vision of Christ in London, during those months so rich with inner experiences, in which Swedenborg's religious crisis approached its climax. During this crisis, he realized that his mission would lead to a higher vision beyond his learned knowledge. But still he had no firm idea what form this new work would take. During autumn of 1744, Swedenborg felt he had received a divine commission to write "a divine book about the worship and love of God," in which "he should weave nothing of other men's material, but which should contain only things that he had from himself and from God, who would show him the right path in the composition of this work."

On 27 October 1744, he received a special illumination, commanding him to begin the work, and he published the first two parts of the book in London the following year. But it remained a fragment: only a few pages in proof and some in manuscript from the third part. In April 1745, his vision of vocation ensued, in which the consciousness of his true divine vision became manifest, and he received his commission to reveal the inner meaning of the divine Word simultaneously with the opening of his vision into the spiritual world. This event curtailed his work on the worship and love of God. The *Adversaria*, which he wrote after his vision of vocation, already contained a critique of the work interrupted by his vocation. He explained that it was "prompted by reason" and can therefore be credited only in those parts that agree with the revelations of Scripture.

In old age, Swedenborg qualified this harsh judgment. When asked whether the work on the worship and love of God should be counted among his canonical works, he said that it was based on truth but still retained a trace of egoism because he had used the Latin language in a playful manner. This self-criticism appears to refer more to style than content, although style and idea are difficult to separate in this work.

The style of the work already reveals that it stands on the threshold between his scientific and visionary periods. Scientific, philosophical, and visionary ideas blend in a unique way. It is a kind of creation poem similar to Milton's *Paradise Lost*, which had an immense influence on Swedenborg's language and perception. However, it is not written in verse but in an elevated prose. The starting point is the biblical account of the creation of the world, the creation of humankind, and paradise. But the Mosaic story of creation is not allegorically indicated as it is in *Adversaria*. The Bible is also neither quoted literally nor expounded. It is remodeled poetically, weaving in the scientific theories of the creation, the structure of the universe, humanity and the soul that Swedenborg had advanced in his chief scientific works like *First Principles of Natural Things* and *Economy of the Animal Kingdom*. The biblical account of creation is a stimulus for his speculation and fantasy, mingling biblical and mythological views in free, poetic speculation. In this work, Swedenborg drew on the full range of his cosmological and metaphysical ideas, gathered through research and confirmed by his illuminations and "assurances."

The Worship and Love of God is a poetic myth of Swedenborg's cosmology and anthropology, in which biblical notions, ancient myths, and erudite scientific speculations combine. Poetic visions alternate with long didactic passages where Adam and Eve converse with the genies, angels, and heavenly intelligences around them. Here one finds the words in Aristophanes' *Birds*, describing how the dark winged night lays a wind-egg, from which Eros hatches to create the universe, or it may be the description of the world's creation and the doctrine of the world-egg in Ovid's *Metamorphoses*. Swedenborg sees in these myths references to his own cosmic theory, according to which the sun was originally surrounded by a crust of material fog that broke up when the sun emerged from its chaos and the various planets of the solar system were formed from its exploding fragments.

The description of paradise presents an imaginative link between Swedenborg's astronomical observations concerning the changing orbital period of the earth and biblical ideas of paradise and the ancient myths of the Golden Age. The realm of the sun in Plato's *Phaedo*, Hesiod's description of the Gardens of the Hesperides, the Garden of Eden in the Bible—in his view, all these myths indicate the pristine state of the earth, in which nature enjoyed its childhood. This was the age when Flora and Ceres rested on their grass bowers; Diana hastened through the forests with her nymphs; Jupiter, Phoebus, and the other gods dwelt with human beings; Pluto came out of the shadows of Tartarus and raped Proserpina; and Venus and her son Cupid were constantly armed. The arcadian scenery in which Adam and Eve conduct their conversations with intelligences, the description of groves and meadows, the dancing games of the intelligences, the wedding of the first couple, and the atmosphere of classical nudity permeate the whole poem with the mood and style of ancient myth.

The visionary experiences, which Swedenborg was granted during his religious crisis, also play a significant role here. Adam and Eve's archetypal understanding, their conversations with the heavenly intelligences, their vision of heavenly Love, and their intuition perfectly match Swedenborg's dream experiences. The reports in his *Dream Diary* serve as a commentary to this work, which reflects the history of his visionary experiences, elevating them to a metaphysical and mythical realm. The basic theme in the preface of *First Principles of Natural Things* is pervasive: what was wistfully described there as the "understanding of Adam," he now feels miraculously emerging in himself. This experience empowers him to sing the life of the first-born man in a hymn. But what is the content of this work, which originated at such an extraordinary point in Swedenborg's development and which he judged so harshly before it was finished?

The preface begins with Swedenborg's seeking to distract his restless thoughts by taking an autumn walk in a London park. He sees the autumn leaves whirling through the air and is seized by a fear concerning the change of the seasons. This fear takes on a cosmic dimension, as thoughts about the changing seasons lead to the stages of human life and thence to the succession of world eras. He sees the whole universe subject to the law of life, which carries things from the state of paradisial youth through gradual maturity to old age and dissolution. The Golden and Silver Ages are past, "now the final age, the Iron Age, is coming, which will soon perish in rust and dust."

Melancholy concerning the aging of the earth leads the author to contemplate the myths of the ancient sages, "whose souls were independent of the body and thus closer to heaven" and who possessed a clearer knowledge of the nobler time at the birth of humankind, when the gods came down from their starry dwellings and lived intimately with the human race. The ancient sages are equated with the prophets of the Old Testament; their wisdom is also due to the opening of inner vision, which brings them closer to heaven. The myth of the golden, Saturnian age as an eternal spring, eternal youth, and innocence suggests to Swedenborg a general law of nature, that "everything begins with spring and blossoms, with childhood and a time of innocence." By considering the primeval myths, he feels moved "to consider the phenomena of the universe, how it is reflected in individual things, and to recognize the destiny of the ages." He entreats the grace and consent of God for this undertaking, "the sole source of wisdom and the supreme sun, from which all truths flow like rays into our thoughts."

The creation of the universe, which forms the content of the first book, includes an exposition of the ancient myths of the world-egg, which Swedenborg daringly links with the biblical story of creation. He sees in the world-egg myth a confirmation of the theory advanced in *First Principles of Natural Things* that all the planets and moons were formed by an explosion of the solar mist, which surrounded the solar core like a crust. Even his description of the development of the individual realms of life, within which the plant kingdom arose from the mineral kingdom and the animal kingdom from the plant kingdom, transforms the evolutionary theory of the *First Principles of Natural Things* into mythical events, whereby the successive orders of life arise from each other like eggs hatched by the sun. All objects and processes of nature are transformed into living figures and scenes. After the creation of the plant kingdom, the earth steps forth like a young bride, in a dress adorned with the most beautiful rosebuds, a garland of rare flowers upon her head, and invites the inhabitants of heaven into her wedding chamber to taste her first fruits. From the vernal warmth of the sun, the trees and the herbs of the earth receive new generative powers and produce eggs, from which the various species of animals emerge.

This mythical notion of all life's originating out of an egg also determines the creation of the first man. Here Swedenborg develops the richest poetic imagination, all the while inspired by ideas acquired through his studies of the organic world and the human organism.

After the animal kingdom had developed the most varied worms, the earth reached "the middle of its spring." All creatures brought their natural talents as wedding presents, in order to celebrate the communal spring festival. All heaven and earth stood revealed to the eye of vision, yet the creature possessing this eye of vision had not been created. "The one who could relate all these joys of the senses to his own personality, that is, to his own consciousness and way of seeing things, and who could have coined the concept of beauty from all these harmonies, he was still missing." "The son of earth or reason in human form was still missing, he who could look up to heaven from his earthly paradise and down to earth, and as it were combine both with an inner sight. By linking both, he could experience the fullness of all joy, and from this original source of joy and love he could honor and worship above all things the giver and creator of all gifts." This is the fundamental theme: the human, the personal spiritual being, "reason in human form," is the creature in which creation is reunited in free adoring love with the Creator. He is the creature, in which life, having individuated on the lower levels of nature in many varied forms of life, turns back in its spiritual form to God the Creator. The nature of humankind is here described as the Adamic intellect was treated in the prologue to the *First Principles of Natural Things*. What was an object of abstract speculation in his earlier work should now be described as a living view of things. The archetypal human appears before Swedenborg's inner vision as a living being, whose origin and development is praised in a hymn to the waxing and waning of divine life. Humankind is the figure in which the created universe is reunited with God and returns to its origin, the highest creative reason, in a vision of the lower and upper world, and so "the cycle predetermined from eternity comes full circle."

In the most temperate region of the earth, Swedenborg relates, there was a grove of fruit trees through which clear brooks flowed, a "paradise in paradise." In its center stood a fruit tree bearing an egg, the most precious thing ever, in which nature had concentrated her highest powers as in a jewel. It concealed within itself the elements of the most perfect corporeality, a "sacred little Ark of all nature's treasures and merits." The Supreme Mind approached this work of nature; and by concentrating its rays, it fashioned out of itself a transcendent figure, the soul, which it lowered into the egg. Thus came about the first marriage of the spiritual essence with the most subtle aura of nature, "in order that the cycle of causes, created from the eternal in the great world-egg and brought down to this smallest egg, should come full circle within nature. Through its link with eternity, it becomes itself eternal, and thus the terrestrial forecourt is linked with the heavenly chamber." As soon as the soul inspires the egg, it immediately begins to envisage its predetermined end with pure ideas and to imagine the universe, and not just the universe of nature, but also that of heaven with its intelligences. It burns with a holy desire to descend "on winged sandals" from its height to the lower atmosphere, the terrestrial paradise, in order to drown its senses in the marvels of this earth and then rise to heaven to tell of the beauties of the terrestrial universe. Nature satisfies its longing; for nature is created for this purpose, and her desire to be the instrument of souls and spiritual beings is thus fulfilled.

With the aid of nature, the soul now constructs for itself a microcosmic body on the model of the Supreme Mind. The soul forms the highest cognitive center of the human being as a mirror of heaven, "a kind of Olympus" in human form, which is intended as the dwelling place of the intelligences and their servants, the sciences. It then forms the tissues and fibers of an organic body with entrails and members and "so fashions the winged sandals or rather the steps, in order to descend from its seat on the highest watchtowers of nature to their base in terrestrial paradise." The descent of the soul is the path of its incarnation. All nature collaborates in this event: the surrounding trees feed their sap to the tree bearing the wonderful egg. The sun approaches, mitigating its heat by shining its rays through the fruits of the trees. Like attentive guardians, the surrounding trees stretch out their arms to carry the burden of the leafy mother. Heaven is present in its mercy: its inhabitants, the spirits, keep watch that no wild animal shall disturb the ripening of the egg. The animals approaching the tree "fall on their knees, as if they wished to worship their prince and Lord."

In the fullness of time, the branch with the egg sinks slowly to the earth. The fetus bursts the prison of its shell and steps spontaneously into the world of paradise, for which it had yearned from the first moment of its life. With his nose and chest, the child inhales the air, greeting it with a light kiss, and fills his inner chambers with the new spirit of life. The whole of nature celebrates the birth of the first-born man. The most choice flowers breathe out their fragrance, and heavenly choirs conclude the scene with resonant dancing lights, while their flames prevent any other lights from shining the first ray upon the newborn.

Swedenborg describes the child by amplifying his ideas on physiognomy and the relationship of corporeality and the soul, already seen in the soul's formation of the human body. The corporeality of the child is the perfect image of his soul. "In its form his face so completely harmonized with the idea of his spirit or soul that every fiber reflected a ray of its glory and simultaneously stood out, so that the spirit revealed itself in human form." The image of God is even apparent in the physiognomy of the first-born. His corporeality is so impressionable that it reflects the subtlest stirrings of the soul. Thus "the soul drives the tender body as a kind of generator, which develops its powers for all it must accomplish." The tender child, the small son of the highest ruler of the world, grows up with the collaboration of nature under the protection of heavenly spirits to whom he is entrusted.

Swedenborg's own visionary experiences are mingled in the description of the child's spiritual growth. Just as Swedenborg had felt the influence of heavenly intelligences deep in his soul through his illuminations, the heavenly spirits not only surround the child outwardly but penetrate into the most secret corners of his soul. "Nothing in nature can resist them. They are in the Highest and also in the Innermost; indeed they can even enter into community and conversation with the soul and the reason." They enter the inner Olympus, the seat of the intelligences of humankind, and admire the spiritual microcosm of the first-born, which analogously reflects within itself the starry firmament. "One could believe that the heavens had served in miniature as a model and are replicated here in a tiny, concentrated form."

The heavenly powers hold a festival to celebrate the first day of humankind. The intelligences perform a dance in the round. They lead the reason of the first-born in a continuous spiral movement from the outermost circle to the innermost. "United with him, forming as it were a divine spirit in their concord," they show him to the Highest One, who sees the end and purpose of his works in the first-born and greets him with signs of grace and favor. Swedenborg's own visionary experience again colors the description of Adam's first encounter with his divine image. The archetypal man is so overjoyed by this vision that "his lungs forgot to breathe, because the spirits of his fibers had fainted in amazement and love. And when he had been led back to the edge of the dance, the wings of his lungs

beat with such joyful, frequent and strong breaths that their movements imitated the last rhythms of the heavenly powers' games."
Swedenborg thus described the physiological state of the archetypal
man at his first vision according to his own experience of how illuminations were attended by a faltering in his outer breath.

But the first-born still lives under the gaze and full control of the
soul, still unaware of his corporeality, in direct and unconscious realization of his *anima*. "For the soul regards everything according to
the purpose and principles of nature, and thus it always works in its
body in accordance with the most secret and inner principles of
causes and effects." It moves the body like the power that drives a
wheel, wholly according to its will; it portrays itself in the form of
the body and forms an image of itself. The senses and intellectual attributes of the human being are then further created under the supervision of the soul. Only now does the individual's consciousness
begin to form. The images of the visible world, which receive their
form from sunlight, are first transformed by the soul into material
and then into intellectual ideas. The soul stores these ideas in the
memory, and they give birth to the soul's own intelligences. The
soul brings them up and shares with them her own light and love.
They form the *mens*, the mind of the newborn. After the newborn
has grown up and has become conscious of himself in his mind, the
soul lays down its sceptre in favor of the *mens*. The soul withdraws to
its dwelling in the cerebellum, whence it directs the unconscious
functions of the organism, while the *mens* rules in the cerebrum.

The youth, awakened to self-consciousness, now converses with
his intelligences, which surround him in the form of nymphs. He is
appointed their king and holds contests of wisdom among them.
However, he cannot learn from them the source of all good and useful things flowing into his brain. He notices that this influx does not
come to him through the senses but along another secret inner path.
Once again the inner experiences of the first-born reflect Swedenborg's own experience. While the youth ponders the origin of goodness and truth so deeply that he almost loses his reason and throws
the dwellings of the intelligences into confusion, he is suddenly entranced by a "full vision." He sees his wisdoms sitting in the lap of

Supreme Love and his intelligences conversing with divine spirits surrounding Supreme Love.

Now he recognizes the true sanctuary, whence the rays emanate to illuminate his inner world. He is seized by a violent longing to hear the highest truth from the mouth of Supreme Love. His fervent wish finds a favorable hearing. He is snatched up to the lap of Supreme Love amidst the choir of the holy beings surrounding her. As he attempts to throw himself to the earth in holiest reverence, he hears the words spoken to him: "My son, I love both you and your wisdoms. My ears tell me—for I hear everything that you say—how much you long to know whence the goodness stems that you perceive and whence it flows into the sphere of your spirit. This I will teach you from my own breast. Seek no further for the source: you are sitting at its true heart. Understand that the love with which you embrace me comes from me. I make you feel it in yourself. Fill and nourish your spirit with the good things, which flow from this source, my little brother." After this instruction by Supreme Love, a thick veil falls over the sight of the first-born. He feels himself brought back to the place where he was enraptured and experiences his returning natural vision as an oppressive fog.

Adam's ecstasy clearly recalls Swedenborg's own vision of Christ. Supreme Love is the Son, the "big brother," the figure in which God personally represents himself in the form of his love. Swedenborg had seen himself enraptured in the lap of the Son and looked him in the face. Supreme Love had spoken to him and taught him about the origin of goodness and truth. Now he translates Adam into the lap of Supreme Love and shows how the first-born receives information about the origin of truth and goodness from the mouth of Love. Simultaneously, Love warns the first-born—Swedenborg experienced this himself also—to drink from the spring of self-love and allows him to glimpse its own heavenly paradise, of which the terrestrial paradise of the first-born is but a shadow and reflection. Even the end of the vision matches Swedenborg's own experiences. He felt "as when we are moved from the brightest light into the shadow." In desperation, the first-born finds himself once again in his former place and believes he has fallen down from heaven. But one of his wisdoms comfort him: he still abides in the lap of God, and it is only a veil before his eyes that stops him seeing heaven. Heaven is in our own inner world, in the soul; but we only become aware of it once the light of the soul has shone into the mind.

Here Swedenborg prophetically describes the state he hopes to attain in the future. In his own vision of Christ, he had seen heaven in a short inspiring flight of rapture and had sat in the lap of Supreme Love. However, afterwards he experienced how a veil sank over his eyes and how the heavenly power of vision deserted him. He also had the sensation of falling down from heaven, but new experiences gave him the comforting awareness that the link with Supreme Love was not broken. He now hoped for the day and hour when the light of heaven would shine into his inner world again. Then his *anima*, the image of the Son, would sink into his mind and open his inner vision into the heavenly world forever as a permanent form of sight. Thus, he interpreted his final vision of vocation in the light of his earlier visionary experiences. This interpretation also typified his view of humanity's spiritual evolution.

In portraying the further development of the first-born, Swedenborg gives a mythical and speculative description of his own religious crisis, whose individual scenes were made clear to him in oppressive and rapturous dreams and visions. The first-born is visited by heavenly beings, whom he has previously seen in the company of his intelligences. They come in the form of naked girls, whose hair is pinned up in a bun with golden needles. They wear precious stones upon their brow and are linked together by garlands of flowers. They portray the secrets of planetary movements in the heavenly dances they perform in circles and spirals around his bier. In conversation with these wisdoms—Swedenborg interpreted the female figures of his dreams as such heavenly wisdoms—Adam learns about the dual influence that our human soul is subject to in the heavenly and natural sun. Here one sees for the first time the metaphysic of love, which forms the basis of all Swedenborg's later visionary theology. There are two kinds of love, the divine kind, which draws us upward, and the worldly, which alienates us from the divine. They both meet in our mind, which becomes their battleground. Here Swedenborg begins to weave in old theological speculations about the origin of evil and its conquest by divine love. God himself made a source of unending life in the natural world and created a lord of this world with subject spirits. But this spiritual prince was misled into arrogance and selfishness by the great power granted to him and rebelled against God and his only-begotten Son. His two captains are self-love and love of the world, who rule over countless commanders, governors, and chieftains, whose dominion extends over the various empires, provinces, and estates of this world, and who implicate the souls in the rebellion against God, namely, Supreme Love. With a single wave, God could have destroyed the universe with all its worlds and thrown the tyrant with all his subject souls into the storm. Burning with righteous anger, God had already armed himself with his thunderbolts, to crash down upon the tyrant and all rebellious humankind. But at the very moment when he wants to hurl his thunderbolts—O, wonders!—his only-begotten Son throws himself between them and embraces the human souls, willing to let himself be torn to pieces by the raging hound of hell rather than hand them over. The Almighty then lowers his thunderbolts. At the request of his Son to spare the naive and innocent beings until they have run their course, the Father promises to spare the world until it has run its course and perished like its mortal inhabitants in winter and night. At the same time, he gives the Son the power to bind and loose the tyrant and enemy of God as he wishes. The power of the devil has been limited ever since, but now death had entered the life of the human children.

Thus, the metaphysical drama of the battle between God and the devil, heavenly love and mundane self-love, is played out on the stage of world events and our soul. Our soul represents the Almighty and reigns like a goddess in her microcosm, which lives through and out of her. The mind with its will and reason is a reflection of love or the only-begotten Son of the Highest One. But natural life is the dominion of the prince of the world, who seeks to conquer the higher centers, to extend his power over the whole spiritual universe of humankind, and to banish God. As long as our self-love does not invade the higher levels of our inner life and seize the sceptre, we are united with God, and the prince of the world cannot harm us but lies completely in our power. Adam himself experienced what Swedenborg saw in his dreams. The captured prince of the world was forced to appear before his eyes and to assume the shapes of all the monsters, in which he is accustomed to deceive the human race. Just as he had appeared in Swedenborg's dreams, he appeared to Adam as a dog, a dragon, a flame, and a lion, whom the first-born grabs in his teeth and claws with encouragement from the heavenly wisdom.

The second part of the work describes the creation, education, and marriage of Eve in a metaphysical paean to love, in which Swedenborg sketches a mythical and philosophical view of marriage, later documented in his work *Conjugial Love*. The first-born once fell asleep in a grove, in whose center stood a magnificent tree, identical in growth and beauty to the Tree of Life. In his sleep there appeared to him a virgin, beautiful in face and body, at the sight of whom he was so inflamed "by a kind of sympathetic warmth," that a gentle fire suddenly glowed in all his loosened fibers. He tries to embrace her, but she escapes him like a shimmering cloud. In his attempt to arrest her flight, he strains his chest cavity so much that it seems as if a rib is torn out of him. When he finally catches her and covers her mouth with kisses, he suddenly awakes and sadly realizes that it was just a dream. However, a mysterious, real process corresponded to the dream. He did not know that the fruit tree, beneath which he was sleeping, was the counterpart of his own mother tree and that it bore an egg, from which his future wife will be born. It was she who appeared to him in the dream. He embraced her egg in sleep and breathed life and soul from his own soul into it through his kiss. In vain he tries to fall asleep again, in order to hold onto the lovely experience, but he feels that he has seen something, whose consequences he will later discover.

The first-born had breathed the soul into the egg with his fiery embrace. Now the soul begins to weave its own body in the fertilized egg, and Eve is born from this egg. She also grows up under the guidance of the heavenly powers. Her spiritual life is also reflected in the form of her body; her ideas, wishes, and thoughts are directly mirrored in her face, where they can be read like handwriting. Through an experience like that of Narcissus, she becomes conscious of herself. When once by chance she bent over the crystal-clear surface of a spring, she saw to her amazement an image and face on the water, which made the same movements as herself. "When she looked more closely, she recognized her own ivory-colored breast, her arms and hands" and began to understand that she was looking at her own image. She now saw in the image of her face everything she was thinking of in her mind, her own amazement and her thoughts about the reflection, and she marveled that all the secrets of her soul were so clear to see in the image before her. In confusion, she hurried to her guardians, who explained to her the secret connection between soul, mind, and corporeality and what they teach us about their inner and outer properties and purpose in the world. Here Swedenborg borrows features of his own intuitive experiences to elucidate those of Eve. In order to memorize the surprising thoughts, she holds her breath.

The heavenly guardians instruct Eve by showing her how all spiritual creatures are created in accordance with the laws of heaven. Here Swedenborg sketches a state for which he so greatly longed himself and which he already glimpsed in fleeting moments of rapture. "They live in constant inspiration. For through the love of heaven, the path is opened on high in their inner world, from the soul to reason, and from reason to the soul. They are constantly receptive to the heavenly light of understanding and to the heavenly fire of wisdom." The other path, however, the lower path between the life of the senses and reason—the path on which Swedenborg had seen himself previously directed in his life and his science—"is so bolted and locked that there is scarcely a chink through which nature can enter. For the door of reason can only be opened outwards, so that the heavenly light can flow into the natural light, but the natural light can never flow backwards and mingle with the heavenly light. The insights of the true and the truth of goodness flow from their source through the single pure vein down to nature, but they cannot return in the same vein to their source until they have been cleansed of all impurity."

The heavenly ones finally tell the astonished virgin about her future husband. They arrange her flowing hair into a bun and clasp it in a golden ring and place a diamond crown upon her head. When the young bride, "who did not yet understand her destiny, nor know what a wedding was or what it meant to share a man's bed" caught a glimpse of her intended, her face became rose red. "Thus

she transformed herself into the image of a naked heavenly grace."
The first-born recognizes with joy the image of his dream, which he
has tried to recall to memory a thousand times. "I see clearly that she
is mine," he says to himself, "for she comes from my own breast and
my own life." One of the heavenly intelligences nods to him that he
should approach. Here ends the second part.

The third, unfinished part describes the marriage of the first couple and begins with a poetic description of the wedding night, in
which the whole universe strives to beautify the hour of their union.
"With this promising start there began in both a new life, which distinguished itself from the earlier life, even if they did not yet grasp
the difference. From now on, nothing should please the one without
producing the same emotion in the other and uniting their joys in
mutual agreement and sympathy, so that the artery of pleasure
flowed into a single heart divided into two chambers. It united there
in a common stream, in which neither of the two knew a pleasure,
without simultaneously feeling that of the other."

A sublime play appears before the lovers' eyes in the morning.
After they have rediscovered themselves in each other, the whole
universe with all its marvels introduces itself to them. "In the early
morning, when the dawn sent the rays of the rising sun like golden
arrows into the vault of heaven, the two awoke from the sweetest
slumber upon their marriage bed. A kind of heavenly flash shone
above their eyes and drew their attention from each other. In the
middle of the sky, a phenomenon appeared, which showed the universe with all its fates and ordinances; the two saw this as in the
broad light of day." There follows a poetic description of the universe in seven pictures, which represent the stages of its development
and the inner structure of the upper and lower world. It begins with
a vision of the spiritual sun, whose light is so strong that the lovers
must close their eyes. Through closed lids, they can still perceive
how the sun spreads its rays through the whole universe. Then they
see how the whole of creation grows out of this center. Finally, there
rises from the middle a human figure, in which all creative energy
condenses and rises up to heaven. Even these pictures reflect
Swedenborg's visionary experiences. Several of his later visions of the
heavenly sun are described in a similar fashion as morning visions, in

which he first sees the beaming light only through closed eyelids. His later ideas included the "Universal Human," who formed heaven and combined in himself the communities of spiritual beings of heaven, as well as his doctrine about the humanity in God, represented in a personal human form. It is quite clear here that these ideas clearly do not derive from a theoretical extension of the old mystical idea of the human being as the microcosm, but from a vision in which the macrocosmic human, the primal figure of divine humankind appeared to him.

After contemplating this sublime vision, the newlyweds begin a conversation, in which they try to explain the meaning of what they have seen. The themes of these conversations largely repeat what has been shown in the preceding story of creation. In these conversations, the newlyweds come to an intellectual understanding of the marvels of the heavenly and terrestrial worlds. The factual, progressive sequence in the first part of the work is now inwardly understood by the couple. They learn that it is a person's destiny to worship the Creator of the universe in free love and that "man is nearer to worship, the more he is united in love with the Creator." The work breaks off in the middle of the explanation of the vision.

We do not know how Swedenborg thought of completing the work. Should the account of the wedding of the first couple have continued with a metaphysical and mythical interpretation of the Fall and the expulsion from paradise, as in Milton's *Paradise Lost*? Or should the work close with a hymn to the wonders of creation seen through the eyes of the first people and a panegyric to their loving reunion with their Creator? Swedenborg broke off under the impact of his vision of God in April 1745. Now he experienced illumination in the form which he had already described as the highest form of understanding in his work on the archetypal human. This special knowledge had already been anticipated in his doctrine of the inner structure of humanity's spiritual personality. Now he felt translated into the state that Adam once had known and for which he had so longed during his visionary experiences. Now he saw the veil lifted from his eyes. The soul streamed into his mind, and he saw heaven with his spiritual eye in ceaseless intuition.

The new work, to which he now turned, took up the same theme that had shortly before been the subject of his poetic and mythical vision: the prehistory of the universe and humankind. But he no longer treated this with that unique blend of intuition, personal visionary experience, and poetic fantasy, or with this strange mixture of biblical creation story and ancient mythology. Now the clarification ensued; his mission stood clearly before him. His calling is the revelation of the inner meaning of the biblical Word with the aid of visions and auditions, which stream down upon him from a contemplation of the spiritual world. Thus, his first visionary work after his vocation is a commentary on the biblical story of creation. The awakening of his visionary gift in its final form superseded the awakening of his poetic and speculative imagination. The poet was awakened before the visionary, the poetic imagination before the visionary sight. In this first phase, the concepts and realities of his scientific period are transformed into mythical figures, the processes of nature into mythical encounters, his ideas into graces, and the movements and laws of thought into the dances of heavenly nymphs. In the second phase, it is spirits and angels who speak to him and proclaim the inner sense of the divine Word.

21

Early Visionary Writings

The eye needs some preparation before entering the wonderful world of Swedenborg's vision. What literary form did his visionary gifts assume in the first works following his conversion? The difference from his earlier works must be particularly obvious in the writings first describing his new insights. The images of the higher world glimpsed by his newly opened eye must be painted in especially powerful colors; they must resonate with the movement of his mind and the exultation of his prophetic mission.

Two works are primarily considered here: the *Adversaria* of 1745 and the *Spiritual Diary*, which appeared in several parts from 1747 onwards. Swedenborg wrote the first work after his vocation as an exegesis of the biblical story of Creation and several other texts from the Old Testament. *Adversaria* was first published by Johann Friedrich Tafel in Tübingen between 1842 and 1853.[1] It has received little scholarly attention until now, as it was printed so late

---

1. For biographical details, see Theodor Müllensiefen, *Leben und Wirken von Dr Johann Friedrich Immanuel Tafel, Professor der Philosophie und Universitätsbibliothekar zu Tübingen* (Basle, 1868). Swedenborg's *Explicatio in Verbum historicum Veteris testamenti* has been translated into English as *The Word of the Old Testament*

and does not present Swedenborg's ideas with the same systematic clarity as his later theological writings. However, this biblical work has the greatest importance for Swedenborg's development. In many respects, it helps one understand his later attitude and doctrine, especially his prophetic persona in this early period of his visionary writing. As the history of Christianity shows, the basic form of visionary literature is a first-person account of some experience or a religious autobiography. "My name is John. . . . It was the Lord's day and the Spirit possessed me, and I heard a voice behind me, shouting like a trumpet"—so begins the revelation of St. John. "The Spirit seized me and carried me through a wild desert. When I began to pray, the heavens opened"—thus Hermas begins the report of his visions. But Swedenborg does not begin his visionary writing with a free account of his experiences, but with a Bible commentary, the traditional genre of theological scholarship.

A Bible commentary from the pen of a man who claims the portals of heaven have parted and God himself has opened his inner vision? Cannot the spirit of revelation express itself more eloquently in visionary terms than in the stale form of a Bible commentary? But this very fact expresses a characteristic feature of his mission. Swedenborg does not want to produce something of his "own" or something "personal." His revelations are not subjective experiences or private intuitions. Rather he feels that he is the harbinger of the one objective, unshakeable, and eternal truth, which has already been revealed in Holy Scripture. He feels he is called to disclose the secret eternal sense of the divine Word. Thus his new work is to be a humble service to the Word, the exposition, revelation, and communication of the hidden truth within the material, historical form of Scripture.

His method of revealing the hidden sense of Scripture is allegorical. It presupposes that every word, every figure, and every event in Holy Scripture "means" something, that it is charged with a higher, spiritual sense. Scriptural exegesis is thus transformed into the

---

Explained, trans. and ed. A. Acton, 9 vols. (Bryn Athyn, Pa.: Academy of the New Church, 1928–1951).

exposition of semiotics. A certain "spiritual sense" is attributed to the same words, persons, actions, objects, colors, and properties, so that the whole of Holy Scripture is overlaid with a network of such meanings.

This type of spiritual exegesis is as old as the exegesis of Christian Scripture. The close relation between the Old and New Testament came about because the Christians of the early Church saw the Christian gospel allegorically anticipated in the Old Testament. They understood the Old Testament as the preparation, exemplar and model for the New Testament beginning with Christ. In his letters, St. Paul allegorically expounded episodes and figures of the Old Testament and related them to Christ and the Church. But Paul was not the inventor of the allegorical method but the follower of a more ancient practice. In the second century BC, this practice flourished at the school of Alexandria among the interpreters of Homer and the ancient myths of the Greeks and Romans. Under the influence of this tradition, Philo of Alexandria, the learned Jewish commentator, expounded on the Old Testament. Origen, the leader of the Christian catechetical school in Alexandria, systematically applied the allegorical method to the Old and New Testaments in the third century, which became a standard practice for all scriptural exegesis in Western Christendom. The great German mystics such as Meister Eckhart—and even the young Luther—used this allegorical method to explain Scripture. The last example from the period before Swedenborg's commentaries was Jacob Boehme's *Mysterium Magnum*, which exhibits an astonishing formal and inner affinity with Swedenborg's *Adversaria*. In Boehme's case too, a special experience of vocation and the opening of his "sight" provided the religious motive for his mystical allegorization of the creation story. His exegesis was driven by an awareness of vocation, which resembled Swedenborg's in many respects.

Despite all these similarities, what distinguishes Swedenborg from his forerunners is that he always refers to visionary experiences, which continuously accompany his exposition, as proof of the correctness of his interpretation of Scripture and the "meanings" he adduces to the historical Word of the Bible. In his case, the interpretation of the hidden spiritual sense of the Word is linked with the opening of the world of spirits, heaven, and hell. He sees himself deemed worthy to keep company with angels, spirits, and the deceased. He sees the mysteries of divine revelation mediated not only through the letters of historical Scripture but through his own vision and experience. Thus, he can illustrate his explanations of the true spiritual meaning of the historical Word with reports of what he has "seen and heard" in the world of spirits. The vision itself thus becomes a commentary and serves to illuminate the hidden sense. His visionary gift is therefore a gift of grace to serve the exposition of the Word.

Let us consider the mystical experiences and first-person accounts in *Adversaria*. They are scattered unsystematically throughout the allegorical exposition of the Creation story, and it is difficult to deduce these personal experiences from the allegorical maze. Visionary report and exposition are never clearly separated but frequently mingle. Only in the later works did a certain method develop: the scriptural exposition at the beginning, intermittently followed by a visionary report under the title "Memorabilia," in which the preceding exposition is clarified on the basis of things "seen and heard." The *Adversaria* does not offer this schematic division, displayed with pedantic regularity in his later writings. It is evident from the numerous first-person accounts in the *Adversaria* how frequently Swedenborg speaks of his prophetic mission and the literal inspiration of his revelations. The work is completely sustained by the exultation of his vocation and his sense of being appointed to a holy office of revelation. Swedenborg therefore thinks it necessary to define this kind of revelation more closely.

First, it is not God himself who speaks to Swedenborg; rather, inspiration comes to him through intermediaries of various kinds: sometimes they are angels, sometimes spirits, sometimes deceased persons. Among the latter, it is the great figures of the Old and New Testament, the patriarchs, the apostles, and the evangelists who play the most important role.

Second, Swedenborg enumerates various degrees of intensity in his revelations and also various degrees in their certainty. This religious peculiarity appears logically meaningless in the first instance, for logic recognizes no gradations of truth. However, religious experience does make this distinction between the various degrees of divine corroboration and their levels of certainty.

Swedenborg claims that the whole of *Adversaria* was inspired by God. If this were true, then logically everything in it would have to be "true." Nevertheless, he notes at numerous places that this or that scriptural exposition is especially attested, for it was thus expressly and literally presented to him, while he admits that he is still in the dark concerning other pieces. He thus distinguishes various degrees of certainty, which depend on the influence of the spirits while he was writing the corresponding passage, as well as on the nature of these spirits themselves.

Writing of the influence of the spirits upon the human being in his exegesis of Genesis 31:12, Swedenborg says that they work from the inside of the person outwards. In the first place, they do not affect language but set the thoughts in motion, which then give rise to the spoken word. He then explains that his writings also came to pass through such an inner influence of the spirits. "Yes, I have even written whole pages, and the spirits did not just dictate the words, but wholly guided my hand and thus wrote themselves; they wrote what I have experienced, even that which I was not thinking, but what the spirits were thinking beyond what they were dictating."

He thereby justifies the inspiration of his writings on the grounds that the spirits are using him as a medium to write down spiritual truths. The instrumental function of the visionary extends so far that the spirits not only awaken thoughts in him but even dictate to him the particular words he should write and think. Ultimately, he becomes a mere instrument, whose hand the spirits guide to write down the truths, which he no longer even thinks. These words flow from the mind of the spirits through his hand, and he only understands them afterwards, when he reflects on what he has written.

However, there seem to have been few cases in which Swedenborg's ego is completely passive during the revelations. According to his statements, the customary form of writing down heavenly revelations involved his ego, insofar as he grasped the dictated words consciously and wrote them down independently, without the spirits "guiding his hand." Thus, he reports in his exegesis of Genesis 33:13: "This was written by my hand as a mere instrument; the Lord

Himself dictated it through the mediation of Abraham. In case men do not wish to accept this, he proclaims a heavy judgment on them although he constantly intercedes for them with the Lord. . . . This was written down by my hand and dictated by Isaac. I can swear a holy oath before God, that not a single word stems from me."

Such heavenly dictation should be distinguished from his records of the conversations he conducts with certain spirits. He writes these down afterwards in the manner of a heavenly reporter and also makes them known as special revelations. These records, including his own comments for and against, form the main component of his visionary reports, not only in the *Adversaria* but also in his later writings. Here one must imagine him immediately writing down such conversations on awaking from a visionary state on a special note. These were then continuously inserted into his work, wherever they made sense according to the context. In his exegesis of Genesis 41:1–49, he makes the following comment: "If it pleased God, I should here insert the conversation I had with the Jew yesterday, which was written down on a special sheet of paper."

The suggestions occur to him through the mediation of angels and spirits. Direct visions of God or Christ, as he experienced at his vocation, are later an exception. Swedenborg perceived that the mediation of his revelations by all kinds of intermediaries could cause doubt about their genuine divine origin and authenticity. He therefore thought it necessary to indicate that his revelations contained only suggestions commanded by the Lord and for which God used angelic mediators in order to give humankind certain knowledge of salvation. He even went so far as to distinguish expressly between heavenly working conversations and heavenly private conversations. He emphasizes in the context of a general explanation of his revelations in an exegesis of Genesis 37: 5 about Joseph's dream: "Yes, what is more, everything recorded here was written down in the presence of an assembly of several long-deceased persons, spirits and angels of God, and moreover, in such a way, that they conversed with me about these things both before and afterwards; but, for the time being, I should only add this: I would not have said anything here, which one of them had orally dictated to me. If this were the case—and this has occurred several times—I would have to strike it out forthwith. I may only write down what God directly gives me through their mediation and what became clear to me as such." According to his perception, the actual revelations do not derive from private conversations with angels and spirits, but from God himself. In *Adversaria*, Swedenborg asserts in his explanation of Moses' prophetic status that God himself is the ultimate author of his revelations and that the mediation of angels and spirits does not prejudice their authenticity and purity. Again and again, he compares God's summons of Moses and God's talks with the lawgiver of Sinai with his own vocation and the nature of his own revelations. The story of the summons in Exodus 3 moves him to comment on God's conversation with human beings with reference to "his own experience, which has now lasted for a whole year with scarcely an interruption." He then enlarges on this: "It is God alone, who speaks through the spirits and angels, for no one has life apart from him, and everything, be they angels or spirits or men, who live on earth, are only instruments. I have also experienced this in the course of a year." Boldly proceeding to his own prophetic status, he continues: "Not a single word that I produce and write down stems from me; this I can solemnly swear. If anyone, whether they be in heaven or on earth, ascribes even an iota of my writings, which are the truth, to me, they are doing God such an injustice, that no one can forgive, unless it be God himself." In his enthusiasm, he goes so far as to make a claim found among the ancient prophets: whoever disbelieves the revelation of the prophet, sins against God. Doubting the authenticity of Swedenborg's revelations is tantamount to a sin against the Holy Spirit.

But Swedenborg had another reason for concern that his revelations came through intermediaries. As it was a fundamental aspect of his prophetic status that he was a "servant of God" and an instrument for God's revelation to humankind, he was loath to grant the angels and spirits a greater role than himself in the mediation of revelations. Knowing he is only a humble instrument, he feels moved in various ways to exhort the spirits and angels to humility. He reminds them that they too are only instruments and not the authors of the divine revelations. Thus, he writes in his exegesis of Moses's summons by God: "Today I spoke with those who were around me about the fact that they and I were simply mere instruments and organs, as was never so plain."

Swedenborg also makes frequent reference to his prophetic status in the further exegesis of Exodus 6, discussing God's revelations to Moses: "Here one should note that many conversations (between God and Moses) go to and fro, as is usual when the Lord speaks with someone, but this conversation occurs through angels, as it did with me, and lasted for several days." In the exegesis of Exodus 34:4, he discusses the question whether it was God or Moses who wrote the Ten Commandments on the two tablets of stone. He answers this question by saying that Moses wrote them simply as the earthly instrument and organ of divine legislation and that God's power had moved his hands. "It has often happened to me that I was writing and my hand was touched by a higher power and sometimes clearly led to write down certain words. I have therefore said that these words were not written by me, but by one apart from me; sometimes I was also given to know by which angel of God these words were written down."

In the exegesis to Exodus 34:28, he says on the same theme: "One reads here, that Moses wrote the words of the covenant on tablets. Thus, one sees that there were certain words and that Moses wrote them, but his hand was directed by an angel. Several of my writings can also confirm this to you. For then my hand was clearly directed to write, and in such a way that the words seemed scarcely written down by my hand. My hands, fingers, eyes, legs, and body were directed in a physical way over a long period, and this often happened. If these things were reported out of context, it would surely cause the greatest amazement to inexperienced and incredulous people; but it must suffice to mention this in a general fashion and solemnly swear it."

All these statements in Swedenborg's first visionary writing betray his eager efforts to clarify the nature and source of his prophetic office. However, they also show the force of his prophetic enthusiasm, which remained with him until the end of his life and escalated in his final writings.

In *Adversaria*, Swedenborg also comments on the limits of his mission. Here he expresses an authentic experience, which recurs among many great visionaries in the history of Christian piety. St. Paul appends this report on his ecstasy in his second letter to the Corinthians 12: "He was caught up into paradise and heard things which must not and cannot be put into human language." Even the earliest commentators of this passage have understood these words in a double sense. Either he heard much that he could not utter, because it could not be grasped in human words; or he heard much that he did understand, but which he could not communicate because other men were not yet ready to grasp these mysteries. The prophet was granted an excess of revelation. These are the limits of prophecy. First, the whole abundance of visionary experience is not reducible to human words and concepts; and furthermore, the divine mysteries are not yet all intended for communication to contemporary humankind because men are not ready to understand them.

Swedenborg also discovered this twofold limit of prophecy. The whole of *Adversaria* is pervaded with accounts of experiences and visions, in which Swedenborg speaks of wonderful insights that he may not yet communicate. It may be that he cannot yet express them conceptually himself, or that God has forbidden him to communicate them, or that he instinctively knows that people of his time are not yet receptive to these revelations.

Swedenborg's caution in communicating his visions proves his authentic experience of the numinous. He experiences the transcendent as a power that is both supernatural and suprarational. The human senses and even the concepts of human reason and human language are insufficient to grasp the immeasurable, transcendental divine numen. Swedenborg makes special reference to the unintelligibility and superabundance of numinous experience, especially in his few visions of God. Thus in the exegesis of Exodus 25:1–2: "God is everywhere, but he is more so in the saints and with another potency than elsewhere. It was granted to me to experience myself this presence through the heavenly grace of God, once in a London square and at home in a Stockholm church. This presence is an inner movement of the mind, which cannot be described at all and which would convey nothing of the real experience if it was described with many words."

What is said here about the supreme experience of God's presence is also true of other experiences of the numinous in the world of spirits. Swedenborg observes in an exegesis of Exodus 28:2 concerning the language of the spirits in the highest heaven: "I can also attest of this language, that I have heard it in a state of waking sleep and that I have understood something of it; but when I thought about, I could not express it. But it cannot be spoken of in such a way that the intellect grasps it, for it lies above that realm." Here too the numinous appears as the ineffable, inaccessible to the reason, vision, and language of humanity. The expression *ineffabile* frequently occurs in his descriptions of the numinous. Especially in his description of the upper heavens, Swedenborg repeatedly speaks of such experiences, which surpass the highest concepts of his capacity to think and leave him in a state of utter amazement. This amazement can embrace two kinds of feeling: supreme joy in experiencing an ineffable heavenly blessing and abysmal terror in experiencing the overwhelming power, awesomeness, and holiness of God. This amazement proves that he has genuinely seen both the beneficent and the fearful aspect of the numen.

Thus Swedenborg writes in his exegesis of Isaiah 24:8 concerning the joys of heaven: "What heavenly joys are only he can know who has learnt it through the heavenly mercy of God. Because I have had this experience, indeed for a long time now, I can only say that they are unutterable; and if they can be uttered, then only their smallest part could be expressed, for one cannot describe them. No man, who has not had the experience himself, could believe this." But he even describes the experience of the fearful side of the numinous; we often see him filled with the fear of explaining it to others. In an exegesis of Jeremiah 50:13 concerning Babel and its destruction, he writes under the impression of terrible visions: "This had been revealed to me by a horde of hellish spirits. When I wrote this and the forgoing, they attacked me violently and instilled black poison into my thoughts, so that it could not be described. This occurred on 9 February 1747."

Numerous statements in *Adversaria* confirm that Swedenborg repeatedly had to wrestle with an excess of revelations and that his records are but a brief indication of what overwhelmed him in superabundance. In his exegesis of Genesis 32:10, he writes that the human race would not have human features but for the appearance of the Son of God and that evil spirits, who turn away from the Lord, lose their human face: "This was made known to me by many experiences. If I were to publish all this, it would fill many pages, indeed whole folio volumes, and it would all be experience, no theoretical speculations." In the exegesis of Genesis 38:24, he notes that all, even the smallest changes of mood, ultimately derive from God. He has experienced this almost continuously for a long time. This process of influx is more wonderful than one can imagine and put in words. "It is a matter of unutterable things, which, if published, would fill whole volumes."

Besides such general experiences of the superabundance of the numinous, Swedenborg also received precise instructions during his visions, which heavenly insights he should communicate to his contemporaries and which he should not. He sees his prophetic office constrained by a kind of higher planning. Not everything is for everybody, and not everything can be said at any time. In many cases, he expressly notes that he has a greater knowledge about this or that matter than he is allowed to say. In the exegesis of Genesis 40:14–15—he is speaking about the various kinds of heavenly language—he explains that he could not acquaint people with the various kinds of heavenly language because "these are so wonderful, that scarcely anyone would believe, if they were explained in detail." Dealing with the various forms of God's speech to human beings in Genesis 37:4, he says he does not want to speak of that here but will report on it elsewhere, "if God should deem me worthy to do this." Sometimes he interrupts the reproduction of conversations with heavenly beings with respect to the understanding of his reader, as in: "Moses said several things, which it is not permitted to append here." Similarly, he concludes the description of a mystical experience characterized as "banishment to the desert" with the words: "Several things befell me here, which I may not tell of, because they contain secrets." On his deathbed, he indicated to his priest, the Swedish pastor Ferelius: "I acknowledge that all my revelations are true and stem from the Lord, and I could have said still more, if I had been permitted" (Tafel, II, doc. 267 (a), pp. 557–558; LL, 87).

He also knew that his own mission within the soteriological advance of revelation was limited. He rarely stated this, except at the beginning of his visionary period. In his exegesis of Genesis 35:14, he wrote: "This was given unto me, but I fear to write it; therefore, it must be proclaimed by those who are permitted to communicate it." Here he evidently expected greater prophets to succeed him. But later he believed he was accomplishing salvation and that the Second Coming of Christ was realized in his writings.

The numerous personal data in *Adversaria* have a special feature in that they make two kinds of reference to time. First, Swedenborg gives the precise date when individual visions were granted to him. He was able to date his most important religious experiences and his registration of specific insights. This remained characteristic of his later work. Even in his final years, he remembers exactly on what occasion, at what time, and with what vision he understood individual teachings. Experiences and insights present themselves to Swedenborg's memory in the form of a spiritual diary, and he duly kept such a record in his *Memorabilia*.

Swedenborg also continuously noted in *Adversaria* how long he had remained in a state of spiritual understanding. These references begin with his vision of God in London in April 1745, which he perceived as his divine vocation. This opening of his visionary gift resonates powerfully through his first visionary work. It seems as if this vision of vocation is every minute before his inner eye as the measure and touchstone of his prophetic integrity. Following this vision, he always gives the date of any demonstration of his visionary gifts.

In the first volume of *Adversaria*, he writes that he is constantly conversing with angels, spirits and the deceased, "for more than eight months now, almost without interruption, save on my journey from London to Sweden, and then again uninterruptedly, while I am writing this work which will now be published." In a later section, giving an exegesis of Genesis 30:39, he says: "There are many, who say they could only credit what I write, if they were themselves permitted to enter heaven and speak with the risen dead. But I swear that, I have now conversed for eight months by the pure mercy and grace of God with those in heaven as if with friends here on earth, and almost without interruption. But this was not all, for I have also been instructed by them in such a fashion that the content of their teaching was attested by living examples and simultaneous discussion. Therefore, I would like to publish all these wonderful things, so that people will believe that I was both in heaven and simultaneously on earth among my friends from the middle of April 1745 to 29 January or 9 February, apart from the month I was traveling to Sweden, where I arrived on 19 August according to the old calendar." Here the date of the decisive London vision of vocation is given as a chronological marker.

References to the London vision of vocation in *Adversaria* are so common that one can even date the composition of its individual chapters. He continually appends to his reports of visions details of how many months his spiritual vision has now been opened. The longer this miracle lasts, the more he is amazed, and he is also increasingly astonished at how this newly gained higher world has become a second reality to him. Thus he writes of Genesis 36:20: "This must be well noted; I know this from several months' experience—nine to date—and indeed the daily frequency of such apparitions is so high that I cannot keep count." After several months have passed since penning his first revelations, he writes in the exegesis of Genesis 49:17–18: "In order that mortals should not fall into error and continually sink from life into death, heaven was opened to me through the heavenly mercy of God, so that I was permitted to converse for almost a whole year with the inhabitants of heaven and thereby gain experience in spiritual matters." In the exegesis of Exodus 23:1, he relates his conversations with the patriarchs of the Old Testament, which "have now lasted for fifteen months. All those with whom I have spoken in the meantime in Sweden will know that this is no fantasy." This exultation of his vocation is also apparent in the continuous datings of the second volume.

Adversaria thus confirms that Swedenborg's religious self-consciousness was wholly sustained by his London vision of vocation. It was the decisive, precisely dateable event of his life, giving all his subsequent action a higher meaning and sanction. It was the starting point of his mission, in which two elements of his vocation are linked: the revelation of the inner sense of Scripture and the opening of his vision into the spiritual world. The *Adversaria* also creates the main genre of his religious literature, namely, visionary commentary. *Arcana Coelestia*, written between 1747 and 1758, is also a visionary commentary on the first two books of Moses. *Apocalypse Explained*, which he wrote between 1757 and 1759, and *Apocalypse Revealed* (1766) are visionary expositions of the Book of Revelation "according to things seen and heard." By the end of the 1760s, these visionary commentaries were increasingly replaced by works in which Swedenborg presented his teachings as a systematic doctrine of the New Church rather than in the form of a running biblical commentary.

Besides this genre, there is a second form of his visionary literature. This is the chronological record of his *Spiritual Diary*, initially intended for only his own use, which is preserved in five volumes from the years 1747 to 1751 under the title *Memorabilia* and was published by Johann Friedrich Tafel between 1844 and 1847. This is a private diary of a special kind, which was not intended for publication. But one looks in vain here for longer entries giving daily impressions, events, personal information, and outlines of his own plans. It would also be mistaken to see the work as one of the numerous spiritual diaries of the pietistic tradition, in which sensitive souls effuse about the state of their heart, make confessions and improving observations, and spread their life before God according to a certain method of spiritual trial. Nor does one find in Swedenborg's diary references to living contemporaries, journeys, letters, the daily round, literary works, and whatever else one usually mentions in diaries.

Swedenborg's *Spiritual Diary* is better compared with Pascal's *Pensées*, for it contains a series of philosophical and theological sketches that may be regarded as fragments of a system of Christian metaphysics, philosophy of religion, and natural philosophy. But even the comparison with the *Pensées* is not wholly correct. Although much of this work consists of philosophical and religious observations, the main part is taken up with visions, dreams, ecstasies, illuminations, evidences, and inspirations. Both the philosophical aphorisms as well as the reports of visions and dreams are precisely dated and as a rule written down immediately or at least on the day of their occurrence. The *Spiritual Diary* therefore offers a surprising insight into the multiform world of Swedenborg's religious life and demonstrates through an unbroken chain of visionary experiences the unique background of his theological thought.

In the first place, these notes make manifest the living religious basis of his doctrine. Whatever is published in abstract and schematic form in his doctrinal writings appears here in its original context of religious experience. His thoughts and doctrines are developed here in direct reference to individual visions, whose mood and emotional content is still resonant. The experiential basis of his religious thought is especially evident here. This is particularly true of notes where fundamental ideas are developed in connection with an angelic conversation or a vision in the spiritual world.

There are frequent references to which of his thoughts have sprung from a direct illumination. Such notes are entitled "Written down in the presence of angels" or "Recorded with agreement of the spirits" or "Written in the gleam of the heavenly light." One is thus reminded that Swedenborg's system is not based on abstract speculation but was constantly nourished by authentic religious experiences, which represent the living element of his thought.

The visions described in the *Spiritual Diary* are more abundant, colorful and emotional than those mentioned in the doctrinal writings. The visionary reports, which Swedenborg presented from time to time as "Memorabilia" at the end of individual chapters in his exegetical or systematic works, frequently have a schematic character; stylistically often colorless, they reflect the preceding learned discussions and are devoid of their original emotional content and authentic color. By contrast, the notes in the diary communicate the direct colorful impact that the visionary experience exercised on the inner senses and leaves a fresh image, rich in surprising details, which does not lack extravagant and burlesque features. Swedenborg wrote here without any of the caution he employed in those works intended for publication. In short, the diary contains the original form of his visions, which he then stylized and polished for his printed works.

But the reports of the diary also distinguish themselves through the abundance of their contents from the accounts in his printed commentaries or doctrinal writings, where the visions are basically described as downright monotonous events. Here he describes how he "is in the spirit" and then sees and hears things that confirm the doctrine just presented. By contrast, the diary offers an insight into the incredible diversity of religious experience. The most varied kinds of illumination, rapture, "being in the spirit," ecstasy, and vision of images appear in juxtaposition; indeed, there are also precise details concerning the time and place of the events. He also records the outer circumstances, whether he had a vision while asleep or awake, and if so whether sitting, lying down, or walking, in the morning or at night. He records physical pains that accompany the individual manifestations, the sensations of taste, smell, and touch he had—things highly significant for the peculiarity of his experiences, which remain largely unmentioned in the printed memorabilia.

The individual notes in the diary are precisely dated, even down to the time of day and hour. This applies not only to the visionary experiences but to all his notes of philosophical thoughts and certain intuitions and evidences. Whatever is communicated in the doctrinal works in a well-ordered, systematic structure is expressed in the diary as a spiritual history with all its tensions, upsets, tragedies, and catastrophes. The dates are informative for relating details to larger contexts. It is evident, for example, that certain thoughts appear more frequently, repeat themselves and intensify throughout a definite period, and reach a certain clarification. Even the connections between specific groups of visions and specific cycles of thoughts in a period can be clearly recognized, as well as the emotions, mood, and physical state of health from which certain trains of thought developed. This is a fruitful field of study for a psychologist.

The diary entries also allow the various shades of Swedenborg's experiences and insights to be graded according to their certainty. Some notes are the result of chance thoughts, some unexpected intuition, some a direct revelation claiming an authoritative validity, some a communication from angels that carry the highest degree of certainty and some as the whispering of spirits, whereby Swedenborg remains uncertain whether this is a matter of temptation or demonic deception. Even the inner connection of individual thoughts is informative. Swedenborg frequently returns to an object of reflection that he has already discussed. Under the impression of new visions and more abundant evidence, he develops new aspects of an earlier idea or makes further unexpected inferences on the basis of earlier insights. Here also the diary gives a much richer and more varied picture than his exegetical and dogmatic works, in which much of the vividness and originality of his visions is lost.

The notes therefore reveal the personal note, the individual color, emotional state, and shade of Swedenborg's world of experience and ideas and offer the most stimulating starting point for any acquaintance with Swedenborg's visionary theology. They portray the visionary in a state of evolution, not yet a hostage to his own system, which later became the case. His own insights are still new to him, and he is investigating their concealed mysteries, while his later works present the greatest miracles of inner life in a normalized conceptual language, repetitive in its monotony, and parceled in numbered paragraphs.

There is finally another aspect of this personal note in the *Spiritual Diary*. However discrete Swedenborg may otherwise be in naming and judging recently deceased persons in his visions, and however general and anonymous is his polemic in his doctrinal works against current trends in philosophy, science, and theology, his attitude in these private notes is correspondingly personal, acute, and frank. In his other writings, reports on historical personalities only seldom surface, and even then they are long dead, such as Luther, Calvin, or Leibniz. But in his diaries, there are copious reports of conversations with recently deceased acquaintances among the political heads of Europe and their cabinets or from the world of contemporary science and theology. These notes are often anything but flattering, as already seen in the case of Hjärne or Polhem. However, their sharp critical tone and the detailed description of the bizarre fate that Swedenborg sees his acquaintances suffering in the world of spirits, enables one to know Swedenborg's views more clearly than is the case in the impersonal account of his thoughts. On the basis of these notes, one can be sure that Swedenborg is talking about specific historical personalities, wherever he obliquely refers in his printed commentaries and doctrinal works to encounters with "a famous figure among recent Churchmen," "a Saxon dictator of the evangelicals," or "a leader from the school of naturalists."

22

Swedenborg's Visions

Science has no trouble playing the part of the famulus Wagner in Goethe's *Faust*, "the dry intriguer spoiling the fullness of the visions." Visionaries of Swedenborg's type can seduce the scientific observer into a merely psychiatric interpretation. Nothing is more tempting, nothing more simple than to treat his visions as phenomena deriving from "an abnormal mental state" and thus "explicable" in terms of psychopathology. Our modern age protects itself so fearfully from all irruptions of the transcendent that it not only would send contemporary representatives of an "abnormal" mental state to the madhouse but would also like to stigmatize in retrospect all earlier possessors of "abnormal" spiritual abilities as psychopaths. They could thus be delivered retrospectively to the mental asylum, and our modern age could even protect itself from the troubling spirits of the past who disturb our rational world picture and could thus upset our extremely insecure self-confidence.

The author of this book is no psychiatrist and would not wish to comment on its methodology. However, he rejects such analysis because one fact clearly emerges from the lives of such religious figures as Luther, Zinzendorf, and Boehme. However clinically justified it may be to explain religious experience as psychopathology, such an explanation ignores the cultural, artistic, literary, or social achievement that derived from this abnormal mental state. The ingeniousness of a person and the spiritual value of intellectual achievement do not depend on whether the achievement sprang from a normal or abnormal mental state. In the area of religion, a realm of incomprehensible encounters with the transcendent, unleashing enormous inner tensions, breakdowns, transformations, and rebirths, the border between normal and abnormal mental states and achievements is highly fluid. Neither St. Paul's vision of Christ nor that of St. Bernard of Clairvaux nor St. Francis' experience of the stigmata nor Luther's experience in the tower nor the apparitions of Ignatius of Loyola sprang from a "normal" spiritual state; yet all five caused profound transformations in the intellectual and social condition of the West. The psychiatric "explanation" of religious geniuses is often merely the translation of this phenomenon into current clinical jargon derived from the observation of the mentally ill.

To be sure, Swedenborg did exhibit various signs that recall the symptoms of schizophrenia. But can one explain Swedenborg's visionary experience and his whole doctrine by characterizing it as schizophrenic? And would this be an objective judgment of Swedenborg's extraordinary influence on the intellectual history of the English-speaking and Scandinavian countries, especially on German Romanticism, German idealistic philosophy, and European literature from Goethe to Balzac and Strindberg? We do not reject a psychopathological interpretation of Swedenborg's personality, but we leave that to the specialists. We will concentrate on describing the various types of visionary experience that Swedenborg recorded and demonstrate their connection with his theology.

Swedenborg established and systematized the possibility and occurrence of visionary states in the most precise way. He therefore takes his place in the tradition of great Western mystics, from Hugh of Saint-Victor (c. 1096–1141) and St. Bernard (c. 1090–1153), even St. Augustine, to the German, French, Spanish, and English mystics of the seventeenth and eighteenth centuries. They all developed a mystical theology to explain their own visionary experiences and theoretically grounded their vision of the transcendent world in a mystical psychology. The mystics have therefore been most important stimuli for Western spiritual teaching.

The recipient of such extraordinary spiritual experiences is highly motivated to reconstruct the incident rationally, to clarify what it was, how it could occur, its consequences, and the preconditions for a possible recurrence. An innate instinct of human nature thus leads from religious experience to a doctrine of God and the human soul.

In the link between religious experience and doctrine, it can be occasionally seen how the derivative intellectual scheme reacts upon the religious experience itself. Once reflective thought has established a conceptual scheme for the course of the religious experience, the ensuing religious outlook as well as religious experience itself will increasingly conform. Religious experience and the theory of the experience complement and determine each other, so that ultimately every new vision confirms the accuracy of the theoretical interpretation that the recipient has developed. The result is that the individual visions are grouped into a thoroughgoing system, which confirms the theoretical scheme the recipient has elaborated concerning the structure of the spiritual and intellectual world. The visions become ever more obedient servants of their recipient and adapt ever more obligingly to his theoretical system, by occurring just as they should according to the scheme. This pattern can be seen in the visions of St. Hildegard of Bingen (1098–1179), Gertrude the Great (1256–1301), and St. Bridget of Sweden (1303–1373). As Friedrich Christoph Oetinger, an expert in this matter, commented, "The corn of heavenly revelation always grows on the stalk of human contemplation."

Swedenborg himself thought the most remarkable thing about his visionary experiences was that they usually occurred in complete wakefulness, in which his daytime consciousness and his sensory perception were fully present. This seemed to him the greatest miracle of his visionary ability: he dwelt simultaneously in heaven and on earth, he conversed with angels and men at the same time. His inner vision superseded and penetrated his outer vision, yet without neutralizing or paralyzing it. His spiritual eye saw the things of the spiritual world as through his physical eye. Earlier visionaries experienced their vision in a state of rapture, in which the earthly person lay as if dead. Their own thoughts, their consciousness, their senses were paralyzed, their physical condition gave the impression of utter rigidity and lifelessness, and their respiration was reduced to a barely perceptible level. However, the alertness of the intellect and the senses was typical in Swedenborg's case.

Swedenborg therefore differentiated the various kinds of visionary experience according to the alertness of his daytime consciousness. In his exegesis of Genesis 32:3, he establishes a model with five grades. The first and highest grade is vision "with open eyes." This occurs with people "who belong to the inner Church to such an extent that they can see the angels as well as men." In this highest state of visionary experience, the onlooker's gaze penetrates the earthly and spiritual worlds in the same instant. Whoever is deemed worthy of this highest form of vision can understand the mysteries of both the upper and the lower world in a fully wakened state. He sees the mundane reality in the light of the spiritual world, understands the spiritual forces forming this sensuous world, sees the influences from above which determine life below, and sees in every earthly figure its corresponding archetypal heavenly form. He glimpses the energies and causes that have led to its present form and also recognizes the latent potencies, possibilities, and goals of future realization and unfolding that lie hidden in every earthly thing.

The second form of vision occurs likewise with waking consciousness and alert senses. However, a kind of separation and loosening of the outer and inner senses takes place. While the outer senses remain directed towards things in the outer world, albeit to a diminished extent, the inner sense focuses on things in the spiritual world and communicates its perceptions to the cognitive center. In this form of vision, the outer impressions are bound to fade in comparison with the dominant experiences of inner vision taking place in the cognitive center.

The third form of vision is closest to the state of wakefulness, "to the extent that the onlooker cannot believe that he is other than awake, while in reality this is not a true state of being awake." In this interim state between sleeping and waking, the consciousness of wakefulness is present in the vision, while in reality the outer senses are resting. This was the case in Swedenborg's highly frequent visions, which occurred between sleep and waking in that intermediate state where daytime consciousness has not quite become fully awake.

The fourth form exists when the visionary "sees apparitions in a state of wakefulness as clearly as in daylight, but with closed eyes."

The final form is represented by dream visions, which are not identical with customary dreams but represent a state of heightened consciousness during sleep.

These forms of vision are graded according to the degree of alertness of consciousness in the onlooker. The five grades demonstrate a progressive lapse of daytime consciousness and alertness. In the first grade, both the outer and the inner person are awake. The wakened spirit and senses simultaneously receive impressions from the mundane and spiritual world and see the incidents of the visible world in the light of the spiritual world; the wall separating both worlds is demolished; the eye penetrates both realms with one gaze. In the lowest grade, by contrast, the inner and the outer person are quite separate. The activity of waking, daytime consciousness and the senses is completely extinguished and the outer being sleeps, while the inner views the spiritual world with waking spiritual eyes. The intermediate grades demonstrate the gradual fading of daytime consciousness and outer perception and the increasing loosening of the outer from the inner person.

Swedenborg noted that he had personally experienced all kinds of vision except for the first. "I can solemnly swear that manifestations of the second, third, fourth, and fifth kind have occurred to me; the second kind frequently, the third kind several times, the fourth kind extremely frequently, and now and again the fifth kind in the course of several years." The assertions of his own reports absolutely confirm this statement. Swedenborg's numerous observations about his visionary state at any one time show that two kinds of vision were most frequent in his case. In one kind, Swedenborg remained aware of being in his room, or on a particular spot in the street, or in church during the visionary experience. The sensory perceptions of his surroundings continued to impinge on his consciousness, while his spirit was directed towards persons and phenomena of the spiritual world, which became partly visible in the context of earthly reality and seemed to intrude into his sensory world of experience. The other frequent kind of vision occurred when he was sitting in a state of complete absorption with closed eyes. His outer sensory perception had completely lapsed, while his spirit perceived events in the realm of other dimensions. By contrast, there are seldom accounts in his reports of pure dream visions. Visions granted to him in a state of "false" wakefulness are relatively few, and as a rule these are expressly noted as such.

This differentiation of various states of consciousness coincides with another list, which he presents in reverse order in his exegesis of Numbers 24. There he describes fantasy as a sight of inner vision, when one seems to receive impressions from outside. But actually this is not a sight of the higher reality, rather a viewing of images that the soul has developed on its own through its imaginative ability. Swedenborg referred to this sight as taking place "inwardly in the natural spirit" (*mens naturalis*). The forms of authentic vision revealing the reality of the spiritual world are distinguished from the sight of fantasy.

Here Swedenborg calls the first and lowest grade the dream vision, in which daytime consciousness and sensory perception are completely inactive.

The second grade of sight occurs with closed eyes in a state of the highest wakefulness, in which things appear as seen in the brightest daylight.

He describes the third grade thus: "It occurs in an interim state between sleeping and waking. In this state, a person believes themselves fully awake because all his senses are active."

The fourth grade consists in sight "which takes place between the time of sleeping and the time of waking, whenever the person wakes up but has not yet broken through sleep with his eyes. This sight is the sweetest of all, for here heaven peacefully works on the reasonable spirit of a person in an intellectual way."

The fifth and final form is "an even more profoundly inward sight," but no further details are given.

In this second list, one can easily recognize the five grades of the first list, but in reverse order. In both sequences, the highest sight appears as a form of understanding beyond the mental capacity of the human being. Both sequences differentiate the other types of vision according to the relationship of inner and outer wakefulness.

Swedenborg's development was thus characterized by the emergence of a certain standard type of vision in the course of the years. This notable development is also related to Swedenborg's didactic model of his visionary experiences.

All the forms of visionary experience, which had already occurred during the period of his religious crisis, initially continued after his vocation. However, Swedenborg now interpreted them in a specific way. Before his vocation, the dreams, illuminations, assurances, apparitions of deceased persons, and demonic temptations were puzzling effects of an unknown power, of which he had only a frightening presentiment in fleeting moments. However, after his vocation, he interpreted these visionary incidents according to the understanding he had now been granted. Henceforth, he was certain that these were revelations of the spiritual world and that he had been deemed worthy of a special gift of grace by God. He now set out to systematize all his visionary experiences on the basis of this insight. Vision and doctrine began to influence and remodel each other reciprocally. His experience of the world of spirits induced him to develop a doctrine of the world of spirits, but the doctrine reacted upon the experience itself. Experience increasingly accommodates itself to doctrine, until he finally succeeded in integrating the whole stream of his irrational experiences into his system. It thus came about that a standard type of vision repressed the other types of visionary experience.

One already sees this in the most original form of his visionary experiences, the "evidence experiences" or confirmations during the period of his crisis. While working on *The Animal Kingdom*, Swedenborg repeatedly experienced how certain insights spontaneously provoked the awareness "It is like that and not otherwise! That is the truth!" and fiery flames or lights appeared. At this early stage, the evidence experiences were isolated incidents, linked with experiences of lights. Even after his vocation, these experiences of lights continued. But now he began to interpret them theologically and to integrate them in his doctrine of correspondences. In his *Spiritual Diary*, he wrote: "The flame is a representation of love, and the lights it emits is the truth. Therefore the flame is a sign of confirmation out of love. Through the heavenly mercy of God I frequently had such manifestations, and moreover in various sizes, colors, and rays; and during several months when I was just writing a work, scarcely a day passed without a flame appearing as vividly as on the hearth, and that was a sign of confirmation. This happened before the time when the spirits began to talk in living voices with me." This manifestation is thereby classified in the system of his correspondences: the flame represents love, its light truth. The manifestation of such a fire therefore signifies a confirmation of divine truth springing from divine love.

This systematization is continued further in the *Spiritual Diary*. There he wrote: "An enormous flaming light appeared unexpectedly before my eye, which it pierced in an indescribable fashion. The flame not only pierced my eye but also the inner vision, which I now clearly perceive. Soon I also saw something dark, dark like a dark cloud, in which there was however something earthly. I felt that this came from the Lord through heaven." A similar vision overcame him in the same month, October 1748: he saw a bright, shining light like a flame in the dark hearth, but it was not wood burning. He interpreted both visions in a similar way: they represent the difference between the wisdom of the angels and the wisdom of lower spiritual beings. The dark cloud, as it were the dark hearth, represents the state of intelligence of lower spiritual powers. The light itself is distinguished according to its type and luminosity: the flaming light of the first vision means the heavenly; the vibrating bright light like a white flame means the spiritual.

Swedenborg was also granted confirmation through a manifestation of light after his vocation. However, this was no longer an isolated phenomenon but linked with longer visionary experiences in the spiritual world. The following sequence occurred regularly in numerous reports. After Swedenborg or an angel had refuted erroneous teachings on this or that point of divine revelation at a meeting in the world of spirits and the true doctrine had prevailed, a shaft of light or a radiant flame-like fire descended from heaven as a sign of divine confirmation. Wonderful changes usually occurred to the spirits in this heavenly light. All who had persisted in their error turned away in dread from the intolerable light, and they were scared into hell. But those who had been seized by the truth and foresworn error were illuminated by the light and were included in a higher and purer community of the heavenly spirits according to their illumination.

A similar systematization and reinterpretation occurred with the "illuminations." While in the midst of his researches on *The Animal Kingdom*, Swedenborg more frequently had peculiar illuminations, in which previously concealed insights and intuitions suddenly came to him, connected with the feeling of inner enlightenment. Such illuminations recurred also after his vocation. But now they no longer referred to objects of nature but to the Word and doctrine. But he continued to interpret them as effects and influences of the world of spirits in a specific fashion.

Even after his vocation, these illuminations have the character of a spontaneous flash of higher insights. But now Swedenborg saw in them manifestations of a higher idea. In his view, the higher the idea, the more universal it is. All ideas are hidden in every idea, the whole truth reposes in each individual truth, and one has the whole and general idea in every particular idea. Our customary human understanding is only able to perceive and understand the individual idea and cannot advance from the individual idea to the general idea concealed within. But whatever the human spirit cannot achieve by itself can be granted by a divine intuition. Then the individual idea becomes transparent, the entire breadth of higher and more general ideas concealed within begins to reveal itself, and the general idea begins to shine through the individual idea. Swedenborg understood his illuminations as an ascent or breakthrough of particular ideas towards the general idea.

Numerous notes in his *Spiritual Diary* express this idea. Thus, he wrote on 20 March 1748: "I was in a general idea, which is as it were the idea of everything, without reference to something specific. Something appeared to me, which I cannot describe, for in the spiritual world one can receive such an idea, that is, it may be granted to men, but men cannot grasp it. Into this idea streamed particular or individual ideas of the spirits, which I clearly perceived within the general idea, while I personally remained in the general idea, and moreover to such an extent, that the individual ideas of others streamed in and I perceived them. I was told, that the idea of several spirits is created thus." The doctrine of ideas is related here to his doctrine of the world of spirits. The higher spirits have a higher and more general idea, and their thought takes place in a higher and more universal light. The illumination, in which Swedenborg felt translated into a higher idea, accordingly means his elevation to the cognitive level of a higher community of spiritual beings. The chain of ideas leads up to the most general ideas, which embrace all lower and particular ideas in themselves and which are in keeping with the cognitive status of the highest angels. The higher the cognitive level into which he feels translated, the more universal is the idea that fills him. He then sees things through the sight of the corresponding choirs of angels.

He described a similar elevation at the beginning of 1748 as follows: "For quite a long time, I remained in a general outlook, which almost led me away from particular or physical ideas. There appeared to me a sort of living, coherent, glittering light, an adamantine light, for quite some time. I cannot describe this light otherwise, for it was general and drew me away from physical ideas, indeed from the body itself. When I was in this state, I saw the physical far below me. I observed it, but it was detached from me and did not belong to me." He described other kinds of transposition into a higher idea in a similar fashion on 23 February 1748: "Today I was clearly shown in an idea, that the Good, which is the Lord's alone, may not be attributed to Evil. . . . This idea can be perceived more clearly than it can be described." Another time he wrote: "For a great part of the night and also during the morning for several hours, I was in the spiritual idea, how man is led by God, and I experienced this in an uninterrupted spiritual idea, which I cannot express." He developed a certain style for introducing such visionary reports, which usually begin with the following sentences: "Out of a general idea, I was given to understand . . . " or "I was in a general idea . . ." In these cases, there is a special state of intellectual sight, which is linked with the experience of an inner illumination. Every time the emergence of such an intuition is combined with a clear feeling of its special nature, he "feels" the illumination. There is another formula of introduction to such accounts: "*viva experientia didici*," "from living experience I have

learned . . . " or "I was shown through living experience." Wherever
Swedenborg speaks of "living experience," he usually means this
process of a perceptible intuitive illumination, a translation into a
higher form of cognition into a higher and more general idea.

But even this type of visionary experience receded. In its place,
there appeared more frequently another kind of communication of
higher insights, namely, direct instruction by spirits and angels living
in the light of the higher idea. The vision of illumination became a
vision of instruction, where specific spiritual communities or angelic
choirs presented to him their heavenly wisdom according to their
cognitive capacity. The spontaneous intellectual mode of observation
is increasingly supplanted by a rational didactic conversation with
spirits and angels, which in turn becomes the standard type of his vision. The purely intellectual experiences of illumination increasingly
recede and appear only as occasional peripheral manifestations in the
standard vision involving an encounter with specific spirits and didactic conversation. In his later works, such experiences of illumination are occasionally discussed as the conclusion of the standard
vision. At the end of a didactic conversation in the world of angels or
spirits, a heavenly light descends into the interior of his mind, pervades him, and translates him into the cognitive level of the angelic
community with whom he was just speaking. But here the illumination is no longer an isolated, independent event, only a decorative
conclusion and the confirmation of a process of understanding completed in the didactic conversation. The formula of introduction also
changes accordingly. Instead of the formula "from living experience
I was told," the new formula already contains the theological interpretation of the visionary process: "This the angels told me" or
"This I thought with the spirits" or "This came to me from the angels via the spirits."

Swedenborg's dream visions developed in a similar way. They
also initially surprised him as inexplicable manifestations. What was
the meaning of his father's nocturnal apparitions, the buildings he
was led into, the landscapes that opened before his gaze, the strange
events he was caught up in, and the animals who attacked him? After
his vocation, this dreamworld is also interpreted and systematized:
now he recognizes it as an influence of the spiritual world. It is the

spirits themselves who influence the inner world of the human in sleep. They awaken in him their intended images and suggestions. In his visions, Swedenborg found confirmation for this interpretation of the causes of dreams. "Tonight I noticed," he wrote in his diary in autumn 1747, "that it is the sprits who produce dreams, and that the dream life is their life, while a person is sleeping . . . ; I clearly understood this when I awoke." These sorts of experiences recur. On 16 September 1748, he wrote: "I was taught through repeated experience how dreams are produced and that it is the spirits who call them forth. When I was in a state of waking and another was sleeping, I was a spirit with the spirits, and I was allowed to dwell with the spirits who produce dreams. I was also permitted to call forth dreams in the other person. I was taught this by experience, for when the other person awoke three or four times after dreams I had given him, I remembered everything that he had known in the dream. The dreams I was allowed to give him were pleasing and happy. I was thus taught who gives dreams to men and how this occurs, namely, through representations, in order to invigorate the sleeping person."

But this very experience, that dreams are induced in men by the spirits, indeed that he himself could induce such dreams, must have made him doubt the revelatory value of dreams. What if it was evil spirits who induced dreams in us to distract us from the truth? How could one distinguish whether the insights of our dreams are true or false, whether they derive from good or evil spirits? The fear of illusion made him mistrust dream revelations and his own dream experiences confirmed him in this view.

Thus he wrote in his report of an experience in the night of 22/23 October 1747: "I had a dream, from which I repeatedly awoke, for evil spirits afflicted me to such an extent that I could not sleep on. After waking several times and I was fully awake, I felt my whole body shake and clearly observed that I was surrounded by a kind of pillar. I could definitely feel it. I waited to see what would happen, believing I could protect myself against the evil spirits in this fashion. I could feel how this pillar was constantly growing and the thought occurred to me that this was the 'wall of bronze' (Jeremiah 1:18), to protect the believers against the evil spirits." Here he feels himself miraculously protected from the influence of the demons.

But not all dreams are linked with such a differentiation of spirits. Where is the threshold between deception, illusion, and truth? Due to these vexations, he saw no certain revelations of the truth in dreams. In his later works, there are fewer and fewer dream reports. One can find only sporadic dream records in his *Spiritual Diary*, and they are not taken up in his doctrinal works.

Even after his vocation, the figure of his father still plays a major role in his dreams. In August 1748, his father appeared to him and said that a son might no longer recognize his father as father once his upbringing was complete and he was standing on his own two feet. As long as the son remained in his father's house, he should recognize his father as God's deputy over him; but once he had left his father's house and made himself independent, he should recognize his father only in the Lord God. Does not this sound like a dream of wish-fulfillment, in which the conflict with his father is resolved and his father retrospectively justifies the stubborn conduct of the son? Is this not the settlement in a wishful dream of a dispute that never found conciliation during the lifetime of old Bishop Jesper? On 1 April 1749, Swedenborg dreamed his father had fallen into the water and been completely submerged, but he pulled him out again and brought him ashore. Swedenborg interpreted this dream to mean that his father was the divine Word, seeing an indication of his prophetic commission in his age, when the Word had sunk into the sea of the world and theology, and he had to fetch it from the depths. But is not the personal interpretation of the dream more appropriate? The painful dependence of the son on the father is here reversed, and the son appears as the savior of the father, who pulls the father out of the water by his own powers, which the father so greatly doubted.

As a result of his scepticism towards dreams, Swedenborg grants them revelatory value only when dream visions are confirmed by daytime visions or when a dream vision directly converts into a daytime vision. Pure dream visions never occur in *Adversaria*, although he expressly emphasizes their genuine revelatory character in his exegesis of Jacob's dreams. However, there are two cases in *Adversaria* when a dream vision leads into a waking vision. In his exegesis of Exodus 36:3, he reports: "Acting out of love means acting out of freedom. Compulsion is irreconcilable with happiness because it does not stem from the love of God. This was proved to me in the clearest way possible by a dream in the night of 27/28 July 1746. After waking, I spoke with the spirits and angels present about the dream and they confirmed this to me." The dream itself is not recounted.

A similar connection between both forms of vision can be found in the exegesis of Exodus 29:42. There Swedenborg talks about the imperfect understanding of the lower spirits, who live in a kind of dream state and cannot distinguish dreams and waking either in themselves or in humans. "I dreamed, and, as sometimes happens, it seemed to me that I was awake and the spirits present were convinced that I was awake and replied to me as to a person awake. But suddenly I awoke and observed that I had been dreaming and that the spirits had been talking to me in my sleep in the belief that I was awake. They were very ashamed about this. One was indignant, another astonished, a third liked it. . . . Thereupon I wrote down the comments on this verse, and so I was allowed to persuade them that they spent their life hitherto in a dream state. They could not say anything to that." Once again, the dream vision spins on into a waking vision. Both are related to each other; the waking vision illuminates and confirms the dream vision, which in this case is particularly delightful as it deals with the different states of consciousness in sleeping and waking.

In the *Spiritual Diary,* there are also dreams that pass through various steps of awakening consciousness, clarifying themselves more and more in each successively more wakeful state. Swedenborg describes the following dream of early November 1747: "In this night, it seemed to me that I was traveling on a ship through a stormy sea. When I woke afterwards, I saw this sea with its towering waves so black that anyone would have been terrified. The violence of the sea seemed to be growing constantly; the waves stormed from left to right, and then they raged towards the shore on which I was standing. There were also several people on the island or cliff who had saved themselves. When I fully awoke, I felt a clearly perceptible movement as before and noticed that I was together with spirits who rose up. I heard that they had previously been chained in the pit but had been redeemed and liberated here by the grace of the God Messiah. It was a large crowd, as I could infer from the noise and other sensory perceptions, and I was told that the seas that rage on Judgment Day or at the millennium mean this and similar things." Here the dream progressively reveals itself with the various steps of waking and explains more and more of what the original dream represented. The allegorical interpretation of Scripture provides a commentary on the dream vision and the waking vision. In the biblical prophecies of the millennium, the stormy sea signifies the wave of unchained spirits from the underworld who hasten towards their liberation.

After his vocation, a third type of visionary experience occurs in ecstasy, a state in which the inner person feels completely liberated from the outer person. We should recall that Swedenborg's religious crisis began with such a state of rapture combined with the feeling of supreme bliss. Externally this state consists in a complete lapse of daytime consciousness and sensory perception and in an extreme reduction of physical functions like respiration and heartbeat. These kinds of states, which he noted in his dream diary brought him to the threshold of death and physical disintegration, are extremely rare later on. Swedenborg distinguishes two forms of this ecstasy. The first is an elevation into the highest sphere of the heavenly world and involves the experience of contact with the Divine itself, but without this contact being described in the style of mystical union as an entry into the divine essence, a unification with the deity, a spiritual wedding. The state is combined with an indescribable feeling of bliss, without being represented in specific, distinct intuitions. There are simply no adequate images or representations for the feeling. He calls this state the *status gloriationis*, the state of glorification, and reports on this at the beginning of February 1748: "In this *status gloriationis*, in which I remained almost a whole day or a half day, I had no particular idea, not even thinking in ideas, which I could have received, for I was in the magnificence of the Lord."

The other form of ecstasy translated him to a lower level of trance. This did not lead Swedenborg into the sphere of divine magnificence but into the state of spirits when they are released from their physical bodies. Here he feels himself a spirit among spirits, released from all physical, earthly influences and forms of knowledge.

In this state, he learns through "living experience" the being of the spiritual world in all its peculiarities. He wrote about this in 1749: "Twice or three times I was translated into the state that spirits occupy, in such a way that I was a spirit among spirits and released from the earthly body. I was with the spirits, talking to them, looking at them, and finding out what distinguishes their life from that of men." While he retained the consciousness of his earthly, physical being in his normal visions, in such rare ecstasies he felt completely taken out of his physical being and wholly translated into the spiritual world's state of being. In one such rapture, he also experienced his own death and described all the degrees of dying, which occur as the inner person is loosened from his outer figure, in such precise detail that he devised an impressive experimental phenomenology of death "on the basis of his own experience."

Besides the experience of supreme bliss exceeding all conscious notions, he describes another state of bliss as "heavenly rest." In this state, all thoughts, images, emotions, and ideas withdraw. He feels himself in a calm, blessed, and contented euphoria. Swedenborg interpreted this state as an experience of heavenly peace and once again distinguished several steps, the experience of heavenly peace itself, and the experience of rest, which emanates from this peace. He thus reported on 11 January 1748: "At first waking, I felt once again, as before, the state of rest, which comes from peace, an exquisite feeling of well-being, but it was not the peace itself." He similarly wrote in the middle of June 1748: "After a deep sleep in the afternoon, I was translated into a state of rest . . . I have remained in this state for a whole hour, and I am still in it." Evidently such euphoria still resonated within him after he had returned from his rapture into daytime consciousness.

These are mystical experiences, where analogies can be found in the accounts of the great mystics of the sixteenth century such as St. Teresa of Avila (1515–1582) and St. John of the Cross (1542–1591), but also in the writings of the medieval mystics. But Swedenborg's piety does not seek the *unio mystica*, but an intellectual way of seeing. He seeks not bliss but understanding. It can be established that he consciously repressed those kinds of blissful experiences. He felt justified in this by a sentiment that other mystics, especially the Spanish and French mystics of the seventeenth century, have expressed. When experiencing such blessed states of bliss, he too was seized by a fear of illusion and devilish deception. His doctrine of the world of spirits came to his aid again here. He recognized the dangerous possibility that such experiences of bliss may stem not from God, but from evil spirits, who want to dazzle him with a false fulfillment of his desire for knowledge and thus distract him from his actual commission. The fear of illusion induced him to regard such experiences with mistrust, all the more when other visions indicated the possibility and the causes of error in such states. Already in April 1745, he related how evil spirits aroused a delicious feeling of bliss in him, which seemed like the feeling of heavenly bliss. However, he was taught that this was just illusion and lies and that the spirits awoke this illusion in him out of a desire to destroy the heavenly part of him.

Similar experiences reinforced his skepticism. In December 1747, he was granted an experience of bliss that was clearly linked with the notion that spirits had the evil intention of placing him in this state. "Today I was surrounded by numerous spirits of various kinds on first waking. Several of them wanted to infuse me with their heavenly joy through cunning, by transferring their joy or bliss onto another. . . . Therefore I had an experience of bliss, which laid hold of my whole body including my entrails to such an extent that I believed I was in heavenly joy among the deceased, for I felt in a delicious state of being poured out, as into a delightful bath. I did not feel the causes of this bliss, namely, that they sprang from a desire to torture and from cunning. . . . Apart from this physical bliss, inner bliss was also instilled in me, and moreover by other spirits, who wanted to give me this bliss." In the same account, he gives his verdict on this kind of experience: "An outer pleasure can be introduced into man in the shape of a heavenly joy, and this is loathsome, although the souls believe that something heavenly is happening."

He was repeatedly made aware of this fact in the following years. At the beginning of 1749, he was informed that "false delights and pleasures can sometimes simulate authentic heavenly delights in such a manner that one cannot possibly distinguish them, unless the Lord has inspired one with the gift of discrimination." Fear of illusion put him off this type of experience and increasingly steered him towards that form of visionary contemplation to which he was best suited and in which he saw the fulfillment of his mission. This was the conversation with spirits in the state of "being in the spirit," the didactic conversation in which the spirits communicated to him the revelations of the transcendental world. In this way, a standard type of vision emerges in his practice, namely, rapture into the world of spirits or angels, vision of the upper realms and their inhabitants, didactic conversation with spirits and angels being its centerpiece. Meanwhile, the other types of vision increasingly recede or merely appear as subsidiary forms of visionary experience within or on the margins of the standard type of vision.

However, there is still another type of vision, which Swedenborg did not list. These are apparitions, in which events take place before his eyes and ears and bear all the characteristics of earthly phenomena. They are apprehended by the consciousness as such, as Swedenborg had in this case no sense of "being in the spirit." However, these events violate all laws of natural behavior and give the onlooker the horrible feeling that something uncanny is afoot. His later works show no evidence for such apparitions of a pseudohallucinatory nature. By contrast, his great vision of vocation seems to have started with such a pseudohallucination.

The description he gave to his friend Robsahm has already been quoted. In his exegesis of Exodus 8:5–7, Swedenborg returns to this subject while discussing the plague of frogs in Egypt. He says that frogs represent unclean spirits of the lowest kind, which govern the lowest parts of the human and incite all lusts of the body and blood. "Such frogs once appeared to me in a similar fashion. They emerged so obviously that I saw them crawling before my eyes. Then they combined into a shape, which caught fire and exploded with such a deafening noise that there was a bang in my ears when they burst asunder. The place was cleaned up afterwards. This happened in London in April 1745. The pores of my skin seemed to perspire some, but on the floor I saw something akin to many wriggling worms in great quantity." Here he perceives apparently sensible events with his earthly senses in a waking state, without his consciousness "being in the spirit." With his eyes, he sees frogs and worms, he sees the smoke emerging from his pores, he hears the bang. At the moment of the vision, he has no idea what it means and only reacts to these wholly abnormal events with the greatest horror. Only subsequently is he instructed in the meaning of the events and their symbolic character is revealed to him.

His later visions, in which these "representations" take place, no longer bear the characteristics of such pseudohallucinations but are granted to him in one of the four listed visionary types while he "is in the spirit." Moreover, a spiritual interpretation usually follows forthwith. The visionary image is no longer isolated but accompanied by an audition, in which Swedenborg learns from the mouth of an angel or spirit what the symbolic image means. Even in the later representations, he sees animals that enact all kinds of transformations before his eyes, but here he perceives visions as inner images rather than incidents in the earthly external world. The sense of horror so typical of the pseudohallucination is also absent. Such manifestations of images usually end with the animals disappearing. Their place is taken by a group of spirits who represent them and then explain the meaning of the incident to Swedenborg in a didactic conversation.

The examples quoted so far already show the close connection between Swedenborg's visions and his interpretation of Scripture. Many visions are nothing else but interpretations of a passage in the Bible. This fact underlines the peculiarity of Swedenborg's visionary gift, the commission of revelation, which he had already recognized in his vision of vocation as his main task. Numerous comments that he appended to his reports of visions concerning the way they begin elucidate this connection between vision and the Word of the Bible.

A great number of Swedenborg's visions actually occurred while he was sitting in his room and reflecting on a particular passage in the Bible. Suddenly he "was in the spirit" and received a vision that illustrated the inner sense of the pertinent passage. This posits a fundamental difference between the Protestant visionary Swedenborg and the Catholic visionaries of the sixteenth and seventeenth centuries. Swedenborg's visions do not occur in church or in the exercise of priestly observances or in connection with the sacrament, but surprise the scholar studying at his desk as he labors over the inner sense of the Bible.

Thus Swedenborg reported his exegesis of the twelfth and thir-teenth chapters of the Book of Revelation: "When I was reflecting on the dragon, the beast, and the false prophets described in Revelation, an angelic spirit appeared to me and asked: 'What are you thinking about?' I said: 'About the false prophets.' Then he spoke: 'I want to lead you to the place where those known as the false prophets are.' I followed him and, lo, I saw a crowd, in whose center were Church leaders who had taught that nothing else besides faith in Christ's re-ward can save man and that good works do not lead to salvation." He was now permitted to enter the temple with a cult image representing the faith of false prophet's followers. A statue of a woman dressed in a scarlet robe carried a gold coin in her right hand and a pearl neck-lace in her left, but neither the temple nor the idol really existed. They were only chimera conjured up through the imagination of the hellish spirits. "When I noticed that they were just illusions, I prayed to the Lord, and immediately the interior of my mind was opened. Instead of the magnificent temple, I saw a ruined house riddled with holes from the roof to the ground. Instead of the woman, I saw there an image with the head of a dragon, the body of a leopard, the feet of a bear, and the muzzle of a lion, just like the beast of the sea de-scribed in Revelation 13:2. Instead of the ground, there was a swamp that teemed with frogs, and I was told that beneath the swamp was a great carved stone, beneath which the Word lay completely hidden" (*True Christian Religion* 187, *Apocalypse Revealed* 926). The eyes of the priest of the temple were similarly opened, so that he did not see the temple of the false faith according to his imagination, but truly in a state of dreadful dilapidation. Thereupon, in contrast, the angels show the seer the true temple of the spiritual heaven, and finally the Lord himself in the third heaven. In the same form that he appeared to the visionary John on Patmos, he is standing on the foundation stone, which is the Word (*True Christian Religion* 187).

The commentary nature of the vision is immediately obvious here. In the Johannine apocalypse, the coming of the false prophet is prophesied. The vision makes it clear to Swedenborg that the false prophet means those Church teachers, who have severed love from faith in their doctrine of redemption through faith alone and thereby corrupted the true evangelical religion. This is revealed to him not in a didactic form but in a vision. He sees for himself the false teachers. He beholds their erroneous doctrine in the form of the temple and its idol, first the way they see the temple and their idol, and then in the light of heaven by whose aid he sees the illusion dispelled. The Word appears to have sunken in the swamp of their false faith under a large stone. For its counterpart, he catches sight of the true heavenly image of the Church, the temple of the spiritual heaven, and finally the Lord himself upon the foundation stone of the divine Word.

The structure and course of the vision, characteristic of numerous other visions, is also worthy of note. As Swedenborg ponders over the sense of a biblical passage, it is no single image like the figure of a false prophet that appears unexpectedly before his gaze. Rather, the vision unfolds according to a definite theatrical progression. An angel appears and asks him about the subject of his thought. He immediately invites him to accompany him and brings him to the place where he will be informed by his observation on the subject of his enquiry. From this point, the vision seems like a film. The visionary and his heavenly guide approach the pertinent group "from afar"; they go up to them; the visionary is permitted to enter their temple and speak with the priest of the temple. The vision does not remain an objective image, but Swedenborg deals and speaks with the figures in his vision as one of their own and moves through the same space as they do. The illusion of the temple is transformed at the moment of Swedenborg's prayer and appears in its true, demonic form. The vision is completed by an ever-rising ascent, culminating in the sight of the Lord.

A great number of Swedenborg's visions came to pass in a similar situation, under similar circumstances, and followed the same structure and course. The vision regularly begins as a demonstration of a biblical passage requiring explanation and ends with a symbolic representation of its inner meaning.

Swedenborg thus described the vision that showed him what the dragon signified in the twelfth chapter of the Book of Revelation. "I spoke with several who are understood to be the dragon in Revelation, and one of them said: 'Come with me and I will show you the amusements of our eyes and hearts'. He led me through a dark wood onto a hill, from which I could see the amusements of the dragon spirits. I saw an amphitheatre built in the form of a circus and surrounded by steep terraced seating on which spectators sat. From afar, those on the lowest rows seemed like satyrs and priapic figures, some covered and some naked. On the seats above sat lewd men and women, as was evident to me from their gestures, and then the dragon said to me: 'Now you shall see our game.' I looked and saw that young bulls, rams, sheep, goats, and lambs had been let into the central space of the circus. Once they were all inside, a gate was opened, whereupon young lions, panthers, tigers, and wolves rushed in and fell furiously upon the herd, tearing them to pieces and killing them. After this bloody massacre, the satyrs strewed sand over the site of the bloodbath. Then the dragon said to me: 'These are the games which delight our souls.' I replied: 'Get thee hence, demon, in a while you will see this amphitheatre turned into a lake of fire and brimstone'"(*True Christian Religion* 388). Everything that Swedenborg sees here the dragon has conjured up through his imagination. He did not really see bulls, rams, sheep, and lambs; rather the demon effected through his magic that the goodness and truth of the Church, which he hated, appeared in the form of these domestic animals, while the wild animals, the lions, panthers, tigers, and wolves represented the evil lusts of the dragon spirits. Even here the vision of the spiritual community representing the dragon does not appear unheralded. It comes after an introductory conversation with a demon of this community and after Swedenborg has gradually approached the dragon community and the actual visionary incident after being led along paths in the world of spirits. The entire sequence of images is an allegorical, spiritual exegesis of the relevant passage in the Book of Revelation. The object of the vision is not the dragon, but the community, which the dragon signifies according to Swedenborg's allegorical exposition.

A third vision may elucidate this kind of allegorical and visionary exposition of the Bible. This one also refers to a theme in the Book of Revelation, namely, Christ's Second Coming. "When I was thinking about the Second Coming of Christ, a shining light suddenly dazzled me, whereupon I looked up, and, lo, the whole sky above me was shining brightly, and from morning unto evening one heard a long hymn of praise, and an angel stood by me and said: 'This hymn glorifies the coming of the Lord and is sung by angels in the eastern and western heavens.'" Swedenborg looks and now hears how all promises of the Lord's coming, which are found in Holy Scripture, are being sung by the various choirs of angels one after another. "When I had heard and understood this, my heart beat in excitement and I went joyfully home, and there I returned from my spiritual state into my physical state, in which I wrote down these things which I had heard and seen." Once again, the vision takes its cue from his consideration of the promise of Christ's Second Coming in the Bible. Even the course of the vision demonstrates the close connection between the visionary event and the text. The returning Lord is glorified by the heavenly choirs, inasmuch as they sing as a heavenly liturgy the messianic prophecies of the Old Testament, which relate to Christ's Second Coming in Church teaching. The angels praise the Lord according to the rules of biblical theology.

The concluding remark is worthy of special note. Swedenborg returns from the world of spirits to his "home" and there leaves his spiritual state and re-enters his physical state. The experience of being "outside of oneself" and "in the spirit" is therefore linked with the specific movements and spatial impressions of leaving and returning to his earthly standpoint, his house and his room. Numerous other observations relate that a spirit from a heavenly community or an academy accompanied him "home."

The relation of vision to Holy Scripture is expressed even more clearly in a second type of vision, frequently described in *Adversaria*. There the allegorical exegesis takes the form of his "being granted by the heavenly grace of God"—the recurrent formula—to speak with the personalities of the Old or New Testament who are either the subject or author of the relevant passage of Scripture he is trying to expound. In his exegesis of Old Testament texts, he converses predominantly with the Jewish patriarchs; in later writings, there are numerous conversations with the apostles. While he is working on the Bible, the authors of the holy books appear to him in spirit and convey to him the true meaning that they long ago disguised in the letters of the Word. Precisely for this reason together with his prophetic self-confidence, Swedenborg's explanations of Holy Scripture thus lay claim to the status of an immediate and authentic testimony.

Again and again, he considered it necessary for the credibility of his interpretations to allude to the personal presence of persons mentioned in the scriptural texts.

Thus he characterized himself as "the lowest servant of God" when expounding Genesis 34:19 in *Adversaria.* "Whom God has accepted, in order that these words might be written down, and moreover in the presence of Abraham. The latter is watching and speaks at this very moment with me. He wishes that this should be attested, as if he had written it himself." Swedenborg finds himself in a similar situation in his exegesis of Genesis 32:8, which describes Jacob's meeting with the angel. Here he notes: "This was written down by my hand as a mere instrument. Spirits similar to Jacob were in attendance, and I do not doubt that he was also there." These references differ from the rest of the text as direct heavenly dictations and are specially identified. They are quite different from the other accounts, which he records as heavenly travel reports from memory at the conclusion of a vision "at home."

Conversations with specific saints of the Old and New Testament constantly accompany his work on the exposition of the Bible. In his commentary on Genesis 50:9–10 dealing with the burial of Jacob, he mentions several discussions with Peter and other apostles and then continues: "I have talked extensively with them for a whole month. I was also permitted to speak with Solomon several times." On another occasion, he wrote in his interpretation of Exodus 3:12, the account of God's summons of Moses: "Moses himself is at this very moment with me and confesses that he had no faith at that time." Other patriarchs frequently approach him in order to commission the writing down of specific revelations. To his exegesis of Exodus 32:5–6, he added: "These words were written down on 8 July 1746 according to the old style. On this day, I also spoke with Abraham, who ordered me to write that nothing can be effected in heaven save through God, whom they worship."

Sometimes Swedenborg flatters himself that biblical personalities court him. Thanks to his special vocation, they regard him as their only means of letting people on earth have the correct interpretation of their words from long ago. The patriarchs often appear moved whenever they see Swedenborg writing about them, and they watch over his shoulder with every indication of pleasure, while he interprets their words. Writing of the passage in II Kings 23 "Josiah was the only king whom God loved," Swedenborg observed: "That is why tears now stream from my eyes, when I read this chapter, because I hear that King Josiah is present here and wishes these words to be written down in his memory. 13 August 1746, Old Style. This should be well noted."

This group of visions that overcome him while interpreting Scripture is followed by a second group, in which the vision follows some meditation on doctrine but without relating to a specific passage of Scripture. These visions do not occur when he is reading the Bible at his desk, but everywhere, during sleep, while walking, and especially in the interim state between sleeping and waking in the morning. They bring a visionary representation of the subject that Swedenborg was absorbed in meditating. The following vision is characteristic of this second group.

> When I awoke from sleep, I sank into a deep reflection about God; and as I looked up, I saw above me in the sky a blinding white light shaped like an egg. When I fixed my eyes on this light, it withdrew to the sides and dissolved in circles of light. And, lo, heaven stood open to me, and I beheld marvelous things. Angels stood in a circular formation at the zenith of the opening. They conversed with each other; and because I was burning with a desire to know what they were saying, I was first permitted to hear the sound of their voices, which was full of heavenly love, and then the content of the conversation itself, which was full of wisdom emanating from that love. They spoke among themselves about the one God, the link with him and the rapture this produces. They spoke unutterable things, most of which cannot be expressed in the words of a natural language. Because I had associated several times with the angels in heaven and because I was in a similar state and could speak like them, I could understand them and infer something from their conversation, which can be set forth through words of a natural language in a rational fashion. (*True Christian Religion* §25)

There then follows an extensive account of the angels' speeches, which concerned the essence of divine being. Later he participates in their conversation:

Afterwards the heavenly light which I had seen earlier retreated above the opening and then gradually descended, filling the interior of my mind and illuminating my ideas of the trinity and unity of God. Then I saw my earliest notions on this subject, which were merely natural, separated from me, just as the winnowing shovel separates the wheat from the chaff, which is carried up by the wind to the northern sky and scattered. (_True Christian Religion_ §26)

According to Swedenborg's notes, this vision occurred in the morning in that peculiar half-waking state, where the imaginative powers of the soul work without hindrance and also display remarkable features. One sees various stages in the vision's onset and fading away. The opening phase is formed by a manifestation of light, which may be caused by the sensory stimulus of light upon the sleeper at the moment of awakening. The vague perception of light—a blinding white light round like an egg, which gradually dissolves into wave-like circles—condenses into specific figures, choirs of angels, which surround the opening into the sky like a heavenly corona. An audition supervenes: initially this is also vague, just a sound, and then gradually become clearer until one can understand words. A new intensification: hearing the angelic conversations leads to Swedenborg's joining in their discussions. Thus he receives an answer to the question whose meditation led to the vision. The vision then fades away gradually in several phases. The divine light laps over the opening in the sky, the angelic choirs vanish, and the vision passes into an illumination. The heavenly light now sinks into the inner mood of the seer and fills him with a direct vision of the divine essence. This illumination leads to the jettisoning of his former erroneous ideas about the divine essence, which stemmed from natural reason and which are now thrown out as the chaff of thoughts from the wheat of intuition in an experience of purification.

Swedenborg's morning visions indicate a similar uniformity. As a rule, they concern a previously considered theological problem, which is solved in visionary objectification. He describes one in this passage: "One morning, when I was woken from sleep, I gave myself over to reflections in the cheerful morning light before complete wakefulness. Through the window, I saw something resembling flashes of light, and soon afterwards I heard something like the roll of thunder. While I was wondering whence this came, I heard from heaven that there were several spirits not far from me who were violently arguing about God and nature." He hears that it is an argument between several angels and demons over the question whether nature itself is God. In order to convince the devils that nature is not God but only a vessel for divine life, the angels lead their demonic conversationalists into heaven under strong guard. In the light of heaven, the devils realize that God exists and that nature was created by him in order to serve life. But as they descend again, their old love of evil returns, closing their understanding to things above and opening it to things below. At their arrival on earth, the ground opens and swallows them up (*True Christian Religion* 77). Here the vision is preceded by a contemplation, already concerned with the topic, which the seer hears "in the spirit" being discussed by the angels and demons. The topic is also one of the fundamental themes of Swedenborgian theology. The debate with Spinoza's pantheism is here conducted on a visionary plane.

Sometimes such morning visions seem to have occurred without any previous conscious meditation on a specific problem. But in such cases, the introductory meditation as a cue for the vision is only apparently omitted. In the productive interim state between sleeping and waking, problems are sometimes solved about which he was thinking on earlier occasions. Thus he wrote once: "When I awoke from sleep one morning, the sun of the spiritual world appeared to me in its shining glory, and beneath it I saw the heavens at a distance like that separating the sun from the earth. From the heavens, unutterable words could be heard, which might be summarily expressed in the following words: 'There is *a* God, who is human and his dwelling is that sun.'" These words descend through the various heavens, but they are transformed by the cadences of their downward fall according to the imaginative capacity of the listeners; and among the lower spirits they are inverted into the erroneous notion of the three gods. Swedenborg engages in a conversation with such spirits and teaches them about their error. "After I had said this, the crowd of spirits around me stepped back, and I noticed that those who really thought of three gods looked into hell and those who imagined *one* God, in whom there is a divine trinity . . . looked up to heaven. To them the sun of heaven appeared, which is God's human aspect" (*True Christian Religion* 135). The vision supplies the answer to the problem of the unity and trinity of God, which had long preoccupied Swedenborg.

Another morning vision similarly appears to induce the visionary state without any preceding contemplation. "When I awoke one morning from sleep, I saw two angels coming down from heaven, one from the southern part of heaven, the other from the eastern, both riding carriages drawn by white horses. The carriage carrying the angel from the south of the heavens shimmered like silver, while the other coming from the east of the heavens shone like gold. The reins they held in their hands were radiant like the flaming light of the dawn. Thus these two angels appeared to me in the distance. But when they came nearer, they no longer appeared in their carriages, but in the form of angels akin to a human. The angel from the east of heaven wore a shining purple robe, while the angel from the south of heaven wore one the color of hyacinth. When they were below the heavens in the lowlands, one ran after the after as if they were trying to overtake each other. They embraced and kissed each other, and I heard that these two angels, when they formerly lived on earth, had been bound by the closest ties of friendship, and that one was now in the eastern heaven and the other in the southern heaven." The two angels discuss the nature of love and wisdom. Swedenborg listens to their speeches and learns "a thousand things, which natural speech cannot express and which cannot even be put into the notions of natural thought." After the angels have finished their discussion, they disappear again. While they ascend, stars appear around their heads, and at a certain distance they appear once again in their carriages (*True Christian Religion* 386). Here the nucleus of the vision is a didactic debate about the nature of love and wisdom and their reciprocal relationship. This is also a central problem in Swedenborg's theology and was a constant theme of his meditations. But the rational and tangible part of this vision is only a tiny section of the exuberant abundance of the unspeakable mystery of love and wisdom.

The relatively rare night visions, which overtook Swedenborg while awake and not when dreaming, also form part of this class of visions. He describes such a night vision as follows: "When I awoke from sleep around midnight, I saw an angel at some height in the east. In his right hand, he held a leaf of paper which was dazzling white in the sunlight with a text in golden letters, and I saw written: 'Marriage of the Good and the True.' A radiance shone forth from the text, forming a corona around the paper. This circle or frame of light appeared like the dawn in spring. Then I saw the angel descend with the paper in his hand, and as he descended, the paper seemed less and less bright, while the text changed from gold first into silver, then into the color of bronze, then iron and finally into the color of rusted iron. The angel seemed to have passed into a dark cloud before alighting below on earth. Now the paper could not been seen, although the angel still held it in his hand." Then a great crowd of spirits gathered. Swedenborg receives a commission from the angel: "Ask those, who are coming hither, whether they can see me, or observe something in my hand." The spirits thus questioned give various replies depending on the state of their understanding and the illumination of their inner person. Some see the angel in a bright splendor, others more dimly, some see the text in this color, some in that color, several not at all. Finally the angel teaches them about the true meaning of the marriage of the Good and the True. He then begins to rise again from the earth, "and after he had risen over the clouds, he went up into heaven, and the paper shone ever more brightly the higher he rose, and, lo, the corona, which had resembled the dawn, descended and scattered the cloud which had brought darkness upon the earth, and all became as bright as sunlight" (*True Christian Religion* 624).

In this heavenly vision, Swedenborg receives an answer to the question of the relationship between faith and love, a problem that ceaselessly occupied him and that he found so inadequately solved in the doctrine of justification taught by his Church. The vision also ends here in an illumination, in which the understanding of the marriage between love and faith penetrates the thick cloud that had prevented its light from reaching the lower levels of the spiritual realm and earth, spreading the truth as a bright light down into the lowest regions. Once again the course and structure of the vision consist in a gradual approach and dispersal of the imagery, while its nucleus is a didactic conversation, in which the seer personally participates.

A vision arising from contemplation does not occur only in morning and night visions, where one imagines Swedenborg lying in bed in a state of complete physical rest and spiritual ecstasy, but also in the course of the day, when he is sitting at home thinking or out walking. When such daytime visions intervened while he was walking, his motor functions seemed to have continued automatically as in a sleepwalker, or else he stood still, seemingly sunk in thought, while the visionary event took place before his spirit. He was rarely more precise concerning their outward circumstances. He only sketches the theme of his contemplation, in order to describe how the vision suddenly developed.

For example: "Once I was thinking with amazement how many people there are who reckon all creation above and beneath the sun a part of nature. When they see something, they say: 'Does this not form part of nature?' I was feeling astonished at the great number of such naturalists, when an angel stepped up beside me and said: 'What are you thinking about?' I replied: 'The great numbers of people who believe that nature is self-generating and thus the creator of the universe.' The angel said to me: 'All hell is full of those who believe this. But I will lead you to the colleges in the southwestern district, where there are such naturalists as are not already in hell.' Then he took me by the hand and led me there, and I saw small college houses, and in their midst a house which looked like the residence of a principal. It was built of pitch black stone and covered with little glass plates shimmering in gold and silver like selenite. We approached and knocked, and soon someone opened the door, bid us welcome, and then ran over to a table to fetch four books." These books contained the doctrines purporting to prove that nature is self-generating and the creator of the universe. A long didactic conversation ensues, during which the angel and Swedenborg instruct the principal of the naturalists concerning the errors of his view of nature. "Afterwards we set off, and he accompanied us as far as the outer court of his college, talking with us about heaven and hell and divine governance on the basis of his newly won spiritual insight" (*True Christian Religion* 35).

This is an example of one of the most common classes of vision, to which Swedenborg attributed his understanding. He is reflecting upon a specific problem. The meditation glides into the vision. An angel goes up to him, asks what he is thinking about, and in answer to his concern, translates him to the realm of such spirits with which Swedenborg was concerned. The angel instructs the messengers of false doctrine. As a spokesman of the truth, Swedenborg joins in the discussion and so helps the former teachers of error to attain true understanding. The whole vision, which gradually leads to the involvement of the seer in the visionary events fades in a similar fashion. The converted spirit accompanies the seer across the outer court of the place where they were talking, and Swedenborg returns "home." The meditation has fulfilled itself in the vision and led to a concluding insight.

This type of vision may be clarified by two particularly graphic examples. Swedenborg relates the first as follows: "One day I was reflecting on the creation of the universe. The angels above my right side who had also pondered this subject several times noticed my interest. One descended and invited me to follow. I entered the spirit and accompanied him. After I had entered, I was led to the prince, at whose court I found about a hundred gathered, with him in the center." The gathering is just at that moment discussing the creation of the universe. Swedenborg joins in the debate and sets forth his own view. "After this had been discussed, when I took my leave sparks fell from the sunlight through the angelic heavens into their eyes and their spirits. Thus they were illuminated, and they applauded my explanations and followed me into the outer court. But my previous companion followed me back to the house where I was staying and thence ascended to his community."

This report shows that Swedenborg was convinced he had immediate access to duly qualified heavenly teachers for whatever questions he was meditating. The angels helped him, as soon as they noticed he was laboring over the solution of a problem, and translated him in spirit to the appropriate heavenly society or academy, which was discussing this question in detail that very moment. There he received the answer of truth, and with its aid, he helped to combat the error of false teachings. At the beginning and the end of the vision, both worlds intersect in a certain way. While retaining the temporal and spatial conception of his physical being, he sees the angels approaching from a location that he can exactly determine from his own standpoint. He then ascends and is conducted by them to a gathering of the spirits and returns "home," whereby the vision comes to an end in the temporal and spatial assumptions of his physical place of residence.

The same theme is discussed in the following vision: "Once, when I was reflecting on the creation of the universe, several of the most famous and wisest philosophers of all time in the Christian world came up to me and said: 'We have noticed that you are thinking about the Creation. Tell us your opinion on the subject.' But I replied: 'First tell me yours.'" One after another, they presented their views in an academic manner. Afterwards they were permitted to speak with the angels. Thanks to this conversation, the philosophers truly understood the Creation and the error of their former view and they exclaimed: "We were mad, we were mad!" But after the angels have departed, they relapsed into their old false view. In its basic type, the vision is identical to the preceding ones. As Swedenborg's writings attest in numerous cases, he receives answers to the same problem in the form of several revelations in various visionary guises.

This kind of vision becomes a regular pattern, which is often repeated to the point of excess. The heavenly spirits ever more willingly assume the role of Swedenborg's eager assistants, who have a ready answer to all his problems. They are constantly prepared to illustrate and lecture on all mysteries their master is pondering or to lead him to heavenly colleges and academies where his questions are presently being discussed. A certain feeling of effortlessness and pleasing convenience seems inherent in these sorts of experience. Scarcely has the seer begun to think about something, and "the aerial, gentle youths" (Goethe, *Faust, Part Two*) are there straightaway, and immediately he learns everything at first hand from the best authorities. This confirms our earlier statement concerning the relationship between the theory and practice of visionary thought. The pattern of the vision reacts on the course of the vision itself, and even the unusual finally becomes a routine.

In the case of the daytime visions, it is noteworthy that Swedenborg is completely master of his visions. They do not unexpectedly overwhelm him in the manner of an epileptic attack, so that he is enraptured while in society or in conversation with visitors, but rather they form an extension of his solitary contemplation at the right time and place. Not one of his friends and visitors report sudden raptures, which might have overpowered him against his will at an unsuitable moment, in company or before witnesses. His vision of the fire of Stockholm appears to be the only exception. But this incident at a party in Göteborg did not involve an extended period of rapture coupled with any externally visible change. Rather, he was granted a momentary instant of clairvoyance, which he reported with all the signs of fright to the company present. As a rule, he had visions only when he was alone and preoccupied with a specific problem or passage of Scripture. Only someone who exceptionally and by chance surprised him, like Count Tuxen, could become the unbidden witness of such an occurrence.

Another point is worthy of mention. The peculiarity has already been noted that, at the beginning and end of the visions, the mundane world and the world of spirits overlap and mingle in the perception of the visionary. He perceives the spirits in a specific spatial relation to his own standpoint in physical space, on the right or left, above or below, nearer or further away; he sees them descending towards him, through an opening in the sky, sometimes coming in through the window; then he ascends with them to higher domains, and finally returns "home" with them. As a rule, then, the visions first lead him away from his mundane location and then back to it, while clearly maintaining normal ideas of time. The deliberations of the heavenly academies, in which Swedenborg joins, often last a considerable time, and he sometimes intervenes to shorten them and help bring the debate to a speedy close before returning to his desk back on earth. He finds just this a speciality of his visionary gift and emphasizes the alertness of his consciousness and senses, which continue to receive impressions of his surroundings during the vision. But actually this alertness is present only at the beginning and the end of his vision, when he glides from rapture back into daytime consciousness.

Sometimes a situation arises when the imagery of his visions relates to tangible objects and impressions, which he then sees on waking or while out walking and they recall the spiritual vision. Thus he glimpses the rising sun in a morning vision. This is the prelude to a heavenly vision of light. Likewise, in the aforesaid vision, he sees a kind of flashing "outside his window" and hears thunder. These perceptions form a transition to an encounter with a society of spirits, who express themselves in these incidents. The following record is particularly informative concerning the intersection of the two worlds: "When I once awoke after dawn, I went into the garden in front of my house and saw the rising sun in its splendor and all around it a ring, which was initially dim but then became brighter and shimmered like gold. Beneath its edge, I saw a cloud rising up, shining like a carbuncle in the flame of the sun." Until this point, he describes the sensory impressions gathered on his morning walk. Then he continues: "I now fell into a reverie about the primeval myths, which portray the dawn with silver pinions and gold in its mouth. While I was taking delight in these thoughts, I came into the spirit and heard several spirits talking with one another and saying: 'May we not speak to the newcomer, who has thrown the apple of Eris among the Church leaders.'" In these words, Swedenborg overhears an allusion to his recently published book *Brief Exposition of the Doctrine of the New Church* (1769). He begins to converse with the spirits, who want a discussion with him as the author, and he presents his views. A vision of light again forms the conclusion. "When I had said this, I looked at them and noticed changes in their faces, depending on the changes in their mood: some looked at me with approval, while others turned away from me. Now on the right, a cloud the color of an opal, on the left a dark cloud, and beneath this a heavy shower of rain as occurs in late autumn, and lower still something like the dew at first spring, and thereupon I ceased to be in the spirit and was back in my body and so returned from the spiritual world back into the natural one" (*True Christian Religion* §112). This vision clearly recapitulates motifs Swedenborg had perceived in the coloration of the rising sun in the cloud, but now the illuminated clouds appear to him as "correspondences" reflecting the state of illumination of the spiritual societies, with whom he has just been talking. Those who are open to his truth appear as a cloud in opal light, but those who turn away from him are a dark cloud. Similar cases, where his own spatiotemporal sensory perceptions pass over into the imagery of the vision, frequently occur in his records.

Only very few visions retain this overlap between the two worlds throughout the entire process, to the extent that Swedenborg remains aware of his room, his furniture, the window during the visit of an angel or spirit. Thus he reports on one occasion: "After receiving permission to do so, a devil once rose out of hell accompanied by a woman and came towards the house where I was. When I caught sight of them, I shut the window but spoke through it to them and asked the devil, whence he came. He said: 'From the community of my kind.' I asked: 'Whence does the woman come?' 'Likewise' came the answer. But she came from the band of sirens, who know how to imitate beauty and grace through all manner and forms of fantasy. The sirens are the courtesans in the world of spirits and devote themselves to fantasies." The devil now elaborates his sensualistic worldview to Swedenborg through the window. In a long conversation, Swedenborg explains the error of his views and conveys to him the true understanding of things. Thereupon, the devil exclaims, "I am mad" and explains that his former errors had made him a devil. But his conversion is not permanent. He reverts to his old spiritual state and describes the things he has just heard from Swedenborg as follies and disappears again into hell (*True Christian Religion* §80). The whole incident takes place as a conversation through a closed window, and the physical conception of space and time remains intact during the whole vision. These kinds of reports may well have led to the legend of spiritual visits in Swedenborg's residence.

But any survey of the *Spiritual Diary* indicates that visions are numerically few in which Swedenborg gives a precise description of their origin, his external circumstances, their onset, and their eclipse. The great majority lacks such stage instructions. As a rule, the reports begin with a formulaic turn of phrase, of which the most frequent are: "Once I saw in the spiritual world . . . ," "I looked out into the spiritual world and saw . . . ," "Once I entered a temple in the world of spirits . . . ," "Once I was strolling in the company of angels in the world of spirits . . . ," "Once, when I was associating with angels in heaven, I saw . . . ," and "One day I wandering through sundry districts in the spiritual world." The formalism of their presentation is already evident in their stylistic expression.

Particular attention should be paid to the scenic structure of the visions. At any given time, the introduction, centerpiece, and end can be clearly distinguished. The previously quoted examples demonstrate two main types of introduction. The introduction either follows from the mediation of an angel, who assumes the role of Beatrice and leads the Swedish Virgil through the higher domains, or it ensues through "correspondences," namely, the occurrence of sounds, figures, and lights, whose inner meaning is revealed in the course of the vision. These correspondences symbolize certain societies of spirits and express their important characteristics. The first type of introduction occurs very frequently, and it is hardly necessary to give further examples.

The second type of introduction is more remarkable. Here light and colors play a large role, especially in the morning visions, and optical perceptions doubtless contributed to their occurrence. The seer might have received such impressions through closed or slightly open eyelids, without registering them consciously. From these uncertain apparitions of light, there then developed angelic figures, whose nature was represented by the color, form, and intensity of perceived light. The angels then communicated specific insights to Swedenborg.

Another time the vision begins with auditions. The societies of spirits make themselves audible through all kinds of sounds, before they reveal themselves to Swedenborg. At any given time, these sounds symbolize their nature and correspond to their activity or doctrine. Sometimes the music of the angelic world reached his ears, on other occasions it was the commotion of hell. Here the earthly and spiritual worlds overlap in such a fashion that he believes he can hear thunder coming from the world of spirits with his physical ears or that he can feel the tumult of the demons beneath his feet.

Two examples may be cited here:

> Once I heard something like the sea raging beneath me, and I wondered what it was. Someone told me that it was a tumult

among those gathered on the lower earth, which is located just above hell. Soon the ground, which had covered them, opened up, and, lo, a multitude of owls flew out through the fissure and scattered overhead. They were immediately followed by locusts, which hopped around on the grass and made everything waste. Soon after I heard several plaintive cries from those owls and to the side a confused shouting as from ghosts in the woods. Then I saw beautiful birds coming from heaven, which flew towards the right. These birds were resplendent with pinions like gold, with markings and plumage like silver, and on their heads they bore coxcombs in the shape of crowns. When I saw this with amazement, a spirit suddenly rose out of the lower earth, whence the tumult came. This spirit was able to change into an angel of light and exclaimed: "Where is he who speaks and writes of order, with whom God the Almighty has made a covenant with men? We have heard of this down below." As soon as he was above ground, this spirit ran along the path. When he reached me, he immediately pretended to be an angel of heaven and said in a voice that was not his own: "Are you the man who thinks and speaks about order?"

Swedenborg then presents to him his theory of divine order in a didactic conversation, which forms the centerpiece of the vision. "When this devil heard this, his face changed, first becoming a leaden gray color, then black." Having metamorphosed back into his hellish form, he curses Swedenborg's teaching. "Forthwith he sank down to his own kind and disappeared. The birds on the left and the ghosts made strange sounds and plummeted into the sea known as the Suph Sea and the locusts jumped after them. The air was cleansed, and the earth was delivered from these wild animals. The tumult below ceased, and it became quiet and serene" (*True Christian Religion* §71). First of all, the noise resounds, which indicates the nature of the spirits represented, then the corresponding animals and figures appear, finally the spirit presents himself, in whose attitude and doctrine all these correspondences are revealed. The process is not unlike the appearance of the devil in Goethe's *Faust*, whose conception of the spirits was indebted to Swedenborg's reports and teachings. First, the monstrous, ghostly animal appears, as large as a cloud, which draws his fiery circle around Faust, then it becomes a poodle, and finally Mephistopheles reveals himself as "the essence of the brute." The vision passes away in a reversed sequence.

Many of Swedenborg's visions proceed according to this scheme of correspondences. He hears a mill clacking. As he approaches, it turns out to be a cave in which an old man is sitting surrounded by mountains of books. He is reflecting on justification by faith and is surrounded by pieces of paper, which he has already covered with writing. In an anteroom, there are numerous clerks, who are collecting and copying the sheets of paper (*True Christian Religion* §161). Thus Swedenborg hears the clatter of theology with his own ears. On another occasion, "I heard a gnashing of teeth and then a blow punctuated by hoarse sounds, and when I asked what this was, the angels who were with me said: 'They are assemblies, known as lodges, in which they are arguing with each other. At a distance their arguments sound like this noise.' I came up and saw a small house woven from rushes and daubed with mud. When I tried to look through the window, there were none, and one could not go in through the door." Finally he receives permission to enter and finds the inhabitants standing on the benches, arguing about faith and love, with the supporters of various theological opinions contradicting each other most violently. For a while, he listens to the quarrelsome discourse and then turns away from this spectacle in disgust.

Only in the rarest cases does Swedenborg experience the old, traditional form of vision known in Christian visionary literature since the Book of Revelation. Here the event takes place directly before the spiritual eye of the seer and the spiritual meaning of the images are proclaimed simultaneously or immediately afterwards. Such visions do not begin with a long introduction or transition, nor do they extend into a long-winded didactic conversation. These visions translate the seer immediately into the visionary event at the first flight of rapture and leave behind the impression of a sacred mystery, which is only gradually unveiled.

This traditional form of vision, in which imagery predominates over didactic content, is found in the following example:

> I was looking out into the spiritual world and saw an army on
> chestnut and black horses. The riders looked like apes, with face

and chest like the croup of the horse and the tail of the horse. Their backs were turned to the horses' heads and manes, and the reins hung round the necks of the riders. They were shouting: "On to battle against the riders of the white horses!" They pulled at the reins with both hands but drew the horses back further and further away from the battle. Then two angels descended from heaven and came to me, saying: "What do you see?" I related what comical riding I saw and asked what it meant and who they were. The angels replied: "They are from the place called Armaggedon, Revelation 16–17. There many thousands have gathered, in order to fight against the faithful of the New Church of the Lord." (*True Christian Religion* §113)

Swedenborg looks at the bearers of demonic resistance to his own preaching and immediately realizes the impotence of their efforts to destroy his work. The angels then explain to him the exact course and meaning of this battle. Here at the instant of rapture, the seer's gaze falls upon the supernatural drama of the demonic rebellion against the new revelation, and the vision is explained only afterwards by heavenly agents. But even this vision is an exegesis of Scripture, relating to the prophecies of the Johannine apocalypse.

A vision, which begins in a similar graphic fashion, delineates the shocking image of the Church, whose love has grown cold. To portray the Swedish Lutheran Church, Swedenborg used the imagery of the wintry landscape of his homeland.

I was conducted in the spirit to the North, to the region where all the land is covered with snow and all water is frozen. It was Sunday, and I saw people, that is spirits who looked like people in this world. On account of the cold they wore over their heads lion skins with the muzzle corresponding to their mouth. The front and back of their bodies were covered down to their loins with leopard skins, and their legs were covered with bearskins. I also saw several traveling on carriages and some carriages in the shape of a dragon with horns sticking out in front. The carriages were drawn by small horses, whose tails had been cut off. They ran like wild animals. The coachman held the reins in his hand and constantly drove them on, whipping them at full gallop. Finally I saw that the crowds were streaming towards a church, which one could not see before, as it was covered with snow. But the guardians of the church shovelled the snow away and cleared a path for the arriving churchgoers. These dismounted and went in. I was also allowed to see the church from inside, and it was opulently lit with lamps and lights. The altar was made of carved stone and behind it hung a tablet bearing the words: "Holy Trinity, Father, Son and Holy Ghost, which are threefold in nature." (*True Christian Religion* §185)

The priest gave a sermon on the justification by faith alone, about the attribution of Christ's justice and other orthodox themes. Thereupon Swedenborg began teaching and preaching in the midst of the congregation and tried to explain to those present about the chilling errors that they had had to hear, but the priest gave him black looks. The obdurate churchgoers departed and again mounted their carriages, "intoxicated with strange assertions, deluded with empty words and satiated with darkness in all matters of faith and redemption" (*True Christian Religion* §185).

This is a vision in the style of St. Hildegard or St. Bridget. Imagery prevails over the didactic and rational content. The chilling effect of dogma, which knows no love, appears in tangible form: the church, which has forgotten love for faith, is covered with snowdrifts and encrusted with frost. The misled believers, who stream towards the church, are shrouded in the skins of animals, which express the demonic character of the errors of their faith. Loveless souls in demonic mummery chase through the gloom towards the snowbound church, in order to be duped anew in their favorite errors, and then they race out into the icy night. The vision is quite self-evident even without long didactic conversations. But such examples are rare with Swedenborg.

This fact is significant. The centerpiece of most of Swedenborg's visions is the didactic conversation with the angels or spirits, which looms ever larger and stifles the imagery. Little action is matched by more talking and teaching. As a rule, the actual event serves only as a frame. Thus it comes about that the accounts are typically very monotonous and are deficient in imagery. There are descriptions of preaching in heavenly temples, debates in heavenly arbors, teaching in heavenly lecture halls, lectures in heavenly academies, judgments in heavenly courtrooms, and books being written in heavenly studies. The vivid element usually forms the stage scenery for long-winded, theoretical discussions, and even this scenery is often quite unreal. Even the world of heavenly learning cannot entirely dispense with dust and boredom, which is evidently an attribute of scholarship both in heaven and on earth.

This conspicuous disparity between imagery and didacticism is evident inasmuch as the didactic conversation with angels, demons, or dead antagonists in theology and philosophy often fill many pages of text, while the description of imagery takes just a few lines. Occasionally, this is dropped altogether, and the didactic conversation is simply reported, which Swedenborg has heard or conducted with the spirits.

Swedenborg distinguishes himself from all earlier visionaries precisely in this preponderance of didacticism over imagery. He can never conceal that he is a seer in the age of Enlightenment, which he may combat but never deny in the style of his thought and writing. The heaven of Swedenborg's accounts is an enormous establishment for the teaching and further education of the spirits. Its regions are classrooms, in which the spirits are led to increasingly higher levels of understanding under the guidance of already more advanced angels, who are in many passages given the title of senior master. What Swedenborg desires and abundantly receives from these spirits and angels is enlightenment and instruction in matters of doctrine. What he wants is theology and moral philosophy. Whenever he begins to speak in heaven and hell, it is in the role of teacher, who does not shrink from instructing long-deceased and prominent dissenters like Luther and Calvin about their errors.

However colorful individual accounts may be, they mostly deal with one and the same situation: the setting is the school or the debate. His heavens and hells are filled with debating groups, schools, or academies.[1] In squares, under trees, in avenues, in great amphitheaters, in lecture halls, caves, grottoes, and dungeons, in palaces and huts, on mountains, meadows and in valleys—everywhere

---

1. See *True Christian Religion* §136 for a debate on the question of God at five colleges.

Swedenborg meets groups of spirits who are hungry for knowledge or take delight in teaching and talking. They discuss problems of faith, questions of Holy Scripture, and often argue with each other. They exhaust themselves with unremitting lectures on their doctrinal position or enrage each other, until they are finally instructed in the correct solution and enlightened by angels of a higher degree or by Swedenborg himself, sometimes with and sometimes without success. Even lovers hastening towards each other on fiery wagons fall into conversation on metaphysical subjects as soon as they meet. There are teachings, proofs, demonstrations, critiques, and rebuttals on every corner. Swedenborg hardly ever comes upon one of his spirits otherwise engaged. If there was too much singing in the heaven of the Pietists, one could say that there was too much discussion in Swedenborg's heaven. The intellectuals are an intimidating majority, and among these the theologians are the most importunate. These theologians would like to spread the old dissenting views they proclaimed from their pulpits when living with dogged consistency in the heavens, or else they come together in synods and Church assemblies and make renewed attempts to have their own opinions adopted as generally valid articles of faith. One cannot help thinking that one would not feel at ease in this contentious heaven full of self-important colleagues.[2]

The doctrinaire character of Swedenborgian visions is also evident in their long chain-like sequences, where the same problem is discussed from various viewpoints. These visions can be separated from each other by long intervals of time, but they recur with the same scenery in the same heavenly spaces and take up the conversation at the same point where it was last left. They thus turn into a kind of heavenly lecture, which is not without a certain pedantry.

But this monotony does not prove that Swedenborg's visions were inauthentic. This monotony only reflects a strange fact that no one has yet fathomed and psychology had not even heeded: the human spirit almost always fails to imagine heaven. We are so made

---

2. [Swedenborg-Verlag note from 1969 edition] It should be noted, however, that there are no self-important theologians in Swedenborg's descriptions of heaven, but an amazing number of them in the world of spirits and in hell.

that only evil stimulates us. Only the rogues are interesting, while goodness bores both imagination and thought in a frighteningly short space of time. Just as Dante's description of *Inferno* fascinates the naïve reader much more strongly than that of *Paradiso*, so too do Swedenborg's visions of hell have a more powerful and vivid effect than his visions of heaven. Our human spirit is so constituted or spoiled that the eternally good and eternally beautiful soon seem tedious and insipid, and even the visions of the greatest visionaries describing heaven tire and bore us in the long run. There seems to be a kind of proof of original sin in this fact. If we wish to indict Swedenborg on this count, we must blame ourselves. The fact that heaven—and not only Swedenborg's heaven—seems boring to us whenever we want to imagine it in any detail is the surest proof that we have lost it.[3]

The extensive comments, which Swedenborg appended to many of his reports, also enable us to answer a significant question. Could he have evoked his visions intentionally? Did he possess the art of conjuring the spirits with whom he wanted to confer? Was he a sorcerer who possessed the key to the world of spirits, which he could manipulate at his pleasure? The temptation to abuse his gift was certainly great in an era when charlatans and magicians controlled kings and princes, and alchemists and Rosicrucians were still in demand at many European courts. In the whole time following his vocation, Swedenborg was never led astray into such abuses and refused the challenge of high potentates to summon certain spirits. But did he nevertheless live in the Faustian consciousness that he was lord of the spirits, able to compel them as he chose?

Several statements actually seem to indicate this. "It pleased the Lord, to open the face of my spirit and so admit me into the spiritual

---

3. [Swedenborg-Verlag note from 1969 edition] On closer inspection, Swedenborg's description of heaven is certainly not "boring." In contrast with the usual representations, Swedenborg's angels are not employed only in praying, singing, praising, and playing harps. Their duties are highly varied. A glance at the contents page of Swedenborg's *Heaven and Hell* gives ample demonstration of this. It is also evident that he has most to say about heaven, for two-thirds of the text is devoted to heaven, while barely 2/9s of the text is concerned with the world of spirits and less than 1/9 with hell.

world and granted me to speak not only with spirits and angels, but also with relatives and friends, even with kings and princes who have ended their days in the natural world." This exultation makes him sound like someone, who knows he possesses the "art," the "Key of Solomon," and can summon and dismiss the spirits at his discretion. "It was granted to me to join the angels and spirits in their world as one of them." These are the words of someone who feels himself endowed with the powers of a necromancer and who could say with Faust:

> "You hover, you spirits, beside me.
> Answer me, if you can hear me!"

Nevertheless there are no grounds for suspecting that he understood let alone used his gift freely to command the spirits and the deceased. Not only did he vigorously reject anyone wishing to use him as a necromancer and magician, but he also regarded each new vision as a fresh gift and charismatic marvel. His numerous reports unanimously confirm that he experienced his visionary gifts as a unique and precious work of divine grace and felt a sacred responsibility towards the donor of this grace. Constantly recurring phrases in the introductions to his reports express this: "It was granted to me to speak with angels and spirits," "It was granted to me to enter heaven," "I was permitted to join the angels in the spiritual world," and "The Lord permitted me to speak with angels and spirits." At no point does he ever attribute to himself the power of summoning a vision or "conjuring" a spirit or receiving a specific answer to a question. Prayer, the fundamental form of all religious life, is his only means of being assigned a revelation or an illumination, and the relationship between his visions and prayer must be examined more closely.

It can no longer be established whether and to what degree prayer played a part in Swedenborg's life in the years before his conversion. Although he describes a fervent life of prayer in his childhood and a breathing technique used to enhance his fervor, he is silent regarding his years of study and maturity. Swedenborg does not appear to have reverted to praying until the religious crisis preceding his vocation. In the Easter vision of 1744, Christ himself puts the words of his first prayer of the heart into his mouth. As his

Dream Diary shows, he lived henceforth in a world of prayer, once again accessible to him, and confronted all outer and inner temptations from now on with prayer. Following his vocation, prayer enables him to experience the proximity and presence of God again and again. It is therefore no wonder that many visions originated for him in prayer. This can be seen especially in the entries of his *Spiritual Diary*. Thus he writes on 20 November 1747: "Whenever I say the Lord's Prayer in the morning and evening, I am almost always raised into an inner sphere, combined with the feeling of a change of state, and nothing is more definite than this feeling after more than two years. After I have finished praying, I am translated back into my normal sphere." From this, it is evident that the Lord's Prayer has become a means of spiritual absorption since his conversion. In the diary entries for 1748, there are further suggestive clues:

> Whenever one reads the Lord's Prayer, which embraces all things in heaven and the spiritual world, one can plunge into such an abundance of details that not even heaven is capable of comprehending. This abundance is accessible to each according to his capacity for understanding and his usefulness. The more one penetrates into one's inner world, the greater the abundance streaming over one, and whatever is understood in the heavens cannot be understood in the lower spheres and remains a mystery to them. Many things can only be understood by intellectual faith, and many things are ineffable. The more heavenly ideas, which all come from God, descend to earth or penetrate a man of lower ability, the more closed it seems, so that it is finally like a hard mass, in which there is little or nothing besides the literal sense of the words.

This is to say that the Lord's Prayer is a dead arrangement of words to the unbeliever or an obtuse person closed to spiritual things. Meanwhile, it offers the most immense abundance of inner life to the person whose heart is receptive, so that he or she can ascend to the heart of God. Swedenborg even reported that he was deemed worthy to judge people's degree of receptivity to this prayer and the inner sphere to which it raised them.

Swedenborg regarded the Lord's Prayer as the most concentrated form of divine loving will, radiating the greatest power and warmth. For him, it summarized everything that God could give to humanity in life, blessing, and exaltation. It was the original revelation communicating the abundance of divine life to angels, spirits, and humankind according to their inner preparation and powers of comprehension. As he says in another passage of the *Spiritual Diary*, this prayer is a powerful whirlpool of ideas, for in each idea there is a multiplicity of new ideas and in each of these more ideas and so on. "The ideas are not closed, but there is an influx from the Lord on the inner path, thus their superabundance." The prayer was for Swedenborg the most important path leading him into the inner realms of life. It also became his means for asking God to clarify specific questions of meditation or scriptural passages.

Thus he once wrote:

> When I was once meditating on conjugial love, my spirit wished to know, what this love was like among those who lived in the golden age . . . , and because I knew that all who had lived well in this age are in heaven, I prayed to the Lord, that he might allow me to speak and be instructed by them. And, lo, an angel came to me and spoke: "I am sent by the Lord, to be your guide and companion. First, I want to lead you to those, who lived in the first age, known as the golden age." He continued: "The way to them is difficult, it leads through a gloomy forest, which no one can traverse without a guide sent by God." I was in the spirit and made ready for the journey, and we turned our faces to the east. . . .

Here the prayer is directed towards a specific object of knowledge. The vision itself is the fulfillment of the prayer. Its course and structure conform to the usual type in that a heavenly guide appears to lead him from his mundane location to a desired object, the most ancient human society, in order to learn about the nature of love in a didactic conversation. Many of Swedenborg's visions took place in a similar fashion, just as various illuminations and evidences occurred during a prayer or at its conclusion.

Prayer seems to have been his only means of establishing contact with deceased persons in the recent or distant past. He does not "conjure" the spirits but beseeches the Lord for understanding or a meeting with a specific spirit. Whenever Swedenborg conversed with famous men of past ages, it is always noted that this meeting came about through God's grace in listening to his prayer. Thus he wrote once:

> Once I prayed to the Lord that I might be granted leave to speak with the students of Aristotle, Descartes, and Leibniz and hear their views concerning the connection of the soul with the body. After the prayer, there were nine men there, three Aristotelians, three Cartesians, and three Leibnizians. They were standing around me, on the left the admirers of Aristotle, on the right the followers of Descartes, and behind me the admirers of Leibniz. At some distance and separated from each other by intervening rooms, there were three figures bearing laurel-wreaths; and thanks to an influx from heaven, I understood that these were the leaders or principal teachers. Behind Leibniz, there stood a man, holding a corner of his garment, and it was said this was Wolff.[4] The nine men then looked at each other, gave the most courteous greetings and began to converse. (*True Christian Religion* §696)

The actual didactic conversation is then reproduced in minute detail.

Such wishes for meetings with specific deceased persons are an extraordinary rarity with Swedenborg. Throughout his whole life, he constantly warned others against any spiritualistic experiments, and he was also personally terrified of undertaking any experiments himself in this direction. He had a fine sense for what he could and could not take upon himself regarding his visionary gift and always lived in fear of losing his gift through abuse. He had too high an estimate of the origin and meaning of this gift to risk profaning it through self-willed use. He could not be moved from this position even by the requests of princes, such as the Landgraf Ludwig IX of Hesse-Darmstadt, who inquired about the fate of several mistresses and war comrades in the next world. This is also characteristic of Swedenborg's general attitude of piety. He knew and felt himself to be a favored instrument, the "servant of God in the lower world," and his mission never tempted him to use the powers granted to him for his own purposes or the satisfaction of others' curiosity.

---

4. Concerning Wolff, see *Spiritual Diary* §§4550, 4727, 4744, 4851, 6018, 6049; and *True Christian Religion* §§90, 335, 696.

One should comment on the literary form of his visionary accounts. It is necessary to indicate several characteristics in order to disprove current errors and misunderstandings. If one regards the visions according to their external arrangement in the works of Swedenborg, it is striking that they never form the starting point of his didactic observations but always come at the end of a section. Swedenborg thereby distinguishes himself from all other visionaries in the history of Christian mysticism. In the case of St. Hildegard of Bingen, visions always form the starting point of the instructive meditation. First, there is a detailed description of the individual images of her visions, which then receive a theoretical explanation through a heavenly interpreter. With Swedenborg, the vision is quite secondary regarding its position in the general presentation of his doctrines or biblical exegeses. The reports of visions are always inserted under the special heading "Memorabilia" at the close of his didactic or exegetical chapters.

This must be understood in the context of the singular nature of his experience of vocation. His visions are and remain commentaries on a theological theme or a passage of the Bible. Their meaning serves to illustrate and corroborate spiritual knowledge. They are not the starting point but the confirmatory conclusion of his biblical exegeses and teachings.

This also explains a second characteristic of the literary use of his visions. They are linked to individual points of doctrine with a certain pedantry. Whenever he is discussing a specific theological problem, he also alludes to the corresponding vision, in which the solution to this problem dawned on him. If he expounds a thought, the pertinent vision occurs to him, and he seldom forgets to mention it, if only by reference to the relevant paragraph of an earlier work. The visionary reports thereby acquire a certain formalism even from a stylistic point of view. Some are literally repeated several times. There is a definite tendency towards literary substantiation, apparent in the revelatory claim of the visions themselves.

This peculiarity even characterizes his work *Heaven and Hell* (1758), which is entirely based on visions. Nothing would seem more natural than first describing the visionary images of heaven and hell in the manner of Dante's *Divina Commedia* and then clarifying

the structure of the transcendental and infernal worlds. But Swedenborg proceeds in quite the opposite way to Dante. He starts with a
systematic presentation of the structure of the spiritual world. At
particular places, a visionary report "from things heard and seen" is
inserted as a conclusion to clarify and confirm various doctrinal
points. Here too it is not the vision but the doctrine that takes the
lead, and the vision follows as a commentary and illustration.

After his vocation Swedenborg wrote prodigiously and quickly.
He explained this uncanny productivity by saying that he composed
his book under direct inspiration, as it were automatically. But even
if one were inclined to credit this marvel, one would have to note
that a hereditary factor favored it. His father Jesper was also incredi-
bly productive. Despite numerous conflagrations, which repeatedly
destroyed his manuscripts, the bishop produced an immense number
of sermons, books of prayer, and improving works and reckoned his
output by the cartload.

As a rule, Swedenborg wrote his manuscripts himself and employed neither secretary nor copyist. According to legend, the manuscripts show no sign of corrections or erasures. In this connection,
there is a story reported by Pernety: "When Ritter von Sandel was
visiting Swedenborg and saw a quantity of manuscripts without corrections or erasures lying on the table, where he was writing, he
asked him, if he took the trouble to make a fair copy himself.
Swedenborg replied: 'I make a fair copy at the first draft, for I am
only a secretary and write what my spirit dictates to me'" (Tafel, I,
doc. 6, pp. 61–62).

The circumstances of this dictation resulted from the visionary
reports themselves. Nowhere does Swedenborg assert that his books
were written straight off in a state of inspiration. On the contrary,
two factors can be distinguished.

Once the visionary reports assumed a special position in his
works. They are committed to paper from memory immediately after
the passing of the vision and the return to normal consciousness. But
several are also automatically written down as dictations during the
ecstasy, and this is usually specially noted. The *Spiritual Diary* contains a collection of such accounts. When composing his exegetical
or systematic works, Swedenborg refers back to these notes and

inserts them in the appropriate place. The "Memorabilia," which he records in a work of 1769, do not therefore necessarily stem from this year but could have occurred years before. There is also no doubt that Swedenborg subsequently altered the original text in stylistic terms. The literary form of the same visionary report, as it first appears in his *Spiritual Diary* and then later in one of his doctrinal works, is never literally identical. But once a visionary report had achieved its final form, he would gladly adhere to that version whenever he referred to that vision even for the third or fourth time.

One must distinguish notes that arose during an ecstasy. They are also numerous. During their committal to paper, Swedenborg had the sense of pure automatism and often absorbed the sense and content of what he had written only after he had subsequently regained daytime consciousness. It has already been indicated how his consciousness was active within this automatism in various stages from purely mechanical reproduction to conscious collaboration in composition. Regarding content, such dictations are less concerned with images as with ideas, which he receives in an intuitive way, or with exegeses of Holy Scripture, which spontaneously occur to him while absorbed in the text. In these cases, there is a frequent annotation "Written in the presence of the angels" or a similar reference. Such intuitions continuously accompanied the composition of his individual works. Here again, one can see that with time inspiration has become a conceptual and literary routine.

It is a further characteristic of his literary production that he did not compose his works on the basis of notes, sketches, and preliminary studies. Two generally useful tools of scholarship were notably missing from his study: bookshelves and a card index. He wrote everything straight down out of his head and belonged to that rare breed of authors who read only their own books. Count Höpken once gave a classic description of Swedenborg's attitude to the literature of his time: "In his latter years, he never read the works of others because he was so busy writing his own books."

The speed of his literary production struck all those who had an opportunity to observe Swedenborg at work. Cuno, an acquaintance in Amsterdam, described his work on *True Christian Religion*: "He is now working tirelessly—indeed, I have to say with amazing and superhuman industry—on his new work. Sixteen sheets with such small letters as his earlier works are already printed! Just imagine! For every printed page, he must fill four pages with writing. Every week he has two pages printed. He corrects them himself. It follows that he must write eight pages a week! And what is completely inconceivable is that he never has a single line prepared. As he says, his work when printed shall be eighty pages long. He has already calculated that it cannot be printed before Michaelmas." On another occasion the same informant speaks of Swedenborg's numerous visitors, and his readiness to accept invitations from friends, although he is still working on the manuscript of *True Christian Religion*. He then continues: "I just cannot understand, how he intends to have two closely written pages printed each week and write ten pages of manuscript, without having a single line already prepared. He says, his angel dictates to him, and he can write sufficiently fast." This literary productivity is amazing and extraordinary in an eighty-year-old man. Only an exaggerated missionary consciousness and a persistent training of his intuition could surely qualify for such an achievement.

23

The Heavenly Mirror

Numerous analogies exist between Swedenborg's visions and the writings of great Western visionaries like St. Hildegard of Bingen and St. Teresa, in respect of their types of vision, images, and symbols. However, Swedenborg's visions differ in assigning a special role to his own person and contain a host of personal incidents. Hildegard of Bingen appears in her own visions only as a spectator. She is enraptured; she sees certain images of events and then hears a heavenly voice that interprets what she has witnessed. It is a general rule that the visionary sees a heavenly scene and then experiences its exposition. Only in the emotional mysticism of love, as with St. Bernard of Clairvaux, is the viewer snatched up into the visionary event. But such instances are very rare and nowhere so systematically developed as in Swedenborg.

His visionary life is exceptionally self-referential. He is not so much concerned with the spirits but rather he appears a highly important personality to the spirits. The debate with them always takes place in a very self-conscious fashion, creating the impression that he is very much at home in the world of spirits, in heaven, and in hell.

Over time, he almost loses that sense of numinous awe that dominates most visionaries.

Almost as a matter of course, Swedenborg enters the heavenly realm with the routine of a pilot starting out on his hundredth transoceanic flight. He descends into hell like a miner who has gone down the shaft a thousand times. Almost three decades of persistent visionary experience have made him an old acquaintance of the spirits, giving his appearances in the next world a confident and unworried air. Indeed, he feels more secure in heaven than on earth because the inhibitions of earthly life disappear there. His speech flows smoothly, his thoughts develop in lucid order, his inspiration and his anger are without restraint, and his words work wonders. The devils he converts change before his eyes, lose their bestial form, and regain their human faces. But spirits who resist the truth of his words show external signs of their inner corruption: their faces are contorted into demonic and bestial masks, and they start to stink and plunge into the abyss. This frequently naïve self-reference deserves special attention.

Swedenborg not only felt unique in his spiritual gift and emphasized his special status vis-à-vis his fellows on earth but constantly indicated this to the spirits and angels. In the *Inferno,* Dante must explain again and again to the amazed inhabitants of this realm why he can dwell as a living man among the damned. On his wanderings through the spiritual world, Swedenborg likewise attracts the attention of its dwellers and frequently uses the opportunity to explain his exceptional status. According to his doctrine, an ordinary person has as little chance of entering the world of spirits as an ordinary spirit has of making itself understood to people on earth. Both realms are separate, and both worlds lack a sense for each other. If Swedenborg feels that he alone possesses this wonderful gift of living in both worlds, it is no wonder that he instructs the spirits and angels in a tone that blends self-confidence, modesty, and condescension.

This leads to curious incidents. Once he went up "in the spirit" to a group of youths in the world of spirits who were strolling in a park and attracted their attention. "You are surely not in our state of life," said one to him. Swedenborg replied with a smile: "I am neither an actor nor a *Vertumnus,* but I alternate between your light and your shadow, so I am a stranger here and yet a native" (*True Christian Religion* §280). Amazed by this riddling talk, the leader of the group asks him: "Who are you?" Swedenborg only now reveals his secret: "I am in the world in which you were, and I am also in the world in which you are, which is called the spiritual world. That is why I can communicate in a natural state with men on earth and in a spiritual state with you. The Lord granted this to me."

This special status of citizen in two worlds has very important consequences. People who are entirely given up to their sensory impressions finally lose all knowledge of the spiritual world, and they become materialists who reject the spiritual realm as mere fantasy. Conversely, the inhabitant of the world of spirits, with whom Swedenborg is talking, has lost all knowledge of the natural world and its earthly mode of being. He has become a pure idealist because he has neither contact with the natural world nor any means of comparison with it. Swedenborg therefore uses his special status to explain the peculiarities of existence in the world of spirits and its contrast to life on earth by reference to his own person. Surrounded by the astonished inhabitants of the spirit world, he arranges a series of experiments in a scientific and methodical fashion.

Swedenborg first instructs the spirits concerning their language. With the aid of various words, he shows them that they use the universal language of the spirits among themselves, while they instinctively speak to him in his own Swedish language. Other experiments relate to the difference between heavenly and earthly writing. One of the spirits is asked to go outside and write a sentence in heavenly characters on a piece of paper. However, he cannot explain it to Swedenborg the man because the few characters of the heavenly alphabet contain countless meanings and allusions that cannot be compressed into human script. Every letter and every stroke of the heavenly script are packed with meaning and ideas to express the essence of any signified thing completely and exhaustively.

Swedenborg finally conducts experimental tests concerning the difference between spiritual and natural thought. Certain spirits must go away, think of something, and then come back and tell Swedenborg what they thought of. But this proves impossible because they have no notion of natural thought to match spiritual thought. They lack concepts to express their ideas to Swedenborg in terms of human thought. Through the repetition of this experiment, the spirits are convinced that "the spiritual thought pictures are supernatural, inexpressible, unutterable, and inconceivable to natural man." It is therefore Swedenborg who first explains to the spirits their previously unconscious ways of being, thinking, and speaking.

These experiments also attract attention in the upper regions of heaven. A voice from above summons one of the participants: "Ascend!" He does so and returns after some time to give Swedenborg the flattering information that even the angels did not previously know the difference between the spiritual and natural realms. Before Swedenborg's arrival in the world of spirits, no one had an opportunity to make comparisons and note the differences in being and understanding with the aid of a man who lives in both worlds. Thus Swedenborg becomes "a spectacle to the angels," as St. Paul once wrote in I Corinthians 4:9.

Similar experiments are repeated several times in his visions. Swedenborg organizes tests for the inhabitants of the spirit realm concerning the different conceptions of time and space in the natural and spiritual worlds. The results are exciting, but it must suffice to mention the fact. How shy and timid was the conduct of the great visionaries of earlier centuries on their appearance in heaven! But here a man of an enlightened age enters the spirit realm, a seer who immediately makes even heaven the object of scientific investigation, and does not shrink from performing experiments with the spirits and angels.

Swedenborg's encounter with the inhabitants of the spirit realm sometimes reminded him of his earlier researches. Although he sees his true vocation in proclaiming the wonders of the higher world to those on earth, he occasionally forgets himself. He hymns the wonders of the earth to the spirits, plays the role of Odysseus in reporting the delights of the marvelous world to the pale wraiths of the underworld, and allows them to drink the sap of the earth in order that they may understand the enchantment of their earlier life. Here speaks the heart of the natural scientist who spent the greater part of his life in the mines, fathoming the mysteries of life by observing plants and animals. This is a man who regarded Swammerdam's

Bible of Nature as a holy book, proclaiming the magnificence of both the Creator and the creation.

Once, when translated to the company of ancient sages in heaven, he explained his special case to them: "Physically I am in the natural world, but spiritually I am in your spiritual world" (*True Christian Religion* §695). The sages start to ask him what people in the earthly world think about the influence of the upper on the lower world. Swedenborg replies that people have no proper understanding of this and explains his own doctrine of influences underlying the metaphysics of life to the amazed colleagues of earlier centuries. Everything earthly is only a receptive organ for the life that streams from the upper world into the earthly sphere where it calls forth an inexhaustible abundance of forms:

> Then I spoke about the marvels that arise from the influence of the spiritual world upon the natural world. For example, how caterpillars become butterflies, the worker bees and drones, and the marvels of plants and how they develop from one seed to a new seed. It is just as if the earth knew how to prepare their raw materials and adapt itself to the fertilizing energy of the seed and entice it out of the germ. It then widens this into a stem, lets branches sprout forth, clothes them in leaves and decorates these with blossoms, from which fruits form. These fruits then bring forth new seeds as their children, in order that a new birth occurs. But due to constant observation and repetition these things have become customary and common, so that one no longer regards them as marvels but mere effects of nature. One only holds this opinion because one does not know there is a spiritual world and that this works inwardly and sets each and every thing in action.

Here Swedenborg is not presenting a theory but a confession of his own feelings when contemplating the wonders of the world. It is a confession of the beauty of this world but also an indication of the path that led the natural scientist into the realm of visionary understanding.

Swedenborg not only attracts attention in the spirit realm through his presence but employs himself there with an energy and passion wholly absent from his earthly conduct. In the spiritual world, he is a lively apologist for himself and uses all the means he would scorn on earth to publish and defend his opinions. Full of confidence in the truth of his doctrine, he participates in all heavenly discussions. No heavenly academy or learned society is safe from him. In a polite but unabashed manner, he asks leave to speak, even when he is only joining in such sessions as a guest or stranger. He intervenes in the debate with a mixture of gentleness and force and frequently has the satisfaction of seeing his own opinion confirmed by a divine sign. The academies of this world may have had little to offer him, but he has every chance to speak in the world of spirits. His philosophical, scientific, and theological opponents in this world may shun any public debate with him or, like Ernesti, dismiss him with malicious reviews and plague him with evil rumors; but in the lecture halls and councils of the spiritual world, they have to listen and learn from him.[1] If he cannot convert them down here on earth, in the other world he at least has the satisfaction of bringing them over from their error, malice, and obduracy. Thus, he can put on record their opposition to the truth, which is his truth and the truth of God. In the world of spirits, he settles all the scientific and theological battles that his enemies on earth avoided, partly due to scorn and partly due to indifference. There he achieves and receives everything that is denied or withheld from him on earth.

Swedenborg flatters himself with the role of teacher to an extraordinary degree in the spirit realm. The professorial chairs there attract him as those at Swedish universities repelled him. The lecterns of the heavenly academies entice him to speak and lecture, while his seat in the Swedish Academy of Sciences induced him to attend as rarely as possible. At the academy, he spoke about the art of marble inlays; but in the spiritual world, he speaks about his real concern, his doctrine, his revelations, his knowledge, for here prevails a freedom that he vainly sought on earth, and things appear without pretense according to their innermost nature. His appearance in the learned societies of the spiritual world gives him as great a satisfaction as the annoyance

---

1. Swedenborg replied to Ernesti's review, a totally uncritical insult, by indicating that it was "contrary to the laws of honor." He refused to answer it in the same tone and "return slanders or refute it with slanders; this would be like common women throwing bread in each other's face when they quarrel. . . ." Swedenborg printed this critique on a special note inserted in his works printed in 1770 and 1771.

produced by visits to their corresponding earthly establishments. He refutes his opponents in the spiritual world with a freedom, daredevilry, and superiority that stand in an inverse proportion to the timidity and reserve he demonstrated in such debates on earth.

We have already observed Swedenborg in an extraordinary role teaching the spirits about their speech, writing, and thought. But his zeal is even greater whenever he meets theological or philosophical colleagues in the other world. Apart from the ancient thinkers, he can meet there countless throngs of theologians and philosophers from all schools over seventeen-and-a-half centuries, so it is no wonder that he meets them at every step. Most frequently, he takes the opportunity of opposing disputatious orthodox Lutherans, who so embittered him on earth and who even in the world of spirits seek to impose their opinion on practically every conference or synod.

Rarely does Swedenborg remain a silent listener. He once came into an academy session at which God's image in man was being discussed. Accompanied by two angels, he was invited to take a seat, but he refused politely and modestly: "I have been conducted here by two angels to see and hear, but not to take a seat" (*True Christian Religion* §48). He remains standing and hears the whole discussion through to its end. On another occasion, he participated at a kind of heavenly synod at which "the wisest of the wise from the Christian religion" had gathered to discuss the act of justification (*True Christian Religion* §390). The doorkeeper admits him to the dilapidated conference hall only on the condition that he will not speak a word. He is therefore silent during the debate and leaves the melancholy place in an angry mood due to the errors of the orthodox believers. But at least he has the satisfaction of seeing the effect of this assembly on those heathens present. As he goes out, he hears one say to another: "These people have no religion whatsoever." Thus the heathens confirm his own verdict that the ostensible spokesmen of religion are frequently the enemies of religion.

Such rare scenes showing him as a silent participant are far outnumbered by visions in which he vigorously intervenes in the debate, indeed takes a leading part and ends the discussion with the complete defeat of his opponents. These reports all conform to a similar type.

Once he came into conversation with several canons and a bishop about the doctrine of the Trinity. After giving several explanations about the spiritual world, "about which they had no prior knowledge," Swedenborg asks the clergy to tell him their views. When the bishop has finished his speech to approving nods from the canons, Swedenborg begins to prove their numerous errors to them with many theological arguments and biblical quotations. He succeeds in convincing his listeners. As he departs, the bishop turns towards him and wants to exclaim: "There is *one* God," in order to recant his previous error regarding three gods in the divinity. But at this very instant, he relapses into his old way of thinking. His intellect prevents his tongue from admitting the truth. To the great merriment of the bystanders, he is forced to confess the three gods with his mouth wide open and against his better knowledge.

Swedenborg pays an even more impressive role in another vision in which he meets with professors of theology and Church teachers, "the intellectual leaders of the whole clergy in Europe." Their spiritual arrogance and conceit are vividly illustrated by their external appearance. They float along in an airship with seven sails in the sky, dressed in purple robes with the laurel of their academic degree upon their brow. Swedenborg hails them. They stop overhead and speak to him from the airship. Swedenborg reproaches them for separating God from humankind and love from faith in their false teaching. He closes with violent invective such as he never uttered to theologians on earth: "I know that your intellect can have nothing in common with anything that proceeds from the Word." After he has given his speech in the elevated role of a judge, he receives a supernatural endorsement. Before his eyes, the illustrious company is shorn of its pomp and display. The airship disintegrates and its passengers tumble down. The gentlemen who had just previously been floating in purple and laurel through the skies are now sitting in rags on the sand, girded with nets, through which their bare flesh is showing! Confronted by the truth from Swedenborg, the theologians' inflationary conceit bursts in the literal sense of the word.

On another occasion, Swedenborg comes upon a circle of theologians who are expounding the doctrine of the three persons in the divinity. First he listens to their speeches and thinks: "O, what stupidity!" Upon the command of the Lord, three angels descend from the upper heaven and join with him "in order that I might speak with greater perception to those under the delusion of three gods." On behalf of God and with the aid of his inspiration, he steps before the assembly of orthodox Church teachers and reveals to them the correct doctrine of the unity of God. At the end, a wonderful apparition corroborates the accuracy of his exposition. Hell appears before all those who adhere to their false opinion according to old habits of thought, while those who have now received the truth gaze up to heaven. "The sun of heaven, in which God assumes human form, appeared to them" (*True Christian Religion* §136). In the world of spirits, true theology is thus separated from false by Swedenborg's teaching. Such experiences illustrate the enormous power of this man's mission.

In another vision, he simultaneously sees five heavenly universities. He approaches one of these, which is swathed in twilight. There an assembly is discussing what is meant by Christ sitting on the right hand of God. Swedenborg listens to several explanations and is astonished that "these educated persons are so ignorant, although they have already been in the spiritual world for some time. So that they should not remain ignorant any longer, I raised my hand, and asked that they grant me an audience for the few words I wished to say on the subject." He then proclaims his teaching on this point with a violent polemic against the decrees of the Council of Nicaea, "which turned the Church into a theater, by hanging up painted scenes where masked figures kept performing new plays." Those present are angered by this condemnation of the major council of Christianity, and there is an excited commotion. Even the chairman objects to the words of the unbidden guest. But Swedenborg sticks to his opinion, asks the chairman to call the assembly to order, and continues with an explanation of biblical texts on the right hand of God. When the tumult rises again, he makes a truly prophetic threat: "Take care," he shouts into the excited crowd, "that a hand does not come down to you from heaven and give you an incredible fright, as it did when it appeared to me." "Scarcely had he spoken, when an outstretched hand appeared beneath the sky, the sight of which terrified everyone so much that they ran in a mass to the doors and some to the windows. They rushed outside and several fell down breathless. But I walked slowly behind them." Forthwith he sees a college covered with a dark cloud, the visible counterpart for a darkening of understanding that prevailed within. No speaker at an earthly conference of theologians has ever had such a splendid exit. He opposes the false teachers, blames them for the decline of the Christian religion, exposes them as directors of a deceptive theater, and deprives their false faith of its basis. When he confronts their dry and abstract notion of the right hand of God with his own true idea, this right hand of God comes down from heaven and chases the opponents out in hasty flight. Meanwhile, the seer who threatened this apparition walks from the place of his victory with dignity.

Another experience proceeds in a similar fashion. Swedenborg sees five heavenly grammar schools and enters the first of them, which is enveloped in a flaming light. Pious spirits are sitting there on benches, talking about active love. The chairman of the assembly stands in front of the lectern, asking questions and allowing one after the other to answer. The most varied views are presented. One says that active love is morality based on faith; another thinks it is piety inspired by compassion; a third thinks it is restricted to assisting one's relatives and friends in every way; a fourth believes in giving alms and supporting those in need; a further person thinks it consists in making the churches more wealthy and benefiting their servants. After all have spoken, Swedenborg steps forth and politely asks if he may present his view, although he is a stranger. He summarizes the views of the preceding speakers and shows that they have spoken only about individual symptoms of active love, not about its actual essence, which he now begins to explain to the illustrious forum. After concluding his speech, "a silence arises, as among those who see and acknowledge something through their inner person." The assembly is so deeply impressed by his exposition that they remain silent in devout emotion. He leaves the assembly in this state and is translated back to his natural state (*True Christian Religion* §459). Can any earthly speaker record a greater success among men than Swedenborg achieves here with the spirits?

For all this, Swedenborg is no more set on success in the world of spirits than on earth. It is enough for him to appear as a witness for the truth, and the spirits should decide for this truth. The wonderful constitution of the heavenly light tolerates neither deception nor pretense, and there all spiritual creatures appear according to their innermost nature and intention. Thus Swedenborg's preaching does serve not only to convert dissenters but also to expose the deceit of those who defend error out of convenience, ambition, or self-deception.

His visit to a surly theologian surrounded by a pile of books on the doctrine of justification has already been described. While he ceaselessly gathers biblical arguments to justify his theology, a crowd of clerks are busy in his anterooms writing out fair copies of their master's works. Swedenborg instructs the old man concerning his errors and reveals to him the true understanding of Christian faith, which must embrace love. Seeing himself cheated of his life's work and fame, the learned man becomes angry, jumps up from his seat, and orders the clerks to eject the irksome man. As Swedenborg hurries off before the clerks can reach him, the old man furiously hurls a heavy book after him. Swedenborg picks it up and notes that the old man had seized the Bible as a missile from among the many books surrounding him! Once again, Swedenborg presents his personal experience and conviction in this visionary experience. This is how he experienced the Bible scholarship of ostensible believers. In the absence of any real arguments, such theologians threw the Bible at anyone who grasped the true meaning of Scripture.

The unmasking of orthodoxy in his era is Swedenborg's favorite employment in heaven as on earth, but his reforming zeal is far greater there than here. Once he met a company of theologians who were discussing justification by faith alone. He intervenes directly in the debate and proves to them "that their faith is false and absurd and leads only to physical security, blindness, sleep, and insanity in spiritual matters and also to the death of the soul." In reply, the incensed opponents boast about their theological learning. "Why should we renounce this? The learned precedence of the clergy over the laity depends on this doctrine of justification." But Swedenborg continues to expose their folly and proves conclusively that they are fulfilling the prophecy of the Johannine apocalypse of the coming Apolyon, the great harbinger of the last days. The theologians answer with a pun: their learning makes them Apollo, not Apolyon. Swedenborg retorts that they are not only Apolyon but Leviathan, and God will punish them with his sharp sword. He receives only scornful laughter in reply (*True Christian Religion* §182).

In this case, his speech is unsuccessful, but at least he has told his opponents in the name of truth what they should think of them- selves and what God thinks of them. Judgment is passed on their ob- duracy by God before the angels and Swedenborg, who ceaselessly proclaims the spiritual aridity of Christianity in his time. He summa- rizes the conclusions of many conversations in the world of spirits concerning this issue in these words:

> I have come to know the desolation of the truth and debilitation of theology in the Christian world today through conversations with many laymen and clergy in the spiritual world. These people are so spiritually impoverished that they scarcely know anything besides the Holy Trinity of Father, Son, and Holy Ghost and that one can be redeemed by faith alone. They only know the evangelists' his- torical accounts of Christ and the rest penetrates their ears no more than the murmuring of the wind or a drum beat. The angels sent by the Lord to attend the Christian congregations lament and say that such stupidity prevails there. There is such gloom in matters of salvation that one might be dealing with a chattering parrot. In spiritual and divine things, they have no more insight than statues.

Swedenborg performs the office of an outspoken witness of the truth with identical vigor towards those philosophical trends that are most opposed to the truth in his view. He speaks against the Spin- ozists and their related schools of natural science, as well as against the sensualists and the atheists, who deny the existence of a spiritual and divine world altogether.

Once, accompanied by an angel, he enters a college of philoso- phers, who assert that nature, not God, is the origin of life. He begins a dispute with one of these sages who has spread out before him a whole library of Spinozist literature from all countries. The scholar initially insists on his opinion, until Swedenborg and the accompany- ing angel explain: "Friend, you are talking nonsense!" He finally con- vinces the Spinozist, who submits first unwillingly and then willingly to their proofs. As a man of courtesy, he accompanies them through the outer court of his college, while speaking to them on other matters with "the newly acquired acuity of his spirit" (*True Christian Religion* §35). It is noteworthy that Swedenborg evidently associates the persons he meets in his visions with specific historical personalities, but he usually does not refer to them by name. He does this honor only to the most famous, like Spinoza himself, Descartes, Newton, Leibniz, or Wolff.[2]

On another occasion, Swedenborg meets with Dutch and English deists. One of these is just giving a lecture to prove that God is bound by his own natural order and can do nothing contrary to the laws of nature. Another turns to Swedenborg and asks him for his comment on this assertion, for its seems a sacrilege to shackle God with his own laws. First Swedenborg prays for divine illumination: "I want to pray to the Lord for his assistance to throw light on this matter." Then he elaborates his doctrine of the Lord, who does not impose a law upon things from outside but whose life is implicit in the law. He implants in everything an inner order as its principle of development, which embraces the redemption of humanity, their ascent to God and deification. His listeners subsequently see a divine sign of corroboration for his teaching: "At these words, a gleam of golden light shone through the roof and gave rise to cherubim floating in the air. Their fiery glow illuminated the temples but not the foreheads of several people present." The philosophers murmur: "We still do not know what omnipotence is." But Swedenborg, sure of the success of the truth he has presented, says to them: "That will be revealed when you are penetrated by some light concerning what has been said." Here too his presence in the world of spirits serves to publish the truth and root out the errors that trouble the spirits in heaven and on earth.

The philosophers in the spiritual world are generally less vindictive and behave more courteously than the disputatious theologians. Swedenborg's heaven is also in this respect a mirror of earthly circumstances. Let us hear his experiences in another heavenly academy, over which a prince presides. Requested to give his views on the

---

2. See, for example, *Divine Love and Wisdom* §82 and the *Spiritual Diary* §6064.

creation of the universe, Swedenborg speaks of the origin of the natural and spiritual worlds and their relation to each other, while referring to his divine illumination on this point. At his departure, sparks of light fall from the sun of the spiritual world through the angelic heavens into the eyes of the assembled company and thence into their souls, "and with this illumination they applauded my speeches." The scholars then accompany him into the outer court, while the spirit who introduced him to this circle descends with him as far as his house in Stockholm and then hastens back to his heavenly congregation.

Swedenborg's egocentricity is conspicuous in these visionary scenes and their literary description, but there are even more glaring examples of his self-confidence in his visionary life. Not only does Swedenborg describe himself as an interesting phenomenon to the inhabitants of the spirit realm, not only does he appear as the teacher of the Church fathers, theologians, and philosophers of all times, but he is also flattered to discover that he is already well known as an author in heaven. Although his works met with hurtful rejection and disregard to some extent on earth, he has the compensation of their being all the more eagerly read and renowned in the world of spirits. The theme of Swedenborg's fame as an author in the spiritual world deserves special attention, for there is no other comparable claim in the history of European thought.

Once he describes how a spirit from a company in the lower earth adjoining hell ascended up to him and challenged him to a debate. "Where is the man," he cries, "who speaks and writes of the order that God the Almighty has bound himself with respect to men? We have heard of this through the surface of the earth!" The demon here alludes to Swedenborg's doctrine that God's omnipotence is realized in the order he has imparted to all things and that the supreme principle of order consists in humankind's being created in the image and likeness of God. The stranger continues: "Are you he who thinks and talks about order? Tell me briefly what order is and what belongs to order." Placed in the happy position of giving a lecture on one of his principal doctrines, Swedenborg begins: "I will tell you the major points but nothing special because you could not grasp this" and then treats seven carefully defined points. But the spirit from the depths, who has meanwhile turned himself into an angel of light, cannot bear the truth. The angelic face he has falsely assumed begins to darken, becomes a leaden hue and then black. Finally he sinks back into his underworld with the cry: "What you say is a unique offence against the doctrine!" (*True Christian Religion* §71). In this fashion, the shaken author learns that his teachings have spread as far as the nether regions of the spirit realm. However, they are rejected there and serve only to demonstrate the obstinacy of the learned societies of the underworld.

Swedenborg's opinion about divine orders even leads to violent disagreement in a heavenly company. During a visionary journey, he meets a party of clergymen, scholars, and intellectuals; several seeing him coming in the distance run up to him and reproach him: "Are you he, who has shackled God with his own laws? What a presumptuous venture! You have destroyed the faith. . . . I have heard that you consider our faith void because it does not attribute order to man." This provocation causes Swedenborg to instruct his opponents angrily "with a raised voice." At his words, "the assembled people wanted to argue abusively, but they did not dare because they saw the heavens open above him and heard a voice saying: 'Listen patiently to the order, which guides God the Almighty.'" After this divine endorsement, Swedenborg continued his speech. He succeeds in winning a part of his audience for the truth of his doctrine. The converted depart and praise God, but the others move off to the left (*True Christian Religion* §74). What a difference in his behavior between the earthly and heavenly worlds! On earth, his answer to questions mostly consisted in referring his inquirers to the appropriate discussions in his books, and he avoided all violent discussion. In heaven, he vigorously and courageously takes up the battle, has the satisfaction of divine attestation for his doctrines, and witnesses the conversion of a part of his opponents, which had never happened in such a demonstrative manner on earth.

His fame in the spiritual world even reached the point that many spirits—not unlike curious readers on earth—feel a strong urge to converse personally with the author of such instructive books. According to his own statement, the rumor of his appearance reached Luther. The reformer desires to speak with the new prophet, even to be taught by him, with the unexpected result that Swedenborg actually convinces him of the error of his doctrine of justification by faith and converts him to his own teaching. Other visions record similar flattering experiences. One morning, absorbed in the sight of the rising sun, Swedenborg hears several spirits saying: "May we speak with the newcomer who threw the apple of Eris among the Churchmen? Many laymen throng around him to lift him up before our eyes." Swedenborg understands immediately that this is an allusion to his newly published *Brief Exposition of the Doctrine of the New Church* (1769). The spirits continue talking about this work and pose the same question, which then concerned the Swedish clergy examining the orthodoxy of Swedenborg's books in the context of an inquisition trial against him. "Is it really so schismatic?" asks one, while another takes the view of the Provost Eckebom of Göteborg and exclaims: "Schismatic? It is heretical!" Others dare to champion Swedenborg's work and explain that he refers to a mass of passages from Holy Scripture. Their remarks show plainly that this spiritual society is a group of theologians and Church princes. Swedenborg begins talking to them. An unnamed Saxon theologian, "a dictator of the Evangelicals," attacks him, saying: "How can you be so presumptuous as to overturn the worship of God, which has been established for many centuries in the Christian world?" His supporters agree with him and take up a fighting stance "like bold warriors on a battleship, when they glimpse the enemy fleet and want to shout: 'Up to battle; the victory is surely ours!'" Swedenborg now begins to defend his work with many interruptions from the Saxon dictator. He substantiates his doctrines of the New Church and cleverly quotes the articles of concordat, in order to strike the camp of orthodoxy with its own weapons. He proves that he does not know the symbolic books properly and is therefore not capable of judging the congruence of Swedenborg's doctrine on Christ with those in the symbolic books. His own heresy trial, in which he displayed so much reserve on earth, he now conducts in the world of spirits with every determination and uses the same arguments to refute Eckebom, which he had sent in a letter to Dr. Gabriel Beyer. Swedenborg concludes his apology in the world of spirits with numerous exegeses of biblical passages. He recognizes the changes in the souls of his opponents in the transformation of their faces. Several look at him with approval, while others turn away from him with dark looks (*True Christian Religion* §112).

This visionary report must have particularly impressed Swedenborg's opponents on earth. He demonstrates his triumph not over any arbitrary opponent but over a "leader of the Evangelicals" and a teacher at the mother university of Lutheranism. The court case currently conducted against him in Sweden is already resolved in his favor in heaven. Swedenborg's truth has long since prevailed in heaven over opponents who hounded him on earth in the name of orthodoxy.

But Swedenborg is not only vindicated before the spirits of theologians of his Swedish Lutheran Church. His prophetic self-consciousness also causes him to challenge the early centuries of the Church. He experiences this in a vision, which counts among his most delightful reports from the world of spirits and subtly indicates how widespread his fame is already there. It is the most recently deceased scholars and theologians who have spread the news of their unusual contemporary. Thus, Swedenborg was once visiting the town Athenaeum located in that part of heaven where the ancient philosophers of Greece and Rome live together in peace. They discuss not only the problems of their own philosophy but also the advance or retreat in knowledge that has occurred on earth since their death. As Swedenborg makes his pilgrimage to the town of the ancient sages, he notices three newcomers—a priest, a statesman, and a philosopher. All three are Christians. After a long-winded welcoming ceremony, they enter the palladium, where the sages of Greece and Rome sit with laurel wreaths at tables and ask the new arrivals, "What's new on earth?" The three first give news of Swedenborg, who is not pleased to be the center of conversation. "The latest thing is," reports the priest, "that someone claims he can talk with the angels and has a face that has been opened into the spiritual world. He is alleging many new things." Thereupon the sages listen to all Swedenborg's astonishing teachings concerning the spiritual world and ask: "What do they think about this on earth?" The priest answers that the people of his class first thought they were genuine visions, then that they were pure inventions, and finally, that he had probably seen ghosts. But the general verdict of his circle is "Believe whoever wants to; we have previously taught that man will not have a new body until the day of the Last Judgment."

The sages shake their heads at the senselessness of contemporary theologians who speak through the words of the priest. They flatter Swedenborg by asking whether there are not at least "some intelligent people" among the theologians on earth who can prove his doctrine of life beyond death and persuade the others of the truth of this fact. The priest thinks there may be some, but they do not insist on their proofs. Most content themselves by explaining that their reason is obedient to their faith, and they believe in the physical resurrection on the day of the Last Judgment. The sages are therefore as indignant as Swedenborg concerning this unreasonable attitude. Swedenborg himself regarded the orthodox teaching that reason should be subservient to faith as the source of all inertia in the Church. The philosophers now show the priest how absurd is the belief that the physical resurrection will not occur until the day of Last Judgment. They explain to him how their own doctrine of the soul's residence in the Elysian Fields is much closer to the truth than these alleged orthodox teachings.

At this point, they turn to the politician who tells them that, when he dwelt on earth, he rejected immortality in every guise. He is now ashamed by these thoughts since he has experienced in his own case that the person actually survives as a person after death. The philosopher also tells a similar story. The ancient sages are very shaken by these frank avowals: "O how stupid are the minds of men on earth nowadays! If only pupils of Heraclitus and Democritus were there, who laugh and cry over everything, we would hear great laughter and crying" (*True Christian Religion* §693). What more can an author experience than the justification in heaven from the mouths of such witnesses! Even Swedenborg the seer was still sufficiently a humanist to value such vindication by the spiritual heroes of his youth.

Let us conclude this account of the heavenly mirror with a vision in which Swedenborg experiences the supreme glorification of his person and endorsement of his teachings together with the glorious finale in heaven of his earthly court case (*True Christian Religion* §461). It is a vision in which Swedenborg is confronted by his opponents and forced to justify himself, thus recapitulating the scene of his trial before a college of judges. Swedenborg sees himself called before a kind of ecumenical council, attended by Christian theologians from ancient times up to the present. On the right side of this illustrious synod sit the apostolic fathers, dignified men with long hair and beards. It was these fathers whose writings William Whiston discovered and published at the time of Swedenborg's studies in London. On their basis, Whiston had proven the apostasy of the Nicene theologians from the faith of the early Church. On the left side sit the modern theologians, "who had become famous through their writings and learning, concerning the present faith and the doctrine of the justification of the elect," in the traditional costume of their age, close-shaven, with flowing wigs and ruffs around their necks. The censor of the century stands before the lectern, his stick in hand. The latter files the complaint concerning the publication of Swedenborg's works before this universal council. With dignity, he steps onto the upper step of the rostrum, gives a heavy sigh and begins after a pause: "Brothers, what a century! Someone from among the laity, a man without an academic gown, without a crown, without a laurel, has stood up and dragged our faith down from heaven and thrown it into the Styx. O, what sacrilege!" Then he describes Swedenborg's person and doctrine: "This man, although advanced in years, is completely blind in the mysteries of our faith." He has understood neither the doctrine of justification nor that of the Trinity. The scholars with the curly wigs and ruffs clap with applause at his accusation and revile the doctrine of Swedenborg.

Then one of the apostolic fathers on the right, a teacher of the authentic ancient Christian Church, rises and intervenes on behalf of Swedenborg. He refutes the modern supporters of the orthodox doctrines of justification and the Trinity and corroborates Swedenborg's revelations on these matters. Then Swedenborg himself steps forward. An angel instructs him to read aloud several passages from the articles of concordat to the orthodox party and then Swedenborg shows the astonished audience that his true doctrine of Christ accords with the symbolic books of the Lutheran Church. They have never properly understood this doctrine, although they are always talking about it (*True Christian Religion* §137). But he has not yet delivered his final blow. He asks the censor on the rostrum about a famous theologian of his acquaintance and receives the reply, that he dwells "near Luther's grave." Then Swedenborg says to him with a smile: "Why do you speak of Luther's grave? Don't you know that he is resurrected and that he has today renounced his false justification through faith. Don't you know that he has joined the deceased in the New Heaven and laughs at his blind adherents, who persist in this nonsense?" Such is the amazing revelation he presents to the Lutherans of his age: Luther himself has renounced them and is now laughing at his own followers!

This disclosure naturally leads to a violent argument, but Swedenborg manages to silence his opponents. The chairman is about to bring the conference to a close when a man breaks through, wearing a crown on his head with a hat over it. He speaks on behalf of Swedenborg's most bitter enemy, Provost Eckebom of Göteborg. In the presence of the assembled Church fathers, he hurls at Swedenborg all the reproaches and accusations Eckebom had printed in his lampoon. "This New Doctrine smells of Mohammedanism," he exclaims. Eckebom had actually leveled this very reproach against Swedenborg, as had the Catholic theologians against Luther in the sixteenth century.

Once again the apostolic fathers begin to speak and intervene on behalf of the attacked visionary. When Swedenborg's slanderer blusters forth so violently, they turn the tables "as if struck by lightning" and shout with great indignation: "O, what a disgrace, O what a century!" Now Swedenborg sees the great moment coming to exonerate himself before the leaders of Christendom. "In order to calm the legitimate rage of the apostolic fathers, I raised my hand and asked for an audience, and when I had achieved this, I spoke: 'I know, that the man in that high office'—he means Eckebom—'wrote some such thing in a letter, which was subsequently printed, but if he had then known, what a great blasphemy this is, he would have torn it up and consigned it to Vulcan for burning.'" Full of self-confidence, Swedenborg then applies the word of the Lord to himself and his case: "Whoever is not with me is against me, and whoever does not gather with me will be scattered." The spokesman of the provost of Göteborg casts his eyes down in shame and says, "I have never heard anything more severe from you." Swedenborg replies that this is only a fair retort to the charges of Mohammedanism and naturalism, which Eckebom leveled against him, "shameful, deceitful, and invented lies and two deadly stigma to distract one from worshiping the Lord."

He then charges Eckebom's spokesman to tell the provost that he should read what is written in the Book of Revelation 3:18 and 2:16. We find there: "I warn you, buy from me white robes to clothe you and cover your shameful nakedness, and eye ointment to put on your eyes so that you are able to see." The second address to his opponents reads: "You must repent, or I shall soon come to you and attack these people with the sword out of my mouth." Once again, the noise rises in the assembly, but it is calmed by a heavenly sign. A light appears, and under its influence, several people cross from the group on the left over to the apostolic fathers on the right. This heavenly light shines into all those on the right, while those on the left deflect it away.

While the war of legal opinions is still being conducted over the Swedenborg case on earth in Göteborg and Stockholm and the outcome of the heresy trial is still undecided, Swedenborg experiences a triumphant vindication in heaven. Not only do the Fathers of the early Church intervene on his behalf before the gathered assembly of modern theologians but also a marvel confirms his doctrine, some of his opponents come over to his doctrine, and his main enemy, Provost Eckebom, is threatened with the judgment of God. This is the seer's response to the persecutions of his opponents! The solitary man of Stockholm must have been filled with such certainty concerning his vocation and the truth of his preaching! This kind of vision must have reassured him that he need not worry about the outcome of the trial, as heaven would look after his affairs.

To some extent at least, Swedenborg's visions are a heavenly mirror of his earthly life and his struggles. It is very likely that even more visions besides those already discussed could be related to specific events in his life. A topsy-turvy world is set to rights for him in the world of spirits. He is attacked on earth, but in heaven he is vindicated. Declared insane on earth, he sees in heaven how his enemies make themselves a laughingstock with their doctrines. Misunderstood on earth, he is granted the highest recognition in heaven. Poorly reviewed, scorned, and ignored on earth, his books are praised in heaven and the subject of heavenly conferences. Declared heretical on earth, his doctrine is defended in heaven by the teachers of the early Church. Opponents who scorn to answer him on earth must attend him in heaven and are persuaded by him to abandon their errors and self-deception. The orthodox clergy who pursued him so hard on earth discover the evil in their hearts and fearfully realize whom they have attacked. Whatever he cannot and will not do on earth, he is empowered to do in heavenly freedom. The quiet scholar, who barely spoke about his doctrines in society, becomes the most zealous preacher and apologist for himself in heaven. The private man of reserve, who enjoyed confidential conversations only with friends on earth, becomes the public spokesman of his revelation in heaven before the councils of theologians and philosophers of all centuries. Not only does he gaze into the heavenly mirror, but he holds it out in each of his works to his contemporaries in order that they may see their true face. Thus, he experiences his life's fulfillment on a higher plane, wages his battles, and celebrates his triumphs in an inner world, which makes it easier for him to renounce victories in the external world.

PART FOUR:

The Doctrine

24

The Doctrine of Correspondences

What are the intellectual foundations of the soteriology described in Swedenborg's visions and his interpretation of Holy Scripture? There have always been two kinds of theological speculation in Christianity. The biblical approach is concerned with concepts of Holy Scripture and tries to arrange them systematically. The metaphysical approach also relates to biblical ideas and images but traces them back to ultimate principles, without being exclusively limited to biblical philology.

Swedenborg is concerned with metaphysical theology. He wants to reveal the true nature of things. The principles of true being are contained as an "inner sense" in the external words of Scripture. The opening of his vision enables him to discern intuitively in their pure form the universal ideas hidden in Scripture. His entire spiritual development led towards this mode of contemplation. Even his study of the various realms of nature contributed towards this. During his scientific period, he had tried to derive the teachings of the Bible from the same basic principles he had understood in the scientific observation of the universe.

After his vocation, Holy Scripture became the sole subject of his contemplation. The decipherment of its inner sense became the only path to understanding. But this "inner sense" is not theology in the meaning of a system of biblical concepts. Rather it relates the teaching of the Bible to ideas endorsed by his visions and intuitions. He used the allegorical method to harmonize the content of his intuitive vision of the universe with the content of Scripture. This method stripped the words of Scripture of their historical, literal meaning and transformed all figures, persons, events, and images into "meanings" and "types," containing a spiritual and metaphysical sense. This method was developed in his doctrine of correspondences. Both Swedenborg's visions and his exegesis of Scripture are dominated by a particular kind of thinking, expressed in his doctrine of correspondences. This fundamental pattern in his way of apprehending reality was evident even before his religious crisis.

The doctrine of correspondences is already expressed in its most general form in several passages of the third part of his work *Economy of the Animal Kingdom*, published in 1740. A year later it was summarized in a manuscript bearing the title *A Hieroglyphic Key to Natural and Spiritual Arcana by Way of Representations and Correspondences*, first printed at London in 1784. In this work, four years before his vision of vocation, Swedenborg is already teaching a fundamental law governing the realization of divine life in the various realms of the universe. There is a concordance between divine, spiritual, and natural things; and consequently, there is also a correspondence between their signs. The relationship between the divine, spiritual, and natural realms is the relationship between archetype, likeness, and shadow. Every natural object is a representation and the correspondence of a spiritual and divine thing. It does not only represent itself but is a shadow indicating its spiritual image. The spiritual image is in its turn the representation of a divine archetype. All things in the lower world proclaim the higher world by reflecting the divine archetype in shadow form. Divine archetype, spiritual likeness, and earthly image relate to each other like a living face, mirror reflection, and silhouette. Thus the sun of the starry firmament does not only represent itself but simultaneously represents the sun of the divine realm, the Lord. The way in which it illuminates the earthly world, pervading it with its light, represents the influence of the Lord on the heavenly and spiritual worlds.

Swedenborgian research has shown that the historical prototype for this doctrine of correspondences is ancient neo-Platonism, an important influence on early Christian theology. This metaphysical tradition describes how divine reason constantly emanates in new self-representations. It can actually be proven that Swedenborg was acquainted with this philosophy through a series of neo-Platonic works including Marsilio Ficino's translation of Plotinus and the neo-Platonist text known as *The Theology of Aristotle*. He also appears to be have been influenced by Jacob Boehme's idea of *signatura rerum*. This doctrine teaches that the spiritual essence of everything is apparent in its external form and that both the outer form and the name of everything expresses its inner essence. These speculations, by whatever means of transmission they came to Swedenborg, became important to him only in the course of his religious crisis. He understood the images of his visions and dreams as mysterious allusions to pressing issues in his scientific research and his inner and outer life. In the light of the doctrine of correspondences, he then applied the subjects of his visions and dreams to the entire perceptible, natural world and his exegesis of Holy Scripture.

His understanding of the correspondences between everything in the world became a basic tenet of his epistemology, the more he pondered the thought that each natural thing is only the shadow of a spiritual thing and that this in turn is only the likeness of a divine archetype. The entire visible natural world was transformed for him in a marvelous way under the sway of this idea. Nothing in this world is only what its form and name proclaim it to be but also points esoterically to the higher realms of being. Every speck of dust preaches the mysteries of heaven. Whoever possesses the key to the correspondences of things can learn the truth of heaven from the dust and be borne from the heavy earth to the realm of heavenly freedom and truth on the wings of vision. A divine mystery slumbers in every least thing. If one could only unlock it, then the stones would preach of God and the transient would reveal the wonders of immortality.

For Swedenborg, this idea was linked to his view of the primeval state of humankind. At the beginning of the world, humans still had the key of correspondences. Things still told the people of that age of their secret inner meaning, and the forms of the natural world revealed their corresponding nobler form in the higher world to the reverent gaze of the observer. In Swedenborg's view, a remnant of this original form of contemplation, this insight into the essence of things, is still present in the hieroglyphs of Egypt. "The Egyptians seem to have elaborated this doctrine, and they identified these correspondences with various hieroglyphs, which expressed not only natural things but also their spiritual counterparts at the same time" (*Arcana Coelestia* §§6692, 7097, 7926; cf. *Spiritual Diary* 6083 [on Hermes Trismegistus]).

As the reference to hieroglyphs indicates, correspondences apply not only to things themselves but also to their signification. For modern people, the word is solely a concept that identifies a certain natural object. Among the ancients, names were not just labels but simultaneously expressed the inner essence, the nobler form and the divine archetype. Words were charged with a representative content, just as hieroglyphs were not only images of things' external appearance but ideograms and representations of their inner, nobler essence. But on this very issue there was a certain ambiguity in Swedenborg. Does the original representative meaning still reside in every word? Have later generations lost the inner meaning? Or have certain words, texts, and books still retained their representative character?

Initially Swedenborg was open to both possibilities. Once he declared that, if we express some natural truth with physical concepts and then substitute the corresponding spiritual concepts, a spiritual truth or a theological dogma emerges that no mortal could ever have guessed if he or she did not know the mysterious symbolic meaning of natural things. Jacob Boehme based his metaphysical philosophy of language and doctrine of the mother language on the idea that a symbolic power and meaning still resides in our contemporary conceptual language. Swedenborg took a more limited view. As time went on, he increasingly regarded the Bible, the divine Word of Holy Scripture, as the only book whose language preserved a symbolic character in a special sense.

In his small sketch of the doctrine of correspondences of 1741, Swedenborg makes a list of biblical words with their symbolic, allegorical meaning. Several kinds of mystical scriptural interpretation were customary on orthodox hermeneutics, and Salomon Glassius had developed these into an extensive system in his *Philologia sacra*. Using these categories, Swedenborg tried to distinguish between "harmonic correspondences," "typical correspondences," "dream correspondences," and "correspondences of divine and human actions." It would lead too far afield to analyze his system of interpretation in detail, especially as the boundaries between the various categories of correspondence are highly fluid in his case and most words in the Bible can be spiritually interpreted in several ways. The crucial point is that Swedenborg was developing his doctrine of correspondences four or five years before his vision of vocation and relating it at the very outset to Holy Scripture, by trying to ascertain its inner sense through an allegorical system of word meanings.

In all these attempts, Swedenborg is pushing at a door in vain because his hieroglyphic key still does not fit the magic lock. He only surmises that the biblical language is a mysterious code, but he is not yet able to decipher its nobler meaning. He is in the same situation as when he had a presentiment of Adamic understanding. He wants to climb higher and confront the mysterious frontier of a higher world of understanding. He sadly realizes that he is still barred from entering this world but is nevertheless consumed by the desire to grasp this original, lost knowledge. His desire is strongest concerning the shrouded mysteries of Holy Scripture. Even his first handwritten sketch concerning correspondences hints that no human method will disclose its true meaning in the present age. The key can be given to the believer only by the grace of God.

Interestingly enough, Swedenborg speaks about a particular dream correspondence with reference to the dreams of Pharaoh or Joseph described in the Bible. The way in which he treats this matter shows how his own experiences compel him to think about the symbolic meaning of images, persons, and events in dreams. What might this uncontrollable world of visions mean, which kept overwhelming him? What secrets did it conceal? Was he already nearer to the truth than he thought? Was it due only to his ignorance that he did not recognize the truth even when it was offered to him? Was he to be condemned to miss the divine truth when it came to him in such a direct fashion and he lacked only the key to decipher the revelation?

Once again, his dream diary is the best commentary on his struggle for this higher understanding. Here there are many attempts to interpret the figures of his dreams allegorically and to ascertain their symbolic meaning. But these interpretations are still fairly uncertain and sometimes Swedenborg lists several possibilities without opting for one or the other. The diary betrays the torment these things caused him. He lives in fear of missing the true meaning of what happened to him and losing his chance of higher understanding. For him, this is no theoretical matter but a matter of life and death, a struggle for the higher, nobler, heavenly understanding, which leads him on to the peaks of hope and bliss and into the depths of disappointment and resignation. No clarification comes until his vision of vocation, granted to him in London in April 1745. Here he receives the commission to disclose the inner sense of Holy Scripture, and he experiences how God makes known to him the spiritual meaning and correspondence of every word in the Bible. Finally he feels he has attained that level of understanding of which he had a dim presentiment in his doctrine of correspondences. Now the words of the Bible reveal their divine meaning to him. Natural things and concepts preach to him about their divine archetypes and heavenly truths. The spiritual and heavenly world is now transparent to him in the text, and he understands the mysterious inner connection between the frequently contradictory statements of the Bible. Now he has received the key to its decipherment from God himself. Now he knows he is finally in possession of the true knowledge of the correspondences. He now sees an inconceivable wealth of intuitions streaming down upon him, where before there was only guesswork.

After his vision of vocation, the doctrine of correspondences becomes a doctrine of the divine Word. This Word, present in Holy Scripture, appears to him as the visible representation of divine truth, tailored to the sensory perception of human beings. The divine truth has descended through all the higher and lower worlds. On its first levels, it even exceeds the angels' capacity to understand. On subsequent levels, it is intelligible to the angels, and below these to other beings of the spiritual world. At its lowest level, the divine truth represents itself in a form intelligible to humankind as the Word of Holy Scripture. The literal sense of the Word is the foundation, envelope, and support of its spiritual and heavenly sense. The physical word is the "container" of its spiritual and heavenly sense, just as the earthly world is the container of the higher spiritual and heavenly life. The literal form is the body of the heavenly Word, veiled in a form accessible to humankind upon earth.

"The heavenly and the spiritual sense (on their own) are not the Word without its natural meaning, for without it they are like spirit and life without a body and resemble a palace that has no foundation" (*True Christian Religion* §213). The literal sense serves as a sentinel to the truth hidden within. It is the cherub with a flaming sword, who stands before the inner paradise of the divine Word. "The sentinel is such that the sense can be interpreted and explained this way or that according to the capacity to understand without its inner sense being damaged. No damage is done by the literal sense of the Word being understood differently by one from another. But damage is done when the divine truth hidden within is twisted, for then violence is done to the Word. The literal sense stands guard so that this does not occur" (*New Jerusalem and Its Heavenly Doctrine* §97). Thus, the divine truth inheres in the literal sense of the Word in its abundance, sanctity, and power. But access to this sanctuary is granted only to those to whom God grants the understanding of true correspondence.

Swedenborg gave systematic expression to these ideas especially in his two works *Doctrine of Holy Scripture* (1763) and *True Christian Religion* (1771). Throughout these works, his conception of the Word is intimately bound up with his own consciousness of vocation and mission:

> A man, who does not know that a certain spiritual meaning inheres in the Word cannot judge the Word by anything else than its literal sense, while this literal sense is but a container containing the valuables of its spiritual meaning. If one knows nothing of this inner meaning, one cannot judge the divine sanctity of the Word any more than one judges a rock that encloses a gem but appears like an ordinary stone. One might liken this to a little box inlaid with

jasper, lapis lazuli, mica, and agate, but which contains diamonds, rubies, onyx, and topaz. But if one does not know its contents, it is not surprising that the box is valued no more highly than that the materials apparent to the eye. The Word is related to its literal sense in a similar way. So that man should not doubt that the Word is divine and supremely holy, the Lord revealed its inner sense to me, which is spiritual in essence and inheres in the outer meaning, as the soul in the body. This meaning is the spirit that animates the letter. This meaning can therefore also bear witness to the divinity and sanctity of the Word and can even convert the natural man, if he only wants to be convinced. (*True Christian Religion* §192)

This spiritual meaning is "inherent in the Word, like the soul in the body, the thought in the eyes, and the feeling of love in the face." For this very reason, the Word is written in correspondences, "in a way of writing found in the prophets and evangelists, which may appear something quite ordinary but contains within it the divine wisdom and all the wisdom of the angels." The revelation of the inner meaning through correspondences represents the immediate link between humanity and God. Swedenborg sees it as his mission to restore this link.

Swedenborg endeavors to work out in detail a sort of encyclopedia of correspondences. On the basis of a compilation of various passages in which the same word or image occurs, he seeks to determine its symbolic meaning or its spiritual sense. For each animal, each color, each figure occurring in the Bible, a unique, definitive spiritual meaning is ascertained, which varies according to the context and is supplied with a positive or negative indication. Wherever this animal, this color, or this figure may occur in the Bible, it always refers to some nuance of its basic spiritual meaning. This is impressive, but it runs the risk of being doctrinaire. Thus, the animal kingdom corresponds to the realm of instincts, desires, and appetites in men, whereby a concrete meaning attaches to each species and type of animal. The same applies to the plant kingdom, which generally corresponds to our knowledge and insights, whereby the individual types of plant have a special meaning. The mineral world corresponds generally and in detail to our fixed principles. In this fashion, the whole of Holy Scripture is transformed into a complex of spiritual meanings, which are woven into a doctrine of salvation.

Swedenborg regarded thinking in terms of correspondences as the archetypal form of thought. He even related the origin of religions to it. In his opinion, people in ancient times knew about correspondences. To them, all things were signs and symbols of the Divine. This ancient religion gradually degenerated into polytheism, where people revered things themselves as holy and divine instead of the divinity they represented:

> The idolatry of the heathens in ancient times derived from the science of correspondences. This came about because all things appearing on earth had some correspondence, not only trees, but also beasts, birds of all kinds, fishes, and everything else. The ancients made themselves images corresponding to the heavenly things and took delight in them because they signified things of heaven and the Church. Therefore, they set them up not only in their temples but also in their houses, not to pray to them, but to remind them of these heavenly things. Accordingly, calves, bulls, snakes, then boys, old men, and virgins were set up as images in Egypt. The calves and bulls were symbols for the desires and powers of the natural man, the snakes were symbols for the cleverness and cunning of the sensual man, the boys for innocence and affection, the old men for wisdom, the virgins for truth, and so on. But when the science of correspondences was lost, they began to worship the images and statues set up by the ancients in and besides the temples as relics and finally as divinities. (*True Christian Religion* §205; cf. §§189–209 for the full context)

The original knowledge of the symbolic character of all earthly forms still underlies all idolatry. The old Word was originally hidden in every religion. It already existed before the Bible was written down and was initially comprehended in the intuitive contemplation of correspondences. From this old Word, "the religions spread out to India and its islands and through Egypt and Ethiopia into the empires of Africa and from the maritime countries of Asia to Greece and thence to Italy. But because the Word could only be written in the form of images denoting things in the world corresponding to heavenly things, the religions of many peoples were transformed into idolatry.

In Greece, they became myths and the divine attributes were perverted into so many gods." Nevertheless, a certain remnant of the ancient knowledge remained in the pagan myths, illustrated by the lore of paradise, the great flood, the sacred fire, and the four ages.

The doctrine of correspondences also induced Swedenborg to classify the books of the Bible. The Word consists only of those parts of Scripture that are written in correspondences, namely, texts whose inner sense can be deciphered by a knowledge of correspondences. On the one hand, he distinguishes the writings of the Old Testament and the gospels; on the other hand, the works of St. Paul and the other apostles. The apostolic works are "only doctrinal texts and are not written in the style of the Word like the writings of the prophets, David, the evangelists and the Book of Revelation. The style of the Word naturally consists in correspondences and thereby produces a direct community with heaven. But the style of the doctrinal texts is quite varied, as they are related to heaven, but only in an indirect way." The apostolic works are therefore not the "Word" itself but already an interpretation of the Word, a translation of its inner sense in correspondences into a "clear and simple language suited to the capacity of all readers to understand." For this reason, Swedenborg never composed a commentary on any of the apostolic works.

As he had already hinted in statements before his vocation, Swedenborg finally explains the origin of numerous heresies in the Christian Church by means of his doctrine of correspondences. The fact that there are such diverse and contradictory interpretations of the divine Word is due to the letter of the Word being adapted to the comprehension of such varied people, while concealing a divine meaning of timeless validity within. Only he to whom this inner meaning is revealed and who masters the science of correspondences has a true understanding of the Word. This view logically leads to the conclusion that only someone inspired by God can understand the true meaning of the divine Word. However, Swedenborg expressed this idea in a more conciliatory way. Holy Scripture is not totally incomprehensible. The spiritual meaning is not so concealed in the literal sense that it is unintelligible to natural powers of comprehension. Following orthodox hermeneutics, Swedenborg differentiates between "manifestations of hidden truth" and "manifestations of unhidden truth."

There are passages in Holy Scripture where the divine truth is unhidden, and from these passages, it is also possible to understand the more obscure passages. But errors come about when teachers of the Word, prejudiced by their intellectual arrogance, cannot distinguish between hidden and unhidden, apparent and authentic truth. They take such apparent truths as their point of departure for an interpretation of the Word, which seems most sympathetic to their personal outlook and taste. Thus heresies arise. It is not sufficient to quote the Bible in order to prove the truth of some knowledge, for "one can derive any arbitrary doctrine from the literal meaning of the Word and seize on everything that pleases one's desires, even the false instead of the true." A word can be truly understood only when comprehended in the light of the whole truth shown to the illuminated.

In the last analysis, this view was based on Swedenborg's sovereign self-confidence that he had the true key of the correspondences, that he had knowledge of the unhidden truth of the Word. However, in marked contrast to other prophets from inspired congregations of his time, Swedenborg was not intolerant of dissenters. Most people cannot help having an incorrect view of the divine Word. How should an ordinary person be able to distinguish where the unhidden truth may be found in Scripture and which words represent only hidden truths? Every person is born into the religion of his or her parents and brought up in it from childhood, retains the outlook of this upbringing, "and cannot rid himself from the falsehood of these views owing to the ways of the world." Who would condemn anyone for this? The error does not condemn the person, but error does become damnable heresy when evil conduct accompanies false knowledge. Error becomes heresy when someone elaborates these errors into a universal system for interpreting the Word, endorses them by reason, and so raises falsehood to truth behind the mask of the divine Word. "Leading an evil life and endorsing the false to the detriment of the truth, this leads to damnation." But the way always lies open for an ordinary person raised in any one of the Christian confessions to be led out of his or her preconceived errors through the truth of the Word. Whatever confession we may belong to, whenever we let ourselves be seized by the unhidden truth of the Word, it will also help us to divest ourselves of our previous errors.

Swedenborg thus combines the idea of tolerance, itself based on his doctrine of correspondences, with his exalted consciousness of election and mission. "Whoever remains in his religion and believes in the Lord, keeps the Word holy and lives according to the Ten Commandments does not swear on falsehood. When he hears the truth and understands it in his way, he can grasp it and so be delivered from falsehood. But not he who has fortified himself in the falsehood of his religion, for endorsed falsehood remains and cannot be destroyed . . . , especially when this is connected with egoism and intellectual arrogance." This aspect of Swedenborg's thought is a characteristic feature of the age of Enlightenment and its idea of tolerance based on the universality of religion.

The same scheme of correspondences used in the exegesis of Holy Scripture also dominated Swedenborg's visions. The encyclopedia of correspondences, which he established in the course of his allegorical exposition of the Bible, can be easily applied to explain his visions. The figures, colors, movements, actions, gestures, and symbols that he sees in his visions have the same representative meaning as they possess in Holy Scripture. This very fact shows most clearly how the doctrine of correspondences is consolidated into a universally valid code that dominates Swedenborg's view of the upper and lower worlds. It also shows how closely vision and exegesis are related.

Swedenborg thus regards the doctrine of correspondences as the universal principle, with whose aid he elucidates the inner unity of the divine life, its self-representation within the various realms of higher and lower being, and the revelation of God in the Word. On all levels of being, the same things and their names have the same spiritual meaning, and they manifest the same spiritual or divine truth, which is concealed in their external form of their shape or their letters.

25

The Metaphysics of Life

Swedenborg's entire view of the lower and higher worlds is based on a metaphysical philosophy of life, derived from a few simple principles. Life is the dominant idea in his view of the motions and forms of the universe. It is a key aspect in his view of God, his doctrine of humankind, and his doctrine of the structure of the spiritual and natural worlds. Despite this systematic and scholarly wording, his idea of life is inspired by the basic experience of simple piety. These basic experiences are combined with ideas that came to him through his scientific researches and his later visionary experiences.

Two points of view dominate his metaphysics of life: the idea of divine origin and the idea of the unity of life. Swedenborg's view of life in the various realms of nature and spirit was already rooted in religious concepts during his scientific period. All life proceeds from God; he is the one and only Creator of life, the source of the great river of life, which flows through the whole universe and realizes itself in an inconceivable abundance of higher and lower forms. All living creatures, be it the highest angel or the smallest worm, bow down in humility before the Creator of life and are nothing, are dead, without him. This religious view of existence runs consistently

through the history of piety: God is everything, and all living creatures are nothing. Whatever creatures have in being and life, they
have from God; it comes from God and flows towards them from
the superabundance of divine life. "All creatures are simply nothing," Meister Eckhart had taught. The whole of nature, the entire
created universe, and even the highest creature of this world, the
human being, is only a vessel and container of life, not its Creator.
From this point of view, one may understand Swedenborg's sharp
polemic against contemporary naturalism in his theoretical writings
as well as his visions. He reproached the advocates of this contemporary view of nature for robbing God of his honor, by attributing to
nature what was due to God.

This perception is significant for Swedenborg's view of religion
and his view of nature. Religion is for him what Friedrich Schleiermacher (1768–1834), the German Romantic theologian, later described as a human being's simple dependence on God, a
dependence that is not only spiritual but extends to the deepest layers of each person's physical existence. In faith, we recognize that we
are dependent on God in everything that we are and have, in every
breath, in the smallest incident of our spiritual and physical being.

This idea is crucial for Swedenborg's view of nature. As a scientist, he had made the acquaintance of God as the Lord and origin of
life in the starry heavens, the miracle of electricity, the iron and copper seams and the subterranean rivers of the mines, the sedimentary
strata of the mountains, and the formation of crystals. God had revealed himself to Swedenborg in powerful visions after the opening
of his sight. The unity of the entire visible and spiritual world was
disclosed to him under the aspect of the unfolding of divine life. The
neo-Platonic doctrine of the ascent and descent of divine being was
refashioned into an organic and personal view of the essence of divine life under the influence of his scientific knowledge and visions.

The fact that God alone is life implies that only divine life has its
own activity and effect. By contrast, all created things have an activity only in the sense of reaction: they are stimulated and set in motion by the influx of divine life. The ideal harmony of life consists in
effect and reaction's being synchronized, co-operating together
without resistance.

This idea also underlies his view of sin. Whenever a creature attributes its life and activity to itself, whenever a person considers himself the origin and author of his life, the inner balance and harmony of effect and reaction are disturbed. Original sin occurs when a person regards what is caused by an influx of divine life as his own activity and believes "that life is his own, whereas he is in reality only a vessel for the reception of life." The person opposes himself to God as his own center of effect, begins to react against God, so that the life he received from God is inflamed in selfish opposition to God.

The divine life can truly unfold only in the person of faith. If he recognizes in faith the basic fact of his existence—namely, that his whole life proceeds from God and that all goodness of life proceeds from the activity of God and all evil from the reaction of the individual—then his reaction becomes an action, and he becomes active in faith with and in God. The life activated by God can thus operate effectively and productively only in the person of faith. Only then does this life lack the guilty character of a reaction against God, the thorn of contradiction against our Creator.

Swedenborg deduced the basic idea of his metaphysics from the story of Creation in the Old Testament. God's breathing life into Adam confirmed that God alone is life, is only the organ of life, and does not derive it from himself. If a person had life from himself, he would be as God, and there would be as many gods as there are people. But there is only a single life, just as there is only a single, indivisible essence of God. "As God alone is life, it follows unquestionably that God enlivens each man from his life. Without this animation, man would be a naked sponge and his bones a bare skeleton, in which there was no more life than a hour-glass. . . . God is life itself. This life is the only real life, from which all angels and men live" (*True Christian Religion* §364). Everything living carries this trace of its divine origin.

> However far the ear, however far the eye extends,
> You find only something familiar, resembling HIM
> (Goethe, *Gott und Welt*)

In contrast to contemporary vitalism, this metaphysics does not start from the lowest and most primitive form of animal life, such as the cell or the amoeba. The origin of life is divine life, in which divine love and divine wisdom flow together, realizing itself in a personal spiritual form, in the human aspect of God. The personal and human are a part of God's nature. In its innermost principle, life is something spiritual and personal. Thus it comes about that God is active in the highest creature and highest form of life in this world: the human being is created in his image. God does not give of himself in a fragmentary way, but with all his love and wisdom, which together constitute divine life, "for the Divine cannot be divided" (*True Christian Religion* §363). Swedenborg thus extends the dynamic view of God found in the mysticism of Nicholas of Cusa, Paracelsus, and Boehme. He assimilates the traditional images of mysticism to clarify the cooperation of love and wisdom in divine life. Just as the sun simultaneously radiates warmth and light, so love and wisdom streams forth from the power that is God. "These two pour into each and everything in the universe and stimulate them in their innermost being."

> What would a God be, who pushes only from without,
> Letting the universe revolve around his finger!
> It becomes him to move the world from within,
> To foster nature in himself, and himself in nature,
> So that whatever lives and weaves and is in him,
> Never misses his power nor his spirit.
>
>   (Goethe, *Gott und Welt*)

Life in itself is therefore created on the part of God, not of creation. Everything that can be and is created is only an organ for the purpose of receiving this life. Because this love is nothing else "but the innermost activity of love and wisdom, which are in God and are God himself, the living power itself," the human being as the image of God is the most suitable organ for its activation. Indeed, the creation of humankind is made necessary by the essence of this life. All love and all knowledge can operate only in another and in being other. God created humanity in his image and likeness in order to lead his life in another, "in his own image" (Genesis 1:27), thereby realizing the love and knowledge within himself.

A double aspect and mystery inhere in this life of humankind.

On the one hand, it is so constituted that a person perceives it as his own, not as something alien. The individual does not perceive himself as a kind of remote-controlled machine, but his love and his knowledge bear his own stamp. The influx of life from God should not, therefore, be considered in the sense of pure determinism. Each person is no passive antenna receiving the rays of divine life and setting the machine of the human organism in motion. On the contrary, this divine life moves the innermost center of personality, the image of God in humankind. This marvel continues without interruption. God willed it because he did not want humankind as a slave but expected free, faithful, loving devotion from us.

Each person receives the life of God as if it were his own. "God grants that this is so perceived by man that the influx stimulates him and is taken up and remains in him." It is God who breathes life into each of us, and only in the free realization of this life does each become active as a spiritual person. The inhalation of life in the human being is the impulse towards his individuation, for divine life requires variety and diversity in order to become conscious of its inexhaustible abundance. "The life of influx is the life which proceeds from God, which is also called the spirit of God, of which it is also said that it illuminates and enlivens. But this life assumes a different form and changes according to the organization, which it receives through his love" (*True Christian Religion* §362).

The miracle in the transfer of life to humankind is the miracle of human freedom. As God is free, he can only realize himself in free love. He therefore does not expect from the creature made in his own image an attitude of slavish submission but free, loving devotion. "Man is an organ of life, and God alone is life, and God allows his life to flow into this organ and its particulars, just as the sun lets its warmth flow into the tree and its particulars. Now God grants that man may feel this life in himself as his own. God wills that he should feel so, in order that man may live according to the laws of the order, which are as many as there are commandments in Scripture, and thus prepare himself to receive the love of God" (*True Christian Religion* §504).

Only this freedom gives dignity to the link between God and humanity. It would be a bad God who was content to squander his life

driving a machine and using his creation as an object of his despo-
tism. He much prefers that the other be free, in whose heart he has
laid an image of his own essence. "Man has free will because he experiences the life within him as his own, and God allows man to feel
thus, in order that a connection can ensue. Such a connection would
not be possible, if it were not reciprocal, and it becomes reciprocal as
soon as man is active in his freedom as if he were independent. If
God had not granted this to man, man would not be man, nor
would he have eternal life. It is the reciprocal connection with God,
which makes man a man and not a beast, just as it also gives him
eternal life after death. Free will in spiritual things cause this."

We might add that this free exchange between God and humankind makes God God, for love can be fulfilled only in the other,
and without human beings, the personal other, the love of God
could not realize itself. But there is also a risk inherent in this freedom that the person forgets the divine origin of his essence and
makes himself a center of effect against God. If the first miracle is
freedom, the second miracle is faith. Only in faith can the divine life
be purely realized in each person. Only when the individual realizes
in faith that his freedom is a gift from God and that he owes everything he has to God can there be an inner harmony of action and reaction between God and the person.

Two things must be distinguished. All life is from God. God pours
his life on good and evil alike, just as he lets his sun shine on good and
bad people. Even those condemned in hell have their life from God, as
long as they are living. What matters is how the person reacts to this
influence (influx). Evil people "block the path and close the door, so
that God does not enter the lower regions of their mind, but good
people smooth the path, open the door and invite God into the lower
regions of their mind, in whose highest regions he dwells. Thus they
prepare the state of their will for the influence of love and affection,
and the state of their intellect for the influence of wisdom and faith,
and thereafter for the reception of God. By contrast, evil people ob-
struct the influence through many appetites of the flesh and spiritual
pollution, which they interpose in order to resist the influx. However,
God dwells in their highest regions with his whole essence and gives
them the capacity to want goodness and understand the true."

But the divine life takes shape wholly only in the faithful, for only the faithful recognize the life of God in this life, realizing itself in their innermost being, and they give it full scope in all spheres of their existence. Only they grasp the mystery of freedom and sacrifice themselves as an instrument of God in free submission. The more they surrender themselves to his love, the more the love grows in them; and the more they surrender to his wisdom, the more the wisdom grows in them. But the unbelievers pervert the divine life through an abuse of their freedom.

The human being becomes the true image of God only in free submission to God. But he loses the image of God in rebellious self-assertion against God; this loss is the spiritual or "second" death, the eternal self-annihilation of the individual, the destruction of his spiritual person. "Man is a vessel for the reception of God, and this vessel is the image of God. Because God is love and wisdom, man is the vessel of the same. The vessel becomes the image of God the more it receives his spirit. Man is a likeness of God by dint of feeling that which comes from God is in him as his own. But this similarity only leads to an image of God when he acknowledges that love and wisdom—or goodness and truth—are not his own, and thus not of him, but are only in God and thus also of God." Each person gives his freedom back to God through faith and thereby becomes a single image with him. He transforms himself into a free collaborator of God, who is permeated with divine life and its associated love and wisdom right down to the externalities of his life.

Swedenborg attempted to describe more precisely the special manner in which divine life was activated in humankind. Just as love and wisdom are joined in the life of God and determine the essence of life, so the innermost life of the human being is not something physical or bestial, but his love and his understanding. In Swedenborg's thought and in his view of humanity, love acts as the determinative impulse of life. Human life receives its first impulse, its direction, goal, and inner form through the love that dominates this life. "The actual life of man is his love, and the whole man is constituted like his love and his life." This ruling love is not altered by physical death and does not dictate only the earthly form of man's existence, but also his spiritual destiny and its continuation in the spiritual world.

Life is primarily a transcendent reality for Swedenborg. All physical life is derived life. The life of each person springs from the innermost center of his or her personality, or "disposition" as Swedenborg calls it. From thence it pervades the whole person and activates itself in the various higher and lower life functions. By "disposition," Swedenborg means the unity of will and understanding, love and wisdom, that innermost center of the person, in which both are yet undivided. "His life dwells in him; the body is only obedient."

Thus Swedenborg can say that it is false to speak of a corporeal life, for if we as spiritual persons have no life from our own, the body has much less. The body is only an organ of human and personal life and an instrument for its realization. Right down through the animal, plant, and mineral worlds, the innermost nature of life is love, which is kindled by a higher life and develops according to levels and hierarchies in specific physical vessels and organs. The inner life, which comes from God and pervades all levels of the universe, is the actual principle of activity and formation of all being. Once it is removed, a thing is destroyed, "like a pearl crumbling into dust." "For what the disposition wants and thinks, it does and speaks through the body as its organ." Life is in everything that is physically and bodily present in the human being. It is not identical with him, but works in him, "without being mingled with him."

The unity of life is the second fundamental theme of Swedenborg's metaphysics.

> And it is the eternal One
> That manifests itself so diversely;
> Small is the great, great the small,
> All according to their own way.
> Ever changing, but holding fast;
> Near and far and far and near;
> So forming, transforming—
> To my amazement I am there.
>
> (Goethe, *Gott und Welt*)

The unity of life is substantiated by the fact that all life derives from God. Swedenborg made the unity of life an object of his research in a particular fashion. All life, the highest and the lowest, is subject to an inner coherence and forms a unity in its origin and goal. Nothing in the earthly and spiritual world is detached from the unfolding divine life. Nothing exists on its own in isolation, but only in the context of the whole. This principle applies to nature as well as the spiritual world. "Each specific thing lives from the common cause; each individual thing lives from its generality." "Everything in heaven and on earth lives in community, and there is no life without community."

It is evident that the neo-Platonic model of ascent and descent prevails in this metaphysics. The life emanating from God unfolds and divides itself like a waterfall into three cadences or realms—heavenly, spiritual and natural, which are all linked together by the same thread. Whatever takes place in the universe, also occurs in the individual. Each person possesses three levels of life from creation: a heavenly, a spiritual and a natural life. Their reciprocal relationship has a dual aspect.

On the one hand, Swedenborg understood the coherence of life from the point of view of its origin. All higher life is the origin of lower life. All natural and bodily life streams forth from the spiritual life of the disposition, and this again has its hidden source in the heavenly life that comes to it from God. The other point of view is that of its goal. All lower life presses for its transformation and reception in higher life. Natural life wants to perfect itself in the life of the spiritual realm; the bestial has an inherent urge to ascend into higher forms of organization. But it is not the case that the lower form gradually produces the higher form out of itself. The higher cannot arise out of the lower, but the higher form is already present from the very beginning in the lower form as an entelechy.

The idea that all lower things are a vessel of higher things also applies to the relationship between the creation and the Creator. On all levels, the creation behaves towards God, the giver of life, as a vessel and organ, through which the mighty stream of life passes, enabling God to work upon the lower through the higher according to a definite hierarchy. "Nothing comes from itself, but from the other." The higher thing initially appears as the other, but ultimately the other from which all life proceeds is God, who is simply life itself. This conception represents the old mystical view, often misunderstood as pantheism: God is indeed in the world as its life, but he is not identical with it. Everywhere he is present as the principle of life and the basis of all effect, but he is not identical with the life of each individual thing and its activity, or with the totality of all living effects. He is present in every individual thing, but he is not exhausted in created existence but stands above them as Creator and Lord. He is everywhere and unfolds everywhere in his characteristic way, but in such a way that one cannot assign him a specific place within the universe nor can one equate the universe in its entirety with him.

Swedenborg used an old image of mystical theology to make this idea clearer. He compared the omnipresence and omnipotence of God in the universe with the omnipresence and omnipotence of the soul in the human body. "The soul or the innermost being of man can be present everywhere in the body. It can direct all its physical functions, thoughts, and whatever pertains to man, however diverse they may be, and thereby maintain their inner coherence and care through its omnipresence. If such providence were not available, everything would collapse within an instant." The same is true of God's relationship to the universe.

Only God possesses and gives life, but this life varies according to the form of the receiving vessel. This is the old mystical image of the well of life. The water of life bubbles forth into various bowls and fills each vessel according to its particular shape. The inexhaustible life of God takes shape in all creatures and reveals itself to them in an inconceivable variety of forms. The destiny of creation is thereby fulfilled, for "all organic forms are destined to receive life." Organic forms are instrumental creations, owing their activity to the plan of divine providence.

The actual organ of realization in which the personal and spiritual life of God has assumed its highest form is the human being. The doctrine of humankind is the kernel of this metaphysical philosophy. It is not derived from the humanistic tradition of Swedenborg's own century but is based on an original exposition of humanity's creation, confirmed by his own visionary experience.

Why are there people? Why has God created this human creature at all? This question has been answered in various ways by pious

Christian thinkers. For St. Thomas Aquinas and his school, the creation of the human race was an act of God's self-love. God created the world and humankind within it for his own glorification, in order to form a Kingdom of God, in which the deceased could proclaim the glory of the Creator in free submission. Our love for God is an echo of God's self-love, which sought to develop its power and glory. This self-love found its highest fulfilment in the creation of humanity; for only a personal spiritual being, created in the image of God, could love its Creator and worship him in the spirit and truth. God created and loves each of us because God loves himself.

Mystics such as Johannes Tauler and Angelus Silesius thought otherwise. The blissful experience of their own love of God, deeply felt and attained by enormous self-denial, is reflected in their view. In unification with God, the mystic experiences a heightening of his own being, which goes far beyond his simply being an instrument of God's self-love. One of the strongest impressions of this encounter with God is that the mystic feels how God longs for the love of the human being and how God desires to fulfill and bless this person and enter his innermost being. God and the individual thus essentially depend on each other; both need each other for their fulfilment. We need God; God needs us. Both can realize themselves only in each other and thus attain perfection, as Angelus Silesius expresses it:

> Without me, God cannot live a moment.
> If I were destroyed, he would give up the spirit.

The key to understanding this idea is the profound mystical interpretation of the biblical statement that the human being is created in the image of God. The words "God created man in his own image, in the image of God He created him" (Genesis 1:27) have the following meaning for the mystic. The human is the image in which God expresses his transcendent unintelligibility and omnipotence in a specific shape and form; man is the image in which he represents himself as a person. God created humankind in his image in order to be able to realize himself as a person. His love is not self-love but by its very nature a love for the other, which wants to fulfill himself in free reciprocal love and therefore needs this other. Love is not being there for oneself, but being there for the other.

Swedenborg developed this idea further under the direct impact of his vision of Christ. For him, humanity is based on the nature of God. Humanity, that is personal life, is not alien to God by essence and nature but is a part of his wholeness. God is dependent on humanity in such a way that humanity belongs from the very beginning to his own nature. The Lord, the Son of God, is God in his humanity.

In his own right, God is a consuming fire and a mighty light, but the inexhaustible exuberance of his nature assumes a form and becomes personal willing, loving, working, and understanding in his humanity. This humanity in God is simultaneously the archetype of all spiritual life. As God in his nature is human, so the humanity in him is simultaneously the archetype of life in all spiritual creatures and not human alone. "On the basis of the fact that God is man, all angels and spirits are men in perfect form."

Swedenborg thought out this idea in all its consequences. Everything is in God that pertains to humanity, but in a spiritual way. A personal creature must necessarily have a corresponding form of corporeality:

> Because God is man, he therefore has a body and everything pertaining to a body. He therefore has a face, chest, abdomen, loins, feet, for without these he would not be man. He also has eyes, ears, nose, mouth, tongue, and also the inner parts of man like the heart and lungs and what depends on them. All this makes man a man. There is a multiplicity in created man, and if one considers all their ramifications, they are countless. There is an infinity in the God-man, and nothing is missing. Thus, there is an infinite wholeness in him. One can make such a comparison of uncreated man, who is God, with created man, because God is man and as he says, man was created in his image and likeness.

The corporeal is not alien to God and does not limit his divine nature but is an expression of his wholeness. The spiritual nature of God is not an abstraction but a bodily thing. The spirit is no abstract being because everything spiritual is personal, and there is no personal being without corporeality. Both humanity and corporeality thus belong to the nature and wholeness of God.

This conception signifies a complete break with the worldview of the Enlightenment. The philosophy of the Enlightenment had totally rationalized the idea of God and utterly rejected the human and physical features of God as found in the Old Testament. All physical and human utterances of God were meticulously interpreted away as nonexistent. The fact of their presence was explained by the naïve representation of God by analogy with humankind. The thinkers of the Enlightenment considered the human characteristics of God in the Old Testament as proof for the view of the ancient rationalists and Euhemerus that we created gods in our own image.

Swedenborg ventures a different teaching. We are human because God is human and because God has created us in the image of his own humanity, and this similarity with God extends to the last and smallest shapes and physical forms of his humanity. Everything in the human being, the highest and the lowest, the most spiritual and the most corporeal, is a reflection of humanity in God. In finite humanity, one can see the infinite humanity in God. God is not an abstract concept, or an idea nor a number or a law, but a living, corporeal spiritual personality. His personal life is his humanity, and this humanity in God is the highest organization and realization of spiritual and personal life. The personality of God fulfills itself in his humanity and is confirmed in his being human.

As proof, Swedenborg adduces not only the visions of the Old Testament in which God appears in human form and the fact of Christ's humanity, but also his own revelations, granted to him in the world of spirits and angels. "God only ever introduces himself as a man in heaven. God himself is man, wherefore the Lord reveals himself as a man, whenever he manifests himself to angels in person." Ultimately, Swedenborg formed this view on the basis of his own experience at the end of his religious crisis. During his scientific period, he encountered God in his unintelligible, transcendent, numinous superabundance, as the hidden Lord of life and the cosmos. But during the period of his religious crisis, he was stirred by the question of personal salvation and his own relationship with the Lord, and he had to acknowledge that his previous life could not withstand the terrible sanctity of this God. At the moment of his deepest remorse, the Holy appeared to him in the form of Christ.

He was permitted to see God in his humanity, to look face to face at Christ. His conception of God took a new form on the basis of this shattering and blessed experience. "That the Divine cannot ever be grasped is evident from the words of the Lord in St. John: 'No man has seen God at any time' (John 1:18) and 'You have neither heard his voice at any time nor seen his shape' (John 5:37). But those who do not think out of themselves nor from the flesh, but out of the spirit of God, think in a specific way about him, that is to say, they conceive God in a human shape. Thus thought the angels in heaven concerning the Divine, and thus thought also the sages among the ancients, to whom the Divine appeared as a divine man." This is also what he encountered in the decisive hour of his life. "Whatever proceeds directly from the Divine, even the angels of the innermost heaven cannot conceive. This is because it is infinite and thereby surpasses even the angels' capacity to understand. But whatever proceeds from the Divine Humanity of the Lord, they can understand because it deals with God as a divine man, and that humanity is conceivable to them."

The idea of the archetypal significance of humanity for all spiritual being led Swedenborg to a conception that seems initially as remarkable as his doctrine of the corporeality of God. Not only does each spiritual creature have human features and form, but the spiritual creatures are grouped and organized in communities, which themselves assume a human shape. The individual angelic communities in human form combine in turn to form a "Universal Human" (*homo maximus*), which constitutes the entire heaven. The humanity in God is, therefore, not only the archetype of the individual spiritual personality, but simultaneously the archetypal form of the community of all spiritual personalities. "Heaven as a whole and in its parts is fashioned like a man," and this heaven "always remains the same down to the last detail."

The notion that the spiritual beings of heaven together form the "Universal Human" or universal man, and that this "Universal Human" is composed of individual men like cells seems pure fantasy to our modern way of thinking. But these ideas of Swedenborg are not so far removed from Christian thought. They are determined by his view of Christ, and it will be remembered that St. Paul refers in his letters to the Church as the body of Christ. One totally fails to understand this idea if one simply takes it as a simile. Even ancient pre-Christian writers compared the state or other communities with the human body and individual social groups with the limbs of the body. St. Paul is not making a mere comparison but saw the individual believers who belong to the Church actually forming the body of Christ. For him, the Church is really a body, for "you are the living stones in the temple of the living God" (II Corinthians 6:16). Here already is the view of a metaphysical, spiritual, and corporeal supra-personality, which embraces a community of diverse individuals. The Church is the body of Christ, Christ is the head, his spirit and blood pulse through the individual limbs and unite the cells and "living stones" of his corporeality, which are in turn living people, into a wholeness permeated by his personality.

Just as St. Paul's statement that "he is the head of the body, the Church" (Colossians 1:18) should not be understood as an image but as a physical fact, Swedenborg really imagines the combination of the various angelic societies in heaven as the universal personality of the "Universal Human." Swedenborg's doctrine is a development of Pauline notions; for humanity in God, the god-man, in which everything is and through whom the superabundance of divine life realizes itself, is for him identical with the Son, Christ and the Lord. The totality of heaven and all spiritual beings appears to him as the body of Christ, which embraces all redeemed spiritual creatures in its spiritual corporeality.

This aeonic being, the "Universal Human," is not identical with God himself, but is the body of God, the form in which redeemed spiritual beings are united and simultaneously the organ through which divine life radiates down into the lower realms of life.

A series of diary entries gives further information on this subject. Thus Swedenborg wrote on 26 March 1748: "Whatever comes by influx from the Lord into the universe also comes into the Universal Human, with a variety corresponding to the various functions, so that neither spirit nor angel can be unaffected by its influence. The lowest and the highest life stream down to the universe from this Universal Human. Even the soul could not give influx in all its varieties into the forms of the body, unless the Universal Human existed, whose life is the Lord." Here it is clearly stated that the "Universal Human" is not the Lord himself, but the image, instrument, organ, and vessel of the life of the Lord. Swedenborg continues in paean-like tone: "From him comes the diversity of individual forms; from him comes the hierarchy of all things according to their uses and goal; from him come the functions of all things as a whole and individually; from him comes the existence of all bodies and their effects; from him comes their maintenance, which is an enduring creation; from him comes the existence of all animal bodies, even the most minute creatures; from him comes the existence of all plants with all their variations."

The doctrine of the "Universal Human" thus expresses the most important aspect of his metaphysics of life. At the beginning, the divine life does not reveal itself in its lowest but in its highest form, which already entails all lower forms as personal, human, and corporeal life. The hierarchy of levels of being and correspondences are also laid down in this combination of the "Universal Human," as is also the form of the future community of redeemed spirits.

The "Universal Human" does not represent a second divine being besides God; rather the "Universal Human" is the first incarnation and self-reflection of divine life in a personal form, from and through which further differentiation proceeds. Swedenborg stated this in a note of 1 October 1748, when the idea and form of the "Universal Human" came to him in a series of intuitions and "living experiences." The "Universal Human" should be understood as something corresponding to the organic and instrumental aspect of the human body, which is stirred by the life of God. It is the Lord alone who animates and activates it because he is the life, for his life is in everything from the first to the last. "Whoever therefore wants to live and work as his own cannot be in the Universal Human, but the more he desires to be himself, the more he is repelled and rejected by him. Thus the whole Universal Human is a suffering or passive power, which is dead in itself. But the Lord alone is an active, effective, or living power. Their cooperation is therefore a marriage, whereby heaven is the bride and the Lord the bridegroom." The "Universal Human" therefore has the same metaphysical meaning for Swedenborg as the "heavenly Sophia" had for Jacob Boehme.

God alone is the creative living power of the universe, but the "Universal Human" is the body or "container" in which the universe receives the effective power of God. Just as the heavenly Sophia is described as the revealer, body, box, mirror, and likeness of the divinity and his heavenly bride, so the "Universal Human" appears to Swedenborg as the revealer and body of the Lord, through which influx of divine life into the universe occurs.

Humanity is not an arbitrary and coincidental section in the multifarious forms of the universe, not just one form of life among countless others but quite simply the archetypal form of life. Humanity carries within itself divine characteristics, the image of the personal spiritual nature of God. It is that aspect of the divine essence in which the unknown, overwhelming, terrible, and numinous nature of God assumes a concrete form.

This conception signifies an extraordinary elevation of the human image and rejects all the errors of modern materialism, the biological philosophy of life, and the theory of evolutionary descent. The highest life is not a product of the lower nor the last link in the chain of evolutionary forms. Rather, it the first and the origin and operates as an archetypal form and entelechy in all forms of life from the very outset. This archetype is represented by the "Universal Human," from which the realization of all life commences and in whom everything combines again at the end in its elevated and redeemed form. "Man is only a particle (*particula*) in the Universal Human, and there is nothing in man, which does not have its correspondence in the Universal Human." "Man cannot exist without corresponding to the Universal Human in all his expressions of life. If this universal man did not exist nor the universal body with its organs, then the individual particles would neither be present nor exist." But the whole also remains present as an archetype and heavenly model in the individual thing. "Although universal, this body or man is simply organic in itself and has its life from God, and in this fashion man is derived from God. A life in man is otherwise unthinkable. All participation lives from its common cause because it is a part of the common cause, and all individual things live from the universal because it is a part of the universal."

This is true not only for people on earth but also for the whole universe. The humanity of this earth is only one special form of the representation of creation. The spirits and angels are also human and have a human face, but in their realm humanity assumes a higher form of corporeality. This physical form is more appropriate to spiritual nature and is a more plastic representation of humanity than in the coarse material of earthly corporeality.

Heaven or the "Universal Human" is the body of God, which bears the stamp of all levels of life in human form. "God fills up the universe as man, and so all things in the universe correspond to him because heaven is God himself. Because God is in everything, so the poles and house of the heavens correspond to him and his limbs." This idea dominates every single vision of Swedenborg and forms the basis of his whole classification of the realm of spirits and angels. Heaven is the *corpus maximum*, the "Great Body," and poses such an exact analogy of the human body that its individual parts, the societies of spirits and angels, cohere in a manner corresponding to the limbs of the human body.

The earthly eye of the human being is blind to this immeasurable form. Only God sees it in its unity and wholeness and recognizes the harmony in the cooperation of its diverse parts within the universal body. "In God's view, the whole heaven forms one man, and even the angels are therefore men, and this occurs as a result of the influx of the divine into heaven. It is the divine human, streaming into heaven which composes heaven. The innermost heaven forms its head, the second heaven the chest, the first heaven the knees and the feet. The correspondence of heaven with each and everything in man is thus self-evident."

A specific principle of community is thereby laid down. Everything depends on community. This does not arise through an amalgamation of separate individuals, but the community is prior and superior to the individual. Just as the individual cells in the human body are bound together in tissues, and these in turn in higher organs, so the spiritual beings unite in structured societies, which together form the "Universal Human," not as its sum, but as its original unity, as the central form and archetype of its life.

The absolute precedence of humanity in the universe is expressed in these thoughts of Swedenborg. The universe is an image of God and is therefore "full of God from God" and created in God, "for God is being itself, and from being must be what is." But as God is human in his innermost essence and his spiritual form is represented in the universal man, so the universe reflects the God-man as the image of God. "The created universe is a likeness of the God-man."

This does not mean that the universe is the God-man himself. "For absolutely nothing in the created universe is substance and form in itself, nor life in itself, nor love and wisdom in itself, nor even man, but everything comes from God, who is man, love, wisdom, substance, and form in himself. He in himself is the uncreated and the infinite, but whatever comes from him is created and finite, because it contains nothing, which is in itself. It represents only the image of that, by which it is and exists. The created universe is not God but comes from God; and because it comes from God, his image is in it, just as the image of a man appears in a mirror, although there is nothing of man in the mirror."

Because humankind and the universe are an image of God, a correspondence must exist between all parts of humankind and all parts of the universe. "Each and every thing existing in the created universe corresponds with each and every thing in man, so that one can say man is also a world. There is a relationship of correspondence between his drives and thoughts and everything in the animal kingdom. There is a correspondence between his will and his intellect and everything in the plant kingdom, and a correspondence of his lowest life with everything in the world of minerals." The human being summarizes all the realms of the universe in the organism of his spiritual and corporeal personality.

This traditional mystical doctrine of the human as microcosm underlies the whole development of modern science from Nicholas of Cusa to Paracelsus, Boehme, Helmont, Kepler, and Newton. However, Swedenborg carried it further, in that it derives from his new conception of human essence and is supported by an abundance of scientific observations. Everything created represents humankind in a certain way. Life in its highest, spiritual form is human life. But lower life also portrays higher life because all lower forms contain a graphical indication of higher life. Humanity is reflected in the most distant and lowest forms and activities of the animal, plant, and mineral kingdoms. All living forms indicate the human being, allude to his form, and are designed with him in mind. Thanks to his scientific knowledge, Swedenborg listed a mass of examples showing how lower creation related to humankind. He could thus demonstrate that the spiritual model of the human being and his organs was everywhere the guiding principle for the development of the diversity in the organs and limbs of the animal and plant kingdoms.

The archetypal character of humanity should be so understood that the archetype itself possesses the power to have a formative influence on the lower forms of life. The lower levels of life have an inherent urge to transform themselves into something higher. Minerals strive to assume the forms of plants, vegetables to become animals, and this drive passes through all levels of creation right up to humanity. This is the mystical chain of the ascent of life to humanity, and from humanity to God, and the powerful counter-movement of the descent of life from God through humanity down into the mineral world. Johannes Arndt expressed the same scheme in his *Book of Nature*, the fourth book of *True Christianity*, and Goethe also speaks of it in his poem "World Soul" dedicated to the monads, the personal living forms of the universe:

> Now everything with divine daring
> Strives to surpass;
> The water wants to green the infertile,
> And every dust speck lives.
> A throng rich in forms soon stirs
> To behold a propitious light,
> And you are astonished to see in the valleys
> The first pair.
> And soon the unlimited striving
> Ceases in a shared blissful glance.
> And so the most beautiful life thankfully
> Receives everything back from everything.

Humankind is the central point of development from above to below and from below to above. "The universal purpose of all parts of creation is the existence of an eternal link between the Creator and the created universe." But

> such a link is not possible, when there are no subjects, in which his divinity cannot exist, dwell, and remain as in himself. These subjects must be able to receive his love and wisdom as if out of themselves in order to become his dwelling places. They must raise themselves up to the creator and be able to connect with him. Without this reciprocal relationship, there is no connection between God and the world. These subjects are human beings, who raise themselves up to God and can assume a connection with him. Through this connection, the Lord is present in each of his created works, for everything created is ultimately there for the sake of humankind. The utility of all that is created increases in stages from the lowest level to the human and through the human to God the Creator, by whom it was created. From the aforesaid one can see, that the final purpose of creation consists in everything returning to the creator and that there is a connection.

Thus the universe is the theater of an enormous transformation of lower being into higher being, as the Divine Comedy of an all-embracing rebirth, in which all creation is humanized by rising through the various stages of creation, and thence from humanity back to its origin in God. The mystery of the descent and ascent of life is incarnation.

These ideas represent the supreme glorification of humanity in the history of European thought. Following his visionary experience of Christ, humanity, as the personal spiritual form inherent in the nature of God, became for Swedenborg the archetypal form and highest formative principle of all living things and all development. There is nothing abstract in the spiritual sphere. In its essence, spirit is not a formal principle but life seeking personalization and incarnation. It can live only in a corporeal and personal form. Divine life wants to become human, wants to become person, wants to create a person, unfold in the personal and develop the divine archetype physically in an individual way. Everything spiritual strives to become history and community, which are not restricted to the theater of this world but are continued and per-fected in a realm of the spirits. They find their conclusion in the Kingdom of God, where the perfect spirits, who have most purely developed the image of God in themselves, return their love to God in eternal worship and contemplation.

26

The Doctrine of the Spiritual World

Swedenborg's doctrine of the spiritual world is an ingenious attempt to revive the view of the hereafter and the Last Things as real events in the spiritual development of humankind. In his time, these theological subjects had faded from Church dogma. In contemporary orthodoxy, the doctrine of Last Things had become just a historical appendix of theology, which played no role in the maintenance of the faith and in practical piety. This relegation of the hereafter and the millennium is all the more remarkable as a belief in the Resurrection, the Last Judgment, and the reality and glory of the Kingdom of God were dominant themes in early Christian piety. How had this decline come about?

The believers of the early Church lived in certainty that Christ would come again on the clouds of heaven, gather his faithful around him, and reign with them. The evangelists and the letters of the apostles show in numerous passages that the faithful of the earliest congregations were filled with a belief in the imminent return of the Lord and still expected this event in their own lifetime. The

Second Coming was still awaited when the community of the baptized began to die off, but many still believed with certain disciples, especially St. John, that they would see the arrival of the Lord: "That disciple should not die . . . but tarry till I come" (John 21:23). The proximity of divine reality with all the great events of Resurrection, the Judgment, and the new creation of heaven and earth must have overshadowed in urgency everything that had previously been important on earth. Earthly life seemed only a temporary span of preparation for the coming, imminent fulfillment, and entry into the holy realm of the Kingdom of God.

This expectation of the millennium faded with the passage of time. Years, decades, centuries passed but fulfillment failed to come. Christ had not appeared on the clouds of heaven, and the disciples of the Lord were dying without having seen the advent of his Kingdom. The Church presented itself as a world power on earth in place of the coming Kingdom of God. Millennial expectations in their original form repeatedly flared up under the impact of historical disasters; but in the absence of their literal fulfillment, these expectations gradually lost their attraction. Whatever does not happen for a long time ceases to be sufficiently important to determine one's life. The wait grew longer and longer; would the end ever come? Later generations of the Church accustomed themselves to reckon that this world would pass away and yet reconciled themselves to the old earth lasting a while longer and the Day of Judgment would be still some time in coming.

The original notions of the Last Things also became increasingly uncertain. What became of the dead in the long intervening period between their death and the distant resurrection? Here theology could give only the evasive answer that the dead were "resting" until the Last Judgment. The Reformation set aside the Catholic doctrine of purgatory but retained the idea of the sleep of souls. But this idea could not satisfy the active religious temperament. According to this doctrine, human destiny seemed highly paradoxical. First, an earthly life full of toil and trouble, which was a matter of eternal salvation. Next came a vacant period of indeterminate, inconceivable duration, while the person "rested" in his grave. Then finally, after a few millennia or tens of millennia—by which time everything that filled life today had become irrelevant—Resurrection, Judgment, and assignment to heavenly bliss or hellish torment! The dark period lasting aeons between the day of a person's death and resurrection was no less terrible than the notion of eternal death to the imagination of the believer. A resurrection that was so long in coming could scarcely assuage the fear of the grave.

Even the expectation of the Last Judgment, seemingly postponed to an immeasurably distant future and no longer an immediate terror, lost its edge for religious and moral sensibility. It became increasingly harder to reject a legitimate consideration of the future against such a protraction in the history of salvation. Theology in the age of the Enlightenment raised a host of objections against the traditional expectation of the millennium. Did it not assume a pettiness on the part of God that, after so many thousand years in a distant future, he would exhume, judge, and punish our superannuated, small sins and vanities? And even if a conclusive, final judgment of humankind by God does ensue at the end of time, is it just in the context of the millennia of world history to grant each person only a single short chance to decide his eternal fate? And is it right that, after this short period of probation, he is detained for an unlimited period of time in the investigative custody of death without any further possibility for action, before finally facing a judgment on this life? Is it just to condemn a person eternally after an interminable period of waiting for wasting the short chance of his earthly life? Why the whole drama of the history of salvation, why the incarnation, why the self-sacrifice of God, why all the events in heaven and earth, when the actual benefit for the individual takes place in such a delayed and superannuated fashion that it creates the impression of injustice?

Swedenborg filled the traditional conceptions of the hereafter with new religious content. He restored to them their original concern for pious individuals by understanding them not as historical events but as events in the spiritual development of humankind, as metaphysical incidents of life in a human context.

The starting point for this new interpretation was Swedenborg's image of humanity. Traditional orthodoxy recognized two kinds of spiritual creature: angels and humans. According to this doctrine, the angels are the first spiritual beings that God created. They are also created in his image. However, their mode of existence is not physical and material, but spiritual and corporeal. Some angels abused their freedom to rebel against God, and they were banned from heaven, led by Lucifer, the light-bringer, who was the first to revolt against God. The expulsion of the rebellious angels created a breach in the original unity of the Kingdom of God, and this necessitated the creation of the earth. The number of fallen angels thrust into the abyss was to be replenished from the ranks of humanity. Adam was to be raised to the throne of fallen Lucifer. But the fallen angel tried to draw this new creature of God into the rebellion. The background of world history is thus a battle between God and Satan, the angels and the demons for humanity.

Swedenborg recognizes no distinction between the several species of spiritual being: there is only *one* spiritual creature and that is the human being. There are no special spiritual beings for this world and for the world beyond, but both are the world of humankind. There are no special angels and demons besides the human, for these are also humans in another, further developed form of their being. Heaven, the spiritual realm, and earth are places for the realization, elevation, and condemnation of humankind. They serve the development, individuation, and representation of humanity in our heights and depths, in our possibilities and specialities, in isolation and in the community. Angels and humans are not distinct like two species of creation, but are two distinct phases of the same species, like a butterfly and caterpillar.

There are numerous references of this nature in Swedenborg's visionary works. In *Heaven and Hell*, he sums it up as follows: "It is completely unknown in Christendom that heaven and hell consist of the human race. It is still believed that the angels were created at the beginning in heaven and that the Devil or Satan was an angel of light. The angels are amazed at this. They want me to confirm that I have it from them that there is not a single angel in the whole of heaven who was created at the beginning nor a devil in hell who was created as an angel of light and was expelled, but that all in heaven and hell are of the human race."

This gives rise to a second, related idea of Swedenborg. The evolution of the human being is not concluded with this earthly life but continued in the world beyond, and moreover immediately following physical death. Life here and there form a single, coherent continuity of personal existence. No interminable night of death intervenes here. A person changes from the state of his physical existence with the entirety of his or her personal life into another, more spiritual form of corporeality.

It is at this point that Swedenborg's ideas of the relationship between spirit and corporeality begin to operate in their full significance. Personal, spiritual life is not dependent on the realization of a physical, fleshly body in the organism. Every person has his or her specific spiritual and corporeal mode of being, in which the "inner person" is represented. During one's physical life on earth this inner person is concealed in the outer as its inner model. Physical death does not touch the "inner person" at all, for it is only a promotion of this individual from the earthly mode to another, more spiritual mode of being. He is thereby transferred to another kind of corporeality, which exhibits other dimensions, other life functions, and other possibilities of understanding and communication.

Dying is thus already resurrection. In death, the inner person is liberated and can represent himself in his pure form, unhindered by the limitations of physical corporeality. He can become what he really is, in accordance with his innermost love:

> A man is said to die when he can no longer function in the natural world. But for all that, man does not die but is only separated from the physical things that served him in this world. The man himself lives. I said the man himself lives because man is not man through his body but through his spirit, as it is the spirit which thinks in man and determines the thought and inclination of man. It is clear from this that, when man dies, he only passes from one world into the other. That is why the inner sense of death in Scripture means resurrection and survival. Being raised from the dead means the departure of the human spirit from the body and its introduction to the spiritual world, commonly known as the resurrection.

The contrast with the traditional doctrine of the Last Things is striking. The ideas of resurrection and the Last Judgment receive through Swedenborg a new spiritualized interpretation and thereby a new relevance for a life of faith. According to the old conception, a single judgment for all the resurrected takes place on Judgment Day. According to Swedenborg, this judgment is not a unique verdict of God on all the resurrected dead at the end of history but takes place directly after the death of each individual person. It does not consist in a heavenly judge giving a verdict on the completed life of the deceased, but the life of the person itself, the realization and representation of his or her innermost striving and desire in this world, on earth, is his judgment. Death signifies the unveiling and revelation of the inner self, which has been realized in the course of one's life. The Hegelian idea that world history is the judgment of the world is anticipated here in its application to the individual and his or her metaphysical destiny.

Swedenborg substantiated this idea through his doctrine of "inner memory." Just as an inner and an outer person work and dwell in the earthly being, unbeknown to him, he also has an inner and an outer memory, which are very different. Outer memory embraces the words of various languages, the objects of external sensory perception, and the things of knowledge pertaining to the earthly world. Inner memory embraces the idea and conceptions of the higher world, which each person receives with his inner eye, and all rational concepts, which constitute thought. During one's earthly existence, both types of memory work together, in such a way that the idea and conceptions of the inner memory unconsciously stream into the outer memory and activate themselves in it. The outer memory is really the organ of the inner memory, whereby its ideas are clothed in concrete notions, images and concepts.

The inner memory is active not only in thinking but also in the processing of sensory impressions. The outer and inner memories are different in the way they store received impressions. The outer memory is very limited in its receptive capacity and retains only a few impressions, which have a greater significance in our life on account of custom, repetition, or an emotional stress in a positive or negative sense. It rejects other impressions and this constitutes forgetfulness. The capacity to organize impressions properly and link them under a general idea is also limited and subject to many errors.

The inner memory is much more perfect. It forgets nothing but stores everything in its proper order by raising all impressions to the level of an idea. "Everything, that a man ever hears, sees, and is stimulated by penetrates into the ideas and purposes of a man's inner memory without him knowing, and remains there, so that nothing is lost, although it fades in the outer memory." Thus a complete and true image of each person is constructed in the inner memory, without the caprice of forgetfulness or the involvement of outer memory. "The nature of the inner memory is such that every single thing a man has ever thought, said or done from earliest childhood to the end of his days is registered there." This inner image is therefore not identical with the image a person has of himself in his outer memory because the outer memory is debased and defective. The person cannot even consciously apprehend the inner image. Unbeknown to him or her, the inner memory preserves the unerring image of that person, in which the smallest detail of thought, desire, stirrings of will, action, impression, and conception is indelibly etched. It is the inner model of the individual himself, the characteristic impress he has received in the course of his life.

Death removes the physical conditions of existence. After death, the inner person begins to reveal himself. He becomes visible in the entirety of his life development from his first until his last days. This unveiling of the inner person before God is the judgment. In the light of the higher world, each person appears revealed as he really is and as his inner memory portrays him. No attempt of the outer memory to forget certain things can cover up the infallible and exact impressions recorded in the inner memory. Death removes the veneer that the outer memory laid over the true inner form of the individual, and gradually his spiritual form emerges in its purity.

In Swedenborg's view, this inner memory, the diary that the relentless inner observer has kept, is the "Book of Life" that is opened in the next life and according to which the individual is judged. No extrinsic judge rules on the person, but each carries his or her own judge within. In the next world, the inner person is also opened to the spirits and angels. Whoever looks into a person's Book of Life can read everything that he has ever thought, done, and felt. "All purposes, which were hidden to man, and all thoughts, but even all conversations and actions right down to the last iota are recorded in that Book, that is in the inner memory, and so often as the Lord permits it, they are as clear as day to the angels. This has been shown to me several times and confirmed by so many experiences, that there is not the slightest doubt concerning it." Death strips away the corporeal curtain, the mask of the flesh, and reveals the true form of the individual to the admiration or disgust of the heavenly observers.

Swedenborg emphasized the revelatory nature of his knowledge through this spiritual interpretation of the Judgment and the Book of Life. "No one yet knows the state of the soul after death with respect to the memory. Through many years of experience I have been granted to know that the individual loses nothing of what was in his memories, both the outer and the inner. Thus one cannot imagine anything, however petty or small, that the individual would not have retained. After death man leaves nothing behind but his flesh and bones, which were animated by the life of his spirit as long as he lived in the world and his purer substance was bound to the physical."

Swedenborg found confirmation for his doctrine of the inner memory in a series of visions. They have the character of psychic tests. On one occasion, he experienced how several angels were granted a glimpse into his own inner memory. They quoted to him literally whole pages from his earlier notes, which he had committed to paper several years before and which he could no longer remember. They thus confirmed to him that the individual "cannot think anything, which will not see the light of day following his death." Later experiences enabled Swedenborg to look into the inner memories of other persons. Thereby he gained insights into secret and hidden things in the lives of his friends, which they had completely forgotten but which they were able to remember when Swedenborg spoke of them. To be sure, this concerned deceased persons; but in a few rare cases, he seems to have been able to read the Book of Life of living contemporaries, as is confirmed by the story with the Queen of Sweden.

A characteristic transformation takes place in the individual with his entry into the spiritual world. This transformation signifies a third revision in the Church doctrine of Last Things. The world beyond no longer appears as a world of eternal punishment or bliss, in which the individual is eternally rewarded for good deeds or eternally punished for offenses in this life, but as a place for the further education of the individual. It is not a place of faceless, bodiless, timeless, sexless, impersonal spiritual beings but the theater of development for active spiritual personalities. It is the place for further individuation of personal life and its combination into higher forms of community. It is the place of diversity of spiritual life, which is also expressed in the external, corporeal multiformity and the wealth of the world beyond.

Of course, this further development of personal life is subject to certain limits. First, the individual develops after death in the world beyond only in the basic tendency of the love that ruled his or her life in this world. Second, he only educates himself further according to the degree of harmony existing between his outer and inner person at his death. The basic tendency, the basic stamp or character, and the span of personal life thus remain intact even after death and determine the further ascent or descent. The development of humanity in the spiritual world is described in the Johannine apocalypse: "He that is unjust, let him be unjust still: and he which is filthy, let him be filthy still: and he that is righteous, let him be righteous still: and he that is holy, let him be holy still" (Revelation 22:11). Here on earth, the basic tendency and the span of future development of the spirits is established in standing or failing the test of this world.

Swedenborg justified the first limitation of this development with a basic idea of his metaphysics. Every person is identical with his or her love. A person *is* whatever he or she loves. Everyone determines his own inner form and his understanding through the object of his love. Swedenborg justified the second limitation in his doctrine of inner memory. During earthly life, the inner person is rooted in the outer person. But the outer person forms himself through his outer memory, with which he constantly receives new impressions and stimuli that influence his basic attitude and determines his character. At his death, the individual is relieved of his earthly mode of existence in time and space. He no longer receives impressions from the earthly world in his outer memory and no more impulses that could react on his inner attitude and inclination:

After death man still has his entire outer or physical memory, or each and every thing which pertains to it. But it can no longer grow, and when this is the case, no new concordances and correspondences (between the inner and outer memory) can be formed. This explains the saying in Scripture: "Where the tree falleth, there it shall be" (Ecclesiastes 11:3). It is not that the good can no longer be perfected; it is perfected in a high degree, as far as the wisdom of the angels, but in proportion to the concordance and correspondence existing between his inner and outer person while he was living in the world. After the death of the body, no one receives outer, but only inner and innermost things. It is the concordance of the inner or spiritual man with the outer or natural man, which "remains where it falls." In the next life, the individual has both; the inner or spiritual extends into his outer or natural person, as in the last life. The inner or spiritual person is perfected in the next life, but only insofar as this corresponds to his outer or natural person. The outer or natural person cannot be perfected in the next life, but retains the character it acquired in the life of the body.

Swedenborg begins his description of the change the individual experiences at death with a bold and startling idea: the dead do not initially notice that they have died. The continuity of consciousness undergoes no interruption, so that the spirit is not at first aware of its change of state. As the dead enter the spiritual life in the fullness of their personality, they do not initially realize that they are in the world of spirits. Their change of state only dawns on them gradually (*Heaven and Hell* §457; cf. *Arcana Coelestia* §§4796, 4797, 4800).

Swedenborg's reports concerning encounters with recently deceased persons belong to the most exciting narratives of his diaries and memorabilia. They also betray a certain literary pleasure in the description of such scenes. The deceased and resurrected persons are so engrossed in their false notions of death, the world beyond, the realm of spirits, and the resurrection that Swedenborg must first prove to them that they have already died and been resurrected, and even then they do not always believe him. Occasionally, he also describes scenes in which he attends with the spirits the funeral ceremonies of well-known contemporary personalities. By confronting his former acquaintances with their own corpses, he makes them

realize the peculiarity of their new existence which they have exchanged in the realm of spirits for their former earthly existence.

Thus he reports the funeral of Polhem, his old teacher, in his
diary of autumn 1751:

> Polhem died on a Monday and spoke with me on the following
> Thursday. As I was invited to his funeral, he saw his coffin and
> everyone present and the whole funeral procession and also how he
> was laid in his grave. While this was going on, he asked me why he
> was being buried when he was still alive. He also heard the pastor
> saying he would wake on the Day of Judgment, when in fact he
> had already been resurrected. He wondered what sort of faith
> stated that one would rise on Judgment Day when he was still
> alive, and that the body would rise at some future time when he
> still felt that he was in his body, and other things besides.

Swedenborg collects encounters of a similar nature in *Arcana
Coelestia*:

> I was talking with several people a few days after they had died. Be-
> cause they had only recently arrived in the world of spirits and
> found its light little different from the light of the world, they
> doubted whether this light was coming from anywhere besides the
> world. Therefore they were raised onto the first level of heaven,
> where the light is more brilliant; and when they spoke to me from
> there, they said that they had never seen such a light. Some of them
> believed that men became ghosts after death, and they were
> strengthened in this view by hearing about spirit apparitions. But
> they only concluded from this that this was something coarsely
> physical initially exhaled by the life of the body, but which then re-
> turned to the corpse and thus expired. But some believed that they
> would rise again at the Last Judgment, when the world was de-
> stroyed. Although their old body had long crumbled into dust, it
> would be gathered together, and they would be resurrected in the
> flesh and bone of their old body. But because they had awaited this
> Last Judgment or the destruction of the world for several centuries
> in vain, they fell into the erroneous opinion that they would never
> be resurrected. But they were taught that a Last Judgment would
> occur for every person when he died and that he would believe he
> was in a body as he was previously in the world. He would possess

all his senses as before, but purer and more refined senses, because the physical would no longer be an impediment and because that which belongs to the light of the world would no longer darken what is the light of heaven. They would then be in a purified body, which would by no means be a body of flesh and bone as in the world because otherwise they would be surrounded by earthly dust again. I talked about these things with several people on the day when their bodies were being buried, and they saw their corpse, the bier, and their interment through my eyes. They said that they had now thrown this body away. It had served them usefully in the world, where they had previously been, but now they lived in a body that would be useful to them in the world in which they now lived. They also wanted me to say this to their relatives, who were in mourning. But I was permitted to answer that, if I told them that, the relatives would only mock because they believed that nothing existed except what they could see with their own eyes, and so they would regard it as a delusion. (*Arcana Coelestia* §448)

Swedenborg distinguishes three levels in the change of state after death. In the first, the individual is still in possession of his external consciousness and does not yet grasp the fundamental change that has occurred in his nature. This state was already described. It "resembles the state of a man in the world, because he is still in the same mode in his exterior. He still has the same physiognomy, the same way of talking and thinking, and the same moral and social life. That is why he still thinks he is in the world, at least until he notices what happens to him and what the angels tell him when he awakens, namely, that he is now a spirit. Thus the one life continues in the next, and death is merely a transition" (cf. *Heaven and Hell* §§470–520).

But soon the individual "is translated into his interior or into the state of inwardness." In describing this change, Swedenborg stated his fundamental ideas on the relationship of spirit and corporeality and developed a system of physiognomy, which exercised a great influence on Johann Kaspar Lavater (1741–1801), the Swiss pastor and pioneer of this esoteric science. These ideas relate to his notion of the archetypal man. The essence of the "most ancient men," the oldest members of humankind, represented by Adam, were characterized by the complete concordance of the inner and outer person. Their corporeality was so plastic that it clearly reproduced every characteristic in the form of their inner person. The concordance was expressed in the whole attitude of the outer person, especially in the face, which was so constituted that the face of inner person completely shone through, "so that the inwardness in him appeared as in a reflecting mirror. One would notice when someone was hostile towards him, for he would reveal his feelings when talking both through his speech and his face. The ancients who belonged to the heavenly Church had such a face, and all angels have such a face, for they want to conceal from others nothing they are thinking because they always mean well towards their neighbor and have no ulterior motive, as if they were doing good to their neighbor only for their own sake" (*Arcana Coelestia* §9306).

In the state of complete correspondence, the physiognomical expression simply becomes the archetypal language. The corporeal exterior of the ancients totally and directly reflected the basic tendency of their being and its individual spiritual and emotional expressions. The outer form was so permeated by the inner form that the face actually signified the interior. "With the ancients, the face characterized the interior because the interior shone through the face. In the most distant times, the face so accorded with the interior, that each person could see the disposition or temperament of another from his face" (see *Arcana Coelestia* §607, 1119, 3527, 3573).

This presupposes a corporeality completely permeated by the inner model of the personality. The outer person is not a mask, but a living form of expression that reflects the slightest stir of the inner life. The deceit, pretense, and lies typical of fallen humankind are not possible because of this complete permeation. Swedenborg particularly emphasized this idea: "Because they were heavenly men, everything that they thought shone out of their face and eyes. Accordingly, they could never affect a countenance other than that which matched their thoughts. They considered pretense, and even more so cunning, as gross wickedness."

The incapacity for pretense was no defect in their nature, but a sign of their inner freedom. Just as the pious person subordinates himself in love as a free personality to God, so the outer person subordinates himself to the inner image of God in the individual and represents its purity. The ancients had nothing to hide, for they wanted only to realize the good in free love and serve God. Therefore

> the ancients of the Church did not speak as latterly and today in words, but like the angels in concepts, which they could express through countless changes of facial expression, mainly through their lips which contained innumerable muscle fibers, which are nowadays no longer developed. As their lips were mobile in those days, within a minute they could express through them ideas, which would take an hour nowadays in articulated tones or words. They could also express them much more completely and clearly for the comprehension of those present than would ever be possible with words and sentences. . . . They were not afraid of others knowing their aim and purpose, for they wanted nothing but the good. (*Arcana Coelestia* §607; §3573)[1]

The original human lives in the love of God; he thinks and wants only the good and therefore has no occasion to conceal anything from his neighbor, for the good is held in common. But in the instant when the individual rebels against God and wants the good for himself, he wants to deprive another of it. A radical transformation of being begins, in which the ego becomes the guideline of thought and desire. The necessity of hiding one's true inclinations, wishes, and thoughts arises from this original fall and estrangement from God. The outer person becomes a cloak covering the hidden designs of the inner person. Through egoism, the face becomes a mask. It is not as if there is no longer any link between the inner and outer person, for everyone bears a mask pertinent to his nature; but a hardening sets in. The plasticity of spiritual expression, the precise concordance of the inner and outer person, is lost. The facial means of expression atrophy, and the face becomes a coarse, ponderous sheath. The face still bears several characteristic runes of the inner person, but its has lost its immediate responsiveness to the infinite expressiveness of the inner person.

---

1. cf. Ernst Benz, "Swedenborg und Lavater: Über die religiösen Grundlagen der Physiognomik," *Zeitschrift für Kirchengeschichte* 57 (1938): 153–216.

People devoted to self-love must hide their thoughts. They cannot let their face do as it will but must restrain it. "The face of such people is contracted, so that it is ready to change as cunning demands. Everything that the individual wishes to hide contracts his face." Earthly physiogmony is under the star of the mask seeking to hide deception. The rigidity characteristic of the mask is the consequence of the original sin of egoism.

This whole development is conceived as a living, never-ending process. The hardening of the face is not final but changeable. It begins and advances with the progressive inclination to evil and abandonment to the ego, while the inclination to good and the overcoming of egoism softens the hardened features and can restore the mirror of the soul. The correspondence between the outer and inner person does not therefore come to a complete end. Even in the apostate, it is the inner person that imprints the outer person and gives him his features, but the immediacy of correspondence is destroyed. The illusion of the ego warps the lines of the inner model, the soul's means of expression are congealed, and the mirror of the soul is transformed into a "lime-wash over the grave."

As his face hardens, the individual also loses the archetypal language, which consisted in the candid expression of his thoughts and feelings in his face. At this point, it became necessary to invent the language of words:

> As long as this sincerity and honesty existed in men, they retained this language of the face. However, as soon as the spirit began to speak other than it thought—and this happened when the individual began to love himself instead of his neighbor—the language of words began to gain ground, while the face remained impassive or was even able to express falsehood. The inner form of the face thereby changed and it contracted, hardened, and began to lose its life. But the outer form began to glow with the fire of egoism and look as if it were animated.

From a physiological and psychological point of view, a third factor intervenes between the divine image in the individual's disposition and his face after the Fall. This is the animus, the self-conscious ego, the degenerate image of the individual, which manifests itself physiognomically in the mask. There is now a correspondence between the face and the animus. By contrast, the correspondence between the face and anima, the actual image of God in the individual, is lost and the innermost core of the personality is encrusted with a hard mask. Swedenborg can therefore write:

> In man, his inward nature is represented in his exterior, principally in his face and its expression. But his innermost being is no longer apparent nowadays, only the inward nature to some extent, if he has not learned from childhood to dissemble. Thereupon he assumes another character, namely, the animus; and, consequently, he puts on another countenance, expressing the animus in his face. Hypocrites are good at this; the better they are at it, the more deceitful they are. (*Arcana Coelestia* §3527)

In consequence, one can read the character, or animus, from many people's faces, but it is difficult to penetrate through the mask to the anima, their innermost image. For this one requires a special gift of the Holy Spirit, the gift of transparent viewing, which consists in looking through a person's mask into the very ground of his being and seeing his authentic image shining through the armor of his deceptive outer form.

This enables us to understand Swedenborg's description of the change in the individual after death.[2] After his translation into the realm of spirits, the deceased retains the form he historically acquired in his lifetime. Initially, the dead appear physiognomically just as they did at death and therefore are recognizable to their acquaintances in the world beyond. But now their mask no longer has a material basis; the encrustation of their inner face cannot last in their new state. Their face again becomes plastic and lively. The lost concordance between the true inner person and the outer person is once again restored and the individual again becomes on the outside what he is within. As Swedenborg personally experienced, "he is translated into the state of his inward man," that is, his inward person now completely determines his external appearance. Once again, his face

---

2. The three states after death are described in *Heaven and Hell* §§491–520.

reflects the inner model of his personality in a pure and unadulterated fashion, and his mask falls away. "Then it is evident, how man was constituted in the world." In this state:

> the spirits appear exactly as they were in the world, and it also becomes evident what they did and said in secret. Because the outer no longer restrains, they speak the same and try to do the same, and they are not afraid of slander as in the world. They are also translated into their various evil states, in order that they may appear to the angels and good spirits as they really are. Thus the hidden is uncovered, and the secret is revealed according to the words of the Lord: "For there is nothing covered, that shall not be revealed; neither hid, that shall not be known. Therefore whatsoever you have spoken in darkness shall be heard in the light; and that which you have spoken in the ear in closets shall be proclaimed upon the housetops" (Luke 12:2–3).

At the same time, there ensues a further decisive turn in the development of the personality. After the innermost essence of the individual is liberated and can unfold in a pure fashion, everyone turns towards the society of his own kind. Everyone is attracted by the special love underlying his or her nature to those bound by the same love. The assignment of spirits to the various societies in the realm of spirits and angels is not arbitrary. Everyone is guided rather by the basic tendency of the individual's inner person, through the tug of the heart towards their own kind. The higher destiny of the individual's earthly life is fulfilled in this assignment to a specific society in the realm of spirits, an assignment that changes again and again with advances in inner development. According to the basic tendency of his inner person, he already belonged to this higher congregation during his earthly life. Now he wholly joins this society:

> Everyone comes to the society where his spirit was in the world, for every man is linked according to his spirit, be this good or evil, to a heavenly or a hellish society. The spirit is gradually led to this society and finally joins it. The evil spirit, when he is in the state of his inward man, turns by steps towards his society and finally takes up his position there, even before this state is complete. But once this

state is reached, the evil spirit throws himself into hell, where his own kind are.

The great separation of the spirits occurs on the second level. As long as the good and the evil are still in their outer form, they are together in this world. But once they are translated into their inward form and the dominant love of their nature becomes an outward feature, the good separate from the evil, and each hastens towards the society to which they are drawn by the kinship of their love. Not only does the individual spirit stand in the light of heaven without hypocrisy and throw his mask away, but also the congregation of spirits embraces only members sharing the same nature and love.

The orthodox doctrine of the Last Things regarded the separation of the sheep from the goats, and their assignment to the right or the left, as a consequence of the Day of Judgment. In Swedenborg's thought, this separation is understood as an incident in the metaphysical unfolding of the human spirit-personality. The individual determines his higher destiny by his love in this earthly life. What is decisive is the basic tendency of his nature, whether his love is directed towards God or his own ego, whether he allows himself to be moved by good or by evil. Everyone's life in the world beyond follows the basic tendency of his earthly life. In the world beyond, his nature and his love are realized without hypocrisy, falsification, and impediment; they become the formative principle of his personality and determine his assignment to a society of his own kind. In the world beyond, the individual becomes the unveiled form of what he is in his innermost man, whatever was covered up, falsified, distorted here on earth and dormant unbeknown to him. In the world beyond, the fruit of the human personality matures; the pull of the heart, which led the individual on earth, is completed there.

Heaven and hell are therefore not realms that await the individual and into which he is translated by a divine verdict after the Last Judgment. There are no angels and no demons apart from human beings. Hell consists of societies of humanity, whose basic tendency is egoism and who have rebelled against God and his Word here on earth. They have exploited their neighbor on earth for the increase of their own power and pleasure, and now they have to realize and practice their perverted basic tendency further in the world beyond. Shackled to each other by the similarity of their depraved nature and their perverted love, they gravitate towards the evil, the focus of their innermost person, and make life hell for each other, by simultaneously punishing each other for the evil they do. The evil person is the devil of the other evil person, and hell consists in their *having* to do evil to each other. By activating their real nature, they torment each other, and each one punishes the vice of the other by practicing it on him.

Similarly, there are no angels and no heaven apart from humanity. Heaven consists of societies of human beings brought together by the same love of God and one's neighbor, who do good towards each other in like-minded love of the good and the true. They perfect themselves in the understanding of truth and constantly progress up towards the Lord their archetype. Humankind is its own angel, and the realization of the love of God in the love of one's neighbor makes the life of each angel and his neighbor into heaven. The loving deed he performs for his neighbor is reciprocated by his neighbor, and every action in the community becomes its own reward, just as it becomes a punishment in hell.

The third state after death, the state of further education, is reserved only for those whose love is directed towards God. "Through instructions, they are prepared for heaven and the path that leads upwards to heaven. There they are given in charge to guardian angels, and then received by other angels, led into the societies, where they have many joys. Hereupon each is brought by the Lord into his own society." In this way, the evil and falsehood that even attaches to the best on earth as a residue of the earthly is increasingly rooted out, until their love permeates their entire nature and they become a perfect member of their heavenly society.

A pervading inner living connection thus links the various realms with each other. In the earthly world, the personal essence, the spiritual person formed in the image of God, is educated into an individual form and moreover in accordance with the basic tendency of his love. In the spiritual world, this basic trait of his essence becomes prominent and drives him towards his own kind. The spiritual realms are made up of heaven and hell. In hell, the human life that has been directed against God unfolds in its eternal self-punishment. In heaven, the redeemed and purified spirits organize themselves as living, active personalities in higher and higher societies within the body of the "Universal Human."

There can be no doubt that this doctrine of heaven and hell is extraordinarily profound. For the first time since the Reformation, it introduced a tangible way of looking at the Last Things, which had become unclear and consciously suppressed in dogmatic teachings. It conceives of heaven and hell as final possibilities and enhancements of the human condition. It regards the development of the personality on earth and in the world beyond as a continuous process. It does not tear the here-and-now asunder into an earthly, corporeal world and a disembodied, spiritual world; but through its view of the spiritual corporeality of the inner person, it maintains the unity of the evolution of personality in the earthly life and into the world beyond. It avoids all the illogical conceptions of the orthodox doctrines of the world beyond. It understands the resurrection, the Last Judgment, the assignment to heaven and hell as incidents founded in the evolution of personality. It requires no first created Satan or devils for its hell, it claims no pre-existing angels for its heaven, but relates heaven and hell to the human sphere. It is people who make their life hell through their evil and people who make their life heaven through their love. Human beings become devils in their temptation for evil and in the punishment of evil or are angels in the perfection in the good and the true and in the elevating power of love. The earth is the theater in which a way is prepared for the separation of souls according to the basic tendency of their nature. Some become obdurate in their egoism against God, while others experience rebirth and devote themselves to the Lord in free love. The world of spirits belongs to the sphere of human life. It is there that the separation of hearts and souls occurs, and it comes to pass in the clear assignment of spiritual beings to societies of the same love. Heaven is the theater of elevated humankind, hell that of self-destructive humankind.

From this viewpoint, several offensive or incomprehensible ideas in the orthodox image of the world beyond are clarified. It is not God but the individual who condemns. By turning against God in the abuse of his freedom and thus excluding himself from the life of God, the individual condemns himself. It is not God who judges the individual, but the individual who judges himself by surrendering to self-love and rejecting divine grace. It is not God who throws men and women into hell, but the person himself hastens there, driven by the evil instinct of his selfish nature towards his own kind. The eternity of hellish torments does not consist in our being eternally punished by an angry God for individual evil deeds committed on earth. Hell consists in the evil's continually practicing their inclination towards evil upon each other after death and each punishing another in his society for the evil done unto him. The bliss of heaven does not consist in elevated humankind enjoying eternal joys as an eternal reward for good deeds on earth. Heaven is the state where the elevated constantly realize their love for the good and the true in an active life among each other, and the eternally renewed practice of this love among them becomes the mutual reward of their love.

27

Marriages in Heaven

The most original feature in Swedenborg's doctrine of the spiritual world concerns marriages in heaven. This idea can already be detected in his earliest visionary works, but it was systematically presented in his work *Conjugial Love*, published at Amsterdam in 1768.

This doctrine has usually been treated as a curiosity and interpreted in a superficial fashion. However, the doctrine has had an extraordinary influence on the religious outlook of the eighteenth and nineteenth centuries, and especially on the view of love and marriage in German Romanticism and theosophy. A recent researcher has presented a purely psychological interpretation in terms of Swedenborg's repressed complexes. According to this theory, Swedenborg never experienced happiness in love, which his strong sex drive led him to imagine as the ultimate earthly bliss; thus, he postponed it to life after death. His doctrine of heavenly marriage was, therefore, the product of wish-fulfilment: in heaven, he was allowed to enjoy the marital happiness denied to him on earth.

This paltry explanation in no way does justice to Swedenborg's ideas concerning marriages in heaven. These ideas are an integral part of a metaphysical tradition of love, centuries old, which runs through the history of Western thought from Plato and the neo-Platonists through Renaissance philosophy and the speculations of Jacob Boehme to the metaphysics of Friedrich Wilhelm Joseph von Schelling (1775–1854) and Franz von Baader (1765–1841). Their authentic metaphysical concern cannot be dismissed with the argument that all these thinkers were trying to sublimate their unfulfilled passions. Undoubtedly, personal life experiences can give the idea a certain direction, influence the choice of themes and the priority of their discussion; but the metaphysical concern is not thereby impugned. Plato's *Symposium*, Franz von Baader's *Erotische Philosophie*, and also Swedenborg's *Conjugial Love* mean more for the history of the human spirit than mere fantasies of disappointed bachelors.

As in Plato, Jacob Boehme, and Franz von Baader, the metaphysics of love in Swedenborg is based on the idea of the androgyne. Like all Christian thinkers, Swedenborg developed this idea from an interpretation of the biblical account of Creation. The archetypal man created in the image of God embraces both the male and female principle within himself. Jacob Boehme and his followers in England, Thomas Bromley, John Pordage, and Jane Leade, who themselves were a strong influence on Henry More and the Cambridge Platonists and on John Milton, held such views. They understood the androgynous wholeness of the archetypal man as a marriage of the heavenly virgin Sophia with the image of God in his soul, so that his personality comprised both sexes. The separation of the sexes ensued only after the original Fall, when the heavenly Sophia, the inner companion, fled from Adam and he was allotted Eve, created from his own body, as his outer, earthly counterimage. Only after man's estrangement from God is the androgynous unity dissolved in the form of a visible, personal differentiation of the sexes, coincident with the descent into carnal, earthly corporeality.

Swedenborg substantiated the androgynous idea in a different way. He did not recognize the doctrine of a single androgynous, archetypal man. In his view, man and woman are created as two different beings from the outset, but together they form *one* person. The allegorical interpretation of the biblical account of Eve's creation from the rib of Adam provides him with a series of allusions showing how man and woman inwardly and outwardly combine to form a higher being.

Swedenborg had already mentioned this idea in his early visionary work *Worship and Love of God*. His doctrine is not only concerned with marriage in heaven but with marriage in general. The beginning should find itself in the end. True marriage is the form of community of man and woman, in which both come together in true perfect love not only in an outer union but also in a spiritual, personal unity embracing all levels of personal life. Together they form a whole person. Thus, he expounds the words of Genesis 2:24 and Matthew 19:5-6, which was also the premise for the speculations of Boehme and his English followers:

> "And they twain shall be one flesh. Wherefore they are no more twain, but one flesh." This explains that woman is created from the man, and that both have the desire and the capacity to unite again in One, and moreover in *one* man, as this is likewise explained in the book of creation, where both together are called "man." For one reads in Genesis 5:2: "In the day that God created man, male and female he created them, and called their name man." It actually says, "He called their name Adam," but Adam and man are the same word in Hebrew. Moreover, both man and woman are together called "man" as in Genesis 1:27 and Genesis 3:22–24. "A man" is signified by "one flesh." (*Conjugial Love* §156a [2])

Marriage exists in a complete sense when man and woman unite in total mutual love to form a whole. "Love is nothing else but the wish and resultant striving for joining in unity. For man and woman are so created that *one* man or *one* flesh can come from two; and when they have become one, then they are considered together *one* man in his wholeness. But without this connection, they are two, and each is like a divided or half man" (*Conjugial Love* §37).

This desire for wholeness is the cause of conjugial love on earth, for it is founded in the nature of man and woman. But rarely and exceptionally is this complete union ever attained in the sphere of earthly life. Only in heaven is it possible. This presupposes that the basic desire of love remains in man and woman even after death. This is the boldest inference in Swedenborg's metaphysics of love.

"As that capacity for union lies hidden inside man and woman, and the ability to form a unity and the desire for it dwells in each, it follows that the mutual and reciprocal love of the other sex remains in man after death" (*Conjugial Love* §37). The union of man and woman is consummated in a true marital unity in heaven, where the innermost essence of man—namely, his love—realizes itself purely and determines his outer form. There reciprocal love unites the couple, so that they increasingly become *one* person, "for in heaven a couple are not two, but *one* angel" (*Conjugial Love* §50, §177). In this union, the original, culpable separation of the sexes is annulled and overcome. Once again, Swedenborg proceeds from his spiritual exegesis of the biblical account of Creation and the creation of Eve from the rib of Adam. The archetypal man, whom God created in his image with freedom, had the potential to turn against God and reverse his love of God, the love of his archetype, into self-love. In order to prevent this degeneration of his self-love, man is confronted with woman as a part of his self in another being. Every marriage reflects the separation of Eve from the man, but their mutual love simultaneously reflects the annulment of their separation and their combination into an original whole.

In this sense, Swedenborg interprets the words of Genesis 2:22–24, which reads: "This is now bone of my bones, and flesh of my flesh":

> The rib of the chest has the spiritual meaning of the naturally true. This explains that woman is created from man by the transfer of his wisdom, . . . and that the love of this wisdom is transferred from man into woman, in order that conjugial love results. This happened in order that man does not love himself but loves his wife, who has the innate predisposition to transform the self-love of a man into love for her. Once one has understood the mystery of woman's creation out of man, one can see that the woman is created or formed from man likewise in marriage and that this happens from the wife, or rather through the wife from God, who has given the wife these inclinations through influx. The wife thereby assimilates the image of the man in herself, appropriating his inclinations and combining the inner will of the man and absorbing the reproductive seeds of his soul. This explains how

woman, according to the inner description in the book of creation, is fashioned into a wife by that which she takes from her husband and his chest and absorbs in herself. Because every man from birth onwards is inclined to love himself, creation made provision that man should not be destroyed by self-love and arrogant self-reliance by transferring this love of man onto woman. Woman was implanted with this love from birth, so that she would love the insight and wisdom of her husband and thus love him. Therefore, woman draws her husband's pride in his own insight continuously towards herself, while extinguishing it in him. She makes it living within herself and transforms it into conjugial love, filling this love excessively with affectionate feelings. The Lord provided for this, in order that the pride of his own insight would not delude man into thinking he was intelligent and wise in his own right and not through the Lord. (*Conjugial Love* §156b ff)

The love of woman "quenches" the self-love of man. He recognizes in woman his own self as a gift and image of the Lord and vice versa. In the mirror of their mutual love, man and woman recognize the image of God, in which they are one. The image of the beloved is in each of the lovers, and thus they are both whole and *one* man in their love:

The spouse sees his spouse in his outer and inner soul, so that each spouse has the other in him or herself. This means that the image and similarity of the man in the soul of the woman and the image and similarity of the woman in the soul of the man are such that one can see the other in him or herself, and so they dwell together in their innermost being.

A fundamental law of the realization of divine life is generally reflected in the differentiation and reunification of the sexes. Swedenborg's idea that man represents wisdom and woman love is directly linked to his notion of God. God has his essence in love and wisdom. He appears to the angels as a sun, radiating warmth and light. Warmth is the radiant divine love and light is the radiant divine wisdom or truth. In the divine being, love is united with wisdom in a shining, warming light. But all life forms and realizes itself only in the other and become aware of itself only in the other. Therefore, in its own image of man, the divine life divided itself into its truth and its goodness, which are once again united through marital love. "That this is so," writes Swedenborg, "was clearly visible from the angels in heaven. Separated from their wives, they are intelligent but not wise. But when they are with their wives, they are also wise. What surprised me is that they attain a state of wisdom as soon as they turn their face towards their wife, for the link between the true and the good in the spiritual world is produced by the look, and woman is the good, while man is the true. When truth turns towards goodness, they animate each other." Thus the mystery of the development of divine life is reflected in conjugial love:

> Marriage was so instituted by the creation: man was created, in order that he should understand the truth, and woman, in order that she should incline to the good. Accordingly, man is the truth and woman goodness. When the understanding of the truth, which is inherent in man, comes to unite with the inclination to goodness, which is inherent in woman, both souls are combined in one. This combination is the spiritual marriage, from which conjugial love stems.

This is the love, which Goethe described in his *Metamorphosis of Plants*: "The holy love strives up to the highest fruit of like convictions, the same view of things, in order that the pair can unite in harmonious regard and find the higher world." Swedenborg's statements about marriages on earth and in heaven are thus rendered intelligible by his metaphysical foundation of conjugial love.

There is one clear conclusion to be drawn from this foundation of marriage in a doctrine of the androgynous nature of the human image. Real marriage leading to a spiritual and corporeal union of man and woman can only be monogamous. For this reason, Swedenborg explicitly distinguishes conjugial and sexual love. Sexual love is selfish and roving, love with varying object, a love "for several and with several." In conjugial love, however, sexual love is elevated into a personal, spiritual form. But at this point, Swedenborg comes into conflict with traditional ecclesiastical notions of the world beyond. Since St. Augustine, the doctrine of angels had been governed by a prudishness, supported by metaphysical notions. Here two of Augustine's basic religious convictions contradict each other. On the one hand, he believed in the resurrection of the flesh. In his view, people would be resurrected as men and women at the Day of Judgment. On the other hand, the sexual domain was simply the sphere of sin. How should one then imagine the state of resurrected people? It must be physical but it is not permitted to be sexual. The chapters of *The City of God* dealing with the resurrection are therefore filled with the most bizarre speculations, describing the transformation of resurrected bodies into a sexless state but which still retain their secondary sexual characteristics. Scholastic theology and Protestant orthodoxy both followed St. Augustine in imagining heaven as the domain of sexless spiritual beings.

Swedenborg overcame this view like his predecessors, who had based their view of love on a doctrine of the androgyne. Sexual differentiation plainly concerns a hereditary factor grounded in the inner form of man, and man and woman are clearly united in a single spiritual personality according to their innermost nature. There must therefore be marriages in heaven; indeed, it is there that the genuine marriages of this earthly world can first realize themselves in a pure form. Sexual differentiation will also continue in heaven in a mode of being appropriate to spiritual corporeality.

However, under the influence of ecclesiastical notions of the next world, Swedenborg initially shrank from the implication of his ideas. He still described heavenly marriages as purely spiritual unions in his work *Heaven and Hell* (1758): "Marriage in heaven is not like marriage here on earth. In heaven, there are spiritual weddings, which cannot be called weddings (*nuptiae*), but spiritual unions between the good and the true. By contrast, one calls them weddings on earth, as they are not only spiritual but also carnal unions. Accordingly, couples in heaven are not called man and wife" (*Heaven and Hell* §382b). Swedenborg refers to the word of the Lord, that the resurrected in the next world "neither marry, nor are given in marriage" (Luke 20:35).

But the traditional doctrine of angels did not long withstand his idea of corporeal spirits. It is characteristic of his view of the world beyond that the whole human is resurrected in his individual personality in the mode of being of the spiritual world, and this includes sexual differentiation. Because the angels and spirits have a corporeal mode of being, sexual differentiation must be evident in their corpo-reality, and conjugial love must also have a sexual nature.

He had already come to this conclusion in his work *Apocalypse Explained* (1759). This idea was then further discussed in his work *Conjugial Love* (1768) without further reference to the customary view:

> Because a human being survives as a human after death and a human is male and female and the male is different from the fe-male, indeed so different that the one cannot be changed into the other, it follows that, after death, the man lives on as a man and the woman as a woman, both as spiritual people. In the man, the male aspect is present in all, even the smallest parts of his body, and also in each concept of his thought and every stirring of his emotion. The same things in woman are all female. And as one cannot be transformed into the other, it follows that after death the man re-mains a man, and the woman remains a woman. (*Conjugial Love* §32)

Even the heavenly union has the character of a real marriage:

> Natural man loves and desires only outer unions and physical pleas-ures from them. But spiritual man loves and desires an inner union, and delightful feelings of the spirit from it. He recognizes that these feelings can only be achieved with a single spouse, with whom he is continuously and increasingly united as one. The more he is so united, the more his feelings of delight are heightened. This is the reason that it is said that the conjugial love of those who come to heaven remains after death. (*Conjugial Love* 38)

How is the earthly marriage related to the heavenly? However ideal his notions of heavenly marriage were, Swedenborg took a real-istic view of earthly marital relations, which already in his time dis-played all the symptoms of modern disintegration and the loosening of monogamy. He knew that monogamous love is the exception rather than the rule. He knew that sexual love had lapsed into self-ishness. Such selfish sexual love seeks and changes its object with caprice and mood, and the roving instinct of insatiability is inherent in it. He also knew that real marriage is a gift of grace. He said that it is divine guidance that determines true lovers for each other from the outset and brings them together and that this union of lovers in a true person can take place only in God:

> The love, which is the love of spiritual marriage, becomes the love of natural marriage, when it descends into the body. Everyone who wishes to can recognize that this is so. Couples who love each other mutually and inwardly in the soul also love each other physically. It is known that all love descends from an inclination of the soul into the body and without this origin no love exists.

Swedenborg knew that only a few marriages are contracted from such an inward love, but that considerations of estate, social usage, the calculation of all possible financial and commercial advantages, and a thousand other selfish motives played a role. He also knew the whole dynamics of physical sexual desire. In *Conjugial Love,* he emphasizes that sexual love cannot be overcome without detriment by very passionate men, if they are not able to marry once they have reached marriageable age. He advises those youths who cannot marry but are incapable of curbing their desires to take a lover in order not to ruin themselves through a disorderly sexual life. In the same degree to which a man prefers conjugial love to a lecherous state, his inner man is in conjugial love. If he nevertheless continues his extramarital relations, then this is a necessity for him. Conjugial love can be hidden in him, as the spiritual is in the natural. But what if the man finds the predestined object of his true love and true wholeness in his lover and not in his legitimate spouse?

Precisely because he saw true marriage on earth so often prevented by external or personal circumstances, Swedenborg emphasized all the more that those who belong together and form a single person will come together in the purer sphere of heaven, even if they did not find each other on earth. He thereby took all possibilities into consideration. If a widower dies, he will be recognized by his wife as long as he appears in the world of spirits in the form he had on earth. The husband rejoins the wife. "They recognize each other, and when they have lived together in the world, so they keep company again and live together for a while" (*Conjugial Love* §47). But then the change of state gradually begins, in which the new spirit is translated into the inward nature of their soul. The mask of his outer nature falls away, and he must be without hypocrisy and pretense, as he actually is in his inner man. Now it will become apparent whether his conjugial love was authentic and whether husband and wife find each other in a heavenly marriage and personal unity. Alternatively, their love would belong only to the outer man, which has no inner spiritual correspondence and is therefore cast off. Swedenborg's insights into the social conditions of his time and country led him to some cool and skeptical considerations. As long as a married couple are in a state of outwardness, "neither knows the inclination of the other to him or herself because this is hidden within. But afterwards, when they come into their inner state, this inclination is revealed. If this is harmonious and sympathetic, they continue their married life; but if it is not harmonious and antipathetic, they separate, sometimes the man from the woman, sometimes the woman from the man, and sometimes both mutually" (*Conjugial Love* §47; see also §49).

Like everything untruthful and false on earth, false marriages do not endure in heaven. The judgment, which takes place after the death of each man in the form of a revelation of his true nature, is also a judgment on his marriage. Those remain together who really belong together and form a whole; the others separate of their own accord. Like all earthly chaos, the marital chaos is brought into order in heaven. When true conjugial love prevailed on earth, however many troubles, temptations, and crises it endured, then both lovers will find each other in an increasingly more perfect unity in heaven. When there was no genuine love, where there was no spiritual and intellectual community, where there was no basic tendency towards a higher unity, then a separation takes place. Nothing that does not belong together is forced together in heaven.

At all events, Swedenborg stated another idea in his work on the soul, which was written in 1741 and thus before his vocation. He says that the punishment for couples who lived with each other in discord on earth consists in their having to argue eternally and torment each in the world beyond. Once their physical desire ceases, the only band that held them together here, there remains only a murderous, immortal hatred that ultimately takes possession of their whole being and "this is the earthly hell, and one can justifiably believe, that one soul will torment another like two Erinyes or Furies in Erebus."

This dreadful idea of divorce in heaven was moderated in later visions: whatever does not belong together breaks up of its own accord. However frightful his visions of hell are individually, he did not hold fast to the vision of eternal marital hell. The outer difficulties frustrating a real marriage on earth seemed too involved with earthly marital chaos for man to deserve an eternal punishment:

> Separations take place after death because the unions on earth are seldom contracted from an inner sentiment of love, but only from an outer, which conceals the inner. The outer sentiment of love has its basis in such things, which pertain to the love of the world and the body. The love of the world relates above all to wealth and property, the love of the body to titles and honors, and apart from these there are many enticing attractions, like beauty and feigned decorum, occasionally even lechery. Moreover, marriages are customarily contracted within the country, the town, or the estate where one was born or dwells. Here there is only a small choice of partners restricted to the families of one's acquaintances, and again only with those in the same class as oneself. Thus it comes about that marriages contracted in the world are mostly outward and not inward, but it is only the inner union of souls that makes the true marriage. This union cannot be perceived until man casts off the outer and clothes himself in the inner, and this occurs after death. Hence separations take place and afterwards new unions with similar and congenial partners, whenever this was not the case on earth, as it is with those who from youth have loved, desired, and prayed to the Lord for loving relations with one beloved, while scorning and abhorring all licentious desires. (*Conjugial Love* §49)

Swedenborg therefore regards a genuine marriage on earth under a double aspect. From God's point of view, true marriages on earth are those in which God has joined those who belong together:

> God's providence, which extends to the smallest detail and embraces everything, ensures that conjugial couples are born for each other. Under the guidance of the Lord, these are constantly educated for their marriage, without the boy or girl knowing it; and after the passage of time, the marriageable virgin and youth come

together somewhere and see one another. Then they immediately recognize as if by instinct that they are and think alike. It is as if an inner voice spoke within and the youth heard: "She is mine," and the virgin heard: "He is mine." When they have considered this in their souls, they talk to each other with intention and become engaged. One says this happens as by fate, through instinct, through inspiration, but one means through a dispensation of divine providence, for so it seems as long as one knows nothing of it. For the Lord reveals their inner similarities, so that they see each other. (*Conjugial Love* §229)

However, this mutual discovery is neither a compulsion nor a law of nature but takes place in the sphere of freedom as far as man is concerned. Such a marriage can be realized only when both partners believe in their hearts and outer behavior in the possibility of such a perfect union. They should also have prepared themselves for it before they become acquainted, and they should have prayed to God for a genuine marriage, and their belief in future unity should have kept the roving sexual instinct in check.

What happens in the world beyond when one spouse died and the survivor enters into a new marriage on earth? What happens if, in the world beyond, a husband is confronted with three or four wives to whom he was successively married on earth? Swedenborg gave a careful and human answer to this question, which plays a large role in pastoral practice. Once again, his distinction between the various states of being in the world beyond is a crucial factor. As long as the husband is still in the state of the outer, he opens relations with all his former wives of this world. But once he enters his inner state, in which his true love emerges without deceit and hypocrisy and in which he also "recognizes the inclinations of love according to their true character," then "he either takes one of them, or he leaves them all." If, after the revelation of his inner nature, he finds among them the true wife corresponding to his nature, he makes the former choice. But if his real love was deceived in all wives, he leaves them. Swedenborg had sufficient experience of men to credit them with marrying the wrong person several times.

In this view, those marriages that represented a true community of soul and spirit on earth assume a special status. Death will not separate these marriages. Whoever lived in such a marriage will not enter into a second marriage. "Two such spouses are not separated by death because the spirit of the deceased partner still lives together with the surviving partner, moreover until the death of the latter, when they come together again, unite, and love each other more tenderly then before because they are in the spiritual world." But even here, outer things can compel the surviving partner to enter a new marriage of convention, "for example, when there are small children one must care for, or when the household expands with domestic servants of both sexes" and other things "which do not concern conjugial love" (*Conjugial Love* §321). Notwithstanding, the husband will find his true wife in the world beyond, to whom he was bound in ties of true love here on earth.

Swedenborg once made an allusion, reported by his followers, which suggests that his view of divorces in heaven was linked to personal expectation. Swedenborg is said to have occasionally mentioned that he had seen his future wife in the world beyond and that she expected him there. On earth, she had been known as Countess Elisabet Gyllenborg. This lady of the Stiernkrona family was the spouse of Fredrik Gyllenborg, a leading Swedish politician, who died in 1759. She was a pietistic lady, who wrote an improving book in two volumes entitled *Mary's Better Part*. Swedenborg had been close friends with her husband and her father since 1733. It is unknown whether he had already indicated his feelings towards her during her lifetime. However, it is a fact that, in his visionary reports, he placed her husband in hell because of his lust for power. Countess Gyllenborg survived her husband by ten years and died in 1769, three years before Swedenborg. Nevertheless, Swedenborg must have known the state of her marriage if he expected her to divorce her earthly husband and marry him; otherwise, he would hardly have mentioned the matter to others who knew the deceased countess.

Genuine marriages stand under the star of higher and higher perfection in heaven. There is no stagnation in heaven, no mere enjoyment but an eternally active realization of love and understanding towards one's neighbor and in community with one's neighbor. This is particularly true of the married state, which aims at union as *one* man and *one* spiritual person. "Because true conjugial love endures eternally, it follows that the wife becomes a wife more and more and the husband becomes a husband more and more. The real cause is because both partners become ever more inward people in a marriage of true conjugial love, for this love opens the interior of their souls; and as this is opened, man becomes more and more a man. To become more a man means the wife becoming more a wife, and the husband becoming more a husband" (*Conjugial Love* §200). But because every transformation of the inner man also corresponds to a transformation of the outer man, an outer change takes place in the world beyond: in the degree to which their love deepens, the lovers return to the state of their youthful perfection. The realm of heavenly love is the realm of eternal youth. Swedenborg discussed the idea of eternal youth most vividly, before Lavater, Romantics like Novalis, and theologians and philosophers of German Idealism like Schleiermacher and Schelling even mentioned it:

> Everyone who is in true conjugial love returns after death as angels to their youth and the onset of their manhood. However much they may have aged, men become youths once again, and women return to the bloom and joys of an age in which conjugial love began to exalt life with new pleasures. The man who in the world avoided adultery as a sin and was led by the Lord into conjugial love comes into this youthful state, at first outwardly and then more and more inwardly. As they inwardly become ever younger, it follows that the true conjugial love constantly increases in them and enters into their delights and blessings, which were prepared for them from the beginning of the world. These delights and blessings of the innermost heaven come from the Lord's love of heaven and the Church and therefore spring from the love of the good and the true. As a result of this inclination, man casts off all the seriousness, despondency, and dullness of age and clothes himself in the liveliness, gaiety, and exuberance of youth. (*Conjugial Love* §137)

The transformation to a higher unity is also impressed in the individual features of the lovers and is reflected in the "inner beauty of the face." "For the man takes from the woman the beautiful blush of her love, and woman takes from man the shining luster of his wisdom, for the two spouses are united in soul and the abundance of their humanity appears in both" (*Conjugial Love* §192).

Swedenborg elucidated in numerous visions the transformations of conjugial life in heaven. These reports are highly vivid and rich in imagery and display a spontaneous vitality and colorfulness by contrast with the monotonous, didactic conversations in heavenly academies. The idylls of contemporary rustic shepherd poetry often influence their poetic style. Even in his visions, he remained a child of his time. His images are mingled with the dreams of Arcadia with eternal spring, eternal youth, eternal innocence, and eternally true love, just as they found lyrical expression in the poetry of the Rococo period. In one vision, he visits the heavenly couples of the golden age of men. On a high plain planted with cedar and olive trees they live in tents, entwined with vines bearing dark blue grapes. The men are clothed in hyacinth-colored coats and white tunics and the women in purple togas. The picture is completed with the decorative white Rococo sheep "symbolizing the innocence and peace of the mountain-dwellers." He feels that the linguistic and stylistic means of poetry are not sufficient to depict this paradise of blissful life. He also expresses this when describing his heavenly visions with the view of Arcadian paths leading through fields of flowers with olive and orange trees, the heavenly beauty of the figures, their costumes, the festivities, the vessels and utensils. Oetinger's comment that the corn of the vision grows on the stalk of human imagination particularly applies here.

This doctrine of Swedenborg culminates in a panegyric to conjugial love and true marriage in a period when marriage was beginning to decline in courtly, aristocratic, and bourgeois society. He extolled marriage as the "nursery of the human race; and as the angelic heaven is composed of the human race, it is also the nursery of heaven," for not only earth but also heaven is filled with living personalities through marriages in this world. "As the human race and its resulting heaven, in which the Divine can dwell as in his own, is the final purpose of the whole creation, and propagation occurs through marriages in accordance with the divine order, so it is clear how sacred marriages are from the point of view of creation and how sacred they should therefore be kept." If one were to succeed in elevating true marriage to the general form of earthly marriage, then the Kingdom of God would be realized on earth and human society would truly correspond to heavenly society, as was the case among men in the golden age in Swedenborg's opinion:

> When the propagation of the human race occurs through marriages, in which the sacred love of the good and the true prevails, then they happen on earth as in heaven, and the realm of the Lord on earth corresponds to the realm of the Lord in the heavens. For the heavens consist of a hierarchy of societies corresponding to all the varieties of heavenly and spiritual inclinations. The form of heaven proceeds from this arrangement, which so incomparably surpasses all forms of the universe. A similar form would exist on earth, if propagation were to occur through marriages, in which true conjugial love prevailed.

The true family on earth would then correspond to the heavenly community. "There are as many identical images of heavenly societies as there are families descended from one ancestor. The families would be of various kinds like fruitful trees, from which as many gardens are formed with their own species of fruit, and all the gardens together would present the form of a heavenly paradise." Conjugial love is the jewel of human life and the source of the Christian religion, precisely because "conjugial love starts in the innermost of man, and in accordance with hierarchy descends into the outer of the body, thus filling the whole man with heavenly love and impresses upon him the form of divine love, which is the form of heaven and an image of the Lord." All beauty in earthly things and all the more in the life beyond has its origin in conjugial love.

The antitype of conjugial love is promiscuity (*amor scortatoria*). This is a love perverted by human selfishness. In promiscuity, the other is not the object of love but the object of selfish pleasure, a mere means for the increase and fulfillment of one's own lust. In this kind of love, the image of God in one's neighbor is completely disregarded and dishonored. The image of God also degenerates in him who submits to this love, and increasingly so the more he lives in this love. It leads to evil people forming couples, abusing each other mutually for their selfish purposes, and thereby descending ever further into their evil.

All those who have succumbed to this selfish opposite of true conjugial love bear out Swedenborg's idea that it is men in the world beyond who mutually make life hell for each other and that each must accord with his innermost love. As soon as those who have surrendered to promiscuity on earth are translated in the world beyond into their inner and true essence begins to realize itself, they feel drawn to their own kind. They hasten to the hellish brothels to satisfy their love with their companions. There they copulate like beasts and tear each other to pieces because they feel only loathing and disgust for each other despite all sensual pleasure.

In their poetic power, Swedenborg's visionary reports concerning adulterers and fornicators can match Dante's imagination. Also in his case, we find confirmation of the strange phenomenon that human imagination is much more plastic and fertile in the description of evil than in the description of good. The fornicators are led in hell to sirens who attract them as beautiful girls but who change into black, frightful monsters at the instant of embrace. If the infatuated are still lured by their mad lust, they plunge into deeper hells, where their passion ensnares them in greater horrors. Their lasciviousness turns into disgust, satiety, and staleness, they and everything in their sphere of activity becomes dirty and smelly, they live in a world of excrement and dirt. The brothels where they reside are filled with refuse and disgusting filth of all kinds. They acquire white faces, which look as if they were made only of skin. Their voices become harsh, screeching and rattling in the throat. Their clothes become ragged; their gait become crooked and bent. Finally, they lose all capacity for fornication, and they are filled with disgust for the other sex, without being able to flee their world of lechery. Here one punishes the other through the realization of his innermost nature, by practicing his special form of perverted love on the other, which constantly lures and holds them fast. Thus they make each other's life an inescapable hell, which is its own terrible punishment.

Swedenborg's doctrine of marriage has great historical significance. Since the sacramental character of marriage was disallowed by the Reformation, the sanctity of marriage was only morally substantiated in the Protestant Church. No orthodox attempt was made to comprehend the religious foundations of marriage through a

Christian understanding of sex. Only Nikolaus von Zinzendorf (1700–1760) and some theosophists, especially followers of Jacob Boehme, pressed forward to a new religious proof for the sanctity of marriage. But none of these doctrines was presented in such clear ideas and images, and none was so directly applied to the religious outlook as Swedenborg's doctrine of conjugial love.

From a historical point of view, his doctrine of marriage represents the final elimination of medieval and monastic notions, which had dominated traditional expectations of the next world. The Reformation had indeed introduced a new theology and morality for the earthly world, but it had no new view of the next world, but rather tended to devalue it. Whenever the next world was discussed as a sort of appendix of theology, this was presented in the traditional concepts of the Catholic Middle Ages. Heaven appeared as a kind of large monastery where sexless angelic beings in an undefined state of abstract happiness praised the Lord in eternal choirs. With Swedenborg, this residue of a monastic piety is overcome. Heaven is also the realm of an endless development of man and humanity and moreover of all his personal talents and energies of both love and understanding. Just as all love reaches its perfect representation and fulfillment there, so too does conjugial love. Even more so, when this union of man and woman in a single spiritual person is an original endowment of human nature and both sexes carry this will for personal unity and wholeness within themselves.

But the third point is even more important. Because his doctrine of the life beyond and heavenly marriage goes into such detail, Swedenborg touched the point at which the expectations of the next world achieve a direct personal significance for every devout person who reflects on the matter. In our later centuries, questions about the Last Things are no longer topical in their original form among individual believers. When will the Day of Judgment come? When will the world end? When is the Second Coming? When will the new heaven and the new earth come? When will the Heavenly City descend to earth? Even the simplest believer, who still believes in the spiritual nature of the personality and in life after death, encounters a burning question in his direct experiences of life: how will my life be after death? As pastoral practice shows, the question of Last Things is equally urgent when death tears our loved ones away and puts an end to our love on earth. Wherever there was genuine love on earth, the question spontaneously arises: will the love for the beloved continue in the next world? Will there be a purification of love, in which a fulfilled, blessed community with the beloved is possible?

The ecclesiastical doctrine of the world beyond had only vague answers for these highly personal questions and thus offered a pale, monotonous, and insipid image of heaven that did not address living religious feeling. Swedenborg's visions and ideas opened a view that stimulated religious sentiment to a high degree by describing heaven as a place of endless activity and the unlimited development, perfection, and elevation of humanity. He portrayed the great potential of future fulfillment of being and community. He did not show bliss in the enjoyment of unspecified delights but rather in the ever higher activation of love and understanding in the realm of an elevated and pure humanity within the circle of a close personal community.

28

The Doctrine of the
Planets and Their Inhabitants

A nother aspect of the doctrine of the spiritual realm still deserves
special attention. Swedenborg related his ideas concerning the
structure and spiritual organization of the higher world to his cosmological and astronomical ideas and thus created a very detailed
doctrine about the inhabitants of the heavenly bodies. Observations
of this kind could be found in numerous works of his visionary
period. There is a systematic description in the work *Concerning the
Earths in Our Solar System called Planets, and the Earths in the Starry
Sky, and on Their Inhabitants, also on the Spirits and Angels There
from What Has Been Seen and Heard* (1758). This work became
known in Germany through a translation, the earliest known German translation of Swedenborg's work. It was edited by Oetinger in
1770 and appeared under the title *Von den Erdcörpern der Planeten
und des gestirnten Himmels Einwohnern, allwo von derselben Art zu
denken, zu reden und zu handeln, von ihrer Regierungs-Form, Policey,
Gottesdienst, Ehestand und überhaupt von ihrer Wohnung und Sitten,*

aus Erzählung derselben Geister selbst durch Emanuel Swedenborg Nachricht gegeben wird. Ein Werk zur Prüfung des Wahren und Wahrscheinlichen, woraus wenigstens vieles zur Philosophie und Theologie, Physik, Moral, Metaphysik und Logik kann genommen werden, aus dem Latein übersetzt und mit Reflexionen begleitet von einem, der Wissenschaft und Geschmack liebt.

To our modern way of thinking, Swedenborg's visionary gift at this juncture seems to have entered the realm of pure fantasy, indeed the wildest delusion, and to undermine the truth that a well-intentioned reader may grant to his doctrines of the world beyond. This subject is usually passed over in silence in modern accounts of Swedenborg, evidently with the intention of not further damaging Swedenborg's reputation, which is already burdened with theological and philosophical criticism.

However, this link between his doctrine of the world of spirits and his cosmology is not as misguided as it might seem. Swedenborg is by no means alone in his ideas of spiritual beings inhabiting the planets in our solar system and other planetary systems. He takes his place in an illustrious company of leading astronomers and natural philosophers, including the founders of the modern scientific worldview, such as Kepler, Huygens, Fontenelle, and above all Kant. They all advanced ideas about the inhabitants of heavenly bodies and tried to find scientific proofs for the existence of intelligent beings on the other planets.

These speculations, arising from the profound change in worldview after Copernicus, Galileo, and Kepler, also effected a revolutionary change in the image of man. According to ancient cosmology, Earth was the center of the universe, humankind was the highest creature of this earth, and our salvation was the central event in heaven and on earth. The ancient view of humanity was shaken by the discovery that Earth is only one planet among others revolving around the sun and that the sun itself is a mere speck within the countless solar systems of the starry firmament. If the inconceivable distances of the stars studied by Halley and Newton increasingly relegated Earth to a dust speck in the macrocosm, how could the human being, a quintessence of dust, still claim that he and his fate were the real object of the universe and divine action? Surely the relegation of our planet must result in an even more crucial devaluation of humankind? Was it not presumptuous and wholly unjustified arrogance still to claim that the human being was the central point of creation? Surely the new knowledge would topple the old Christian view of humanity.

The view of salvation, the basis of the Christian faith, was also threatened by the new worldview. Salvation was a cosmic event in both medieval and Reformation theology. The redemptive act of Christ held a universal meaning for the whole universe, for all sensible and insensible creation. Not only humankind, but "the whole of creation groans for the Day of Fulfilment" and as Jacob Boehme writes, the blood of the Lamb "tinges" the whole world. But according to the new worldview, Earth was no more than an inhabited rock in the middle of an ocean studded with countless, larger inhabited islands. Confronted with this fact, the importance of Christ began to pale and the divine act of redemption in the Incarnation seemed a trifling episode in the history of an insignificant little star. What megalomania on the part of the inhabitants of this miserable rock to proclaim this episode the central event of the universe and to assume that God would have alighted on just this wretched island! But even if this were so, the redemption of this particular planet would be of no consequence given its diminutiveness in the crowded universe.

Astronomers such as Newton and Huygens pointed their sophisticated instruments into the depths of the universe with feelings of awe and reverence. They now undertook to count and measure the stars, to calculate the rotation periods of the planets, and to establish their properties in order to oppose this devaluation in the image of humankind and the universal facts of salvation. These men, devout Christians, saw themselves as having to harmonize the new perspective on the universe with their belief in humanity's divine destiny and our identity with the image of God.

The comparison of the other planets with Earth gave rise to the idea that human life is not restricted to our planet but extends to the other planets and even other planetary systems of the galaxy. This hypothesis made it possible to uphold the universality of the divine act of redemption. It was possible to implicate the whole universe in the cosmic event of salvation, if the heavenly bodies were dwelling places for spiritual beings of a human kind, who were developing further and impatiently awaiting the great day of God.

These speculations on the part of Huygens, Fontenelle, Kant, and many other researchers did not arise from a playful imagination. They were greatly concerned to protect the Christian view of humankind from the nihilistic consequences of a materialistic interpretation of the new worldview in the estimation and self-regard of the individual. There was wide scope for speculation, and it was all the harder to observe the boundary between fantasy and exact research when the technical means available for the observation of the planets was still so limited. The temptation was all the greater to fill the gaps in observation with speculation. Kant took so much delight in ideas about the inhabitants of other planets that he constantly had to wag his finger to himself, as it were, to recall himself to the solid basis of facts. The chief motive of these speculations was not a desire to invent stories, which has so much in common with literary imagination, but a religious desire to save humankind.

In my book *Swedenborg in Germany* (1947), I discussed in detail the ideas of Kepler, Huygens, and Fontenelle concerning the inhabitants of other planets. It will therefore suffice to restrict this study to Kant, especially as he knew Huygens and Fontenelle and frequently referred to them.

Kant's ideas about the inhabitants of other planets are found in his work on the structure of the universe, *Allgemeine Naturgeschichte und Theorie des Himmels, oder Versuch von der Verfassung und dem mechanischen Ursprunge des ganzen Weltgebäudes, nach Newtonischen Grundsätzen abgehandelt* [Universal Natural History and Theory of the Heavens, or an Essay on the Constitution and Mechanical Origin of the Whole Universe, discussed on Newtonian Principles] (1755), which was published three years before Swedenborg's work *Concerning the Earths in our Solar System*. Generally speaking, only certain parts of this work are known: the first part consisting of an "outline of a systematic constitution among the fixed stars, likewise of the plurality of such fixed star systems" and the second part dealing "with the first state of nature, the formation of the heavenly bodies, the causes of their motion and their systematic relation to the planetary system, regarding the whole creation." By contrast, the third part, "containing an essay on a comparison between the inhabitants of various planets, based on the analogies of nature," is hardly known. Kant was inspired to write this work not only by Huygens and Fontenelle but also by the poetic visions of Alexander Pope, who is frequently quoted and supplied the motto for this part:

> Whoever knows the relationship of all worlds, of one
>> part to the other,
> Whoever knows the multitude of suns, and every
>> planetary orbit:
> Whoever recognizes the various inhabitants of each star.
> He alone is permitted to understand why things are as
>> they are
> And to explain them to us.

To be sure, Kant is sufficiently cautious not to ascribe scientific status to his theory of the inhabitants of the planets. He presents it rather as a hypothesis, which possesses a certain degree of probability on the basis of the location and formation of the other planets in relation to our earth:

> It might well appear, that the freedom to imagine has no limits and one can give as full rein to one's fantasy about the nature of the inhabitants of remote worlds, as a painter in the representation of the plants or animals of undiscovered lands, and that such ideas can neither be proved nor disproved. But one must admit that the distance of the planets from the sun imply certain circumstances that would have an essential influence on the various forms of intelligent life residing on them.

But once he has salved his philosophical conscience with this comment, Kant proceeds to speculate on the enticing theme with all the more delight.

Kant prefaces his discussion with an idea, which Swedenborg also mentioned in his *First Principles of Natural Things*. The organization of the celestial sphere does not support the assumption that all the planets must be simultaneously inhabited. Rather, the appearance of such inhabitants evidently depends on the state of the planets, which have their youth, maturity, and old age, as observation confirms, without this evolution occurring simultaneously on the different planets. One observes young and old planets next to each other. Therefore,

> it is not necessary to declare that all planets must be inhabited, although it would be an absurdity to deny this in the case of all or even most. With the abundance of nature, where worlds and systems are but specks of dust with respect to the whole of creation, there could well be desolate and uninhabited regions, which would not serve the purpose of nature most precisely, namely, the reflection of intelligent beings. Perhaps not all heavenly bodies have yet finally evolved. Jupiter still seems to be in this process. The remarkable changes of its form at various times have long led astronomers to speculate that it must still endure great upheavals and that its surface is not sufficiently tranquil for it to be an inhabited planet. . . . But one can only say with satisfaction that, if it is now uninhabited, then it will be at some future time, when the period of its evolution is complete. . . . If a planet takes a thousand years to reach this stage of completion, this is not prejudicial to the purpose of its existence. It will on this account remain longer in this completion of its nature, once it has attained it.[1]

According to Kant, the distance of the individual planets from the sun is decisive for the development and modification of their life forms. "The matter composing the inhabitants of the various planets, indeed even their plants and animals, must be of a lighter and finer nature, and the elasticity of the fibers together with the advantageous design of their construction must be more perfect, the further they are away from the sun" (Kant, 36). This passage applies not only to their physical organization but also to their intellectual power. Not only the physical but also the spiritual perfection of the inhabitants of the planets increases with their distance from the sun:

---

1. Immanuel Kant, *Von den Bewohnern der Gestirne*, in *Kants Populäre Schriften*, edited by Paul Menzer (Berlin, 1911), 28f. All subsequent citations to this work will be cited within the text.

We can conclude with more than probability that the excellence of intelligent beings, the swiftness of their ideas, the clarity and liveliness of concepts, which they receive through outward impression, together with the capacity to integrate them, finally even the agility in their practice, in short the whole range of their evolution is governed by a certain rule, that these will be more excellent and perfect in proportion to their distance from the sun. (Kant, 37)

There is therefore a definite hierarchy upon the planets within our solar system, in which the inhabitants of our Earth occupy a middle position according to their distance from the sun. Kant says of them:

They are excited to jealousy by the idea of the most sublime classes of intelligent creatures, which inhabit Jupiter or Saturn, and are humiliated by the knowledge of their own lowliness, but the sight of the low levels to which human nature has fallen on Venus and Mercury reassures them and makes them content. What an astonishing prospect! To one side, we see intelligent beings, among whom an Eskimo or a Hottentot would be a Newton, to the other side, those would regard Newton as an ape. (Kant, 37f)

Observations concerning the various diurnal periods of the planets seems to confirm Kant in this view:

If Jupiter is inhabited by more perfect creatures, who combined more elastic energies and a greater agility in practice with a more subtle formation, one can believe that these five hours (the length of their day reckoned in earth time) would be the same and more than the twelve hours of the day for the lower class of men. . . . According to the calculation of its rotation, Saturn has an even shorter division of day and night and this leads one to ascribe even more superior abilities to the nature of its inhabitants.

Like Huygens and also Swedenborg in his *First Principles of Natural Things* (1734) before him, Kant speculated on the greater longevity of inhabitants of those planets further from the Sun with quicker times of rotation:

Although transience erodes even the most perfect natures, one may believe that the excellence in the subtlety of the matter, the elasticity of the vessels, the facility and efficacy of the humors, which compose those more perfect beings living on the most distant planets, delay far longer this decrepitude, which is a consequence of the inertia of coarse matter. These creatures have a longevity proportional to their perfection, so that the frailty of human life has a direct relationship to its worthlessness. (Kant, 42)

While these ideas still build on a comparison between the material constitution of the individual planets and their position with respect to the Sun, Kant enters the realm of pure speculation when he wonders whether sin prevails among the more perfect inhabitants of the more distant planets. At any rate, Kant is aware of this:

Who would be so bold to risk an answer to this question, whether sin extends its dominion even to these other planets, or if virtue alone holds sway?

"Perhaps the stars are the seat of transfigured spirits,
As wickedness here prevails, there is virtue master."
(Albrecht von Haller)

Does not a certain intermediate position between wisdom and irrationality appertain to the unfortunate capacity for sin? Who knows whether the inhabitants of those remote planets are not too sublime and wise to stoop to the folly inherent in sin, but those who dwell on the lower planets are too attached to matter and equipped with such meager spiritual capacities to be held accountable for their actions? In this fashion, only Earth and perhaps Mars (so that we are not denied the comfort of a companion in misfortune) would lie in the middle range, where the temptation of sensual attractions has a strong capacity to mislead the governance of the spirit. But I prefer to leave this reflection to those who find more reassurance in indemonstrable knowledge and more inclination to take on its responsibility. (Kant, 45)

With these speculations about the stars as the possible "seat of transfigured spirits," Kant is moving close to Swedenborg's visions. But he completely abandons scientific demonstrability when he wonders whether the heavenly bodies serve as waiting rooms for the deceased and whether the stages of perfection, which the inhabitants of the outer planets assume, are not after all steps in the perfection of human spirits after their death:

Should the immortal soul in the eternity of its future longevity, which the grave does not interrupt but only transforms, remain fastened to this point of the universe, to our earth for ever? Should it never participate with a closer look at the remaining marvels of the creation? Who knows, perhaps the soul is intended to become closely acquainted with those distant globes of the universe and the excellence of their institutions, which have already aroused its curiosity from afar? Perhaps still further globes are forming in our planetary system, in order that new dwelling-places in other heavens are ready for us at the end of the time allotted for us on earth. Who knows: are those moons revolving around Jupiter, in order to give us light at some future time? (Kant, 46f)

Here Kant is approaching religious ideas of the next world. He also hints at the idea that the more perfect planets of the celestial sphere form the heaven, appointed to souls of this earth as a place of perfection and bliss. But Kant revokes this wandering speculation, if only to exchange the idea for another that seems more reasonable to him:

It is permitted, it is proper, to amuse oneself with these sorts of ideas. Only no one will base his hopes of the future world on such uncertain images of the imagination. After vanity has claimed its share of human nature, the immortal spirit will soar over everything mortal with a single leap and continue its existence in a new relationship with all nature, which springs from a closer link with the supreme being. This elevated nature, which has the source of happiness within itself, will no longer scatter itself in external objects, in order to seek comfort among them. (Kant, 47)

Instead of a world beyond based on the translation of souls to more perfect stars, Kant suggests a next world that expects a release from earthly being after death, a new relationship with all nature, and a closer link with God. Here the human being no longer directs his mind towards outer things but has the source of happiness within himself in a state if elevated nature. Although Kant accused Swedenborg of fantasies in his *Dreams of a Spirit-Seer*, his own worldview has much in common with that of Swedenborg, who described in his visions nothing but the release from earthly being, the new relationship that humankind assumes after death towards nature, and the closer link with the Supreme Being. It was Swedenborg rather than Oetinger who first drew attention to the close parallels existing between his own visions of the inhabitants of other planets and the speculations of Huygens or Fontenelle (Swedenborg did not know those of Kant). He referred to the question of inhabitants on other planets before the emergence of his visionary gift. Scholarship has tended to overlook the fact that, in the cosmological and astronomical studies of his early scientific period, Swedenborg expressed ideas similar to those of Kant.

Swedenborg mentioned these ideas especially in the third volume of his *First Principles of Natural Things* of 1734, ten years before his vocation. They reflect the enormous impression made on Swedenborg by the infinite depths and multiplicity of the starry heavens, awakening in him a humble feeling for all living creation: "Look at this immeasurable grandeur and abundance, and compare yourself at the same time with it, dear little man, and what a tiny part of the heaven and the world you seem! Your greatness can only consist in your being able to worship such greatness and infinity." This wondering worship of infinity culminates in the already cited hymn to the rushing, inexhaustible river of life that pervades the whole universe and produces the inconceivable variety of worlds. Following this hymn, he sketches the picture of worlds beginning and passing away, of suns newly kindled and dying out, of new planets forming and disintegrating. "When other worlds arise, and moreover arise from the same causes and conditions as our planet arose, then one can assume that a newly arisen world would appear in its youth like our world in its youth." As Kant would later, Swedenborg saw new worlds continuously arising in the universe. As one enters its youth, some have reached their prime, while others have reached maturity, and yet others their old age. One must assume that the inhabitants of the new planets develop under similar conditions. Like Kant, Swedenborg senses that such ideas take him beyond what can be proven by exact research or analogy: "Nevertheless, one cannot conclude from the fact that something can be that it also is so. In matters of divination, the spirit can expand into infinity. But we must return from conjectures to realities."

Even so, Swedenborg did not remain on the level of observable facts but turned again to speculation. The life forms on other heavenly bodies are not the same as here, but one must assume that the other worlds have their characteristic creatures, corresponding to their special position in the universe and the composition of their elements:

> Nature cannot assume the same form in one world as in another, and the beings in one world cannot be modified in the same way as the beings in another. Their mechanism presents itself in another way because it is ordered according to other ideas, forces, and stages. Everything develops (in the various worlds) in a different way, and analysis thus exhausts all its analogies. There the air or whatever is similar to ether does not vibrate in the same way. The trembling movements act differently upon the organs of sight and hearing, and perhaps our organs are not even capable of receiving their wave movements because they are not formed according to that principle of motion and the movements of those elements. The machines of one sort are perhaps constructed according to other rules and other applications of energy. The boastful Archimedes, who wanted to turn the earthly world upside down with his mechanism, would speak more modestly if he were placed on another world. He would ask where his art and mechanism were and would not know how he must apply his leverage. If he did want to try it anew there, he would have to learn anew the phenomena of that world from first principles and elements. All movements there are related to their equilibrium with the aid of other analogies and figures. Other ways, other contingencies, other causes combine there to produce phenomena. In comparison with our phenomena, these phenomena would appear to us as miraculous. The learned men of those worlds would be a laughing stock to the learned of our world before they had established their causes.

These are also ideas that recur in Kant but which he inverts in a comical fashion to demarcate earthly knowledge and summarizes in a quotation from Pope:

> "When the sages above recently saw
> What a mortal man among us
> Had not long ago amazingly done
> And he derived Nature's law, . . ."

they were astonished,

> "That such should be possible
> Through an earthly creature
> And beheld our Newton,
> As we look at an ape."   (Kant, 38)

When contemplating the various worlds, Swedenborg glimpses an inexhaustible differentiation and individuation in the forms and motions of life, an insight into the profundity of being, both fascinating and awful. But he also tries to abandon this view and call to mind what is humanly knowable:

> We do not even know the thousandth part of any fragment of our own world! What do we know of the elementary world? At best, several reactions. In the mineral, vegetable, and animal world, we know as good as nothing in comparison with all we are ignorant of. Whatever the senses do not grasp remains unknown to the soul. What should we then know of other worlds, whose mere numbers are inconceivable? What do we really know, when one considers that the infinite has been able to multiply the simple primal energy in infinite ways . . . and therefore been able to produce countless other worlds and heavens? The greatest wisdom consists in knowing that we know only too little.

The sight of other worlds and their potential leads Swedenborg to the limits of our knowledge, but this very experience inflames his desire to surpass these limits. Here on earth we know only what our senses recognize, and this knowledge is partial even concerning our own Earth. If we had the Adamic intellect, the glimpse into the essence, we could penetrate the infinity of the worlds and recognize the other systems of geometry and mechanics, the other life forms, and the enormous wealth of higher and lower life in the universe. It is the desire for more perfect knowledge that constantly induces Swedenborg to soar up from his scientific observations to divinatory contemplation.

Thoughts about the inhabitants of the heavenly bodies also occur in his treatment of the changes in Earth's period of rotation, which served him as a scientific explanation for ancient legends of a golden age. On the basis of astronomical measurements and geological observations, he believed that the Earth revolved more swiftly around the Sun in earlier times. At that time, the longevity of human beings was greater, as biblical references to the age of the patriarchs testify. Regarding the shorter rotational periods of Mercury and Venus, similar conditions must prevail on these planets. "When the ancients counted as many summers as the inhabitants of Mercury and Venus, they had a greater number of years than us, but in the same time." But even here Swedenborg almost forces himself to avert his gaze from such fascinating images and concludes that he mentions this only in passing.

But his longing for a higher form of knowledge persisted, as did his tendency to dwell on the far reaches of the universe. After his vocation, Swedenborg devoted himself intensively to visionary intuition. He now felt redeemed by God's grace from the state in which wisdom consists in knowing how little we know, and heaven opened up to him. His urge for knowledge, hitherto laboriously suppressed, now wanders freely in realms formerly inaccessible to him. Now he speaks personally with the spirits of the inhabitants of Mars, Jupiter, and Venus, with the spirits of the fixed star systems and elaborates a picture of life on distant heavenly bodies in his work *Concerning the Earths in Our Solar System called Planets*.[2]

He does not undertake space voyages in order to talk with the inhabitants of the planets. Instead, he meets them in the world of spirits and angels, and they tell him about the worlds on which they previously dwelt. The world of spirits and angels includes beings not only from Earth, but from all the heavenly bodies. Swedenborg's reports concerning the other worlds and their inhabitants are, therefore, only a section of his general view of the world beyond.

The inner coherence of these visions with his scientific researches

---

2. It is rarely noticed that this work is nothing but a revised excerpt from *Arcana Coelestia* (London, 1749–1756), in which Swedenborg intersperses his views on the inhabitants of the planets between the individual chapters of his exegesis of Exodus. For some unknown reason, the discussions of the sixth planet in the heavens at the end of chapters 38–40 are omitted. The first references to the inhabitants of the planets occur at the beginning of his exegesis of Genesis, in a volume published in 1753 (*Arcana Coelestia* §607), as well as in the *Spiritual Diary*.

is clear to see. The same arguments recur in Swedenborg's conversations with the spirits, which the great astronomers of his century had already advanced for the existence of life on the planets and which he had adopted in the period before his vocation. Now the spirits themselves tell him what he had formerly hinted. They confirm to him that

> anyone of sound intellect can deduce from many facts known to him that there are many worlds and people living on them. For it is reasonable to infer that such vast bodies as the planets, some of which are larger than the earth, are not empty masses, created merely to circle the sun and shine their feeble light for the benefit of one world, but they must have some more important purpose than this. The planets visible to our eyes, because they lie within the bounds of the solar system, can be plainly known to be worlds, as being bodies made of earthly matter. This is plain because they reflect sunlight and, when seen through telescopes, do not show the redness of flame as stars do but are mottled with dark patches like lands on Earth. They also rotate about their axes in the same way as the Earth, thus causing days and the different periods of the day, morning, midday, evening, and night. Moreover, some of them have moons, which are called satellites, traveling around their orbits with fixed periodicity, like the moon around the Earth. The planet Saturn, being the furthest from the sun, has also a great shining ring which supplies that world with a great deal of light, even if it is reflected light. Can anyone knowing this and able to think rationally still claim that these are empty masses? (*Arcana Coelestia* §6697; *Earths in the Universe* §3)[3]

Numerous scientific observations are interlaced in these visions, for example, when he writes that, although Mercury is nearer to the Sun, the heat there is not too great, for "temperature is not the result of proximity to the Sun but depends on the thickness and density of the atmosphere, as is plain from high mountains being cold even in hot climates. Temperature is also regulated by the directness or obliquity of the incidence of the Sun's rays, as is evident from the seasons of winter and summer in any one region" (*Arcana Coelestia* §7177; *Earths in the Universe* §45).

---

3. Goethe's last conversation with Eckermann repeats this idea almost word for word.

But all these scientific arguments are intended only to demonstrate the precedence of humankind in a universe infinitely extended by the new cosmology:

> Anyone who believes, as each of us should, that the Deity's sole purpose in creating the universe was to bring into existence the human race, and from this to people heaven—the human race being the seed-bed of heaven—must inevitably believe that, where there is a world, there must be human beings. . . . I have moreover discussed with spirits the argument that one can be led to infer that the universe contains more than one world from the fact that the starry sky is so immense and contains countless stars, each of which is a sun for its own region or system, resembling our sun, though differing in size. Anyone who correctly weighs these facts must conclude that the whole of this immense structure is a means to serve the ultimate purpose of creation, the establishment of a heavenly kingdom in which the Deity can dwell with angels and human beings. For the visible universe, that is, the sky shining with countless stars, each being a sun, is but a means to the creation of worlds and human beings to live on them, from whom the heavenly kingdom may be formed. These facts must inevitably lead a reasonable person to think that so immense a means designed for so great a purpose could not have been made for the benefit of the human race, and the heaven from it, coming from one world. How would this appear to the Deity, who is infinite, to whom thousands, or rather tens of thousands, of worlds, all full of inhabitants, would seems trifling and almost negligible? (*Arcana Coelestia* §6698; *Earths in the Universe* §§3, 4)

It is unnecessary to repeat Swedenborg's description of the inhabitants of the individual planets. It is sufficient to mention that the scheme of these visions is dominated by two ideas. The basic concern of his metaphysics of life is reflected in the first of these ideas. The nearer or more distant heavenly bodies are the places of humanity's further individuation and perfection, and moreover to a degree far beyond the earthly constraints of humankind. Just as all possible functions of animal life in the animal kingdom experience a unique specialization in endless forms and as all possibilities of perception, communication, reproduction, adaptation, and forming groups are

represented in living species, so the inhabitants of the planets special-
ize, refine, and perfect the capacities and possibilities of human understanding and love. This was another idea shared with Kant.

Thus Swedenborg describes the level of knowledge among the
people of Mercury as a specialization of thought, on whose basis
they do not grasp material things but the spiritual realities reflected
in the things. "They do not look at the outer wrapping, but what is
inside." They "dislike speaking aloud because it is a physical process.
So, when there were no spirits to act as intermediaries, I was only
able to talk with them by a kind of thought activation. Their memory, being of ideas, not of purely material pictures, presents these
more directly to their thinking. For thinking above the pictorial level
needs abstract ideas as its object" (*Arcana Coelestia* §6814; *Earths
in the Universe* §17). Accordingly, they do not know the written
word and are amused at our way of communicating knowledge
through books, "poking fun at us as if papers knew things that
people do not."

One peculiar characteristic of the inhabitants of Mars is their
physiognomical language, whereby they reflect their thoughts in
their face, which is more mobile and expressive than the face of
people on Earth:

> Their speech has little sound but is almost silent, following a
> shorter path to penetrate the inner hearing and sight. Being of such
> a nature, it is more perfect, more full of the concepts of thought,
> and so closer to the speech of spirits and angels. The actual affec-
> tion in the speech is pictured in their faces, and the thought in their
> eyes; for with them, thought and speech, as well as affection and fa-
> cial expression, act as one. They consider it a crime to think one
> thing and say another, or to wish for one thing and show some-
> thing else by facial expression. (*Arcana Coelestia* §§7360, 7361;
> *Earths in the Universe* §87)

Swedenborg encounters an even higher form of communication
among the inhabitants of Jupiter, whose physiognomical language is
most highly developed:

> I was also shown how thoughts are expressed by means of the face.
> A person's looks display the affections his love produces and their

changes; and variations in their inward form express thoughts. It is impossible to describe these more fully. The inhabitants of Jupiter also use verbal speech, but it does not sound so loud as ours. One way of speaking assists the other, and facial speech gives life to verbal speech. (*Arcana Coelestia* §4799, §8247; *Earths in the Universe* §54)

The differentiation of the humans on the planets concerns not only their forms of knowledge and speech but all life functions, the physical as well as the spiritual and mental, community life, the types of marriage, the nature of religious observance, and links with the world of spirits. This is evident from the long title of Oetinger's German translation of *Concerning the Earths in Our Solar System.*

The second idea of Swedenborg that dominates the individuation of human life among the inhabitants of the planets is similarly indicated in his metaphysics of life. All spiritual beings of the near and distant heavenly bodies not only possess a human form, but together they form the "Universal Human," the cosmic universal man, and in such a way that a planetary spiritual congregation represents a specific organ or limb in this universal body. Their totality forms the body of God. The spiritual congregations of the individual worlds form the living cells, from which his outer and inner organs are constructed. Their special association and organic purpose within the Universal Human is expressed in their spiritual corporeal nature and also determines the state of the physical mode of being, together with their society and life form on their respective planet.

The description of these communities thus changes into a kind of anatomical atlas of the Universal Human, an anatomy of the universal figure of heaven. Indeed, Swedenborg conceived of the macrocosm as a human body, and the individual communities correspond to parts of the brain, the skeleton, individual muscles, tissues, and glands. Here again the scientific view of Swedenborg from his earlier period of research combines with the visionary intuition of his later period. The anatomical and physiological knowledge acquired while preparing his *Animal Kingdom*, recurs in his visionary anatomy of heaven.

It is important to establish the scientific bases of his heavenly anatomy. On reading *Concerning the Earths in Our Solar System*, it is easy to think that its hastily sketched ideas are a dilettante attempt to conceive of the ancient macrocosm as the Universal Human. However, his earlier anatomical and physiological writings show that an exact science lay behind this speculation. Swedenborg really did imagine heaven, as a whole and in its parts, as the Universal Human, whose corporeal, mental, and spiritual organism exactly corresponded to the image of the human being. The specialized and individualized organs of the Universal Human again consisted of persons and spiritual communities. Thus, the spirits of our Earth represent the skin, the organ of external sensory perception, in the Universal Human, while the spirits of Mercury represent the memory of abstract things in the Universal Human and display a corresponding individuation of their form of knowledge. Swedenborg proceeds along similar lines in interpreting inhabitants of other planets, always relying on his earlier anatomical studies. He writes of the spirits of the moon, that they "answer in the Universal Human to the scutiform or xiphoid cartilage, to which the ribs are connected in front, and from which the *linea alba* descends, which is the fulcrum of the abdominal muscles" (*Earths in the Universe* §111). Other planetary spirit communities are localized in this special anatomical fashion; and the peculiarities of their nature, knowledge, social groups, marriage, language, and view of God are related to their special macrocosmic function.

However absurd these notions might individually appear if separated from their context, they confirm Swedenborg's fundamental thought that the archetypal and highest form of life was human. In humanity, he saw the supreme principle of organization and activity in the universe, both from a spiritual and a physical point of view. The universe is not only *like* a human, *but is itself* human. The miracle of the human spirit, soul and body are simultaneously miracles of the heavenly universal person, in which all spiritual and personal life is summarized. The miracles of the anatomy of the human organism reveal at the same time the miracles in the structure and multiform unity of the macrocosm. The miracle of life is reflected in the smallest and the largest, and the meaning of this miracle is the human, the image of God, the spiritual corporeal form in which the life of God unfolds in an inconceivable wealth of individual forms.

One may make whatever one will of Swedenborg's visions of the inhabitants of the planets. In any case, they represent the most searching systematization of the idea of humankind as the image of God and the highest involution of the idea of incarnation in the history of Western thought. It is difficult to avert one's gaze from the fascinating abundance of visions that Swedenborg elaborates to demonstrate the individuation of humanity in all spheres of life. One should mention only his portrayal of religion among the inhabitants of the planets, for it shows how strong were his theories of religious experience and how much his own vision of Christ dominated his visions.

Christ had appeared to him in London on Easter Eve in his glorified humanity. He looked at the Lord face to face in his transfigured form. Henceforth he lived in the elevated consciousness of having seen the Divine Man with his own eyes. He continually had before his eyes the holy features of this face, which reflected the archetypal form of God. This experience was also crucial for the insight that the Lord has not appeared only on our Earth in the form of the Divine Man and that the divine archetype has not revealed himself in human form only to us on Earth. Rather, the Lord fills and pervades the whole universe with his humanity and realizes himself continually in new and various epiphanies in all heavenly regions. Christ is really the Lord of all worlds, who fills the whole universe with his humanity.

But he does not need to reveal himself everywhere in the same form of incarnation as he appeared on Earth. Although he appears to each inhabited world according to its form of knowledge, he appears everywhere in human form. The incarnation itself, his realization in a physical body, is the special form of his appearance on this Earth, for we on Earth know through sensory perception, which is geared to seeing external, physical things. The particular earthly form of perception made it necessary for the Lord to come to us on Earth in the flesh and communicate his Word to us in a way that was audible to human ears and conceivable to human senses and notions. It also made it necessary that his Word should be written, printed, and preached because our understanding of truth lives in the concept: "The chief cause [why the Lord was pleased to be born and take on human nature in our world and not in another] was for the sake of the Word, which could thus be written in our world; and once circulated, could be preserved for all posterity, thus enabling it to be made plain that God became man" (*Arcana Coelestia* §9351f; *Earths in the Universe* §113).

The inhabitants of other planets are granted another form of the Lord's epiphany and another kind of communication of the Word corresponding to the level and nature of their knowledge. Thus, Swedenborg asserts of the men on Mercury that they need no books because they are not acquainted with the veiling of the inner meaning of the Word in letters. The Word is therefore accessible to them through an immediate intuitive grasp of its real inner content, and they need neither the incarnation of the Word nor the Bible. The Lord also appeared to them, but in a form appropriate to their mode of seeing, that is, not in the flesh but in the transfigured form of the Divine Man.

Even the inhabitants of Jupiter live from the direct view of the Lord in his epiphany as a man, but in another form. The Lord instructs them by engraving the truths of the Word in their minds, so that they have a living tradition of the divine Word without a book, letters, or theology. Swedenborg wrote of them:

> I asked them whether they knew that their One and Only Lord was a man. They answered that everyone knows he is a man because many people on their planet have seen him as a man. He teaches them about truth, preserves them, and confers everlasting life on those who out of goodness worship him. They said further that he has revealed to them how they ought to live and what they ought to believe. This revelation is handed on from parents to children, so that the teaching spreads to all families, and thus to the whole tribe who have a single ancestor. They went on to say that it seems to them as if they had that teaching engraved on their minds. They reach this conclusion from the fact that they instantly perceive and acknowledge, as it were spontaneously, whether what others relate about a person's heavenly life is true or not. They do not know that their One and Only Lord was born as a man in our world. They

remarked that this was of no interest to them, only that he was a man and the ruler of the universe. (*Arcana Coelestia* §8543; *Earths in the Universe* §65)

Swedenborg reports of the inhabitants of planetary systems of other distant stars that they had no immediate view of the Lord corresponding to the level of their knowledge but that the Word—that is, its inner meaning—was communicated to them by an angel. Others imagine God as two different beings according to his transcendental and his human form. They worship "a visible and an invisible God, the visible in human form and the invisible in no form. But I recognized from their language and the notions they communicated to me that the visible God is our Lord, as they also called him Lord."

Thus, the religion of the individual planets differentiates itself in various ways of regarding the Lord, according to the form of knowledge and the special function of the pertinent spirit community within the macrocosmic Universal Human. But everywhere religion develops into a worship of the Divine Man. It became clear to Swedenborg in several visions, in which the spirits of various planetary societies discussed their worship of God, that the object of worship, prayer, and vision in all starry worlds is the One Lord and the various forms of the deity's manifestation is the realization of the One Lord. Indeed, he frequently describes himself in such visionary reports as the teacher of other planetary spirits, who explains to them that their knowledge indicates the same Lord who was revealed to people of this earth through the incarnation and the Word of Holy Scripture.

These discussions about the religion of the inhabitants of the planets show most clearly Swedenborg's chief concern: God is present everywhere in the universe as the Divine Man. His salvation is not restricted to our minute planet. He is the One Lord, who appears as the Redeemer in various forms to the spiritual beings of all worlds. The revelation of his Word is not tied to the book but expresses itself in beings of a higher order in an intuitive illumination of the spirit or the mind. His epiphany does not need to occur in the flesh, for it can consist in his transfigured humanity among spiritual beings, who have already overcome the lower form of sensory

perception. Thus did Swedenborg personally experience the manifestation of the Lord, thus was the Word granted to him, and thus did
he feel himself empowered to strike the living waters of inner meaning from the rock of the letter. The basic view of his religious
thought was formed in this vision of Christ: the Lord is present
throughout the whole universe in the form of the Divine Man.
Everywhere he brings about the transformation of creation into elevated spiritual beings, which come together in the body of the Universal Human as the Church of the redeemed and the heavenly bride
of the Lord. Here the Christian idea of incarnation is understood as
a universal cosmic principle of the development and perfection of all
living things.

29

Ideas on the History of Humankind

Swedenborg's visionary preaching should be regarded as a new soteriological doctrine, the doctrine of the "New Church." Like any other doctrine of salvation, his describes the path of salvation for the believer to follow, as well as the history of salvation and its various eras.

Swedenborg considered the history of humankind essentially as the history of the Church of God. This should not be taken to mean that he saw world history as the history of a specific Church or in various confessions. For him, the history of the Church is rather the history of the gradual realization and development of the perfect human community. This is the community in which the influence of God and influx of heaven occurs in human hearts and people practice the worship of God in a life of faith and love. When Swedenborg speaks of the Church, he does not mean a specific, legally organized authority or historical institution of his time, but this true community. He also calls this true community the "spiritual Church," the archetype of the human community and goal of world history.

Through the various eras of humankind and history, the Church presents itself in varying forms adapted to individual ages. These changes are related to the overall development of humankind. Swedenborg's view of the Church's historical changes was influenced by the idea of decline, an idea that had formed part of the scholarly Christian view of history long before his time. Every religious community, even the best, declines with the passage of time and betrays its original mandate either consciously or unconsciously. This is the essence of human nature, whose egoism repeatedly prevails over the love of God. If religion were left to human beings, it would completely degenerate, and the wildest cult of idols and demons would usurp the proper worship of God, and the most reckless self-destruction would replace true community life. The inner history of humankind proceeds in such a way that God constantly founds new Churches in order to lead an errant humanity surrendering itself to the powers of darkness back to himself, and so God realizes the foundation of his kingdom. The history of the salvation of humankind consists in the mysterious succession of new Churches, which constantly counter the decay of religion and community life.

The idea of decline dominated the historical worldview of medieval sects. Luther took it from them and applied it in a revolutionary fashion to the history of the medieval Catholic Church. Spiritualists such as Sebastian Franck (1499–1542) then extended the idea to the new confessions emerging from the Reformation, and finally Gottfried Arnold (1666–1714) made this idea the basis of his view of the Christian religion in his *History of Church and Heresy* (1700).

In principle, Swedenborg's idea of decline does not differ from that of his spiritualist and pietistic contemporaries. What is original in his case is the periodization and division of Church history into eras and its extension into the prehistory of humankind.

First, he addresses the question whether humankind can be perfected and attain its intended divine purpose without a Church. Is it absolutely necessary that a Church should exist at all times? The answer is to be found in Swedenborg's view of divine revelation. God does not reveal himself to humanity as he is in himself, not in the supernatural majesty and omnipotence of his essence, for this sight would kill us, but through an appropriate means for our nature and intellectual capacity, through his Word, which contains the revelation of the eternal Kingdom of God in a way that is understandable to human beings. Through the Word, we receive an influx of life forces, which alone enable us to establish a sustainable community life and to realize our inherent divine destiny. Through the Word, God therefore creates life, community, and order in humankind. However, the Church is the bearer, herald, and guardian of the divine Word. Thus

> the Church of Lord on earth is like the heart. The human race, even people outside the Church, receive life from the Church. The whole of the human race on earth behaves like a body with all its parts, in which the Church is like the heart. If there were no Church, with which the Lord was united by heaven and the world of spirits as with a heart, a separation would occur. If the human race were separated from the Lord, then it would immediately be ruined. This is the reason that a Church always existed since the creation of humankind and the reason that it always remained among a few, whenever it was destroyed. The world cannot exist without a Church, in which the Word is and in which the Lord is known, for heaven cannot be linked to the human race without the Word and the knowledge and recognition of the Lord. The divinity emanating from the Lord cannot then flow with new life. In the absence of a link to heaven and thereby to the Lord, the human race would not be human, but a beast. Thus it comes about that the Lord continually provides for a new Church, whenever an old Church comes to an end. (*Arcana Coelestia* §§637, 2054, 9276)

Swedenborg sees the forces leading to decline as rooted in human nature. The fundamental cause is human egoism, the wanting to be oneself, the self-assertion of humanity against God, which constitutes the actual essence of sin. This selfishness, the inveterate tendency to subordinate all divine arrangements to oneself, is the chief cause of the Church's decline. Therefore, God must always intervene in the history of humankind with new institutions of salvation, for

> if man were left to his own devices, he would plunge into ruin of himself and all, for he longs for nothing but his own and everyone else's destruction. His original order should be that one loves the

other as oneself, but now each loves himself more than the others and thus hates the others. If God did not take pity on man and offer him a link through the angels, man would not even survive for a minute. (*Arcana Coelestia* §637)

The Church always begins to decay whenever selfishness has conquered love. This event can assume the most varied forms. Swedenborg's presentation of the eras of Church history and the Christian confessions impressively depicts these phases of degeneration. Swedenborg distinguishes five eras in the history of humankind, corresponding to five Churches. Their description interweaves the ancient mythological view of history with its declining sequence of the Golden, Silver, and Iron Ages with the Christian idea of history, which understands world history as a struggle between God and Satan proceeding through many dramatic episodes until the final triumph of God and the establishment of the Kingdom of God. Swedenborg calls the five eras the First or Most Ancient Church, the Second or Ancient Church, the Third or Israelite Church, the Fourth or Christian Church, and finally, the Fifth or New Church.

It is evident from a survey of these five eras that Swedenborg sees the closest connection between the inner development of humanity and the inner development of the Church. Church history is the spiritual history of humankind. Its phases correspond to humanity's levels of understanding in its progress towards a spiritual being. Whatever occurs as a redemptive event in the soul of the individual is also realized as a world historical drama in the history of humankind's salvation.

The Most Ancient Church corresponds to the state of the primal human in his natural perfection in accordance with creation. Everything said of Adam in Genesis is interpreted typologically with reference to the First Church. All the themes of the doctrine of the primal being are carried over to the Most Ancient Church. It is the archetype of the human community; its period is the golden age; here heaven is still completely united with the earth; and there is still a direct influx of heaven through the inner and outer person. All ordinances of religion and love among people are realized from within in voluntary, joyful surrender. The community has neither priests nor a holy book and does not need them. It is instructed in heavenly matters and everything relating to eternal life through direct association with the angels. The division separating the human world from the world of angels and spirits has not yet occurred. The people of this Church are illuminated by heaven and have the gift of speaking with angels. The Word therefore does not require written form but may be grasped intuitively. The truth of the Word is constantly strengthened by continuous new perception in each person. "Thus the Word is engraved in their hearts."

The worship of this Church is of an inner and spiritual nature and consists in the ceaseless contemplation and adoration of the Lord. This spiritual worship indicates the characteristic attitude the most ancient people assume towards external reality. Each external thing has a significance for them not only in itself but through its correspondence, whereby every object in the outer world represents and reflects something in the inner world, towards which it directs the soul. Thus, all things in the external world constantly indicate their archetype and Creator, and contemplation of such a thing changes into an intuition and a prayer:

> When they saw a high mountain, they did not imagine the mountain, but the notion of height. This awoke in them the notion of heaven and the Lord, whereby the Lord is called the Highest and the Most Sublime and later the service of the Lord was held on mountains . . . ; when they observed the morning, they did not think of the actual time of day, but of heaven, which is like the morning and dawn in the mind, whereby the Lord is also called the morning, sunrise and the dawn. Similarly, when they saw a tree and its fruits and leaves, they did not notice the fruits and leaves as such, but saw the person reflected in the tree, love and affection in the fruit and faith in the leaves. (*Arcana Coelestia* §920)

The people of the Most Ancient Church were therefore endowed with an intuitive type of understanding. With them, the knowledge of the individual thing was transformed into the knowledge of the idea reflected in the thing. They ascended from the idea of the particular to the universal. They apprehended the supreme universal truth in contemplating something specific. Everything earthly is only a parable of heaven. The type of understanding in the Most Ancient Church is therefore identical with the gift Swedenborg received after his vision of vocation, the *intellectus adamicus*, the glimpse into the essence.

The knowledge of the true and good is not accessible to these people as something alien, but "the good was implanted in their will; from the good they became aware of the true." Assent to the good is not submission to an outward command but a free act of adoption and assimilation. This is what is meant when Swedenborg says that these people needed no instruction. The desire of the good and the knowledge of the true flows continuously from God to the human being and fills him with immense joy.

This corresponds exactly to Swedenborg's own perception of the special grace of God after his vision of vocation. His knowledge is also an "awareness," a "living experience." He lived thereafter in the consciousness, that his longing for Adamic knowledge, expressed in the preface to *First Principles of Natural Things*, had been fulfilled in him through an inconceivable act of divine grace. In the midst of a degenerate world, the original vision of ancient humankind and the First Church, the gaze of Adam had come to life again in him, and the original link between heaven and earth was restored. Everything in between is decay, which can only be arrested by God's salvation. Swedenborg sees himself not as an unusual or inhuman exception but rather as the fulfillment of the initial destiny of the human being to see God, to understand his truth in gratitude and reverence, and to praise his glory.

The Most Ancient Church expired with the Flood. It collapsed because egoism became stronger than the love of God and the love of one's neighbor. In this context, Swedenborg expresses ideas that strikingly anticipate the ideas of Rousseau. The lust of power entered into the hearts of people:

> Those who would not submit aroused hostility and attack, and so tribes, houses and families were compelled to unite into states and placed a person over them, whom they initially called judge, and later prince and finally king and emperor. Then one began to defend oneself with towers, ramparts and walls. The lust for power

increasingly infiltrated people from the judge, prince, king, and emperor like an infectious disease, as from the head into the body. Thus there arose gradations of honors and dignities and with them egoism grew and the insistence on one's own cleverness.

Willfulness and the lust for power led to the stratification and organization of authority.

A similar classification and distinction also arose in the social sphere:

> The same thing happened with the love of wealth. In the most ancient times, there was no other love of wealth besides the desire to own only as much as was necessary for the requirements of life. But after the sovereign authority was torn down and had destroyed the commonwealth, the appetite to own more than one needed also gained ground and developed to such an extent that they wanted to own the goods of everyone else.

The organization of property came about, the distinction of rich and poor, and with it the struggle between rich and poor.

The Ancient Church begins after the Flood, that is, after the great judgment of ancient humankind following their decadence. Typologically, Swedenborg associates this Church with the figure of Noah. It represents a regression with respect to the Church of the golden age, when the love and knowledge of people degenerated. The power of intuition also lapses with the extinction of pure love. While wanting and knowing, feeling and seeing indivisibly mingle and nourish each other among people of the First Church, will and knowledge are split asunder in the Second Church. This is the era governed by consciousness. Swedenborg justifies this split because increasing egoism disturbs the center of the will in the human being. Likewise, the understanding, which used to receive the true from the good implanted in the center of will, is weakened. The people of the Ancient Church no longer experience the truth through "awareness," but in faith. Faith still embraces both the act of understanding and its practical realization in a life of love, but knowing and desiring the good are already secondary and occur through the medium of thought.

The worship of the Ancient Church still required no external cult. The believers form a spiritual Church. To them, the entire creation is a living sermon on the glory and greatness of God and his redemptive will. But they no longer spontaneously understand the authentic sign language of creation. The mountains no longer directly speak of the sublimity of God; the morning no longer directly proclaims the rise of the Kingdom of God; the tree no longer preaches the realization of love. Only through tradition do people know about the lost vision of the Most Ancient Church. Tradition and doctrine replace intuition:

> The human race was no longer in that state when the things of the world served as a means to recognise heavenly and spiritual things of the Kingdom of God. But, notwithstanding, the ancient people after the Flood knew from traditions and reports that the inner and the heavenly were signified by the outer, and they considered such signs as sacred. This Church was no longer in the state of awareness, but in a state of knowledge and was already in the dark by comparison with the Oldest Church.

Their view of the universe was transformed into a system of signs, images, emblems, and hieroglyphs, and a particular form of writing developed, which can be characterized as symbolic, emblematic, or hieroglyphic. The chief practice of this symbolic form of writing consisted in the "representation of things through persons and words, by which they understand something quite different." Heavenly and spiritual events are clothed in historical accounts, in which specific heroes step forth and fulfill their destiny. A compilation of such emblematic stories is available in the oldest books of Holy Scripture, which are not to be understood literally but typologically and their figures and events do not relate to historic but spiritual matters. Swedenborg also relates ancient mythology to this era.

According to Swedenborg, the decay of the Ancient or Second Church came about because its leaders wanted to use the true key of the hieroglyphs for themselves and their own power. They perverted their priestly office into magic. Their knowledge tempted them to transform their pre-eminent position into the selfish dominion of a priestly caste. The Tower of Babel is the work of this degenerate Church, which abused its spiritual power for the domination of the upper and lower worlds.

The sacrificial cult and idolatry commence with the loss of the true inner meaning of the Word. People no longer know that the various properties of God were symbolized by various names and figures in the secret mythical language of the ancients. With the decline into paganism, the ignorant take the symbols themselves for gods and worship them as such. Polytheism arises with the loss of the unity of divine life. Its spread is encouraged by power-hungry leaders of the Ancient Church, who allow themselves to be worshiped as gods, while they should be no more than interpreters of the divine Word and instruments of revelation and God's will. At the same time, the faith loses its original character. The initial unity of knowledge and moral realization dissolves. Instead, there is a formal recognition of the doctrine formulated by the priests and a strict observance of prescribed and outward ceremonies, while charity is neglected and the perverted religious attitude is expressed only in the cult and compliance with priestly rules. People began "to worship the external with no inner feeling, and because they digressed from charity, heaven digressed from them, and in its place spirits came up from hell to lead them." This degeneration occurred among all peoples, Jews and Gentiles alike. Swedenborg linked not only Greek mythology but also the development of Egyptian hieroglyphs with his doctrine of prehistory. The hieroglyphs date back to the period of the Old Church and its mythic and symbolical style of thinking. They originally signified spiritual, heavenly things and represented genuine correspondences. The Egyptians still knew how to interpret and understand correctly the secret meaning of these signs. But even in their case, the authentic view of God changed into magic, sorcery, and idolatry. They used their knowledge to forge links with evil spirits and "thus perverted the divine order." The hieroglyphs became demonic signs. Thus the true knowledge of God was taken from them, and they succumbed to the dominion of demons, which they represented in their art.

But even the Third Church, the Church of Israel, is not spared from decline. Swedenborg's portrayal of the Third Church is intended to link the history of the Christian Church not only with its Jewish antecedents but with the general prehistory of humankind. In Swedenborg's historical view, the third Israelite Church represents a further stage of decline by comparison with the First and Second Churches. Its law and cult still externally represent the inner meaning of the divine Word and heaven; but in reality, it is only a fossil of the true Church. External symbols and signs were salvaged from the Ancient Church for the religion of the law and sacrifice. In its symbols and traditions, the worship of the Israelite Church is still a genuine hieroglyph of the divine truth from the prehistory of humankind. The authentic divine truth is hidden in its objective forms of representation and thus preserved by a trick of reason for posterity and a later generation of humankind. After people had degenerated so far that they no longer understood the inner meaning of the divine Word, at least an outer sign and symbol of true religion had to be maintained amid the general desecration of religion. The Israelite Church was a last resort in the era of the general decay of religion, which served to maintain the externalities of the Ancient Church without desecrating its inner world. In this way, Judaism is only outwardly significant as the prehistory of the Christian Church. In its essence, Christianity is directly linked to the Ancient and Most Ancient Churches (*True Christian Religion*, chap. 14).

30

Critique of the Confessions

S wedenborg considered the history of the Christian Church as the
history of its decline, an idea he took up from the German and
English spiritualists of the seventeenth and eighteenth centuries. The
spiritualist critics of the Church, such as Gottfried Arnold, Johann
Georg Gichtel (1638–1710), Friedrich Breckling (1629–1711), and
Johann Konrad Dippel (1673–1734) differ only on the point in time
at which this decline began. Some agreed with Luther in regarding
the dominance of the medieval papacy as the real period of decline,
while others dated it back to the eighth century, and others to Con-
stantine the Great. In comparison with all these predecessors,
Swedenborg's critique was especially radical. According to his
prophetic judgment, the decline of Christianity had already begun in
the most ancient era of the Christian Church.

According to his doctrine, the coming of Christ signified the fulfillment of the history of salvation. "The preparations and symbols
were annulled when the Lord came into the world." He "abolished
the exemplars, which were all external, and founded a Church, in
which everything was inward. Thus the Lord suspended the exemplars and revealed the archetypes themselves, just as someone

drawing a curtain or opening a door, so that one not only sees the interior but can also approach it."

However, this did not lead to the Golden Age, the true fulfillment of history because this divine intervention occurred among a human race that had long since fallen from the height of its original destiny and could neither grasp nor realize the gospel of the Son of God. "The new light mingled with the shadows of darkness and falsehoods" in a humankind that was demonic and selfish at the time of Christ.

Swedenborg's critique of the Church of the New Testament is no less severe than that of the Church of the Old Testament. The early period of Christianity already exhibits symptoms of the original Fall from God. Swedenborg is so radical that he exempts from decline only the apostolic congregation consisting of the disciples the Lord himself called, regarding this as the true Church. This was really a new light, which opened a new view of heavenly truth and knowledge and a new community of love. But the first love soon cooled, so that the early Church "was soon a Christian Church only in name, but not in fact."

In the initial phase of his visionary period, Swedenborg turns fiercely against St. Paul. Numerous statements show that he does not regard the letters of the apostle as the Word but only as an interpretation combined with many individual teachings. Visionary experiences recorded in his *Spiritual Diary* confirm him in this view. In 1749, Swedenborg reports that it is well known in the other world that the letters of St. Paul did not posses the "inner meaning." Paul's insatiable selfishness prior to his conversion did not diminish afterwards but was only converted into spiritual aspiration. From now on, Paul wanted to be the greatest in heaven and judge the tribes of Israel. Swedenborg also frequently recorded in his visionary experiences that the other apostles would have nothing to do with St. Paul in heaven and would not recognize him as one of them. "If I wanted to write everything that I know about Paul, it would fill volumes. The fact that he wrote epistles does not prove that he was as he appears in them, for even the godless can give good sermons and write good letters."

But his main reproach against St. Paul is an idea that recurs in his critique of contemporary Protestantism and the orthodox theology of justification by faith. Through his doctrine of the only saving faith, St. Paul separated faith from love and thereby devalued love in Christian piety, "while everything actually resides in love." In this way, Paul accelerated the degeneration of the Church and the development of a hard-hearted theological formalism.

In his fervent criticism of the dogma of justification by faith alone, Swedenborg initially held St. Paul responsible for this teaching. Later on, he realized that the blame may lie not so much with St. Paul as with his ecclesiastical commentators. Thus, his critique of St. Paul turns into a critique of the commentators in his chief theological work, *True Christian Religion*. He writes in his exegesis of Romans 3:28:

> It is thought in the Church that Paul had the doctrine of the Trinity in mind in the cited passage. This error came about because the Church recognized no other faith in the fourteen centuries following the Council of Nicaea, and consequently knew of no other, so that it regarded it as the sole faith, besides which there could be no other. Whenever one encounters the word "faith" in the New Testament, one imagines it refers to one's own notion of faith and interprets the content of the passage accordingly. In consequence, the sole faith, which can save men, the faith in God the Savior, was lost and so many fallacies and absurd dogmas contrary to reason crept into their teachings. . . . In St. Paul's words in Romans 3:28, by "faith," one should not understand faith in God the Father, but faith in his Son. By the works of the law, one should not understand the laws of the Ten Commandments, but the Mosaic law book for the Jews, which is evident by the ensuing passage and in similar statements of St. Paul in his Epistle to the Galatians 2:14f. But thereby the foundation of modern faith crumbles and the temple built upon it collapses like a house sinking deep into the earth, so that only the roof-top protrudes.

A further cause of decline lies in the misunderstanding of the true essence of God. According to Swedenborg's view, the errors leading to the doctrine of the triune personality of God and the doctrine of Christ's two natures already arose in the ancient Christian Church. After faith had separated from love, the doctrine of faith became a playground of all possible errors, leading ever further from the truth.

According to Swedenborg, the betrayal of the original gospel of Christ was ecclesiastically legitimated in dogma. All subsequent Church synods have done nothing but further develop the initial, fundamental error and "propagate error upon error." The teachers of the Church immured themselves ever more securely in the prison cell of their errors. They "stand there as in a cave, with spectacles on their nose and a candle in their hand and close their eyes to the spiritual truths in the light of heaven. Their efforts to gain knowledge resemble a blind person tapping around by day, or a sighted person at night—neither sees the ditch before he falls into it."

Swedenborg sees this decline first being overcome through his own mission of proclaiming the New Church. This is the climax of his self-confidence to which his prophetic enthusiasm has raised him. The conclusion of Church history, the great renewal, consists in the revelation of the true, original, and previously hidden meaning of the divine Word, in the doctrine of the "New Church." Since the third century, but especially since the Council of Nicaea, the Church was in a process of increasing decline until the year 1757 finally arrived on earth. Then the Day of Judgment was held in the spiritual world and that great transformation occurred in heaven, which paved the way for a transformation on earth and the victory of the New Church through its prophet and evangelist Swedenborg:

> That the (inner) meaning (of the Word) is now revealed for the first time came about because Christianity only existed earlier in name and as a shadow with many. But because the true Christianity now arises and because the New Church, which is meant by the New Jerusalem in the Book of Revelation, is now founded by the Lord, and God the Father, the Son, and the Holy Ghost is worshiped as one person, it therefore pleased the Lord to reveal the spiritual meaning of the Word, in order that this Church should attain to the real salvation of the sacraments, baptism and Holy Communion.

Swedenborg is not alone in his critical attitude towards dogma in his century, although the criticism of dogma unleashed by Deism had overcome and abandoned its initial radicalism by his time. The struggle for free criticism of ecclesiastical doctrinal tradition had been fought with revolutionary violence in England since John Toland published his *Christianity not Mysterious* (1696). Toland had made his appearance as a propagandist in Dublin coffeehouses and asserted that it was pagan philosophers converted to Christianity who had, through their metaphysical concepts and philosophical distinctions, elaborated the simple and reasonable teaching of Jesus into dogma and thereby corrupted it. A year earlier, John Locke had published *The Reasonableness of Christianity* (1695). Locke distinguished the few fundamental articles of Christian faith necessary for salvation, to which one should expressly assent and whose reasonableness could be proved, from the numerous other truths of faith, whose acceptance is necessary only if we have recognized them as coming from God. Locke thereby made all historical dogma the object of free criticism and questioned its previous authoritative validity.

This dispute was still reverberating in London when Swedenborg arrived there in 1710. At that time, the trial of William Whiston was in progress. Whiston had claimed the right of free criticism and had proved on the basis of "apostolic constitutions" that the dogma of the Trinity in the sense of the Council of Nicaea was unknown to the early Church. It is therefore nothing new that Swedenborg dared to criticize Church dogma, but he does set a precedent in basing his criticism on visions rather than historical arguments.

Swedenborg comes into conflict with Church dogma on two issues: the doctrine of the Trinity and the doctrine of justification by faith. In both cases, he expresses himself with great vehemence in all his visionary works. In both cases, he takes up familiar arguments against dogma, but the intrinsic motive of his critique should be sought in his direct religious experience, in the special nature of his religious development, and in his prophetic mission.

The story of Swedenborg's conversion shows how he investigated all provinces of nature in his search for the final cause of existence and finally discovered that life is ultimately not of an animal nature but has a spiritual, human, and personal nature. He discovered that God himself, the Lord of life, had revealed himself in human form as Christ, thereby renewing the fallen image of the human being on this earthly world. The Father is the divine in the Lord, and the Son is the human in the Lord. Both unite in God and permeate each other like body and soul. Both are comprised in the unity of God, which is the unity of a person. His divinity is evident in the creation and maintenance of nature and its hierarchies, while his humanity is prominent in the work of salvation. The Holy Ghost is the emanation of God into human hearts, the divine truth that leads men to God. Therefore, God is One but reveals himself in these three ways in the universe and in history.

On this unshakeable foundation of his religious experience, confirmed in his moment of vocation, Swedenborg opposed the traditional doctrine of the triune personality of God. The more he compared his own knowledge of God, founded on "living experience," with the views of the Church, the more convinced he became that these formulae concealed the true divine essence. His own view of God thus developed in a struggle against the Church dogma of the Trinity. The theoretical content of his criticism is surprisingly reminiscent of Whiston's reasoning, and it seems that the latter's ideas had already made an impression on him in London.

In *True Christian Religion*, Swedenborg meticulously presented his own view corresponding to his religious experience. Father, Son, and Holy Ghost are the three ways in which the One God can work and appear, and their unity should be understood like the unity of body, soul, and effectiveness in a person. Like Whiston, he asserts that this triune unity in God first emerged with the creation of the world. The three forms of being are basically only various forms of the One God's conduct in nature and history. He explains that this doctrine corresponds with the views of the apostles and the Church fathers. Above all, it corresponds with the oldest creed of the Church—this was also argued by Whiston— from which one could see "that the apostolic Church knew nothing whatsoever of a personal trinity or of three persons of eternity." The false teaching of the three persons was dragged into the Church only during the Arian controversies. The doctrinal resolutions at the Council of Nicaea had destroyed the original apostolic view of God and introduced the belief in three Gods, which still confuses people up to the present:

> I appeal to each, layperson and clergy, the masters and doctors with their laurels, as well as the consecrated bishops and archbishops, the cardinals in their purple robes, even the Pope himself, that the only triune unity taught in the Christian Church nowadays is that of the three Gods. One can never be made from these three, even if the mouth says that the three are one.

Swedenborg chiefly blames the religious indifference of his age on the fact that such an irrational doctrine was given in reply to questions about God. For when one has listened to this nonsense for a while, one thinks that there is neither one nor three Gods. "The naturalism prevailing today has no other causes." In the last analysis, the doctrine of the three persons in the Godhead was the impetus for modern atheism and naturalism.

But what distinguishes Swedenborg from Whiston and other critics of the Church doctrine of the Trinity—we should not forget that Newton was also considered an anti-Trinitarian—is the fact that he not only uses historical arguments but refers to his visions in his critique of dogma. In numerous passages of his writings, he reports from "living experience" that the doctrine of the triune personality of God "is utterly repugnant" to heaven and its inhabitants. No one is able to think it there, let alone utter it. The heavenly air, in which the thoughts of the heavenly spirits float and travel as waves, as sounds do in earthly air, resist this doctrine and conduct it no further. Only the hypocrite can utter the doctrine there, but "the sound of his speech grates in the heavenly air like a tooth rubbing against another, or screeches like a raven wanting to sing like a songbird."

The view of the frozen Church, which Swedenborg describes in *True Christian Religion*, is his most impressive vision illustrating the decline of the Church due to its false view of God. In this vision, he encounters the "northern spirits," namely, "those who had put their reason to sleep from an aversion to reflecting on spiritual matters and were at the same time too indolent to be useful." He explicitly referred to conditions in the Church of Sweden, a country where, as he wrote to Gabriel Beyer, "theology is in its winter state and the duration of the spiritual nights is longer nearer the North Pole than in southern climes." The scenic construction of this vision has

already been described. Wrapped in the skins of wild animals, the
northern spirits hasten in a frantic drive through the night towards
the church completely covered in snow. The churchwardens shovel
the snow away and make a path for the arriving churchgoers through
walls of snow and ice. Behind the altar of the church hangs a tablet
with the inscription: "Holy Trinity, Father, Son, and Holy Ghost,
which are One God in essence but three persons." At the altar stands
a priest, who bends his knee three times before the tablet, then ascends the pulpit with a book in his hand, and gives a sermon on the
Holy Trinity. He describes the triune personality of God as a mystery, which reason cannot grasp. Then he preaches on a range of
other orthodox articles of faith, the attribution of divine justice, divine election, and the complete bondage of humankind in spiritual
matters. He cannot support these doctrines except for the argument
that they are mysteries, which the Christian must accept by subjecting his reason to the obedience of faith. "Blessed are you who have
listened and understood nothing, for thence comes your salvation!"
Swedenborg feels induced to contradict the preacher in the ice
church. "Master, I heard you preaching about mysteries. If you only
know that there are mysteries but know nothing of their contents,
then you know absolutely nothing, for they are like wardrobes shut
with three bolts. If you do not open these and look within—which
reason compels—you do not know whether precious, trifling, or
dangerous things are inside. There could be adders' eggs or spider's
webs inside, as Isaiah 59:5 describes" (*True Christian Religion*
§185). But Swedenborg's counterplea is unsuccessful. The priest
gives him black looks; and the churchgoers depart, mount their
sleighs, and chase off into their polar night.

This vision shows how Swedenborg perceived the ecclesiastical
orthodoxy of his country and what thoughts and images haunted
him when he occasionally attended church services. Even on the
level of visionary contemplation, he basically remained a rationalist.
He perceived the blind repetition of incomprehensible dogmas as
the stifling of a rational desire for knowledge, thereby extolling spiritual indolence as a theological virtue. But while Swedenborg calmly
went home after such sermons on earth, he finds it appropriate in

the world of spirits to speak up against these harbingers of incomprehensible dogmas.

The most instructive of all Swedenborg's visions dealing with the doctrine of the Trinity is a sort of anti-Nicaean Council in heaven. He sees in the spirit a splendid palace, in whose center stands a temple with an enormous cupola. Within it stands a golden table, on which lies the divine Word, guarded by two angels. Three rows of chairs surround the table, the first covered with purple silk, the second with sky-blue silk, and the third with white cloth. Below the cupola and above the table a canopy is spread out, which flashes with precious stones, giving off rays "like a rainbow, when the sky brightens up after rain." A procession of figures in priestly vestments approaches; they are delegates in a Church assembly convoked by the Lord himself. A voice from heaven opens the proceedings with the words: "Deliberate!" The clergy begin by praying for heavenly illumination. Then light flows down from heaven upon them, illuminating first the back of their heads, then their temples, and finally their faces. Then they begin to proclaim the individual articles of faith on the basis of numerous passages of Holy Scripture. A teacher of the Roman Catholic Church intercedes for the doctrine of Nicaea, but he is instructed by one of the illuminated delegates on the seats and refuted. Finally, the council resolution is proclaimed: "In the Lord God Our Savior Jesus Christ is a Holy Trinity, consisting of the original Deity called the Father, the Divine Human called the Son, and the proceeding Deity called the Holy Ghost." After the solemn finale, the Church Fathers rise; the angel attendant emerges from a chamber, in which costly clothes lie ready and brings shining vestments embroidered with gold thread to all those sitting on the chairs, saying: "Take these wedding clothes!" The Church Fathers are then led into heaven (*True Christian Religion* §188).

Here the critique of the Church doctrine of the Trinity is not embodied in historical arguments but in a vision. The seer sees a heavenly anti-Nicaean Council, in which the announcers of the traditional Church doctrine are refuted by the saints of heaven in the presence of the divine Word and holy angels. The voice from heaven confirms the truth of the doctrine of the council. This doctrine is the doctrine of Swedenborg. What occurs here is a unique undertaking in the history of the Western Church: appealing from earth to a heavenly council and then playing off this heavenly council against an earthly council. What powerful missionary consciousness must have filled the spirit of this man, enabling him to oppose the Church doctrine of his time with calm confidence in the undoubted victory of his viewpoint. This unshakeable assurance sprang from the certainty that he represented the doctrine of heaven and that this doctrine had long prevailed in the realm of heavenly truth. People on earth might still hanker after their old errors for a while, but they will not be able to hold up the truth once Swedenborg has helped it to victory through the printing of his books. This prophetic son of the Enlightenment greatly believed in the effectiveness of the written word.

Although his critique of Trinitarian dogma concerned all Christian Churches, Swedenborg subjected the doctrinal beliefs of the great historical confessions to an extensive critique. This primarily concerned the Roman Catholic Church and the Churches of the Reformation in the form of the Lutheran Church of Sweden, to which he belonged as the son of a Lutheran bishop.

The criticism Swedenborg makes of the Roman Catholic Church relies on the conventional pattern of Protestant anti-Catholic polemics and apologetics of his age. The reasons for this are easy to understand. All his life Swedenborg had little to do with the Catholic Church. On the basis of imperial law, there were no Catholics in Sweden, and he came into contact with no Catholics in England, as the Catholic rite was forbidden there likewise. On his journeys to Italy, he visited Rome, but his meetings with Italian mathematicians and scientists and his admiration of the classical architecture of Rome took up all his time. Hints in his travel diaries show that the journey to Rome strengthened him in his Protestant aversion to the papacy. He chiefly understood his prophetic mission as a duty towards the Church of his own country; his systematic and historical criticism was essentially directed against the Lutheran orthodoxy of his age. By contrast, the Catholic Church plays only an incidental role in his thought, as well as in his visions.

A glance at his description of the "papists" in the spiritual world and their judgment in his exegesis of the Johannine apocalypse confirms that his criticism of the Roman Catholic Church mainly repeats the traditional Protestant arguments. He sees the Catholic Church represented by the "woman riding a beast," which occurs in the seventeenth chapter of the Book of Revelation. Rome is for him the Church of abuse of spiritual authority. From its original spiritual mandate, it has since become a principle of earthly power and dominion.

The degeneration did not commence at the outset even in the Catholic Church but gained ground in the course of Church history. In the beginning, the Word was still sacred to the Catholic bishops, but "when they saw that they could rule though the holiness of the Church, they deviated from the Word and attributed a holiness comparable to the Word to their edicts, regulations, and statutes; and finally they assigned all the authority of the Lord to themselves." All this reflects the current view of the papacy and its history among Protestant theologians. Original themes occur only in the visions, which Swedenborg summarized in his report "Concerning the papists in the spiritual world" (*True Christian Religion* §817ff).

There a "convention of papists" is trying to invent artificial heavens for the believers. In their confessional boxes and sermons on earth, the priests have promised a pleasant heaven to the credulous crowd. Now, in the spiritual world, they are at pains to redeem their promises; and according to the taste of the believers, they arrange various events where there is plenty of merriment. There are dances, musical entertainment, processions, plays, and theatrical performances. The priests show their inventiveness: in one heaven, all kinds of splendor is conjured up through their imagination; in others, there are jokes and tomfoolery; in others, one can have friendly conversations on religious matters, domestic affairs, and all kinds of exuberance. In short, there is something here for all human needs, abilities, and expectations. But all these pleasures suffer from earthly mortality and become flat and boring within a short while. The credulous and easily satisfied folk, who were enticed by their priests into these heavens, are seized by a deadly nausea and hasten out of these heavens, whose futility is so depressingly evident to them. The deceit of the papists' unscrupulous promises of salvation is thus exposed in their realization, and the expected bliss becomes a hell of boredom and ennui.

But one is not eternally condemned to the wearisome enjoyment of such insipid pseudoheavenly pleasures. There is also a possibility of conversion for the papists in the spiritual world. This work of conversion proceeds from those devout persons who have already found the true faith in the Lord. The converted are then introduced to a large society in which all who have turned away from their previous errors are united. When they arrive there, "they feel like those waking from a deep sleep, or like those coming from the harshness of winter into the delights of early spring, or like a sea voyager reaching port."

The Protestant tradition of criticism is most evident in Swedenborg's estimation of the Catholic saints. Swedenborg knew from personal experience that sanctification can give a powerful impetus to human self-confidence and that human egoism can culminate in the presumption to be like God. He therefore regarded sanctity based on one's own moral achievement before God as the expression of the Promethean arrogance of man, which recognizes no limits in its striving to equal God. The person who yields to this egotism, even under the illusion of sanctity, "fancies himself as Atlas carrying the earth upon his shoulders, or as Phoebus driving the sun with his horses around the earth." The human heart is so unfathomable that it can even cloak self-deification in the mantle of humility. For Swedenborg, the saint who considers himself holy is thus the embodiment of arrogance. All those who sought the glory of sanctity on earth fly into a rage in the spiritual world. They roar and rave that they are deprived of veneration in the world beyond where they expected their glorification, and they become livid at the exposure of their egoism.

However, Swedenborg was too knowledgeable in matters of piety not to know that there is a genuine and innocent form of sanctity, in which people are seized by the spirit of God in a state of humility and self-conquest. They are the true saints of heaven. In the spiritual world, they are hidden from the papists in order to spare them the false veneration of saints, which would destroy their true humility. Swedenborg gives impressive reports of both types of saints in numerous visions.

His actual criticism concerns the Swedish Lutheran Church and is directed at the heart of its doctrine, namely, justification by faith. Here again Swedenborg is not alone in his criticism. All ecclesiastical and sectarian forms of pietism during the seventeenth and eighteenth centuries had rejected the orthodox hardening of this view, which saw only the formal reckoning of the rewards of Christ in the justification by faith. Since this whole controversy is now unfamiliar in our modern age, a brief explanation of this doctrine follows.

The doctrine of justification by faith alone sprang from a religious attitude that saw a legal contract in the link between God and humanity. God, the Creator and lawgiver, has a legal claim on humankind. He has laid down a law of life and conduct for humankind to fulfill, and he watches over the observance of this law. Here the religious and moral fervor of Old Testament godliness is evident. Two of the most profound Christian minds experienced the burden of this law when they sought to fulfill it: St. Paul, when he was at pains to fulfill the Jewish Law and comply with God's demands on humankind; later, Luther the monk, who was confronted by the law in the form of the Catholic sacrament of repentance. Both men recognized the impossibility of fulfillment and suffered unspeakably from their inability to comply with God's demands. After a struggle bringing them to the limits of despair, both men experienced liberation from the oppressive burden of the law and came to feel that grace is stronger than the law. Paul and Martin Luther found similar interpretations for their experience of grace. By taking the sins of humanity upon himself through his propitiatory death, Christ made a gift of his justice to them and allowed them to share in his own justice: "The blood and justice of Christ, these are my finery and ceremonial dress." Both St. Paul and Luther felt the experience of justification was identical with the experience of rebirth: they were lifted out of their old lives and implanted in a new God-given life, which is the life of the Lord himself. God had taken up his abode in them, and they felt immersed in his justice. Luther conceived his doctrine of justification from the intensity of his experience, but his followers, who were not granted the original experience of rebirth, made it into a theological scheme. In believing in Christ, Luther had experienced how the Son entered into him. He now shared in the justice of Christ, who was present and effective in faith. The legalistic mind of a century versed in jurisprudence made a formal precedent of it. One taught that Christ had fulfilled the legal claim of God against humankind in our place; through his propitiatory death, God had atoned for our violations of the law. We are justified before God in our faith, in being granted the justice of Christ.

Like many other devout persons of his century, Swedenborg regarded this doctrine as the death of all Christian life. The pietistic reforming movement is an attack on the externalization of the Lutheran doctrine of justification. It sought to overcome the crippling effect of this comfortable "drinking at Christ's expense" by steering people towards the necessity of personal rebirth. Swedenborg belongs to a great series of combatants who protested against the orthodox scheme in the name of religion from the beginning of the seventeenth century. His own religious outlook could not envisage the relationship between God and humankind as a legal arrangement. He found God initially in nature as the Lord of creation and life. The universe appeared to him as the container of this overflowing source of life. In his conversion, he encountered God as his redeemer, who approached him in love, lifted him up, and revealed himself face to face. He had experienced the depths of remorse and contrition, the feeling of being lost to the powers of inner and outer destruction, and had felt how Christ had lifted him up from the abyss of alienation and drawn him to his breast. In humble worship, it dawned on him that the divine life is mercy and love.

The traditional Church interpretation of Christian salvation appeared to Swedenborg the product of ignorance, which knew nothing of the grace of rebirth and excluded humankind from the abundance of divine mercy by a legal device. The advocates of the doctrine of justification therefore seemed to him the real enemies of religion, who sought to keep people at a distance from the true experience of God.

His polemics are never more caustic than when he inveighs against the doctrine of justification by faith. For him, the faith of the Christian is not a comfortable legal transaction by which we can rid ourselves of our sins. Swedenborg could not regard redemption as some cheap and easy exploitation of a legal loophole created by

Christ's act of satisfaction, whereby the charge sheets for our own crimes are burned before we come to trial. The fundamental experience of faith is rather the feeling of the profound restoration of humankind through God, the blessed influx of divine life into humankind, the newly creative influence of the spirit of God on all spheres of human life, and the activation of the individual's life forces, his illuminated reason and his love. Precisely because Swedenborg had been granted the abundance of new life in such a unique and overpowering form, the spiritual laziness of justification by faith must have seemed a particularly wicked misrepresentation.

A small Latin fragment by Swedenborg from the time of his first encounter with Christ appears among the preparatory studies of *The Animal Kingdom*. This essay shows how he thought about faith before his vision of vocation and closely relates his viewpoint to his physical and scientific ideas. He begins by accepting the general evangelical idea: "There is no doubt that faith saves man and that the performance of works without faith cannot achieve this." But the question is whether faith without works can also save, if humankind is given the opportunity to do such works, "as the Lutherans assert this." He therefore has the extreme opinion in view that good works are injurious to salvation and that such works, if one could do them, easily deflect one from the grace of God. Swedenborg recognized the chief evil of Protestant devoutness, the separation of faith from love, in this doctrine of justification—which actually no longer formed the basis of Lutheran orthodoxy in his time. This conception of redeeming faith "could be reconciled neither with the revealed divine Word nor with reason." Both Holy Scripture and reason taught rather "that a faith without works is void and if there were such a faith, it would lead to damnation and not to salvation."

Swedenborg refers not only to the Bible but also to physical proofs in examining the concepts of effect, will, faith, and love. He defines effect as the consequence of the will or the operative will. In itself, it is something mechanical or physical, similar to a machine. But the essence of the effect is the will active within it. Just as physics interprets motion as consecutive impetus, will is consecutive, continuous will. Will and effect are one. Will does not derive its impulse from itself but from its principle, which gives it direction and the necessary active force. Thus, the will is only the medium through which its principle realizes itself in the act. At any given time, a principle is that which determines the will, giving it a particular constitution and inducing it to specific actions.

Swedenborg distinguishes several such principles: physical, corporeal, rational, and divine. Divine principles are those that steer the will towards a goal higher than that attainable in this life. A higher principle is not dependent on us and is to be considered as a higher will. Faith is of this nature. When this principle penetrates the human will and realizes itself through the will in an action, then this action cannot be considered in regard to itself, but to the principle of faith which caused it. Faith is not theoretical but is a principle of effect, and its power of realization is love. Faith and love are indivisible; they belong together like heat and light in the flame. To whom God gives faith, he also gives love, and both grow with each other to the same extent. Only when faith is linked with love can one speak of a true faith. But the historical faith is only a form of knowledge or cognizance, not an operative principle. Even the demons can have such a faith.

In order to demonstrate the realization of faith and love, Swedenborg uses a simile from physics. When drawn, a bow has the elastic energy or propensity to return to its former position. But if prevented by an obstacle, it remains in constant tension. What if it were given the possibility to work, and it did not? Can one still maintain that it has elastic energy or tension? No, for as the effect shows, it does not work, although it could work once the obstacle was removed. This is a sign that principles are either opposed to its tension or they have destroyed its elastic energy. The relationship between faith and will, respectively, faith and love, is similar. Granted that faith is the principle of the will and that will is the principle of action, if the action does not ensue when it could, where is the will? Either it is void, or it is governed by a principle opposed to faith. Therefore, one can recognize faith by works alone. Faith without love is a broken bow, a bow whose string has been cut.

The love of God necessarily comprises the love of one's neighbor. But neighborly love is the same as performing good works. It is all the same whether we show our love to such persons as are loved by God or to such as are not. We have no idea who is loved by God and who is not, and the judgment of that is a matter for God alone, not for us, wherefore one says: "Judge not, so that you may not be judged." Therefore it is sufficient that we help our neighbor who needs our help out of love for God or true faith. We should not make distinctions in our good deeds and think that this person is dearer to God than the other. It is our affair to judge actions according to their usefulness for human society, and it is God's affair to judge the principles giving rise to them. In conclusion: there is no love of God without love for one's fellow beings, and thus there is no faith without good works. If there are no works, there is no faith, even if faith or love was present earlier, for then it has been destroyed by principles inimical to the love of God and faith. This concept of faith without works is a contradiction in terms and cannot exist.

Swedenborg's entire theology is contained in this chain of reasoning, which also indicates his attitude towards the Protestant orthodoxy of his age. For him, the supporters of this orthodoxy are people whose true faith has lapsed or whose faith is hindered and suspended by a hidden, ungodly, opposing force. They appear to him as the real enemies of the Christian religion, as they cut the strings of true faith and advocate a formal life of faith lacking any love. This attitude explains the passionate nature of his polemics, apparent not only in his theoretical writings but also in his gloomy and shocking visions.

Faith without love appears to Swedenborg in wintry visions.

It was given to me to know through living experience, that this faith is like the winter light. . . . For several years, spirits of various faiths have passed by me; and whenever such approached who had separated faith from charitable works, such a coldness overcame my feet and gradually also my thighs and finally my bones that I thought my body would lose all its powers of vitality. This would have happened if the Lord had not taken these spirits away again and delivered me from them. But it seemed strange to me that these spirits felt no coldness in themselves, which they also confirmed. Therefore, I compared them with fish under ice, which also feel no cold because their life and thus their nature is cold in itself. At that time, I realized that this coldness streams forth from the will-o'-the-wisp of their faith, precisely because this happens in marshy and sulphurous places during winter, after the sun has gone down. Wanderers see such a cold will-o'-the-wisp now and again. One can compare them with mountains made of pure ice, which when torn away from their places in northern regions drift around in the ocean and of which I have heard it told that, when ships approach them, all on board tremble with cold. The congregations of those persons who have a faith separated from charity may be compared with those icebergs and could be called such. It is known from Holy Scripture that faith without love is dead. But I will tell whence his death comes. It originates in coldness under whose influence this faith exhales its life like a bird in a hard winter. The bird first loses his sight, then his power of flight, and finally his breath, and then he suddenly falls off the branch into the snow below and is buried. (*True Christian Religion* §385)

These visions are among the most dramatic experiences granted to him. They confirm that this was the essential concern of his proclamation. They include visions of truly prophetic grandeur. Once Swedenborg was placed in that department of hell occupied by theologians who had taught justification by faith alone on earth. The clergy, who had compensated for their lack of love on earth through ecclesiastical activities, are in hell completely taken up with compulsive activity, which manifests itself in an excessive zeal for building:

Whenever they wanted to build, a whole pile of dressed stones, bricks, posts, and boards, heaps of reeds and rushes, clay, chalk, and pitch appeared before them; and as soon as they saw these, their desire to build was inflamed. They began to build a house and took stone, then wood, then reeds and laid them one on the other. They arranged them in a higgledy-piggledy fashion but thought it was all in order. But whatever they built by day fell down overnight. On the following day, they would gather the collapsed wreckage from the debris and build again anew. . . . This happens, because in their earthly life they had assembled pure falsehoods to prove salvation through faith alone, and these falsehoods contribute as little to the construction of the Church [as their activity in hell].

But the hell of those who verbally proclaimed the orthodox doctrine of faith, denied God in their hearts, and derided the sanctity of the

Church consists in being entangled in endless theological disputes with each other and tormenting each other to the utmost with their dialectical arts. "They do nothing but argue, tear their clothes, climb on tables, lash out, insult each other, and because one may not hurt anyone here physically, they threaten each other with their tongue and their fists. Everything is impure and dirty there." Thus, the *furor theologicus*, with which many pastors harassed their own kind and their flock in their lifetime, becomes the sting of their own torment. They make a hell for themselves with their theology.

In another vision, Swedeborg sees a splendid harbor with ships of all kinds, in which boys and girls are sitting. Suddenly, turtles come swimming up from all directions, with young turtles sitting on their shells. The male turtles have two heads, a large one with a human face, and a small ordinary turtle head, which they can withdraw within the large head. When they arrive, they stick out their large head, talk with the boys and girls on the thwarts, and lick their hands, whereupon they are fed with cakes. It is revealed to Swedenborg that these turtles are symbols for the clergy. The small head is their real, private opinion concerning matters of faith, while the large head with the human face is their official Church doctrine. When they withdraw their small head into the large head, they attach to their words a meaning that they have formed in their private opinion, namely, that one must do good works and charity "not for the sake of God, heaven or salvation, but simply for public and private welfare." "But because they are able to talk elegantly about the Gospel, the Holy Ghost, and salvation, they appear to their listeners as fine people, superior in wisdom to all others in the world" (*True Christian Religion* §462). Their fate in hell corresponds to their dry nature and their inner, unloving aridity: these preachers of a lifeless faith shrink and become mummies whose hard skin corresponds to the interior of their spirit.

The most impressive vision concerning the doctrine of justification occurred in 1764. In this vision, worthy of an Old Testament seer, Swedenborg sees his own destiny as a prophet and the destiny of the enemies of his teaching. He reports that, when he was working on the explanation of the eleventh chapter of the Book of Revelation, he was suddenly overcome by an almost fatal illness. For four-and-a-half days, he lay in his bed; but he imagined that he was lying in this state on a street in Stockholm. Around him he heard voices, which said, "See, he is lying there in the street of our city, he who had preached penance for the forgiveness of sins and Christ." He then heard his enemies asking several clergy of the city: "Is he worth burying?" These reply: "No, he can stay there on display." He hears the wicked talk, without being able to reply because he is lying there as dead. But after four-and-a-half days, his spirit revives. He walks from the street where he was lying into the city and says once again, "Repent and believe in Christ, and your sins will be forgiven and you will be saved; if not, you will be lost. Did not the Lord himself preach repentance for the forgiveness of sins and teach that one should believe in him? Did he not command his disciples that they should preach the same? Is not a complete security of life a result of your doctrine of faith?" But the people of Stockholm say, "What are you chattering about? Has not the Son given satisfaction that the Father credits to our account if we believe this? Will we be led thus from the spirit of grace? What has become of the sin in us? What has death to do with us? Did you conceive this gospel, you herald of sin and repentance?" Swedenborg's call for repentance is supported by a voice from heaven, which turns against the self-assured followers of the doctrine of justification by faith: "The faith of those unprepared to repent is dead. The end is coming, the end is coming upon you, you Satans, who feel innocent in your eyes and justified in your faith!" A deep abyss then suddenly opens in the center of the city, which keeps on widening. One house after another plunges into the abyss, until all are swallowed up. Boiling water immediately bubbles up out of the gorge and floods everything. Afterwards, Swedenborg wishes to know the fate of those who have gone down. Immediately, the water disappears, and he sees the unrepentant advocates of false justification running around on sandy ground between piles of stones and wailing that they were cast down out of their city. Full of indignation, they boast about their faith in the satisfaction given by Christ and its propitiation. Then a voice is heard, this time from the side, which says, "You are those to whom the Lord said: 'Then you will rise up and say: We have eaten and drunken before you, and you have taught on our streets!' But he will say: 'I tell you, I do not know you. Get away from me, you evildoers!'" Thereupon all will be driven into their hells (*Apocalypse Revealed* §531; *True Christian Religion* §567).

This vision gives the clearest indication of Swedenborg's religious concern: what he wants and sees as his mission with respect to the Church is the renewal of the old prophetic call for repentance, for the real inner rebirth. He sees that the doctrine of justification in the formal interpretation of late orthodoxy had weakened the evangelical view of repentance and hindered any genuine rebirth. But his compatriots do not understand him. They hold fast to their comfortable conception, until heaven uncovers their self-assured hypocrisy and exposes their unrepentant nature.

This vision shows that Swedenborg was esssentially striving for a renewal of the gospel and clearly identified this as the principal task of his religious mission. An authentic experience of repentance and conversion lies behind his visionary experience. The heart of his visionary proclamation is the cry: "Repent, for the kingdom of heaven is at hand!" After experiencing for himself the essence of repentance after a long struggle, he realizes with horror that prevailing Church doctrine deters the devout from true repentance. "It is amazing," he writes in the same vision, "that the Protestants have a deep-seated hesitation, indeed resistance towards true repentance, which is so great that they cannot examine themselves, see their sins, and confess them before God. It is as if a feeling of dread overcomes them, whenever they want to do this."

An impressive summary of Swedenborg's criticism of contemporary ecclesiastical life is found in *Apocalypse Revealed*. The fundamental theme of this work is that the Last Judgment on the confessions and the establishment of the New Church are revealed in the words, figures, and events of the Book of Revelation.

Swedenborg understood the Johannine apocalypse as a prophecy of a judgment on the confessions in the present, in the year 1757, not in some distant future. This fact explains why he inverted the chronological sequence, seeing the judgment on the Protestant Church in chapters 7–16 and on the Catholic Church in chapters 16–22. He also diverges from the historical type of interpretation, found in the apocalyptic commentary of Albrecht Bengel or the

Siegesgeschichte der christlichen Religion of Heinrich Jung-Stilling (1740–1817). In their cases, the events of the apocalypse are related to the whole course of Church history. The individual figures in the secret revelation signify the periods of the Christian Church and its most important personalities in a historical sequence. By contrast, Swedenborg takes no account of this. In his view, the apocalypse does not reveal the events of Church history from beginning to end, but the state of the Church at the instant of its Last Judgment. Swedenborg received a special revelation that this would occur in the year 1757 and expose the confessional division of the Church, as well as its inner and outer decay. Swedenborg is in no way constrained by the logic of his exposition to follow the chronological sequence of the individual images and figures but simply sees the "spiritual meaning," which he relates to one or the other confession.

Thus, he understands the opening of the seven seals (chapters 6–8) as the Lord's examination of the Church at the time of its greatest decay. The result of this examination is cataclysmic. When the apocalypse records that there was silence on heaven for about half an hour, this signifies the shocked silence of the angels at the revelation of the true state of the Christian Church on earth.

The seer initially turns his gaze towards the Protestant Church. As a Protestant, Swedenborg was particularly pained by its failings. He felt stirred by his mission to censure its decline especially severely and to refer it to the forgotten gospel of love. The long-censured deficiencies noted by the pietistic and spiritualist reformers of the seventeenth and eighteenth centuries are cited here as signs of decline. Faith and love are separated from each other; by faith, one understands only adherence to a mere doctrine; good works are rejected as popish prejudices; all charity is stifled by dogmatic formalism. Thus, even faith loses its meaning; it lacks inner life because it is no longer realized practically. Love separated from faith also degenerates and loses its purpose: people become a prey to hellish love.

The Judgment now reveals that no one can receive life who only possesses an external formal doctrinal faith without a spark of love. These people no longer even understand that faith aims at the manifestation of love. Arrogance and reliance on one's own knowledge prevail instead of divine influx. Thus "many men died of the waters, because they were made bitter" (Revelation 8:11), that is, their spiritual life was extinguished because the truths of the Word were falsified.

One accusation Swedenborg levels against the clergy and the professors of Lutheran orthodoxy in his time is particularly impressive. They are described in the apocalypse as "scorpions" because "'scorpion' means a fatal art of persuasion, and 'scorpions of the earth' mean an art of persuasion in Church affairs. When the scorpion stings a man, his limbs grow rigid; if he is not treated, death ensues. Their arts of persuasion have a similar effect upon the intellect." These Church leaders are symbolized by the apocalyptic locusts, which have human faces because they seem wise, learned and scholarly while disseminating demonically distorted knowledge. The armor plating of these locusts symbolize the false proofs and fallacies they employ to support their false doctrines, which they regard as irrefutable. The rustling of their wings symbolizes their sermons in which they give the impression that their doctrines and proofs are founded on the full truth of the Word. Their scorpion tails signify the corrupted truths of the Word with which they confuse people, bewitch their reason, and thus captivate them.

The Johannine apocalypse is interpreted word for word in this fashion from the eighth to the sixteenth chapter, while its basic theme is varied with constantly new images. Decline consists in love growing cold and in the falsification of faith through its transformation into a system of clever doctrinaire definitions. These serve only to flatter the vanity of their author, of whom the apocalypse states, "Their power was in their mouth."

Most striking are the conversations that Swedenborg conducts in the spiritual world with the great reformers of the sixteenth century, the founders of the Protestant Church. The spiritualist reformers had indeed criticized Luther and reproached him for not carrying his Reformation through to its conclusion. However, their attacks concerned only this alleged shortfall and not his doctrine of justification. However, Swedenborg attacks not only the doctrine of justification of contemporary orthodoxy but also the reformers themselves, and moreover in the form of visions that gave great offense on publication. He claims to produce authentic reports of encounters with the reformers in the world beyond, and these reports contain the most unexpected news of their further development.

"I have spoken with the three main leaders, who were reformers of the Christian Church, Luther, Melanchthon, and Calvin; and I am therefore informed about their life in the spiritual world from the beginning up to the present day" (*True Christian Religion* §796). These promising words introduce an extensive chapter, "Supplement to the True Christian Religion," which forms the conclusion to his last work. Here one learns astonishing information concerning Luther's life and his intellectual development after leaving this earth (*True Christian Religion* §796f).

Following his entry into the world of spirits, Luther remained what he had been on earth: the champion of his Reformation doctrine. He found a house there, similar to the one he had occupied during his lifetime at Wittenberg. He sits enthroned upon a raised seat in the central room of this house. Through the open gate, listeners are admitted and arrange themselves in rows. Luther preaches to his visitors, intermittently allowing those present to ask him questions, thus successfully continuing his teaching in the world of spirits. However, a certain degeneration sets in with the passage of time. Luther is the victim of his own theology, which gradually demonizes him. His initial success in the world of spirits eventually tempts him not to preach his faith but to force it upon others. His sermons turn into a demonic art of persuasion. Finally he is forbidden to avail himself of such demonic means. He thus reverts to his earlier style of preaching "from memory and reason." This state of affairs lasts until the Last Judgment, which takes place in the spiritual world in the year 1757. Afterwards, he is transferred to another house and another state. There he hears of Swedenborg's appearance. Accompanied by several friends, he comes to Swedenborg and hears from his own mouth that the confessional era of Christianity has come to an end and that the New Church is now beginning.

Informed that his own Reformation is now obsolete, the reformer understandably flies into a rage and bursts into violent abuse, reminiscent of the boorish style of his earthly polemics. But when he notices that his audience is constantly decreasing, he gradually becomes reflective and begins to talk more confidentially with

Swedenborg, and even listens to his teachings. Swedenborg proves that his principal doctrine of justification by faith does not stem from the Word of God but is an invention of Luther's own intellect. Then he instructs Luther in the doctrine of the New Church concerning the Lord, love, true faith, free will, and redemption. Under Swedenborg's influence, Luther ultimately becomes a good Swedenborgian. Swedenborg even induces him to ridicule his own earlier doctrines and give the following lecture to the infuriated Lutherans, who have not yet grasped the latest tack of their reformer: "You should not be surprised that I took up justification by faith, robbed charity of its spiritual being, denied free will to people in all spiritual matters, and taught many things that depend on the doctrine of mere faith like the hook on a chain. My intention was to disengage from the Roman Catholic Church, and I could not achieve and maintain this goal otherwise. I am not surprised that I went astray, but I am surprised that one fool can make a fool of so many others." "At these words," Swedenborg continued, "he threw a sideways glance at several dogmatic writers, who were celebrated and loyal adherents of his doctrine in their time."

Several angels, who are watching over Luther's further spiritual development, then tell Swedenborg that Luther is now already in a state of conversion, unlike the many adherents of his doctrine by justification. In his early youth and before his reforming activity, he had already absorbed the doctrine of the importance of charity over mere faith. Thus, he bore such eloquent witness to love in his later writings and sermons. The belief in justification was instilled only in his outer, natural person.

While Luther experiences a conversion in Swedenborg's account, things are going worse for Melanchthon in the world beyond (*True Christian Religion* §797). On arrival in the world of spirits, he also found his old house waiting for him. In his room are the same objects as during his lifetime in Wittenberg: the same table, the same stationery cupboard with pigeonholes, and even the same bookshelves. At once, he sits down at his table and proceeds to write on— what else but—the justification by faith "without mentioning a word on charity." Questioned on the one-sided dogmatism of his work, he exclaims that charity is not an essential attribute of the Church, for otherwise humankind could take the credit for justification and rob faith of its spiritual being. After several weeks, the objects in his room begin to grow dim and finally disappear. Finally there is nothing besides the table, the papers, and the inkwell. Melanchthon appears clothed in a coarser robe, the walls of his room look as if coated with lime, and the floor is strewn with yellow brick-dust. He learns that his ban on charity in the Church is the reason for this peculiar transformation. If love is dead, then the inkwell is the sole source of theology.

But because he will not accept this insight, Melanchton is transferred beneath the earth into the society of his followers, with whom he argues about his theology. From time to time, he is brought back to the table with paper and inkwell in his frosty room in order to continue writing his work on faith. The intellectual frigidity of his theology affects not only others but also him. He appears wrapped in a coarse fur coat "because faith without love is frosty." If he ever starts to write about love for a change, his notes keep disappearing and are obliterated of their own accord.

The Last Judgment of the year 1757 and the beginning of the New Church also bring about a change for Melanchthon. He sees that the divine Word, which he had previously interpreted so one-sidedly according to his dogma, deals with the love of God and one's fellow beings. Now he begins to write about love from inner conviction. Whatever he writes no longer disappears from the paper, but it is still dim, so that one can read only it with difficulty. As love has not completely taken hold of his being, his account of love is not yet convincing.

While Swedenborg leaves Melanchthon at least in a state of incipient conversion, he finds Calvin incorrigibly pig-headed and fanatical. Neither the angels nor Swedenborg can dissuade him from his doctrine of predestination (*True Christian Religion* §798f). After his death, he does not even believe that he has died and tries to prove to the angels that he is still living on earth, so meager is his insight into the peculiar life of the spiritual world. Later he roams around and tries to find the prophets of predestination who lived before him. He gets into an assembly of several pupils of Gottschalk, the precursor of predestination in the ninth century; but in the passage of time, he becomes weary of these partisans and finally joins a society of complete simpletons, among whom there are many truly devout persons. When he notices that these know nothing of predestination, he angrily takes himself off to a corner and hides there for a long time. Finally he is discovered by several contemporaries of Swedenborg who are adherents of the doctrine of predestination presented at the Dordrecht Synod, and once again he falls in with a group of his own kind. While these new friends are banished to hell at the establishment of the New Church and the related Last Judgment, Calvin comes to a brothel where he stays for some time. Swedenborg becomes acquainted with him in these strange circumstances and tries to instruct him in his new revelation. But Calvin begins to rave so that the angels accompanying Swedenborg have to seal his lips. Finally and with great persistence, he professes an avowal of his old doctrine: predestination is the sole basis of religion. Taken on its own, the Word of Holy Scripture is the book of all heresies, "a weather-vane on roofs and ships, which blows here and there according to the wind." It acquires its true meaning only through his doctrine of predestination. Thus, Calvin returns unconverted to the place where his followers are making life hell for each other. Afterwards Swedenborg learns something about the true fate of Calvin and his pupils. They have all fallen out with each other there, and each is trying to injure the other, "for this is their pleasure in life."

In these images, Swedenborg's critique of the Protestant Church is more vivid than in his systematic statements. These images disclose the innermost concern of his practical desire for reform and the strongest impulse of his prophetic mission. Swedenborg's critique of the confessions ultimately raises the question how he would practically behave after his vocation towards the Church he summoned to repentance and how the contemporary Church would respond towards his preaching. The ecclesiastical battles, which filled the final years of Swedenborg's life, provide an answer to this question.

PART FIVE:

Swedenborg and the
Church of His Time

31

The Visionary and the Church

Swedenborg had pursued his own religious path through youth and early manhood, and his relationship with traditional Christianity initially necessitated no open breach with the Church. However, the situation changed completely once he emerged as the harbinger of new revelations and proclaimed a "New Church" that would eventually replace and abolish the "old" Churches. The vocation of many devout persons before and since Swedenborg had led them to found congregations or sects and turn away from their former Church. Nothing would have been more natural for Swedenborg than gathering his own congregation around him in order to pave the way for the realization of his New Church, as had his famous English contemporary John Wesley (1703–1791).

But Swedenborg deliberately avoided this. He never outwardly severed the bond connecting him to the Swedish Church, nor did he ever attempt to establish his own Church or sect. He had plenty of opportunities for this during his stays in the Netherlands and England, where he was surrounded by numerous followers and where freedom of religion had already won the right of tolerance. Despite these prospects, he remained the quiet, private scholar who lived in his visions. He never proselytized his doctrine among friends but only alluded to it in conversation with the same reserve that a scientist would speak of his discoveries.

This attitude is unique in the modern history of religion. A seer and a prophet, inspired by his religious mission, Swedenborg restricted himself to printing his revelations while disparaging the sermon that others considered the most effective instrument of instruction and publicity. One might point to Jacob Boehme, whom Swedenborg resembles in several respects. Both perceived their vocation as a divine commission to write down their visions and insights; both remained true to this commission to the end of their lives by carrying out their prophetic office despite many difficulties. But this comparison is not wholly appropriate, as in social rank and educational background Swedenborg had an entirely different potential for public effectiveness. Boehme remained active as a tradesman, while Swedenborg retired from his profession and lived solely for his new task.

Contemporaries were struck by his lack of reforming zeal, public engagement, and sectarianism. Antoine-Joseph Pernety writes of him: "He was not dominated by that egoism which one observes in those who bring to light new opinions about doctrine. Nor did he seek to make converts and he only shared his ideas and views with those whom he believed were honestly inclined to listen to him, capable of understanding him, and who were lovers of the truth" (Tafel, I, doc. 6, pp. 58–59). Thomas Hartley, who had an opportunity to observe him over many years and knew many founders of English sects in London, said of Swedenborg:

> He did not strive for honor, but refused it. He pursued no worldly interest, but used his fortune for travel and printing costs, in order to instruct and to benefit humanity. He had no ambition to found a sect and wherever he stayed on his travels, he remained solitary and almost unapproachable, although he enjoyed wide social acquaintance in his own country. He encouraged no one to leave the Church. There was nothing timorous in his manner, nothing melancholy in his temperament, and nothing bordering on enthusiasm in his conversation and writings. He was so far removed from wanting to be the leader of a sect that his multi-volume theological

works were published anonymously until almost the end of his life. He loved all good men in every Church, while simultaneously taking account of the innocence of involuntary error. (Tafel, II, doc. 259, pp. 502–503)

Swedenborg was naturally aware that his preaching contradicted contemporary Church doctrine. His inspired revelation of the advent of the New Church showed at every step how antiquated he thought the present forms of ecclesiastical Christianity. It is all the more striking that he exercised his prophetic office in such an academic fashion.

The basic motive for this strange attitude lies in his religious worldview. Even the young Swedenborg was repelled by loud polemics, which characterized the intellectual debate of ecclesiastical and sectarian groups. He detested theological know-alls who from the pulpit branded their opponents as the sons of hell. One of his major criticisms of traditional Church doctrine was that love of disputation and quarrels had driven out true Christian love. He did not want to make heretics but restricted himself to literary evangelization and left it to his readers to accept or reject his ideas.

His high estimation of the written word was entirely characteristic of the Enlightenment. Swedenborg was a child of his age in his confident belief that publication was all that was necessary to promote the truth. Only a child of the Enlightenment could believe that a seer and prophet in a dressing gown could proclaim a new world era of truth and a new Church through some Latin books written in a garden pavilion. This confidence in the automatic victory of truth the moment it is published explains his peculiarly uncontentious behavior, which Pernety describes: "He didn't want to engage in debate on religious matters. If one placed him in a position of having to defend them, he did it with a few gentle words. If one persisted, he withdrew and said: 'read my writings carefully and without prejudice! These will answer for me and you will change your ideas and opinions.'"

He was unshakeably convinced of the truth of his mission, but his outlook on its future was that of a scholar of the enlightened age. He thought that falsehood cannot persist in the long run but perishes of its own accord and that truth will prevail of its own accord, even if outside influence and the trumpet of propaganda is absent. Certain of victory, he limited himself to writing and printing his books.

His friend Carl Robsahm once asked him how he imagined the future of his doctrine and whether he believed that his theological system would be accepted in Christendom. He received the characteristic answer: "I can say nothing about that; but I suspect that it will be accepted in good time, for otherwise the Lord would not have revealed what has remained hidden up until the present day" (Tafel, I, doc. 6, p. 39). Gabriel Beyer wanted to know when one should expect the New Church. Swedenborg wrote in reply: "The Lord is presently preparing a new heaven from such people as believe in him and recognize him as the true God of heaven and earth and also look up to him in their life while fleeing evil and doing good. Just as this heaven is being established gradually, beginning and growing, in the same way the New Church is beginning and growing."

Swedenborg was also a child of his enlightened age in his belief in the efficacy education and learning. He thought that the way can be paved for wisdom through lectures at universities and academies and the books of professors. As knowledge of the new natural sciences emanated from university lecterns and learned societies, Swedenborg thought that the truth of his writings could spread through the universities and gain an increasingly firm hold among scholars. But as he despondently notes, the old disputatious theology is still being taught at the universities where it infects the minds of pastors and teachers. Therefore, it is precisely the universities that should first adopt the new doctrine and cast aside old errors. For this reason he wrote his books for scholars and in Latin, the language of scholars. "The universities of Christendom must first be instructed; then will come the teachers, for the new heaven has no influence upon the old spirituality which is based securely on the doctrine of justification by faith alone," he wrote to Beyer in February 1767.

For this reason, Swedenborg regularly sent free copies of his works on publication to universities in Sweden and abroad, as well as to well-known Church leaders and professors. He experienced many disappointments as a result: scholars were among his worst readers. Several notes of thanks from professors at the Universities of Oxford and Cambridge are still preserved. They all sound very similar. The recipient expresses thanks for the consignment of the interesting book but regrets that, as a result of his workload, he is not presently in a position to study the book with the diligence it deserves and promises a benevolent assessment in due course. Of course, this never happened. Despite such experiences, Swedenborg expected a further promotion of truth from each new work by this means, and the old optimism moved him time and again to take up his pen. Thus, he wrote in a letter following publication of his *Brief Exposition of the Doctrine of the New Church* (1769): "I am often asked when the New Church will commence to which I answer: 'By and by, in as much as the doctrine of justification and attribution dies out, which will probably be accomplished by this work. It is well known that even the Christian Church did not immediately establish itself after the Ascension of Christ, but grew gradually.'"

Believing that his truth would be spread by scholars, he emphasized the didactic character of his works over time. His works are meticulously divided into paragraphs and sections and all are cross-referenced. The various visionary interpretations of biblical books are always followed by short systematic summaries of new ideas, such as his *Prophets and Psalms* (1761), his *Doctrine of the Lord* (1761–1763), then his *Brief Exposition of the Doctrine of the New Church* (1768–1769), and finally his major systematic work *True Christian Religion Containing the Universal Theology of the New Church* (1769–1771). Swedenborg was granted the rare pleasure of being able to present his ideas exhaustively and to bequeath a complete life's work. Like Christian Wolff, he was one of those Enlightenment scholars who produced a coherent sequence of systematic works. Whenever fate granted such scholars long life and acuity in old age, they succeeded in apprehending the whole realm of reality concerning God and the world in "reasonable thoughts." This is in contrast to the following era of the fragmentists who prevailed in the age of Romanticism.

However, conflicts with the Church were inevitable in all countries where Swedenborg's ideas and revelations had become well known, especially in England and Sweden.

32

Conflicts in London

Swedenborg had most of his works printed in London. He regularly resided there during the preparation of new publications, and it was there that his works were first distributed. His friends and acquaintances in London were largely members of the Swedish community. In order not to provoke his Church-minded compatriots, he attended the church services of the Swedish congregation and paid courtesy visits to the Swedish clergy, Mathesius and Ferelius. While he quickly befriended Arvid Ferelius, he was bluntly rejected by Mathesius. The latter was an advocate of strict orthodoxy and was especially vexed that a prophet and visionary appeared in his expatriate congregation. The personal animosity, clearly felt on both sides, deepened their doctrinal opposition and was exacerbated by tensions within the community. It was only natural that Swedenborg's personality and doctrine would attract greater interest in an expatriate community than in Stockholm. He would be conspicuous in London, whether he wanted to be or not.

His conduct towards the bishops of the Church of England was also a cause of conflict. Swedenborg had regularly sent his new publications to the Anglican bishops but rightly guessed that they would not respond with enthusiastic agreement to his visions and doctrines. Before his departure for Göteborg in 1766, he wrote to Beyer: "I am travelling from here to England, where some commotion has probably occurred, as the English bishops are drawn very severely in the *Spiritual Diary*, but necessity demanded it." In fact, he had not treated them with forbearance. What he wrote about them in *Apocalypse Revealed*, published in London by John Lewis in 1766, was calculated to anger the princes of the Church. Swedenborg felt justified in attacking them as a result of the following incident.

His works *Heaven and Hell, New Jerusalem and Its Heavenly Doctrine, Last Judgment, White Horse,* and *Earths in the Universe* were all published at London in 1758; and he had sent free copies to numerous bishops and lords in England but received no reply from any of the illustrious recipients. At a time when Wesley's Methodism and other sects were growing, the bishops thought it best not to draw attention to a new prophecy. They believed they could suppress the new spirit by ignoring it. Swedenborg was greatly taken aback by this conduct and felt compelled to make a statement.

In *Apocalypse Revealed,* he describes—one can hardly believe this was a vision and not a literary satire—how he meets the ungrateful recipients of his works in the spiritual world. In heaven, he elicits a comment on his doctrine from the same men who had so carefully avoided a debate with him on earth. The bishops appear as obdurate in the world of spirits as on earth. They tell him that they had received his books at that time and even read them. "Although they are well written," they attached no importance to them and had done their best to prevent their becoming well known. The offended author inquires about their motive, but the bishops "pour forth blasphemies as before in the world." However, Swedenborg soon receives a heavenly compensation. The bishops are read the sixteenth chapter of the Book of Revelation, in which verses 12–16 describe the dragon, the beast from the abyss, and the three unclean spirits. They are then told that these descriptions refer to them and their unchristian conduct. At this instant, the king of England comes forward. One of those present tells the astonished monarch about the anti-Christian activity of his bishops and "exposed the priestly authority, to which some of them aspired and which they exercise and maintain through a close coalition of all the members of their estate." Although Swedenborg's works were published in London and sent gratis to the bishops, their priestly conspiracy ensured that the books were shamefully dismissed and considered unworthy of review. The king is horrified that such a thing could occur in his freedom-loving realm. Then a light from heaven falls upon the bishops. The interior of their spirit is exposed in all its corruption, so that the king shouts aghast: "Get away from here!" He then appoints an inquiry to investigate why the clergy of his land are so submissively obedient to their bishops. He is informed that it is due to the bishops' having the right to nominate a single candidate for all vacant parishes, instead of three as in other countries. In this fashion, they are able "to promote their dependants to higher offices and incomes according to their obedience." This priestly authority could eventually lead to "government becoming its sole function and religion a mere outward formula." The bishops' lust for power is finally exposed by the angels, and "one saw that their lust for power far exceeded those with secular authority." Nothing could have been more insulting than compromising the English bishops before their monarch in heaven. However, there were no repercussions from this incident, as his opponents continued their tactic of ignoring new revelations.

However, there was a clash with Mathesius. Initially, Swedenborg had tried to forge friendly links with him and presented him with a copy of *Arcana Coelestia*, which had been published in London in 1761. On reading this work, Mathesius disavowed Swedenborg completely and began a campaign of slander against him among his Swedish and English acquaintances. He took the easiest means of defaming Swedenborg by declaring that he was insane and found support from a member of the Moravian Brethren called John Brockmer. The latter had been incensed that Swedenborg had described the Moravian Brethren in his writings as an example of spiritual rigidity and sectarian fanaticism. Brockmer now told everyone who cared to listen that he had personally seen Swedenborg have an attack of madness, claiming that he was sent to preach to the Jews and lead them back to faith in the Gospel; Swedenborg had even dragged him into the street to join in such a sermon to the Jews. On the way, Swedenborg had plunged into a big puddle and rolled around in it. Brockmer had pulled him out with difficulty and led him home, "whereupon Swedenborg had demanded from him twelve napkins, in order to dry himself." It is evident from the behavior of John Wesley, the founder of the Methodist Church, that these rumors were effective. To begin with, Wesley initally made positive statements concerning Swedenborg and also seemed prepared to believe in the truth of his revelations for a while.[1] However, he was influenced by such rumors and finally published the story of his alleged madness in his *Armenian Magazine* in 1781. "While living in the house of Mr Brockmer, Baron Swedenborg had a violent fever; in the height of which, being totally delirious, he broke from Mr. Brockmer, ran into the street stark naked, proclaimed himself the Messiah, and rolled himself in the mud."[2]

As Swedenborg's friends could easily and convincingly show, these unpleasant rumors were groundless and appear to have accomplished little, even in the circles for which they were intended. Swedenborg's personality and lifestyle were the best refutation. Commercial Councillor Springer even reported that the attitude of the English bishops towards Swedenborg noticeably improved and that "they met him with the greatest courtesy" on his return to London in 1769.

However, the slanders did not cease and were fed by new rumors soon after Swedenborg's death in London: he was said to have recanted his entire doctrine on his deathbed. It was claimed that he had disavowed everything he had written from 1743 onwards and that he had formally made this recantation in the presence of the Swedish pastor who gave him his last Communion. He was said to have told this clergyman that nothing in his theological works was communicated by the Lord or his angels. In this way, Swedenborg's preaching could be retrospectively devalued once the author of the new doctrine could no longer defend himself. This attack was a great deal more dangerous because a large congregation of followers had already formed in England. Everything they revered in their master

---

1. John Wesley, *Journal*, Part XV, 84 (28 February 1770)
2. Concerning the slanders of the London Moravians and John Wesley against Swedenborg, see Tafel, II, Doc., 270, pp. 581–612.

was now supposed to be recanted by him as falsehood! The rumor even reached Sweden and caused a great sensation among friend and foe alike.

This legend has also been refuted beyond all doubt, both by friends and acquaintances of Swedenborg who were with him during his final days as well as by pastor Ferelius, who gave him his final Communion. All eyewitnesses have made statements under oath concerning the events of his final days, and they unanimously report the following account. Swedenborg consented to the entreaties of his servants that they fetch the Swedish clergy. He rejected the suggestion of asking Mathesius. His former landlord Provo then ran to Ferelius and returned with him to the sickroom. Ferelius asked him several confessional questions in the usual fashion and then came to speak of his doctrines. "I suggested, as quite a number of people thought that his sole purpose in giving out his new theological system had been to make a name for himself or become famous—which he had indeed accomplished—he would do well, if that were so, to deny the whole or part of what he had presented, especially as he could not expect any more benefit in this world, which he would shortly depart. Upon hearing these words, Swedenborg half rose in his bed, placing his sound hand upon his breast, and said with great earnestness: 'As truly as you see me before your eyes, so true is everything that I have written. When you enter eternity, you will see everything, and then you and I shall have much to talk about.'" The question of recantation was therefore actually raised in a confessional examination but rejected by Swedenborg in this impressive fashion. The sick man then received Holy Communion.

This last confession of Swedenborg is also confirmed by the testimony of his follower Hartley. In view of the approaching demise of his revered friend, he also wanted to reassure himself how Swedenborg now regarded his doctrines and revelations. On a visit three or four days before his death, he asked him solemnly in the presence of witnesses whether "he would frankly declare that everything he had written was true or whether some or several parts should be excluded." Swedenborg replied: "I have written nothing but the truth, and you will be increasingly strengthened therein throughout all the days of your life, provided that you always keep close to the Lord and serve him alone, by fleeing all evil as a sin against him and searching diligently in his holy Word, which gives an irrefutable account of the truth of the doctrines, which I have given to the world." The friends regarded this attestation as a great reassurance, and a reference to this statement frequently recurs in the correspondence of Swedenborg's followers after his death. Thus, Imperial Councillor Count von Höpken expressly wrote to General Tuxen on 21 May 1773: "The late Swedenborg did not recant his writings on his deathbed. I especially informed myself on this matter."

33

Conflicts with the Swedish Church

The conflict with the Church in his Swedish homeland was more serious. The course of Swedenborg's controversy with the Lutheran Church of Sweden cannot be understood without reference to his personal relations with its leaders. His father had been one of the most popular bishops, and Swedenborg himself was related by blood or by marriage to many other bishops. The Church of Sweden was dominated by a patriarchal family hierarchy, also typical of the German state churches. During the seventeenth century, for example, the numerous sons-in-law and brothers-in law of the disputatious Professor Calow (†1686) sat in the orthodox Lutheran faculties of Germany and held superintendent positions in Prussia and Saxony. Calow ultimately became the patriarch of German orthodoxy as a result of the swift successive death of five wives, who bore him a total of thirteen children. His relations by marriage formed an absolute majority of the theological faculty at Wittenberg. The university and Church life of the eighteenth century also had examples of scholarly and clerical dynasties, while orthodoxy itself appeared to have the hereditary tendency of the caliphate.

Swedenborg writes about his relatives in his short biographical sketch:

> Concerning my relatives, I had four sisters. One of these married Erik Benzelius, who later became Archbishop of Uppsala, and thereby I am the brother-in-law of two succeeding archbishops, who were his younger brothers. My other sister married Lars Benzelstjerna, who was invested with the dignity of provincial governor. These brothers-in-law are now dead. However, there are two bishops living, who are my brothers-in-law. One is called Filenius, Bishop of Östergötland, who presently deputizes for the sick archbishop as president of the clerical estate in the Riksdag at Stockholm. He married a niece of mine. The other is called Benzelstjerna and is Bishop of Västmanland and Dalecarlia. He is the son of my second sister. Moreover, I can say that in my fatherland all ten bishops and sixteen Imperial Councillors as well as other great men love me and I live on an intimate footing with them as a friend.

This network of close relationships explains why the ecclesiastical attacks planned in Sweden against Swedenborg were so slow in coming and why the trial in the last years of his life was shelved at a critical moment. Here the exception proves the rule. His brother-in-law Petrus Filenius, Bishop of Östergötland, whom Swedenborg called "Judas Iscariot," tried to take proceedings against him following Swedenborgian disturbances in Göteborg, but even this action was ineffectual. Swedenborg would have had to contend with much more persecution in any other country but Sweden, where he was either friendly or related to everyone who could have condemned him. No other heresy trial in contemporary Europe could have reached the verdicts uttered by the judges in his trial: he was an honest, educated man, who did good to all men; besides, he printed his books abroad and wrote them in Latin so that only scholars and not the common people could understand them; their contents were quite good, if only one disregarded the remarkable visions.

In his letters, books, and conversations, Swedenborg portrayed the contemporary Swedish Church as an institution that stubbornly maintained a traditional form of doctrinal orthodoxy. Its conservative spirit was represented by the consistories in Church government, the theological faculty in Uppsala, and the deputies of the clerical estate in the Swedish Riksdag. This inertia of the universities and Church authorities provoked Swedenborg's most violent criticism, and he fell unwittingly into the same one-sidedness as his opponents.

At the time of Swedenborg's vocation, the Swedish Church had long ceased to be as he described it. To be sure, the Swedish Church was a Lutheran state Church with a strictly orthodox character. In 1686, a law proclaimed the Concordat Book the symbolic book of the Swedish Church. Clergy, professors, and teachers had to take an oath that they would respect its doctrine. However, the Swedish Church had long ago assimilated pietistic ideas of reform. The incorporation of Pietism in public Church life had been achieved with less friction than in other European states and national Churches. This was because this religious movement had come to Sweden not in its radical separatist form but based on the model of August Hermann Francke, the energetic founder of Prussian Pietism.

Francke's influence had reached Sweden on an unusual detour through Siberia. After the defeat at Poltava in 1709, a great number of evangelical Swedish officers and soldiers were captured and interned in Siberia. Through the pietistic clergy of German congregations in Russia, who were largely his pupils, August Hermann Francke was able to make contact from Halle with the prisoners in Tobolsk. Francke wrote and sent literature to Colonel Wreech, the leader of the captured Swedes, and a religious revival movement of lasting moment spread among the prisoners. Once these military men were sent back to Sweden after the conclusion of peace, the spirit of Halle Pietism was introduced to Swedish Lutheranism without pietistic sects being founded. The copious distribution of writings by Philipp Jakob Spener, Johannes Arndt, and Christian Scriver among many clergymen also awakened sympathy for the pietistic renewal of life.

Conflicts arose only when Swedish Pietism assumed separatist forms and threatened the unity of the Swedish Church. The cue was provided by the appearance of the most vehement "stormer of Babel." The German physician Johann Konrad Dippel, under the pseudonym "Christianus Democritus," had made a name in all Europe through his attacks against degenerate Church life and his ideas had spread in Sweden. Dippel's ideas met with approval in the renewal circles of Sweden. When the devout no longer wanted a pact with "Babel" but felt compelled to foreswear public Church life, the Swedish Church authorities intervened. In 1726, the so-called Conventicle Bill was proclaimed, which forbade all private pietistic meetings. This measure attempted to gather the new religious currents within the fold of the Swedish Church, prevent their separatist development, and expel revolutionary elements. But the tension between orthodoxy and the pietistic groups intensified. During the 1730s, new extreme groups formed, with a result that a new religious edict was issued against radical Pietism in 1735. The Swedish Church was assisted in this struggle by the Moravian Brethren, which had sought good relations with the state Church from the outset. The Moravians succeeded in gradually leading the radical and separatist elements within Pietism back into the Church.

During the whole period of this controversy, orthodoxy had asserted itself in the consistories and in the clerical estate of the Riksdag. Its unbroken dominance led to biased statements by Swedenborg who was piqued by his personal experience that no prophet is ever recognized in his own country. His friend Pernety reports a conversation in which he was asked "why so few clergy in Göteborg accepted his ideas about Holy Scripture." "Because," answered Swedenborg, "their prejudice in favor of the doctrine of faith alone was strengthened during their studies at the university and schools. Once one is fortified in a false view, one no longer sees the bad as an error. But although they feel that I am speaking the truth, their ambition, egoism, honor, and interests prevent them from acknowledging it openly."

A certain resignation is audible in these words. He cannot help thinking how difficult it is to reform academic tradition by new ideas. In 1766, he wrote the following warning words to Dr. Beyer, Consistorial Councillor of Göteborg, who wanted to publish a collection of sermons in the Swedenborgian spirit: "I assume that you will take all necessary precautions in this work, as the time has not yet come when the basic doctrines of the New Church can be accepted. The clergy, grounded in their doctrines of faith in the universities, cannot be easily persuaded. All foundations in theological matters are firmly glued in the brain so to speak, and they can only be removed with difficulty. So long as they remain, truth can find no space."

But his disappointment is clearest in a confidential letter written in a humorous mood to his friend Beyer, after the trial against his doctrine had begun:

> There are only few in Sweden whose intellect is receptive to true theology. Therefore, they do not take up the light given to them by the Word of God because true theology is still in its wintry state here in Sweden, and the duration of spiritual night is longer nearer the North Pole than in southern regions. One can therefore expect those who stand in the darkness to fight and kick against everything in the New Church, which proceeds from unprejudiced reason and insight. However, we must at the same time admit that there are exceptions in the clergy to whom this observation does not apply. I turn to the words that Our Savior addressed to his disciples: "Behold, I send you forth as sheep in the midst of wolves: be ye therefore wise as serpents, and harmless as doves" (Matthew 10:16).

Swedenborg did not allow such feelings of resignation to depress him, but indefatigably used his numerous connections with Swedish Church leaders, professors, and clergy to familiarize them with his new doctrine. He neither provoked the Church nor offended ecclesiastical custom. But he repeatedly tried to engage the Church leaders in a free and open debate about the relationship of his doctrine to Church dogma and the degenerate aspects of Lutheran orthodoxy. Characteristic of these endeavors is the letter he wrote in 1766 to Archbishop Menander. Referring to *Apocalypse Revealed*, he lists seven points on which the prevailing faith appears to deviate from the Gospel. All seven concern the orthodox doctrine of justification, whose one-sided interpretation he especially blames for the decline. The frankness and integrity of his criticism proves that Swedenborg by no means regarded himself as standing outside the Church. He saw himself as a scholar—he did not make a single allusion in this letter to his divine vocation—who claims the right, like any other member, to lay his personal conviction before the head of his Church.

In view of the intellectual "endarkenment" of contemporary theology, Swedenborg saw himself as a scholarly prophet influencing the learned Church leaders. The prophets of earlier times addressed all and sundry. The prophet of the age of Enlightenment justified the rational and systematic nature of his preaching on the grounds that he addressed learned contemporaries in a time of erroneous reason. The lance that caused the wound should also heal it again. Thus, he could write to Oetinger from Stockholm on 11 November 1766: "Falsehoods grounded in reason have closed the Church, wherefore truths grounded in reason shall open it again. The dogma inherited from the papists and accepted by the Protestants that intellect should be subordinate to the obedience of faith in theological matters has shut the Church again. What else can open it but reason illuminated by the Lord?" He understood the office of seer in a very rational sense with a special application to the "blind" theologians of his age.

Given these circumstances, he was not exactly an enthusiastic churchgoer. When his friend Robsahm reported, "He rarely went to church, partly because he could find no edification in sermons, which were so different from his revelations, and partly because he was plagued by pains caused by stones," the first reason was decisive. Above all, he avoided church services held by argumentative clergy interested in polemics and preferred to attend those where he would find a man in the pulpit closer to his own views. This confirms a delightful episode told of him:

> Several days before receiving Holy Communion he asked his old domestic servant which preacher he should visit for the sacrament, as he did not know his pastors well. The elder chaplain was suggested, but Swedenborg answered immediately: "No, he is a fervent man and a zealous preacher. I have heard him with much displeasure thundering from the pulpit." Then they suggested his assistant, the second chaplain, who was not so well liked by the congregation as the former. "I will go to him," said Swedenborg, "for I have heard that he speaks as he thinks and that is why he has lost the confidence of the congregation, as is usual in this world."

Purely apologetic or polemic sermons were particularly distasteful to him. The malaise that he felt on those occasions also manifested itself in his visions. It must have given the seer a certain satisfaction that the angels and spirits, invisible and inaudible to the congregation, could express their displeasure much more freely than was possible for him in his church pew. Thus, Ferelius, the Swedish pastor in London, relates of him: "Although he attended the Swedish church in London several times and afterwards dined with me or another Swede, he said that he had no peace in the church from the spirits, who contradicted what the preacher was saying, especially when he was dealing with the three persons in the Godhead." Such disturbances made church services rather uncomfortable for him, and it seems that he persisted more out of regard for his friends than out of inner necessity—he did not want to give others the example of an arrogant apostasy from the Church.

This attitude is especially apparent in his view of the sacrament, which changed quite markedly during his religious crisis of 1743–1744. Swedenborg did not mistake the significance of Holy Communion and gave it a profound interpretation in his writings. But once heaven was opened to him by the Lord, he was reluctant to take the sacrament in a form burdened by hundreds of theological controversies and quite possibly from the hand of a disputatious clergyman. His absence was noticed and widely discussed. His relatives ensured that the matter was settled without an ecclesiastical summons or public censure. Two bishops related to Swedenborg made friendly remarks about his conduct when he attended the Riksdag of 1760. He replied that taking Communion was not as important for him as for others because he was constantly in the company of angels and spirits ever since he had been called by the Lord. But the bishops indicated that he should not set a bad example to others. Swedenborg could not ignore this point of view and took Holy Communion afterwards in the church, which had been temporarily built for the congregation of St. Mary's Church after the fire of 1759.

Swedenborg maintained this custom up until his death. Several days before his passing away, he received the sacrament in his lodgings. The wigmaker Richard Shearsmith, whose house in Cold Bath Fields was his home during his last stay in London, relates: "When the deceased found that his end was approaching and expressed the desire to receive Holy Communion, someone who was with him suggested sending for Mr. Mathesius, the pastor on duty at the Swedish Church. But this man was a declared enemy of Baron Swedenborg and had taken sides against his writings. He was the man who had spread that false rumor that Baron Swedenborg was mad. Baron Swedenborg refused to take the sacrament from him and actually received it from another clergyman of his fatherland, called Ferelius."

Another witness, his former landlord Provo, added that Swedenborg asked the pastor who gave him Communion if he might only say or read the blessing (that is, the sacramental words) over the wafer and leave the administration of the sacrament to him, as he knew what it meant and what it was. Ferelius complied with this request, and Swedenborg, who was fully conscious throughout the whole procedure, said at the end: "Now everything has been done as it should be."

Ferelius himself gave the most detailed account:

> In response to my question whether he wished to take the Lord's Last Supper, he replied with gratitude that I meant well. Although he did not need this sacrament as a member of another world, he did want to receive it, in order to demonstrate the community existing between the Church above and that below, and asked me if I had read his views concerning the sacrament of the altar. Asked if he acknowledged himself a sinner, he answered: "Certainly, as long as I carry this sinful body around with me." With much devotion, folded hands and bared head he made a confession of his sins and received the Holy Sacrament.

Conflicts were inevitable despite Swedenborg's moderate conduct towards the Swedish Church. Many pastors simply considered him insane on account of his visions. They found sufficient facts for their charges and could refer to all kinds of stories and rumors circulating about him. Ferelius reported, for example, how he had one day visited Swedenborg, accompanied by a Danish preacher. "He sat writing at a round table in the middle of the room. The Hebrew Bible, which made up his entire library, was lying before him. After he had greeted us, he pointed across the table and said: 'The apostle Peter was just here and stood there, and not long ago all the apostles were here with me. They also pay me frequent visits.'" Assuming that the Danish pastor was unprepared for his encounter with this strange man and heard these words from Swedenborg's own mouth, it is easy to imagine what he would have told his acquaintances afterwards.

Rumors of Swedenborg's insanity led Dr. Beyer to seek his closer acquaintance. He met him at a party and "as the rumors of his madness had influenced him like other scholars of the land, he was astonished to observe that Swedenborg spoke very rationally, without giving any sign of the weakness of which he was suspected." On the strength of that, he invited him to dine the next day with him and Dr. John Rosén at his house, which marked the start of the close friendship between the consistorial councillor and the seer.

Alleged insanity was no reason in itself for the Church to take proceedings against Swedenborg, as he was not a clergyman but a private scholar. Because he was not subject to ecclesiastical jurisdiction, laborious proceedings had to be initiated through the Riksdag against him as a member of the Riksdag. There were insufficient grounds for this, while the imperial councillors and many of the Church leaders were averse to making a public scandal of the case. Thus, Swedenborg remained undisturbed by the Church until the last years of his life. The official attack came in 1768, only four years before his death.

Initially, there was little objection to the doctrinal content of his writings, as his main demand that the Christian faith should be realized in a life of practical Christian love could easily be harmonized with the demands of pietistic reform, already recognized by the Church. However, his visions did arouse the opposition of the clergy. Not only theologians but also his friends among the imperial councillors asked him why he inserted these strange "memorabilia" in his otherwise rational and edifying books. These "memorabilia" only served to make him ridiculous or give him the reputation of a madman and prejudice the effect of his good ideas.

The infuriation of the Swedish clergy at the visions was well justified, for they portrayed the representatives of orthodoxy in a very poor light. Even if these accounts were not regarded as revelations but as literary satires, they still made the Lutheran Church teachers an object of mirth and damaged their authority. Added to this,

Swedenborg was not always discrete in conversations. As Robsahm relates:

> When a certain preacher died in Stockholm, whose church services were always full on account of his eloquence and gushing sermons, I asked Swedenborg if he was now in a blissful state. "This man," said Swedenborg, "went straight to hell and is in the company of hypocrites there, for he was only spiritual in the pulpit, but otherwise he was proud of his natural gifts and his earthly fortune, an arrogant man." "No, no," he added, "no dissimulation and deceit can help there, for all that vanished with death, and man involuntarily shows himself as he is, good or wicked."

Whenever such stories circulated, they would not engender sympathy from the clergy.

Proper ecclesiastical proceedings were first initiated against him only once his followers formed a sort of congregation. The trouble began in the year 1766, initiated by the emergence of a group of Swedenborgians in Göteborg. Swedenborg frequently stayed there and a circle of followers belonging to the clergy had formed around him. Among them were two well-known personalities, Dr. Gabriel Beyer, member of the consistory, and Dr. John Rosén, a professor at the Göteborg grammar school. Both supported his doctrines in their publications. Rosén was the first to publicize his visionary literature in Sweden by a review of *Apocalypse Revealed*, which he published in *Clerical News*, his monthly church periodical at Göteborg, and which caused a sensation. In 1767, despite Swedenborg's reservations, Dr. Beyer published a collection of sermons in the spirit of Swedenborg under the title *New Interpretations at Explaining the Texts for Sundays and Holidays*, which he recommended as the basis for preaching.

Both publications aroused the strongest opposition of the Göteborg clergy. At an assembly in September 1768, Dean Aurelius of Grimeton demanded that the consistory take the most severe measures to suppress the circulation of such writings, whose doctrines violated the Word of God and the symbolic texts of the Church. Dean Kollinius of Seglora expressed himself more moderately in his memorandum of 12 October, suggesting that, as referees for theological questions, the bishop and the members of the consistory should apprise the clergy as to what extent Swedenborg's writings contradicted Church doctrines. In case Swedenborg's writings proved orthodox, this explanation would prevent their false condemnation. Should it be established that they actually deviated from proper doctrine, then one should proceed officially against them, especially against such followers of Swedenborg holding public teaching appointments who could use their position to win converts for these doctrines. This was clearly directed against Beyer and Rosén.

However, initially the majority of the consistory was not inclined to accede to these proposals. Bishop Eric Lamberg did not even want proceedings in the form of an ecclesiastical inquisition. It turned out that almost no one actually knew the writings of Swedenborg. Most members did not feel competent to give a final verdict until they had obtained these writings and studied them thoroughly. It was already apparent that proceedings against Swedenborg would actually help to spread his ideas.

At the request of the consistory, Dr. Beyer first prepared a report in which he asserted that Swedenborg enjoyed the general reputation of a God-fearing, virtuous, calm, peace-loving, and respected citizen and was known for his distinguished scientific achievements and his boundless reverence for the divine Word. One could not casually condemn such a man without first undertaking a careful examination of his works. Until this examination was concluded, the consistory was not authorized to classify his works as forbidden books.

The opposition was not satisfied with this. Their leader, Provost Olof Ekebom, undertook to draw up deliberations in the style of the time against Swedenborg, characterizing his doctrines as "pernicious, heretical, dangerous, and extremely objectionable," and present them to the consistory. Ekebom reproached Swedenborg for claiming divine inspiration, for overturning the entire biblical exegesis of the Church with his doctrine of correspondences and his alleged visions, for renewing Arian and Socinian errors in his concept of the Holy Trinity, and above all for violating the orthodox doctrine of justification. Everything in Swedenborg's doctrine was "diametrically opposed to the revealed Word of God" and "extremely heretical, mostly Socinian and objectionable in every sense." On these grounds, Ekebom demanded that the whole diocesan clergy must be put on its guard against Swedenborg's pernicious writings. Furthermore, Pastor Kollinius should be authorized to prepare a list of all Swedenborgians in Göteborg, in order to protect the innocent from suspicion and expose the guilty to punishment. The bishop should present the issue as a matter of importance for the whole Church to the deputies of the clerical estate at the next Riksdag, in order that measures could be taken to condemn Swedenborgian doctrine and punish its disseminators.

It is noteworthy that from the outset no measures against Swedenborg's own person were demanded but that the whole procedure was directed against his followers. These submitted new affidavits, Beyer on 30 March, Rosén on 5 April 1769. Beyer cited a passage from the work *Conjugial Love*, in which Swedenborg had summarized his doctrine of the New Church, in order to prove its congruity with the Lutheran idea of the Church. Beyer declared that he saw no reason to submit the question of Swedenborgianism to an ecclesiastical court. If the consistory should decide to take such a step, he suggested one should obtain an immediate decision from the king. This seemed an attractive alternative, as he knew that the monarch personally favored Swedenborg.

Swedenborg knew nothing of the whole affair, as he was staying in Amsterdam. Beyer first drew his attention to the threat of danger. Through the offices of Peter Hammerberg, a Göteborg merchant and banker, Swedenborg received a copy of Ekebom's deliberations and immediately prepared a rejoinder. Under the pressure of events, Bishop Lamberg saw himself compelled to travel to Stockholm in order to start proceedings against Swedenborgianism.

In the middle of October, Swedenborg finally returned from Holland. At first, he attributed little importance to the uproar, and the conduct of his illustrious patrons must have confirmed him in this view. After his arrival in Stockholm, he received many signs of the court's favor, was invited to dine with the crown prince, and had a long conversation with the crown princess. Meetings with the senators and leading members of the clerical estate convinced him that there would be no serious proceedings against him.

The situation was aggravated by a embarrassing incident. Swedenborg had sent to Sweden several copies of his work *Conjugial Love*, which he had published during an earlier stay in Amsterdam. These copies had been confiscated on arrival. It could not be established who had ordered this. Swedenborg immediately tried to obtain the release of the books but in vain. This did not represent any great loss to Swedenborg, for he had already brought thirty-eight copies with him and sent them to various bishops, members of the clerical estate, to the king and queen, and to several senators and imperial councillors. But this confiscation made him more cautious, for he presented only a single copy of his newly published work *Brief Exposition of the Doctrine of the New Church* to Bishop Benzelstjerna, his brother-in-law, insisting that he show the book to no one else.

Swedenborg now tried to clarify the misunderstandings by having his letter to Beyer containing a detailed defense printed at Göteborg. This publication resulted in a new intensification of the conflict, as it referred to the "wintry" state of theology in Sweden. This criticism was cleverly used by his opponents to vindicate their worst fears and caused a great uproar in the Riksdag. From Stockholm, Bishop Lamberg reported to his consistory, speaking of the "indescribable scandal" and ascribing to Swedenborg the worst motives, amounting to the overthrow of the existing Church. But the greatest scandal of the infamous letter was its printing at Göteborg, the seat of the bishop and the consistory. In a private letter of 16 November, the bishop wrote even more harshly and described Swedenborg's doctrine as "Mohammedan heresy." Until now, he had regarded it as so absurd that no reasonable person would waste his time on it, but the lamentable spread of the movement now made it necessary to oppose this "worst of all nonsense" vigorously.

The bishop's greatest anger was directed at Beyer, who as dean of the consistory had given official permission for the letter to be printed. Swedenborg himself again remained in the background. Ekebom was now the first to attack Swedenborg. He asked Bishop Filenius, the most active combatant in the struggle against Swedenborgianism, "to use the most severe measures to stifle, punish, and extirpate the Swedenborgian renewal and error" and to swiftly ensure "that the wild boar that devastates our land and the wild beast that torments our land is driven forth with a firm hand." Filenius was eager to comply with this challenge. On 28 December 1769, he informed Aurell of the measures to be introduced against Swedenborgianism. He also spoke of Swedenborg's infamous letter with the censure that it contained a list of all Swedenborg's published works to help spread the heresy. He described his doctrine as an "abominable plague," which was not built on sound arguments, was contrary to the Word of God, rested solely on deceptive visions, and was beginning to spread like a cancer. He called the visions "delirious fantasies" and "hallucinations of a human spirit, disturbed by imagined visions and fables." One must prevent this nonsense from spreading further "in these turbulent times of Zion" by the most severe means. "It is a matter of the deepest regret that Assessor Swedenborg, who was always generally honored and who had hitherto distinguished himself through his knowledge on mining technology and physics, should have in advanced years succumbed to a second childhood and been so violently possessed by a perverse imagination that he is no longer capable of tolerating contradiction or amenable to enlightenment." Filenius succeeded in having the whole matter referred to the imperial court and the chancellor of justice for decision.

Swedenborg regarded the development of the affair with dignified composure. In a letter of 29 December to Beyer, he said that such uproar was as necessary as the fermentation of wine when all impurities settle. He abstained from undertaking any action himself, for "I know that Our Savior defends his own Church." He was also fortified by a vision: "The Lord told me through an angel, I could rest safely on my arm in the night, where night signifies the state of the world in view of Church affairs."

The chancellor of justice greatly disappointed Swedenborg's opponents. After careful consideration, he sent a memorandum to the king on 29 December 1769 that clearly sought to prevent Swedenborg's doctrines from becoming an object of a Riksdag decision and closed with the advice: "It is sometimes more clever to leave erroneous and absurd ideas alone. As experience shows, such an investigation can make them better known and spread them further." The king accepted the suggestions of his chancellor and announced them in a resolution of 2 January 1770. The opponents had expected a severe decree against Swedenborgianism. Instead, a diffidently worded edict was sent to the Göteborg Consistory that contained no decision against Swedenborg and his supporters, simply the demand to hand in a memorandum "of your view of the doctrines of the above-mentioned Swedenborg, and in the event that you consider them false, what measures should be used to prevent their spread."

Basically, this signified a defeat for the consistory, and Swedenborg's person still remained untouched. The descriptions of his doctrines as heretical, dangerous, and objectionable were not taken up. The resolution spoke only of the possibility of errors, that is, unintentional offenses rather than heresies, meaning intended deviations from valid Church doctrine, thus denying the proceedings the status of a heresy trial. The opponents in Göteborg could not accept this turn of events. Ekebom prepared a counter-declaration to Beyer's apology. The proceedings should begin all over again, this time with the charge of heresy.

In the meantime, unfounded rumors of the removal of Beyer and Rosén from office had reached Swedenborg, who wrote a long letter of consolation to Beyer on 12 April. He recommended him to travel to Stockholm, in order to conduct his own case, and referred him to influential friends. The estate of the Swedish Church had no right whatsoever to condemn his doctrine. Only the king and a plenary sitting of the Riksdag could make that decision. He thereby disputed the ecclesiastical authorities' competence to make a legal decision and assigned such competence to the king and the imperial councillors who were well disposed towards him.

The endeavors of Swedenborg and his supporters actually succeeded in having the dispute settled by the privy council rather than by the ecclesiastical authorities. The deliberations of the senate led to two resolutions, which treated the "disturbances" at Göteborg and Swedenborg's writings as separate issues but still did not involve Swedenborg personally. In the second resolution to the Göteborg consistory, Beyer and Rosén are censured for spreading Swedenborg's doctrines, which have proved "manifest errors"—the expression *heresy* is again avoided—but the official reprimand did not conclude with the expected dismissal and banishment.

The other resolution, which concerned Swedenborg's writings and was signed by the king himself, authorized the department of the Chancellery College concerned with books and writings containing errors of doctrine to establish the nature of Swedenborg's books and how they had entered the country. The necessary measures for their confiscation must also be taken, and the relevant booksellers and publishers should be referred to the existing laws concerning theological literature. A corresponding directive went to the seaports.

It was not until the early days of May 1770 that Swedenborg heard of these two resolutions. He now decided to intervene personally. At the end of May or at the beginning of June, he wrote to the king, asking for his protection. He first presented the background of the whole case and emphasized the injustice of the previous proceedings in that they had taken place in his absence and behind his back and that he had been given no opportunity to comment on the accusations. He contrasts his divine mission with the reproaches of his accusers and artfully recalled the earlier favor of the royal dynasty: "That Our Savior revealed himself to me and commanded me to do what I have done and will still do and that he allowed me to converse with angels and spirits, I have declared before all Christendom and not only in England, Holland, Germany, Denmark, Paris, and Spain, but also on various occasions before Your Royal Majesties and especially when I had the favor on dining at the table of Your Royal Majesties, when the whole royal family and five imperial councillors were present and nothing but this was discussed. Afterwards, I explained it before many imperial councillors, among whom Imperial Councillors Count Tessin, Count Bonde, and Count Höpken really understood the truth of this matter, as Imperial Councillor Count Höpken, who has an illuminated intellect, still does, not forgetting others at home and abroad, where this likewise occurred before kings and princes." He then continued that he had learned through rumor that this divine truth of his doctrine had been described as falsehood by the office of the chancellor of justice. But as his visionary gift "cannot be transferred into other heads" nor "can miracles be accepted in the present age," reason itself should establish that his doctrine is true. He therefore humbly requests the king to read his writings and volunteers to give a sworn disposition concerning the truth of all his doctrines. Should the rumor of the condemnation of his doctrine be true, he fears that this could lead to his imprisonment. "For this reason, I take refuge in Your Royal Majesty's protection, as something has befallen me that no one up until now has experienced in Sweden since the coming of Christianity, still less since the introduction of freedom, namely, that proceedings have been taken against me, without anyone giving me the slightest hearing."

He also requested justice for his two friends Beyer and Rosén and noted "that they have become martyrs solely through the heartless persecutions of the local bishop and cathedral provost." He also asks the same for his books, "which I regard as my *alter ego*, while the cathedral provost of Göteborg has poured out pure calumnies and untruths against them."

He received no reply to this letter. It is not difficult to guess the reason. Up until now, the king and the imperial councillors had done their best to spare him. The case had been planned as a heresy trial and the rumormongers in Stockholm were already predicting the arrest of Swedenborg. However, despite the zeal of his opponents, the proceedings had slackened, so that Swedenborg was not involved and his friends in Göteborg had not even been dismissed. The censorship of his writings and the confiscation of books imported without authorization were the minimal measures that the government was obliged to take. Things would have gone worse for Swedenborg in any other European country. When Swedenborg still protested at this minimal penalty, the king passed over the matter in silence.

Swedenborg was unsatisfied with this quiet settlement of the dispute and therefore made a further attempt at public rehabilitation. He requested that the king summon the consistories of the kingdom to examine his writings and deliver a verdict on their contents. No opinion was expressed, but the king was kind enough to give Swedenborg at least some personal satisfaction. Pernety recounts: "When the king met Swedenborg, he said to him: 'The consistories have kept silent regarding that request and your writings.' Laying his hand on his shoulder, he added: 'We may conclude that they found nothing reprehensible in them and that you wrote them in accordance with the truth.'" Thus the matter rested. As planned, Swedenborg left Sweden unhindered at the end of July, in order to travel to Amsterdam to have *True Christian Religion* printed.

The trial thus ended in vain, and Robsahm surely hits the mark when he writes: "His enemies did not dare to put their persecution into practice because they remembered that Swedenborg was related to the most prominent families in both the House of Nobles and in the clerical estate." It is remarkable that Swedenborg never actually had the opportunity to defend himself publicly, and it is obvious that neither Church nor government circles desired this. His friends did not want to cast him in the role of martyr or founder of a new faith. For his part, Swedenborg had waged the struggle, convinced of his divine vocation and the truth of his revelations. He used a further argument with the king, which links him to the enlightened minds of his age, by referring to the "freedom" accomplished by the Reformation. He thereby gave an enlightened, liberal interpretation to the Reformation, which met with the approval of the freethinking king, if not the Swedish Church.

His use of the Church's symbolic books was also remarkable. Both in his reply to Ekebom and his letter to the king, Swedenborg alluded to the congruity of his doctrines with the Formula of Concord. However, he was surely aware that he went beyond the doctrinal wording of the symbolic books of his Church on various points and indicated these differences clearly enough in his own works. He prefaced his exegesis of the Johannine apocalypse with two chapters in which he printed, word for word, the Catholic doctrine of faith next to the Formula of Concord. He intended to show that these versions had been hitherto valid, but now he, Swedenborg, brought the true revelation of the Word and the pure doctrine of the New Church, which rendered all earlier doctrine obsolete.

Swedenborg's doctrines concerning God, freedom, the incarnation, and justification by faith all clearly deviated from the Lutheran symbolic books. During the trial, he wrote to Beyer on 30 October 1769 that the Formula of Concord "was no proper explanation of the Holy Trinity in God the Savior." His subsequently published work *True Christian Religion* is full of critical comments about the symbolic books. He writes there of the Formula of

Concord: "When the clergy are ordained, they swear on this book and thereby on this faith. The reformed Churches have a similar faith. But what man with reason and religion would not consider these things absurd and ridiculous?" In a later passage, he calls the denial of free will in the Formula of Concord "a madness contrary to universal human reason." The relevant doctrinal sections are quoted verbatim, in order to demonstrate the contrast with the doctrine of the New Church even more clearly, "as this happens with paintings where an ugly face is placed beside a beautiful face, in order that the ugliness of one and the beauty of the other is evident at the same instant."

His attitude towards the symbolic books is reflected in his visions. At a debate on free will in the world of spirits attended by numerous theologians of earlier centuries, Swedenborg witnesses the following scene. A man steps panting into the center of the assembly, "carrying under his arm a book called the Formula of Concord, on whose orthodoxy, as he calls it, the Lutherans presently swear an oath." He reads out the sections concerning the constraint of man and his complete depravity, whereupon the audience breaks out shouting: "This is truly orthodox!" But Swedenborg "burns in the spirit" and proclaims to the assembled Church fathers his own doctrine of the freedom of will. They contradict him with scornful words, but a lightning flash falls from heaven and "in order that it does not consume them, they rush out and flee away, each to his own house."

This text had already been sent to the printer when Swedenborg referred Ekebom and the king to the congruity of his doctrine with the symbolic books of the Swedish Church! This attitude is common to many theologians of the Enlightenment, who can no longer reconcile their scientific knowledge and personal faith with official Church doctrine. Theologians such as Johann Salomo Semler in Halle made a distinction between a "public" and a "private" religion. Public religion concerns the constitutional form of official Church life set down in the symbolic books. Beside this stands private religion, namely, that personal religious conviction that the devout individual has acquired through religious experience, education and critical insight. Its validity rests on the freedom of conscience.

One can therefore hardly reproach Swedenborg for having conflicting views at a time when "private religion" was emancipating itself from ecclesiastical indoctrination. On the one hand, he criticized the symbolic books vis-à-vis his personal beliefs by reference to his inner vision; but in the context of a state trial using the symbolic books as a legal norm, he referred to the congruity of his doctrine with these symbolic books. In this situation, he behaved like the turtles with two heads, recounted in an earlier vision, which retract their smaller head within their larger head. This separation of public and private religion reflects the general transformation of modern religious consciousness in the Enlightenment. Here Swedenborg is a representative figure of his age.

Swedenborg did not return from his journey but passed away on 29 March 1772 in London, after receiving Holy Communion from the hand of the Swedish pastor Ferelius. On 5 April 1772, he was interred under the altar of the Swedish Church in London. However, the mortal remains of the seer had to endure some strange adventures before they reached their final resting place. In 1816, twenty-four years after his death, on the occasion of a burial in the vault, Swedenborg's skull was stolen from his coffin by one Captain Ludwig Granholm. The motive for this theft is unknown, but the case was not unknown at a time when the phrenology of the doctor Franz Joseph Gall excited scholars and dilettantes. It became a great fashion to assemble whole collections of skulls. Wealthy enthusiasts not only financed the theft of skulls of prominent deceased personalities but also made provision to secure the skulls of famous living people. When Granholm was lying on his deathbed, he summoned his pastor, Johann Peter Wåhlin, confessed his robbery with remorse, and handed over Swedenborg's skull. For four years, the skull remained in the custody of Pastor Wåhlin and Charles August Tulk, a member of the House of Commons, who owned a phrenological collection. In 1823, the skull was returned to the coffin in the presence of Wåhlin, Tulk, and Nils E. Nordenskjöld, a mining expert from Finland, the father of Adolf E. Nordenskjöld, the famous North Pole explorer. In 1908, Swedenborg's bones were solemnly brought home to Sweden and laid to rest in Uppsala Cathedral on 19 May 1908. Thus, the mortal body of the seer found final peace at the place where the Swedish kings, archbishops, and princes of science including Olof Rudbeck and Carolus Linnaeus are buried.

Conclusion

The portrayal of Swedenborg in this book seems to justify the summary of the man and his works as follows:

1. Swedenborg was a true charismatic visionary. This charismatic type can be traced through the entire history of Christian prophecy from the author of the Book of Revelation through Hermas and the medieval visionaries like Joachim of Fiore up until the seventeenth and eighteenth centuries. If one wishes to dismiss his revelations as madness because they are based on visions, one would have to reject all Christian visionaries, including the author of Revelations, as madmen.

2. Swedenborg became a specifically Christian visionary on the basis of a Christian experience of repentance and conversion, which was decisively influenced by a vision of Christ.

3. The emergence of visionary charisma in Swedenborg is linked with a genuine prophetic experience of vocation. If one wishes to deny the authenticity of this experience of vocation, one would have to question the authenticity of all similar experiences of vocation in the Old and New Testament.

4. Swedenborg was not a spiritualist. It is wrong to abstract a system of spiritualism from his visionary theology and dismiss its specifically Christian impulses as superfluous or irrelevant. His vision and his teachings about the transcendental world and its relationship to the earthly world cannot be separated from his view of Christ, his exegesis of the Bible, and the Christian content of the doctrine of the New Church.

5. Swedenborg expressed the genuine nature of his conversion and the authenticity of his visionary gift by seeking a practical realization of Christian love in his own life wherever possible. He declared such love an integral part of Christian faith. His experience of conversion and vocation signified not only a new form of knowledge but a new kind of life.

6. As his preaching directly concerned the Church, Swedenborg proved himself an authentic Christian prophet. His doctrine is no abstract philosophy but is directed at the Church of his time. The heart of his preaching renews the oldest part of the Gospel: Repent, for the Kingdom of Heaven is at hand.

7. Swedenborg is more specifically a Protestant visionary and prophet, as his piety is nourished not primarily by the sacrament and liturgy but by the divine Word and is elaborated in an exegesis of the Bible. His visions are not free expressions of spontaneous visionary activity but commentaries on Holy Scripture.

8. Swedenborg is a Protestant visionary and prophet, as his revelation and prophetic critique are directed at the Swedish Lutheran Church, to which he belonged up until his death. From a historical point of view, Swedenborg's criticism of the Church in his time was justified. This is proven by the contemporary criticism of Swedish Pietism and spiritualist sects, which was similarly directed against the ossification of the doctrine of justification by faith and its spirit of polemic, lovelessness, and self-righteousness.

9. Swedenborg's special charisma lay in his development from a philosopher and scientist into a visionary. He had a thorough mastery of almost all sciences in his age and furthered many of them. On the basis of his research into all branches of human knowledge, he had already developed a metaphysical worldview before his conversion and vocation, which affected the nature of his visionary charisma.

10. It is not true that all theoretical elements of Swedenborg's later visionary thought were simply borrowed from his philosophy. Elements of his earlier philosophy certainly appear in his visionary theology, but they are refashioned by his experience of Christ and relate to a new, personal view of God.

11. Swedenborg is a representative visionary of the age of Enlightenment. This is evident in the way that he arranges and systematizes his own visionary experiences and underpins them with a theory of knowledge. He is not a complete exception in the history of Christian visionaries, for the beginnings of such a schematic approach can be found in earlier visionaries with a

philosophical background. St. Teresa of Avila notably developed a psychology of religious experience on the basis of her visions.

12. Swedenborg is a visionary of the age of Enlightenment because he shares his age's faith in the power of the book. He considered that it is sufficient to print a truth to assure its victory. He therefore renounced the spoken word as a means of proclaiming his revelations. He also favored learned scholarly publication in Latin, in the expectation that the doctrine of the New Church would spread of its own accord.

13. The fact that many elements of Swedenborg's earlier philosophical views are blended with his visionary theology, if only in a modified form, and the systematization of his visionary experiences do not vitiate their authenticity. The history of Christian prophets and visionaries shows from the very outset that "the corn of visionary or prophetic intuition grows on the stalk of human contemplation" (Friedrich Christoph Oetinger). The preponderance of the didactic element in Swedenborg may, to use the same metaphor, suggest more stalk than corn. But it is wrong to declare that it is all stalk, because one then denies a priori that the corn of prophetic vision can grow on the stalk of human contemplation. The fact that he was a philosophical prophet in the Enlightenment should not mislead one into thinking that he had no authentic visionary and prophetic charisma.

14. Swedenborg understood the course of salvation as a history of the degeneration of divine revelation through humankind. His idea that this decline could be overcome by the opening of an inner, spiritual sense of revelation could easily lead to his interpretation as a messianic figure. But he never saw himself as such and sought neither the role of a saint nor a founder of a sect. He clearly stated that Christ's Second Coming would not ensue in the Savior's return on the clouds of heaven but in a disclosure of the true, inner, spiritual meaning of the divine Word. To this extent, he did relate his own divine task to a spiritualized conception of the Second Coming. If several of his followers saw him as the founder of a sect, this contradicts the fact that Swedenborg did not think in terms of imminent expectation or

a historical date for salvation, but in the scheme of evolution and progression. He did not regard himself as the founder of the New Church but as an important step beyond traditional doctrinal types of Christianity towards a New Church. Through the disclosure of the spiritual meaning of the divine Word, the New Church would once again relate faith to love and achieve a new phase in the realization of the Divine Man. This would initiate a new era in the history of the Church as the perfect community of humanity with God.

15. Swedenborg's proclamation was necessary for the Church of his time. The Last Things, the reality of the Kingdom of God and its coming, the nature of life after death, the resurrection, the Last Judgment, heaven and hell: this whole complex of truths embraced by the original piety of the early Church had faded in the Protestant orthodoxy of his time. "Last Things" had been relegated as an appendix to dogma because they could no longer be maintained in their original, realistic form and because ecclesiastical theology did not venture to consider these questions anew. It is Swedenborg's enduring achievement to have provided a new answer to these questions on the basis of his visionary experiences. As a result, these themes were shifted back to the center of religious thought and personal piety.

16. Swedenborg's charismatic gift had been awakened through a Christian experience of conversion and vocation, and this gift was linked to an exceptional universal education. He sought to honor the moral demands of his teaching in his own life responsibly and to the best of his ability. There is no reason to reject his doctrine of the Last Things because they were grounded in Christian missionary consciousness. He gave rise to strong impulses for the renewal of the Church view of the Last Things, as Friedrich Christoph Oetinger, Johann Kaspar Lavater, Franz von Baader, Heinrich Jung-Stilling, and many other devout individuals in the age of Pietism and Romanticism confirm.

17. Neither theology nor philosophy has hitherto had the means for a sound examination of Swedenborg, which could separate the wheat from the chaff. In philosophy, Kant's premises negated the very possibility of insight into the transcendental world.

Protestant theology accepted Kant's philosophy but failed to draw appropriate conclusions. The beginnings of the Church and theology go back to visions of the resurrected Christ before his disciples, and St. Paul traces his own vocation for the apostolic office and gospel back to a vision of Christ. In this case, the church of Kant's time should have referred its evangelists and apostles to the same lunatic asylum to which Kant directed Swedenborg. Today's Church should try to develop a new attitude toward the phenomenon of charismatic gifts displayed by prophets and visionaries. Such a new approach would elucidate and assess these phenomena, which are so important and relevant to both the origin and purpose of the Church. Only a critical phenomenology of the visionary experiences that have occurred in the Church from its beginnings until the present could achieve this. Oetinger began this project in a critical discussion with Swedenborg and other visionaries over many years and stated important principles of a "prophetic theology" to assess and investigate charismatic phenomena in the life of the Church. "Test, test, and keep the best!" The challenge he issued regarding the works of Swedenborg has not yet been fulfilled.

Bibliography

Acton, A. *An Introduction to the Word Explained, a study of the means by which Swedenborg the scientist and philosopher became the theologian and revelator.* Bryn Athyn, Pa., 1927.

Alm, H. *Swedenborgs hus och trädgord.* Stockholm, 1938.

Ballet, G. *Swedenborg, Histoire d'un visionaire du dix-huitième siècle.* Paris, 1899.

Benz, E. *Swedenborg in Deutschland. F.C. Oetingers und Immanuel Kants Auseinandersetzung mit der Person und Lehre Swedenborgs. Nach neuen Quellen bearbeitet.* Frankfurt a. Main, 1947.

———. "Swedenborg und Lavater. Über die religiösen Grundlagen der Physiognomik," *Zeitschrift für Kirchengeschichte* 57 (1938): 153–216.

Bergson, H. *Matière et mémoire.* Paris, 1900.

Bonjour, D. *Les Rêves.* Lausanne, 1920.

Chevrier, Ed. *Etudes sur les Religions de l'Antiquité.* Paris, 1880.

Driesch, H. *Psychical Research.* London, 1933.

Flammarion, E., ed. *Hypnotisme et Spiritisme.* Paris, 1916.

Flournoy, Th. *Esprits et Médiums.* Geneva, 1911.

Geymuller, H. de. *Swedenborg und die übersinnliche Welt.* Revised and expanded by H. Driesch. Stuttgart, 1936; reprint Zurich, 1966.

Hitchcock, E. A. *Swedenborg: A Hermetic Philosopher.* New York, 1858.

Hoffmann, R. A. "Kant und Swedenborg," *Grenzfragen der Nerven- und Seelenlebens,* H. 69, 1909.

Horn, F. *Schelling und Swedenborg.* Zurich, 1953.

———. *Schelling and Swedenborg: Mysticism and German Idealism.* Translated by George F. Dole. West Chester, Pa.: Swedenborg Foundation, 1997.

Jaspers, K. *Stringberg und van Gogh. Versuch einer pathographischen Analyse, unter vergleichended Heranziehung von Swedenborg und Hölderlin.* Bremen, 1949.

Lamm, M. *Swedenborg. Eine Studie über seine Entwicklung zum Mystiker und Geisterseher.* Leipzig, 1922.

———. *Emanuel Swedenborg: The Development of His Thought.* Translated by Tomas Spiers and Anders Hallengren. West Chester, Pa.: Swedenborg Foundation, 2000.

Matter, M. *Swedenborg, sa vie, ses écrits, sa doctrine.* Paris, 1863.

Mittnacht, A. *Emanuel Swedenborgs Leben und Lehre. Urkunden.* Frankfurt a.Main, 1880.

Nathorst, A. G. *Emanuel Swedenborg as a geologist.* Stockholm, 1907.

Nordensköld, E. *History of Biology.* New York, 1936.

Pratt, J. G. *Towards a Method of Evaluating Mediumistic Material.* Boston, 1936.

Scholem, G. *Major Trends in Jewish Mysticism.* New York, 1946.

Schrödinger, E. *What is Life?* New York, 1945.

Sigstedt, C. O. *The Swedenborg Epic.* New York, 1952.

Smithson, J. H. *The Spiritual Diary of Emanuel Swedenborg.* London, 1846.

Stroh, A. *Origin of Swedenborg's Conceptions concerning the Functions of the Brain.* Uppsala, 1911.

——. *The Sources of Swedenborg's Early Philosophy of Nature.* Stockholm, 1911.

Tafel, R. *Swedenborg as a Philosopher and Man of Science.* Chicago, 1867.

Toksvig, S. *Emanuel Swedenborg: Scientist and Mystic.* New Haven, Conn., 1948.

Viatte, A. *Les sources occultes du romantisme (Illuminisme–Théosophie 1770–1820).* 2 vols. Paris, 1928.

Wetterberg, G. *Jesper Swedbergs lefwernes beskrifning.* Lund, 1941.

Wunsch, W. F. *An Outline of New Church Teaching.* New York, 1926.

Bibliography of the Works of Emanuel Swedenborg

Apocalypse Explained. 6 vols. Translated by John Whitehead. 2nd ed. West Chester, Pa..: The Swedenborg Foundation, 1994–1998.

Apocalypse Revealed. 2 vols. Translated by John Whitehead. 2nd ed. West Chester, Pa.: The Swedenborg Foundation, 1997.

Arcana Coelestia. 12 vols. Translated by John Clowes. Revised by John F. Potts. 2nd ed. West Chester, Pa.: The Swedenborg Foundation, 1995–1998. The first volume of this work is also available under the title *Heavenly Secrets.*

Charity: The Practice of Neighborliness. Translated by William F. Wunsch. Edited by William R. Woofenden. West Chester, Pa.: The Swedenborg Foundation, 1995.

Conjugial Love. Translated by Samuel S. Warren. Revised by Louis Tafel. 2nd ed. West Chester, Pa.: The Swedenborg Foundation, 1998. This volume is also available under the title *Love in Marriage,* translated by David Gladish, 1992.

Divine Love and Wisdom. Translated by John C. Ager. 2nd ed. West Chester, Pa.: The Swedenborg Foundation, 1995.

Divine Love and Wisdom/Divine Providence. Translated by George F. Dole. THE NEW CENTURY EDITION OF THE WORKS OF EMANUEL SWEDENBORG. West Chester, Pa.: The Swedenborg Foundation, 2002.

Divine Providence. Translated by William Wunsch. 2nd ed. West Chester, Pa.: The Swedenborg Foundation, 1996.

Four Doctrines. Translated by John F. Potts. 2nd ed. West Chester, Pa.: The Swedenborg Foundation, 1997.

Heaven and Hell. Translated by John C. Ager. 2nd ed. West Chester, Pa.: The Swedenborg Foundation, 1995.

————. Translated by George F. Dole. THE NEW CENTURY EDITION OF THE WORKS OF EMANUEL SWEDENBORG. West Chester, Pa.: The Swedenborg Foundation, 2000.

The Heavenly City. Translated by Lee Woofenden. West Chester, Pa.: The Swedenborg Foundation, 1993.

Journal of Dreams. Translated by J. J. G. Wilkinson. Introduction by Wilson Van Dusen. New York: The Swedenborg Foundation, 1986. See also *Swedenborg's Dream Diary.*

The Last Judgment in Retrospect. Translated by and edited by George F. Dole. West Chester, Pa.: The Swedenborg Foundation, 1996.

Miscellaneous Theological Works. Translated by John Whitehead. 2nd ed. West Chester, Pa.: The Swedenborg Foundation, 1996. This volume includes *The*

New Jerusalem and Its Heavenly Doctrine, Earths in the Universe, and The Last Judgment and Babylon Destroyed, among others.

Posthumous Theological Works. 2 vols. Translated by John Whitehead. 2nd ed. West Chester, Pa.: The Swedenborg Foundation, 1996. These volumes include the autobiographical and theological extracts from Swedenborg's letters, additions to *True Christian Religion, The Doctrine of Charity, The Precepts of the Decalogue,* and collected minor works, among others.

Swedenborg's Dream Diary. Edited by Lars Bergquist. Translated by Anders Hallengren. West Chester, Pa.: The Swedenborg Foundation, 2001. See also *Journal of Dreams.*

True Christian Religion. 2 vols. Translated by John C. Ager. West Chester, Pa.: The Swedenborg Foundation, 1996.

Worship and Love of God. Translated by Alfred H. Stroh and Frank Sewall. 2nd ed. West Chester, Pa.: The Swedenborg Foundation, 1996.

————. Translated by Stuart Shotwell. The New Century Edition of the Works of Emanuel Swedenborg. West Chester, Pa.: The Swedenborg Foundation, 2002.

Collections of Swedenborg's Writings

Conversations with Angels: What Swedenborg Heard in Heaven. Edited by Leonard Fox and Donald Rose. Translated by David Gladish and Jonathan Rose. West Chester, Pa.: Chrysalis Books, 1996.

Debates with Devils: What Swedenborg Heard in Hell. Edited by Donald Rose. Translated by Lisa Hyatt Cooper. West Chester, Pa.: Chrysalis Books, 2000.

A Thoughtful Soul. Translated by and edited by George F. Dole. West Chester, Pa.: Chrysalis Books, 1995.

Way of Wisdom: Meditations on Love and Service. Edited by Grant R. Schnarr and Erik J. Buss. West Chester, Pa.: Chrysalis Books, 1999.

Index

ONE SYSTEM